A-Z BRISTOL & BATH De Luxe Street Atlas

CONTENTS

REFERENC

Motorway M5

A Road A4

Under Construction

Proposed

B Road B4058

Dual Carriageway

One-way Street
Traffic flow on A Roads is indicated by a heavy line on the driver's left.

Pedestrianized Road

Restricted Access

Track / Footpath

Residential Walkway

Railway — Tunnel, Level Crossing, Station

Built-up Area — HIGH STREET

Local Authority Boundary

Posttown Boundary

Postcode Boundary
Within Posttown

Map Continuation 12 — Large Scale 4

Beaches

Car Park (Selected)

Church or Chapel

Electricity Transmission Line

Fire Station

Hospital

House Numbers (Selected Rds.) 4 22 36

Information Centre

National Grid Reference 360

Places of Interest

Police Station

Post Office

Toilet

Toilet with Disabled Facilities

Large Scale City Centres Only

One Way Roads
Traffic flow is indicated by a blue arrow.

Educational Establishments

Hospitals & Health Centres

Leisure & Recreational Facilities

Places of Interest

Public Buildings

Shopping Centres & Markets

Other Selected Buildings

SCALE

Map Pages 6-95, 98-157
1:10,838 approx 6 inches to 1 mile
0 — ¼ Mile
0 — 250 Metres

Map Pages 4-5, 96-97
1:5,419 approx 12 inches to 1 mile
0 — ⅛ Mile
0 — 250 Metres

Geographers' A-Z Map Company Limited

Head Office :
Fairfield Road, Borough Green, Sevenoaks, Kent TN15 8PP
Tel: 01732 781000 (General Enquiries & Trade Sales)

Showrooms :
44 Gray's Inn Road, London WC1X 8HX Tel: 0171 242 9246
Tel: 020 7440 9500 (Retail Sales)
www.a-zmaps.co.uk

Edition 1 1998
Edition 1A 2000

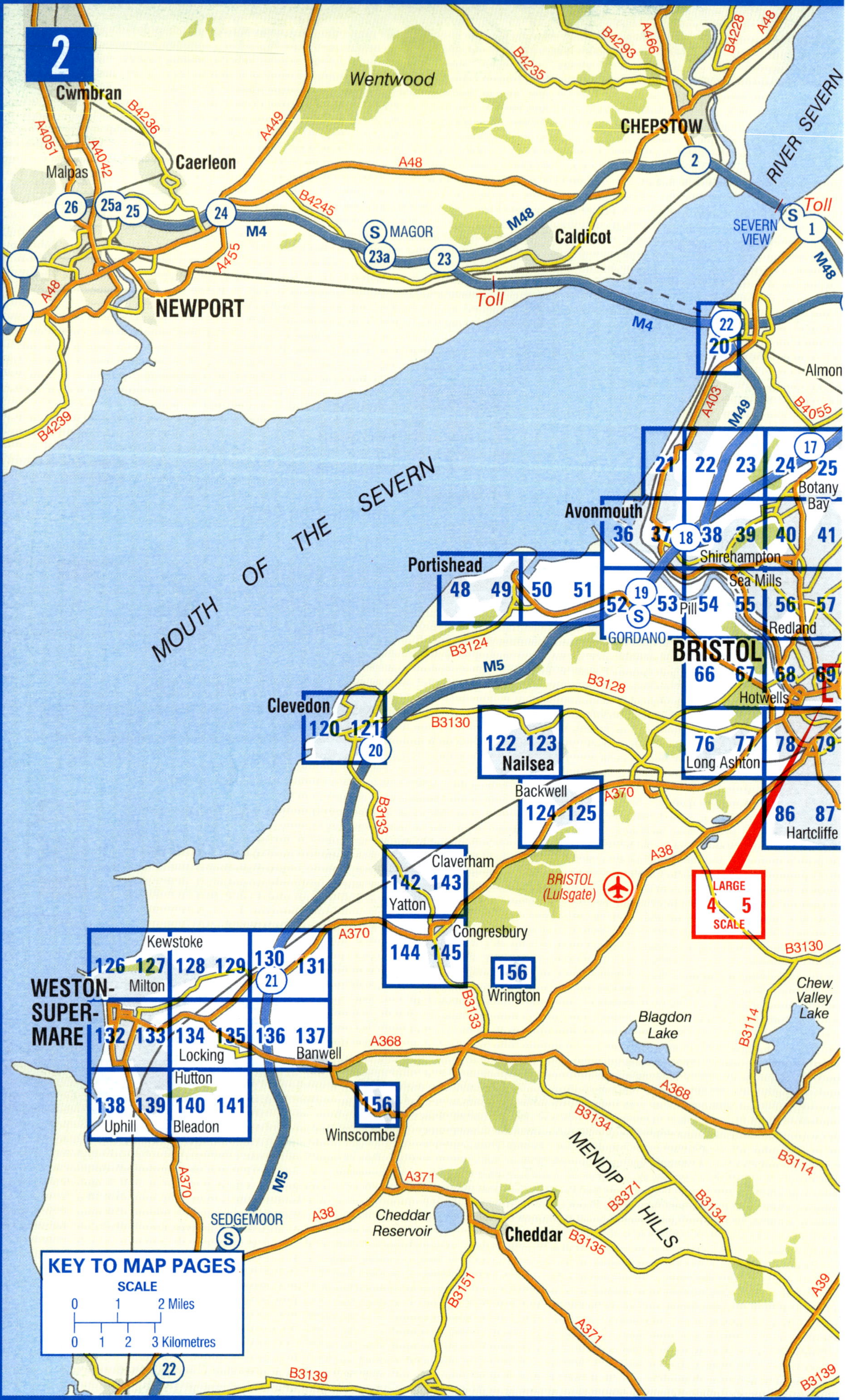

Cwmbran
Caerleon
Malpas
Wentwood
CHEPSTOW
Caldicot
MAGOR
NEWPORT
RIVER SEVERN
SEVERN VIEW
Toll
Toll
M4
M48
A48
A449
A4051
A4042
B4236
B4245
A455
B4235
B4293
A466
B4228
B4239
A403
M49
B4055
Almon
MOUTH OF THE SEVERN
Avonmouth
Portishead
Shirehampton
Sea Mills
Botany Bay
Redland
Pill
GORDANO
BRISTOL
Hotwells
Long Ashton
Hartcliffe
Clevedon
Nailsea
Backwell
Claverham
Yatton
Congresbury
Wrington
BRISTOL (Lulsgate)
LARGE 4 5 SCALE
Kewstoke
WESTON-SUPER-MARE
Milton
Locking
Banwell
Hutton
Uphill
Bleadon
Winscombe
SEDGEMOOR
Cheddar Reservoir
Cheddar
Blagdon Lake
Chew Valley Lake
MENDIP HILLS
M5
B3124
B3128
B3130
B3133
A370
A38
A368
B3114
B3134
B3371
B3135
A371
B3151
A39
B3139
21 22 23 24 25
36 37 38 39 40 41
48 49 50 51
52 53 54 55 56 57
66 67 68 69
76 77 78 79
86 87
120 121
122 123
124 125
142 143
144 145
156
126 127 128 129 130 131
132 133 134 135 136 137
138 139 140 141
KEY TO MAP PAGES
SCALE
0 1 2 Miles
0 1 2 3 Kilometres

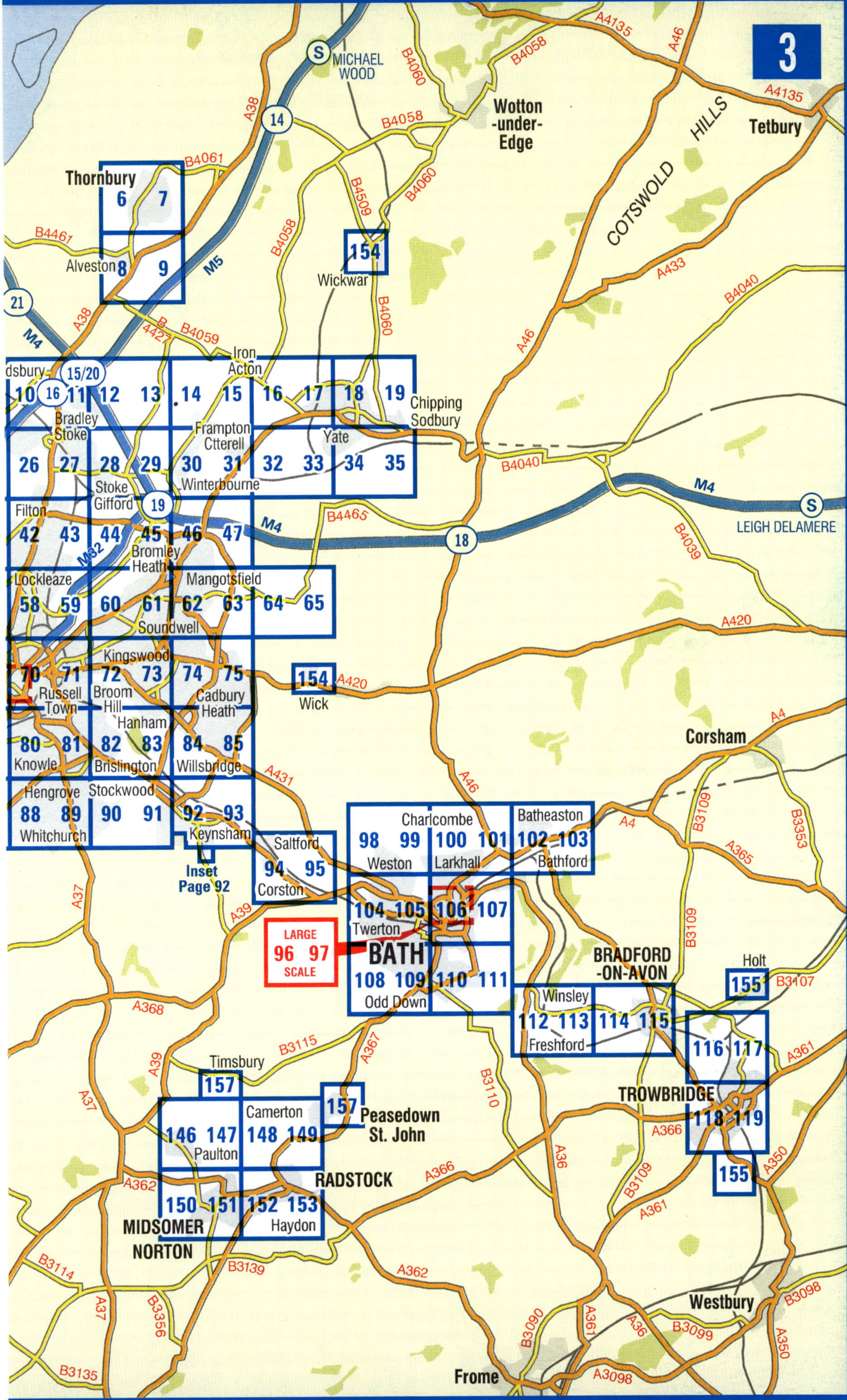
MICHAEL WOOD
Wotton -under- Edge
Tetbury
COTSWOLD HILLS
Thornbury
Alveston
Wickwar
Iron Acton
Chipping Sodbury
Bradley Stoke
Frampton Cotterell
Yate
Stoke Gifford
Winterbourne
Filton
Bromley Heath
LEIGH DELAMERE
Lockleaze
Mangotsfield
Soundwell
Kingswood
Russell Town
Broom Hill
Cadbury Heath
Wick
Hanham
Knowle
Brislington
Willsbridge
Corsham
Hengrove
Stockwood
Whitchurch
Keynsham
Inset Page 92
Saltford
Corston
Charlcombe
Weston
Larkhall
Batheaston
Bathford
Twerton
BATH
Odd Down
LARGE 96 97 SCALE
BRADFORD -ON-AVON
Holt
Winsley
Freshford
TROWBRIDGE
Timsbury
Camerton
Paulton
Peasedown St. John
RADSTOCK
Haydon
MIDSOMER NORTON
Westbury
Frome
M4
M5
M32
A4135
A46
B4058
B4060
A38
B4061
B4509
B4461
B4058
A433
B4040
B4059
B4427
B4465
B4039
A420
A4
A431
A37
A39
A368
B3115
A367
B3110
A36
B3109
B3353
A365
B3107
A361
A366
A350
A362
B3114
B3356
B3139
B3090
B3099
B3098
A3098
B3135
6 7 8 9 10 11 12 13 14 15 16 17 18 19 15/20 21
26 27 28 29 30 31 32 33 34 35
42 43 44 45 46 47
58 59 60 61 62 63 64 65
70 71 72 73 74 75 154
80 81 82 83 84 85
88 89 90 91 92 93 94 95
98 99 100 101 102 103
104 105 106 107 108 109 110 111
112 113 114 115 116 117 118 119 155
146 147 148 149 150 151 152 153 157

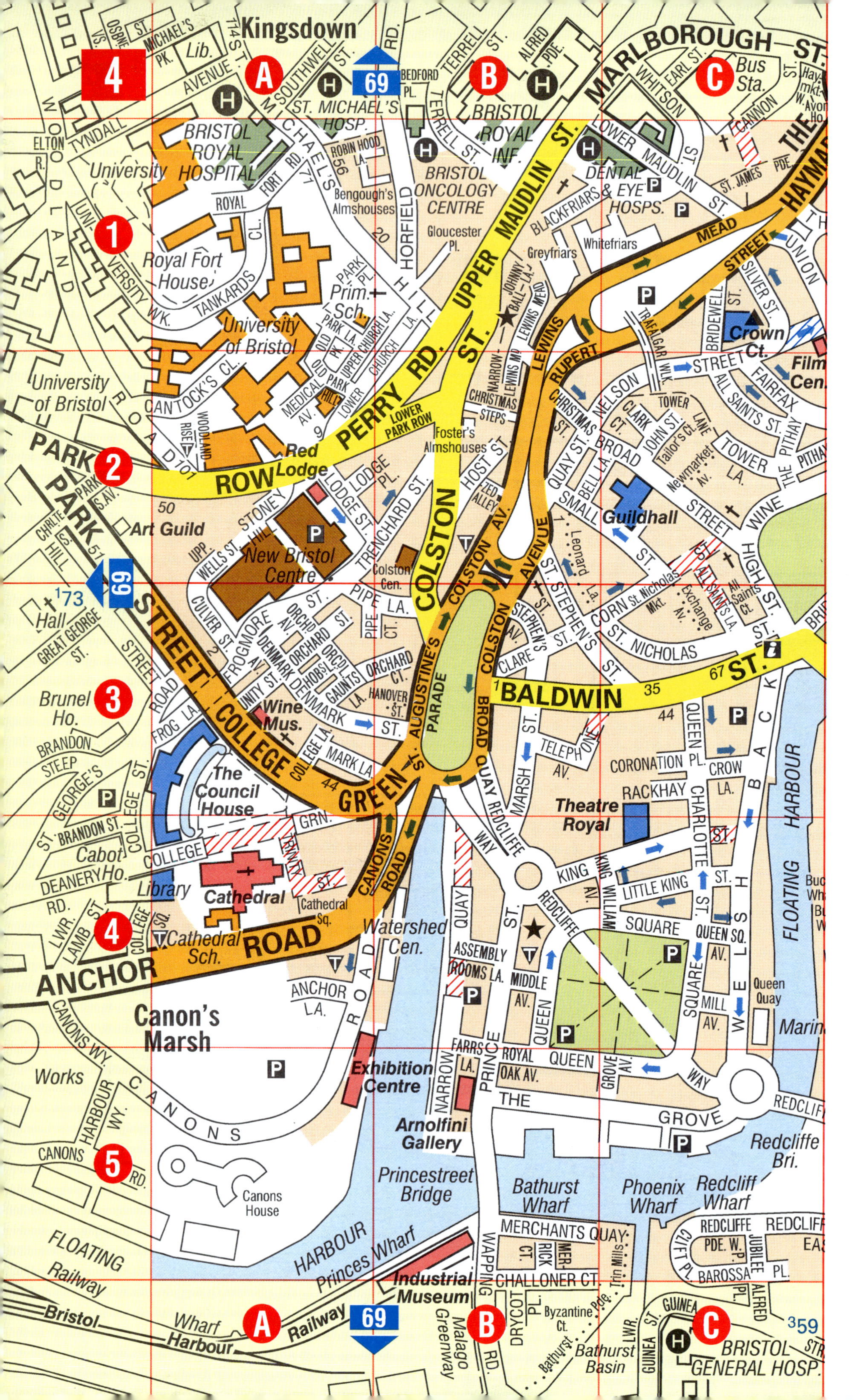
4
Kingsdown
A
B
C
69
Bristol Royal Hospital
University
Bristol Royal Inf.
Bristol Oncology Centre
Marlborough St.
Bus Sta.
Haymarket
Dental & Eye Hosps.
Blackfriars
Greyfriars
Whitefriars
Royal Fort House
University of Bristol
Upper Maudlin St.
Perry Rd.
Lower Park Row
Park Row
Red Lodge
Foster's Almshouses
Bengough's Almshouses
Gloucester Pl.
Christmas Steps
Lewins Mead
Rupert St.
Nelson St.
Crown Ct.
Film Cen.
Union St.
Broad St.
Tower La.
Wine St.
Guildhall
Park St.
Art Guild
New Bristol Centre
Colston St.
Colston Av.
Colston Cen.
Pipe La.
Small St.
Corn St.
St. Nicholas Mkt.
St. Nicholas St.
All Saints Ct.
High St.
Baldwin St.
Hall
Great George St.
Brunel Ho.
College Green
Frogmore St.
Denmark St.
Orchard St.
Wine Mus.
St. Augustine's Parade
Broad Quay
Marsh St.
Telephone Av.
Coronation Pl.
Queen Charlotte St.
Back
Welsh Back
King St.
Theatre Royal
Rackhay
Crow La.
Little King St.
King William Av.
Queen Square
Queen Sq. Av.
Mill Av.
Queen Quay
Floating Harbour
Brandon Steep
St. George's Rd.
Brandon St.
Cabot Ho.
The Council House
College Sq.
Library
Cathedral
Cathedral Sq.
Trinity St.
Canons Road
Deanery Rd.
Lwr. Lamb St.
Cathedral Sch.
Anchor Road
Anchor La.
Watershed Cen.
Quay St.
Assembly Rooms La.
Middle Av.
Prince St.
Redcliffe Way
Canon's Marsh
Canons Wy.
Harbour Wy.
Works
Canons Rd.
Canons House
Exhibition Centre
Arnolfini Gallery
Narrow Quay
Farrs La.
Royal Oak Av.
Queen Square Av.
The Grove
Grove Av.
Redcliffe Bri.
Princestreet Bridge
Bathurst Wharf
Phoenix Wharf
Redcliff Wharf
Merchants Quay
Princes Wharf
Industrial Museum
Challoner Ct.
Redcliffe Pde. W.
Jubilee Pl.
Barossa Pl.
Floating Harbour
Railway
Bristol Harbour Railway
Wharf
Malago Greenway
Wapping Rd.
Drycot Pl.
Byzantine Ct.
Bathurst Basin
Guinea St.
Lwr. Guinea St.
Bristol General Hosp.
359
173

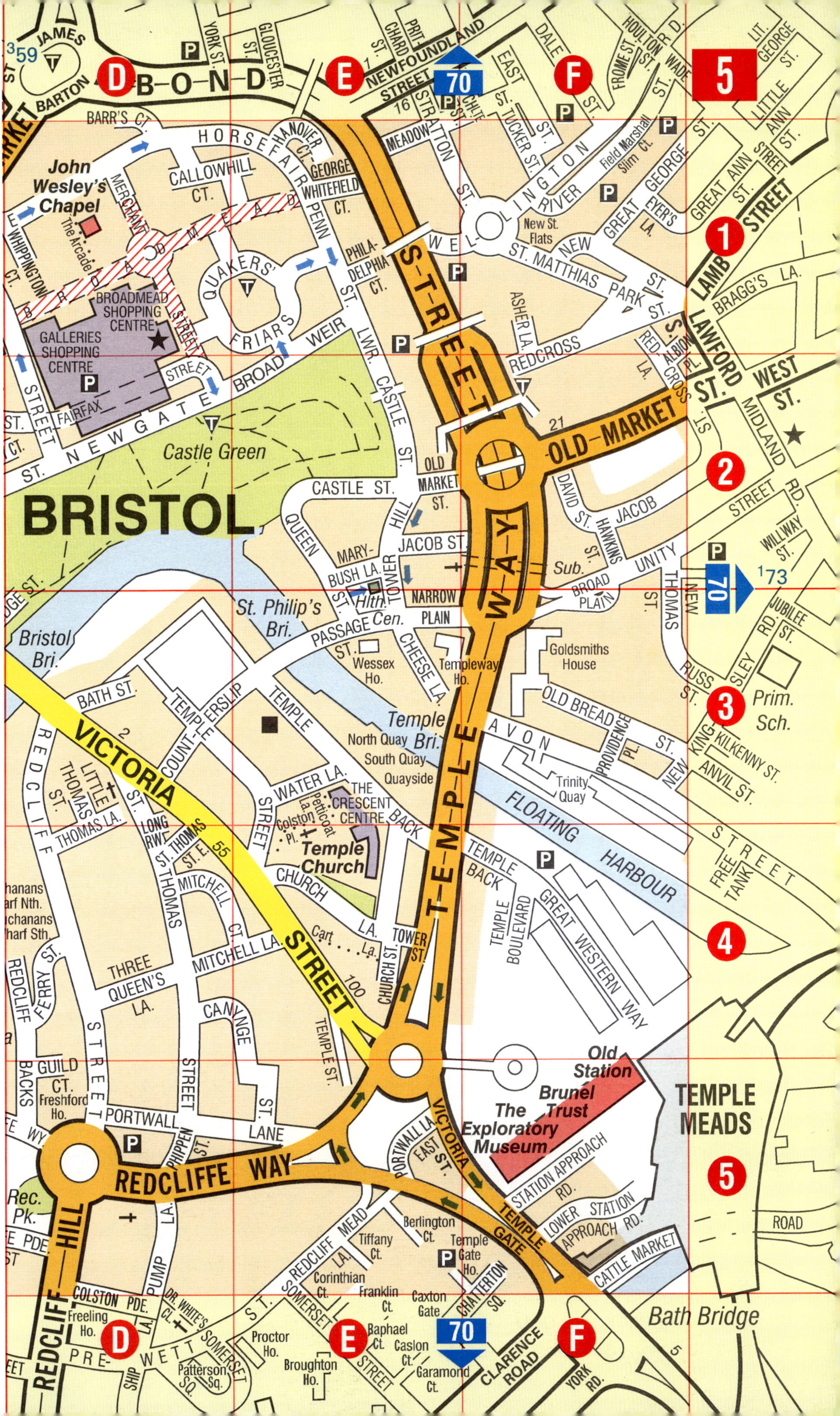

5
59
70
173
D
E
F
1
2
3
4
5
BOND ST
BARTON
JAMES
NEWFOUNDLAND STREET
DALE ST.
HOULTON ST.
FROME ST.
WADE ST.
LITTLE GEORGE ST.
LITTLE ANN ST.
GREAT ANN ST.
ANN STREET
LAMB STREET
BARR'S CT.
HORSEFAIR
CALLOWHILL CT.
HANOVER CT.
GEORGE WHITEFIELD CT.
MEADOW ST.
STRATTON ST.
EAST ST.
ST. TUCKER ST.
WELLINGTON RD.
RIVER ST.
Field Marshall Slim Ct.
GREAT GEORGE ST.
EYER'S LA.
New St. Flats
NEW ST.
ST. MATTHIAS PARK
John Wesley's Chapel
The Arcade
MERCHANT ST.
BROADMEAD
PENN ST.
QUAKERS FRIARS
PHILADELPHIA CT.
WHIPPINGTON CT.
BROADMEAD SHOPPING CENTRE
GALLERIES SHOPPING CENTRE
FAIRFAX ST.
BROAD WEIR
NEWGATE
LWR. CASTLE ST.
STREET
ASHER LA.
REDCROSS ST.
RED CROSS LA.
ALBION PL.
LAWFORD ST.
WEST ST.
MIDLAND RD.
BRAGG'S LA.
Castle Green
BRISTOL
OLD MARKET
OLD MARKET ST.
CASTLE ST.
QUEEN ST.
MARY-BUSH LA.
JACOB ST.
TOWER HILL
NARROW PLAIN
Hlth. Cen.
PASSAGE ST.
Sub.
BROAD PLAIN
DAVID ST.
HAWKINS ST.
JACOB STREET
UNITY ST.
THOMAS ST.
NEW THOMAS ST.
WILLWAY ST.
JUBILEE ST.
SLEY RD.
RUSS ST.
KING ST.
KILKENNY ST.
ANVIL ST.
Prim. Sch.
St. Philip's Bri.
Bristol Bri.
Wessex Ho.
CHEESE LA.
Templeway Ho.
Goldsmiths House
OLD BREAD ST.
PROVIDENCE PL.
AVON ST.
Trinity Quay
NEW ST.
BATH ST.
VICTORIA STREET
TEMPLE ST.
COUNTERSLIP
TEMPLE BACK
Temple Bri.
North Quay
South Quay
Quayside
FLOATING HARBOUR
WATER LA.
THE CRESCENT CENTRE
Colston Pl.
Petticoat La.
Temple Church
CHURCH LA.
TEMPLE WAY
TEMPLE BACK
TEMPLE BOULEVARD
GREAT WESTERN WAY
FREE TANK ST.
REDCLIFF ST.
LITTLE THOMAS ST.
THOMAS LA.
LONG RW.
ST. THOMAS ST.
ST. THOMAS ST. E.
MITCHELL CT.
MITCHELL LA.
Cart La.
TOWER ST.
CHURCH ST.
Buchanans Wharf Nth.
Buchanans Wharf Sth.
FERRY ST.
THREE QUEEN'S LA.
CANYNGE ST.
REDCLIFF BACKS
GUILD CT.
Freshford Ho.
PORTWALL LANE
PHIPPEN ST.
Old Station
Brunel Trust
The Exploratory Museum
TEMPLE MEADS
REDCLIFFE WAY
VICTORIA ST.
PORTWALL LA. EAST
STATION APPROACH RD.
LOWER STATION APPROACH RD.
CATTLE MARKET
ROAD
Rec. Pk.
PDE.
REDCLIFF HILL
PUMP LA.
REDCLIFF MEAD LA.
Tiffany Ct.
Berlington Ct.
Temple Gate Ho.
TEMPLE GATE
Corinthian Ct.
Franklin Ct.
Caxton Gate
CHATTERTON SQ.
Bath Bridge
COLSTON PDE.
Freeling Ho.
DR. WHITE'S CL.
PREWETT ST.
SOMERSET SQ.
SOMERSET STREET
Proctor Ho.
Raphael Ct.
Caslon Ct.
Garamond Ct.
CLARENCE ROAD
YORK RD.
Broughton Ho.
Patterson Sq.
SHIP LA.

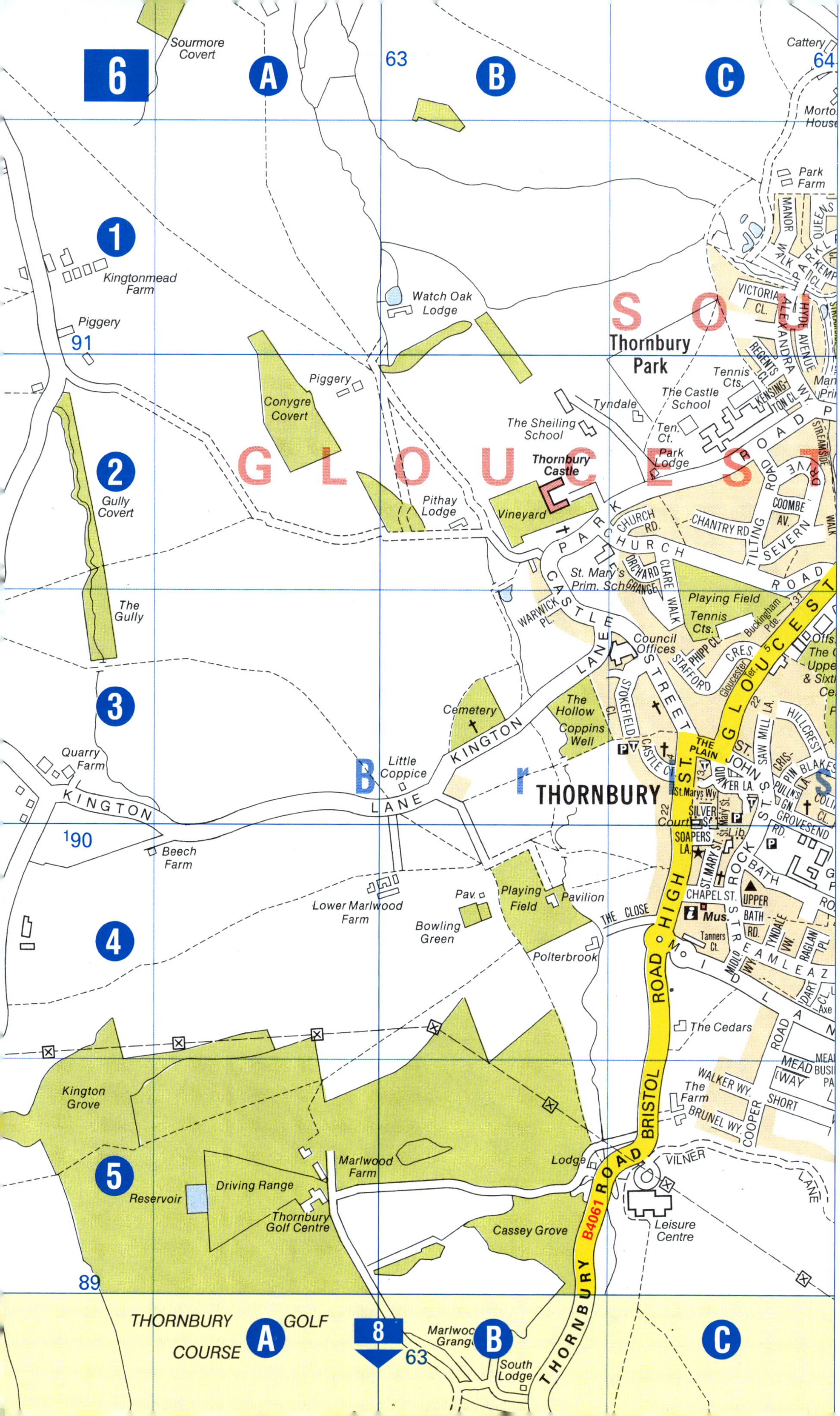

Sourmore Covert
A
63
B
C
Cattery
64
Morton House
Park Farm
1
Kingtonmead Farm
Piggery
91
Watch Oak Lodge
Thornbury Park
Tennis Cts.
The Castle School
Tyndale
The Sheiling School
Ten. Ct.
Park Lodge
Piggery
Conygre Covert
2
Gully Covert
G L O U C E S T
Thornbury Castle
Pithay Lodge
Vineyard
PARK
CHURCH RD.
CHURCH ROAD
CHANTRY RD
COOMBE AV.
SEVERN
TILTING ROAD
St. Mary's Prim. Sch.
ORCHARD GRANGE
CLARE WALK
Playing Field
Tennis Cts.
Buckingham Pde.
CASTLE
WARWICK PL.
The Gully
Council Offices
PHIPP CL.
CRES.
STAFFORD
GLOUCESTER
Gloucester Ter.
Offs.
3
Cemetery
The Hollow
Coppins Well
STOKEFIELD CL.
STREET
CASTLE CT.
THE PLAIN
ST. JOHN ST.
SAW MILL LA.
HILLCREST
CRISPIN LA.
BLAKES
PULLIN'S GN.
COLIN CL.
GROVESEND RD.
Quarry Farm
KINGTON
Little Coppice
KINGTON LANE
THORNBURY
QUAKER LA.
St. Marys Wy
SILVER ST.
St. Mary St.
Court
Lib.
SOAPERS LA.
ROCK ST.
BATH RD.
190
Beech Farm
Lower Marlwood Farm
Pav.
Playing Field
Pavilion
THE CLOSE
CHAPEL ST.
Mus.
UPPER BATH RD.
TYNDALE AV.
RAGLAN PL.
Tanners Ct.
4
Bowling Green
Polterbrook
HIGH ST.
MIDLAND WY.
STREAMLEAZE
MIDLAND ROAD
DART CL.
Axe
The Cedars
MEAD WAY
SHORT WAY
Kington Grove
WALKER WY.
The Farm
BRUNEL WY.
COOPER RD.
BRISTOL ROAD
Lodge
VILNER LANE
5
Reservoir
Driving Range
Thornbury Golf Centre
Marlwood Farm
Leisure Centre
Cassey Grove
B4061
89
THORNBURY GOLF COURSE
8
63
Marlwood Grange
South Lodge
THORNBURY ROAD

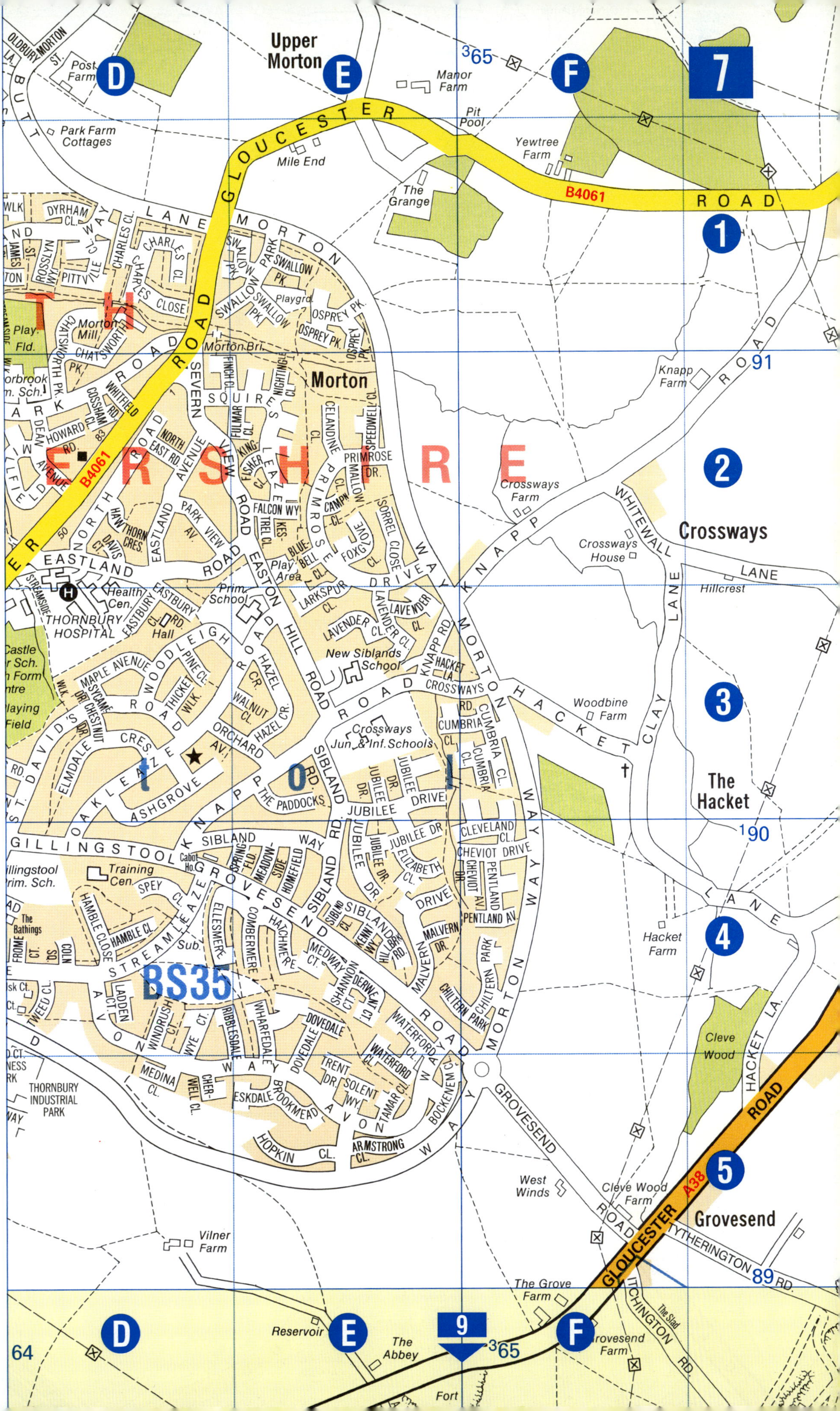

7
Upper Morton
Post Farm
Park Farm Cottages
Mile End
Manor Farm
Pit Pool
The Grange
Yewtree Farm
GLOUCESTER ROAD
B4061
ROAD
MORTON LANE
Morton
Morton Mill
Morton Bri.
Knapp Farm
KNAPP ROAD
Crossways Farm
Crossways
Crossways House
WHITEWALL LANE
Hillcrest
CLAY LANE
Woodbine Farm
HACKET
The Hackett
Hacket Farm
HACKET LA.
Cleve Wood
Cleve Wood Farm
West Winds
Grovesend
GROVESEND ROAD
TYTHERINGTON RD.
ITCHINGTON RD.
A38
The Grove Farm
Grovesend Farm
Reservoir
The Abbey
Fort
Vilner Farm
THORNBURY INDUSTRIAL PARK
THORNBURY HOSPITAL
Health Cen.
Prim. School
Hall
New Siblands School
Crossways Jun. & Inf. Schools
Training Cen.
Castle Sch.
Playing Field
Play. Fld.
Play Area
Playgrd.
BS35
MORTON WAY
KNAPP ROAD
SIBLAND ROAD
SIBLAND WAY
GILLINGSTOOL
GROVESEND ROAD
STREAMLEAZE
AVON WAY
EASTLAND ROAD
PARK ROAD
NORTH ROAD
SEVERN ROAD
EASTON HILL ROAD
SQUIRES LEAZE
PRIMROSE DRIVE
JUBILEE DRIVE
CHEVIOT DRIVE
CLEVELAND CL.
CHILTERN PARK
MALVERN DR.
WOODLEIGH ROAD
ORCHARD AV.
ASHGROVE
OAKLEAZE
ELMDALE CRES.
ST. DAVID'S
MAPLE AVENUE
DYRHAM CL.
CHARLES CL.
CHARLES CLOSE
SWALLOW PK.
OSPREY PK.
CHATSWORTH PK.
COSSHAM CL.
WHITFIELD RD.
HOWARD RD.
HAWTHORN CRES.
DAVIS CT.
EASTLAND AV.
PARK VIEW AV.
FALCON WY.
FISHER CL.
KESTREL CL.
BLUEBELL CL.
FOXGLOVE CL.
SORREL CLOSE
LARKSPUR CL.
LAVENDER CL.
KNAPP RD.
HACKET LA.
CROSSWAYS RD.
CUMBRIA CL.
THE PADDOCKS
HAZEL CR.
WALNUT CL.
PINE CL.
THICKET WLK.
SYCAMORE DR.
CHESTNUT DR.
SPEY CL.
HAMBLE CL.
HAMBLE CLOSE
FROME CT.
COLN
ELLESMERE
COMBERMERE
HATCHMERE
MEDWAY CT.
SHANNON CT.
DERWENT CT.
WATERFORD CL.
TRENT DR.
SOLENT WY.
TAMAR CL.
BOCKENEM CL.
DOVEDALE
WHARFEDALE
RIBBLESDALE
WYE CT.
WINDRUSH CT.
LADDEN CT.
TWEED CL.
MEDINA CL.
CHERWELL CL.
ESKDALE
BROOKMEAD
HOPKIN CL.
ARMSTRONG CL.
PENTLAND AV.
ELIZABETH CL.
SPRINGFIELD
MEADOWSIDE
HOMEFIELD
Cabot Ho.
Sub.
The Bathings
D
E
F
1
2
3
4
5
9
365
91
190
89
64

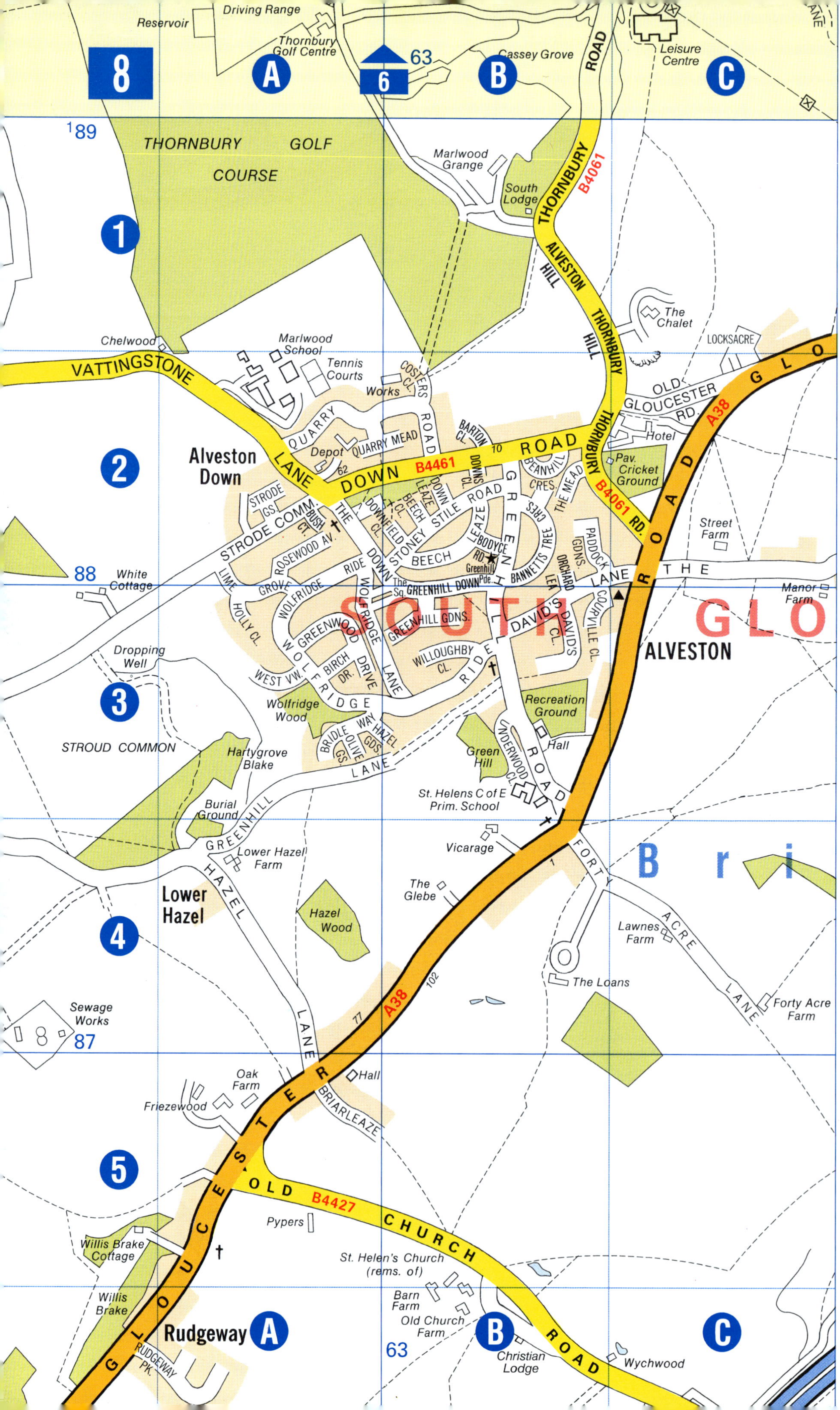
8
6
63
A
B
C
1
2
3
4
5
189
88
87
63
Reservoir
Driving Range
Thornbury Golf Centre
Cassey Grove
Leisure Centre
ROAD
THORNBURY GOLF COURSE
Marlwood Grange
South Lodge
THORNBURY
B4061
ALVESTON HILL
THORNBURY HILL
The Chalet
LOCKSACRE
Chelwood
Marlwood School
Tennis Courts
Works
COSTERS CL.
VATTINGSTONE LANE
QUARRY
Depot
QUARRY MEAD
ROAD
BARTON CL.
DOWN ROAD
B4461
OLD GLOUCESTER RD.
Hotel
Pav.
Cricket Ground
THORNBURY RD.
B4061
A38
GLO
Alveston Down
STRODE GS.
STRODE COMM.
BUSH CT.
THE DOWNFIELD CL.
BEECH CL.
DOWN LEAZE
DOWNS CL.
STONEY STILE ROAD
BEANHILL CRES.
THE MEAD
GREEN HILL
CRES.
PADDOCK GDNS.
Street Farm
ROSEWOOD AV.
RIDE
THE DOWN
BEECH
LEAZE
BODYCE RD.
Greenhill Pde.
BANNETTS TREE
ORCHARD LEA
THE LANE
White Cottage
LIME GROVE
WOLFRIDGE
The Sq.
GREENHILL DOWN
DAVID'S CL.
DAVID'S
COURVILLE CL.
Manor Farm
HOLLY CL.
GREENWOOD
WOLFRIDGE
GREENHILL GDNS.
SOUTH GLO
ALVESTON
Dropping Well
WOLFRIDGE
BIRCH DR.
DRIVE
LANE
WILLOUGHBY CL.
RIDE
WEST VW.
Wolfridge Wood
Recreation Ground
STROUD COMMON
Hartygrove Blake
BRIDLE WAY
OLIVE GS.
HAZEL GDS.
LANE
Green Hill
UNDERWOOD CL.
ROAD
Hall
Burial Ground
GREENHILL
St. Helens C of E Prim. School
Lower Hazel Farm
Vicarage
FORTY
Bri
Lower Hazel
HAZEL
The Glebe
Hazel Wood
Lawnes Farm
ACRE
The Loans
LANE
Forty Acre Farm
Sewage Works
A38
LANE
Oak Farm
Hall
Friezewood
GLOUCESTER ROAD
BRIARLEAZE
OLD CHURCH ROAD
B4427
Pypers
Willis Brake Cottage
St. Helen's Church (rems. of)
Barn Farm
Willis Brake
Old Church Farm
Rudgeway
RUDGEWAY PK.
Christian Lodge
Wychwood

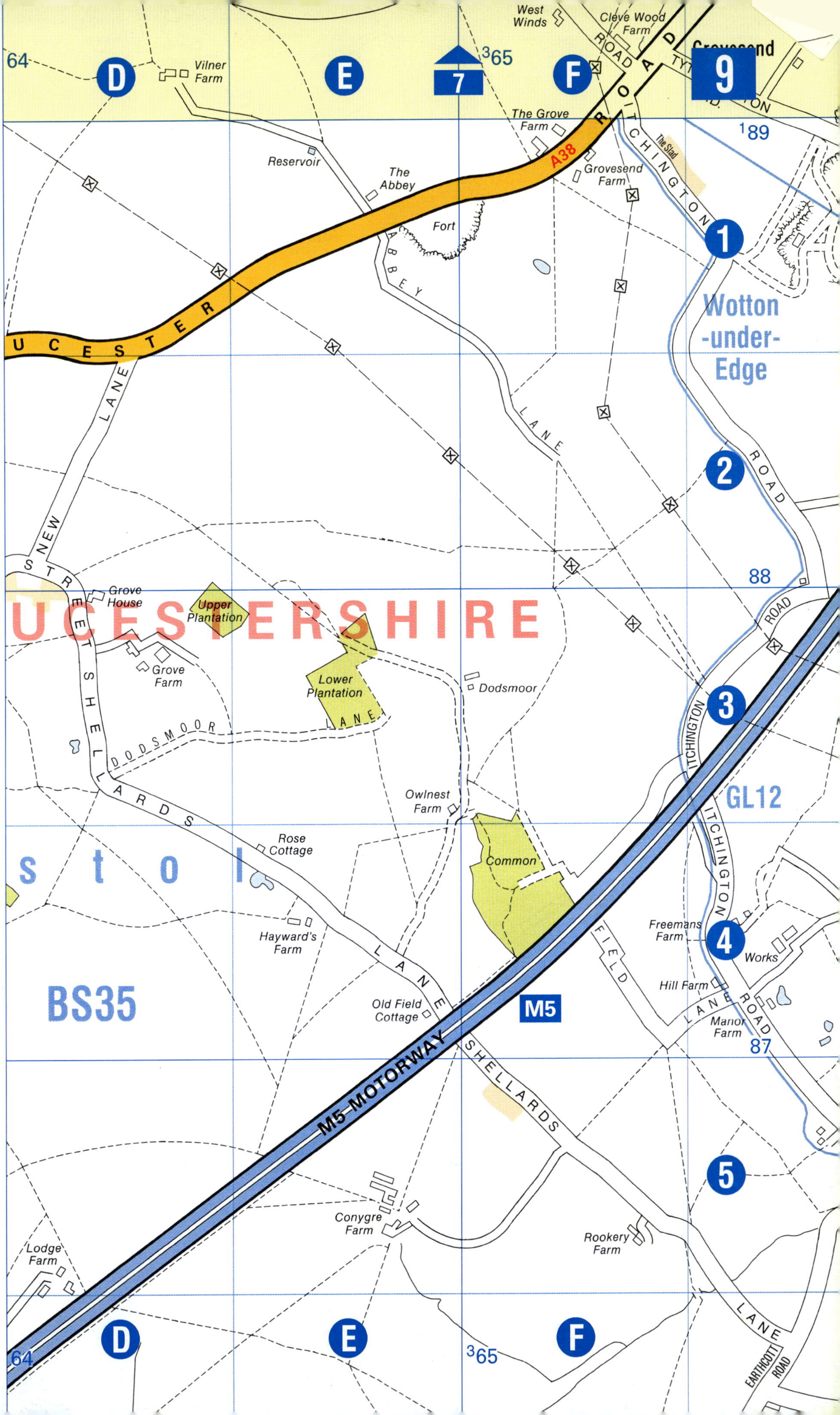

9
7
D
E
F
64
365
189
88
87
1
2
3
4
5
West Winds
Cleve Wood Farm
Grovesend
Vilner Farm
The Grove Farm
Reservoir
The Abbey
Grovesend Farm
The Slad
Fort
A38
GLOUCESTER ROAD
ABBEY LANE
TYTHERINGTON ROAD
ITCHINGTON ROAD
Wotton -under- Edge
NEW LANE
STREET
Grove House
Upper Plantation
GLOUCESTERSHIRE
Lower Plantation
Grove Farm
Dodsmoor
DODSMOOR LANE
SHELLARDS LANE
Owlnest Farm
Rose Cottage
Common
GL12
Bristol
Hayward's Farm
Freemans Farm
Works
Hill Farm
FIELD LANE
Manor Farm
BS35
Old Field Cottage
M5
M5 MOTORWAY
Conygre Farm
Rookery Farm
Lodge Farm
EARTHCOTT ROAD

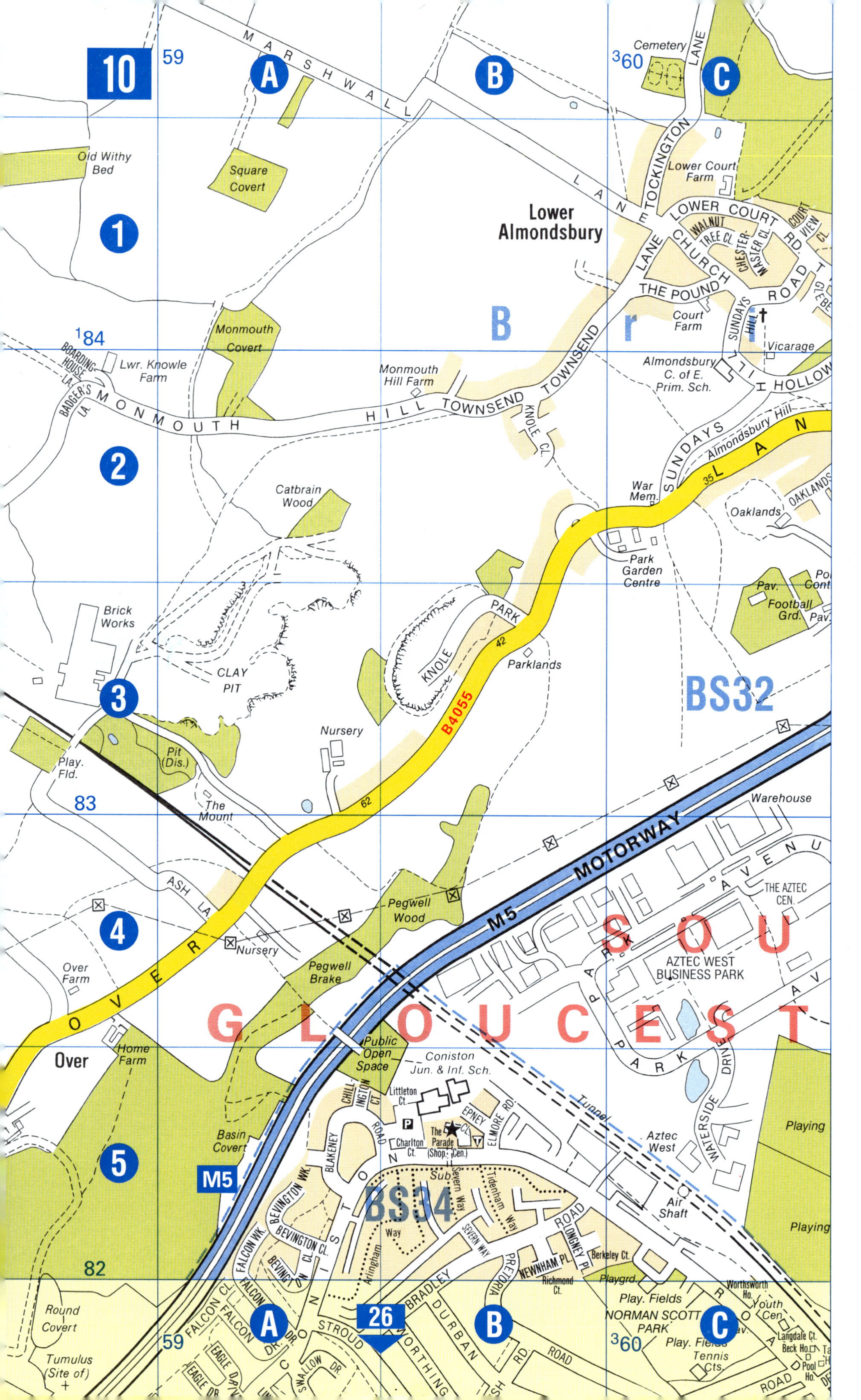

59
A
B
C
360
184
83
82
1
2
3
4
5
MARSHWALL LANE
Cemetery
LANE
Old Withy Bed
Square Covert
TOCKINGTON
Lower Court Farm
LOWER COURT RD.
COURT VIEW CL.
Lower Almondsbury
WALNUT TREE CL.
CHESTER-MASTER CL.
CHURCH ROAD
LANE
THE POUND
GLEBE
Court Farm
SUNDAYS HILL
Vicarage
Almondsbury C. of E. Prim. Sch.
HOLLOW
B
r
Monmouth Covert
BOARDING HOUSE LA.
Lwr. Knowle Farm
BADGER'S LA.
MONMOUTH HILL
Monmouth Hill Farm
TOWNSEND
TOWNSEND
KNOLE CL.
SUNDAYS
Almondsbury Hill
LANE
35
War Mem.
Oaklands
OAKLANDS
Catbrain Wood
Park Garden Centre
Pav.
Football Grd.
Pav.
Brick Works
PARK
KNOLE
42
Parklands
CLAY PIT
BS32
B4055
Nursery
Play. Fld.
Pit (Dis.)
The Mount
62
Warehouse
MOTORWAY
AVENUE
THE AZTEC CEN.
ASH LA.
Pegwell Wood
M5
SOU
Nursery
Over Farm
PARK
AZTEC WEST BUSINESS PARK
Pegwell Brake
OVER
GLOUCEST
AV
Over
Home Farm
Public Open Space
Coniston Jun. & Inf. Sch.
PARK
Tunnel
CHILLINGTON CT.
Littleton Ct.
ELMORE RD.
EPNEY CL.
DRIVE
WATERSIDE
Basin Covert
BLAKENEY
ROAD
Charlton Ct.
The Parade (Shop. Cen.)
Aztec West
Playing
M5
BEVINGTON WK.
Severn Way
Tidenham Way
Air Shaft
BS34
BEVINGTON CL.
Way
SEVERN WAY
ROAD
LONGNEY PL.
Playing
FALCON WK.
BEVINGTON CL.
Arlingham
PRETORIA
NEWNHAM PL.
Richmond Ct.
Berkeley Ct.
Playgrd.
Worthsworth Ho.
Round Covert
FALCON CL.
FALCON DR.
BRADLEY
Play. Fields
Youth Cen.
NORMAN SCOTT PARK
Av.
Tumulus (Site of)
EAGLE DRIVE
EAGLE DR.
CL.
SWALLOW DR.
STROUD
26
NORTHING
DURBAN
RD.
ROAD
Play. Fields
Tennis Cts.
Langdale Ct.
Beck Ho.
Pool Ho.
ROAD

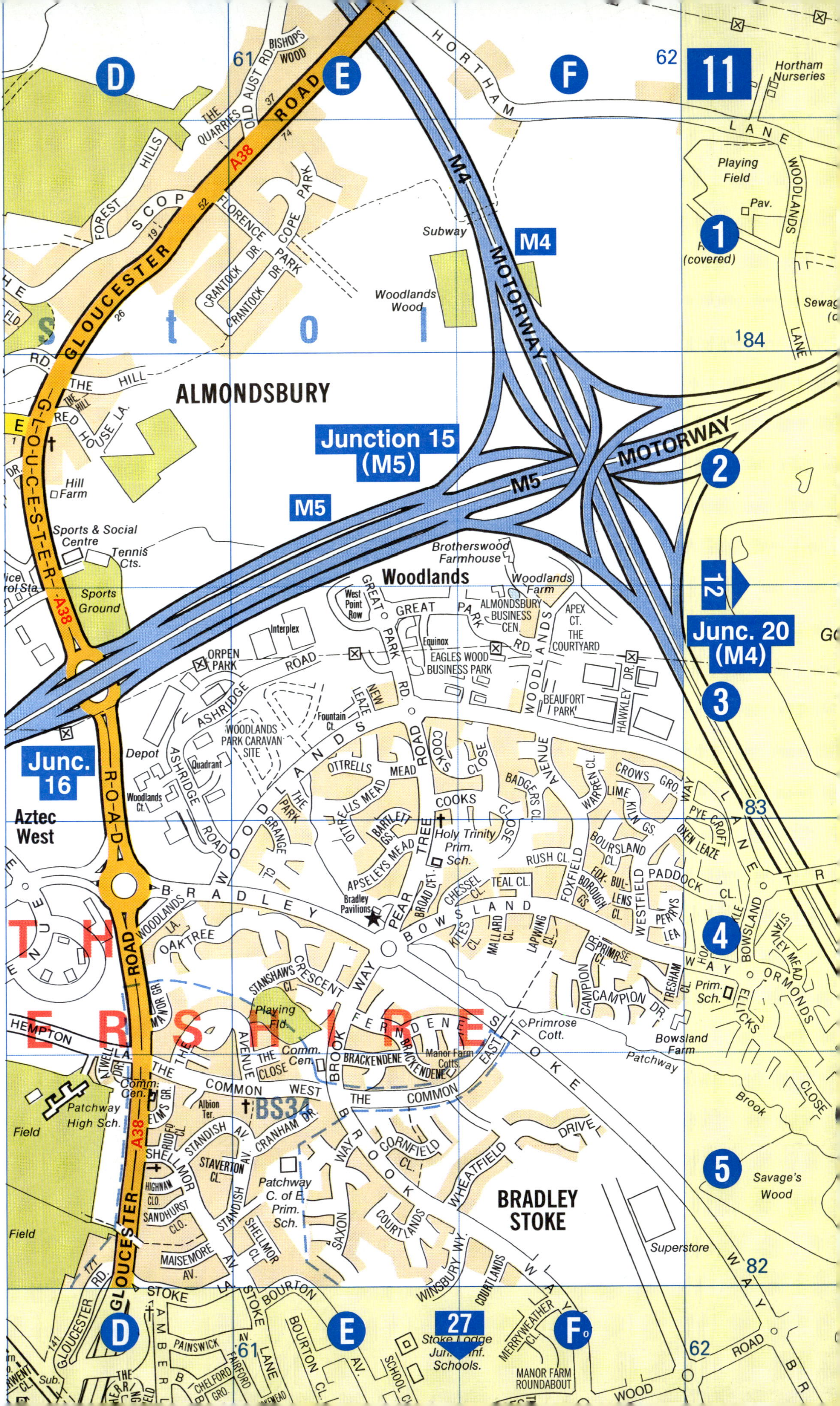
ALMONDSBURY
Junction 15 (M5)
Junc. 16
Junc. 20 (M4)
M4
M5
MOTORWAY
GLOUCESTER ROAD
A38
HORTHAM LANE
Hortham Nurseries
Playing Field
Pav.
(covered)
WOODLANDS LANE
Subway
Woodlands Wood
Woodlands
Brotherswood Farmhouse
Woodlands Farm
ALMONDSBURY BUSINESS CEN.
APEX CT.
THE COURTYARD
EAGLES WOOD BUSINESS PARK
Equinox
Interplex
ORPEN PARK
BEAUFORT PARK
WOODLANDS PARK CARAVAN SITE
Quadrant
Depot
Aztec West
Sports & Social Centre
Tennis Cts.
Sports Ground
Hill Farm
THE HILL
RED HOUSE LA.
FOREST HILLS
SCOP
THE QUARRIES
OLD AUST RD
BISHOPS WOOD
FLORENCE PARK
COPE PARK
CRANTOCK DR.
WOODLANDS ROAD
ASHRIDGE ROAD
GREAT PARK RD.
West Point Row
NEW LEAZE
Fountain Ct.
OTTRELLS MEAD
COOKS CLOSE
BADGERS CL.
AVENUE
WARREN CL.
CROWS GRO.
LIME KILN GS.
PYE CROFT
OXEN LEAZE
BOURSLAND CL.
PADDOCK CL.
Holy Trinity Prim. Sch.
APSELEYS MEAD
BARTLETT GS.
PEAR TREE ROAD
Bradley Pavilions
BRADLEY STOKE WAY
BOWSLAND WAY
CHESSEL CL.
TEAL CL.
RUSH CL.
FOXFIELD
BOROUGH GS.
WESTFIELD CL.
PERRYS LEA
KITES CL.
MALLARD CL.
LAPWING CL.
PRIMROSE CL.
CAMPION DR.
TRESHAM CL.
Prim. Sch.
ELLICKS CLOSE
STANLEY MEAD
ORMONDS CLOSE
Primrose Cott.
Bowsland Farm
Patchway Brook
Savage's Wood
OAKTREE
STANSHAWS CL.
CRESCENT
Playing Fld.
FERNDENE
BRACKENDENE
Manor Farm Cotts
Comm. Cem.
THE CLOSE
THE COMMON WEST
THE COMMON EAST
HEMPTON LA.
ATWELL DR.
Patchway High Sch.
Field
Albion Ter.
BS34
CRANHAM DR.
STANDISH AV.
STAVERTON CL.
HIGHNAM CLO.
SANDHURST CLO.
MAISEMORE AV.
SHELLMOR AV.
Patchway C. of E. Prim. Sch.
SAXON WAY
BROOK WAY
CORNFIELD CL.
COURTLANDS
WHEATFIELD DRIVE
BRADLEY STOKE
Superstore
WINSBURY WY.
STOKE LANE
BOURTON AV.
BOURTON CL.
PAINSWICK AV.
FAIRFORD
CHELFORD GRO.
SCHOOL CL.
Stoke Lodge Jun. & Inf. Schools.
MERRYWEATHER CL.
MANOR FARM ROUNDABOUT
WOOD ROAD
GLOUCESTER RD.
27
12
61
62
184
83
82
1
2
3
4
5
D
E
F

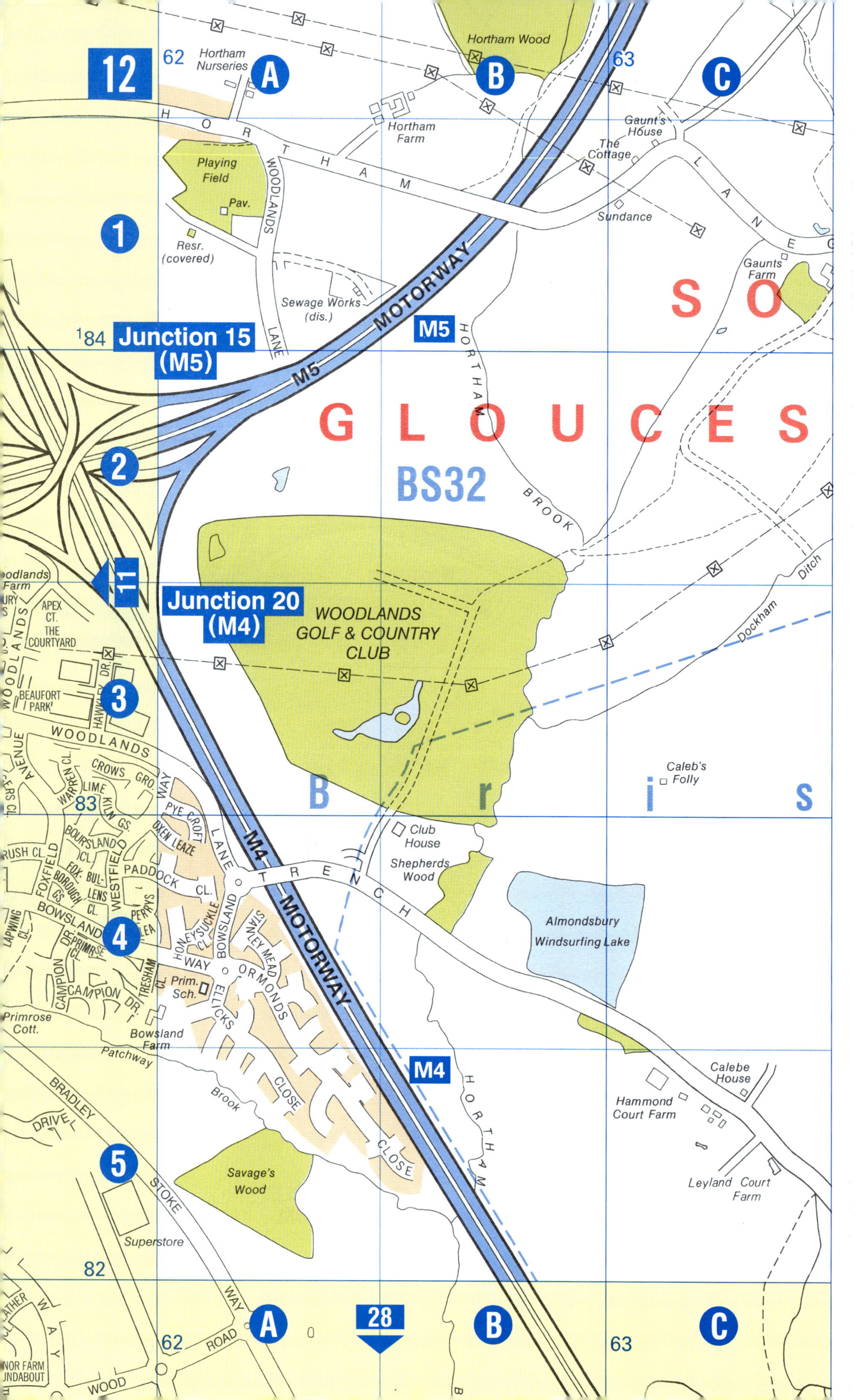
62
63
A
B
C
1
2
3
4
5
184
83
82
Hortham Nurseries
Hortham Wood
Hortham Farm
Gaunt's House
The Cottage
Sundance
Gaunts Farm
HORTHAM LANE
Playing Field
Pav.
Resr. (covered)
WOODLANDS LANE
Sewage Works (dis.)
M5 MOTORWAY
M5
Junction 15 (M5)
HORTHAM BROOK
GLOUCES
SO
BS32
11
Junction 20 (M4)
WOODLANDS GOLF & COUNTRY CLUB
Dockham Ditch
Caleb's Folly
Bris
Woodlands Farm
APEX CT.
THE COURTYARD
BEAUFORT PARK
HAWKLEY DR.
WOODLANDS
AVENUE
WARREN CL.
CROWS GRO.
LIME KILN GS.
BOURSLAND CL.
PYE CROFT
OXEN LEAZE
LANE
M4
TRENCH
Club House
Shepherds Wood
Almondsbury Windsurfing Lake
RUSH CL.
FOXFIELD
FOX BOROUGH GS.
BULLENS CL.
WESTFIELD
PADDOCK CL.
PERRYS LEA
HONEYSUCKLE CL.
BOWSLAND
STANLEY MEAD
LAPWING CL.
BOWSLAND DR.
PRIMROSE CL.
CAMPION CAMPION DR.
TRESHAM CL.
WAY
Prim. Sch.
ORMONDS
ELLICKS
M4 MOTORWAY
Primrose Cott.
Bowsland Farm
Patchway Brook
CLOSE
M4
HORTHAM
Calebe House
Hammond Court Farm
Leyland Court Farm
BRADLEY DRIVE
STOKE
Savage's Wood
Superstore
WAY
ROAD
WOOD
28
MANOR FARM ROUNDABOUT

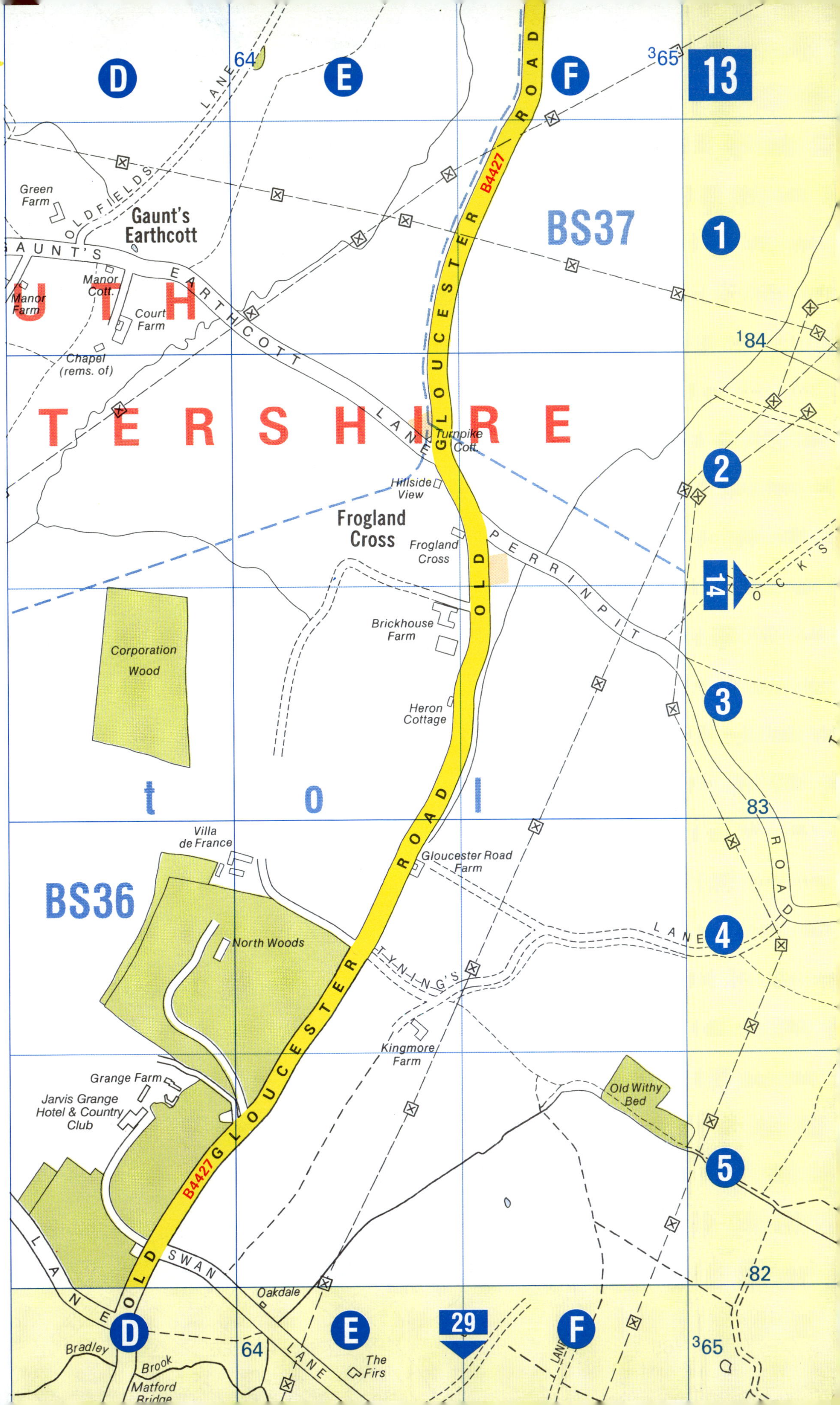

13
D
E
F
64
365
184
83
82
LANE
OLDFIELDS
Green Farm
Gaunt's Earthcott
GAUNT'S EARTHCOTT LANE
Manor Cott.
Manor Farm
Court Farm
Chapel (rems. of)
OLD GLOUCESTER ROAD
B4427
BS37
1
2
3
4
5
Turnpike Cott.
Hillside View
Frogland Cross
Frogland Cross
PERRINPIT
14
Brickhouse Farm
Heron Cottage
Corporation Wood
Villa de France
BS36
Gloucester Road Farm
North Woods
TYNING'S LANE
ROAD
Kingmore Farm
Old Withy Bed
Grange Farm
Jarvis Grange Hotel & Country Club
SWAN LANE
Oakdale
29
Bradley Brook
Matford Bridge
The Firs

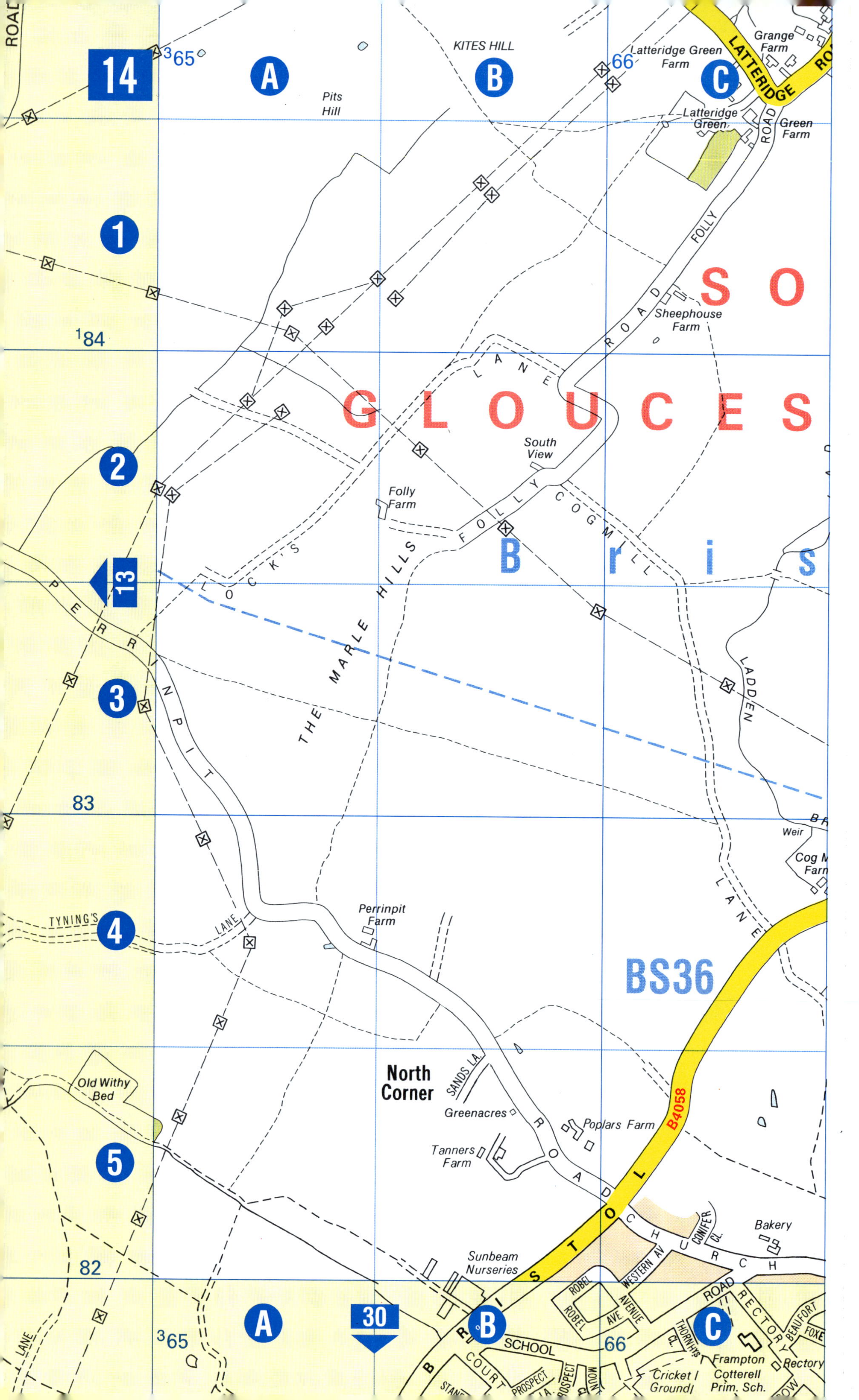

14
13
30
A
B
C
1
2
3
4
5
365
66
184
83
82
KITES HILL
Pits Hill
Latteridge Green Farm
Grange Farm
LATTERIDGE ROAD
Latteridge Green
Green Farm
ROAD
FOLLY ROAD
Sheephouse Farm
SO
GLOUCES
LANE
South View
Folly Farm
FOLLY
COGMILL
LOCK'S
THE MARLE HILLS
Bris
PERRINPIT
LADDEN LANE
Weir
Cog M Farm
TYNING'S
LANE
Perrinpit Farm
BS36
North Corner
SANDS LA.
Greenacres
Poplars Farm
Tanners Farm
ROAD
B4058
BRISTOL
Old Withy Bed
Sunbeam Nurseries
CHURCH
CONIFER CL.
Bakery
WESTERN AV.
ROBEL AVENUE
ROBEL AVE.
SCHOOL
COURT
PROSPECT LA.
RECTORY
BEAUFORT
FOXE
THORNHYS CL.
Frampton Cotterell Prim. Sch.
Rectory
Cricket Ground

15
D
E
F
67
68
Home Farm
Lower Farm
Latteridge
LATTERIDGE B4059
Laddon Bows Bri.
Crossing Cottage
NORTHMEAD LANE
ROAD
BROOK
Acton Court
LATTERIDGE ROAD
B4059
Acton Lodge
184
UTH
TERSHIRE
t o l
B4058
The Green
LATTERIDGE RD.
PARK ST.
Meadow Side
HIGH STREET
Iron Acton
Hill House
Lamb Leaze
WOTTON RD.
Iron Acton C of E Prim. Sch.
16
Sports Ground
HOLLY
Cemy.
CHILWOOD CL.
ALGARS DR.
Laddenside Farm
Elm Farm
Bridge Farm
BRISTOL ROAD
BS37
ROAD
FROME
Station House
STATION ROAD
Algars Manor
Brake Farm
B4058
RIVER
83
Chill Wood
HOVER'S
END
Mill
1
2
3
4
5
Tubbs Bottom
FRAMPTON
ROAD
MAYS
LANE END
Mayshill
Weir
MILL LANE
Frampton End
82
Mayshill Farm
Church Bri.
Works
CHURCH CL.
WINCHCOMBE RD.
BROOKSIDE DRIVE
MEAD
WAY
31
Framptonend Farm
Oakleigh
FRAMPTON

68
A
B
C
69
CHAINGATE LA.
Chaingate House
Jasemin Cottage
North Barn Cottage
Backfield House
Backfield Farm
Two Pools Farm
Greenlane Farm
Sunnyside Farm
DYER'S LANE
ROAD
LATTERIDGE ROAD
1
B4058
WOTTON ROAD
Acton Lodge
Splott House
184
Hillview
Rose Cottage
MISSION
Holbr Cott
Hill House
Lamb Leaze
The Green
LATTERIDGE RD.
2
Iron Acton
PARK ST.
Meadow Side
HIGH STREET
15
Hollans Holme
SOUTH GLOU
Bris
WOTTON RD.
Iron Acton C of E Prim. Sch.
Isle of Rye
Virginia Cottage
YATE ROAD
HOLLY HILL
Holly Hill Farm
Poplar Farm
Park View
Cemy.
NIBLEY LANE
Pool Farm
LANE
Bradf Far
3
CHILWOOD CL.
ALGARS DR.
Berkeley Cottage
B4059
DYER'S ROAD
Onepool Farm
WADE RD.
Algars Manor
Robins Wood
Lavenham Farm
ARMS
YATE R.
WADE R.
STOVER ROAD
LODGE RD.
83
BRIDGE RD.
BRIDGE ROAD
Chill Wood
East View
The Laurels
ROAD
4
Stov Brid
Weir
HOPE
Mill Race
FROME
Mill
Tubbs Bottom
RIVER
Nibley
MAYS HILL
BS36
5
A432
BADMINTON
Nibley Farm
NIBLEY
Mayshill
Chestnut Farm
Cemy.
82
Mayshill Farm
Far End
Depot
32
Sayscourt Bungalow

Engine Common
Goose Green
Stover
Yate
YATE
BS37
WESTERLEIGH COMMON
GREAT WESTERN BUSINESS PARK
NORTHAVON BUSINESS CENTRE
STOVER TRADING ESTATE
BADMINTON ROAD TRADING ESTATE
BEECHES IND. EST.
Sports Ground
Playing Fields
Tennis Courts
Pavilion
Brinsham Green Sch.
North Road Prim. Sch.
Civic Ammenity Site
Cranleigh Court Inf. Sch.
Frome Bank Jun. Sch.
King Edmund's School
Yate Leisure Centre
Kingsgate Inf. Sch.
Stone Mill
Goosegreen Farm
Crowther's Farm
Bradford House
Craigaffie
Orchard View
Rose Cottage
ENGINE COMMON LANE
WATERY LANE
NORTH ROAD
BROAD LANE
BROAD GREEN
GOOSE GREEN WAY
B4059
A432
STATION ROAD
BADMINTON ROAD
LODGE ROAD
RANDOLPH AVENUE
LONG CROFT
CRANLEIGH COURT ROAD
GREEN WAYS
HALIFAX ROAD
MOUNTBATTEN CL.
CELESTINE ROAD
BLENHEIM DRI.
RIVER ROAD
WESTERLEIGH ROAD
STANSHAWES DRIVE
BROOKTHORPE
Superstore
Factory
Works
Warehouse
Depot
Playing Field
Bowling Green
Comm. Cen.
Liby.
18
33

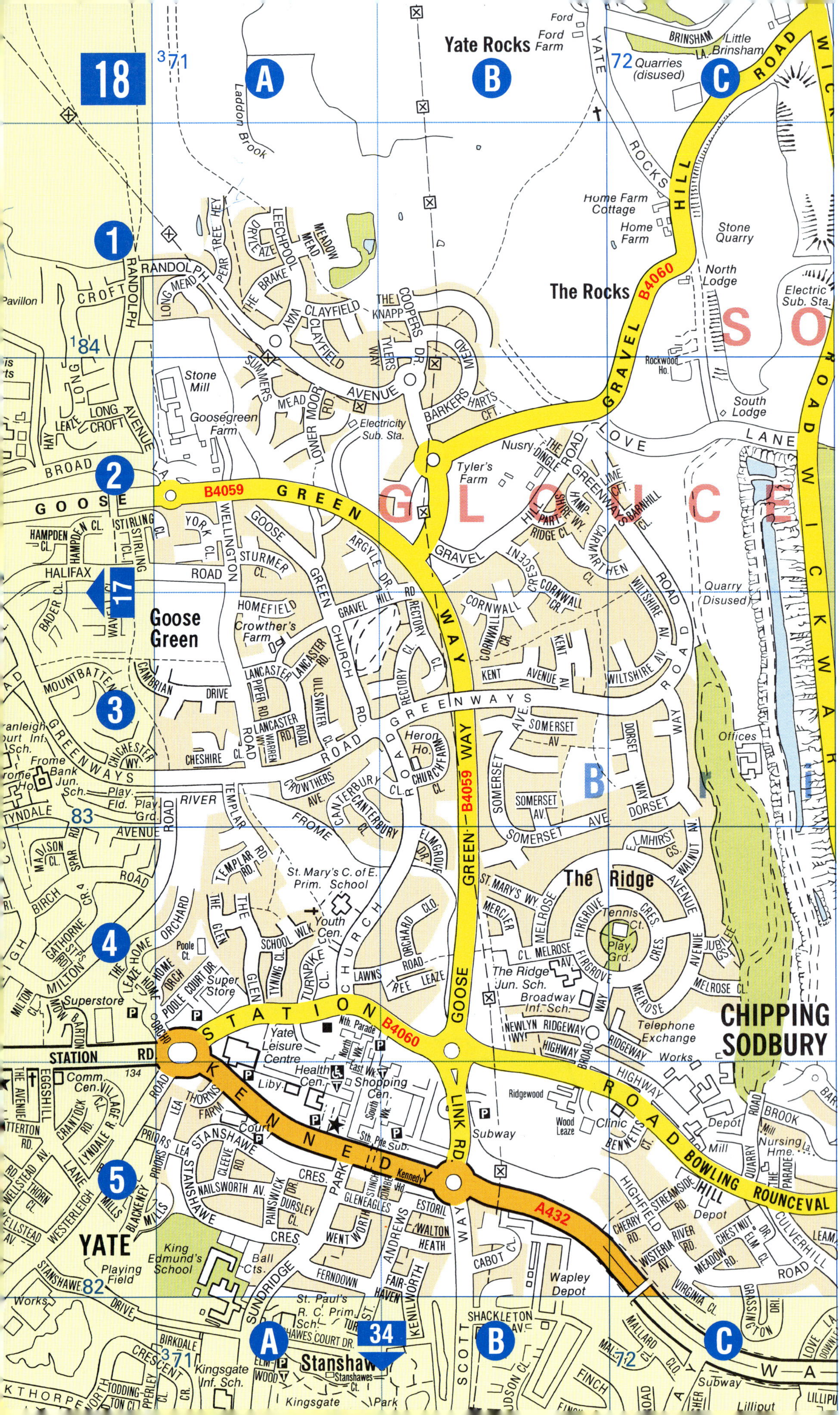
Yate Rocks
Ford
Ford Farm
YATE
Quarries (disused)
BRINSHAM LA.
Little Brinsham
HILL ROAD
WICKWAR
ROCKS
Ladden Brook
Home Farm Cottage
Home Farm
Stone Quarry
North Lodge
The Rocks
B4060
GRAVEL
Electric Sub. Sta.
RANDOLPH
CROFT
Pavilion
LONG MEAD
PEAR TREE HEY
DRYLEAZE
LEECHPOOL WAY
MEADOW MEAD
THE BRAKE
CLAYFIELD
THE KNAPP
COOPERS DR.
TYLERS WAY
MEAD
Rockwood Ho.
South Lodge
SUMMERS MEAD
LOWER MOOR RD.
AVENUE
Electricity Sub. Sta.
BARKERS MEAD
HARTS CFT.
Stone Mill
Goosegreen Farm
LONG CROFT
HAY LEAZE
AVENUE
BROAD
LOVE LANE
Nusry
THE DINGLE
Tyler's Farm
GOOSE
B4059 GREEN
HAMPDEN CL.
STIRLING CL.
YORK CL.
WELLINGTON
GOOSE GREEN
STURMER CL.
ARGYLE DR.
HALIFAX ROAD
GRAVEL HILL RD
RECTORY CL.
GRAVEL HILL CRESCENT
GREENWAYS
RIDGE CL.
CARMARTHEN CL.
BARNHILL CL.
LIME CFT.
SHIRE WY.
HAMP.
CORNWALL CR.
CORNWALL
WILTSHIRE AV.
Quarry Disused
BADER CL.
WAVELL CL.
Goose Green
HOMEFIELD
Crowther's Farm
CHURCH RD.
WAY
KENT AVENUE
17
MOUNTBATTEN
CAMBRIAN DRIVE
LANCASTER RD.
PIPER RD.
ULLSWATER CL.
GREENWAYS ROAD
SOMERSET AVE
Offices
CHICHESTER WY.
Frome Bank Jun. Sch.
Play Fld.
Play Grd.
CHESHIRE CL.
LANCASTER RD.
WARREN WY.
Heron Ho.
CHURCHFARM CL.
B4059
DORSET WAY
TYNDALE
83
AVENUE
RIVER
TEMPLAR
CROWTHERS AVE.
CANTERBURY CL.
FROME
SOMERSET AV.
DORSET
MADISON CL.
SPAR RD
ROAD
TEMPLAR RD.
ELMGROVE DR.
ELMHIRST GS.
WALNUT W.
BIRCH
St. Mary's C. of E. Prim. School
GREEN
The Ridge
ST. MARY'S WY.
MERCIER
MELROSE
FIRGROVE
Tennis Ct.
AVENUE
Play Grd.
CRES.
GATHORNE CR.
ORCHARD
THE GLEN
Youth Cen.
ORCHARD CLO.
JUBILEE GS.
Poole Ct.
SCHOOL WLK
TYNING CL.
TURNPIKE CL.
LAWNS ROAD
TREE LEAZE
GOOSE
The Ridge Jun. Sch.
Broadway Inf. Sch.
MELROSE CL.
CHIPPING SODBURY
MILTON
HOME ORCH.
POOLE COURT DR.
Super Store
Superstore
BARTON
GLEN
STATION
Nth. Parade
B4060
NEWLYN WY.
RIDGEWAY
HIGHWAY
BROADWAY
Telephone Exchange
Works
STATION RD
Yate Leisure Centre
Health Cen.
East Wk.
Shopping Cen.
North Wk.
134
Comm. Cen.
VILLAGE
EGGSHILL
THE AVENUE
Liby.
THORNS FARM
LEA
KENNEDY
South Wk.
LINK RD.
Ridgewood
Subway
Wood Leaze
Clinic
BENNETTS CT.
ROAD
BROOK
Depot
Mill
QUARRY
Nursing Hme.
THE PARADE
CRANTOCK
LYNDALE RD.
Court
STANSHAWE
PRIORS LEA
CLEEVE RD.
Sth. Pde Sub.
BOWLING HILL
ROUNCEVAL
5
Kennedy Wd.
STANSHAWE
NAILSWORTH AV.
CRES.
PARK
GLENEAGLES
ESTORIL
HIGHFIELD
STREAMSIDE RD.
Depot
WELLSTEAD AV.
THORN CL.
WESTERLEIGH
MILLS
BLACKENEY
PAINSWICK DR.
DURSLEY CL.
WENTWORTH
ANDREWS
WALTON HEATH
A432
CHERRY RD.
WISTERIA AV.
RIVER RD.
CHESTNUT DR.
ELM CL.
CULVERHILL ROAD
YATE
King Edmund's School
Ball Cts.
Playing Field
CRES.
SUNDRIDGE
FERNDOWN
FAIR HAVEN
KENILWORTH
CABOT CL.
Wapley Depot
MEADOW RD.
VIRGINIA CL.
GRASSINGTON DRI.
STANSHAWE 82
Works
DRIVE
St. Paul's R. C. Prim. Sch.
TURNBERRY
STANSHAWES COURT DR.
34
SHACKLETON AV.
SCOTT
MALLARD CL.
CLOY
LOVE LA
DOWNLEAZE
BIRKDALE
CRESCENT
371
Kingsgate Inf. Sch.
ELM PK.
WOOD
Stanshawe
Stanshawes Ct.
Kingsgate
Park
HUDSON CL.
FINCH
MALLARD 72
Subway
Lilliput
LILLIPUT
TODDING TON CL
PERLEY
KTHORPE
A
B
C
1
2
3
4
371
72
184

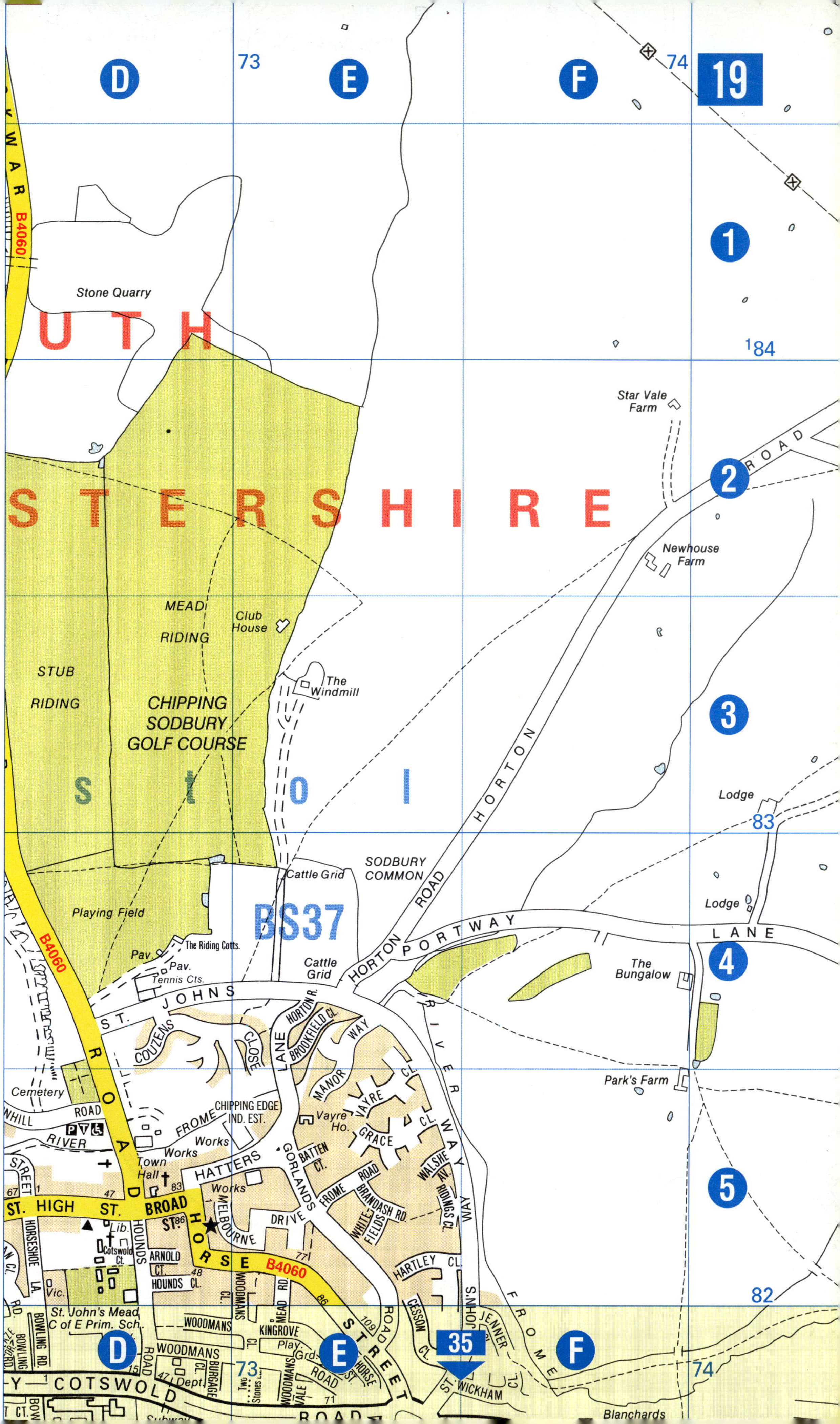
D
E
F
73
74
1
2
3
4
5
184
83
82
B4060
Stone Quarry
UTH
STERSHIRE
Star Vale Farm
ROAD
Newhouse Farm
MEAD RIDING
Club House
STUB RIDING
CHIPPING SODBURY GOLF COURSE
The Windmill
HORTON
Lodge
SODBURY COMMON
Cattle Grid
BS37
Playing Field
Pav.
The Riding Cotts.
Tennis Cts.
HORTON ROAD
PORTWAY
LANE
The Bungalow
ST. JOHNS
COUZENS
CLOSE
LANE
HORTON R.
BROOKFIELD CL.
WAY
MANOR
VAYRE
CL.
RIVER
WAY
Park's Farm
Cemetery
ROAD
RIVER
FROME
CHIPPING EDGE IND. EST.
Vayre Ho.
GRACE
CL.
Works
Town Hall
HATTERS
GORLANDS
BATTEN CT.
WALSHE AV.
STREET
ST. HIGH ST.
BROAD ST.
HORSE
Lib.
Cotswold Ct.
HOUNDS
ARNOLD CT.
HOUNDS CL.
MELBOURNE
DRIVE
FROME
ROAD
BRANDASH RD.
WHITE FIELDS
RIDINGS CL.
HARTLEY CL.
Vic.
HORSESHOE LA.
St. John's Mead C of E Prim. Sch.
WOODMANS
KINGROVE
MEAD RD.
Play. Grd.
E
STREET
ROAD
CESSON CL.
ST. JOHN'S
JENNER
FROME
35
BOWLING RD.
WOODMANS
ROAD
BURGAGE
Dept.
Two Stones La.
WOODMANS VALE
ROAD
HORSE ST.
ST. WICKHAM CL.
COTSWOLD
ROAD
Blanchards
Subway

A
B
C
54
355
1
2
3
4
5
86
185
84
Northwick Warth
Hotel
The Glen
The Pill
Rifle Range
Sewage Works
Severn Lodge Farm
New Passage
Bland's Cottages
REDWICK ROAD
B4055
Redwick
Junction 22
Woodbine Cottages
Nursery
M4
M4 MOTORWAY
B4064
LANE
GREEN
Bristol
SHAFT ROAD
Salthouse Farm
SALTHOUSE FARM CARAVAN PARK
RIVER SEVERN
AVENUE
ROAD
BEACH
OSBORNE RD.
BEACH
BEACH B4064
COVER ROAD
LITTLE GREEN LANE
GORSE
M49 MOTORWAY
BS35
CHURCH ROAD
M49
ROAD
RUSTIC PARK CARAVAN SITE
SOUTH
CHURCH
BEACH RD.
STATION ROAD
RIVERSIDE PK.
STRIDE CL.
ABLETON
Playing Field
Pav.
SEVERN BEACH
Severn Beach
RD.
School
Ableton Ct.
GLOUCESTERSHIRE
ALBERT
VICTORIA CR.
SCHOOL WY.
DENNY ISLE DR.
PROSPECT RD.
ABBOTT RD.
SEVERNWOOD GDS.
A403
SEVERN ROAD
Victoria
Grove Farm
Westholme
LANE
A
B
C
54
355

21
D
352
E
F
53
Stup Pill
SEVERN RD.
82
Fuel Storage Depot
Stuppill Gout
DOCKS INDUSTRIAL ESTATE
1
MOUTH OF THE SEVERN
Warehouses
ROAD
BANK
WORTHY
GREENSPLOTT
ROAD
2
CHITTERING RD.
WASH
LANE
A403
Tanks
Fuel Storage Depot
Mitchell's Gout
Transport Depot
22
81
Rockingham Farm
Warehouse
Hallen Marsh Junction
LAWRENCE
3
Holes Mouth
Tanks
BRISTOL
SMOKE
WESTON
BURCOTT
ROAD
Rockingham Works
Madam Farm
Kites
IRONCHURCH ROAD
DEAN ROAD
Bristol
4
HUMBER WAY
ROAD
SEVERNSIDE TRADING ESTATE
Reservoir
180
BS11
A403
Fuel Depot
KINGS WESTON
Mere
5
ST. ANDREW'S ROAD
St. Andrew's Road
Chemicals Plant
Bank
Piers
D
E
37
F
352
Smelting Works
53
LANE
Rhine

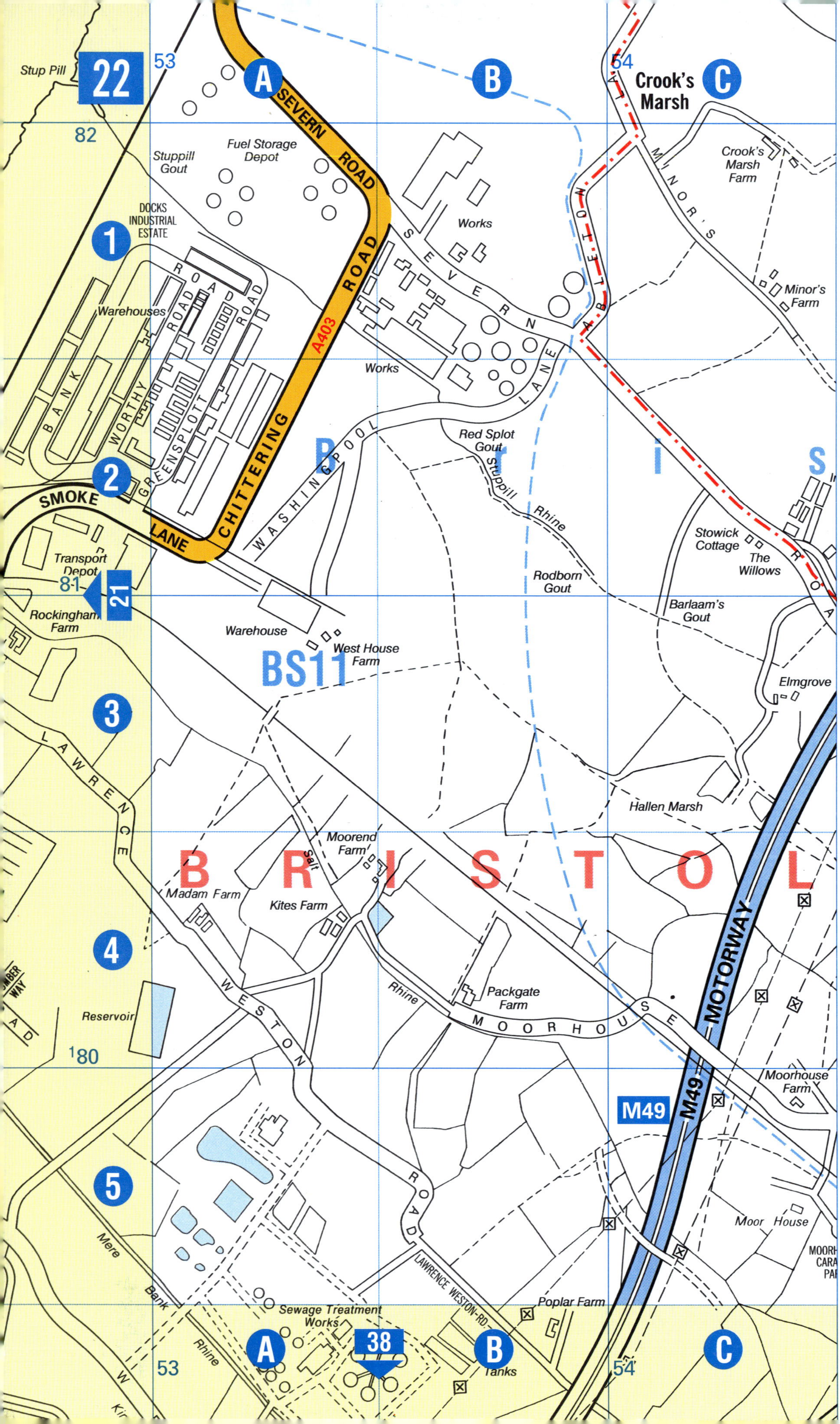
22
Stup Pill
53
82
A
B
C
54
Crook's Marsh
SEVERN ROAD
Fuel Storage Depot
Stuppill Gout
DOCKS INDUSTRIAL ESTATE
1
Works
Crook's Marsh Farm
MINOR'S
Minor's Farm
ROAD
Warehouses
GREENSPLOTT ROAD
A403
CHITTERING ROAD
BANK
WORTHY
SEVERN
ABLETON LANE
LANE
Works
Red Splot Gout
Stuppill
Rhine
WASHINGPOOL
2
SMOKE LANE
Transport Depot
81
21
Rockingham Farm
Warehouse
West House Farm
BS11
Stowick Cottage
The Willows
ROAD
Rodborn Gout
Barlaam's Gout
Elmgrove
3
LAWRENCE
Hallen Marsh
Moorend Farm
Salt
B R I S T O L
Bristol
Madam Farm
Kites Farm
4
MOTORWAY
Packgate Farm
Rhine
MOORHOUSE
WESTON
Reservoir
180
Moorhouse Farm
M49
M49
5
ROAD
Mere
Moor House
Bank
LAWRENCE WESTON RD.
Sewage Treatment Works
Poplar Farm
Rhine
A
38
B
C
53
54
Tanks

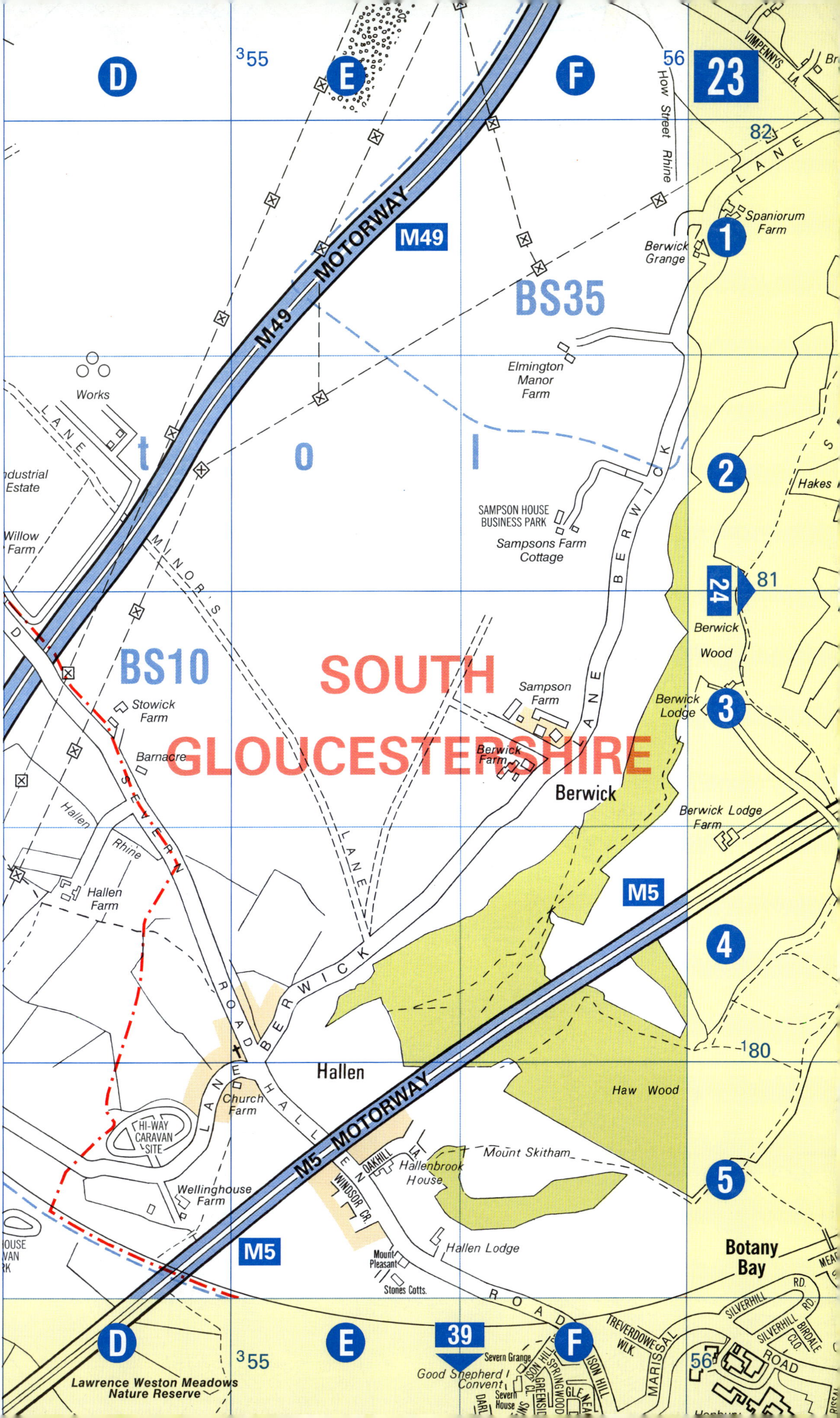

D
E
F
355
56
VIMPENNYS LA.
82
LANE
How Street Rhine
Spaniorum Farm
Berwick Grange
1
M49
M49 MOTORWAY
BS35
Elmington Manor Farm
Works
LANE
t
o
l
Industrial Estate
Willow Farm
2
Hakes
SAMPSON HOUSE BUSINESS PARK
Sampsons Farm Cottage
BERWICK
MINOR'S
24
81
Berwick Wood
BS10
SOUTH GLOUCESTERSHIRE
Stowick Farm
Sampson Farm
LANE
Berwick Lodge
3
Barnacre
Berwick Farm
Berwick
SEVERN
Hallen Rhine
Berwick Lodge Farm
LANE
Hallen Farm
M5
4
BERWICK
ROAD
180
Hallen
Haw Wood
Church Farm
HI-WAY CARAVAN SITE
LANE
HALLEN
M5 MOTORWAY
OAKHILL
Mount Skitham
Hallenbrook House
WINDSOR CR.
5
Wellinghouse Farm
Botany Bay
M5
Hallen Lodge
Mount Pleasant
Stones Cotts.
ROAD
SILVERHILL RD.
BIRDALE CLO.
39
TREVERDOWE WLK.
MARISSAL
ROAD
Severn Grange
Good Shepherd Convent
Severn House
SPRINGWOOD
Lawrence Weston Meadows Nature Reserve
D
E
F
355
56

Brookland Villa
VIMPENNYS LANE
Lyde Brook
Ford
Church Farm
CHURCH RD.
FARM LANE
Rectory
Compton Greenfield
Bishops Farm
BOWSTREET LANE
Spaniorum Farm
Berwick Grange
BERWICK LANE
Compton House
Street Rhine
BS35
Manor Farm
Spaniorum Hill
Briery Brake
The Lyde
Hakes Brake
Hakes Hill Wood
Bangley Wood
Hollyhill Wood
HOLLYWOOD LANE
Hollywood Tower
Tower
Chandler's Brake
Bristol
Berwick Wood
Langett
South Hill Wood
Camp
Mayfield
Cribbs Lodge
Compton Lodge
BS10
Berwick Lodge
M5
M5 MOTORWAY
Catbrain
CRIBBS CAUSEWAY CENTRE (IND. EST.)
A4018
Berwick
Berwick Lodge Farm
Elmsleigh
Cribbs Causeway
Highdene School (The Laurels)
Brent Knoll
Cribbs Farm
SOUTH GLOU
Kingsheath
Deorham
Rugby Football Ground
Sports Ground
CRIBBS
PASSAGE ROAD
THE CLOSE
Weir
BERWICK DRIVE
North Hill Cottage
Rugby Football Grd.
(Course of Roman Road)
CRIBBS CAUSEWAY
WYCK BECK ROAD
Haw Wood
B4055
STATION RD.
GIFFORD RD.
TORMARTON ROAD
WOLFRIDGE GDNS.
SWANMOOR
TRANMERE AVE
BRISTOL
MEADOWLAND RD.
NETTLESTONE CLO.
GREENLANDS WY.
CRANDELL CLO.
LOVERINGE CLO.
BICKERTON CLO.
FITCHETT WLK.
PASSAGE RD.
SLYMBRIDGE AV.
TRANMERE GRO.
CHARLTON
SILVERHILL RD.
Botany Bay
TRATMAN WALK
TREVERDOWE WLK.
MARISSAL ROAD
COTRITH GRO.
MODECOMBE GRO.
DOLMAN CLO.
LOWLIS CLO.
VAUGHAN CL.
CHAMPNEYS AV.
MACHIN CL.
LYPPINCOURT
STOULTON GRO.
ROSE ACRE
356
57
82
81
180
A
B
C
1
2
3
4
5

23
40

Easter
Compton
B4055
ROAD
OVER
B4055
Over
Brook
LANE
Fish Pond
BS32
Round
Covert
Tumulus
(Site of)
Lodge
Oak Covert
BLACKHORSE
HILL
Blackhorse Wood
Webb's
Brake
M5
St. Swithin's
Chapel
(Remains of)
St. Swithin's
Farm
M5 MOTORWAY
OLYMPUS
BRITANNIA
ROAD
Hypermarket
BS34
PATCHWAY TRADING EST.
PATCHWAY
TRADING
ESTATE
Warehouses
FALCON
FALCON DR.
EAGLE DRIVE
CONISTON
LINNET CL.
MARTIN CL.
BEVINGTON
Home
Farm
B4055
CRIBBS CAUSEWAY
Lodge
Junction
17
HIGHWOOD
ROAD
CENTAURUS
ROAD
PEGASUS
ROAD
Reservoir
(Covered)
JUPITER RD.
CONCORDE
ROAD
CAUSEWAY
MERLIN
Trym
Warehouse
Warehouse
WAYFARER
RD.
LINK RD. WEST
ROAD
CRIBBS RETAIL
PARK
CRIBBS CAUSEWAY
SHOPPING CENTRE
(Proposed)
HIGHWOOD
ROAD
LYSANDER
CATBRAIN
Dove
Farm
Henbury
HILL
FILTON AIRFIELD
CESTERSHIRE
58
59
82
81
180
26
PAYNES
ORCHARD
CARAVAN
PARK
CHARLTON
COMMON
Charlton
Common
Sports
Ground
ROAD
WEST WAY
Tunnel
CHARLTON
GDS.
CHARLTON
PENSFIELD PARK
TERESLAKE GREEN
MEAD
PARKERS CL.
BADGERS DR.
Charlton Mead Ct.
HILL
Due South
FISHPOOL
LANE
Kensington
Dairy Farm
BINDON DR.
DRIVE
307
CHARLTON
CHARLTON PL.
MATFORD CL.
NORTHWOODS WLK.
DRIVE
STREAM CLO.
Golf Course
Cottages
FILTON
GOLF COURSE
MEAD DR.
OKEBOURNE
CLO.
ROAD
TREVISA
GRO.
RD.
DORESTER
CLO.
BRACEWELL
GDNS.
BENSAUNT GRO.
TURNBRIDGE
RD.
REDSHELF
WALK
CHAKESHILL
CHAKESHILL CL.
CHARLTON
ROCKSTOWES WY.
WYECROFT CL.
BRIARSIDE
41
Brentry
Primary
School
Oakhill
Sch.
OKEBOURNE
OKEBOURNE
LANE
GILSLAKE AV.
ST. JOSEPH'S
BREWERTON
CR.
171

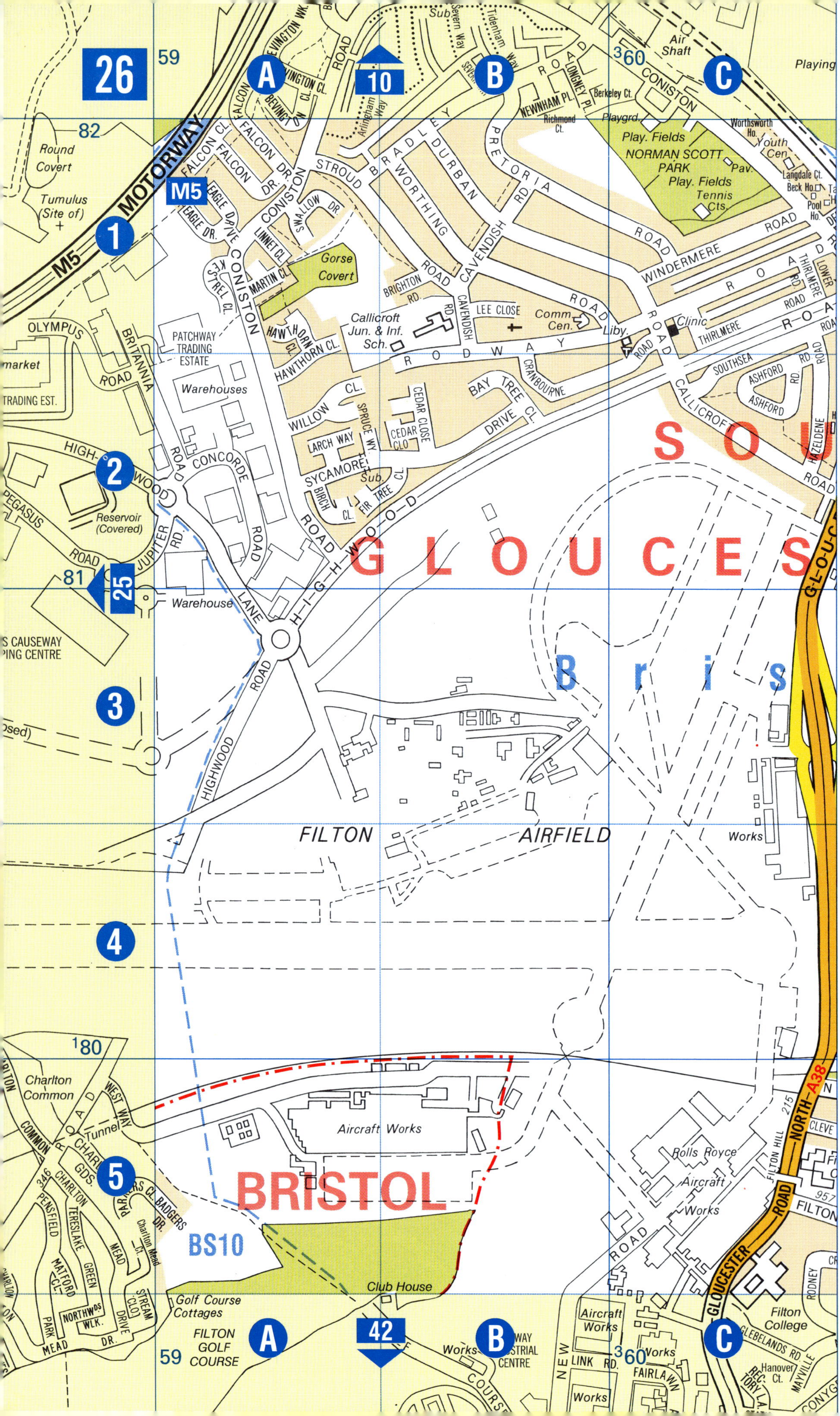
10
42
25
59
360
82
81
180
A
B
C
1
2
3
4
5
M5 MOTORWAY
M5
Round Covert
Tumulus (Site of)
OLYMPUS ROAD
BRITANNIA
TRADING EST.
HIGHWOOD ROAD
PEGASUS ROAD
JUPITER RD.
Reservoir (Covered)
Warehouse
Warehouses
PATCHWAY TRADING ESTATE
CONCORDE ROAD
CONISTON ROAD
FALCON CL.
FALCON DR.
EAGLE DRIVE
EAGLE DR.
KESTREL CL.
LINNET CL.
MARTIN CL.
SWALLOW DR.
Gorse Covert
HAWTHORN CL.
STROUD ROAD
BRADLEY
WORTHING
DURBAN
PRETORIA RD.
BRIGHTON RD.
CAVENDISH RD
LEE CLOSE
Callicroft Jun. & Inf. Sch.
Comm. Cen.
Liby.
Clinic
RODWAY ROAD
CRANBOURNE
BAY TREE CL.
DRIVE
CEDAR CLOSE
CEDAR CLO
SPRUCE WY.
WILLOW CL.
LARCH WAY
SYCAMORE
BIRCH CL.
FIR TREE CL.
Sub.
HIGHWOOD ROAD
LANE
Arlingham Way
Severn Way
Tidenham Way
NEWNHAM PL.
LONGNEY PL.
Berkeley Ct.
Richmond Ct.
Playgrd.
Play. Fields
NORMAN SCOTT PARK
Pav.
Tennis Cts.
Worthsworth Ho.
Youth Cen.
Langdale Ct.
Beck Ho.
Pool Ho.
Air Shaft
Playing
WINDERMERE ROAD
THIRLMERE
THIRLMERE RD.
LOWER
SOUTHSEA
ASHFORD RD.
HAZELDENE
CALLICROFT ROAD
SOU
GLOUCES
Bris
FILTON AIRFIELD
Works
GLOUCESTER ROAD NORTH
A38
Charlton Common
COMMON
WEST WAY
Tunnel
CHARLTON
GDS.
PARKERS CL.
BADGERS DR.
Charlton Mead
PENSFIELD
TRESLAKE
GREEN
MEAD
MATFORD CL.
NORTHWDS WLK.
PARK MEAD
DRIVE
DR.
STREAM CLO.
Aircraft Works
Rolls Royce Aircraft Works
BRISTOL
BS10
Club House
Golf Course Cottages
FILTON GOLF COURSE
NEW LINK RD.
FAIRLAWN
FILTON HILL
CLEVE
FILTON
215
957
Filton College
GLEBELANDS RD.
RODNEY
Hanover Ct.
MAYVILLE
REC. TORY LA.

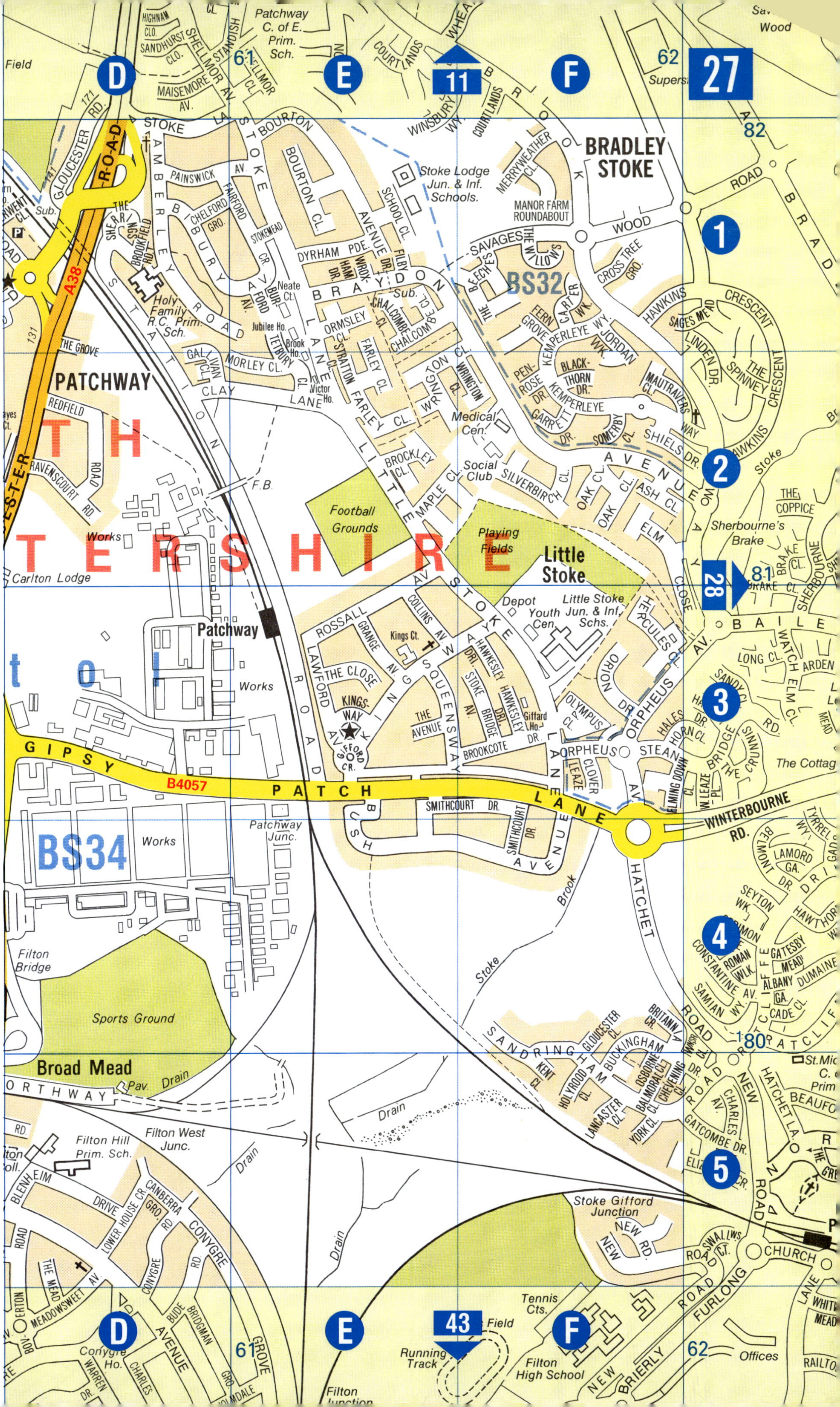

BRADLEY STOKE
PATCHWAY
Little Stoke
Patchway
Broad Mead
BS32
BS34
Stoke Lodge Jun. & Inf. Schools.
Patchway C. of E. Prim. Sch.
MANOR FARM ROUNDABOUT
Holy Family R.C. Prim. Sch.
Football Grounds
Playing Fields
Medical Cen.
Social Club
Little Stoke Jun. & Inf. Schs.
Youth Cen.
Depot
Sports Ground
Filton Bridge
Patchway Junc.
Filton West Junc.
Filton Hill Prim. Sch.
Stoke Gifford Junction
Filton High School
Tennis Cts.
Running Track
Field
Works
Carlton Lodge
Sherbourne's Brake
The Coppice
GIPSY PATCH LANE
B4057
A38
WINTERBOURNE RD.
LITTLE STOKE LANE
BRAYDON AVENUE
SAVAGES WOOD ROAD
BRADLEY STOKE WAY
BAILEYS COURT ROAD
CLAY LANE
NORTHWAY
HATCHET ROAD
CONYGRE GROVE
SANDRINGHAM RD.
KINGSWAY
QUEENSWAY
LAWFORD AV.
SMITHCOURT DR.
ORPHEUS AV.
11
43
28
61
62
81
82
180
D
E
F
1
2
3
4
5

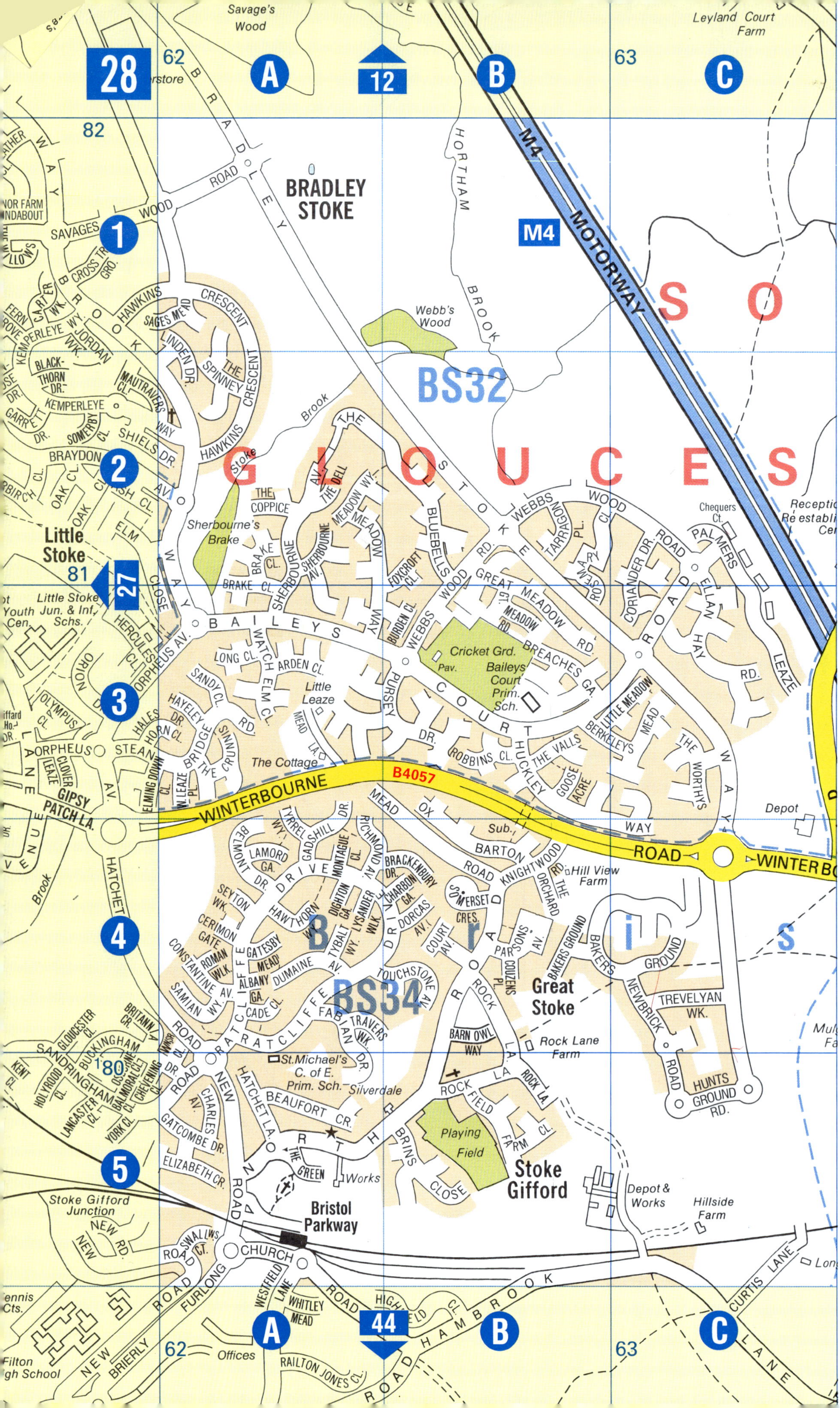
Savage's Wood
Leyland Court Farm
12
62
63
A
B
C
82
81
80
1
2
3
4
5
BRADLEY STOKE
M4
MOTORWAY
SO
GLOUCES
BS32
BS34
Bris
Webb's Wood
Little Stoke
27
Little Stoke Jun. & Inf. Schs.
Youth Cen.
Sherbourne's Brake
Cricket Grd.
Pav.
Baileys Court Prim. Sch.
Little Leaze
The Cottage
B4057
WINTERBOURNE ROAD
BRADLEY STOKE WAY
BAILEYS COURT RD.
WOOD ROAD
SAVAGES WOOD ROAD
HORTHAM BROOK
HAWKINS CRESCENT
THE SPINNEY
SAGES MEAD
LINDEN DR.
MAUTRAVERS CL.
SHIELS DR.
KEMPERLEYE WAY
BRAYDON AV.
BLACKTHORN DR.
JORDAN WK.
FERN GROVE
CARTER WK.
CROSS TREE GRO.
GARRETT DR.
SOMERBY CL.
OAK CL.
ELM CL.
CLOSE
ORPHEUS AV.
HERCULES CL.
ORION DR.
OLYMPUS CL.
ORPHEUS
GIPSY PATCH LA.
STEAN BRIDGE
HALES HORN CL.
HAYELEY DR.
SANDY CL.
LONG CL.
ARDEN CL.
WATCH ELM CL.
THE CRUNNS
BRIDGE
W. LEAZE PL.
ELMING DOWN CL.
THE COPPICE
BRAKE CL.
SHERBOURNE AV.
THE DELL
MEADOW WY.
MEADOW
FOXCROFT CL.
BLUEBELLS
BURDEN CL.
WEBBS WOOD RD.
PURSEY DR.
MEAD LA.
GREAT MEADOW RD.
MEADOW CT.
BREACHES GA.
ROBBINS CL.
HUCKLEY WAY
THE VALLS
GOOSE ACRE
BERKELEYS MEAD
LITTLE MEADOW
THE WORTHYS
TARRAGON PL.
ROSEMARY CL.
CORIANDER DR.
WOOD ROAD
PALMERS LEAZE
ELLAN HAY RD.
Chequers Ct.
Reception Re establi Cen
Depot
OX MEAD
Sub.
BARTON ROAD
KNIGHTWOOD RD.
THE ORCHARD
Hill View Farm
TYRREL WY.
GADSHILL DR.
RICHMOND AV.
MONTAGUE CL.
BRACKENBURY DR.
CHARBON GA.
BELMONT DR.
LAMORD GA.
DRIVE
SEYTON WK.
HAWTHORN WY.
DIGHTON GA.
LYSANDER WLK.
TYBALT WY.
DORCAS AV.
COURT AV.
SOMERSET CRES.
PARSONS AV.
COUZENS PL.
BAKERS GROUND
NEWBRICK ROAD
TREVELYAN WK.
HUNTS GROUND RD.
CERIMON GATE
ROMAN WLK.
GATESBY MEAD
ALBANY GA.
DUMAINE AV.
CONSTANTINE AV.
SAMIAN WY.
CADE CL.
RATCLIFFE DR.
FABIAN DR.
TRAVERS WK.
TOUCHSTONE AV.
ROCK LA.
BARN OWL WAY
Great Stoke
Rock Lane Farm
ROCKFIELD
FARM CL.
Playing Field
BRINS CLOSE
Stoke Gifford
Depot & Works
Hillside Farm
St.Michael's C. of E. Prim. Sch.
Silverdale
BEAUFORT CR.
NORTH ROAD
HATCHET LA.
THE GREEN
Works
Bristol Parkway
HATCHET ROAD
NEW ROAD
CHARLES AV.
GATCOMBE DR.
ELIZABETH CR.
GLOUCESTER CL.
BUCKINGHAM
BRITANNIA CR.
SANDRINGHAM
BALMORAL CL.
CHEVENING CL.
OSBORNE CL.
HOLYROOD CL.
LANCASTER CL.
YORK CL.
KENT CL.
Stoke Gifford Junction
NEW RD.
SWALLOWS CT.
CHURCH ROAD
FURLONG ROAD
NEW BRIERLY
WESTFIELD LANE
WHITLEY MEAD
HIGH FIELD CL.
HAMBROOK ROAD
CURTIS LANE
44
Offices
RAILTON JONES CL.
Filton High School
Tennis Cts.
Long
Mul Fa
Brook
LANE
AVENUE
Ho.
DR.

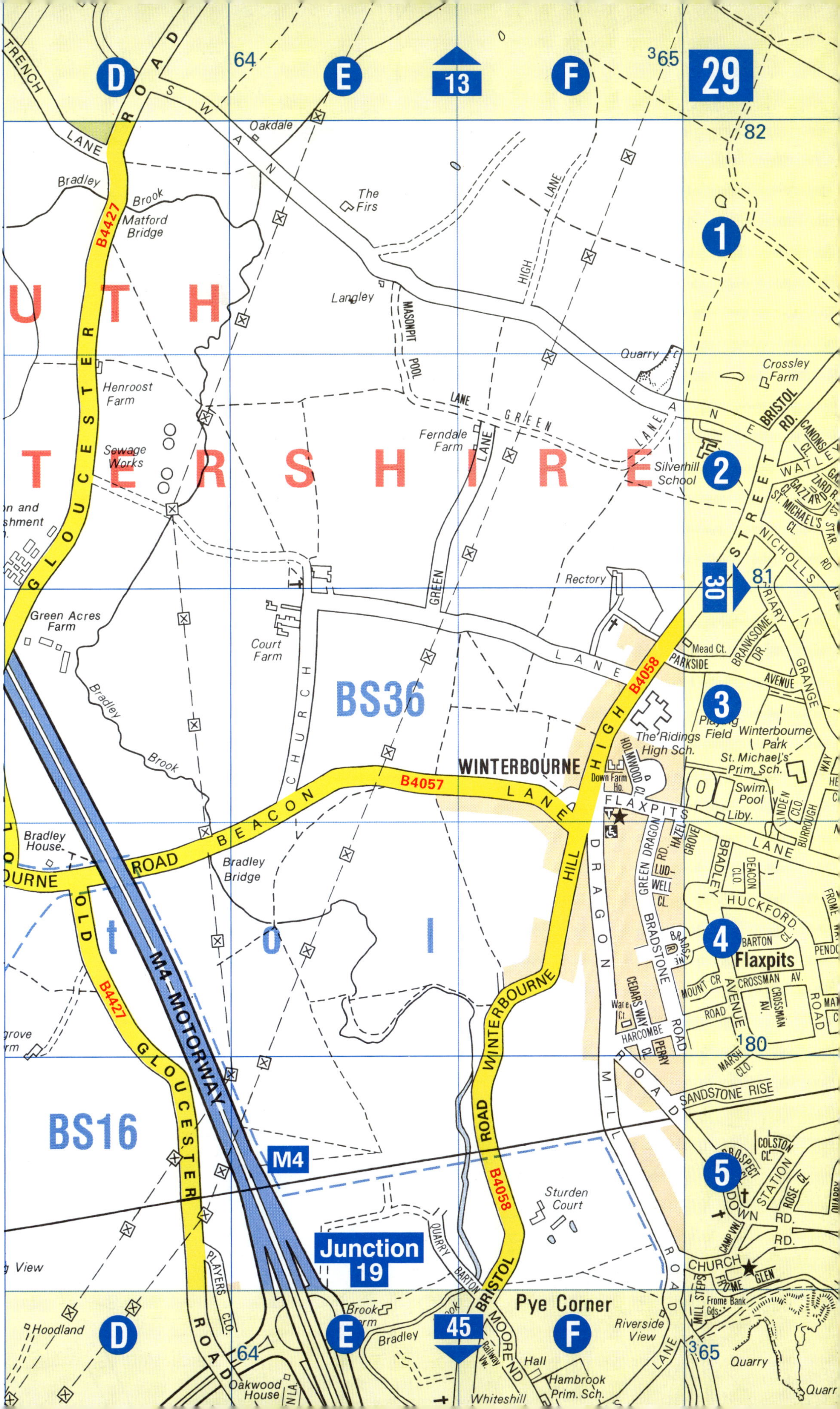
13
D
E
F
64
365
82
81
80
1
2
3
4
5
TRENCH LANE
SWAN LANE
Oakdale
The Firs
Bradley Brook
Matford Bridge
B4427
Langley
MASONPIT POOL LANE
HIGH LANE
Quarry
Crossley Farm
BRISTOL RD.
CANONS CL.
WATLEY
GAZZARD RD
ST. MICHAEL'S CL.
STAR
NICHOLLS RD
GREEN LANE
Ferndale Farm
Silverhill School
Henroost Farm
Sewage Works
GLOUCESTER ROAD
SOUTH GLOUCESTERSHIRE
Rectory
30
Green Acres Farm
Court Farm
CHURCH ROAD
LANE
B4058
Mead Ct.
BRANKSOME DR.
BRIARY
PARKSIDE
AVENUE
GRANGE
BS36
The Ridings High Sch.
Playing Field
Winterbourne Park
St. Michael's Prim. Sch.
Swim. Pool
Liby.
WINTERBOURNE
HOLMWOOD CL.
Down Farm Ho.
B4057
BEACON LANE
HIGH ST
FLAXPITS LANE
GREEN DRAGON RD.
HAZEL GROVE
LUDWELL CL.
BRADLEY CL.
DEACON CL.
HUCKFORD
Bradley Brook
Bradley House
Bradley Bridge
ROAD
BRADSTONE ROAD
BARTON CL.
Flaxpits
MOUNT CR.
CROSSMAN AV.
AVENUE ROAD
PERRY RD
OLD GLOUCESTER ROAD
M4 MOTORWAY
WINTERBOURNE ROAD
CEDARS WAY
Ware Ct.
HARCOMBE CL.
MARSH CL.
DRAGON ROAD
SANDSTONE RISE
MILL ROAD
BS16
M4
COLSTON CL.
PROSPECT CL.
STATION ROAD
ROSE CL.
DOWN RD.
Sturden Court
Junction 19
QUARRY BARTON
B4058
CAMP VW.
CHURCH RD.
FROME GLEN
MILL STEPS
Frome Bank Gds.
PLAYERS CL.
Brook Farm
BRISTOL ROAD
Pye Corner
Riverside View
Hoodland
Bradley
45
MOOREND RD
Railway Vw.
Hall
Hambrook Prim. Sch.
Whiteshill
Oakwood House
LANE
Quarry

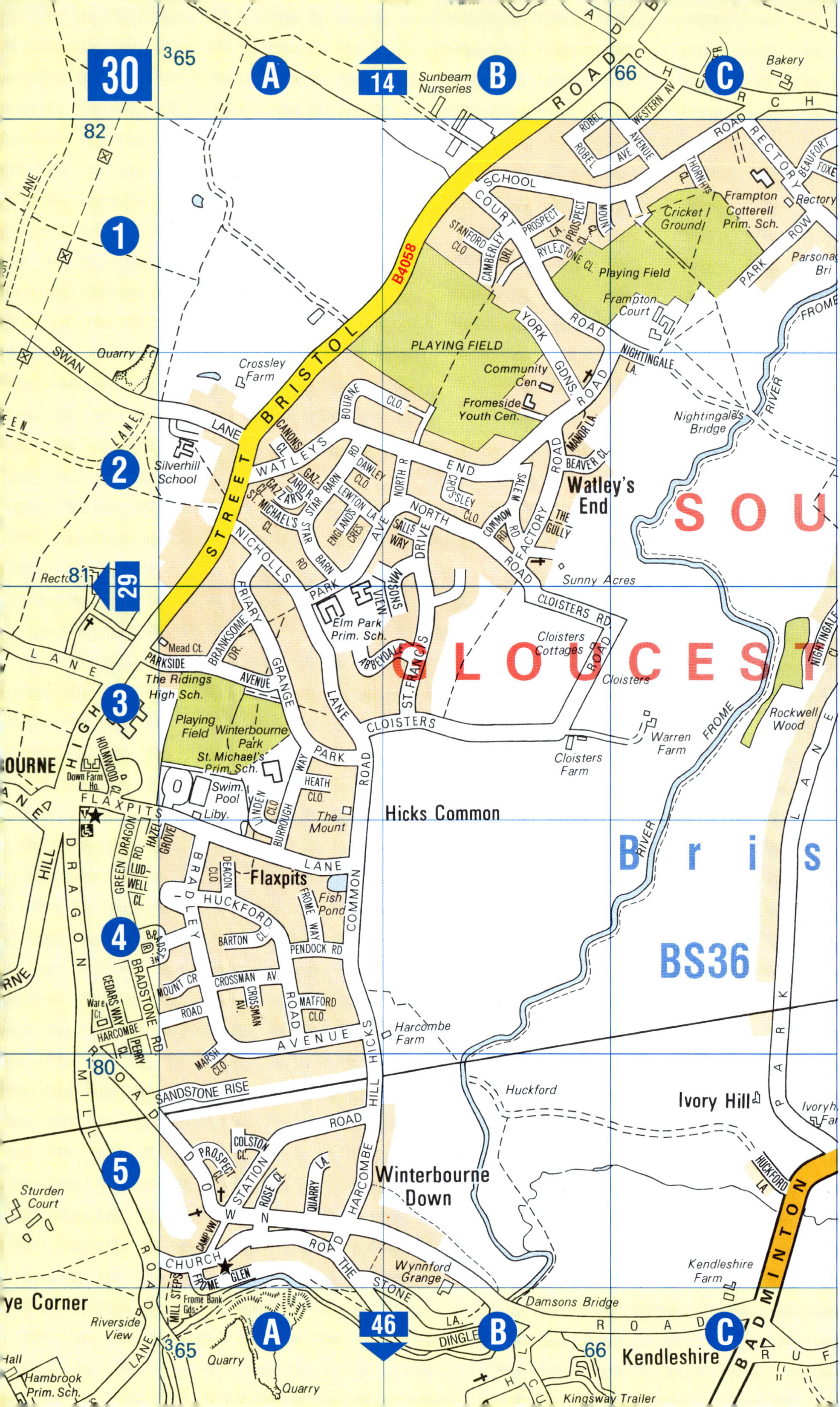
30
365
A
14
Sunbeam Nurseries
B
66
C
Bakery
82
1
2
3
4
5
81
29
180
LANE
SWAN LANE
Quarry
Crossley Farm
Silverhill School
Rectory
LANE
Mead Ct.
PARKSIDE
The Ridings High Sch.
BOURNE
HIGH
HOLMWOOD CL.
Down Farm Ho.
FLAXPITS
HILL
DRAGON
GREEN DRAGON RD.
HAZEL GROVE
LUDWELL CL.
BRADSTONE RD.
CEDARS WAY
Ware Ct.
HARCOMBE CL.
PERRY
MILL
ROAD
Sturden Court
Riverside View
Hall
Hambrook Prim. Sch.
ye Corner
BRISTOL STREET
B4058
ROAD
CHURCH
WESTERN AV
ROBEL AVE
AVENUE
SCHOOL
COURT
STANFORD CLO.
CAMBERLEY DRI.
PROSPECT LA.
PROSPECT CL.
MOUNT CL.
RYLESTONE CL.
Cricket Ground
Playing Field
Frampton Cotterell Prim. Sch.
Rectory
RECTORY
BEAUFORT
FOXE
THORNHYS CL.
ROW
PARK
Parsonage Bri
Frampton Court
YORK GDNS.
ROAD
NIGHTINGALE LA.
FROME
RIVER
Nightingale's Bridge
PLAYING FIELD
Community Cen.
Fromeside Youth Cen.
CANONS CL.
BOURNE CLO.
WATLEY'S END
GAZZARD RD.
GAZZARD CL.
ST. MICHAEL'S CL.
STAR BARN RD
DAWLEY CLO.
LEWTON LA.
NORTH RD
ENGLANDS CRES.
AVE
CROSSLEY CLO.
SALEM RD.
MANOR LA.
BEAVER CL.
Watley's End
THE GULLY
COMMON RD.
FACTORY ROAD
NORTH DRIVE
SALLS WAY
NICHOLLS RD
PARK
MASONS VIEW
Elm Park Prim. Sch.
Sunny Acres
CLOISTERS RD.
Cloisters Cottages
ROAD
Cloisters
ABBEYDALE
ST. FRANCIS DR.
FRIARY GRANGE
BRANKSOME DR.
AVENUE
Playing Field
Winterbourne Park
St. Michael's Prim. Sch.
Swim. Pool
Liby.
LINDEN CLO.
BURROUGH WAY
PARK
HEATH CLO.
The Mount
CLOISTERS
Cloisters Farm
Warren Farm
Rockwell Wood
NIGHTINGALE
SOUTH GLOUCESTERSHIRE
Bristol
BS36
LANE
ROAD
Hicks Common
LANE
BRADLEY
DEACON CLO.
Flaxpits
Fish Pond
FROME WAY
COMMON
HUCKFORD RD.
BARTON CL.
PENDOCK RD
MOUNT CR
CROSSMAN AV.
ROAD
MATFORD CLO.
AVENUE
MARSH CLO.
SANDSTONE RISE
Harcombe Farm
HICKS HILL
Huckford
Ivory Hill
Ivoryhill Farm
PARK LANE
HUCKFORD LA.
BADMINTON ROAD
ROAD
COLSTON CL.
PROSPECT CL.
STATION
ROSE CL.
QUARRY LA.
HARCOMBE
Winterbourne Down
DOWN
ROAD
CAMP VW.
CHURCH
FROME GLEN
MILL STEPS
Frome Bank Gds.
THE STONE LA.
Wynnford Grange
Damsons Bridge
Kendleshire Farm
DINGLE
Quarry
A
46
B
66
HILL
C
Kendleshire
Kingsway Trailer

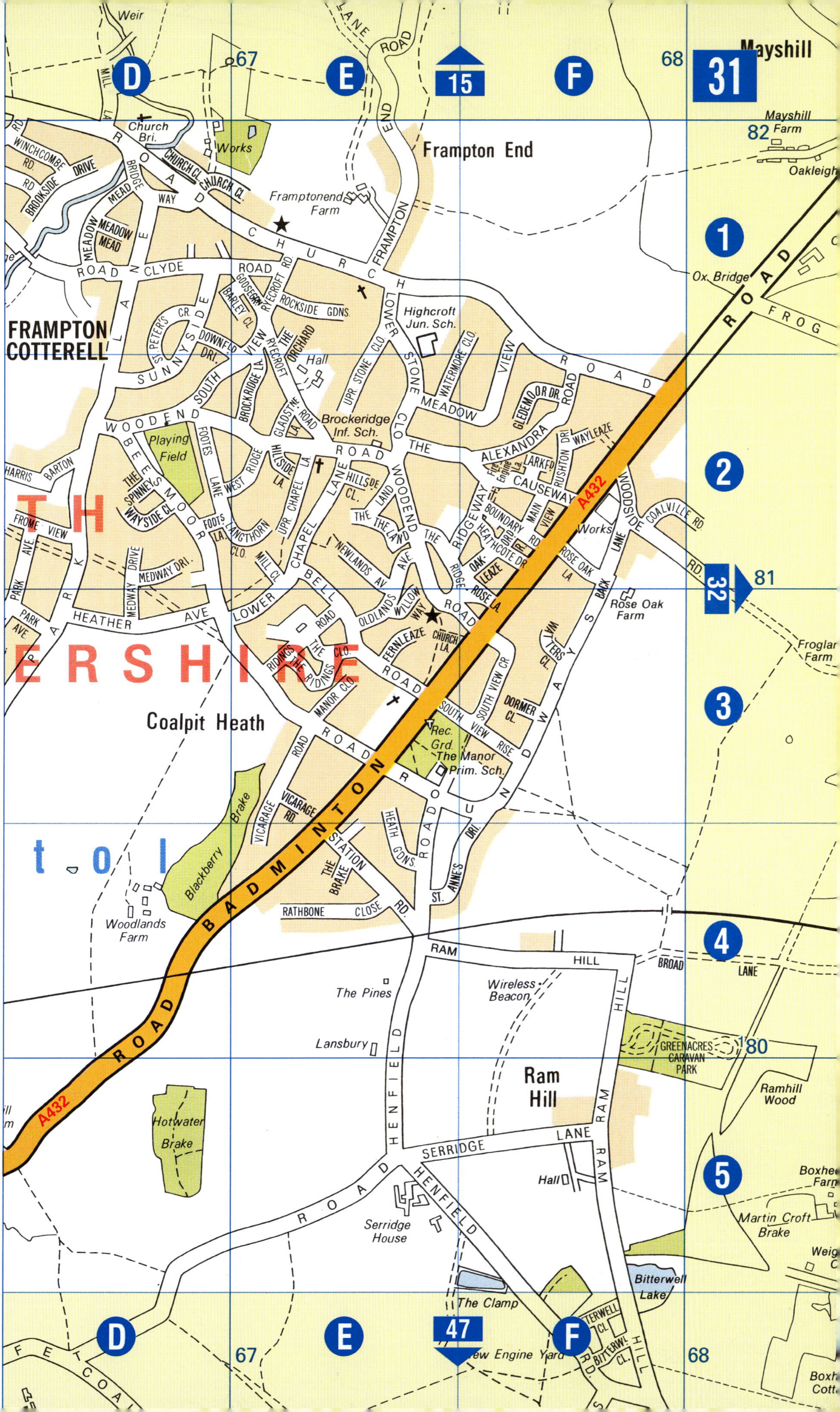

31
15
32
47
D
E
F
1
2
3
4
5
67
68
82
81
80
Mayshill
Mayshill Farm
Oakleigh
Frampton End
Framptonend Farm
Weir
Church Bri.
Works
FRAMPTON COTTERELL
Coalpit Heath
Ram Hill
Highcroft Jun. Sch.
Brockeridge Inf. Sch.
Hall
Playing Field
Ox Bridge
FROG ROAD
Rose Oak Farm
Froglar Farm
Rec. Grd.
The Manor Prim. Sch.
Blackberry Brake
Woodlands Farm
The Pines
Lansbury
Wireless Beacon
GREENACRES CARAVAN PARK
Ramhill Wood
Hotwater Brake
Serridge House
The Clamp
Bitterwell Lake
New Engine Yard
Martin Croft Brake
A432
BADMINTON ROAD
CHURCH ROAD
CLYDE ROAD
WOODEND ROAD
THE CAUSEWAY
ALEXANDRA ROAD
LOWER ROAD
BELL ROAD
ROUND ROAD
BACK LANE
SERRIDGE LANE
HENFIELD ROAD
RAM HILL
BROAD LANE
COALVILLE RD.
HEATHER AVE
PARK AVE.
BEESMOOR ROAD
RATHBONE CLOSE
STATION RD.
VICARAGE RD.
WINCHCOMBE DRIVE
BROOKSIDE
MEADOW MEAD
SUNNYSIDE LANE
ST. PETER'S CR.
ROCKSIDE GDNS.
RYECROFT RD.
THE ORCHARD
LOWER STONE CLO.
UPR. STONE CLO.
WATERMORE CLO.
MEADOW VIEW
GLEDEMOOR DR.
WAYLEAZE
LARKFD.
RUSHTON DRI.
HILLSIDE LA.
CHAPEL LA.
UPR. CHAPEL LA.
THE SPINNEY
WAYSIDE CL.
MEDWAY DRI.
FOOTES LANE
LANGTHORN CLO.
NEWLANDS AV.
OLDLANDS AVE.
WILLOW WAY
FERNLEAZE
CHURCH LA.
ROSE LA.
ROSE OAK LA.
OAKLEAZE
HEATHCOTE DR.
BOUNDARY RD.
RIDGEWAY
THE RIDINGS
MANOR CLO.
SOUTH VIEW RISE
SOUTH VIEW CR.
DORMER CL.
WALTERS CL.
HEATH GDNS.
ST. ANNE'S DRI.
THE BRAKE
BITTERWELL CL.
ENGINE COMMON LANE
WESTERSHIRE
Bristol

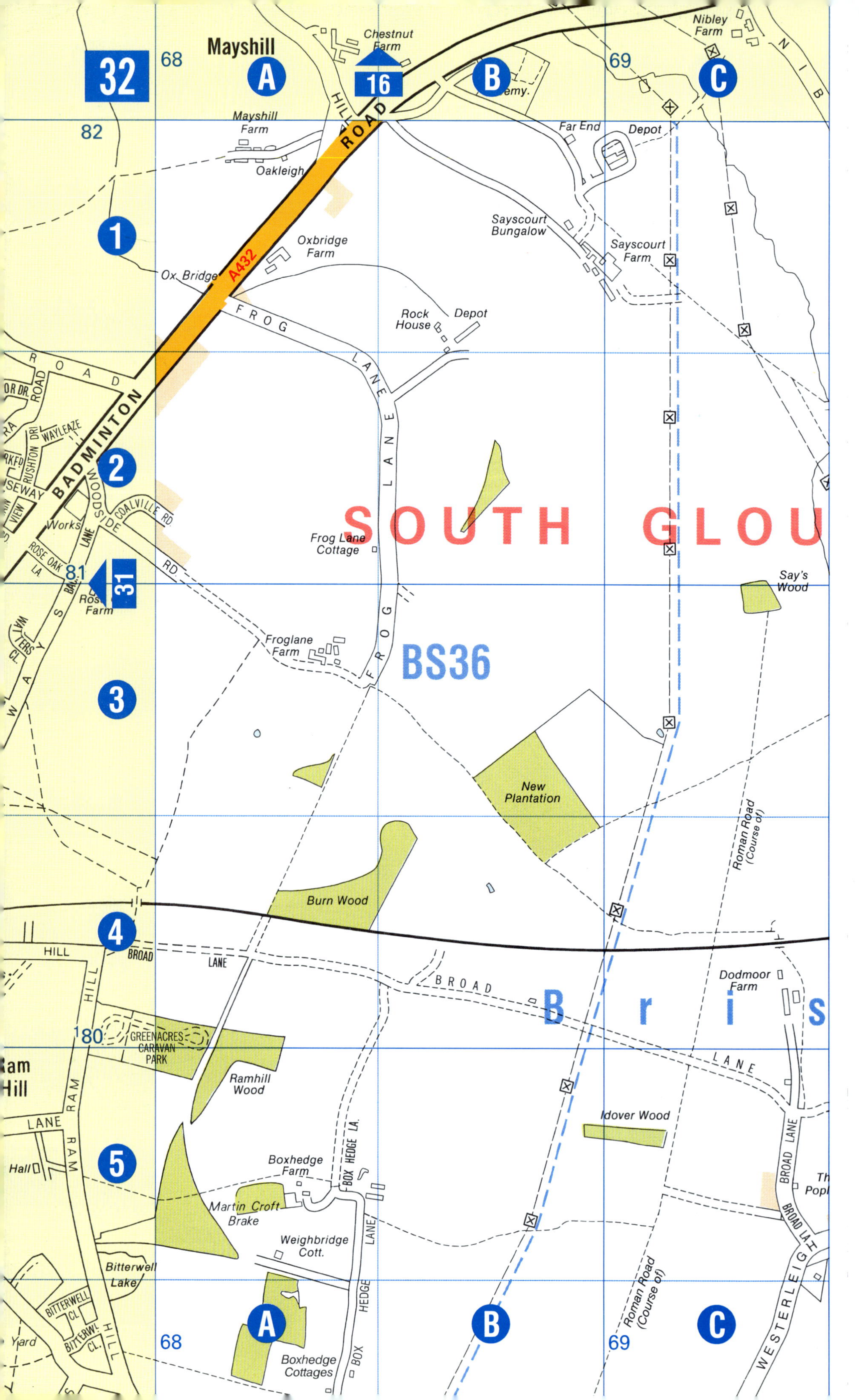
Mayshill
Chestnut Farm
16
68
69
A
B
C
82
81
180
Nibley Farm
Mayshill Farm
Oakleigh
HILL ROAD
Far End
Depot
Sayscourt Bungalow
Sayscourt Farm
Oxbridge Farm
Ox Bridge
A432
FROG LANE
Rock House
Depot
BADMINTON ROAD
WAYLEAZE
RUSHTON DRI
WOODSIDE
COALVILLE RD.
Works
ROSE OAK LA
SOUTH GLOU
Frog Lane Cottage
31
Say's Wood
Froglane Farm
BS36
New Plantation
Roman Road (Course of)
Burn Wood
HILL
BROAD LANE
BROAD LANE
Dodmoor Farm
Bris
GREENACRES CARAVAN PARK
Ramhill Wood
RAM HILL
LANE
Ram Hill
Hall
Idover Wood
BOX HEDGE LA.
Boxhedge Farm
Martin Croft Brake
Weighbridge Cott.
BROAD LANE
BROAD LA
Bitterwell Lake
BITTERWELL CL.
BITTERWELL CL.
BOX HEDGE LANE
Roman Road (Course of)
WESTERLEIGH
Boxhedge Cottages
Yard
1
2
3
4
5

Warehouse
D
E
F
370
17
Playing Field
YATE
71
Playing Field
Ball Cts.
82
STANSHAWES DR.
Works
NAILSWORTH AV.
PAINSWICK DR.
DURSLEY CL.
WELLSTEAD AV.
THORN CL.
BLACKENEY MILLS
WESTERLEIGH COMMON
Kingsgate Inf. Sch.
Stanshawes Ct. Sch.
BIRKDALE
CRESCENT
TODDINGTON CL.
APPERLEY CL.
COLESBORNE CL.
CHALFORD CL.
HIGHWORTH
BROOKTHORPE
LYDBROOK CL.
SAINT BRIAVELS
QUEDGELEY
ELMORE
PRESCOTT
WOODMANCOTE
NORTHFIELD
LONGFORD
SANDHURST
ROAD
PRESTBURY
LANSDOWN
Subway
DRIVE
SUNDRIDGE
SANDY LODGE
CHATCOMBE
HATHERLEY
WESTERLEIGH
DEERHURST
BARNWOOD
Rodford Inf. & Jun. Schs.
GLENFALL
BISLEY
Sub.
PITCHCOMBE
CRANHAM
HARDWICK
CHARGROVE
St. Nicholas Cen.
Prinknash Ct.
Monks Ho.
Abbey Ho.
Friars Ho.
Comm. Cen.
ABBOTSWOOD
RODFORD WAY
CHEDWORTH
Beech Hill
RODBOROUGH
WITCOMBE
BREDON
BLAISDON
Subway
WOODCHESTER
CESTERSHIRE
Wapley Court (Home for the aged)
KELSTON CL.
Glevum Sch.
34
81
Rodford
Abbotswood County Infs. & Jun. Schs.
BROCKWORTH
Wellersley Prim. Sch.
EDGEWORTH
BADGEWORTH
KINGSCOTE
CHERINGTON
MAISEMORE
WESTERLEIGH
Elm Farm
LANE
BS37
The Old Parsonage
Westerleigh Tabernacle
The Sign of the Dolphin
Westerleigh West Junction
Pool Farm
Wapley Bushes
Wapley Common
SODBURY LANE
BESOM LANE
Wapley Rank
Copp Hill
Grove Farm
Works
Wapley Hill
80
CROSSING
DODMORE
Works
Wychwell Farm
Brook Farm
The Quadrangle
Church Farm
Westerleigh
MILL CRES.
NEWMAN CL.
Ivy Terrace
THE QUADRANGLE
SHORTHILL ROAD
Wapley
WAPLEY HILL
Beanwood Farm
Playing Field
Brice's Farm
OLD MILL CL.
Mill House Farm
Vale View
Bean Wood
Bush's Far
D
E
F
370
71
Hareswood Cottages
Beanw Cotta
Electr Sub.
WAPLEY

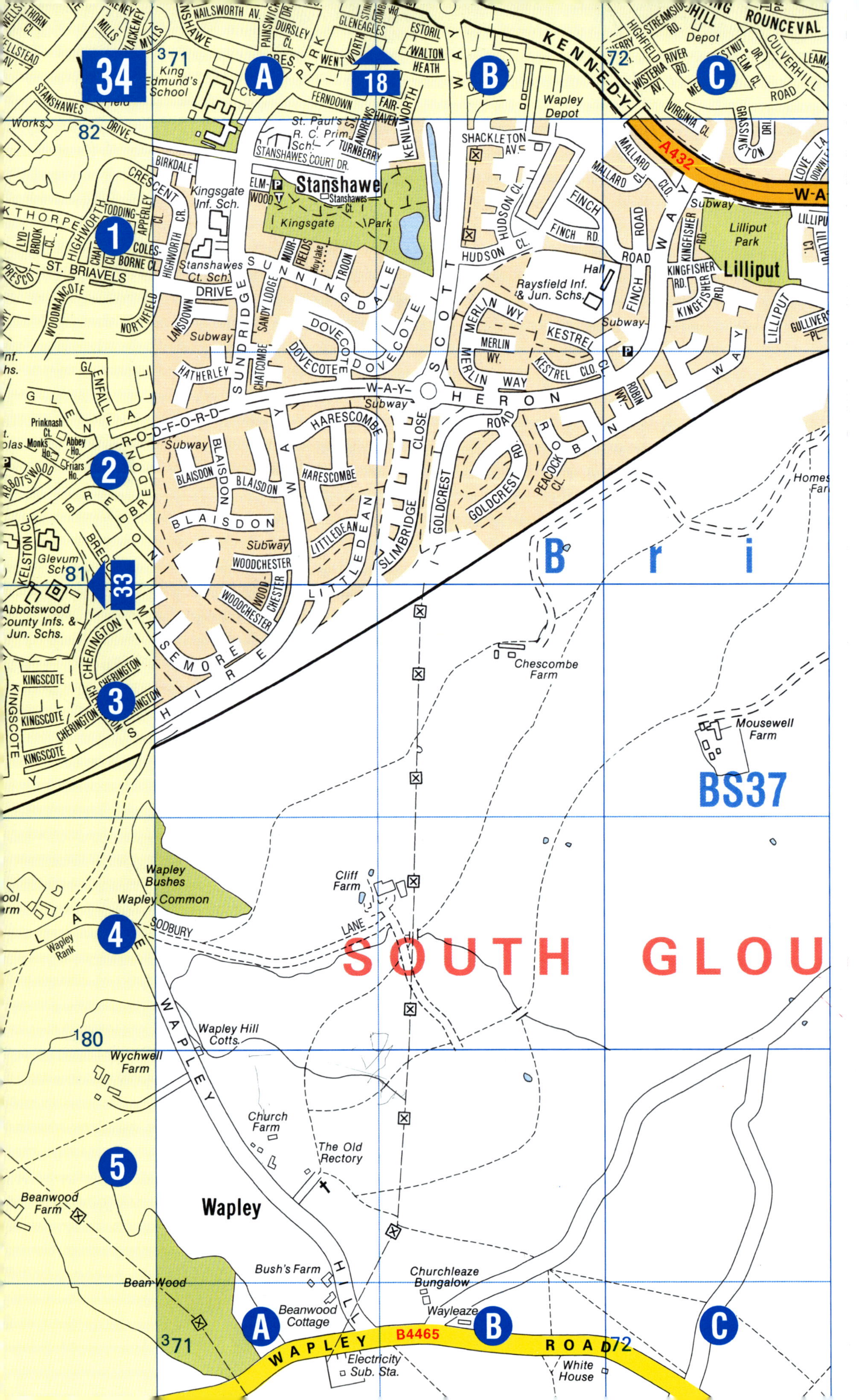
34
18
33
A
B
C
1
2
3
4
5
371
72
82
81
180
Kennedy Way
A432
Rounceval
Culverhill Road
Highfield Rd.
Streamside
Wisteria Av.
River Rd.
Virginia Cl.
Grassington Dri.
Depot
Nailsworth Av.
Painswick Dr.
Dursley Cl.
Gleneagles
Wentworth
Estoril
Walton Heath
Park
King Edmund's School
Stanshawes Drive
Works
Ferndown
Fairhaven
Kenilworth
St. Paul's R. C. Prim. Sch.
Andrews
Turnberry
Stanshawes Court Dr.
Stanshawe
Stanshawes Ct.
Kingsgate Park
Kingsgate Inf. Sch.
Birkdale
Crescent
Elmwood
Muirfields
Hoylake
Troon
Sunningdale
Wapley Depot
Shackleton Av.
Hudson Cl.
Finch Rd.
Finch Road
Mallard Cl.
Mallard Clo.
Subway
Lilliput Park
Lilliput
Kingfisher Rd.
Gullivers Pl.
Raysfield Inf. & Jun. Schs.
Hall
Merlin Wy.
Merlin Way
Kestrel Clo.
Kestrel Cl.
Heron Way
Robin Way
Robin Wy.
Peacock Cl.
Goldcrest Rd.
Goldcrest
Scott Way
Slimbridge Close
Littledean
Harescombe
Dovecote
Chatcombe
Sundridge
Sandy Lodge
Lansdown
Hatherley
Rodford Way
Stanshawes Ct. Sch.
Highworth Cr.
Apperley Cl.
Todding
Coles-borne Cl.
Highworth
Kinthorpe
Lydbrook Cl.
Prescott
St. Briavels Drive
Woodmancote
Northfield
Glenfall
Prinknash Ct.
Monks Ho.
Abbey Ho.
Friars Ho.
Abbotswood
Bredon
Kelston Cl.
Glevum Sch.
Abbotswood County Infs. & Jun. Schs.
Blaisdon
Woodchester
Maisemore
Cherington
Kingscote
Shire Way
Homes Farm
Chescombe Farm
Mousewell Farm
Bri
BS37
Wapley Bushes
Wapley Common
Sodbury Lane
Wapley Rank
Cliff Farm
SOUTH GLOU
Wapley Hill Cotts.
Wychwell Farm
Church Farm
The Old Rectory
Wapley
Wapley Hill
Beanwood Farm
Bean Wood
Bush's Farm
Churchleaze Bungalow
Beanwood Cottage
Wayleaze
B4465
Wapley Road
Electricity Sub. Sta.
White House

D
E
F
73
74
19
82
81
180
1
2
3
4
5
ST. HIGH ST.
BROAD ST.
HORSESHOE LA.
Lib.
Vic.
HOUNDS RD.
ARNOLD CT.
HOUNDS CL.
HORSE ST.
MELBOURNE
DRIVE
FROME
GRANDASH RD.
WHITEFIELDS
GORLANDS RD.
HARTLEY
CESSON
WAY
River Frome
St. John's Mead C of E Prim. Sch.
Play. Fld.
BOWLING RD.
WOODMANS CL.
WOODMANS
WOODMANS ROAD
KINGROVE
MEAD RD.
Play. Grd.
CRESCENT
HORSE ST.
STREET
B4060
JENNER CL.
ST. JOHN'S CL.
WICKHAM CL.
BURGAGE CL.
Dept.
Two Stones La.
WOODMANS VALE
COTSWOLD ROAD
Subway
BADMINTON ROAD
A432
Blanchards Farm
Colt's Green
BOWLING RD.
Chipping Sodbury School
GAUNTS RD.
KINGROVE ROAD
GRN. HAYES
SMARTS GREEN
BLANCHARDS
STATION CL.
AVE.
DODINGTON RD.
Stanbourne Cotts
Playing Field
CLAYPIT HILL
Kingrove Farm
KINGROVE ROAD
Lower Kingrove Farm
MILL LANE
KINGROVE COMMON
DODINGTON LANE
Ham Wood Farm
Branchley Farm
Ham Wood
Dodington Manor
CESTERSHIRE
The Grove
Lydes Farm
Down Farm
Lean Tom Plantation

36
350
A
B
51
C
Fuel Depot
1
Oil Jetty (disused)
West Wharf
Lighthouse
179
Fuel Depot
B R I
North Pier
Lighthouse
Graving Dock
2
South Pier
Entrance Lock
AVONMOUTH DOCKS
Mill
Swash Channel
Royal Edward Dock
KING ST.
NAPIER SQ.
QUEEN ST.
CLAYTON ST.
EAST ST.
MEADOW ST.
RICHMOND
GLOUCESTER
East Pier
3
RESERVOIR
West Pier (Disused)
B r
Junction Cut
Lock
Avonm
78
SEA BANK ROAD
Sea Bank East
RIVER ROAD
River Quay
Avonmouth Old Dock
Lock
Nelson Point
RIVER
4
ROYAL PORTBURY DOCK
BS20
Gordano Quay
GORDANO RD.
St. George's Quay
ROAD
Sheephouse Farm
5
NORTH SOMERSET
ST. GEORGE'S
51
SHEEPHOUSE CARAVAN PARK
MARSH LA.
Old Sea Ba
77
WEST DOCK RD.
52
PORTBURY SAWMILLS ESTATE
Rhyne

St. Andrew's Road
Chemicals Plant
Smelting Works
Slag Heap
INTERNATIONAL TRADING ESTATE
ST. ANDREWS INDUSTRIAL ESTATE
HASLEMERE INDUSTRIAL ESTATE
Barracks Cotts
Industrial Estate
Works
BS11
AVONMOUTH
Avonmouth Park
Lib.
Industrial Estate
Electricity Transmission Station
Shirehampton Rhine
AVONBRIDGE INDUSTRIAL ESTATE
Junction 18
M5
Bowling Green
Avon County Primary School
Bowl. Grn.
Rugby Gd.
Robin Cousins Sports Centre
Avonmouth Primary School
Mill
AVON GORGE INDUSTRIAL ESTATE
AVON BANK INDUSTRIAL ESTATE
AVON
Saltings
Avonmouth Bridge
M5 MOTORWAY
Cycle Path
Drill Hall
Shirehampton Jun.& Inf. Sch.
Cemetery
Hlth. Cen.
Sedgewick
Barwick
Penpole Rhine
KINGS WESTON LANE
AVONMOUTH ROAD
ST. ANDREW'S ROAD
AVONMOUTH RELIEF ROAD
PORTWAY
LOWER HIGH STREET
KINGS WESTON AVE.
BALLAST LANE
21
38
53

21
38
53

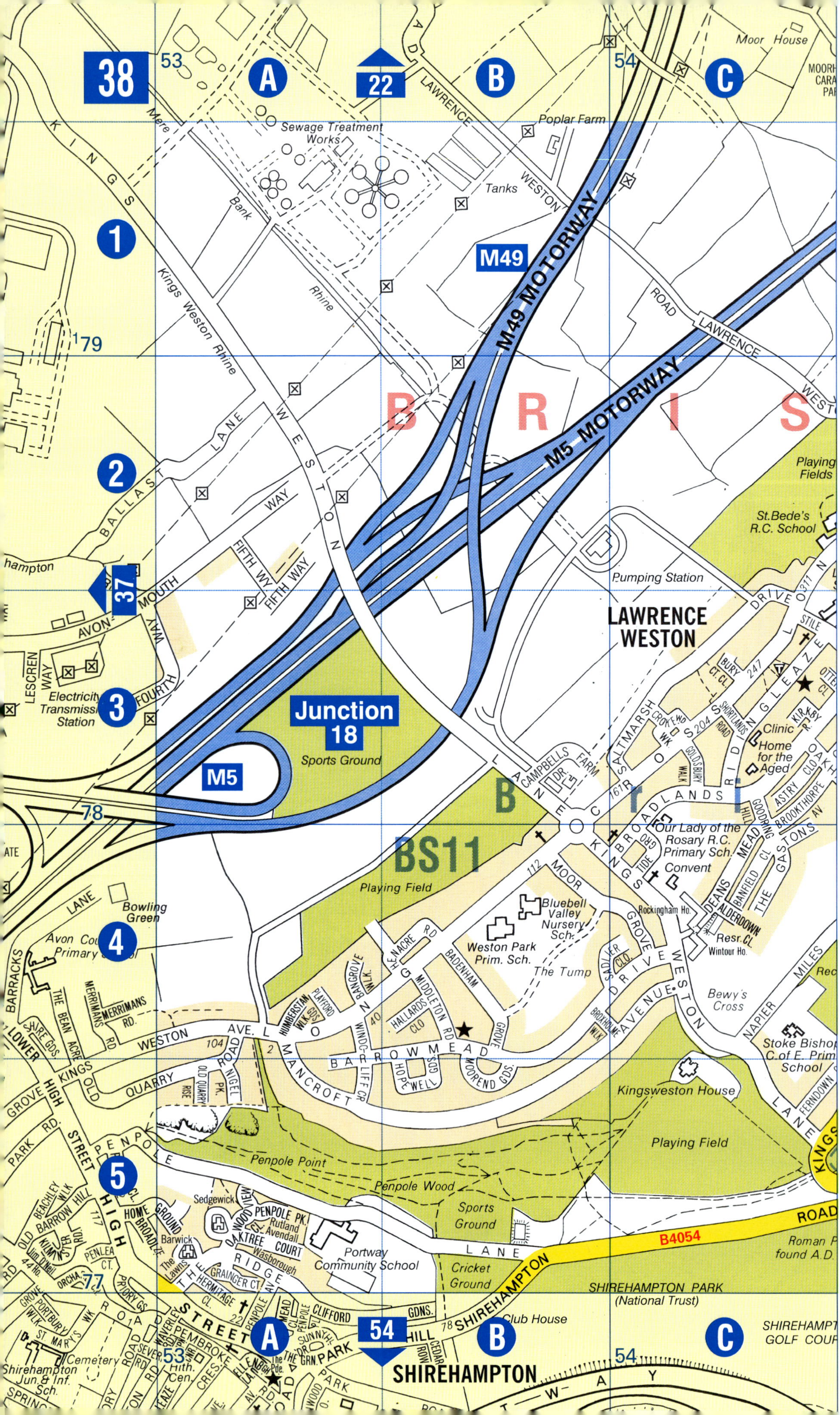

53
A
22
B
54
C
Moor House
Sewage Treatment Works
LAWRENCE
Poplar Farm
Tanks
WESTON
Mere
KINGS
Bank
Rhine
Kings Weston Rhine
M49
M49 MOTORWAY
ROAD
LAWRENCE
WESTON
179
B R I S
M5 MOTORWAY
LANE
WESTON
WAY
BALLAST
FIFTH WY
FIFTH WAY
Playing Fields
St.Bede's R.C. School
Pumping Station
LAWRENCE WESTON
37
MOUTH
AVON
WAY
LESCREN WAY
Electricity Transmission Station
FOURTH
Junction 18
Sports Ground
M5
78
BS11
Playing Field
CAMPBELLS FARM
DR.
SALTMARSH
BROADLANDS
CROFTS END
GOLDSBURY WALK
SHORTLANDS ROAD
Clinic
Home for the Aged
RIDINGLEAZE
KIRKBY RD
ASTRY CLO.
BROOKTHORPE AV
GOODRING HILL
GASTONS
Our Lady of the Rosary R.C. Primary Sch.
Convent
MEAD
BANFIELD CL
THE
DEANS
ALDERDOWN
Resr.
Wintour Ho.
Rockingham Ho.
KINGS
MOOR
112
GROVE
Bluebell Valley Nursery Sch.
Weston Park Prim. Sch.
The Tump
SADLIER CLO.
DRIVE
AVENUE
WESTON
BROXHOLME WLK
Bewy's Cross
NAPIER
MILES
Stoke Bishop C.of E. Prim. School
FERNDOWN
Bowling Green
Avon Primary School
BARRACKS
LOWER
THE BEAN ACRE
MERRIMANS RD.
SHIRE GDS.
WESTON
AVE.
104
HUMBERSTAN WLK.
PLAYFORD GDS.
BANGROVE WLK.
WINDCLIFF CR
HALLARDS CLO
MIDDLETON RD
BADENHAM
BARROWMEAD
HOPEWELL GDS
MOOREND GDS.
GROVE
MANCROFT
KINGS
OLD
QUARRY
RISE
OLD QUARRY
PK.
NIGEL
ROAD
GROVE
HIGH
PARK
RD.
STREET
PENPOLE
Penpole Point
Penpole Wood
Kingsweston House
Playing Field
LANE
Sports Ground
ROAD
B4054
Roman found A.D.
Sedgewick
WOODVIEW
PENPOLE PK.
Rutland
Avendall
COURT
Wasborough
Portway Community School
LANE
OAKTREE
RIDGE
Barwick
The Lawns
GRAINGER CT.
HERMITAGE
Cricket Ground
SHIREHAMPTON
SHIREHAMPTON PARK (National Trust)
HOME GROUND
BROADLEAZE
BARROW HILL
BEACHLEY WLK
KILMINSTER RD.
PENLEA CT.
PRIORY GS
77
OLD
ORCHARD
GROVE
PORTBURY WLK
ST MARY'S WK
Cemetery
Shirehampton Jun.& Inf. Sch.
SPRING
STREET
PEMBROKE
Hlth. Cen.
CRES.
WAVERLEY
SEVERN
53
A
PENPOLE
MEAD
CLIFFORD
GDNS.
54
HILL
CEDAR ROW
78
SHIREHAMPTON
Club House
B
The Grn.
PARK
SHIREHAMPTON
54
C
SHIREHAMPTON GOLF COURSE
WAY

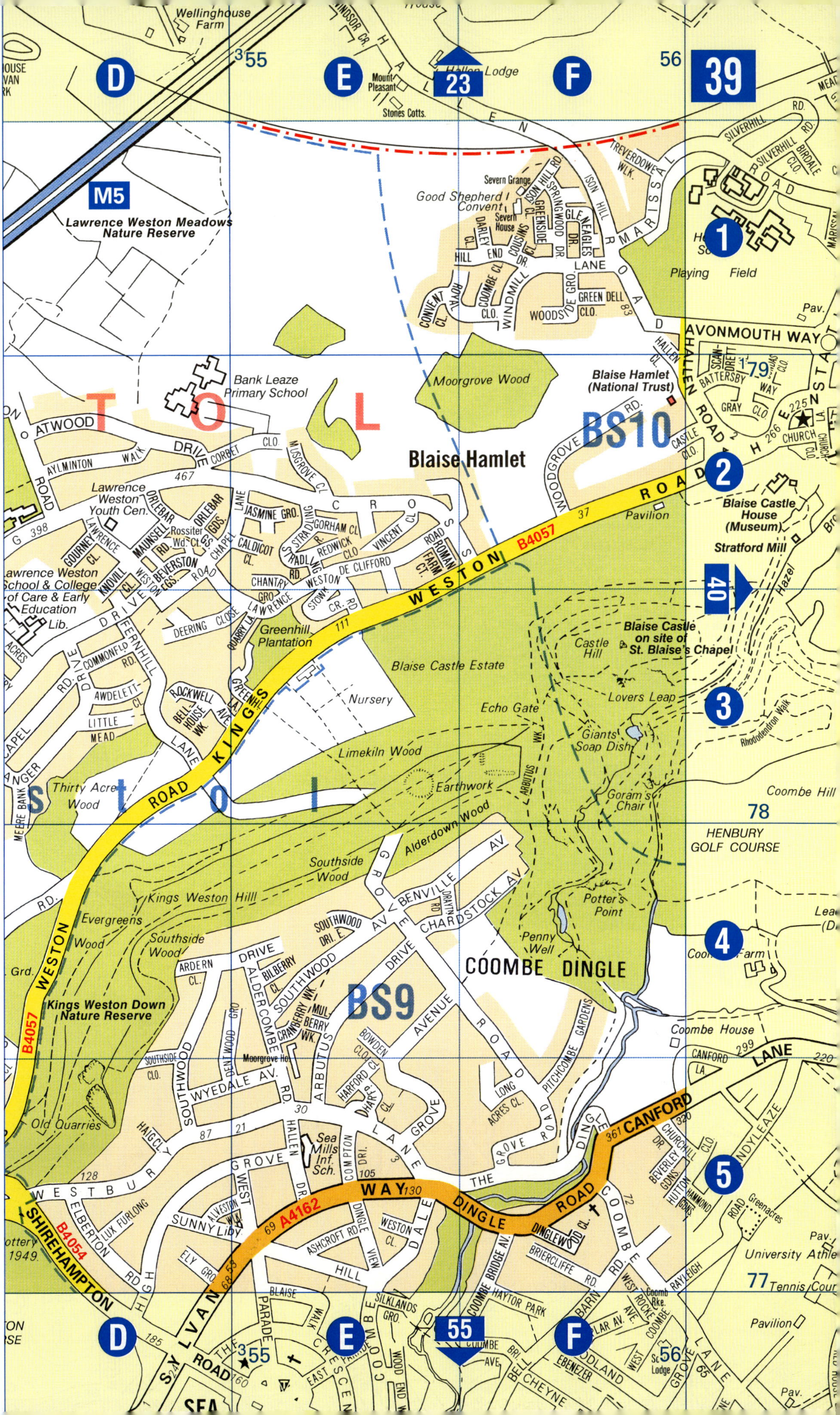
D
E
F
355
56
23
40
55
1
2
3
4
5
78
77
Wellinghouse Farm
Hallen Lodge
Mount Pleasant
Stones Cotts.
M5
Lawrence Weston Meadows Nature Reserve
Severn Grange
Good Shepherd Convent
Severn House
Playing Field
Pav.
AVONMOUTH WAY
Bank Leaze Primary School
Moorgrove Wood
Blaise Hamlet (National Trust)
BS10
Blaise Hamlet
BRISTOL
Lawrence Weston Youth Cen.
Lawrence Weston School & College of Care & Early Education
Lib.
Blaise Castle House (Museum)
Stratford Mill
Pavilion
WESTON ROAD
KINGS WESTON ROAD
B4057
Greenhill Plantation
Blaise Castle Estate
Nursery
Castle Hill
Blaise Castle on site of St. Blaise's Chapel
Lovers Leap
Echo Gate
Giants Soap Dish
Rhododendron Walk
Limekiln Wood
Earthwork
Goram's Chair
Coombe Hill
HENBURY GOLF COURSE
Thirty Acre Wood
Alderdown Wood
Southside Wood
Kings Weston Hill
Evergreens Wood
Potter's Point
Penny Well
COOMBE DINGLE
Kings Weston Down Nature Reserve
BS9
Moorgrove Ho.
Coombe House
Old Quarries
Sea Mills Inf. Sch.
A4162
DINGLE ROAD
CANFORD LANE
B4054
SHIREHAMPTON ROAD
WESTBURY LANE
University Athletic
Tennis Cour
Pavilion
HENBURY ROAD
Greenacres
ATWOOD DRIVE
MARISSAL ROAD
HALLEN ROAD
GROVE ROAD
AVENUE
SYLVAN WAY

24
56
39
A
B
C
1
2
3
4
5
356
57
179
178
177
Botany Bay
HENBURY
WESTBURY ON TRYM
BS9
Coombe Dingle
Henbury School
Playing Field
Blaise Hamlet (National Trust)
Blaise Castle House (Museum)
Stratford Mill
Blaise Castle on site of St. Blaise's Chapel
Castle Hill
Lovers Leap
Giants Soap Dish
Goram's Chair
Potter's Point
Coombe Hill
Club House
HENBURY GOLF COURSE
Lead Mines (Disused)
Coombe Farm
Coombe House
River Trym
Henbury House
Chesterfield House
Recreation Ground
Henbury Gardens
Blaise Primary School
Henbury Manor Sch.
Westmoreland Farm
Swimming Pool
Bowling Grn.
Henbury Ct. Jun. & Inf. Sch.
Henbury Court
Barlands House
Brookridge House
Machin Youth Cen.
Lib.
Clinic
Manor Nursing Home
College
Frances Greeves Ct.
Sheepwood Park
Sheep Wood
Cricket Ground
Pavilion
Gatehouse
C. of E. Prim. Sch.
Canford Cemetery
Canford Park
Mini Rlwy.
Chapel
Tennis Courts
University Athletic Ground
Sports Ground
Red Maids School
Playing Field
South Lodge
Greenacres
AVONMOUTH WAY
STATION ROAD
HENBURY ROAD
CROW LANE
KINGS WESTON ROAD
HALLEN ROAD
MARISSAL ROAD
PASSAGE ROAD
WYCK BECK ROAD
CHARLTON
KNOLE
BRENTRY HILL
THE RIDGEWAY
CANFORD LANE
CANFORD RD.
FALCONDALE ROAD
WESTBURY HILL
HIGH ST.
DINGLE ROAD
COOMBE
A4018
A4162
B4055
B4057

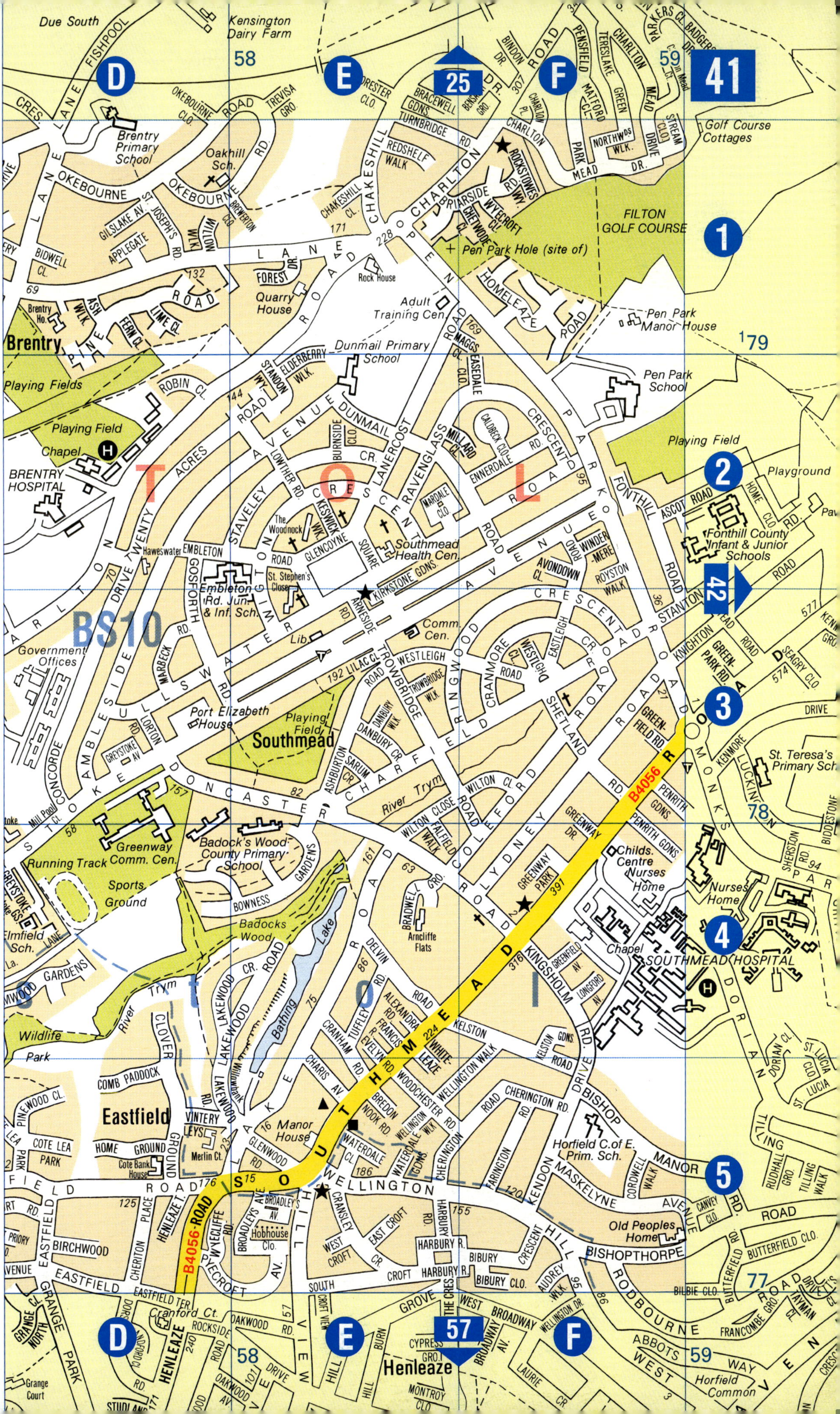

Due South
Kensington Dairy Farm
25
Brentry Primary School
Oakhill Sch.
FILTON GOLF COURSE
Golf Course Cottages
Pen Park Hole (site of)
Rock House
Quarry House
Adult Training Cen.
Pen Park Manor House
Brentry
Playing Fields
Dunmail Primary School
Pen Park School
Playing Field
Chapel
BRENTRY HOSPITAL
Playground
Fonthill County Infant & Junior Schools
The Woodnock
Southmead Health Cen.
St. Stephen's Close
Embleton Rd. Jun. & Inf. Sch.
BS10
Government Offices
Lib
Comm. Cen.
42
Port Elizabeth House
Southmead
Playing Field
St. Teresa's Primary Sch.
Greenway Comm. Cen.
Running Track
Sports Ground
Badock's Wood County Primary School
Badocks Wood
Arncliffe Flats
Childs. Centre
Nurses Home
SOUTHMEAD HOSPITAL
Chapel
Wildlife Park
Bathing Lake
Eastfield
Manor House
Merlin Ct.
Cote Bank House
Horfield C.of E. Prim. Sch.
Old Peoples Home
Hobhouse Clo.
B4056
Henleaze
Grange Court
Horfield Common
57

26
58
41
A
B
C
1
2
3
4
5
59
60
79
78
77
BS10
BS7
SOUTH
FILTON
BRISTOL
Club House
Golf Course Cottages
FILTON GOLF COURSE
GOLF COURSE
FAIRWAY INDUSTRIAL CENTRE
Works
Aircraft Works
LINK RD.
FAIRLAWN AV.
HOMESTEAD ROAD
NEW LANE
Filton College
GLEBELANDS RD.
Hanover Ct.
RECTORY LA.
STATION
CHURCH RD.
Stoke Hill
Cotswold Vw.
NORTH ROAD
GLOUCESTER ROAD
A38
STATION RD.
SHELLARD
Pen Park Manor House
Pen Park School
PEN PARK
FONTHILL ROAD
Playing Field
Playground
Pavilion
Sports Ground
Tennis Cts.
Library
HOLLYLEIGH AV.
CHARLTON AV.
Buckingham Ho.
Britannia Ho.
Concorde Ho.
BEVAN CT.
SPRINGFIELDS
Youth Cen.
Ten. Cts.
Rec. Cen.
RECREATION GROUND
CHARBOROUGH RD.
Charborough Rd. Prim. Sch.
B4056
HOME CLO.
Fonthill County Infant & Junior Schools
STANTON ROAD
WINDERMERE
AVONDOWN CL.
ROYSTON WK.
CRESCENT ROAD
FELSTEAD ROAD
KNIGHTON
GREENPARK RD.
SEAGRY CLO.
KENMORE CRES.
KENMORE DRIVE
BRAEMAR CRES.
DUNKELD
RANNOCH
RANNOCH RD.
CLYDE GRO.
ELGIN AV.
LOMOND RD.
BRONCKSEA RD.
Filton Park School
THE WICKETS
Sinclair Ho.
ELM PARK
GAYNER ROAD
PINE GRO.
FERNDALE RD.
Clin.
SHIELDS AVENUE
THIRD AV.
FOURTH AVENUE
Shield Rd. Prim. Sch.
Pavilion
Playing Field
Northville
NORTHVILLE
Cabot Ct.
BRAEMAR AVENUE
BELMONT PK.
CROPTHORNE RD.
FIFTH AV.
EDEN
St. Teresa's R.C. Primary School
LUCKINGTON
BIDDESTONE RD.
Monk's Park School
Up. Horfield Primary Sch.
SHERIDAN
SHELLEY WAY
ELIOT CL.
MACAULAY RD.
AUSTEN GRO.
SHERSTON RD.
YATTON
Tennis Cts.
MONK'S PARK AVENUE
NORTHWICK RD.
ST. ALDWYN'S CLO.
ST. GREGORY'S RD.
DUDLEY GRO.
SHAKESPEARE AVENUE
GREEN CLO.
EMERSON SQ.
GREENFIELD AV.
Childs Centre
Nurses Home
SOUTHMEAD HOSPITAL
GRITTLETON
ALDERTON RD.
PRIORY GDS.
MONTREAL
TORONTO ROAD
BEVERLEY
BOSTON RD.
DOONE RD.
HAZEL AVENUE
BEECH CROFT
BRIDGE WLK.
BUXTON WLK.
MELTON ROAD
RUSKIN GRO.
DORIAN ROAD
DORIAN CL.
ST. LUCIA CLO.
ST. LUCIA CR.
INKERMAN CLOSE
Sports Ground
CAINE RD.
LAXEY
RAMSEY RD.
MANX RD.
JOCELYN RD.
NORLEY RD.
DOUGLAS RD.
Prospect Pl.
Post Office Comp. and Engineering Centre
REYNOLDS WLK.
Library
HOTTOM GDNS.
FILTON AVENUE
DORCHESTER
KENDAL
TAUNTON WLK.
NEWBURY RD.
LUDLOW RD.
CAMBORNE ROAD
SANDLING
KEYS AVENUE
OAKLEY RD.
Filton Avenue Nursery, Inf. & Junior Schs.
WORDSWORTH ROAD
TILTING ROAD
RUDHALL GRO.
TILLING WALK
T.A. Centre
Horfield Comm.
WESSEX
BAYSWATER RD.
HIGHBURY
COURT
Horfield C. of E. Prim. Sch.
BISHOP MANOR
MASKELYNE AVENUE
CANVEY CLO.
Old Peoples Home
BISHOPTHORPE
BUTTERFIELD RD.
BUTTERFIELD CLO.
RODBOURNE
ABBOTS WAY
BILBIE CLO.
FRANCOMBE GRO.
KELLAWAY AV.
Horfield Common
LOCKLEAZE
Horfield Hlth. Cen.
CHEDWORTH
BLAKENEY
HOLTON RD.
Sports Ground
Pavilion
Gas Holder
FILTON

GLOUCESTERSHIRE
Filton
Filton Junction
Running Track
Sports Field
Tennis Cts.
Filton High School
Playing Field
Pav.
Drain
AVONSMERE RESIDENTIAL PARK
Stoke Gifford Junction
Offices
Parkway
Moat
The Paddocks
Harry Stoke Farm
Harry Stoke
Superstore
Superstore
Superstore
Newleaze
Newleaze House
BS34
Hall
Works
Subway
A4174
ROAD
FILTON ROAD
Filton Abbey Wood
M.O.D. (Abbey Wood)
Splatts Abbey Wood
Factory
Sports Field
UNIVERSITY OF THE WEST OF ENGLAND (Frenchay Campus)
Stanley Farm
Sports Ground
Pav.
Sports Grounds
Sports Ground
Pavilion
Playing Field
Tennis Cts.
Lockleaze School
Play. Fld.
Long Barrow
Adventure Playground
Long Wood
Hermitage Wood
Barn Wood
Star Hill
Obelisk
STOKE PARK
BS16
Lockleaze
The Bristol Home
Edward Bird Ho.
Condor Ho.
Comm. Cen.
Pastime Centre
Pale Plantation
Pond Field
M32 MOTORWAY
BURD HOSPI
Conygre Ho.
CONYGRE GROVE
BLENHEIM DRIVE
CANBERRA GRO.
MEADOWSWEET AV.
THE MEAD
BRIDGMAN GRO.
HOLMDALE RD.
SHANKLIN DR.
BRANKSOME CR.
BRANKSOME DR.
WARREN DR.
CHARLES RD.
HUNTERS WAY
VENTNOR RD.
SANDOWN RD.
STATION RD.
MACKIE ROAD
MACKIE GROVE
MACKIE AV.
ROYCROFT RD.
BRABAZON RD.
STANLEY AV.
STANLEY CR.
WALLSCOURT ROAD
ELEVENTH AVENUE
NINTH AV.
SEVENTH AV.
KIPLING RD.
MORTIMER RD.
WALLSCOURT RD. STH.
NUTFIELD GROVE
PILKINGTON CL.
NEW RD.
GREAT STOKE WAY
NEW ROAD
BRIERLY FURLONG
FOXDEN ROAD
LIME KILN CL.
STOKE ROAD
WESTFIELD ROAD
HARRY STOKE RD.
FILTON LA.
COLDHARBOUR LANE
CHURCH LANE
EIGHTH AVENUE
EMERSON SQ.
BONNINGTON WALK
HOGARTH WALK
EASTLAKE CL.
STOTHARD RD.
NASH DR.
HIGHMORE GDNS.
BRANWHITE CL.
ROMNEY AVENUE
CROME RD.
THORNYCROFT CLO.
HERKOMER CLO.
GAINSBOROUGH SQ.
CAMERON WALK
FLAXMAN CL.
LANDSEER AV.
ROWLANDSON GDNS.
CONSTABLE ROAD
MERRETT CT.
COPLEY GDNS.
TURNER GDNS.
D
E
F
1
2
3
4
5
27
44
59
61
62
77
78
79
311
246
526

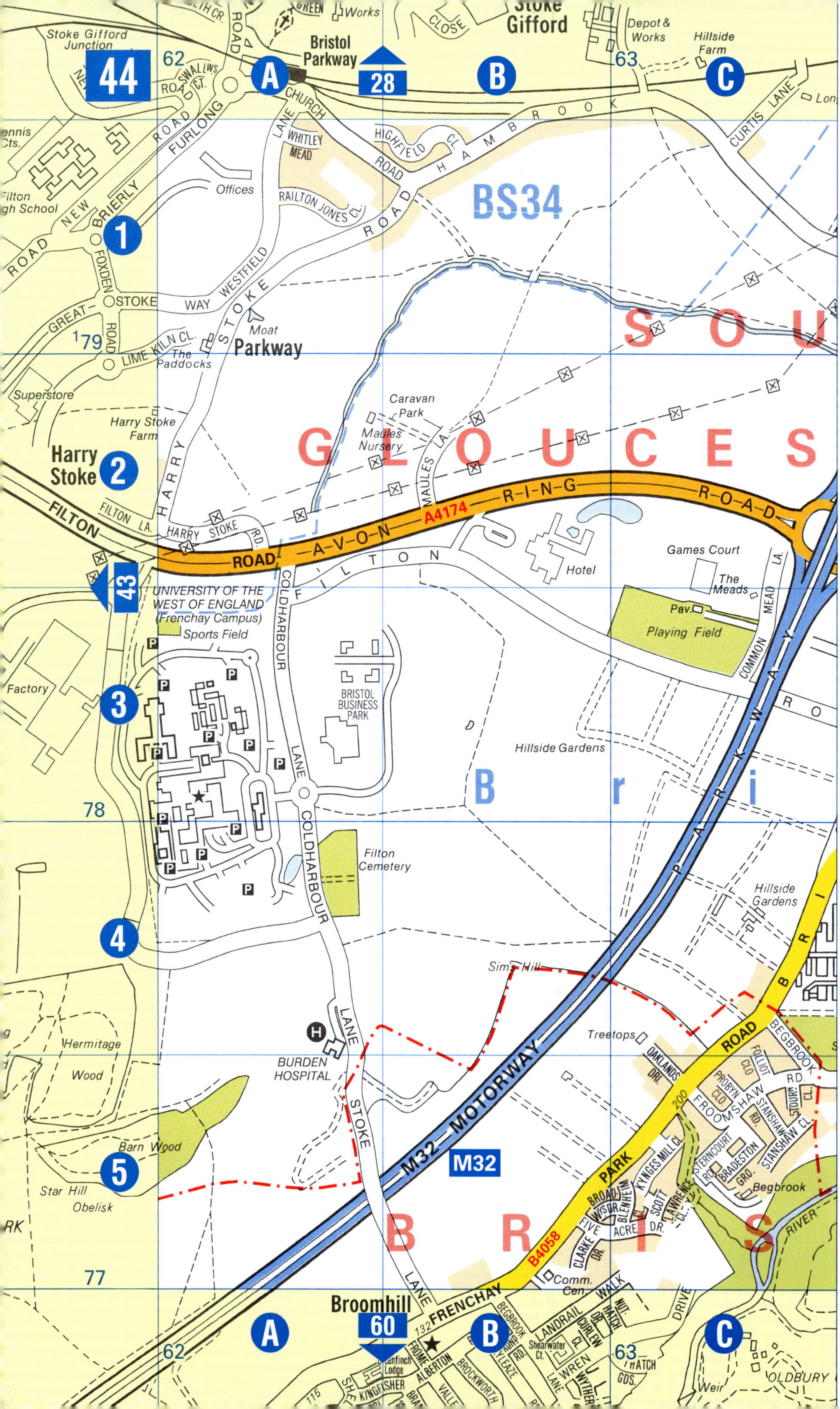

44
Stoke Gifford Junction
Bristol Parkway
28
Stoke Gifford
Depot & Works
Hillside Farm
A
B
C
62
63
SWALLOWS CT.
FURLONG ROAD
CHURCH LANE
WHITLEY MEAD
HIGHFIELD CL.
HAMBROOK ROAD
CURTIS LANE
Offices
RAILTON JONES CL.
BS34
Filton High School
NEW ROAD
BRIERLY
FOXDEN ROAD
STOKE ROAD
GREAT STOKE WAY
WESTFIELD
Moat
Parkway
179
LIME KILN CL.
The Paddocks
Superstore
Harry Stoke Farm
Harry Stoke
Caravan Park
Maules Nursery
MAULES LA.
GLOUCES
SOU
FILTON
FILTON LA.
HARRY STOKE RD.
AVON RING ROAD
A4174
Hotel
Games Court
The Meads
MEAD LA.
Pav.
Playing Field
COMMON
43
UNIVERSITY OF THE WEST OF ENGLAND (Frenchay Campus)
Sports Field
COLDHARBOUR LANE
Factory
BRISTOL BUSINESS PARK
Hillside Gardens
PARKWAY
B r i
78
Filton Cemetery
Hillside Gardens
Sims Hill
Treetops
Hermitage Wood
BURDEN HOSPITAL
STOKE LANE
M32 MOTORWAY
M32
Barn Wood
Star Hill Obelisk
OAKLANDS DRI.
PARK ROAD
B4058
200
FROOMSHAW RD.
BEGBROOK DR.
FOLLIOT CLO.
PROBYN CLO.
STANSHAW CL.
BRADESTON GRO.
Begbrook
RIVER
KYNGES MILL CL.
BLENHEIM
FIVE ACRE DR.
CLARKE DR.
LAWRENCE CL.
SCOTT
BRIS
77
Comm. Cen.
Broomhill
FRENCHAY
60
BEGBROOK
LANDRAIL
WALK
NUT HATCH DR.
CURLEW CL.
WREN DR.
Shearwater Ct.
HATCH GDS.
OLDBURY
Weir
ALBERTON
BROCKWORTH
KINGFISHER
115
132

D
E
F
64
365
29
61
46
1
2
3
4
5
179
78
77
Pye Corner
Sturden Court
Brook Farm
Bradley Brook
Junction 19
Junction 1
M32
M4
M32 MOTORWAY
M4 MOTORWAY
Hoodland
Oakwood House
The Priory
Works
Whiteshill Common
Whiteshill
Hambrook Prim. Sch.
Riverside View
Quarry
Fort
Waterfall Farm
WORRELLS LANE
MOOREND RD.
BRISTOL RD.
WHITESHILL
GLOUCESTER ROAD
B4427
B4058
SUNNYSIDE LANE
STURDEN LA.
MAPSTONE CL.
OLD PLAYERS CLO.
Hambrook Grove
Hambrook Farm
Hambrook
THE STREAM
The Homestead
Weir
HEATH ROAD
The Elms
CHURCH
MILL ROAD
MILL STEPS
FROME GLEN
Frome Bank Gds.
BROMLEY HEATH RD.
AVON RING ROAD
A4174
Lyntonfields
FENBROOK CLO.
FILTON RD.
LYNTON WY
The Willows
The Rowans
The Hornbeams
BECKSPOOL
HARFORD DRIVE
PENN DRIVE
Pond
CRESCENT
BRYANTS CLO.
ELLIOTT AV.
PARK
MARLBOROUGH DR.
WELLINGTN PL.
THE PARK
The Elms
MANOR PL.
BERKY DRI.
WADHAM DRI.
MALMAINS DRI.
BEAUFORT PL.
Manor House
RIVERWOOD RD.
GROVE BANK
Playing Field Pav.
Bromley Heath
Bromley Farm
SCANTLEBERRY CL.
BRAMPTON DR.
QUAKER'S RD.
QUAKERS CLO.
WEDGEWOOD CL.
WENMORE CL.
QUEENSHOLM
GREENLEAZE AV.
GREENLEAZE CLO.
QUEENSHOLM AVE
GREYSTONES
FOUR ACRES
SANDRINGHAM RD.
Hall
Bromley Heath Inf. & J. School
SANDHOLME CLO.
TANNERS CT.
HOMESTEAD GDS.
FRENCHAY HOSPITAL
Cedar Hall
CLEEVE ROAD
GRANGE PARK
RIVER FROME
Mill House
CLEEVE WOOD PK.
CLEEVE QUARRY
Sports Ground
Pavilion
BROMLEY HEATH AV.
PILGRIMS WY.
DOWNLEAZE
OAKDALE ROAD
HEATH GDNS
OAKDALE AV.
BS16
Frenchay House
Tennis Crts.
Sports Field
BECKSPOOL
Frenchay Common
Tuckett Ho.
Frenchay
Frome Villas
CHAPEL LA.
CHAPEL LANE
TUCKETT LA.
Frenchay C of E Prim. Sch.
Westbourne Cotts.
CHURCH
QUARRY RD.
THE COMMON
Westbourne
Newlands
THE NEWLANDS
PEARCES HILL
CLIFF COURT DR.
PARK
FRENCHAY HILL
Lincombe Barn Woods
MARSHFIELD PARK
WOODSIDE RD.
CLEEVE GDNS.
CLEEVE DALE
AMBERLEY CLO.
AMBERLEY RD.
ROCKLAND ROAD
CLEEVE WOOD RD.
HEATH WALK
HEATH WLK.
HEATH COURT
CLEEVE LAWNS
CLEEVE PARK RD.
CLEEVE HILL
A4017
Frenchay Mill
Weir
FROME
RIVERSIDE DR.
GLENSIDE CLO.
FROMESIDE PK.
FRENCHAY CLOSE
Oldbury Court Jun. & Inf. Sch.
Tennis Courts
Pond
Downend
BADMINTON RD.
BADMINTON WK.
WINDSOR CT.
SANDRINGHAM PK.
CLEEVE AV
FARM RD
CLEEVE LODGE RD
The Firs
COURT ESTATE
PENDOCK
BROOKE
WHITTINGTON RD.
BARTON MDW. EST.
SIDELANDS ROAD
FIELD ROAD
OVERNDALE
WOODLANDS RISE
CLEEVE HILL EXTENSION

46
30
45
62
A
B
C
1
2
3
4
5
365
66
179
78
77
Winterbourne Down
Sturden Court
Corner
Riverside View
Hambrook Prim. Sch.
Worrells Lane
Waterfall Farm
The Elms
Church Road
Frome Glen
Mill Steps
Frome Bank Gdns.
Wynnford Grange
The Stone Dingle La.
Damsons Bridge
Kendleshire Farm
Kendleshire
Kingsway Trailer Caravan Park
Quarry
Fort
Bury Hill
Bury Hill
Cuckoo Lane
Mill Road
Moorend
Church Lane
SOUTH GL
Buryhill Farm
M4
M4 Motorway
Ring Road
Avon Ring Road
A4174
A432
Badminton Road
Folly Brook
Bromley Heath Rd.
Bromley Heath
Baugh Farm
Playing Field
Chantry La.
Chepstow Pk.
Wincanton Cl.
Kempton Cl.
Fontwell Dr.
Wetherby Ct.
Haydock Cl.
Plumpton Ct.
Epsom Cl.
Redcar Ct.
York Ct.
Ripon Ct.
Lingfield Pk.
Goodwood Gdns.
Aintree Dr.
Sandown Cl.
Sedgefield Gdns.
Beverley Av.
Ascot Cl.
Church La.
Trident Clo.
Village Park (Prop.)
Queensholm Dri.
Queensholm Ave.
Queensholm Clo.
Queensholm Cres.
Greystones
Four Acre Rd.
Fouracre Cres.
Baugh Gdns.
Baugh Rd.
Greenleaze Clo.
Greenleaze Av.
Wedgewood Rd.
Wenmore Cl.
Quakers Road
Quakers Clo.
Bromley Drive
Pilgrims Wy.
Leap Bridge
Blackhorse Lane
Blackhorse
Blackhorse Rd.
Bridge Leap Rd.
Rockside Gdns.
Rockside Av.
Leap Valley Cres.
Leap Vale
Playing Field
Play. Field
Blackhorse Prim. Sch.
Beaufort Ct.
Hall
Sandringham Road
Sandringham Av.
Sandringham Pk.
Bromley Heath Inf. & Jun. School
Sandholme Clo.
Four Acre Av.
Oakdale Road
Oakdale Av.
Oakdale Ct.
Oakdale Clo.
Glendale
Downleaze
Bromley Heath Av.
Heath Gdns.
Heath Road
West Valley
Chine Vw.
Westbourne
Lulworth Cres.
Lychet Dr.
Valley Gdns.
Berkeley Clo.
Beaufort Road
Dibden Cl.
Dibden Rd.
Mendip Cres.
Wakeford Rd.
Vinny Ave.
Walker Clo.
Boscombe Cres.
The Meads
The Folly
Meadow Clo.
Avenue
St. Augustine of Canterbury R.C. Prim. Sch.
Badminton Road Play. Field
Kimberley Clo.
Garnett Pl.
Bowden Pl.
Downend Sports Centre
Downend Sch.
Windsor Ct.
Sutherland Av.
Badminton Wk.
Farm Ct.
Cleeve Park Rd.
Cleeve Av.
Cleeve Ct.
Cleeve Lawns
Cleeve Hill
Cleeve Rd.
Cleeve Lodge Rd.
Cleeve Lodge Cl.
Heath Court
Heath Walk
Heath Wlk.
Bromley Heath Road
Tennis Courts
Pond
Downend
Cemetery
King George's Field
Pav.
Westerleigh Road
Westerleigh Cl.
Woodhall Clo.
Stockwell Hill
Stockwell Glen
Stockwell Cl.
Stockwell Dri.
Stockwell Av.
Kingston Cl.
Kingston Dri.
Springfield Avenue
Springfield Cl.
Springfield Rd.
Springleaze
Elm Tree Ave.
Dibden Lane
Training Centre Hall
Playing Field
Play. Fld.
Jubilee Cres.
Cherry Gro.
Blackhorse Drive
Stanbridge Rd.
Stanbridge Prim. Sch.
Graham Rd.
Brook Rd.
East View
Stream
West Vw.
Deanna Ct.
The Firs
Barley Close
Peach

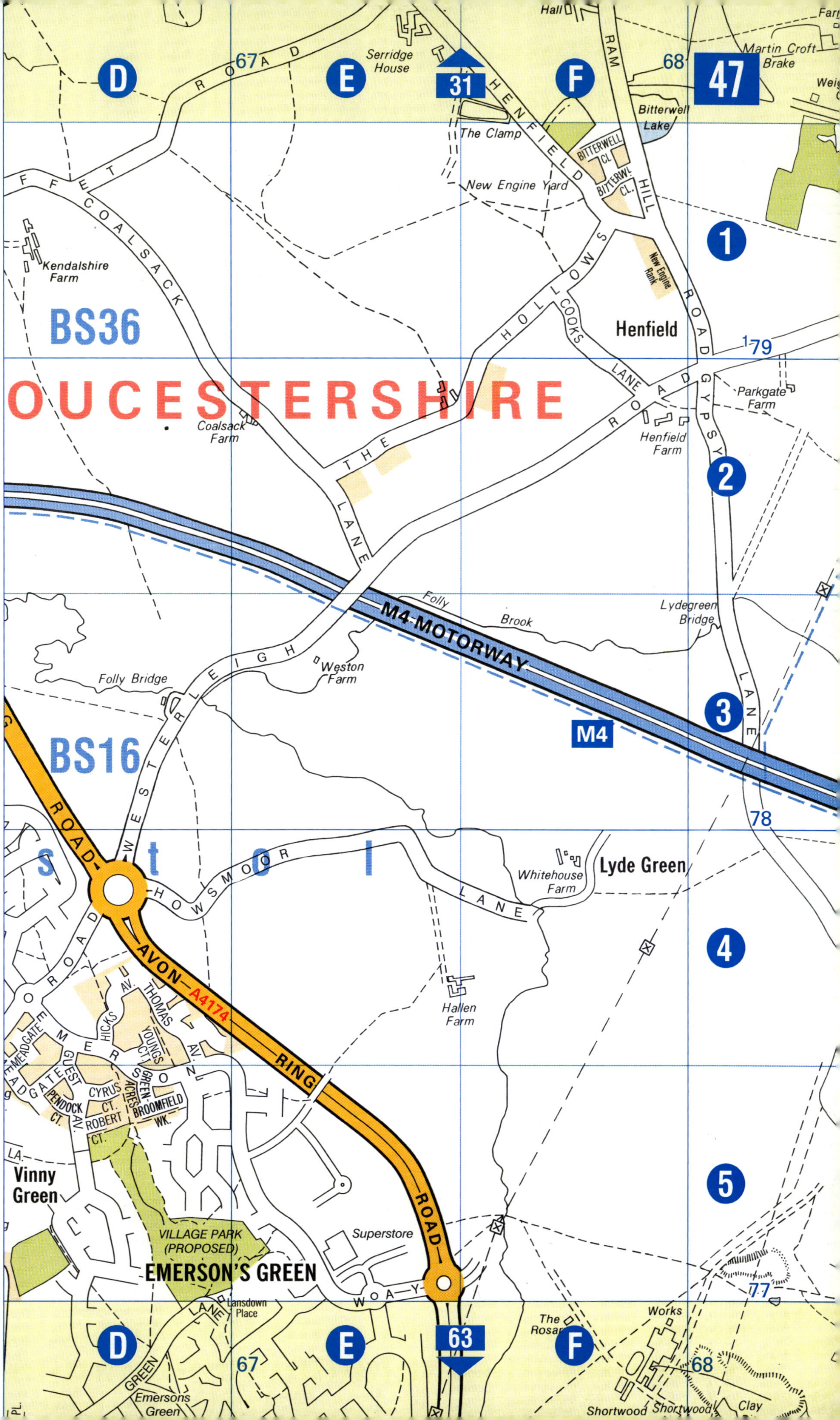
D
E
F
31
63
67
68
79
78
77
1
2
3
4
5
BS36
BS16
GLOUCESTERSHIRE
Bristol
Serridge House
Hall
Martin Croft Brake
Bitterwell Lake
The Clamp
New Engine Yard
BITTERWELL CL.
BITTERWL. CL.
New Engine Rank
RAM HILL
HENFIELD
ROAD
FEET ROAD
COALSACK
Kendalshire Farm
Coalsack Farm
HOLLOWS
THE LANE
COOKS LANE
Henfield
Henfield Farm
Parkgate Farm
GYPSY LANE
M4 MOTORWAY
M4
Folly Brook
Lydegreen Bridge
Folly Bridge
Weston Farm
WESTERLEIGH ROAD
HOWSMOOR LANE
Whitehouse Farm
Lyde Green
Hallen Farm
AVON RING ROAD
A4174
THOMAS AV.
YOUNGS CT.
HICKS AV.
EMERSONS GREEN
MEADGATE
GUEST
PENDOCK CT.
CYRUS CT.
ROBERT CT.
GREEN ACRES
BROOMFIELD WK.
LA.
Vinny Green
VILLAGE PARK (PROPOSED)
EMERSON'S GREEN
Superstore
WAY
Lansdown Place
LANE
GREEN
Emersons Green
The Rosary
Works
Shortwood
Clay

MOUTH OF THE SEVERN
Sugar Loaf Beach
APPROACH GOLF COURSE
Black Nore
Lighthouse
MARINERS PATH
Playing Field
Swimming Pool
The Lodge
NORTH
Redcliff Bay
POLICE H.Q.
PORTISHEAD DOWN
BS20
Caravan Park
Manor Farm
Nightingale Valley
Down Cottage
Brockley Cottage
Black Rock Quarry (disused)
DOWN ROAD
VALLEY ROAD
NORE ROAD
DOWN ROAD
DENNY VIEW
MENDIP
DRAKES
SEAVIEW ROAD
HILLCREST
HILLSIDE ROAD
NEWHAVEN ROAD
PEMBROKE RD.
BEECHWOOD RD.
DEVONSHIRE DR.
SOMERSET RD.
KINGSWAY
KING'S RD.
QUEEN'S RD.
WEATHERLY DRIVE
BADGER RISE
BROCK END
HIGHFIELD DRIVE
BLACKBERRY LA.
NIGHTINGALE RISE
MERLIN PARK
TOWER ROAD
HIGH VIEW
ASHDOWN RD.
BELTON RD.
NICHOL'S RD.
SEAVIEW RD.
FROBISHER CL.
CABOT RS.
BRENDON
DOWNLEAZE
BRUTON AV.
PINECROFT
GLENWOOD RISE
SEVERN MEAD
NORE PARK DR.
RIVERLEAZE
HAWTHORN CL.
MEADOWS CL.
NEWPORT CL.
MONMOUTH CL.
GAUNTS CL.
RANCHWAY
HARMONY DR.
HILL GAY CL.
CEDARHURST RD.
HOMESTEAD
NORTHFIELD RD.
REDCLIFFE CL.
CHESLEFIELD
WATERSIDE
SAGE CL.
WOODSIDE GDNS.
ST. AUGUSTINE'S CL.
QUEEN'S WY.
COMBE WK.
BRAMS
A
B
C
1
2
3
4
5
44
345
77
76
175

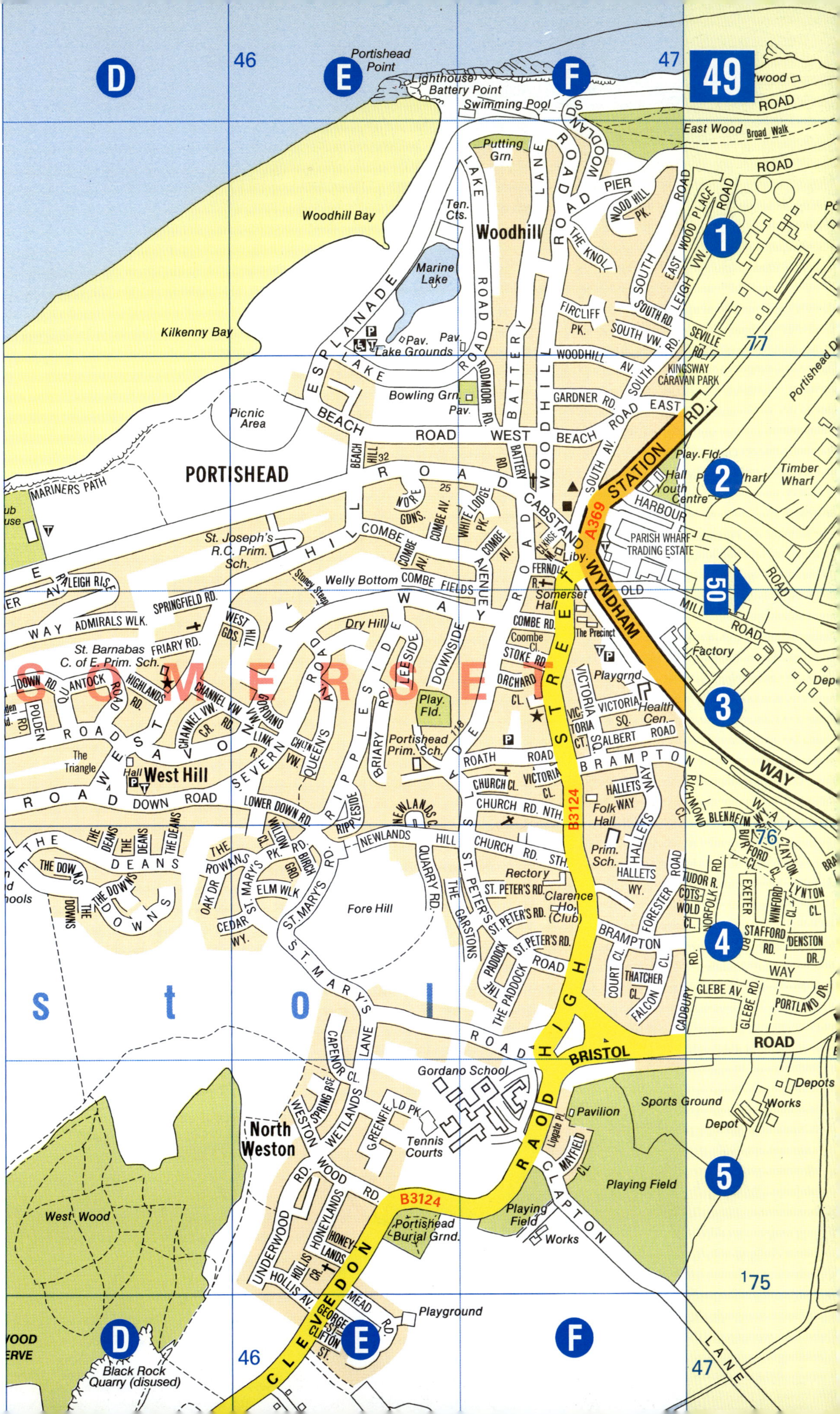
Portishead Point
Lighthouse
Battery Point
Swimming Pool
Woodhill Bay
Kilkenny Bay
Marine Lake
Lake Grounds
Putting Grn.
Ten. Cts.
Woodhill
ESPLANADE
LAKE
Bowling Grn.
BEACH ROAD WEST
BEACH ROAD EAST
Picnic Area
PORTISHEAD
MARINERS PATH
St. Joseph's R.C. Prim. Sch.
Welly Bottom
COMBE FIELDS WAY
Dry Hill
RALEIGH RISE
ADMIRALS WLK.
SPRINGFIELD RD.
FRIARY RD.
St. Barnabas C. of E. Prim. Sch.
SOMERSET
Play. Fld.
Portishead Prim. Sch.
West Hill
The Triangle
DOWN ROAD
RIPPLESIDE
HIGH STREET
B3124
A369
STATION RD.
WYNDHAM WAY
PARISH WHARF TRADING ESTATE
OLD MILL ROAD
Factory
Timber Wharf
Play. Fld.
Youth Centre
HARBOUR
Health Cen.
Playgrnd
The Precinct
Somerset Hall
Coombe Cl.
Rectory
Clarence Ho. (Club)
Folk Hall
Prim. Sch.
BRAMPTON WAY
Fore Hill
ST. MARY'S ROAD
THE DEANS
THE DOWNS
NEWLANDS HILL
CHURCH RD. STH.
BRISTOL ROAD
Gordano School
North Weston
Tennis Courts
Pavilion
Sports Ground
Playing Field
Works
Depot
Depots
Portishead Burial Grnd.
CLEVEDON ROAD
CLAPTON LANE
West Wood
Black Rock Quarry (disused)
Playground
KINGSWAY CARAVAN PARK
East Wood
Broad Walk
WOODHILL ROAD
PIER ROAD
FIRCLIFF PK.
LAKE ROAD
BATTERY LANE
46
47
77
76
75
D
E
F
1
2
3
4
5
50

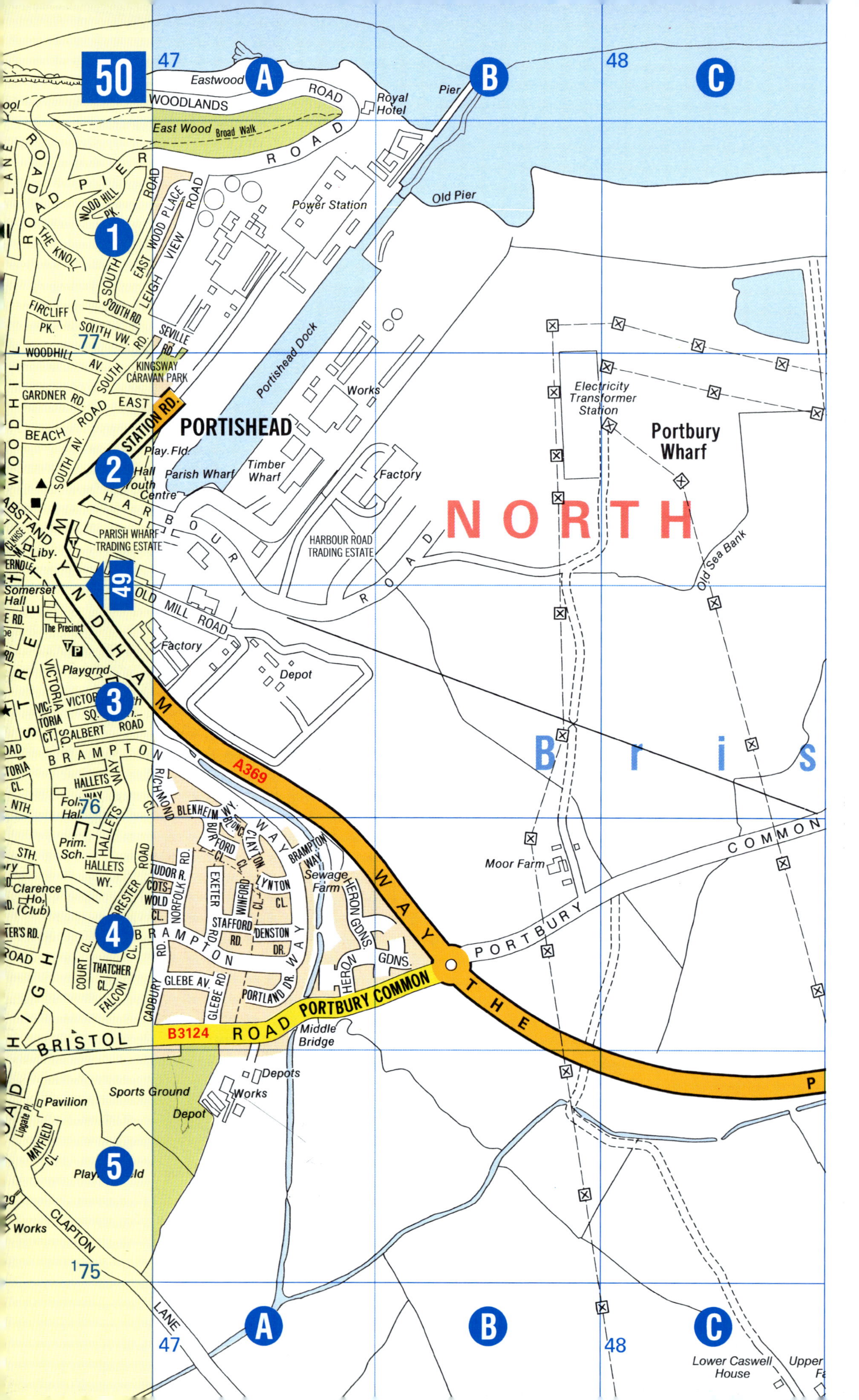
47
48
A
B
C
Eastwood
WOODLANDS ROAD
Royal Hotel
Pier
East Wood
Broad Walk
ROAD
Old Pier
Power Station
PIER ROAD
WOOD HILL PK.
THE KNOLL
SOUTH RD.
EAST WOOD PLACE
LEIGH VIEW ROAD
FIRCLIFF PK.
SOUTH VW. RD.
SEVILLE RD.
77
WOODHILL AV.
KINGSWAY CARAVAN PARK
SOUTH RD.
GARDNER RD.
EAST ROAD
BEACH RD.
SOUTH AV.
STATION RD.
PORTISHEAD
Portishead Dock
Works
Play. Fld.
Hall
Youth Centre
Parish Wharf
Timber Wharf
Factory
Electricity Transformer Station
Portbury Wharf
NORTH
HARBOUR ROAD
PARISH WHARF TRADING ESTATE
HARBOUR ROAD TRADING ESTATE
CABSTAND
Liby.
Somerset Hall
49
WYNDHAM
OLD MILL ROAD
The Precinct
Factory
Depot
Old Sea Bank
Playgrnd.
VICTORIA
VICTORIA SQ.
VIC. TORIA CT.
ALBERT ROAD
HIGH STREET
BRAMPTON WAY
A369
Bris
HALLETS WAY
76
Prim. Sch.
Clarence Ho. (Club)
RICHMOND CL.
BLENHEIM WY.
BURFORD CL.
CLAYTON CL.
BRAMPTON WAY
Sewage Farm
TUDOR R.
NORFOLK RD.
EXETER RD.
WINFORD CL.
LYNTON CL.
COTSWOLD CL.
STAFFORD RD.
DENSTON DR.
HERON GDNS.
Moor Farm
COMMON
PORTBURY
WAY
THE
FORESTER ROAD
BRAMPTON
COURT CL.
THATCHER CL.
FALCON CL.
GLEBE AV.
GLEBE RD.
CADBURY RD.
PORTLAND DR.
PORTBURY COMMON
B3124
ROAD
BRISTOL
Middle Bridge
Depots
Sports Ground
Works
Depot
Pavilion
Lipgate Pl.
MAYFIELD CL.
Play Field
Works
CLAPTON
LANE
175
P
1
2
3
4
5
Lower Caswell House
Upper

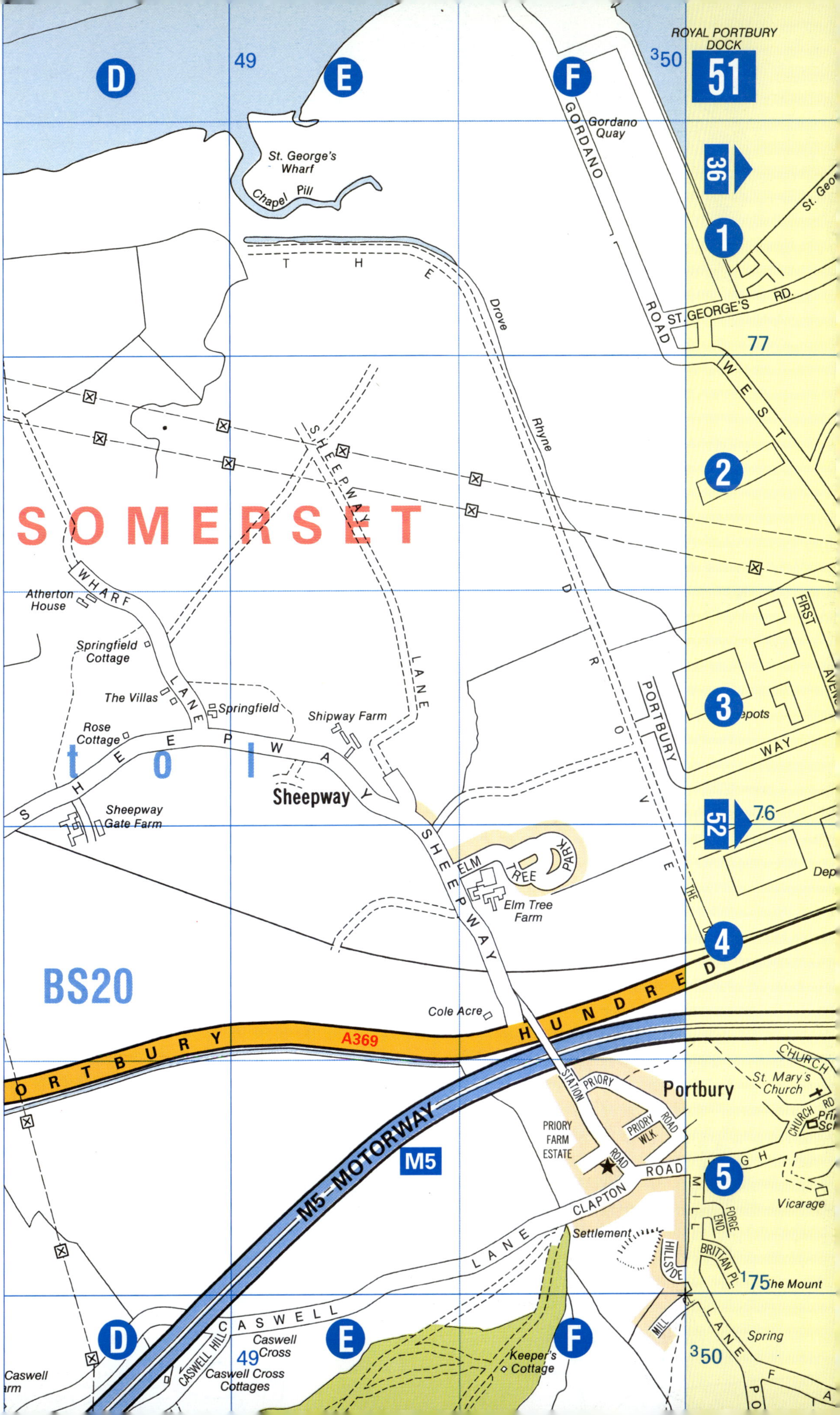

ROYAL PORTBURY DOCK
D
E
F
49
350
Gordano Quay
GORDANO ROAD
St. George's Wharf
Chapel Pill
36
1
St. George's RD.
THE Drove
Rhyne
77
WEST
2
SOMERSET
SHEEPWAY
Atherton House
WHARF LANE
Springfield Cottage
The Villas
Springfield
Shipway Farm
LANE
Rose Cottage
DROVE
PORTBURY WAY
FIRST AVENUE
Depots
3
SHEEPWAY
Sheepway
Sheepway Gate Farm
52
76
ELM TREE PARK
Elm Tree Farm
Dep
4
BS20
Cole Acre
PORTBURY HUNDRED
A369
STATION ROAD
PRIORY ROAD
Portbury
St. Mary's Church
CHURCH RD
PRIORY WLK.
PRIORY FARM ESTATE
M5 MOTORWAY
M5
ROAD
5
HIGH
CLAPTON LANE
Vicarage
MILL
FORGE END
Settlement
HILLSIDE
BRITTAN PL.
175
The Mount
CASWELL LANE
CASWELL HILL
Caswell Cross
Caswell Cross Cottages
Keeper's Cottage
MILL
Spring
Caswell Farm

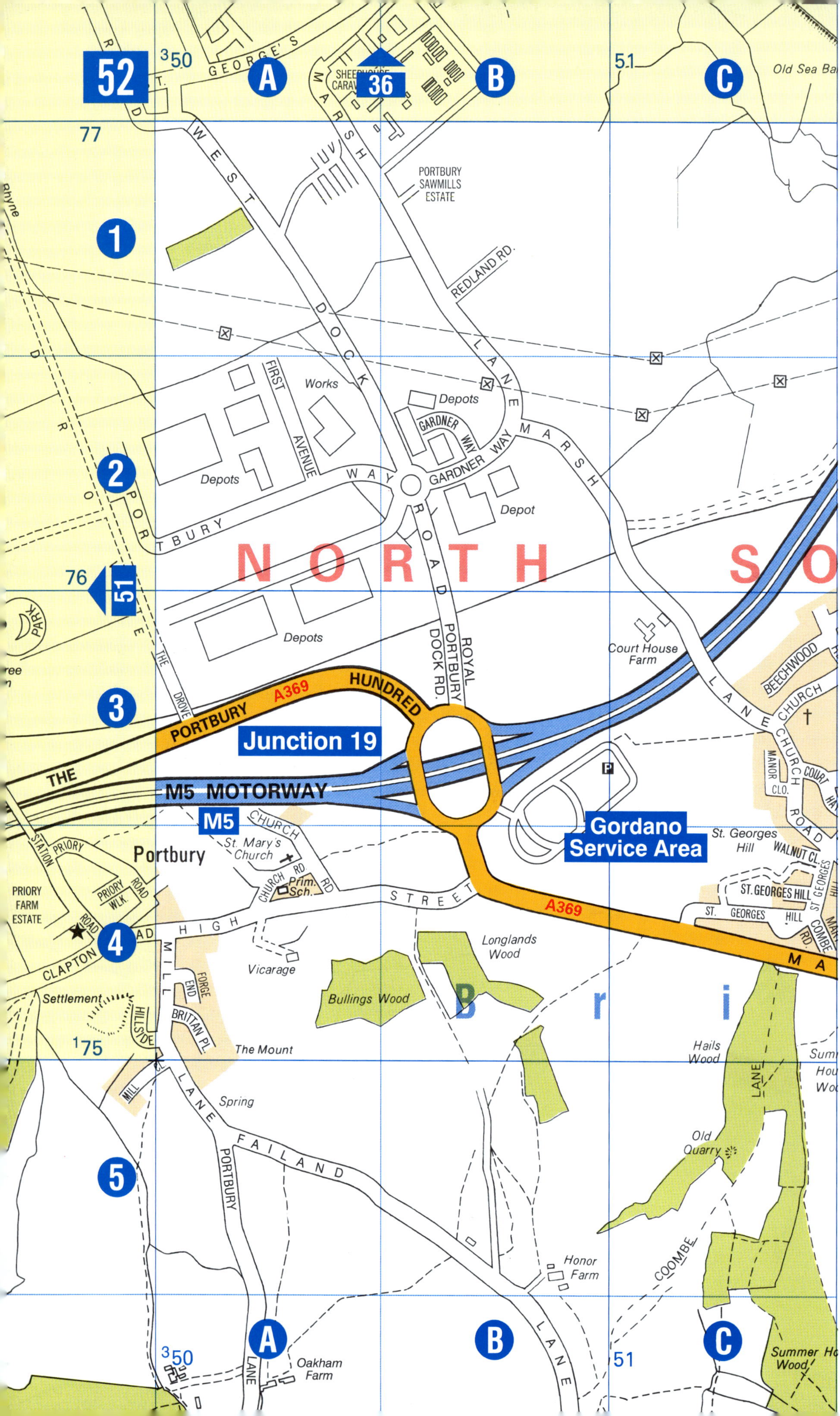

52
36
51
A
B
C
1
2
3
4
5
350
51
77
76
175
ST. GEORGE'S RD
Old Sea Ba
WEST DOCK ROAD
MARSH LANE
PORTBURY SAWMILLS ESTATE
REDLAND RD.
Rhyne
FIRST AVENUE
Works
Depots
Depot
GARDNER WAY
PORTBURY WAY
ROYAL PORTBURY DOCK RD.
NORTH SO
PARK
THE DROVE
Court House Farm
BEECHWOOD
CHURCH LANE
CHURCH ROAD
MANOR CLO.
COURT HAY
THE PORTBURY HUNDRED
A369
Junction 19
M5 MOTORWAY
M5
Gordano Service Area
St. Georges Hill
WALNUT CL.
ST. GEORGES HILL
ST. GEORGES RD.
COMBE
STATION ROAD
PRIORY ROAD
PRIORY WLK.
PRIORY FARM ESTATE
Portbury
CHURCH RD
St. Mary's Church
Prim. Sch.
HIGH STREET
CLAPTON ROAD
MILL LANE
FORGE END
BRITTAN PL.
HILLSIDE
Settlement
Vicarage
Bullings Wood
Longlands Wood
B r i
The Mount
Hails Wood
LANE
Old Quarry
Spring
FAILAND LANE
PORTBURY LANE
COOMBE LANE
Honor Farm
Oakham Farm
Summer House Wood

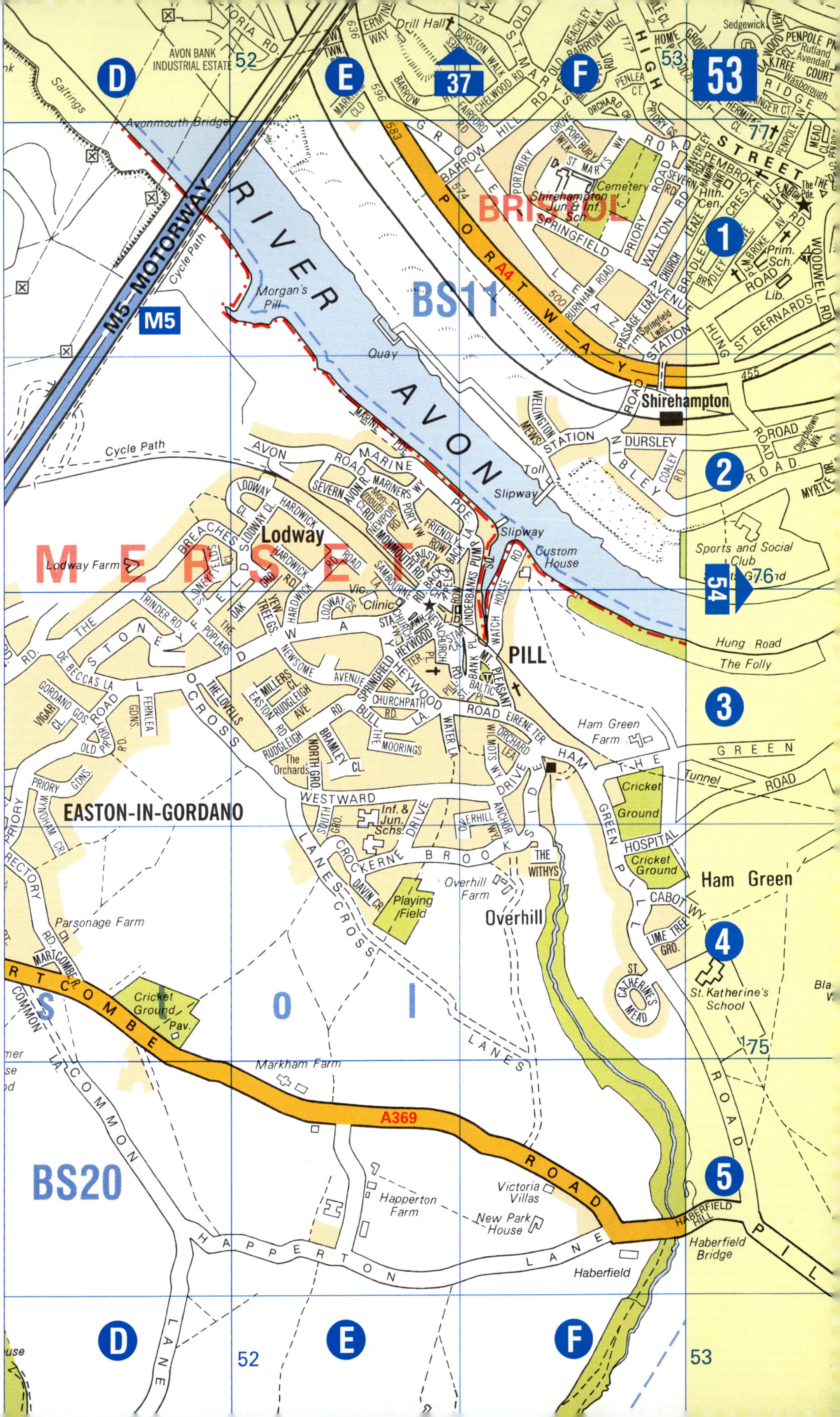
53
37
54
D
E
F
1
2
3
4
5
52
53
AVON BANK INDUSTRIAL ESTATE
Saltings
Avonmouth Bridge
M5 MOTORWAY
M5
Cycle Path
RIVER AVON
Morgan's Pill
Quay
BS11
BRISTOL
PORTWAY
A4
Drill Hall
CORSTON WALK
CHELWOOD RD
FAIRFORD RD
BARROW HILL
GROVE LEAZE
ST. MARY'S RD
OLD BARROW HILL
HIGH STREET
HOME GROUND
PENLEA CT.
ORCHARD CR.
PRIORY GS
PORTBURY GROVE
PORTBURY WLK
ST. MARY'S WK
Cemetery
Shirehampton Jun & Inf. Sch.
SPRINGFIELD
PRIORY ROAD
WALTON ROAD
SEVERN RD
WAVERLEY RD
PEMBROKE RD
Hlth. Cen.
CHURCH LEAZE
BRADLEY CRES.
BRADLEY AVENUE
BURNHAM ROAD
PASSAGE LEAZE
Springfield Lwns.
STATION ROAD
Prim. Sch.
Lib.
ST. BERNARDS RD
WOODWELL RD
HUNG ROAD
PENPOLE PK
Rutland Avendall
OAKTREE COURT
Wasborough
PENPOLE RIDGE
HERMITAGE CL.
Sedgewick
The Pde.
Shirehampton
WELLINGTON MEWS
STATION ROAD
DURSLEY
NIBLEY RD
COALEY RD
ROAD
Churchdown Wlk.
MYRTLE DR.
Sports and Social Club
Toll
Slipway
Slipway
Custom House
Hung Road
The Folly
Ham Green Farm
GREEN
THE TUNNEL
ROAD
Cricket Ground
HOSPITAL
Cricket Ground
Ham Green
CABOT WY
LIME TREE GRO.
ST. CATHERINE'S MEAD
St. Katherine's School
ROAD
PILL
Haberfield Bridge
HABERFIELD HILL
Haberfield
Cycle Path
AVON ROAD
MARINE PDE
MARINE
MARINERS WY
SEVERN
AVON
Monmouth Ct.
NEWPORT RD
PORT VW
FRIENDLY ROW
LODWAY CL.
LODWAY
HARDWICK
Lodway
BREACHES GATE
STONEYFIELDS
Lodway Farm
MERSET
SOMERSET
MONMOUTH RD
SAMBOURNE LA
BACK LA
CRUSTY LA
CHAPEL ROW
BACK RD.
UNDERBANKS
PUMP SQ.
HOUSE RD
WATCH HOUSE
Vic. Clinic
Lib.
STATION
HEYWOOD RD.
NEWCHURCH PL
STAR LA
BANK PL
MT. PLEASANT
BALTIC PL
PILL
TRINDER RD.
THE STONEY
FIELD
THE POPLARS
OAK
YEW TREE GS.
HARDWICK RD.
LODWAY GS.
AVENUE
NEWSOME AVENUE
DE BECCAS LA
GORDANO GDS.
VIGAR CL.
OLD PRIORY RD.
FERNLEA GDNS.
CROSS
THE LOVELLS
MILLERS CL.
EASTON RUDGLEIGH AVE.
RUDGLEIGH RD.
SPRINGFIELD
HEYWOOD TER.
CHURCHPATH RD.
BULL LA.
THE MOORINGS
WATER LA.
PILL ST.
ROAD
EIRENE TER.
ORCHARD LEA
WILMOTS WY
DRIVE
HAM
SIDE
BRAMLEY CL.
The Orchards
NORTH GRO.
WESTWARD
SOUTH GRO.
Inf. & Jun. Schs.
DRIVE
OVERHILL
ANCHOR WY
BROOK
CROCKERNE
THE WITHYS
Overhill Farm
Overhill
DAVIN CR.
Playing Field
LANES CROSS
PRIORY GDNS.
WYNDHAM CR.
PRIORY
EASTON-IN-GORDANO
RECTORY RD.
Parsonage Farm
MARTCOMBE RD.
MARTCOMBE
COMMON
Cricket Ground
Pav.
LANES
Markham Farm
A369
ROAD
COMMON LA.
BS20
Happerton Farm
Victoria Villas
New Park House
HAPPERTON LANE
LANE
175
455
500
574
583
596
636
73
77
117
52
76

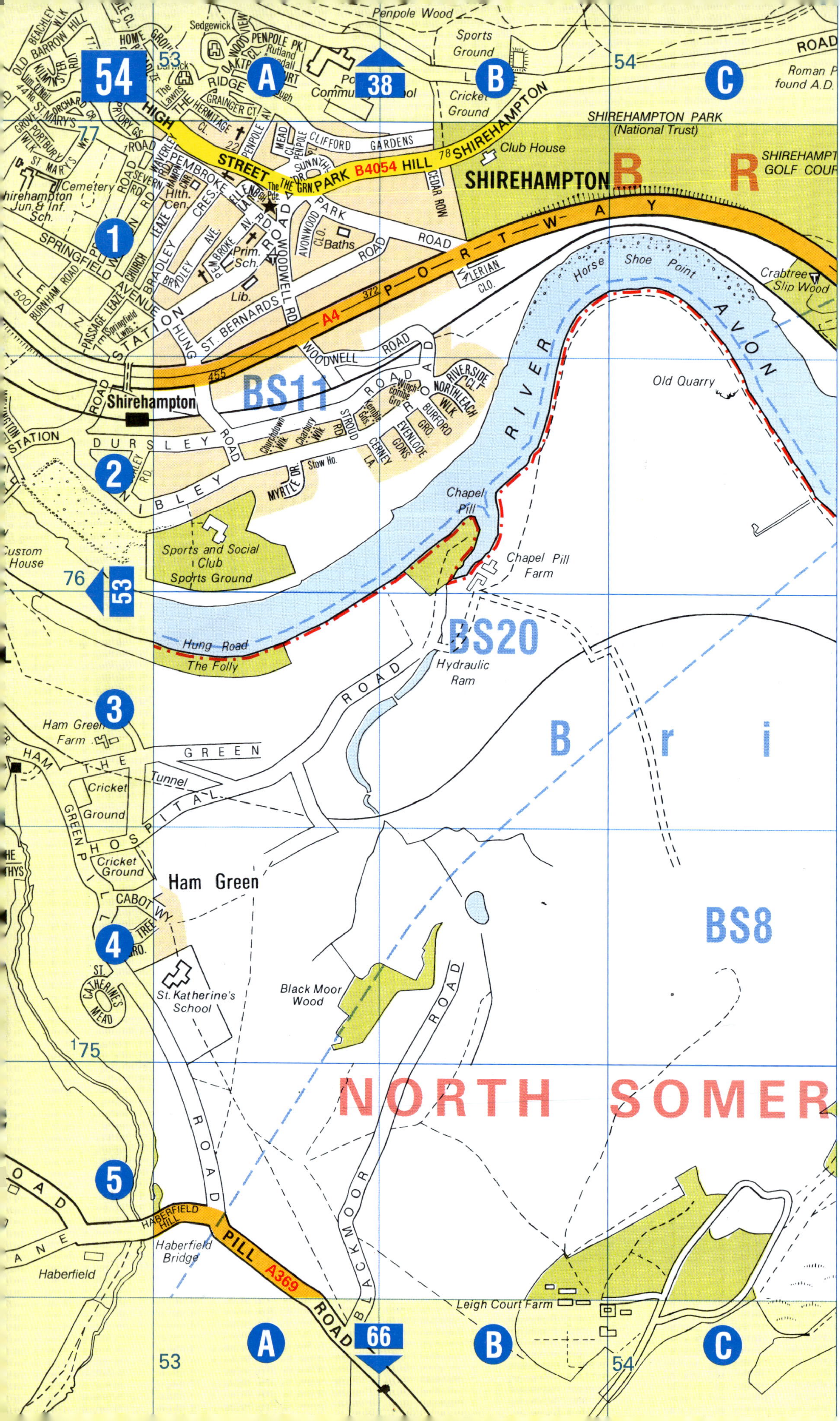

Penpole Wood
Sedgewick
HOME
PENPOLE PK.
Rutland
OAKTREE
RIDGE
GRAINGER CT.
THE HERMITAGE
The Lawns
HIGH STREET
PENPOLE AV.
CLIFFORD GARDENS
SUNNYHILL
THE GRN.
PARK
B4054
HILL
SHIREHAMPTON
Club House
Sports Ground
Cricket Ground
ROAD
Roman P
found A.D.
SHIREHAMPTON PARK
(National Trust)
SHIREHAMPTON
SHIREHAMPT
GOLF COUR
B
R
38
53
54
77
A
B
C
OLD
BEACHLEY WLK.
BARROW HILL
KILMINSTER RD.
ORCHARD
ST. MARY'S
GROVE
PORTBURY WLK.
PRIORY GS.
Cemetery
Shirehampton Jun. & Inf. Sch.
SEVERN RD.
WAVERLEY
PEMBROKE
Hlth. Cen.
CRES.
ELLENBOROUGH
The Pde.
CEDAR ROW
AVONWOOD CLO.
Baths
PARK ROAD
WOODWELL RD
Prim. Sch.
Lib.
BRADLEY AVE.
BRADLEY
LEAZE
CHURCH
AVENUE
SPRINGFIELD
BURNHAM ROAD
PASSAGE LEAZE
Springfield Lwns.
STATION
HUNG
ST. BERNARDS
A4
372
PORTWAY
VALERIAN CLO.
Horse Shoe Point
Crabtree Slip Wood
RIVER AVON
Old Quarry
500
455
WOODWELL ROAD
ROAD
BS11
Shirehampton
RIVERSIDE CT.
NORTHLEACH WLK
BURFORD GRO.
Winchcombe Gro.
Kemble Gdns.
STROUD RD
Churchdown Wlk.
Charbury Wlk.
EVENLODE GDNS
CERNEY LA
Stow Ho.
MYRTLE DR.
DURSLEY ROAD
NIBLEY
STATION
ROAD
1
2
Chapel Pill
Chapel Pill Farm
Custom House
Sports and Social Club
Sports Ground
76
53
Hung Road
The Folly
BS20
Hydraulic Ram
ROAD
3
Ham Green Farm
HAM
THE GREEN
Tunnel
HOSPITAL
Cricket Ground
GREEN PILL
Cricket Ground
Ham Green
CABOT WY.
TREE
4
ST. CATHERINE'S MEAD
St. Katherine's School
Black Moor Wood
ROAD
B r i
BS8
175
NORTH SOMER
ROAD
BLACKMOOR ROAD
5
ROAD
LANE
HABERFIELD HILL
Haberfield Bridge
Haberfield
PILL
A369
ROAD
Leigh Court Farm
A
B
C
53
54
66

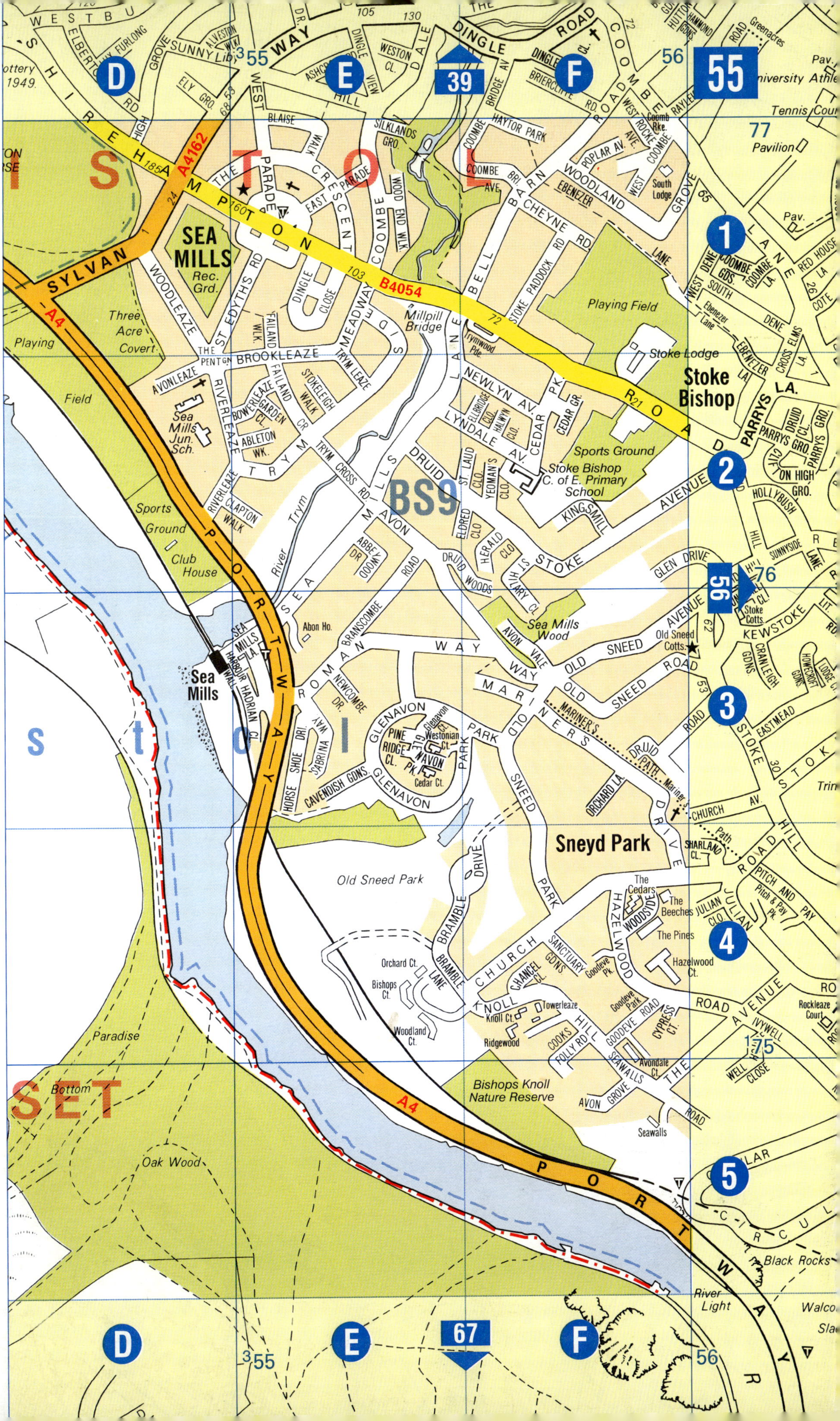
39
67
56
D
E
F
1
2
3
4
5
SEA MILLS
Rec. Grd.
Sea Mills
Stoke Bishop
Sneyd Park
BS9
B4054
A4162
A4
SYLVAN
SHIREHAMPTON ROAD
PORTWAY
Three Acre Covert
Playing Field
Sea Mills Jun. Sch.
Sports Ground
Club House
River Trym
Millpill Bridge
Stoke Lodge
Stoke Bishop C. of E. Primary School
Sea Mills Wood
Old Sneed Park
Old Sneed Cotts.
Abon Ho.
Bishops Knoll Nature Reserve
Paradise
Bottom
Oak Wood
Black Rocks
River Light
Seawalls
University Athle
Tennis Cour
Pavilion
South Lodge
WOODLEAZE
BROOKLEAZE
AVONLEAZE
RIVERLEAZE
TRYM
TRYM CROSS RD.
SEA MILLS LA.
HADRIAN CL.
ROMAN WAY
MARINERS DRIVE
DRUID HILL
DRUID WOODS
STOKE AVENUE
GLEN DRIVE
OLD SNEED AVENUE
OLD SNEED ROAD
GLENAVON PARK
CAVENDISH GDNS.
HORSE SHOE DRI.
SABRINA WAY
NEWCOMBE DR.
SNEED PARK
BRAMBLE DRIVE
BRAMBLE LANE
CHURCH ROAD
KNOLL HILL
HAZELWOOD ROAD
JULIAN ROAD
THE AVENUE
AVON GROVE
SEAWALLS
DINGLE ROAD
COOMBE LANE
WOODLAND GROVE
CHEYNE RD.
STOKE PADDOCK RD.
NEWLYN AV.
LYNDALE AV.
CEDAR PK.
KEWSTOKE
PARRYS LA.
MARINER'S PATH
STOKE HILL
PITCH AND PAY
Hazelwood Ct.
The Pines
The Beeches
The Cedars
Rockleaze Court
Orchard Ct.
Bishops Ct.
Woodland Ct.
Knoll Ct.
Ridgewood
Towerleaze

BS9
BS8
Stoke Bishop
Sneyd Park
Westbury Park
DURDHAM DOWN
University of Bristol (Halls of Residence)
Trinity Theological College
Wills Hall
Churchill Hall
Badock Hall
Hiatt Baker Hall
Stoke Abbey Dairy Fm.
Cote Lodge
Playing Field
Sports Ground
Tennis Courts
Pavilion
Red Maids School
St. Ursula's High Sch. & Convent of Mercy
Badminton School
Elmlea Jun. Sch.
Elmlea Inf. Sch.
New Cote Nursing Home
St. Monica (Home of Rest)
Water Tower
Roman Road (Course of)
Black Rocks
River Avon
PORTWAY
A4018
B4054
B4055
B4056
A4176
A4
40
55
68

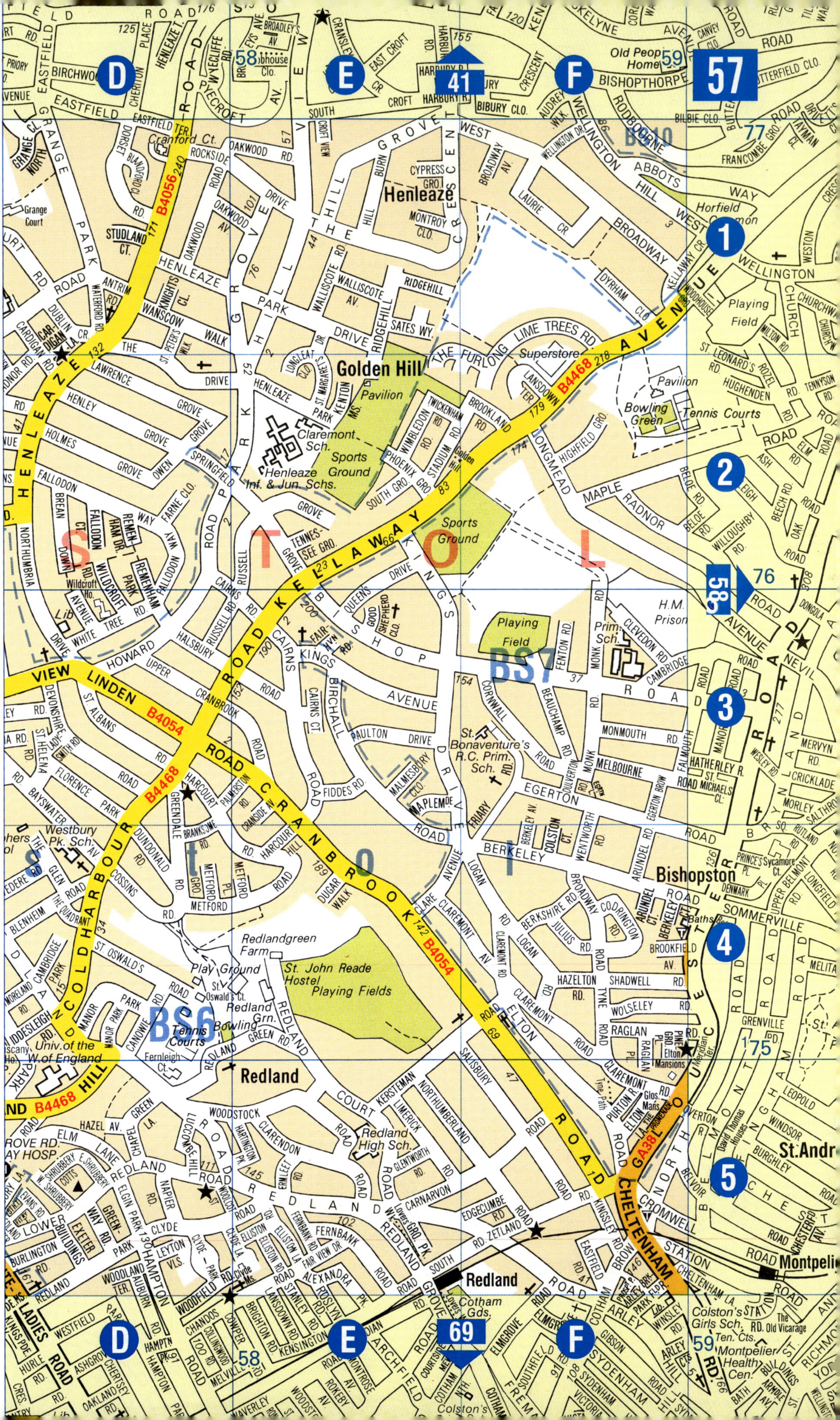
Henleaze
Golden Hill
Redland
Bishopston
Horfield Common
H.M. Prison
BS7
BS6
Sports Ground
Playing Field
Superstore
Pavilion
Bowling Green
Tennis Courts
Claremont Sch.
Henleaze Inf. & Jun. Schs.
St. Bonaventure's R.C. Prim. Sch.
Westbury Pk. Sch.
Redlandgreen Farm
St. John Reade Hostel Playing Fields
Play Ground
Redland Grn.
Univ. of the W. of England
Redland High Sch.
Redland
Montpelier
Colston's Girls Sch.
Cotham Gds.
Grange Court
Old Peoples Home
HENLEAZE ROAD
KELLAWAY AVENUE
CRANBROOK ROAD
COLDHARBOUR ROAD
LINDEN ROAD
B4056
B4468
B4054
A38
CHELTENHAM ROAD
GLOUCESTER ROAD
WELLINGTON HILL WEST
REDLAND ROAD
BISHOP ROAD
LONGMEAD AV.
SALISBURY ROAD
ZETLAND ROAD
REDLAND GROVE
ELTON ROAD
BRISTOL
41
69
58
59
76
77
175
D
E
F
1
2
3
4
5

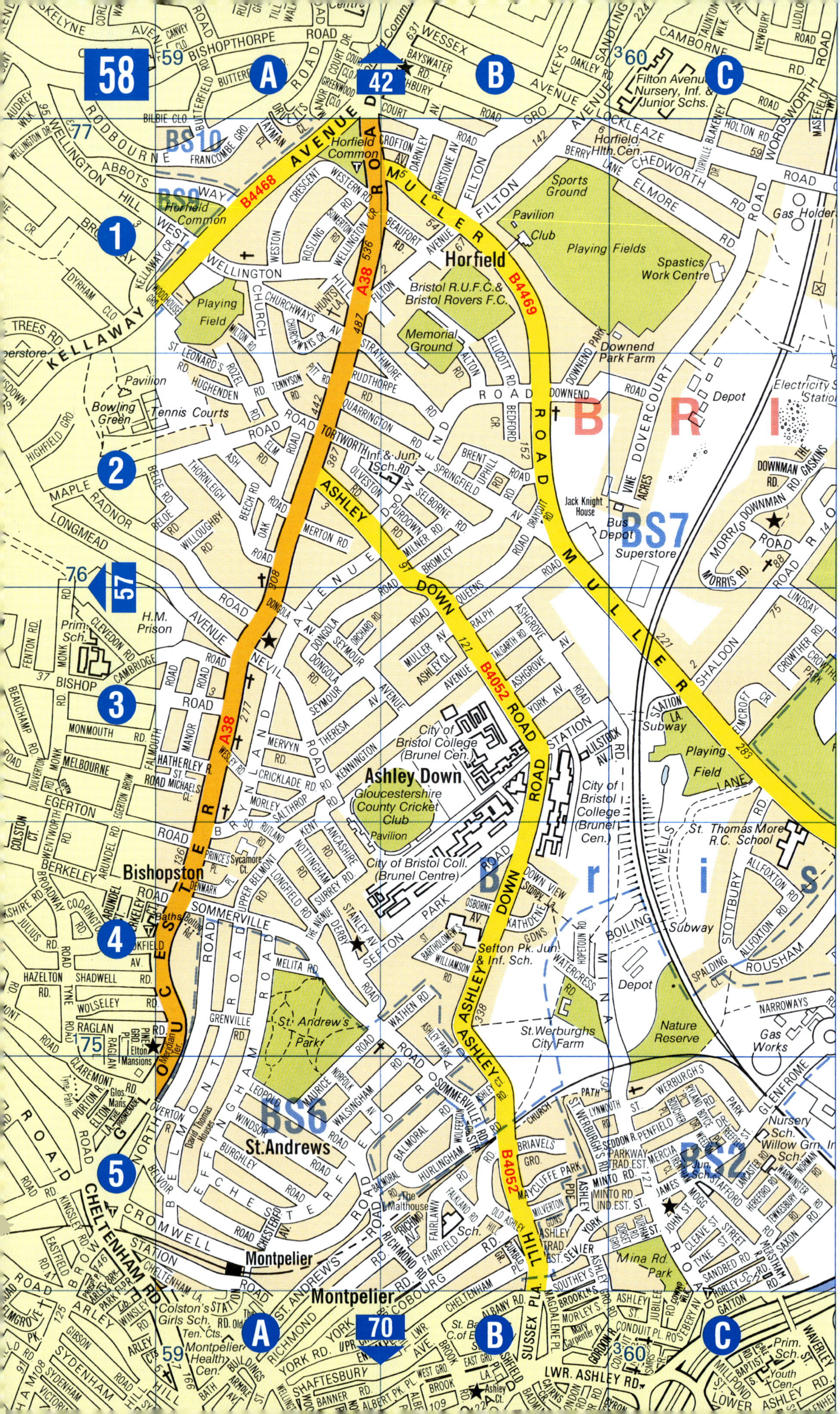

42
70
57
A
B
C
1
2
3
4
5
59
60
77
76
75
BS10
BS9
BS7
BS6
BS2
B R I
B r i s
Horfield
Horfield Common
Ashley Down
Bishopston
St.Andrews
Montpelier
Bristol R.U.F.C.& Bristol Rovers F.C.
Memorial Ground
Playing Fields
Playing Field
Sports Ground
Pavilion
Club
Spastics Work Centre
Horfield Hlth.Cen.
Filton Avenue Nursery, Inf. & Junior Schs.
Downend Park Farm
Depot
Electricity Station
Gas Holder
Jack Knight House
Bus Depot
Superstore
H.M. Prison
Bowling Green
Tennis Courts
City of Bristol College (Brunel Cen.)
Gloucestershire County Cricket Club
City of Bristol Coll. (Brunel Centre)
St. Thomas More R.C. School
Sefton Pk. Jun. & Inf. Sch.
St.Werburghs City Farm
Nature Reserve
Gas Works
St. Andrew's Park
Mina Rd. Park
Colston's Girls Sch.
Montpelier Health Cen.
Nursery Sch.
Willow Grn. Inf. Sch.
Prim. Sch.
Youth Cen.
Subway
B4468
B4469
B4052
A38
GLOUCESTER ROAD
MULLER ROAD
ASHLEY DOWN ROAD
KELLAWAY AVENUE
WELLINGTON HILL WEST
FILTON AVENUE
CHELTENHAM RD.
CROMWELL ROAD
STATION ROAD
SOMMERVILLE ROAD
BELLEVUE ROAD
SEFTON PARK ROAD
BOILING WELLS
MINA ROAD
ASHLEY HILL
CHURCHWAYS AV
NEVIL ROAD
LONGMEAD
MAPLE
RADNOR
BISHOP ROAD
BERKELEY ROAD
EGERTON ROAD
STATION RD.
ST. ANDREW'S ROAD
WERBURGH'S PARK
GLENFROME
SUSSEX PLA.
LWR. ASHLEY RD.

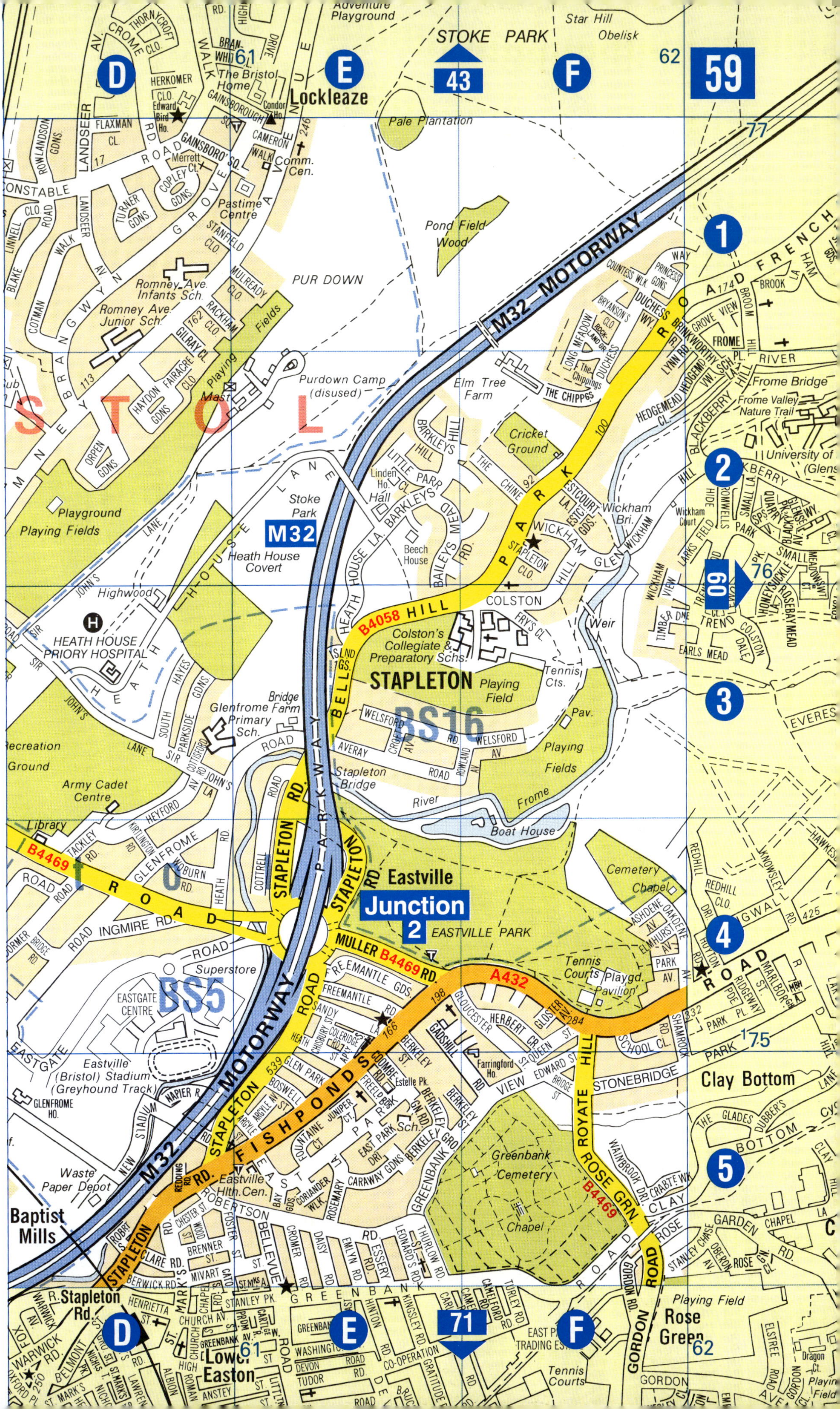

Adventure Playground
STOKE PARK
Star Hill
Obelisk
43
62
D
E
F
Lockleaze
The Bristol Home
Edward Bird Ho.
Condor Ho.
Pale Plantation
Pond Field Wood
PUR DOWN
M32 MOTORWAY
Romney Ave. Infants Sch.
Romney Ave. Junior Sch.
Pastime Centre
Comm. Cen.
Purdown Camp (disused)
Mast
Playing Fields
Elm Tree Farm
Cricket Ground
Linden Ho.
Hall
Beech House
Stoke Park
M32
Heath House Covert
Playground
Playing Fields
Highwood
HEATH HOUSE PRIORY HOSPITAL
Wickham Bri.
Wickham Court
Frome Bridge
Frome Valley Nature Trail
University of (Glens
B4058 HILL
Colston's Collegiate & Preparatory Schs.
STAPLETON
BS16
Playing Field
Tennis Cts.
Pav.
Weir
Playing Fields
Glenfrome Primary Sch.
Bridge Farm
Stapleton Bridge
River Frome
Boat House
Recreation Ground
Army Cadet Centre
Library
B4469
Eastville
Junction 2
EASTVILLE PARK
Cemetery Chapel
Tennis Courts
Playgd.
Pavilion
Superstore
EASTGATE CENTRE
BS5
MULLER B4469 RD.
A432
FISHPONDS RD.
Farringford Ho.
Estelle Pk.
Sch.
Eastville (Bristol) Stadium (Greyhound Track)
GLENFROME HO.
Waste Paper Depot
Eastville Hlth.Cen.
Greenbank Cemetery
Chapel
B4469
ROSE GRN
ROYATE HILL
Clay Bottom
Baptist Mills
Stapleton Rd.
Lower Easton
71
Rose Green
Playing Field
Tennis Courts
EAST TRADING EST.
Dragon Ct.
Playing Field
60
76
77
75
1
2
3
4
5
61

Star Hill
Obelisk
62
A
44
B
63
C
77
M32 MOTORWAY
M32
Broomhill
Begbrook
Comm. Cen.
STOKE LA.
PARK
FRENCHAY
ROAD
B4058
Greenfinch Lodge
KINGFISHER
ALBERTON
BROCKWORTH
BEGBROOK
DRYLEAZE
ANDRAIL
WALK
CURLEW
NUTHATCH GDS.
WREN
WYTHERLIES DR.
VALLEY
BRAMBLING WLK.
FROME
RIVER
Weir
OLDBURY
Begbrook Prim. Sch.
Snuff Mills Park
Playing Fld.
PERRYMANS CLO.
COMYN WALK
LANE
DRIVE
BEGBROOK
GROVE VIEW
FROME PL.
RIVER VIEW
BLACKBERRY HILL
Frome Bridge
Frome Valley Nature Trail
University of the West of England (Glenside Campus)
BLACKBERRY HILL HOSPITAL
Playing Field
Manor Gardens Ho.
Sports Grnd
Univ. of the W. of England
COLLEGE
COLLEGE CT.
GLASSDALE
CLAVERHAM RD.
HOMEFIELD DR.
BS16
ELFIN RD.
COLLEGE RD.
Inf. Sch.
VICTORIA PARK
MANOR ROAD
156
207
44
1
COUNTESS WLK.
PRINCESS GDNS.
DUCHESS WY.
BRYANSON'S CLO.
LONG MEADOW
The Chippings
THE CHIPPINGS
PARK
LYNN RD.
HEDGEMEAD CL.
100
Wickham Bri.
ESTCOURT GDS.
WICKHAM HILL
WICKHAM
2
76
59
Wickham Court
LARKS FIELD
HIDE
CROMWELLS
SMALL LA.
QUARRY
PARK
SMALL LANE
TRENDLEWOOD
LENWOOD
HONEYSUCKLE
ROSEBAY MEAD
FOXGLOVE CL.
PENNYROYAL GRO.
KITE HAY
Snowdon House
SNOWDON
POUND DRI.
POUND LA.
EASTBURY RD.
NORTH DEVON RD.
Guinea Lane
AMBROOK RD.
FISHPONDS
Weir
TRENDLE
COLSTON DALE
EARLS MEAD
Manor Ct.
Whitefield Fishponds School
Playing Field
Marshall Ho.
Callard Ho.
CHANNON'S HILL
ADELAIDE PL.
ADELAIDE T.
COURTFIELD GRO.
Jun. Sch.
ELMDALE GS.
HINTON RD.
GUINEA LA.
786
729
BEECHW
CORONATION AVE
BROOK
Tennis Cts.
Pav.
Playing Fields
3
EVEREST
LOWER GROVE RD.
NEW BUILDINGS
Hall
Works
STATION AVE.
Lib.
CHAPEL
Vine Cotts.
GRAEME CLO.
NEW STATION RD.
Works
Depots
EVEREST AV
ROAD
GROVE RD.
GROVE PK. TER.
ALEXANDRA PARK
PURDY
672
HOCKEYS LA.
LWR. STATION
WHARF RD.
NEW STATION WAY
FILWOOD
B
PARK
LANGDALE RD.
FEATHERSTONE RD.
LODORE RD.
GROVE AV.
STOKE VIEW RD.
609
ALBERT TER.
BAWNS PL.
JUSTICE RD.
Factory
BRENTRY
ELMGROVE
HAWKESBURY
KNOWSLEY
REDHILL
REDHILL CLO.
A432
ERNESTVILLE RD.
LODGE
B4048
PARNALL RD.
GOODNESTON RD.
Factory
Cemetery
Chapel
STAR LA.
DRUMMOND RD.
DUNKIRK RD.
Warehouse
HINGWAL
425
FISHPONDS
492
ALCOVE RD.
MIDLAND TER.
4
OAKDENE
Tennis Courts
Playgd.
Pavilion
PARK AV.
HUYTON RD.
MARINA GDNS.
Upper Eastville
Bristol Lido
LAKE VIEW
HALSTOCK AV.
Works
BALACLAVA RD.
MENDIP
Chester Pk. Schs.
ENFIELD
ABINGDON RD.
MARLBOROUGH ST.
RIDGEWAY
PDE
LAKESIDE
DOMINION RD.
ROAD
RIDGEWAY
PARK PL.
PARK
832
GLOSTER AV.
284
HILL
ROAD
75
SCHOOL CL.
SHAMROCK RD.
GREENS
HILL
Ridgeway
VERA RD.
IRENA RD.
MADELINE RD.
MOORLANDS RD.
HONITON RD.
Gospel Hall
ACTON RD.
Mayfield Park
POPLAR PL.
MAYFIELD AV.
EDWARD ST.
BRIDGE ST.
STONEBRIDGE
Clay Bottom
LANE
Cycle Walkway
TIVERTON WLK.
ABINGDON
ROWAN CLO.
MOORLANDS RD.
MAYFIELD PARK
ROYATE
HILL
THE GLADES
DUBBER'S
BOTTOM
Works
BS5
FISHPONDS TRADING ESTATE
ATLAS CL.
HOLLY
HOLLY
LODGE
RD.
ROAD
173
MAGGS LA.
OAK
ANTHEA RD.
FISHPONDS TRADING EST.
CLAY HILL
5
ROSE GRN
CLAY
ROSE
CHAPEL LA
Clay Hill
LANE
FOUNDRY LA
WHITEWOOD RD.
Speedwell Day Cen.
DEAN DR.
B4465
120
Longhills Hostel
DUNCOMBE
Hall Cl.
STANLEY CHASE
OBERON AV.
ROSE GREEN CL.
KNAPPS LANE
Works
T.A.V.R. Centre
PIT
RD
ROAD
ROAD
GORDON RD.
GORDON
Playing Field
Rose Green
DEEP
CROFTS END
72
Works
FERNHURST
WHITEWOOD RD.
WHITEFIELD
Baths
WHITEFIELD AV.
Playing Field
Speedwell School
Speedwell
C
A
B
ELSTREE ROAD
GORDON
Dragon Ct.
Playing Fields
Crofts End
BROOK
RD.
MALLARD CL.
Lavender Ct.
POPLAR RD.
Roegate Ho.
155
63
PONTING CL.
178
GREEN CROFT
KINGSMEAD
62
Tennis Courts
GORDON
EAST PARK TRADING ESTATE

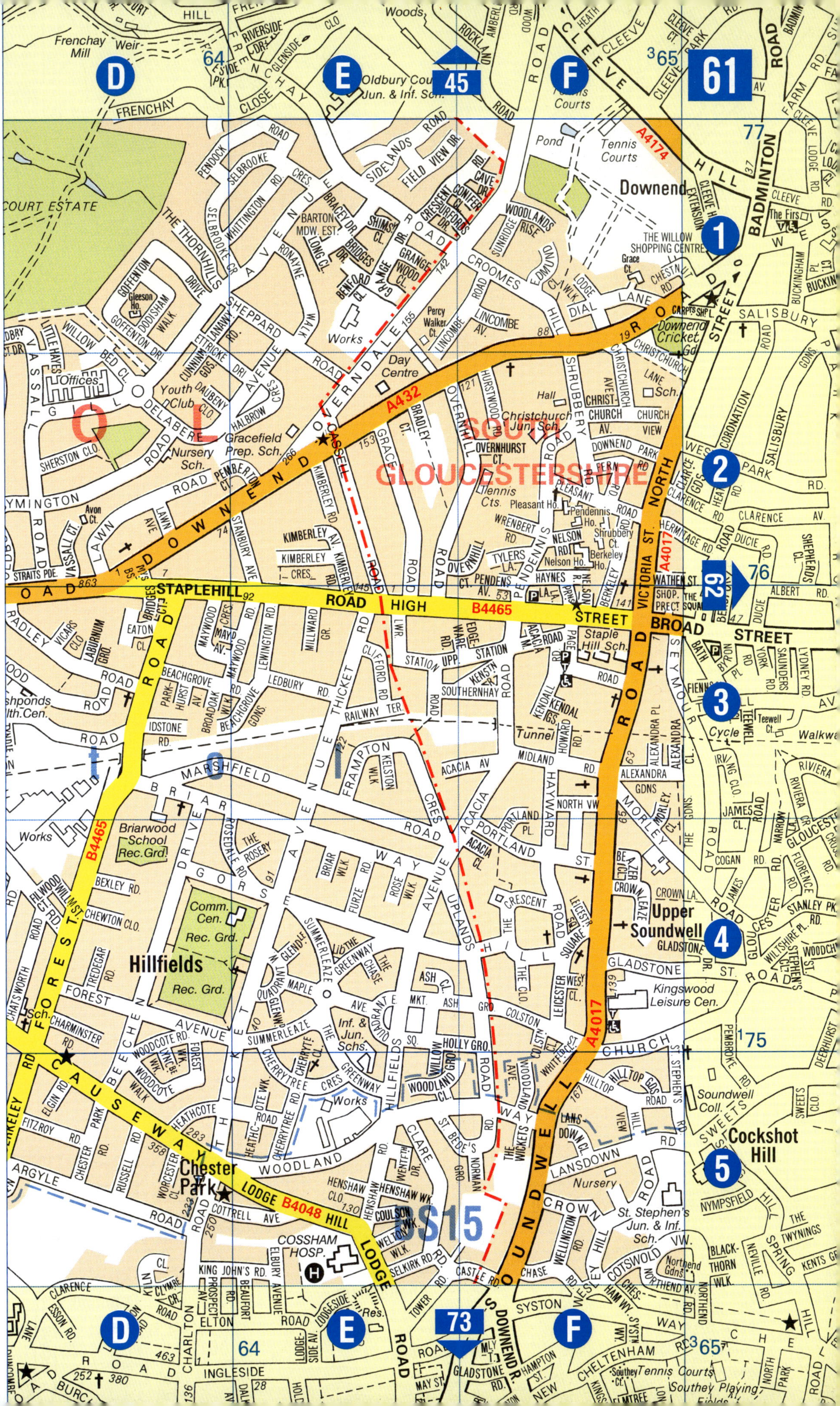

Frenchay Mill
Weir
FRENCHAY
D
E
F
45
Oldbury Court Jun. & Inf. Sch.
Tennis Courts
Downend
CLEEVE HILL
A4174
BADMINTON ROAD
THE WILLOW SHOPPING CENTRE
1
COURT ESTATE
SELBROOKE CR.
SHEPPARD ROAD
OVERNDALE ROAD
DOWNEND ROAD
A432
Day Centre
Works
Youth Club
Nursery Sch.
Gracefield Prep. Sch.
Christchurch Jun. Sch.
SOUTH GLOUCESTERSHIRE
OVERNHURST CT.
Tennis Cts.
2
SALISBURY
CLARENCE
DUCIE RD.
STAPLEHILL ROAD
HIGH STREET
B4465
BROAD STREET
VICTORIA ST.
NORTH ROAD
A4017
62
76
Staple Hill Sch.
3
Cycle Walkway
Tunnel
MIDLAND RD.
MARSHFIELD
FRAMPTON CRES
ACACIA AV
Briarwood School Rec.Grd.
Works
B4465
FOREST ROAD
Comm. Cen.
Rec. Grd.
Hillfields
Rec. Grd.
Upper Soundwell
GLADSTONE ST
4
Kingswood Leisure Cen.
CHURCH RD
175
Inf. & Jun. Schs.
Works
Soundwell Coll.
Cockshot Hill
5
SOUNDWELL ROAD
CAUSEWAY
Chester Park
LODGE B4048 HILL
WOODLAND
Nursery
St. Stephen's Jun. & Inf. Sch.
BS15
COSSHAM HOSP.
LODGE
73
D
E
F
64
365
CHELTENHAM
GLADSTONE
Southey Tennis Courts
Southey Playing Fields

62
46
74
61
A
B
C
1
2
3
4
5
65
66
76
77
175
Downend
MANGOTSFIELD
SOUTH GLOU
Staple Hill
Upper Soundwell
Soundwell
Lower Soundwell
Cockshot Hill
New Cheltenham
Siston Common
Rodway Hill
BS15
A4017
A432
A4175
B4465
CLEEVE HILL
BADMINTON RD.
WESTERLEIGH ROAD
STATION ROAD
MANGOTSFIELD
STREET
BROAD STREET
TEEWELL HILL
CHARNHILL
SALISBURY ROAD
PARK ROAD
NORTH STREET
SOUNDWELL
CHURCH ROAD
SISTON COMMON
DOWNEND ROAD
KING GEORGE'S FIELD
Cemetery
Downend Sports Centre
Downend Sch.
Stanbridge Prim. Sch.
Barley Close Prim. Sch.
Playing Field
Downend Lower Sch.
PAGE PARK
The Tynings Sch.
Kingswood Leisure Cen.
Soundwell Coll.
Lees Hill Playing Field
St. Stephen's Jun. & Inf. Sch.
Staple Hill Sch.
Downend Cricket Gd.
THE WILLOW SHOPPING CENTRE
Tennis Courts
Pond
Factory
Works
Sistonhill Farm
Old Quarries
Charn Hill
Rodway Hill House
Cycle Walkway
Southey Tennis Courts

EMERSON'S GREEN
VILLAGE PARK (PROPOSED)
EMERSON WAY
Superstore
AVON RING ROAD A4174
47
The Rosary
Works
Lansdown Place
LANE
GREEN
EMERSONS
Emersons Green
HORSE PL.
Shortwood Farm
Shortwood House
Clay Pit
ROAD
CATTYBROOK
Subway
B4465
Meadow Farm
PLAYING FIELDS (PROP.)
Sports Pitches (Prop.)
The Vale
CATTYBROOK RD.
Rec. Grd.
Ham Cottage
Hall
ELMLEIGH CLO.
OAKLANDS CL.
ELMLEIGH AV
GLOUCESTERSHIRE
POMPHREY ST.
Sports Ground
Pav. (Prop.)
BS16
Pomphrey
HILL MAIN B4465 ROAD
SHORTWOOD HILL
Shortwood
64
76
BRISTOL
BRIDGE ROAD
Ten. Cts.
Mangotsfield School
Play. Fld.
Running Track
AVON RING ROAD (UNDER CONSTRUCTION Estimated Completion Feb. 2001)
HILL
Works
Pav.
Sports Ground
Bridge Farm
CARSONS RD.
Syston Farm
MANGOTSFIELD GOLF COURSE
Lodge Farm
Club House
Sussex Haven
Glenfern
Withy Bed
75
Cherry Cottage
The Hawthorns
Cherry Orchard Farm
Mill Farm
Weir
Seven Winds
SISTON
(GOOSE GREEN)
Goose Green
Siston Hill
Bonny Mount Farm
Green HILL
Little Brook Farm
Brook Farm
(UNDER CONSTRUCTION)
D
E
F
1
2
3
4
5
67
68
77

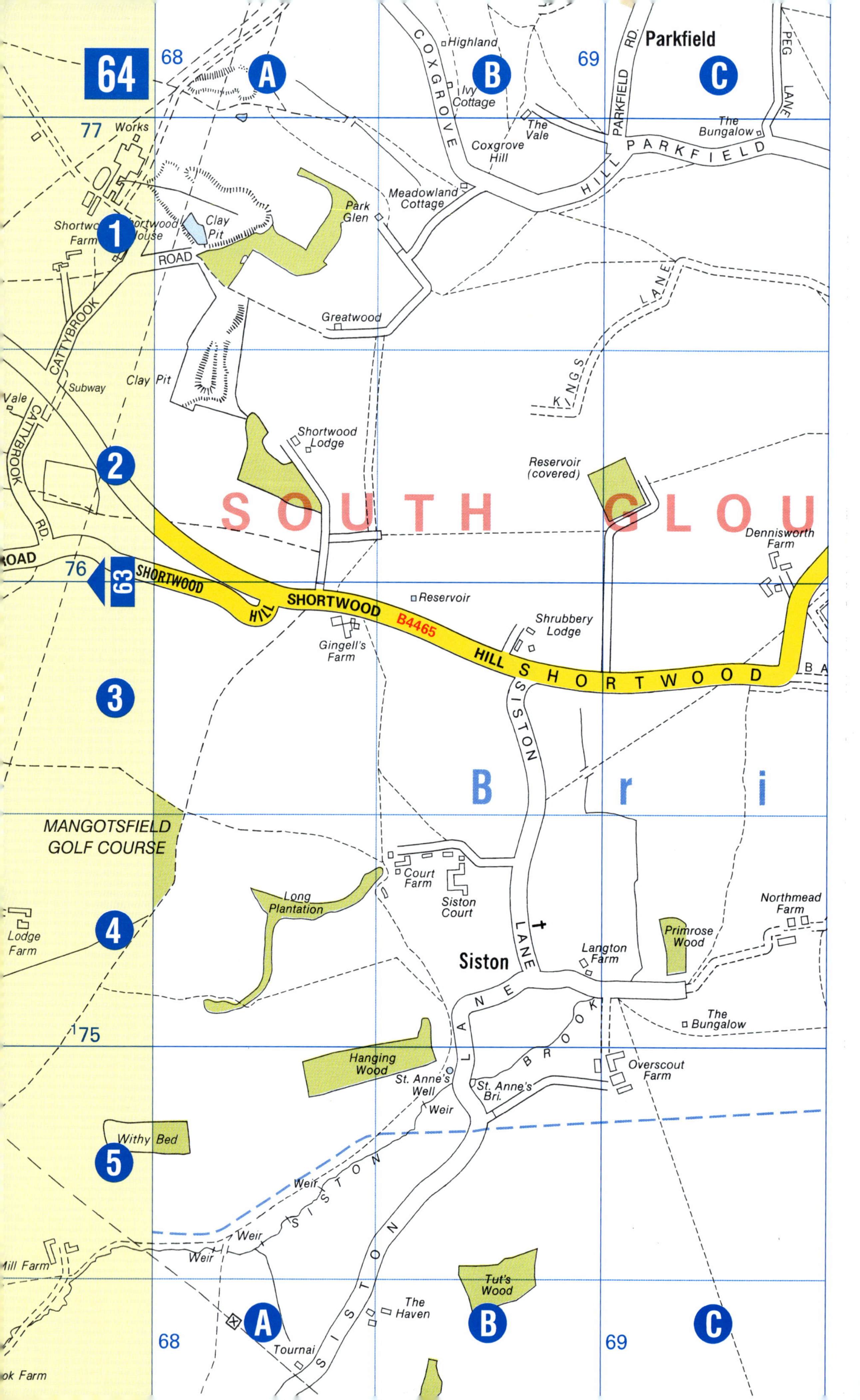
64
68
69
77
76
175
A
B
C
1
2
3
4
5
Parkfield
Highland
Ivy Cottage
COXGROVE
The Vale
Coxgrove Hill
PARKFIELD RD.
PEG LANE
The Bungalow
PARKFIELD
HILL
Works
Shortwood Farm
Shortwood House
Clay Pit
Park Glen
Meadowland Cottage
ROAD
CATTYBROOK
Greatwood
KINGS LANE
Subway
Vale
Clay Pit
CATTYBROOK RD.
Shortwood Lodge
Reservoir (covered)
SOUTH GLOU
Dennisworth Farm
ROAD
63
SHORTWOOD
HILL
SHORTWOOD
B4465
Reservoir
Gingell's Farm
Shrubbery Lodge
HILL SHORTWOOD
BA
SISTON
B r i
MANGOTSFIELD GOLF COURSE
Court Farm
Siston Court
Long Plantation
Lodge Farm
LANE
Siston
Langton Farm
Primrose Wood
Northmead Farm
LANE
BROOK
The Bungalow
Hanging Wood
St. Anne's Well
St. Anne's Bri.
Overscout Farm
Weir
Withy Bed
SISTON
Weir
Weir
Weir
Mill Farm
Tut's Wood
The Haven
Tournai
SISTON
ok Farm

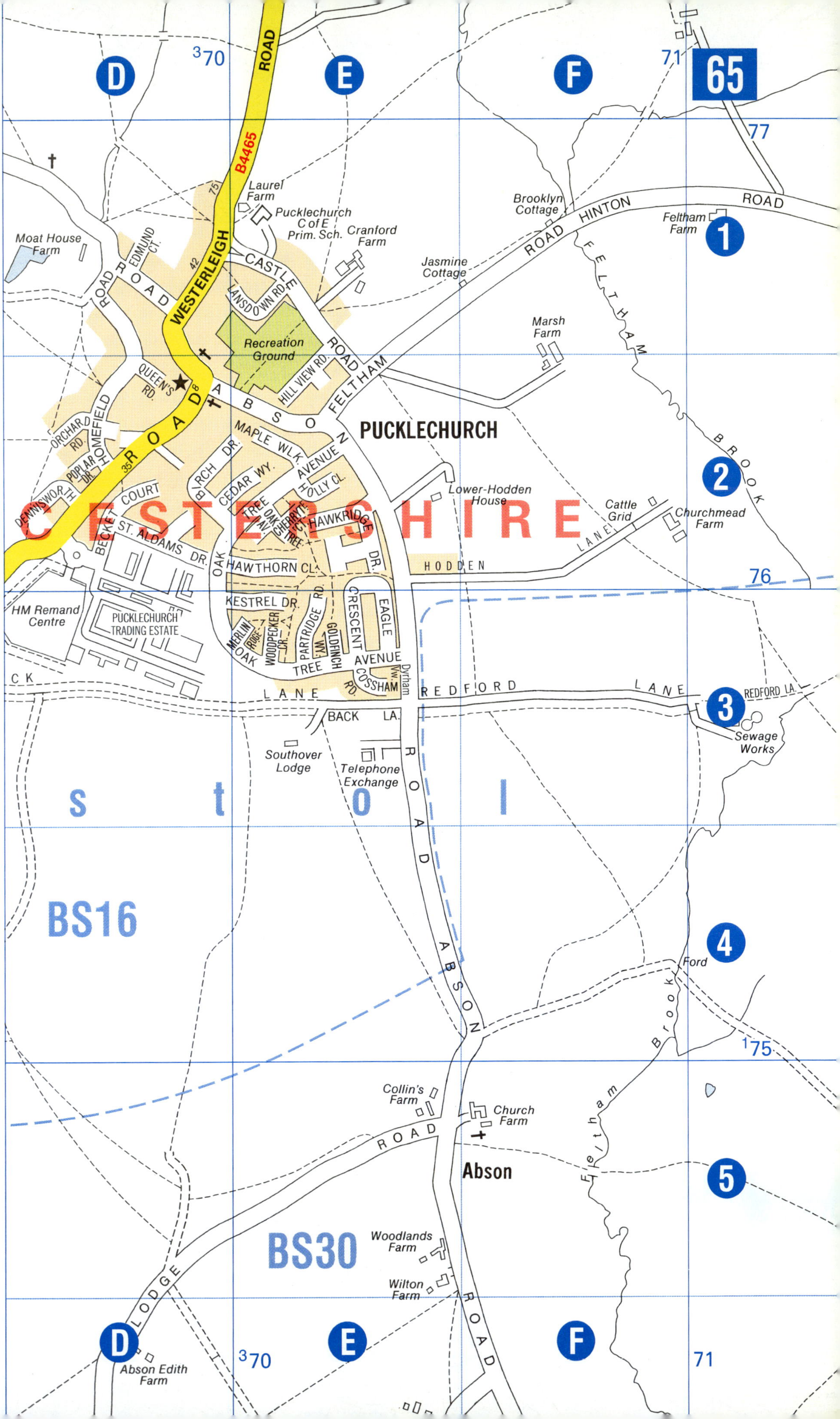
D
E
F
370
71
77
76
175
1
2
3
4
5
B4465
WESTERLEIGH ROAD
Laurel Farm
Pucklechurch C of E Prim. Sch.
Cranford Farm
Moat House Farm
EDMUND CT.
ROAD
CASTLE ROAD
LANSDOWN RD.
Recreation Ground
HILL VIEW RD.
FELTHAM ROAD
QUEEN'S RD.
ABSON ROAD
HOMEFIELD
ORCHARD RD.
POPLAR DR.
DENNISWORTH
MAPLE WLK.
AVENUE
BIRCH DR.
CEDAR WY.
HOLLY CL.
COURT
BECKET
ST. ALDAMS DR.
TREE AV.
OAK TREE
CHERRYTREE CT.
HAWKRIDGE DR.
HAWTHORN CL.
KESTREL DR.
EAGLE CRESCENT
MERLIN RIDGE
WOODPECKER CR.
PARTRIDGE RD.
GOLDFINCH WY.
OAK TREE AVENUE
COSSHAM RD.
Dyrham Vw.
HM Remand Centre
PUCKLECHURCH TRADING ESTATE
PUCKLECHURCH
Brooklyn Cottage
HINTON ROAD
Feltham Farm
Jasmine Cottage
FELTHAM BROOK
Marsh Farm
Lower-Hodden House
Cattle Grid
Churchmead Farm
HODDEN LANE
CK LANE
REDFORD LANE
REDFORD LA.
Sewage Works
BACK LA.
Southover Lodge
Telephone Exchange
ABSON ROAD
s t o l
BS16
Ford
Feltham Brook
Collin's Farm
Church Farm
Abson
ROAD
BS30
Woodlands Farm
Wilton Farm
LODGE
Abson Edith Farm
ROAD

66
54
76
A
B
C
1
2
3
4
5
53
54
74
73
72
HABERFIELD HILL
Haberfield Bridge
PILL ROAD
A369
BLACKMOOR RD.
Leigh Court Farm
Vowles Bottom
OLD PARK
Old Park Wood
Old Park House
Three Cornered Wood
Glen Farm
Glen House
Poundbatch Farm
DENNY VIEW RD.
KNIGHTCOTT RD.
GLEN AV.
HARRIS LANE
MANOR LANE
CHURCH ROAD
Abbots Leigh
Parish Hall
The Priory
THE MANOR CL.
Manor House
ABBOTS
Playing Field
NORTH
Snakes Well Wood
Abbot's Pond
FISH POND WOOD
SANDY
East Tanpit Wood
Snake's Well Plantation
Scutche's Plantation
Yew Tree Plantation
WEIR LANE
Warren House Plantation
Bristol
MANOR
Round Hill Clump
Round Hill Leg
Quarry Plantation
BS8
Sports Ground
Kingcott Farm
BRISTOL & CLIFTON GOLF COURSE
FIFTY ACRE WOOD
B3129
Club House
BEGGAR BUSH LANE
Pavilion
Sports Ground
Resr. (covered)

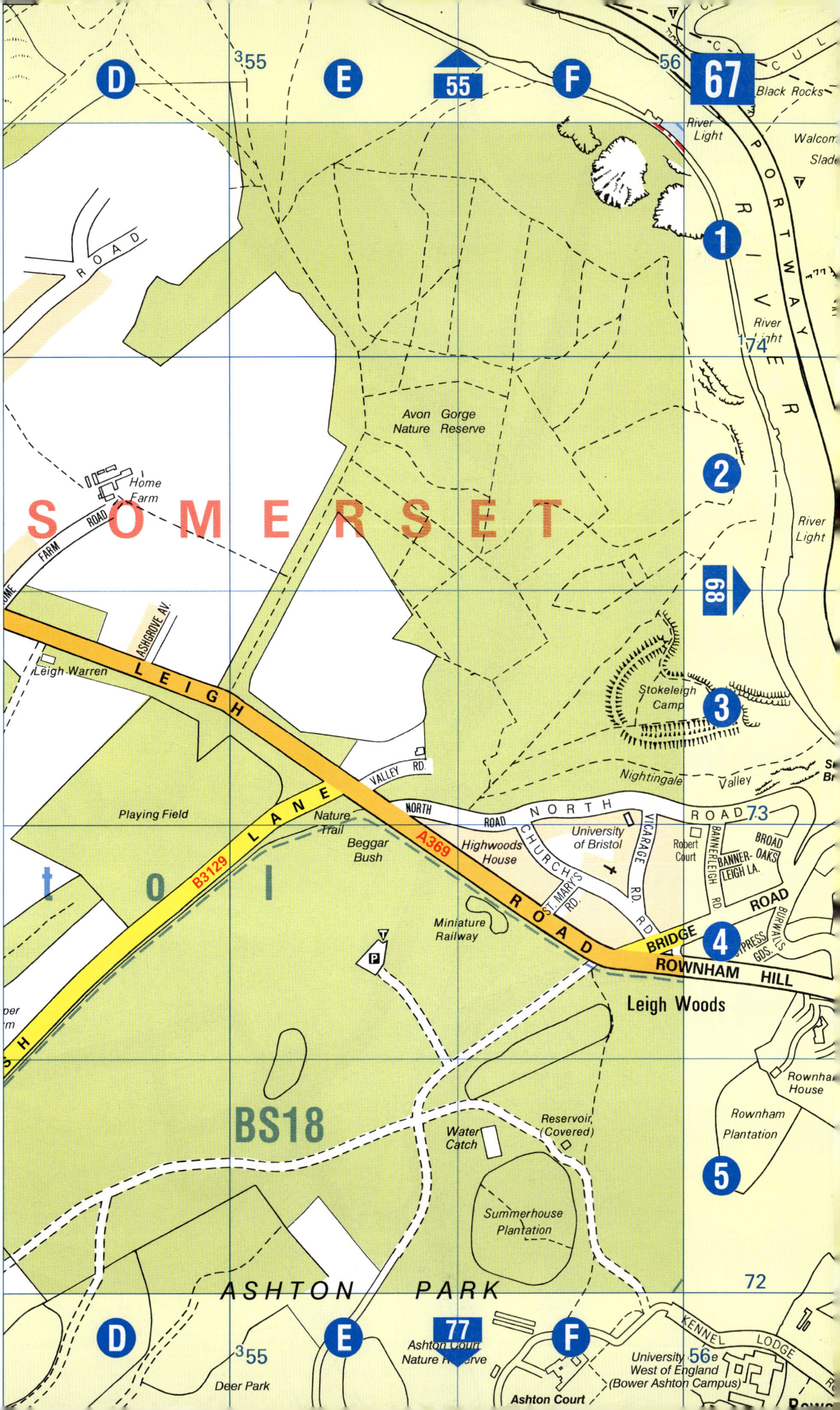

D
E
F
355
56
55
Black Rocks
River Light
Walcombe Slade
PORTWAY
RIVER
River Light
74
ROAD
Avon Gorge Nature Reserve
Home Farm
SOMERSET
HOME FARM ROAD
River Light
68
ASHGROVE AV.
Leigh Warren
LEIGH ROAD
Stokeleigh Camp
VALLEY RD.
Nightingale Valley
NORTH ROAD
Playing Field
LANE
Nature Trail
Beggar Bush
A369
Highwoods House
University of Bristol
CHURCH
VICARAGE RD.
Robert Court
BANNERLEIGH RD
BROAD OAKS
BANNER-LEIGH LA.
73
B3129
ST. MARY'S RD.
ROAD
BURWALLS
Miniature Railway
BRIDGE
CYPRESS GDS.
ROWNHAM HILL
Leigh Woods
Rownham House
BS18
Reservoir (Covered)
Water Catch
Rownham Plantation
Summerhouse Plantation
ASHTON PARK
72
KENNEL LODGE
77
Ashton Court Nature Reserve
University of the West of England (Bower Ashton Campus)
Deer Park
Ashton Court
1
2
3
4
5

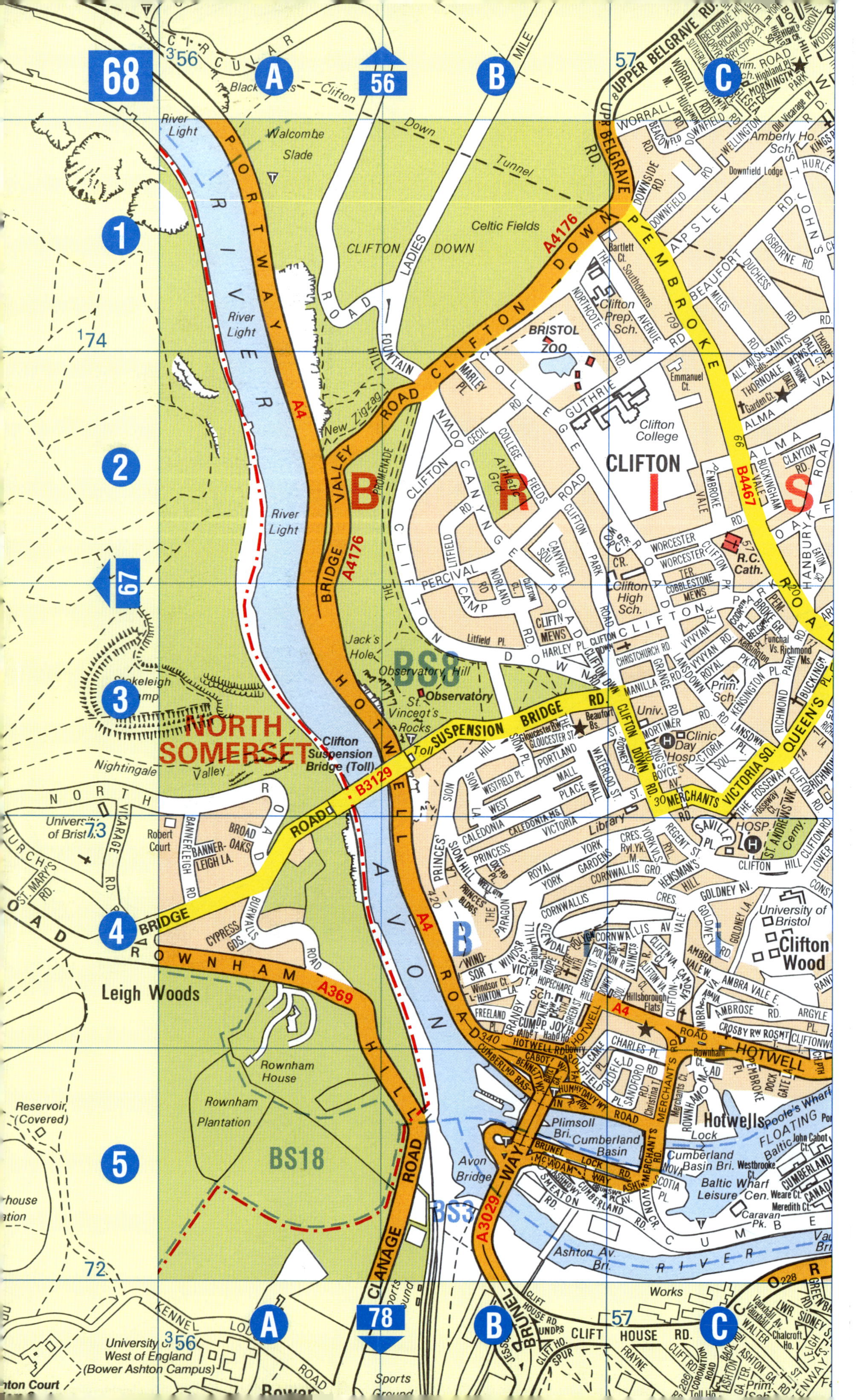

68
56
67
78
A
B
C
1
2
3
4
5
CLIFTON DOWN
Celtic Fields
Clifton Down Tunnel
LADIES MILE
CIRCULAR ROAD
Walcombe Slade
River Light
PORTWAY
A4
RIVER AVON
BRIDGE VALLEY ROAD
A4176
CLIFTON DOWN RD.
UPPER BELGRAVE RD.
PEMBROKE RD.
B4467
BRISTOL ZOO
Clifton College
Clifton Prep. Sch.
CLIFTON
BRISTOL
R.C. Cath.
Clifton High Sch.
BS8
Observatory Hill
Observatory
St. Vincent's Rocks
Jack's Hole
New Zigzag
SUSPENSION BRIDGE RD
Clifton Suspension Bridge (Toll)
B3129
NORTH SOMERSET
Stokeleigh Camp
Nightingale Valley
NORTH ROAD
BRIDGE ROAD
University of Bristol
Robert Court
BANNERLEIGH RD
BROAD OAKS
CYPRESS GDS.
BURWALLS RD.
ROWNHAM HILL
A369
Leigh Woods
Rownham House
Rownham Plantation
BS18
Reservoir (Covered)
CLANAGE ROAD
HOTWELL ROAD
HOTWELLS
Hotwells
Cumberland Basin
Plimsoll Bri.
Avon Bridge
BS3
A3029
BRUNEL WAY
Baltic Wharf Leisure Cen.
FLOATING HARBOUR
Cumberland Basin Bri.
Ashton Av. Bri.
CUMBERLAND RD.
Clifton Wood
University of Bristol
Clifton Day Hosp.
Univ.
QUEEN'S RD
VICTORIA SQ.
CLIFTON HILL
Library
Hillsborough Flats
CLIFT HOUSE RD.
University of West of England (Bower Ashton Campus)
KENNEL LODGE ROAD
Sports Ground
Works

D
E
F
57
58
59
Redland
Montpelier
Cotham
BS6
BS2
BS1
Kingsdown
Tyndall's Park
Clifton Down
Victoria Park
Canon's Marsh
Southville
Cotham Grammar Sch.
Cotham Grammar School
Colston's Girls Sch.
Colston's Prim. Sch.
University of Bristol
Broadcasting House
Bristol Royal Hosp.
Royal Infirmary
Bristol Royal Infirmary
City Museum & Art Gallery
Queen Elizabeth's Hosp. Sch.
Cabot Tower
Brandon Hill Nature Park
Georgian Ho.
Cathedral
Cath. Sch.
Watershed Cen.
Exhibition Centre
Arnolfini Gallery
Princes Street Bridge
S.S. Great Britain
Maritime Heritage Centre
Albion Docks Boatyard
Industrial Museum
Bristol General Hosp.
Theatre Royal
Guildhall
Red Lodge
Art Guild
New Bristol Cen.
Broadmead Shop. Precinct
Castle Green
Bristol Bri.
Floating Harbour
Queen Quay
Redcliffe Wharf
Bathurst Wharf
Phoenix Wharf
Princes Wharf
Canons House
Nine Tree Hill
Arts Cen.
Bus Sta.
Horsefair
Kings Sq.
Queen Square
Victoria St.
Baldwin St.
Marlborough St.
Perry Rd.
Park Row
Park St.
Whiteladies Rd.
Queen's Rd.
Jacobs Wells Road
Anchor Road
Cotham Hill
Cotham Rd.
St. Michael's Hill
Cheltenham Rd.
Redcliffe Wy.
Cumberland Rd.
Coronation Rd.
A4018
A4
A370
B4051
B4053
B4466
70
79
73
72
74

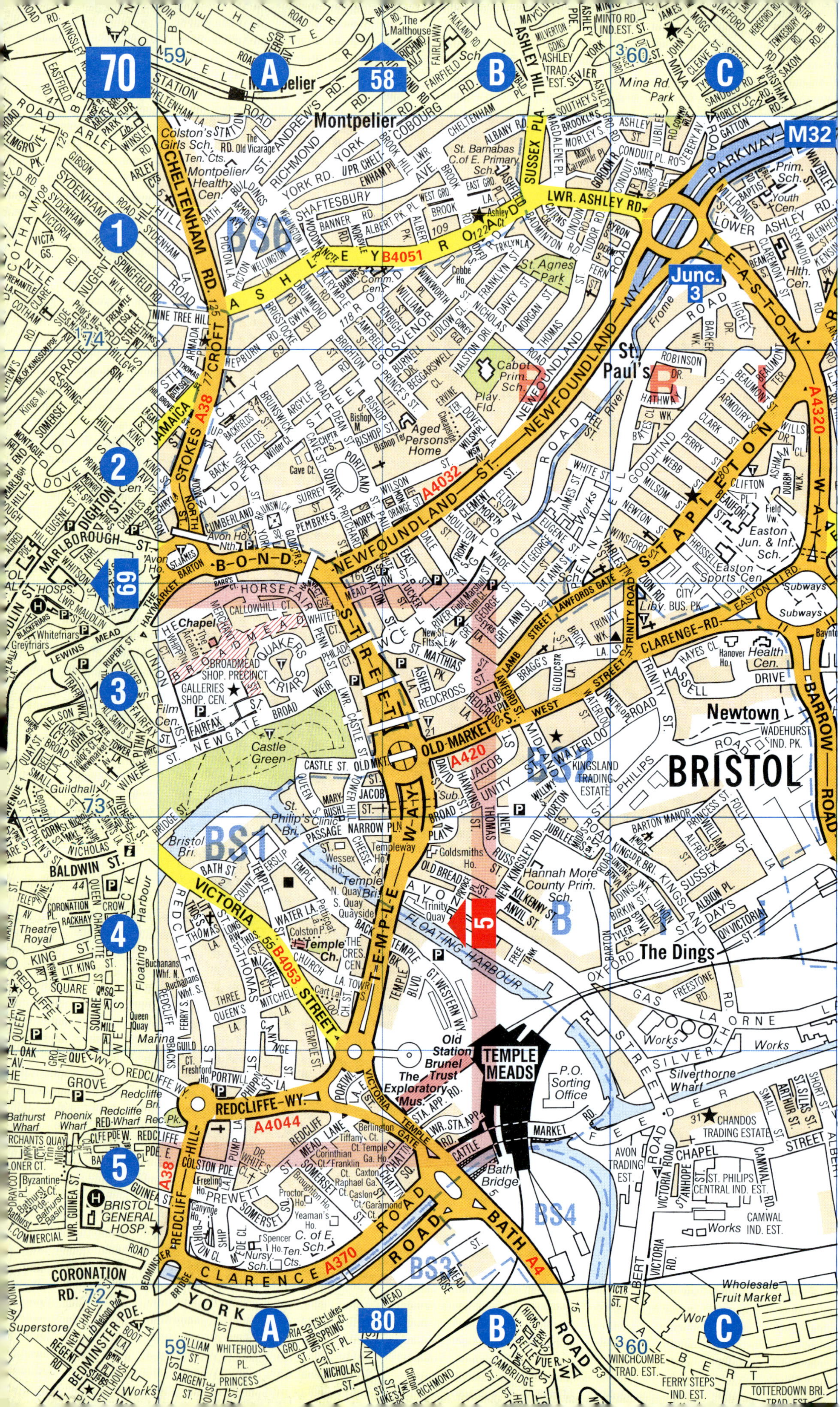
58
80
69
5
A
B
C
1
2
3
4
5
Montpelier
BS6
BS1
BS2
BS3
BS4
St. Paul's
Newtown
BRISTOL
The Dings
M32
Junc. 3
TEMPLE MEADS
Castle Green
Floating Harbour
CHELTENHAM RD.
STOKES CROFT
ASHLEY RD.
LWR. ASHLEY RD.
NEWFOUNDLAND ST.
NEWFOUNDLAND WY.
BOND ST.
HORSEFAIR
BROADMEAD
BROADMEAD SHOP. PRECINCT
GALLERIES SHOP. CEN.
NEWGATE
STAPLETON RD.
EASTON WAY
BARROW ROAD
CLARENCE RD.
TEMPLE WAY
OLD MARKET ST.
VICTORIA STREET
REDCLIFFE WY.
REDCLIFF HILL
CLARENCE ROAD
BATH ROAD
YORK RD.
CORONATION RD.
BALDWIN ST.
MARLBOROUGH ST.
DIGHTON ST.
KINGSLAND TRADING ESTATE
CHANDOS TRADING ESTATE
ST. PHILIPS CENTRAL IND. EST.
CAMWAL IND. EST.
AVON TRADING EST.
Wholesale Fruit Market
BRISTOL GENERAL HOSP.
Old Station
Brunel Trust
The Exploratory Mus.
P.O. Sorting Office
Temple Ch.
Bristol Bri.
Bath Bridge
Cabot Prim. Sch.
St. Agnes Park
Aged Persons Home
Hannah More County Prim. Sch.
Easton Jun. & Inf. Sch.
Easton Sports Cen.
Theatre Royal
Queen Square
Superstore
A38
A4032
A4320
A420
A4044
A370
A4
B4051
B4053
59
60
72
73
174

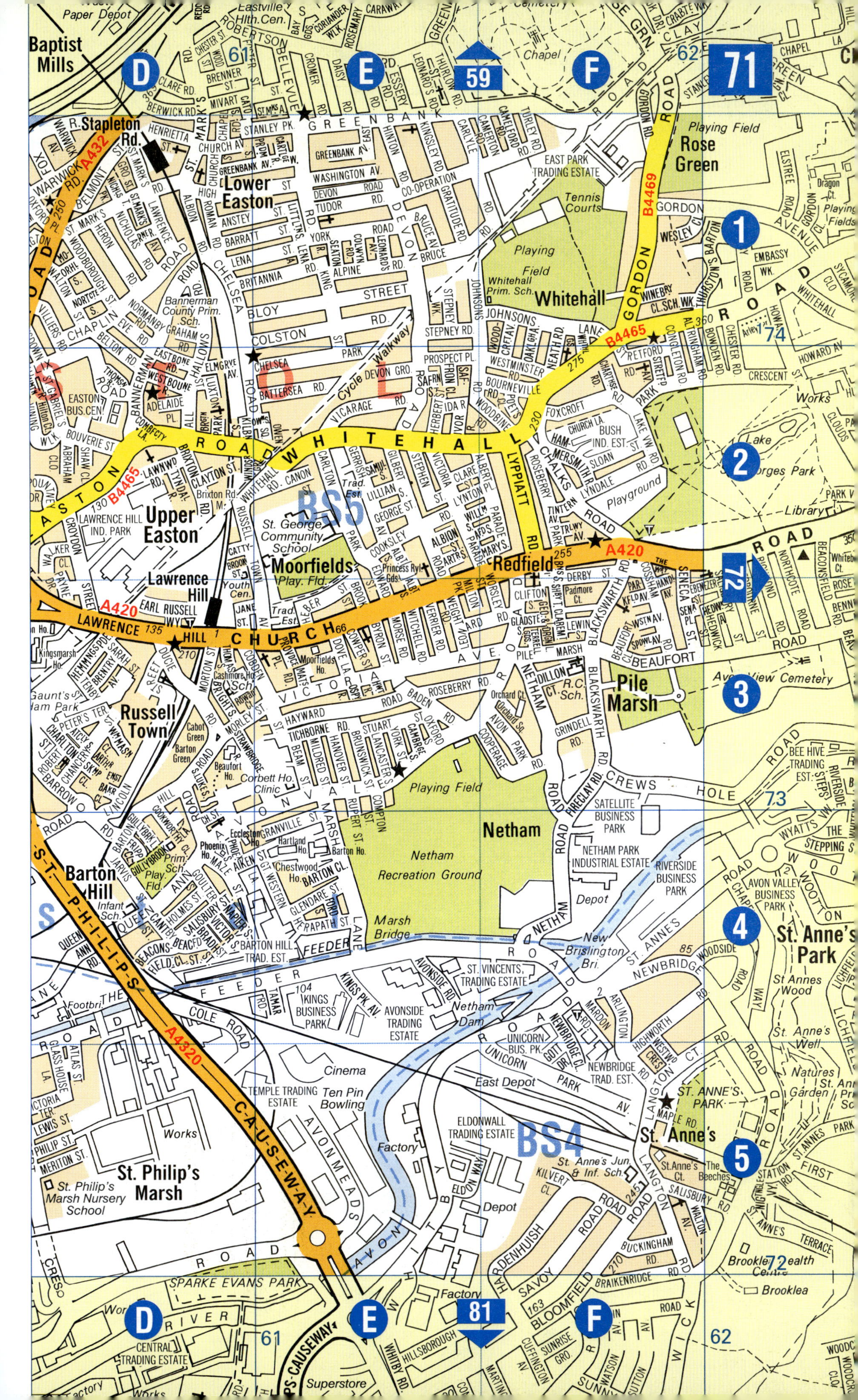

Baptist Mills
D
E
F
59
61
62
Stapleton Rd.
Lower Easton
Rose Green
Whitehall
Upper Easton
Lawrence Hill
Moorfields
Redfield
Pile Marsh
Russell Town
Barton Hill
Netham
St. Anne's Park
St. Anne's
St. Philip's Marsh
BS5
BS4
A432
A420
A4320
B4465
B4469
WHITEHALL ROAD
CHURCH ROAD
GORDON ROAD
LAWRENCE HILL
EASTON ROAD
FEEDER ROAD
CAUSEWAY
CHALKS ROAD
CREWS HOLE ROAD
NETHAM ROAD
Netham Recreation Ground
Playing Field
Marsh Bridge
New Brislington Bri.
Netham Dam
East Park Trading Estate
Kings Business Park
Avonside Trading Estate
St. Vincents Trading Estate
Riverside Business Park
Netham Park Industrial Estate
Satellite Business Park
Avon Valley Business Park
Bee Hive Trading Est.
Temple Trading Estate
Eldonwall Trading Estate
Unicorn Bus. Pk.
Newbridge Trad. Est.
Barton Hill Trad. Est.
Lawrence Hill Ind. Park
Central Trading Estate
Avonmeads
Cinema
Ten Pin Bowling
Superstore
Sparke Evans Park
St. George Community School
Bannerman County Prim. Sch.
Whitehall Prim. Sch.
St. Philip's Marsh Nursery School
Avon View Cemetery
St. Annes Wood
St. George's Park
72
73
74
81

Clay Hill
60
Rose Green
Playing Field
Speedwell
Speedwell School
Crofts End
WHITEHALL ROAD
BROOK ROAD
WHITEFIELD ROAD
B4465
SPEEDWELL
St. Georges Park
Lake
Library
CHURCH ROAD A420
CLOUDS HILL ROAD
BELL HILL ROAD
SUMMERHILL ROAD A431
AIR BALLOON RD.
NAGS HEAD
St. George
Whiteway
Sports Gnd.
BRISTOL
Crew's Hole
BS5
Avon View Cemetery
Pile Marsh
71
CREWS HOLE
RIVER
Troopers Hill
White's Hill
St. Anne's Park
BS4
St. Annes Wood
St. Anne's Well
Natures Garden
St. Anne's
Dundridge Recreation Ground
Conham
Conham Valley
CONHAM RIVER PARK
Jeffries Hill
Brooklea Health Centre
82
NETHAM PARK INDUSTRIAL ESTATE
RIVERSIDE BUSINESS PARK
AVON VALLEY BUSINESS PARK
SATELLITE BUSINESS PARK
NEWBRIDGE TRAD. EST.
New Brislington Bri.
BEE HIVE TRADING EST.
Old Peoples' Home
Dauphine's of Bristol
Butler Ho.
Hlth. Cen.
Air Balloon Inf. & Jun. Schools
Inf. & Jun. Sch.
St. Anne's Pk. Prim. Sch.
Chichester Ho.
Malvern Ct.
Whitehall
Nursery Sch.
Roegate Ho.
T.A.V.R. Centre
Speedwell Day Cen.
A B C
1 2 3 4 5
62 63
73 74

61
83
74
D
E
F
1
2
3
4
5
BS15
SOUTH GLOUCESTERSHIRE
KINGSWOOD
HANHAM
Twomile Hill
Burchells Green
Potterswood
Magpie Bottom
Stone Hill
Cocks Hill
Kingswood Park
A420
A431
A4017
B4046
B4048
MILE HILL
REGENT STREET
HIGH STREET
SOUNDWELL ROAD
DOWNEND ROAD
LODGE ROAD
CHARLTON ROAD
INGLESIDE ROAD
HANHAM ROAD
COURT ROAD
MOUNT HILL ROAD
BRYANTS HILL
HIGH STREET
STONEHILL
AVON RING ROAD
CHURCH ROAD
FOREST ROAD
BRITANNIA ROAD
ELLESMERE ROAD
CECIL ROAD
DOUGLAS ROAD
WOOD ROAD
SCHOOL ROAD
HOLLOW ROAD
LOWER CHAPEL RD.
TABERNACLE ROAD
WOODYLEAZE
BIRDWOOD
WILSHIRE AV.
HOLLYGUEST ROAD
SOUTHEY AVENUE
CHELTENHAM RD.
SYSTON WAY
GILBERT RD.
KING'S CHASE SHOP. CEN.
COSSHAM HOSP.
Sports Club
Sports Ground
Two Mile Hill Inf. & Jun. Schools
John Cabot City Technology College
Works
Council Depot
Playing Field
Beacon Rise Prim. School
Prim. Sch.
Our Lady of Lourdes R.C. Prim. Sch.
Abraham Fry Ho.
Kingsway Shopping Precinct
Hanham Folk Cen.
Liby.
Hanham Abbots Jun. & Samuel Whites Infant School
HANHAM BUSINESS PARK
AVON VALLEY PARK
Greenbank Playing Fields
Stonehill Nursery
Kingsfield
Civ. Cen.
Hlth. Cen.
Council Offices
Ten. Cts.
Bowl. Green
Tennis Courts
Plowright Ho.
Pavilion
Nursery
St. Stephen's Jun. & Inf. Sch.
64
65
72
73
174

74
62
84
73
A
B
C
1
2
3
4
5
Cockshot Hill
New Cheltenham
Siston Common
Warmley Hill
KINGSWOOD
BS15
Woodstock
Mount Hill
Barrs Court
Stone Hill
A420
A4175
A4174
HIGH STREET
CHELTENHAM ROAD
HOLLY HILL
DEANERY ROAD
COURTNEY ROAD
COCK ROAD
AVON RING ROAD
ORCHARD ROAD
SOUTHEY AVENUE
TENNIS COURT ROAD
GRIMSBURY ROAD
MOORLAND ROAD
MARSHAM WAY
CRAVEN WAY
FISHER ROAD
TIBBERTON
KING'S CHASE SHOP. CEN.
Kingswood Park
Falconride Prim. Sch.
The Park Prim. Sch.
Woodstock Sch.
Courtney Prim. School
Our Lady of Lourdes R.C. Prim. Sch.
Beacon Rise Prim. School
Barrs Court Prim. Sch.
Holly Guest Fruit Farm
Kingsfield Farm
Industrial Estate
Hypermarket
Sports Ground
Playing Fields
Southey Playing Fields
Greenbank Playing Fields
Warmley Brook
Old Grange
Grimsbury Farm
Cockroad Bottom
Gee Moor
The Farm
Council Offices
Health Cen.
365
366

63
85
D
E
F
67
68
1
2
3
4
5
174
73
72
Seven Winds
Cherry Cottage
The Hawthorns
Cherry Orchard Farm
Mill Farm
Weir
Goose Green
SISTON (GOOSE GREEN) HILL
Myrtle Farm
Bonny Mount Farm
Goose Green
Siston Hill
The Firs
Little Brook Farm
Brook Farm
WEBBS HEATH
Webb's Heath Farm
Meadow Farm
Moundscourt Farm
SISTON LA.
Varniters
Webbs Heath
Bridge Farm
Springfield Farm
AVON RING ROAD (UNDER CONSTRUCTION Estimated Completion Feb. 2001)
A4174
A4175
A420
COMMON RD.
HOBBS LA.
NORMAN ROAD
FIREWORK
Cycle / Walkway
CAPEL CL.
FAWKES CL.
DEANERY CL.
CRANE CLO.
STANLEY RD.
NORMAN
CHAPEL LA.
CHAPEL CL.
STATION CL.
HIGH ST
LONDON ROAD
BADEN RD.
CROWN GDNS.
Siston Brook
TOWER ROAD NORTH
STATION RD.
WINFIELD RD.
Works
ST. BARNABAS CL.
Bridgeyate
WEBBS HEATH
WARMLEY
Grimsbury Park Sch.
The Grange School
Bakery
CHURCH AV.
BRUNEL CLOSE
CROWN INDUSTRIAL ESTATE
CROWN RD.
Bridgeyate Common
Manor Farm
ST. IVEL WAY
BELFRY
SUNNINGDALE
MONTROSE DR.
ST. PIERRE DR.
GLENEAGLES
HOYLAKE DR.
TROON DR.
TURNBERRY
ST. ANDREWS
KINGSWAY TRAILER PARK
MILLBROOK CL.
ASHCOMBE CR.
ASHBRIDGE
MILLFIELD
ULLSWATER CL.
HAWESWATER CL.
GRASMERE GS.
THIRLMERE CT.
WINDERMERE WAY
CONISTON CL.
TWEENY LA.
HINTON DR.
CHERITON PL.
TOWER LANE
JEFFERY CT.
HADLEY CT.
LINTERN CRES.
Football Grd.
Cadbury Heath
BS30
DRIVE
CHARGROVE
HIGHCROFT DR.
WILLOW CL.
North Common
CANN LANE
Woodfield
Meadow Edge
Cann Farm
Orchard Lodge
ROY KING GS.
HAZELBURY
MARISTON WAY
Prim. Sch.
POPLAR CL.
BUSINESS CEN.
ALBANY WAY
NEADS DR.
POPLAR RD.
SAMUEL WRIGHT CL.
VALLEY RD.
TORRANCE CL.
SOUTHWAY DR.
MILL LANE
HEATH ROAD
ARMSTRONG DR.
Wesley La.
ST. DAVID'S AVE
AVENUE
VICTORIA ROAD
QUANTOCK CLO.
CHILTERN CLO.
SUMMERHAYES
LEES LA.
LEWIS CL.
ATHERSTON
HEATH RISE
Coronation Park
Youth Cen.
ROGERS CL.
SOUTH ROAD
MALVERN DRIVE
EXLEY CL.
DUVEY CT.
MAKIN CL.
FALLOWFIELD
HARDWICK CL.
NICHOLETTES
THE KEEP
Cycle / Walkway
Playing Field
BATH ROAD
BATH STREET
HIGH STREET
CHEVIOT WAY
PENNINE RD.
THE DELL
HAWKINS CL.
PULLIN CT.
Harver's Lye
Hall
COWHORN HILL
Warmley Golf Course (Pitch & Putt)
BRANDON CL.
CLOVERLEA
COOK CL.
COOMBES WY.
BATLEY CT.
Red Lodge Prim. Sch.
Weston Court Farm
BRERETON WAY
QUEENS
STANLEY GDS.
Brook
NORTH
OLDLAND
HIGH

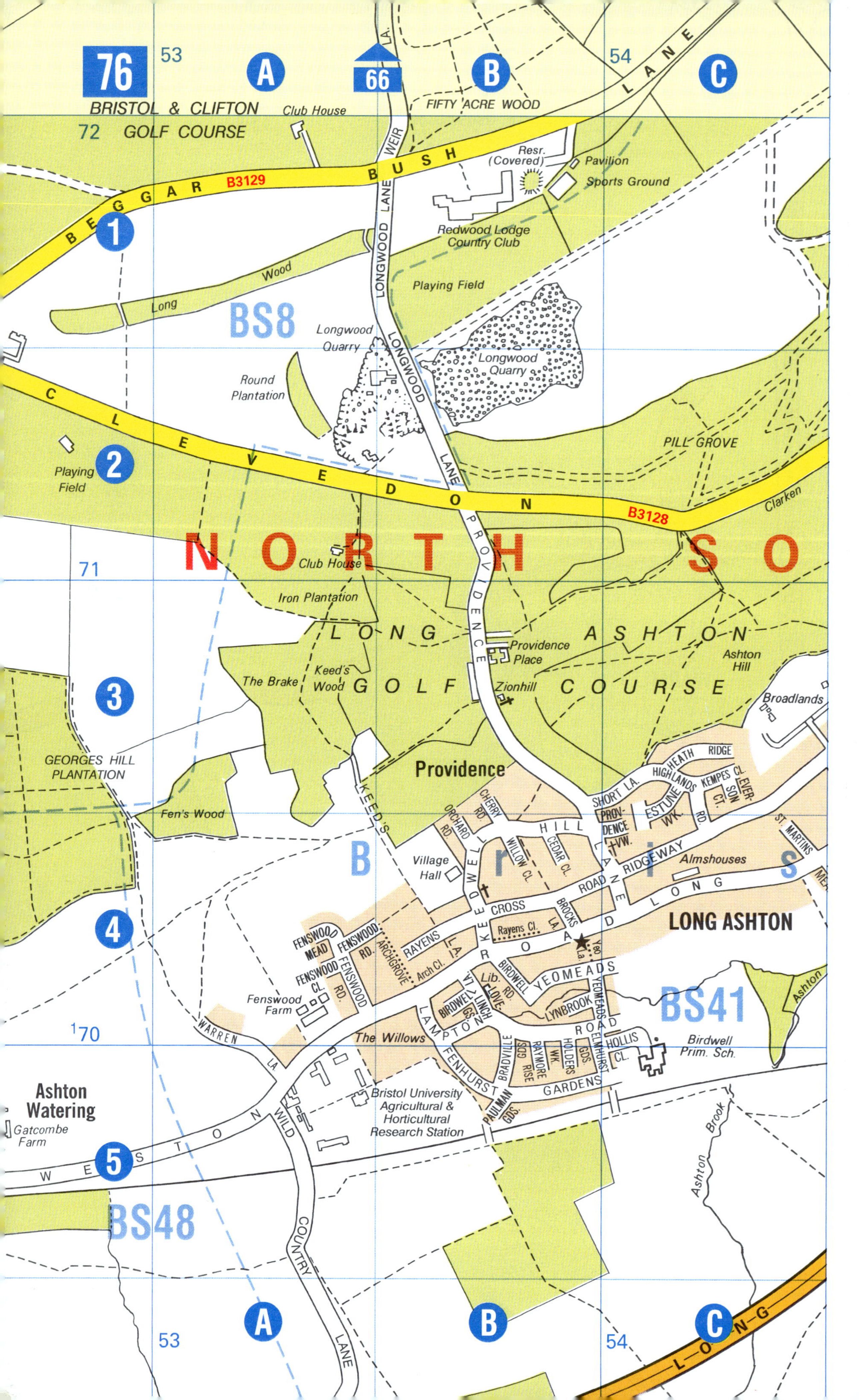

76
66
53
54
72
71
170
A
B
C
1
2
3
4
5
BRISTOL & CLIFTON GOLF COURSE
Club House
FIFTY ACRE WOOD
LANE
BEGGAR BUSH
B3129
WEIR LA.
Resr. (Covered)
Pavilion
Sports Ground
Redwood Lodge Country Club
Playing Field
Long Wood
BS8
Longwood Quarry
LONGWOOD LANE
Round Plantation
CLEVEDON
B3128
Clarken
PILL GROVE
Playing Field
NORTH SOMERSET
Club House
Iron Plantation
LONG ASHTON GOLF COURSE
PROVIDENCE
Providence Place
Ashton Hill
The Brake
Keed's Wood
Zionhill
Broadlands
GEORGES HILL PLANTATION
Fen's Wood
Providence
HEATH RIDGE
HIGHLANDS
SHORT LA.
KEMPES CL.
EVERSON CT.
PROVIDENCE VW.
ESTUNE WK.
RD.
CHERRY RD.
ORCHARD RD.
HILL
WILLOW CL.
CEDAR CL.
ST. MARTINS
KEED'S
Village Hall
RIDGEWAY
Almshouses
Bristol
LONG ASHTON
KEEDWELL
CROSS
BROCKS
LA.
ROAD
LONG ASHTON ROAD
Rayens Cl.
Yeo La.
FENSWOOD MEAD
FENSWOOD RD.
FENSWOOD CL.
ARCHGROVE
RAYENS LA.
Arch Cl.
BIRDWELL RD.
YEOMEADS
Lib.
LINCH LA.
LOVE
BIRDWELL GDS.
LYNBROOK
BS41
Fenswood Farm
WARREN LA.
The Willows
LAMPTON ROAD
FENHURST
BRADVILLE GDS.
RAYMORE RISE
WK.
HOLDERS GDS.
ELMHURST
HOLLIS CL.
GARDENS
PAULMAN GDS.
Birdwell Prim. Sch.
Ashton
Ashton Watering
Gatcombe Farm
WESTON
WILD COUNTRY LANE
Bristol University Agricultural & Horticultural Research Station
Ashton Brook
BS48
LONG

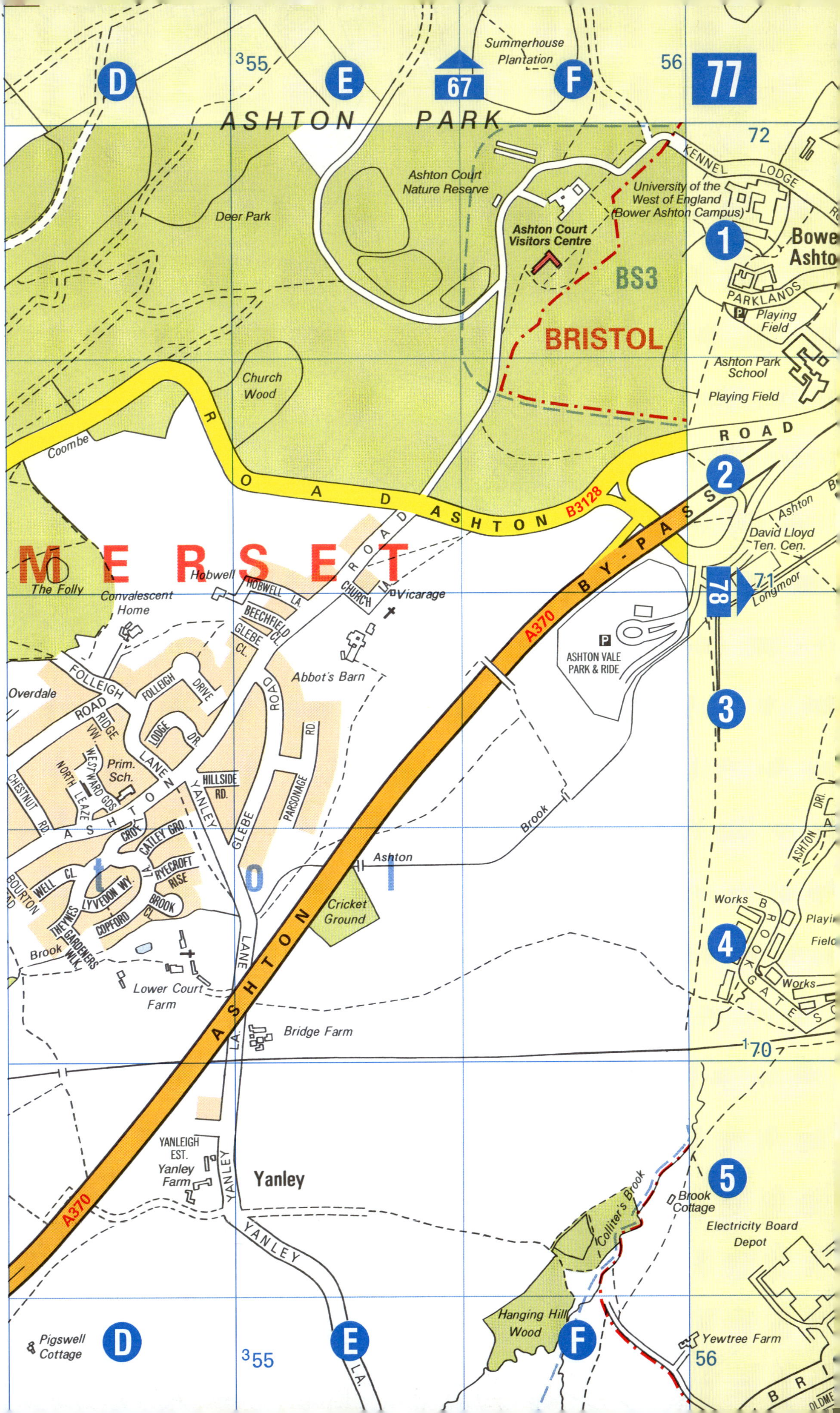
77
67
78
71
D
E
F
355
56
72
70
1
2
3
4
5
ASHTON PARK
Summerhouse Plantation
Ashton Court Nature Reserve
Deer Park
University of the West of England (Bower Ashton Campus)
KENNEL LODGE
Bower Ashton
Ashton Court Visitors Centre
BS3
BRISTOL
PARKLANDS
Playing Field
Ashton Park School
Playing Field
Church Wood
Coombe
ROAD
ASHTON ROAD B3128
BY-PASS
A370
Ashton
David Lloyd Ten. Cen.
Longmoor
MERSET
The Folly
Hobwell
Convalescent Home
HOBWELL LA.
CHURCH LA.
ROAD
Vicarage
BEECHFIELD CL.
GLEBE CL.
Abbot's Barn
ASHTON VALE PARK & RIDE
Overdale
FOLLEIGH ROAD
FOLLEIGH DRIVE
RIDGE VW.
LODGE DR.
LANE
ROAD
RD.
Prim. Sch.
WEST WARD GDS.
NORTH LEAZE
CHESTNUT RD.
HILLSIDE RD.
YANLEY
GLEBE
PARSONAGE
ASHTON
Brook
CRO.
CATLEY GRO.
RYECROFT RISE
LA.
Ashton
BOURTON
WELL CL.
YVEDON WY.
BROOK CL.
Cricket Ground
Works
BROOKGATE
Playing Field
Works
THEYNES
GARDENERS WLK.
COPFORD
Brook
LANE
ASHTON
Lower Court Farm
Bridge Farm
LA.
YANLEIGH EST.
Yanley Farm
YANLEY
Yanley
A370
YANLEY
Colliter's Brook
Brook Cottage
Electricity Board Depot
Hanging Hill Wood
Pigswell Cottage
LA.
Yewtree Farm
BRI
OLDMERE

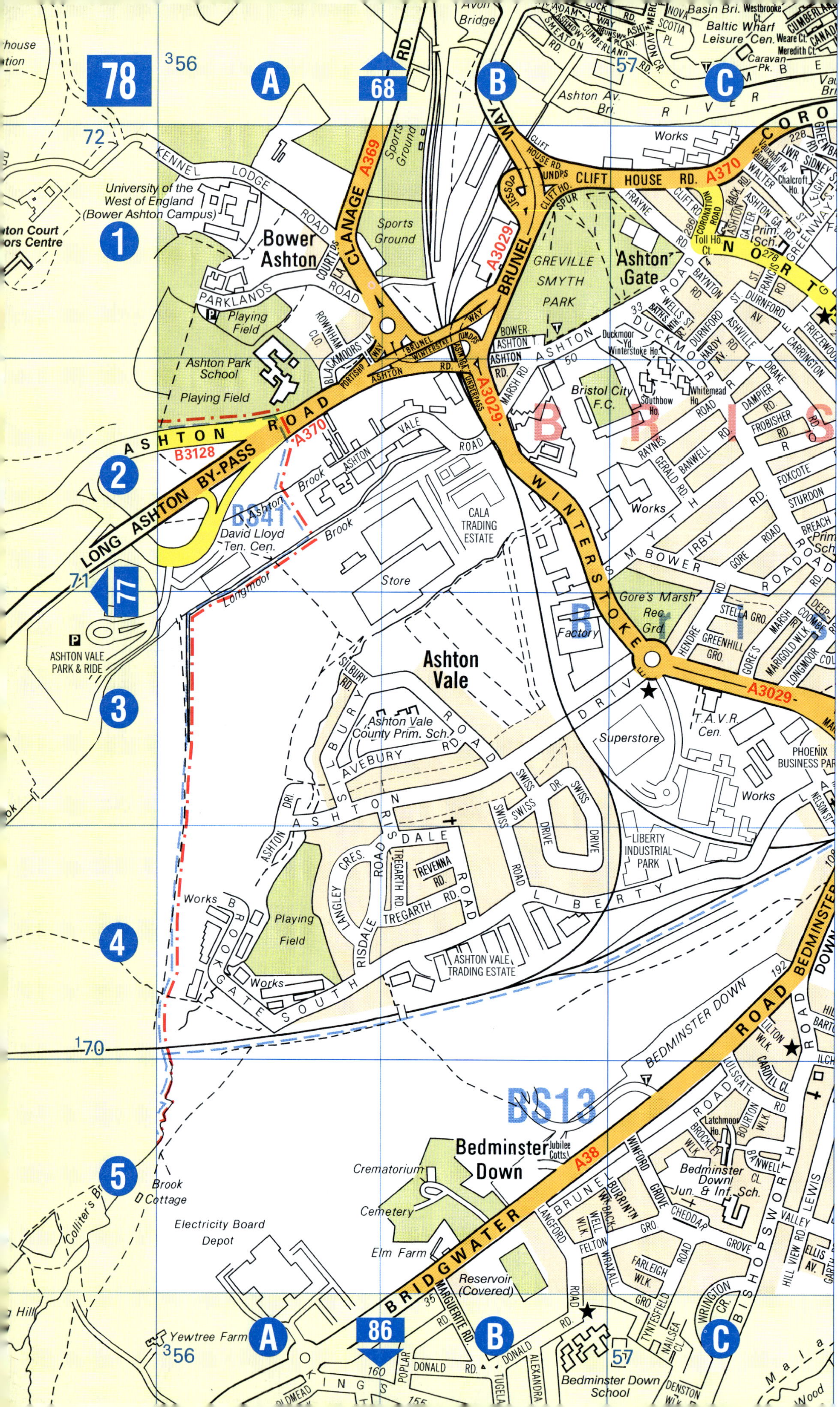
78
68
77
86
A
B
C
1
2
3
4
5
356
57
72
71
170
University of the West of England (Bower Ashton Campus)
Bower Ashton
Kennel Lodge Road
Parklands
Playing Field
Ashton Park School
Playing Field
Clanage Rd.
A369
Sports Ground
Sports Ground
Brunel Way
A3029
Clift House Rd.
A370
Greville Smyth Park
Ashton Gate
Coronation Road
Ashton Road
B3128
Long Ashton By-Pass
David Lloyd Ten. Cen.
BS41
Ashton Vale Park & Ride
Cala Trading Estate
Store
Winterstoke Road
Bristol City F.C.
Works
Ashton Vale
Ashton Vale County Prim. Sch.
Silbury Rd.
Avebury Rd.
Risdale Road
Swiss Drive
Liberty Industrial Park
Superstore
T.A.V.R. Cen.
Phoenix Business Park
A3029
Ashton Vale Trading Estate
Playing Field
Works
South Liberty
Langley Cres.
Tregarth Rd.
Trevenna Rd.
Bedminster Down
BS13
Bedminster Down Road
Crematorium
Cemetery
Elm Farm
Reservoir (Covered)
Bridgwater Road
A38
Brook Cottage
Electricity Board Depot
Yewtree Farm
Bedminster Down Jun. & Inf. Sch.
Bedminster Down School
Bishopsworth Road
Cheddar Grove
Winford Grove
Marguerite Rd.
Donald Rd.
Poplar
Alexandra
Kings
Denston Wlk.
Wrington Cr.
Nailsea Cl.
Tyntesfield
Farleigh Wlk.
Felton Gro.
Langford Road
Brunel Wlk.
Valley Road
Hill View Rd.
Lewis

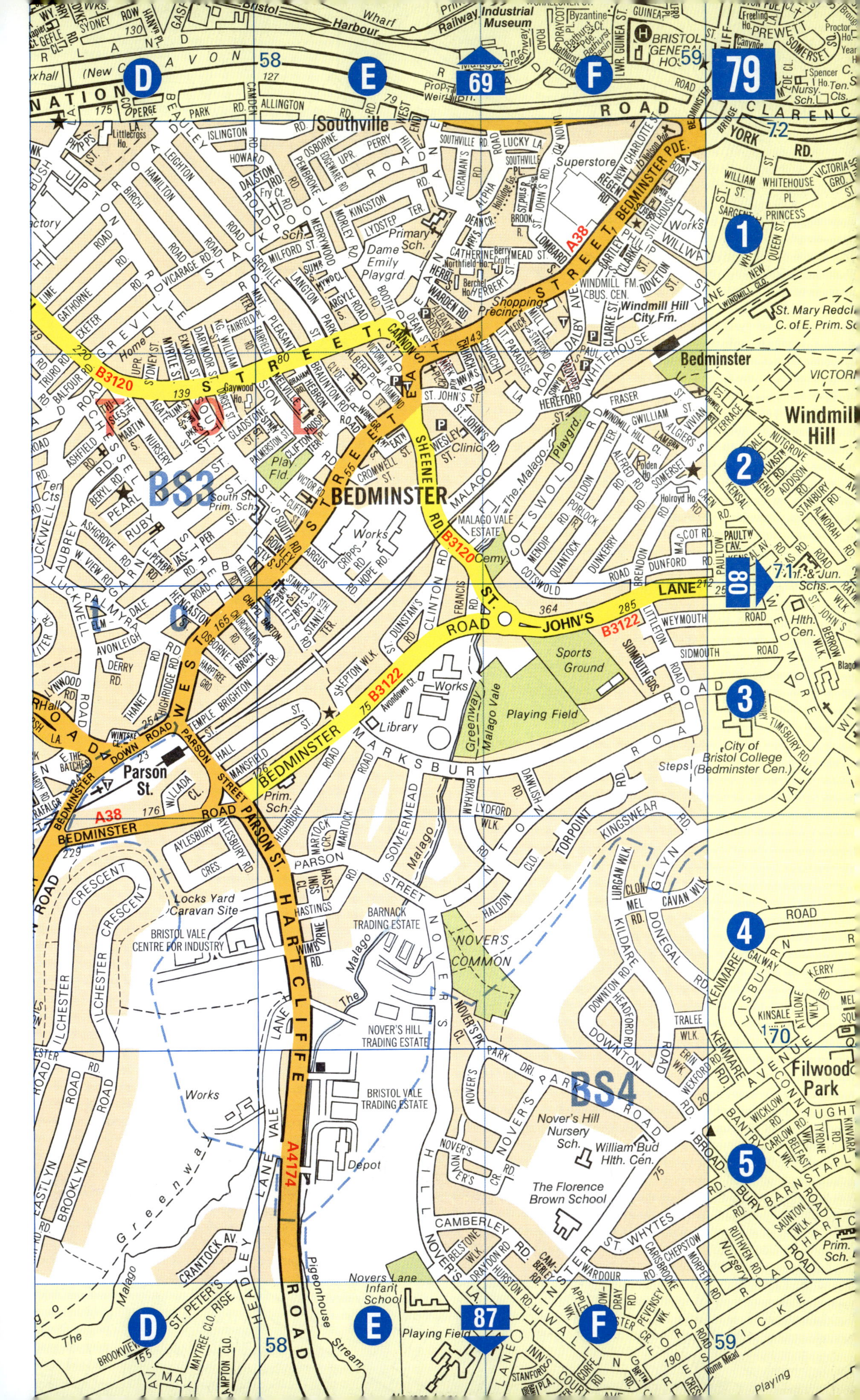
79
69
87
80
D
E
F
1
2
3
4
5
58
59
Industrial Museum
Harbour
Wharf
Railway
CUMBERLAND ROAD
NATIONAL
AVON
Southville
BRISTOL GENERAL HOSP
CLARENCE ROAD
YORK RD.
Superstore
BEDMINSTER PDE.
A38
Primary Sch.
Dame Emily Playgrd.
Shopping Precinct
Windmill Hill City Fm.
Bedminster
St. Mary Redcliffe C. of E. Prim. Sch.
Windmill Hill
B3120
NORTH STREET
EAST STREET
BS3
BEDMINSTER
South St. Prim. Sch.
Play Fld.
Works
MALAGO VALE ESTATE
The Malago
Playgrd.
Cemy.
SHEENE RD.
COTSWOLD RD.
ST. JOHN'S LANE
B3122
Sports Ground
Playing Field
Greenway
Malago Vale
Library
BEDMINSTER ROAD
MARKSBURY ROAD
City of Bristol College (Bedminster Cen.)
Parson St.
A38
BEDMINSTER DOWN ROAD
WEST STREET
PARSON ST.
Prim. Sch.
PARSON STREET
Locks Yard Caravan Site
BRISTOL VALE CENTRE FOR INDUSTRY
BARNACK TRADING ESTATE
NOVER'S COMMON
NOVER'S HILL TRADING ESTATE
BRISTOL VALE TRADING ESTATE
HARTCLIFFE ROAD
A4174
Works
Greenway
Depot
BS4
Nover's Hill Nursery Sch.
William Budd Hlth. Cen.
The Florence Brown School
Filwood Park
Novers Lane Infant School
Playing Field
Pigeonhouse Stream
Malago
Inf. & Jun. Schs.
Hlth. Cen.
Prim. Sch.
WINDMILL HILL
WHITEHOUSE
KENMARE RD.
BROADBURY RD.
WEDMORE VALE
NOVER'S LANE
NOVER'S HILL
CAMBERLEY RD.
WHYTES
ILCHESTER CRESCENT
BROOKLYN ROAD
CRANTOCK AV.
ST. PETER'S RISE
LYNTON
SOMERMEAD
TORPOINT
KINGSWEAR
DAWLISH RD.
DUNKERRY
MENDIP RD.
QUANTOCK
PORLOCK
SIDMOUTH ROAD
WEYMOUTH ROAD

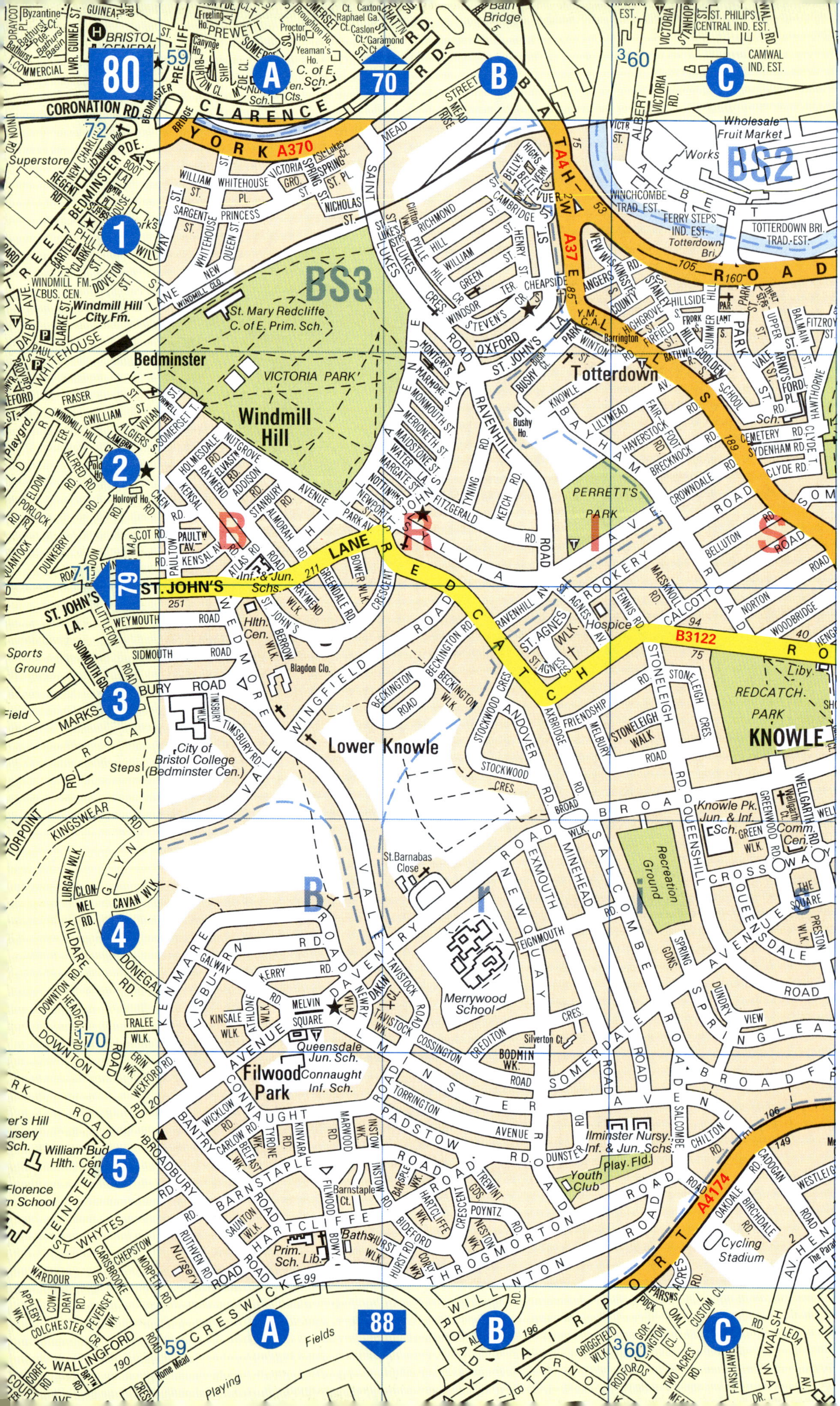
80
70
79
88
A
B
C
1
2
3
4
5
BS3
BS2
Bedminster
Windmill Hill
VICTORIA PARK
St. Mary Redcliffe C. of E. Prim. Sch.
Windmill Hill City Fm.
Totterdown
Lower Knowle
KNOWLE
REDCATCH PARK
Filwood Park
Bristol
Bath Bridge
Totterdown Bri.
CORONATION RD.
CLARENCE RD.
YORK RD. A370
BATH RD. A4
WELLS RD. A37
ST. JOHN'S LANE 211
REDCATCH RD. B3122
AIRPORT RD. A4174
WHITEHOUSE ST.
WINDMILL HILL
VALE LANE
WEDMORE VALE
BROADWALK
SALCOMBE RD.
SOMERDALE AV.
THROGMORTON RD.
HARTCLIFFE RD.
BARNSTAPLE RD.
CRESWICKE RD.
CONNAUGHT RD.
KENMARE RD.
INNS COURT AV.
ST. AGNES AV.
SYLVIA AV.
NORTH ST.
Superstore
Sports Ground
Steps
City of Bristol College (Bedminster Cen.)
Merrywood School
Queensdale Jun. Sch.
Connaught Inf. Sch.
Knowle Pk. Jun. & Inf. Sch.
Ilminster Nursy. Inf. & Jun. Schs.
Youth Club
Play. Fld.
Recreation Ground
Cycling Stadium
Wholesale Fruit Market
Works
St. Barnabas Close
Hospice
Hlth. Cen.
Inf. & Jun. Schs.
Fields
Playing
Melvin Square
Bushy Ho.
PERRETT'S PARK
Barnstaple Ct.
Baths
Prim. Sch. Lib.
Nursery
CAMWAL IND. EST.
ST. PHILIPS CENTRAL IND. EST.
WINCHCOMBE TRAD. EST.
FERRY STEPS IND. EST.
TOTTERDOWN BRI. TRAD. EST.
Lby.
Comm. Cen.
Silverton Ct.

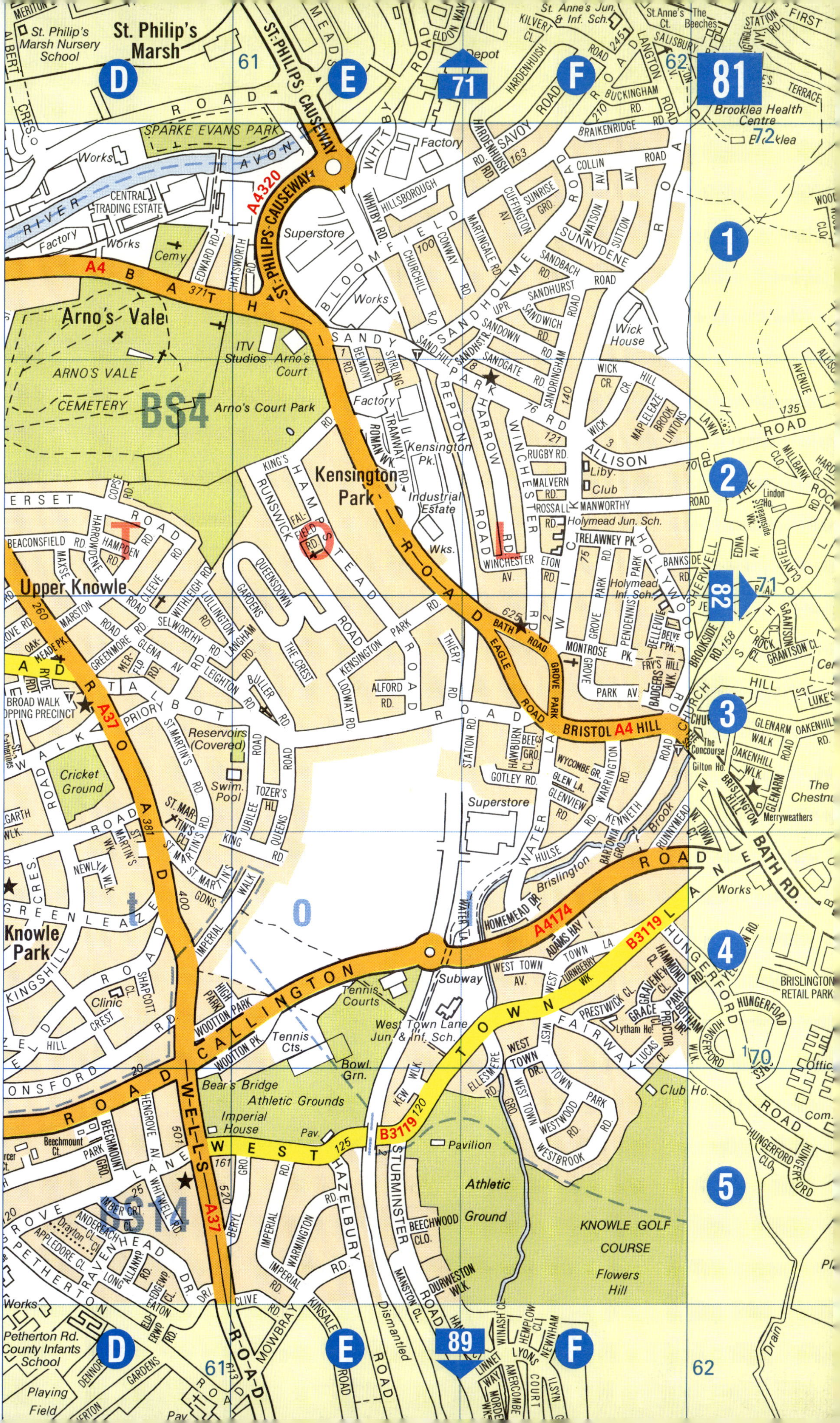
St. Philip's Marsh
St. Philip's Marsh Nursery School
Sparke Evans Park
River Avon
Central Trading Estate
Works
Factory
Cemy
A4320
St. Philips Causeway
Superstore
A4 Bath Road
Arno's Vale
Arno's Vale Cemetery
BS4
ITV Studios
Arno's Court
Arno's Court Park
Bloomfield Road
Sandy Park Road
Sandholme Road
Hillsborough
Whitby Rd.
Churchill Rd.
Conway Rd.
Martingale Rd.
Cuffington Av.
Sunrise Gro.
Sunnydene
Sandbach Rd.
Sandhurst Rd.
Sandwich Rd.
Sandown Rd.
Sandgate Rd.
Sandringham Rd.
Wick House
Wick Cr.
Wick Rd.
Allison Road
Rugby Rd.
Malvern Rd.
Rossall Rd.
Manworthy Rd.
Liby.
Club
Holymead Jun. Sch.
Holymead Inf. Sch.
Trelawney Pk.
Kensington Park
Kensington Pk.
Industrial Estate
Wks.
Harrow Road
Winchester Rd.
Repton Road
Eagle Road
Grove Park Rd.
Bristol A4 Hill
Brislington Hill
Upper Knowle
Beaconsfield Rd.
Somerset Road
Hampden Rd.
Marston Road
Greenmore Rd.
Selworthy Rd.
Leighton Rd.
Priory Road
Buller Rd.
Queensdown Gardens
The Crest
Lodway Rd.
Alford Rd.
Thiery Rd.
Station Rd.
Broad Walk Shopping Precinct
Cricket Ground
Reservoirs (Covered)
Swim. Pool
St. Martin's Rd.
Jubilee Rd.
Tozer's Hl.
Queens Rd.
A37
Wells Road
Superstore
Gotley Rd.
Water La.
Brislington Brook
Hulse
Homemead Dr.
A4174
West Town Lane
B3119
Subway
Tennis Courts
Tennis Cts.
West Town Lane Jun. & Inf. Sch.
Knowle Park
Kingshill
Clinic
Callington Road
Wootton Park
Bear's Bridge Athletic Grounds
Imperial House
Pav.
Bowl. Grn.
Pavilion
Athletic Ground
Knowle Golf Course
Flowers Hill
Fairway
Club Ho.
Hungerford Road
Brislington Retail Park
Bath Rd.
Works
Merryweathers
The Chestnuts
St. Luke's
Hazelbury Rd.
Sturminster Road
Dismantled
Beechwood Clo.
Durweston Wk.
Westbrook
BS14
Petherton Rd.
Petherton Rd. County Infants School
Playing Field
Wells Road
Mowbray Rd.
Kinsale Road
Hemplow Cl.
Lyons Court
Newnham
Amercombe
D
E
F
D
E
F
1
2
3
4
5
61
62
71
72
82
70
89

72
90
81
A
B
C
1
2
3
4
5
62
63
Conham
Jeffries Hill
CONHAM RIVER PARK
Conham Ferry
Broom Hill
Home for the Aged
Playground
Tunnel
Eastwood Farm
East Wood
Brooklea Health Centre
Brooklea
Wick House
BS4
BRISTOL
VICTORY PARK
Cemetery
BRISLINGTON
Oakenhill Farm
The Chestnuts
Merryweathers
Broomhill Cnty. Inf. Sch.
Broomhill Junior School
Youth Centre
Fox House
BONVILLE BUSINESS CENTRE
BRISLINGTON TRADING ESTATE
WILVERLEY INDUSTRIAL ESTATE
BRISLINGTON RETAIL PARK
FLOWERS INDUSTRIAL ESTATE
Trading Cen.
Offices
Warehouse
Com. Cen.
Works
Heath Farm
Swiss Cottage
St. Brendan's R.C. College
The Beeches
Ckt. Grd.
Pav.
Playing Field
Brislington House Nurses Home
Lodge Cottage
PARK & RIDE
Cemetery
Nursery
Eudon House
Scotland Bungalow
Tennis Courts
Brislington School
Scotland House Farm
Pavilion
Playing Fields
KNOWLE GOLF COURSE
Flowers Hill
BS14
Scotland
Bottom
Drain
Club Ho.
Holymead Jun. Sch.
Liby.
Club
BRISTOL HILL
CALLINGTON ROAD
BATH ROAD
A4
B 3119
BROOMHILL ROAD
STOCKWOOD ROAD
HUNGERFORD ROAD
IRONMOULD LANE
WICK ROAD
ALLISON ROAD
BIRCHWOOD ROAD
EASTWOOD ROAD
JERSEY AVENUE
WYNDHAM CRESCENT
CONHAM ROAD

HANHAM
Greenbank Playing Fields
Playing Field
Liby.
Hanham Folk Cen.
HIGH STREET
STONEHILL
A431
73
72
Stone Hill
Stonehill Nursery
HANHAM BUSINESS PARK
AVON VALLEY PARK
Hanham Abbots Jun. & Samuel Whites Infant Schools
Playing Field
Pavilion
Christchurch C. of E. Prim. Sch.
Higham High Sch.
HANHAM HALL HOSPITAL
Hanham Hall
Indust. Esta
Hencliff Wood
Hanham Common Rec. Grd.
Pavilion
Sports Ground
SOUTH GLOUCESTERSHIRE
A4174
RING ROAD
Hanham Cross
84
71
BS15
BS30
Hanham Green
Castle Inn Farm
Woodlands
The Batch
Court Farm
Riverside Cottages
COURT FARM ROAD
Bickley Wood
Towing Path
Hanham Court
Hanham Mills
Hanham Lock
BATH & NORTH EAST SOMERSET
Earthworks
Ferry
Sewage Bed
Hicks Gate
Works
Hicks Gate Farm
Hicks Gate House
BS31
A4
KEYNSHAM BY-PASS
A4175
DURLEY HILL
Durley Park House
91
Roman Villa
64
365
70
1
2
3
4
5
D
E
F

Barrs Court
Greenbank Playing Fields
Health Cen.
Barrs Court Sch.
Barrs Court
74
A
B
C
365
66
72
71
70
83
1
2
3
4
5
BS15
Stone Hill
Stonehill Nursery
Stone Hill
Industrial Estate
Coach Works
Industrial Estate
RING ROAD
A4174
A431
BATH ROAD
STONEHILL
AVON
MARSHAM WAY
ALDERMOOR WAY
KINGSFIELD
EMPIRE CR.
HALE CL.
HEADINGTON CL.
MEADOWS CL.
WHITTUCKS CL.
ILES CL.
STEPHEN'S
COPLEY CT.
COLTHURST DRIVE
SKIPPON CT.
DEVEROSE CT.
CAUSLEY
SCOTT CT.
HARDY
SASSOON CT.
LAURIE LEE CT.
DYLAN THOMAS
CHURCH
NEWTON RD.
CORONATION CLOSE
HAMPTON CLO.
EARLSTONE DRIVE
EARLSTONE CL.
Parkwall Prim. Sch.
Lib.
Alfred Lovell Gds.
CRESCENT
QUEENS
HOME MEAD
THE GROVE
THE WARNS
HORWOOD CT.
HASKINS CT.
STOKES CT.
PARKWALL
ALLINGTON DR.
COX CT.
BRAMLEY CT.
WOODWARD
MOORLAND
PRINCES CT.
SQUIRES CT.
FRANCIS PL.
REED CT.
LAPHAMS CT.
FOX CT.
ARCHER CT.
BRAYNE CT.
ISLEYS CT.
POYNTZ CT.
FARM
STEEL
HICKS CT.
STIBBS CT.
TINDELL CT.
DRUMMOND
DRIVE
GREAT LEAZE
MARYGOLD LEAZE
LONG
HANDSTONES
RUSHY
CALIFORNIA ROAD
BEAUFORT CL.
RUTHERFORD CL.
ELDERWOOD DR.
BURBANK CL.
BAKERSFIELD
BEACH
FAIRDAKS
EDGEWOOD CL.
REDWOOD CL.
LONG AVENUE
ORLAND WY.
FERNDALE
CLOVER
DALE DR.
RAVENS
FIELD LANE
WATSON'S RD.
SHELLARDS
Longwell Green
BAGWORTH DR.
WILLIAMS CLO.
Longwell House
Community Centre
Recreation Ground
SOUTH GLO
Longwell Green Prim. Sch.
A431
PENN GROVE
SPRINGVILLE CL.
COTTONWOOD DR.
PALMDALE CL.
BEACH
ROSEVILLE
SHERIDAN
AVENUE
WAY
GREENVIEW
AVONDALE CT.
LONG ROAD
DAVEN PORT CL.
STANHOPE RD.
SANDRINGHAM RD.
BALMORAL RD.
PEARSALL RD.
LARKSLEAZE
BELLACOMBE
STANHOPE
WINDSOR RD.
CERES CL.
KILNHURST CLO.
RUTLAND AV.
Oldbury Chase
Willsbridge Mill Visitor Centre
WILLSBRIDGE
Stout's Hill
Willsbridge House
Willsbridge
FARM ROAD
Court Farm
Drain
SALLY BARN CL.
Tennis Courts
COURT ROAD
FERRY ROAD
B r i
Hanham Court
Hanham Mills
Cleeve Wood
Towing Path
River Avon
Ferry
Towing Path
Keynsham Hams
BS31
BATH & NORTH EAST SOMERSET
Londonderry Farm
Londonderry Wharf (Disused)
A4175
KEYNSHAM ROAD
Roseneath
Drain
Drain
Somerdale Factory
NORTH ROAD
SOMERDALE ROAD
Path
Recreation Ground
Pavilion
Bowling Green
Tennis Courts
CHANDOS RD.
CROSS ST.
KEYNSHAM BY-PASS
92
Towing
Mead
365
66

D
E
F
75
68
67
Coronation Park
Youth Cen.
HEATH RD.
ROGERS CL.
SOUTH
PARK
ALVERN
CHEVIOT WAY
DRIVE
COWHORN
EXLEY CL.
DOVEY CT.
MILLERS
THE DELL
HARDWICK CL.
FALLOW
THE KEEP
NICHOLEY
Walkway
Playing Field
Harver's Lye
72
Hall
Weston Court Farm
Redfield Edge Prim. Sch.
PULLIN CT.
NOBLE AV.
COOMBES WY.
BATLEY CT.
HAWKINS CL.
BRANDON CL.
PENNINE RD.
GRAMPIAN CL.
CLOVERLEA
COOK CL.
NORTH STREET
OLDLAND
Railway
A4175
1
Warmley Golf Course (Pitch & Putt)
Siston Brook
BRERETON WAY
QUEENS RD
BOULEVARD
STANLEY GDS.
MAPLE CLO.
CEDAR CLO.
GLENWOOD
GLENWOOD DR.
FAIRWAY
WESTCOURT DR.
WESTLAND
Wincroft
WINCROFT
HIGHLEAZE RD.
HILL
VIEW CL.
WEST STREET
Sir Bernard Lovell Sch.
Oldland Common
SIMPLEX INDUS. ESTATE
NORTH CROFT
Redfield Farm
REDFIELD HILL
LOVELL AV.
ORCHARD
CALIFORNIA RD.
BROOKLEA
HENFIELD CR.
Valley
Recreation Ground
Green Gables
STOCKTON CL.
HANDFORD WY.
BERENDA DR.
BS30
ROAD
COURT
DRIVE
THE CROFT
GOOCH CT.
HIGH
CASTLE RD.
THE CLAMP
Avon
TUDOR CLO.
BROOKFIELD WLK.
COURT
GILROY CL.
AUBURN AV.
Oldland Common
2
FONTANA CL.
GRANGEVILLE CL.
Vic.
St. Anne's C. of E. Prim. Sch.
MEADOW
SCHOOL
GLOUCESTERSHIRE
Works
CHEQUERS CLO.
Park Farm
HOPLAND CL.
ROAD
SUNNYVALE DR.
CHERRY WOOD
DRIVE
71
RAVENDALE DR.
Oldland Bottom
CHERRY
OAKLANDS DR.
ST. ANNES
ST. HELENS
LODGE DR.
THE BEECHES
Earthwork
Lower Cullyhall Farm
Upper Cullyhall Farm
3
DRIVE
WARWICK
DUNSTER GDS.
GARDEN
HARLECH WY.
OAKLEIGH GDS.
BARRY
Cherry Garden Primary School
Turnpike Cottage
LUDLOW
ST. FAGANS CT.
LUDLOW CL.
KENILWORTH
HIGHFIELD GDS.
WITHINGTON CL.
LANE
Ronalds Elkstone Wk.
OAKHILL
CHERRY GARDEN RD.
CALDICOT CL.
Valley
Avon
RYEDOWN LANE
LANE
CLOSE
LUDLOW CT.
CARMARTHEN GRO.
Fonthill Way
STANWAY
VERWOOD DR.
WALTON RD.
CORFE PL.
DRIVE
Bitton Sta. Railway Cen.
PINES
PENDOCK CL.
Roman Road (Course of)
HILL
BATH ROAD
CHERRY GDS.
BARRY CLO.
Kimber Coombe
Bitton Hill
4
The Lons
Hill Farm
THE PARK
Roman Road
A431
The Croft
Pavilion
Knights Folly Farm
70
Playing Fields
LA.
COLA
Weir
Works
Granville Nursery
Avon Valley Railway
Cycle Walkway
The Meadows Primary School
CROFT CL.
TAYMAN RIDGE
5
ROAD
ELDGROVE
Barrow Lodge
KINGS SQUARE
MILL LA.
Earthwork
Wks.
Bitton
Works
HIGH ST.
CHURCH
Field Grove Farm
Barrow Hill
Tumulus
CHURCH FARM PAD.
CHURCH LA.
The Old Vicarage
Avonside Ho.
93
HOLMMEAD
River
ROAD

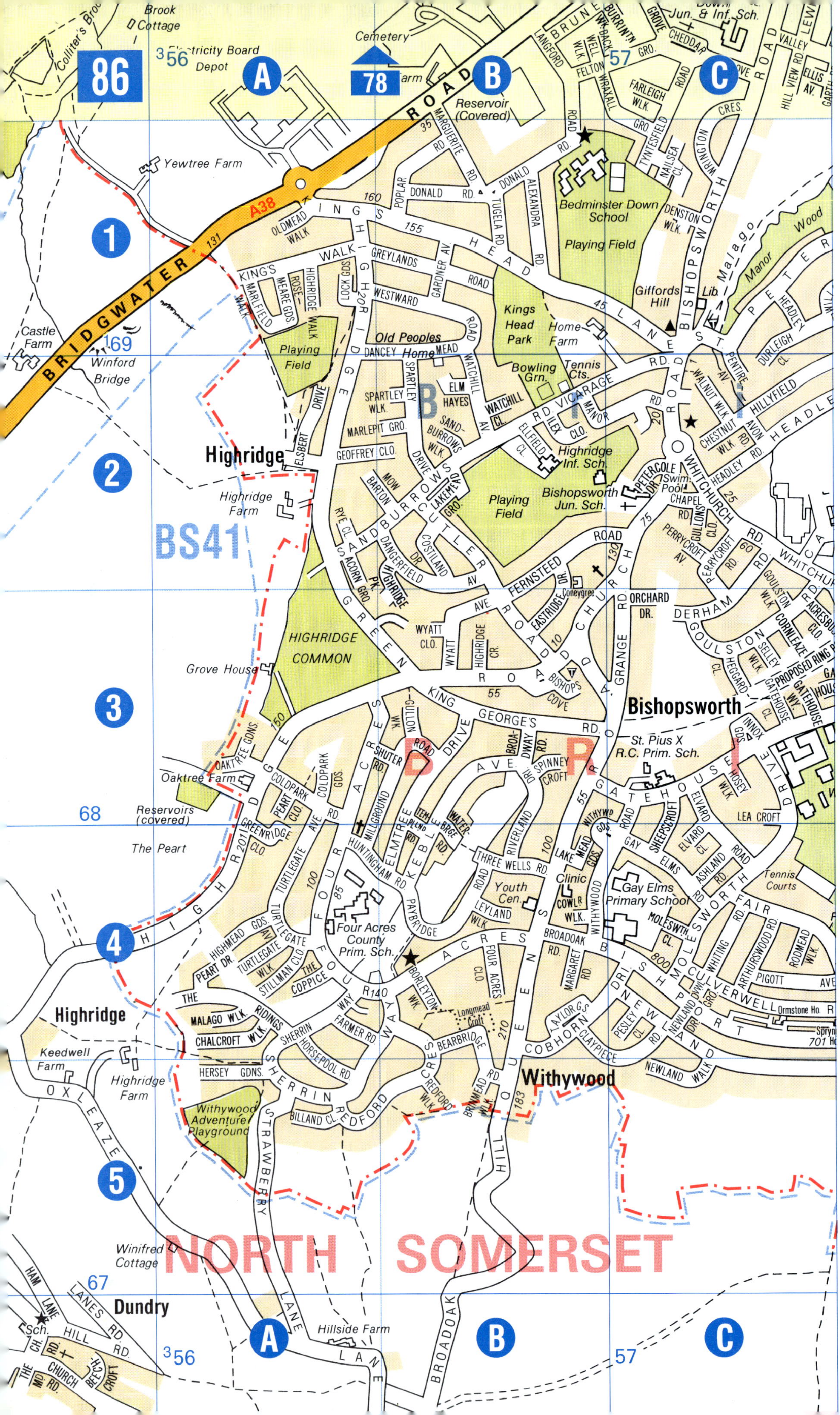
78
Brook Cottage
Colliter's Brook
Electricity Board Depot
Cemetery
Jun. & Inf. Sch.
Reservoir (Covered)
Yewtree Farm
BRIDGWATER ROAD
A38
KINGS HEAD LANE
Bedminster Down School
Playing Field
Giffords Hill
Lib.
Malago
Manor Wood
Castle Farm
Winford Bridge
Kings Head Park
Home Farm
Old Peoples Home
Bowling Grn.
Tennis Cts.
VICARAGE RD.
Highridge
Highridge Farm
Highridge Inf. Sch.
Bishopsworth Jun. Sch.
Swim. Pool
BS41
HIGHRIDGE GREEN
HIGHRIDGE COMMON
WHITCHURCH ROAD
Grove House
KING GEORGE'S RD.
Bishopsworth
St. Pius X R.C. Prim. Sch.
GATEHOUSE AVE.
Oaktree Farm
Reservoirs (covered)
The Peart
HIGH RIDGE
FOUR ACRES
Four Acres County Prim. Sch.
Youth Cen.
Clinic
Gay Elms Primary School
MOLESWORTH DR.
Tennis Courts
Highridge
Keedwell Farm
Highridge Farm
OXLEAZE
Withywood Adventure Playground
STRAWBERRY LANE
Withywood
QUEENS HILL
BROADOAK
Winifred Cottage
NORTH SOMERSET
Dundry
Hillside Farm
Sch.
LANE
356
357
67
68
169
A
B
C
1
2
3
4
5

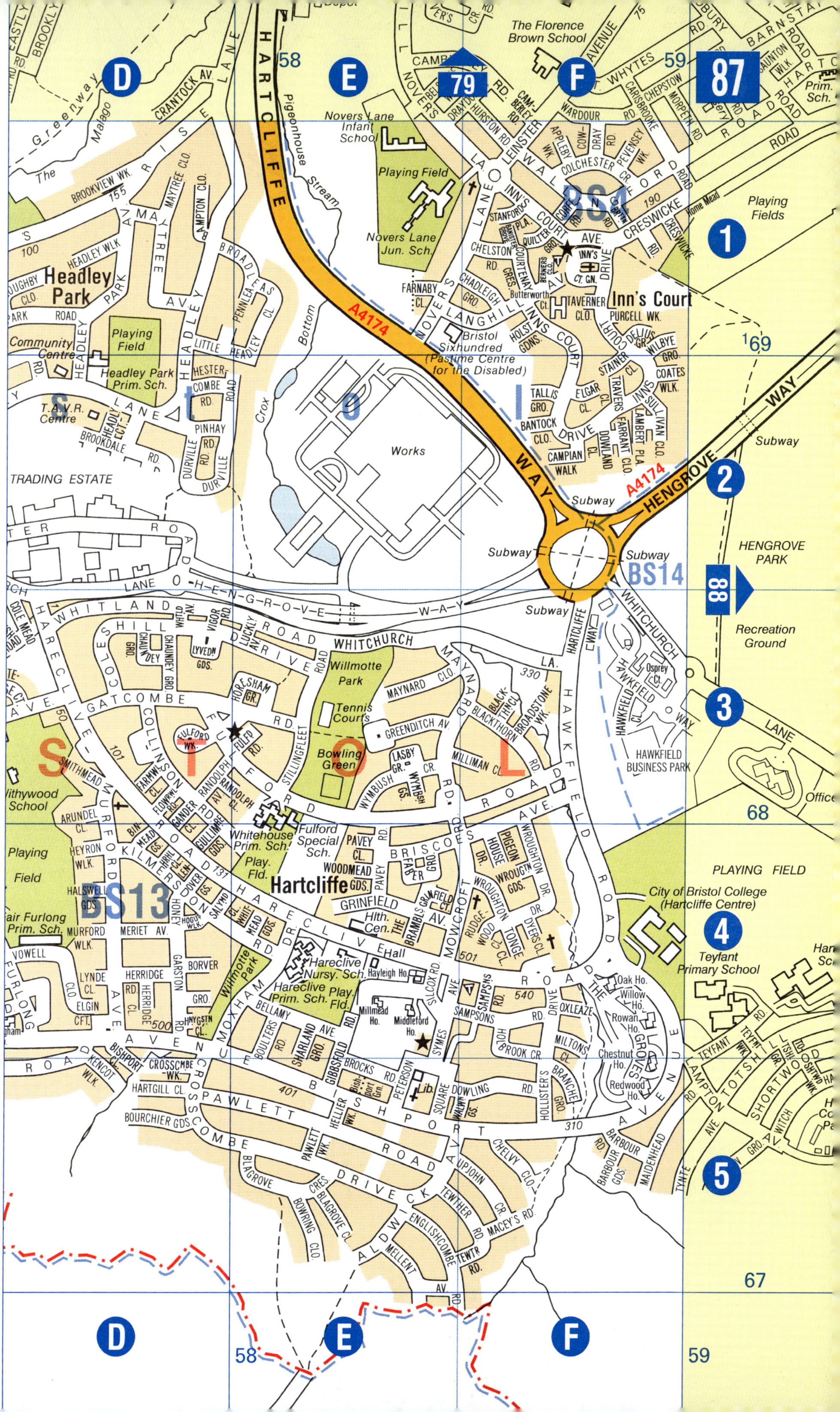

87
79
88
D
E
F
D
E
F
1
2
3
4
5
58
59
169
68
67
58
59
BS4
BS13
BS14
The Florence Brown School
Novers Lane Infant School
Playing Field
Novers Lane Jun. Sch.
Headley Park
Community Centre
Playing Field
Headley Park Prim. Sch.
T.A.V.R. Centre
TRADING ESTATE
Works
Bristol Sixhundred (Pastime Centre for the Disabled)
Inn's Court
Playing Fields
Subway
HENGROVE PARK
Recreation Ground
HAWKFIELD BUSINESS PARK
PLAYING FIELD
City of Bristol College (Hartcliffe Centre)
Teyfant Primary School
Willmotte Park
Tennis Courts
Bowling Green
Whitehouse Prim. Sch.
Fulford Special Sch.
Play. Fld.
Hartcliffe
Hlth. Cen.
Hall
Hareclive Nursy. Sch.
Hareclive Prim. Sch.
Play. Fld.
Lib.
Withywood School
Playing Field
Fair Furlong Prim. Sch.
Willmotte Park
HARTCLIFFE WAY
A4174
HENGROVE WAY
WHITCHURCH ROAD
HAWKFIELD ROAD
WHITCHURCH LANE
HARECLIVE ROAD
BISHOPORT AVENUE
FULFORD ROAD
GATCOMBE RD
CROSSCOMBE DRIVE
PAWLETT ROAD
ALDWICK AVENUE
DUNKERRY ROAD
CRESWICKE AVE.
NOVERS LANE
LANGHILL AV.
INNS COURT DRIVE
HEADLEY LANE
MAYTREE AV.
Pigeonhouse Stream
Crox Bottom
Malago
Greenway

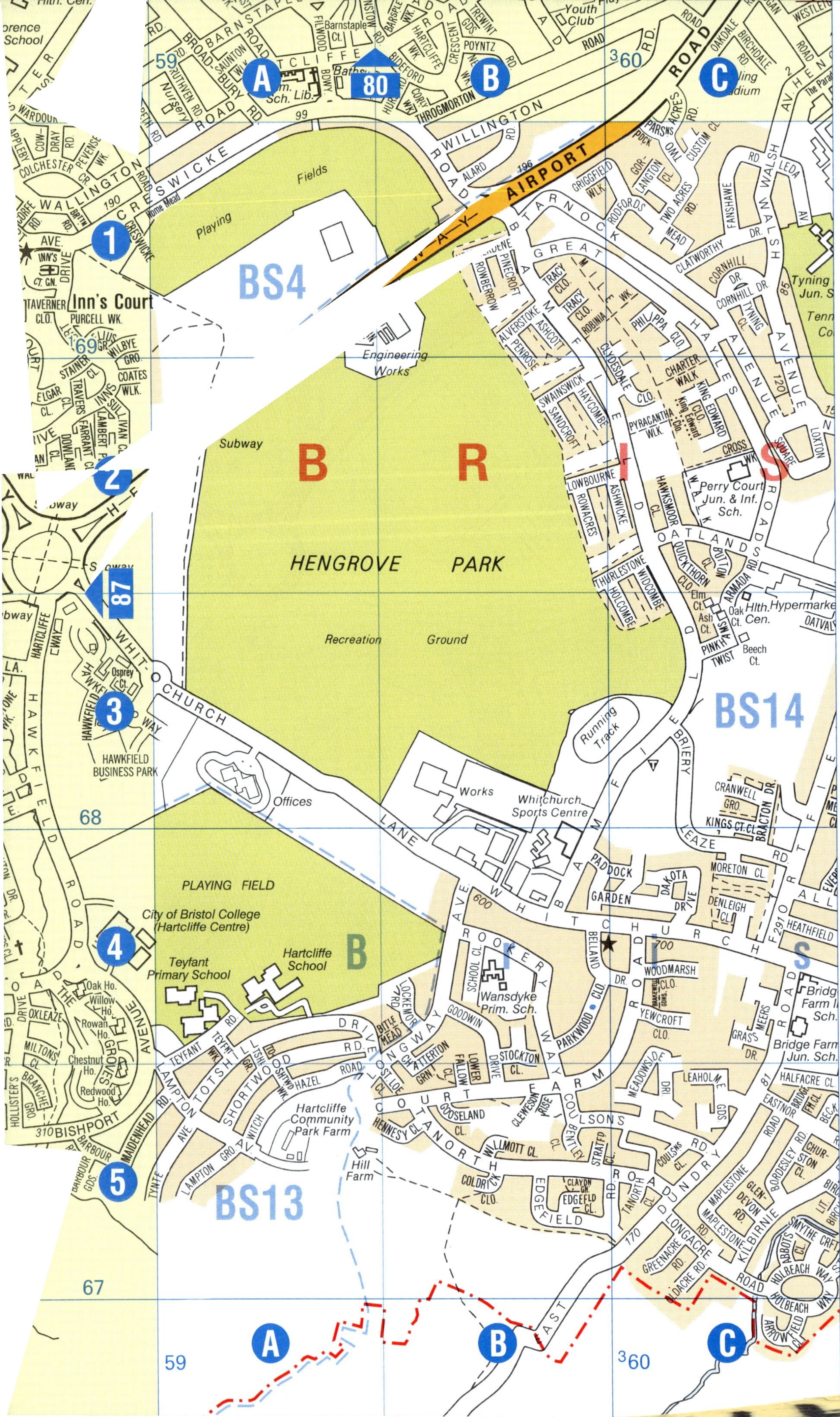

BS4
BS13
BS14
HENGROVE PARK
Recreation Ground
Playing Fields
PLAYING FIELD
Engineering Works
Subway
Running Track
Works
Whitchurch Sports Centre
Offices
City of Bristol College (Hartcliffe Centre)
Teyfant Primary School
Hartcliffe School
Hartcliffe Community Park Farm
Hill Farm
Wansdyke Prim. Sch.
Perry Court Jun. & Inf. Sch.
Hlth. Cen.
Hypermarket
Bridge Farm Jun. Sch.
HAWKFIELD BUSINESS PARK
Inn's Court
Youth Club
Baths
AIRPORT ROAD
WHITCHURCH LANE
HAWKFIELD ROAD
HARTCLIFFE WAY
BISHPORT AVENUE
TEYFANT RD.
HAZEL GROVE
CRESWICKE ROAD
WILLINGTON ROAD
THROGMORTON
GREAT HAYLES ROAD
HAYLES ROAD
WALSH AVENUE
TYNING
BRIERY LEAZE RD.
OATLANDS AVENUE
ROOKERY WAY
FARM COURT
TANORTH ROAD
DUNDRY ROAD
EAST DUNDRY ROAD
LONGACRE RD.
HOLBEACH WAY
80
87
59
360

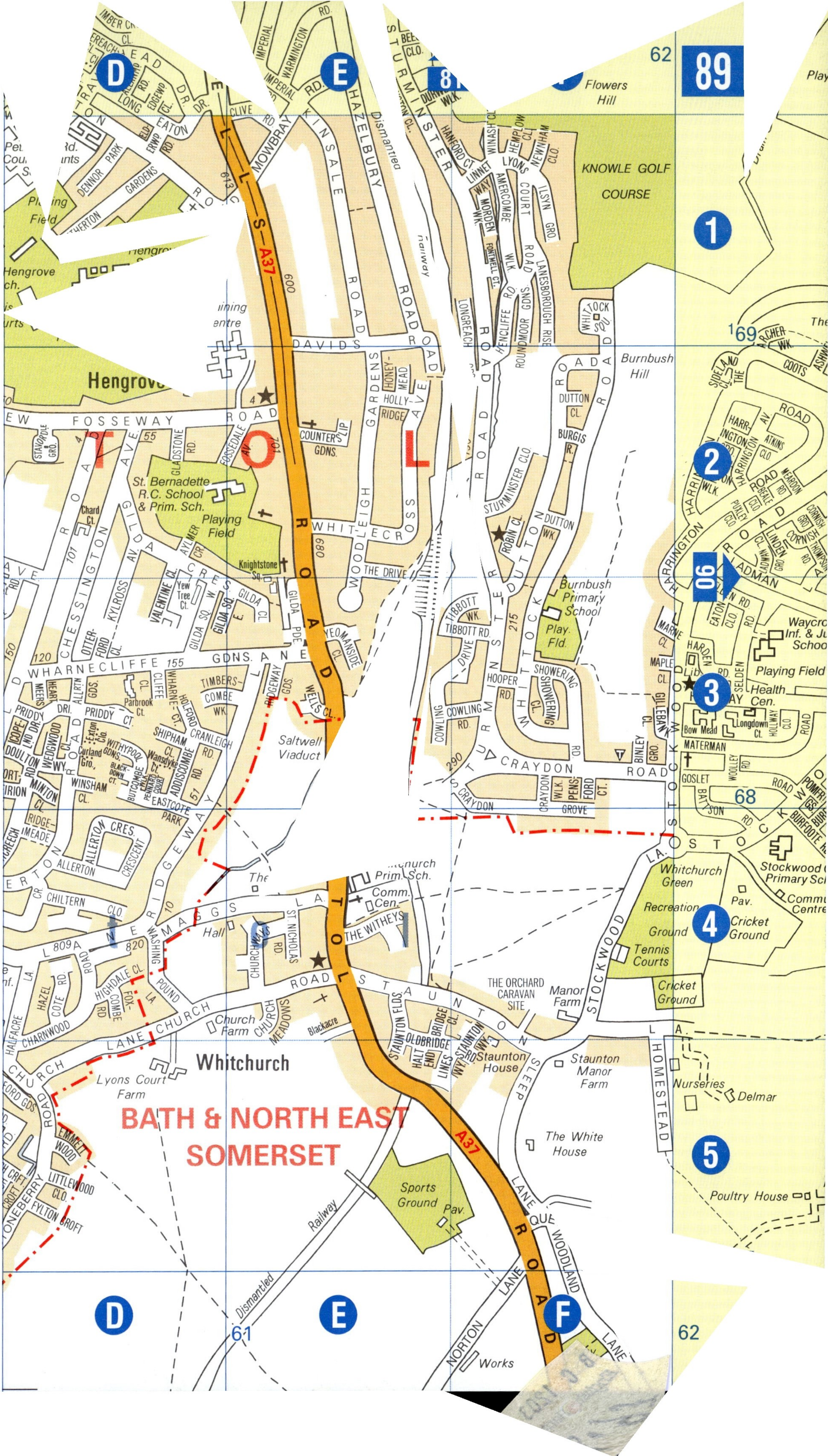

Flowers Hill
KNOWLE GOLF COURSE
Hengrove
Playing Field
St. Bernadette R.C. School & Prim. Sch.
Knightstone Sq.
WELLS ROAD
A37
FOSSEWAY
WHARNECLIFFE GDNS.
WHITECROSS AV.
HAZELBURY ROAD
KINSALE ROAD
STURMINSTER ROAD
LONGREACH
LANESBOROUGH RISE
Burnbush Hill
Burnbush Primary School
DUTTON ROAD
CRAYDON ROAD
CRAYDON GROVE
HARRINGTON ROAD
STOCKWOOD ROAD
STOCKWOOD LA.
Saltwell Viaduct
MAGGS LA.
CHURCH LANE
CHURCH ROAD
STAUNTON LA.
Whitchurch
Whitchurch Green
Recreation Ground
Tennis Courts
Cricket Ground
Stockwood Primary Sch.
Comm. Centre
Health Cen.
Playing Field
THE ORCHARD CARAVAN SITE
Manor Farm
Staunton House
Staunton Manor Farm
The White House
Lyons Court Farm
Nurseries
Delmar
Poultry House
HOMESTEAD
SLEEP LANE
QUEEN CHARLTON LANE
WOODLAND LANE
NORTON LANE
Works
Sports Ground
Pav.
Dismantled Railway
BATH & NORTH EAST SOMERSET
BRISTOL
61
62
68
69
D
E
F
1
2
3
4
5
81
90

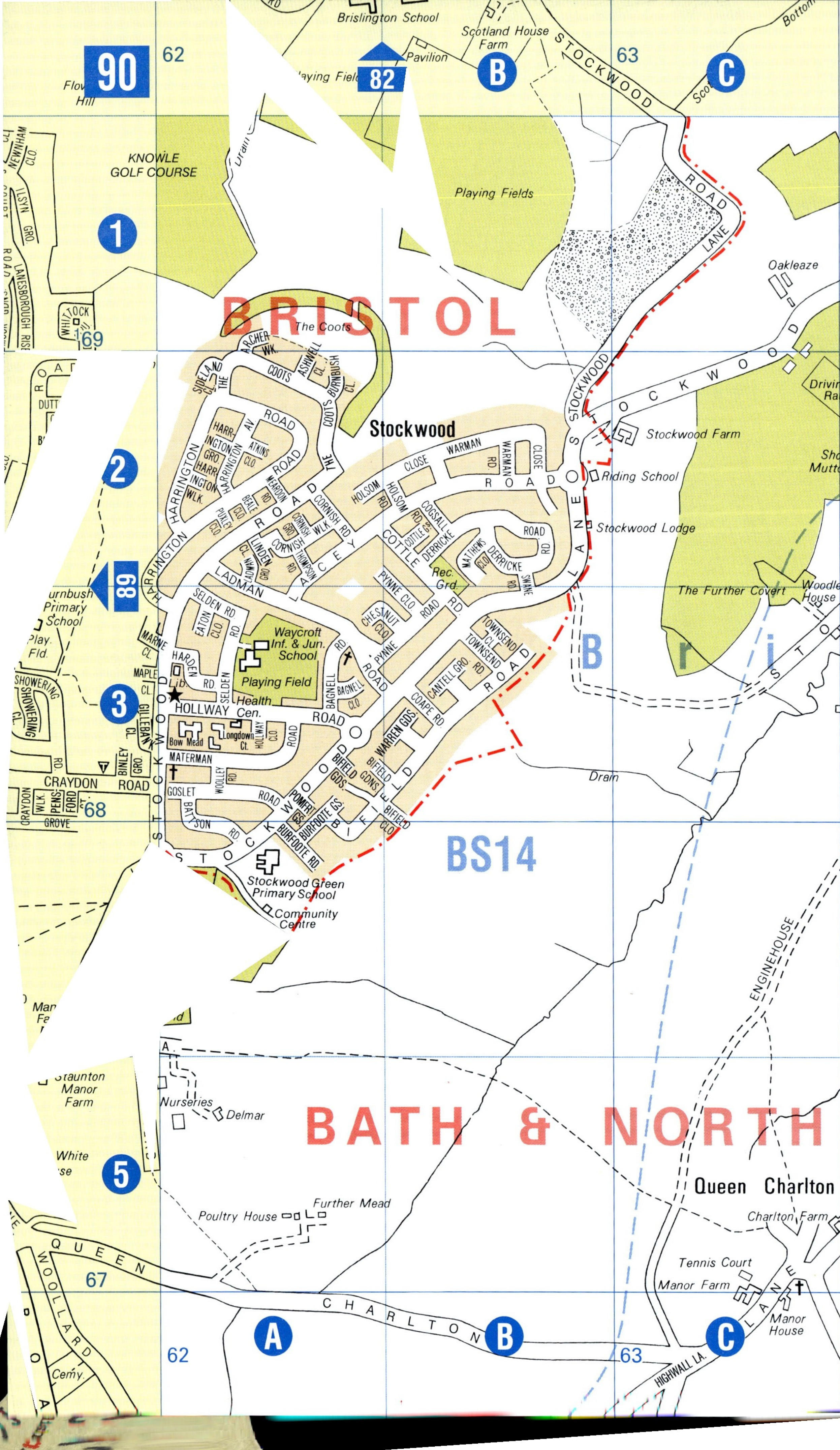
82
89
62
63
B
C
A
1
2
3
5
69
68
67
BRISTOL
BATH & NORTH
BS14
Brislington School
Scotland House Farm
Pavilion
Playing Fields
KNOWLE GOLF COURSE
STOCKWOOD ROAD
STOCKWOOD LANE
Oakleaze
The Coots
Stockwood
Stockwood Farm
Riding School
Stockwood Lodge
The Further Covert
Woodleigh House
Waycroft Inf. & Jun. School
Playing Field
Health Cen.
Lib.
Rec. Grd.
HARRINGTON ROAD
LADMAN ROAD
LACEY ROAD
HOLLWAY ROAD
CRAYDON ROAD
CRAYDON GROVE
BIFIELD ROAD
TOWNSEND ROAD
WARMAN ROAD
COTTLE ROAD
PYNNE ROAD
SELDEN RD.
MEARDON ROAD
BURNBUSH CL.
THE COOTS
Stockwood Green Primary School
Community Centre
Drain
Staunton Manor Farm
Nurseries
Delmar
White House
Poultry House
Further Mead
Queen Charlton
Charlton Farm
Tennis Court
Manor Farm
Manor House
QUEEN CHARLTON LANE
HIGHWALL LA.
WOOLLARD LANE
ENGINEHOUSE LANE
Cemy.

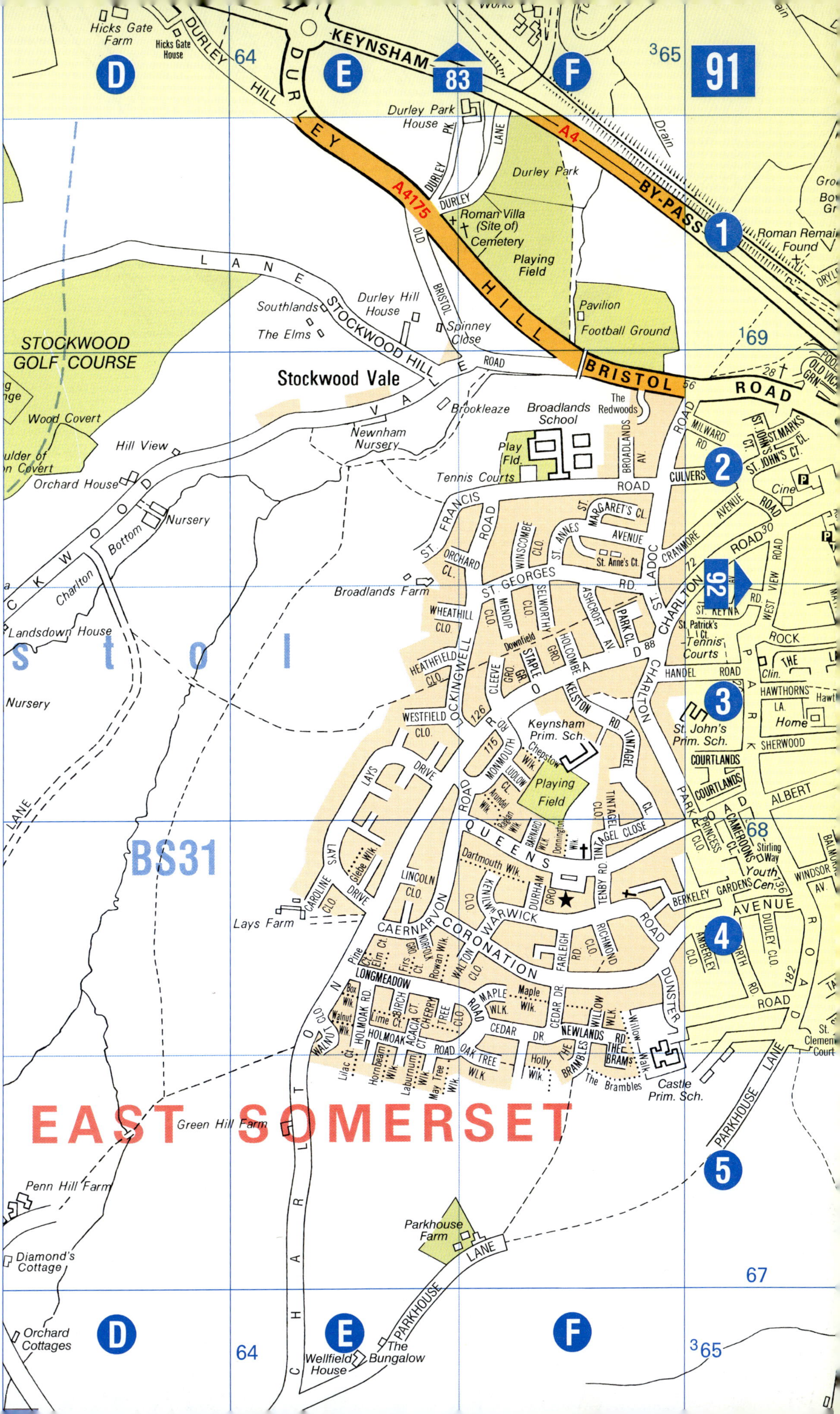

Hicks Gate Farm
Hicks Gate House
DURLEY HILL
KEYNSHAM
83
BY-PASS
A4
A4175
Durley Park House
DURLEY PK.
DURLEY LANE
Durley Park
Roman Villa (Site of)
Cemetery
Playing Field
Pavilion
Football Ground
Roman Remains Found
OLD BRISTOL HILL
BRISTOL ROAD
STOCKWOOD HILL
STOCKWOOD GOLF COURSE
Wood Covert
Southlands
The Elms
Durley Hill House
Spinney Close
Stockwood Vale
STOCKWOOD VALE
LANE
Brookleaze
Newnham Nursery
Hill View
Orchard House
Nursery
Charlton Bottom
Landsdown House
Broadlands School
The Redwoods
BROADLANDS AV.
Play Fld.
Tennis Courts
MILWARD RD.
ST. JOHN'S CT.
ST. MARKS CL.
ST. JOHN'S CT.
CULVERS ROAD
Cine
ST. FRANCIS ROAD
ORCHARD CL.
WINSCOMBE CLO.
ST. ANNES AVENUE
ST. MARGARET'S CL.
St. Anne's Ct.
ST. LADOC RD.
CRANMORE AVENUE
ROAD
WEST VIEW ROAD
92
Broadlands Farm
ST. GEORGES RD.
WHEATHILL CLO.
MENDIP CLO.
SELWORTHY CLO.
ASHCROFT AV.
PARK CL.
CHARLTON ROAD
ST. KEYNA RD.
St. Patrick's Ct.
Tennis Courts
ROCK
HEATHFIELD CLO.
LOCKINGWELL ROAD
CLEEVE GRO.
Downfield
STAPLE GR.
HOLCOMBE GRO.
KELSTON RD.
TINTAGEL CL.
HANDEL ROAD
THE HAWTHORNS
Clin.
LA.
Home
St. John's Prim. Sch.
SHERWOOD
WESTFIELD CLO.
Keynsham Prim. Sch.
Chepstow Wlk.
MONMOUTH RD.
LUDLOW CL.
Arundel Wlk.
Raglan Wlk.
Playing Field
COURTLANDS
ALBERT
PARK ROAD
LAYS DRIVE
QUEENS ROAD
BARNARD WLK.
Donnington Wlk.
TINTAGEL CLOSE
TENBY RD.
PRINCESS CLO.
CAMERONS CL.
Stirling Way
Youth Cen.
BALMORAL
WINDSOR AV.
Glebe Wlk.
Dartmouth Wlk.
KENILWORTH CLO.
DURHAM GRO.
LINCOLN CLO.
CAROLINE CLO.
Lays Farm
CAERNARVON ROAD
WARWICK ROAD
BERKELEY GARDENS
AVENUE
CORONATION
FARLEIGH RD.
RICHMOND CLO.
AMBERLEY CLO.
DUDLEY CLO.
Elm Ct.
Pine Ct.
Firs Ct.
NORFOLK GRO.
Rowan Wlk.
WALTON CLO.
LONGMEADOW
Maple Wlk.
MAPLE WLK.
CEDAR DR.
WILLOW WLK.
DUNSTER
Box Wlk.
HOLMOAK RD.
BIRCH CT.
Lime Ct.
ACACIA CT.
CHERRY TREE CLO.
Walnut Wlk.
HOLMOAK ROAD
OAK TREE WLK.
NEWLANDS RD.
THE BRAMS
Willow Walk
Lilac Ct.
Hornbeam Wlk.
Laburnum Wlk.
May Tree Wlk.
Holly Wlk.
THE BRAMBLES
The Brambles
Castle Prim. Sch.
St. Clements Court
PARKHOUSE LANE
BS31
EAST SOMERSET
Green Hill Farm
Penn Hill Farm
Diamond's Cottage
Parkhouse Farm
Orchard Cottages
Wellfield House
The Bungalow
CHARLTON ROAD
LANE
D
E
F
64
365
169
68
67
1
2
3
4
5

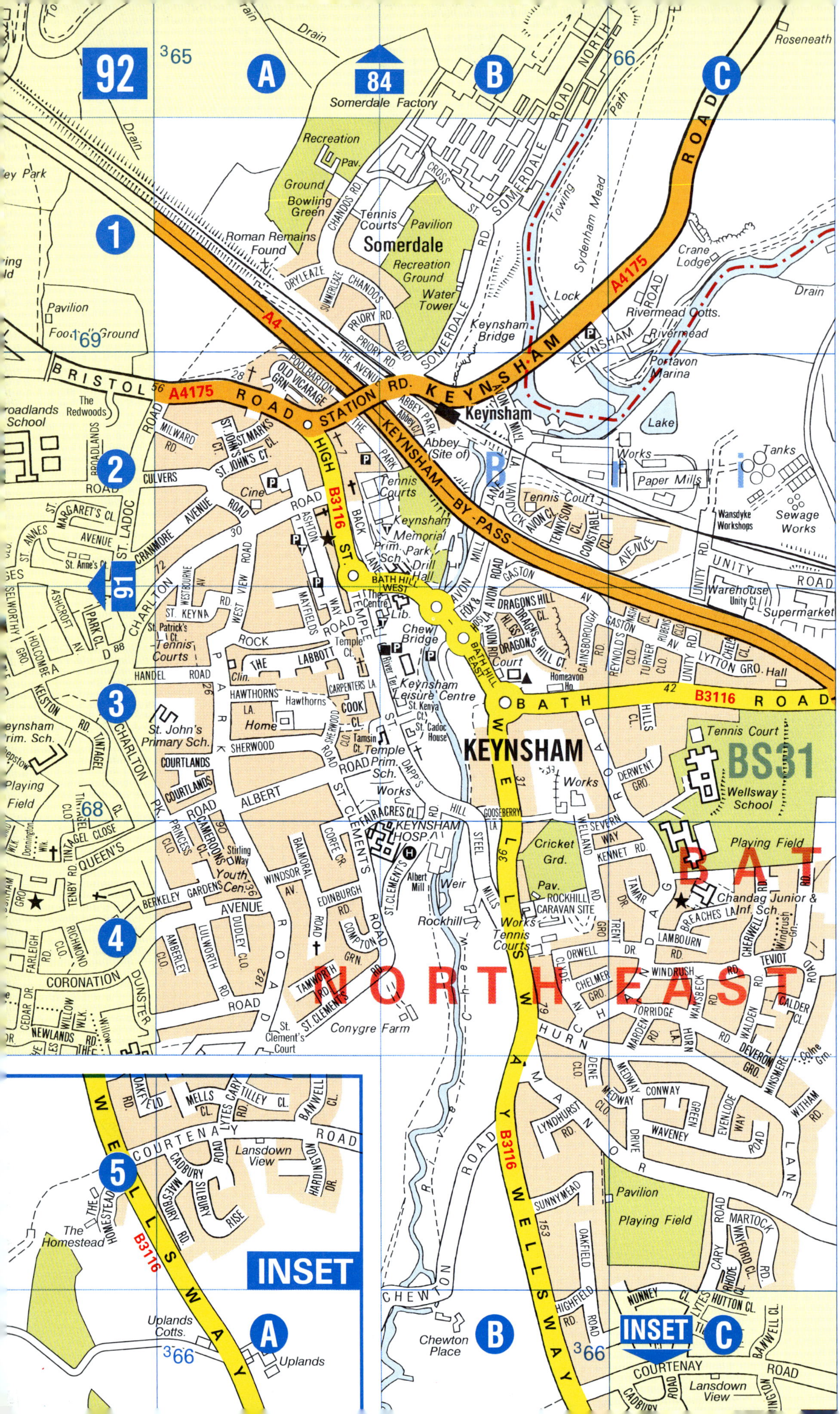
84
Somerdale Factory
A
B
C
Roseneath
Drain
Recreation Ground
Pav.
Bowling Green
Tennis Courts
Pavilion
Somerdale
Recreation Ground
Water Tower
Roman Remains Found
Pavilion
Football Ground
1
2
3
4
5
A4
A4175
BRISTOL ROAD
STATION RD.
KEYNSHAM RD.
KEYNSHAM-BY-PASS
SOMERDALE ROAD NORTH
SOMERDALE RD.
CROSS ST
CHANDOS RD
DRYLEAZE
SUMMERLEAZE
PRIORY RD.
THE AVENUE
POOLBARTON
OLD VICARAGE GRN.
Keynsham Bridge
Keynsham
Towing Path
Sydenham Mead
Lock
Crane Lodge
Drain
Rivermead Cotts.
Rivermead
Portavon Marina
Lake
Works
Tanks
Paper Mills
Sewage Works
Wansdyke Workshops
UNITY RD.
UNITY ROAD
Warehouse
Unity Ct.
Supermarket
Hall
Abbey (Site of)
Tennis Court
Tennis Courts
Keynsham Memorial Park
Drill Hall
Prim. Sch.
BATH HILL WEST
BATH HILL EAST
Lib.
Chew Bridge
Keynsham Leisure Centre
St. Kenya Ct.
St. Cadoc House
HIGH ST.
B3116
TEMPLE WAY
ROCK ROAD
CHARLTON ROAD
PARK ROAD
St. Patrick's Ct.
Tennis Courts
HANDEL ROAD
St. John's Primary Sch.
Temple Prim. Sch.
Works
KEYNSHAM
BATH ROAD
WELLSWAY
Works
BS31
Tennis Court
Wellsway School
Playing Field
Cricket Grd.
Pav.
ROCKHILL CARAVAN SITE
Chandag Junior & Inf. Sch.
KEYNSHAM HOSP.
Albert Mill
Weir
Rockhill
Works
Tennis Courts
NORTHEAST
BATH
River Chew
Conygre Farm
St. Clement's Court
CHARLTON ROAD
QUEEN'S ROAD
CORONATION ROAD
DUNSTER ROAD
Keynsham Prim. Sch.
Playing Field
68
ALBERT ROAD
WINDSOR AV.
EDINBURGH RD.
ST. CLEMENT'S ROAD
Stirling Way
Youth Cen.
MANOR ROAD
CHEW ROAD
Pavilion
Playing Field
HURN
DEANE DRIVE
66
69
65
INSET
Lansdown View
COURTENAY ROAD
Homestead
The Homestead
Uplands Cotts.
Uplands
Chewton Place
CHEWTON
INSET
91

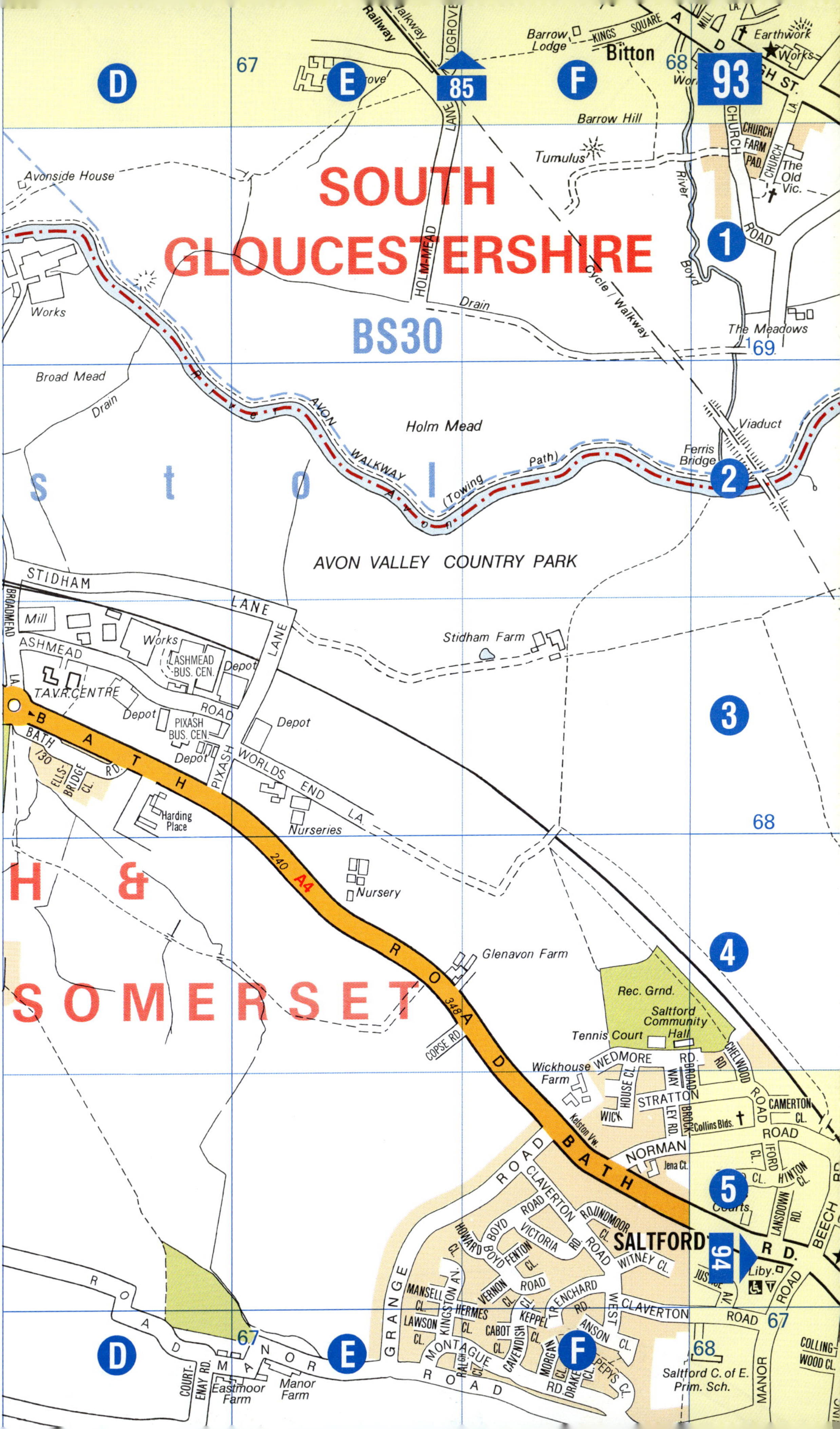

SOUTH GLOUCESTERSHIRE
BS30
Bitton
Barrow Lodge
KINGS SQUARE
Earthwork
Works
Barrow Hill
Tumulus
CHURCH FARM PAD.
CHURCH RD.
The Old Vic.
River Boyd
ROAD
The Meadows
Avonside House
Works
HOLM-MEAD LANE
Drain
Cycle / Walkway
Railway Walkway
85
Broad Mead
Drain
River Avon
AVON WALKWAY
Holm Mead
(Towing Path)
Viaduct
Ferris Bridge
AVON VALLEY COUNTRY PARK
STIDHAM LANE
BROADMEAD LA.
Mill
ASHMEAD ROAD
Works
ASHMEAD BUS. CEN.
Depot
LANE
Stidham Farm
T.A.V.R. CENTRE
Depot
PIXASH BUS. CEN.
Depot
PIXASH LA.
WORLDS END LA.
ELLSBRIDGE CL.
Harding Place
Nurseries
Nursery
BATH ROAD
A4
240
348
Glenavon Farm
COPSE RD.
BATH & NORTH EAST SOMERSET
Rec. Grnd.
Saltford Community Hall
Tennis Court
Wickhouse Farm
WEDMORE RD.
BROAD WAY
WICK HOUSE
STRATTON
BROCKLEY RD.
Collins Blds.
CHELWOOD ROAD
CAMERTON CL.
ROAD
Kelston Vw.
NORMAN
Jena Ct.
IFORD CL.
HINTON CL.
LANSDOWN RD.
Courts
BEECH RD.
SALTFORD
94
Liby.
JUSTICE AV.
CLAVERTON ROAD
ROUNDMOOR CL.
WITNEY CL.
HOWARD CL.
BOYD
BOYD FENTON CL.
VICTORIA RD.
MANSELL CL.
KINGSTON AV.
HERMES CL.
VERNON CL.
LAWSON CL.
CABOT CL.
KEPPEL CL.
TRENCHARD RD.
WEST
ANSON CL.
CAVENDISH CL.
MONTAGUE
RALEIGH CL.
MORGAN CL.
DRAKE CL.
PEPYS CL.
GRANGE ROAD
MANOR ROAD
COURTENAY RD.
Eastmoor Farm
Manor Farm
Saltford C. of E. Prim. Sch.
MANOR
COLLINGWOOD CL.
D
E
F
1
2
3
4
5
67
68
169

93
Farm
Rec. Grnd.
Tennis C
Wickhouse Farm
WEDMORE RD.
WICK HOUSE CL.
WAY
BROAD RD.
BROCKLEY RD.
CHELWOOD RD.
STRATTON
CAMERTON CL.
Collins Blds.
Kelston Vw.
NORMAN ROAD
Jena Ct.
IFORD CL.
IFORD CL.
HINTON CL.
Tennis Courts
LANSDOWN RD.
BEECH RD
CHESTNUT WLK.
HIGH STREET
HIGH ST.
QUEEN SQ.
Saltford Court
THE BATCH
HOMEFIELD CL.
HOMEFIELD RD.
AVON LA.
Vine Cottage
MEAD LANE
THE SHALLOWS
Bristol
SALTFORD
BATH ROAD
A4
527
510
528
559
561
CLAVERTON RD
ROUNDMOOR CL.
WITNEY CL.
JUSTICE AV.
Liby.
TRENCHARD RD
WEST CLAVERTON ROAD
ANSON CL.
DRAKE CL.
PEPYS CL.
MONTAGUE RD.
Saltford C. of E. Prim. Sch.
MANOR ROAD
MANOR RD.
COLLINGWOOD CL.
TYNING ROAD
RODNEY ROAD
UPLANDS ROAD
UPLANDS DR.
HARCROFT CL.
FAIRWAYS
HASELBURY GRO.
LANE
GOLF CLUB
Hill Farm
BERESFORD CL.
SOMERVILLE CL.
THE FOLLY
THE GLEN
Club House
BS31
Kelston Lock
Marina
Boat Houses
Tennant's Wood
Bitton - Ba
RIVE
SALTFORD GOLF COURSE
Folly Wood
Ashton Leaze
Avonmead Cottage
Avonwood
North Breach
Ashton Hill
South Breach
BA2
Homemead
CORSTON
BATH & NORTH
Brigadoon
GOOLD CL.
Swiss Cottage
Windy Ridge
THE BARTON
CORSTON
Church Farm
Church Farm
Manor Farm
Batchelor's Farm
WELLS ROAD
A39
13
Lime Works
Corston Field
Woodenhouse Covert
A
B
C
1
2
3
4
5
66
67
68
69
165

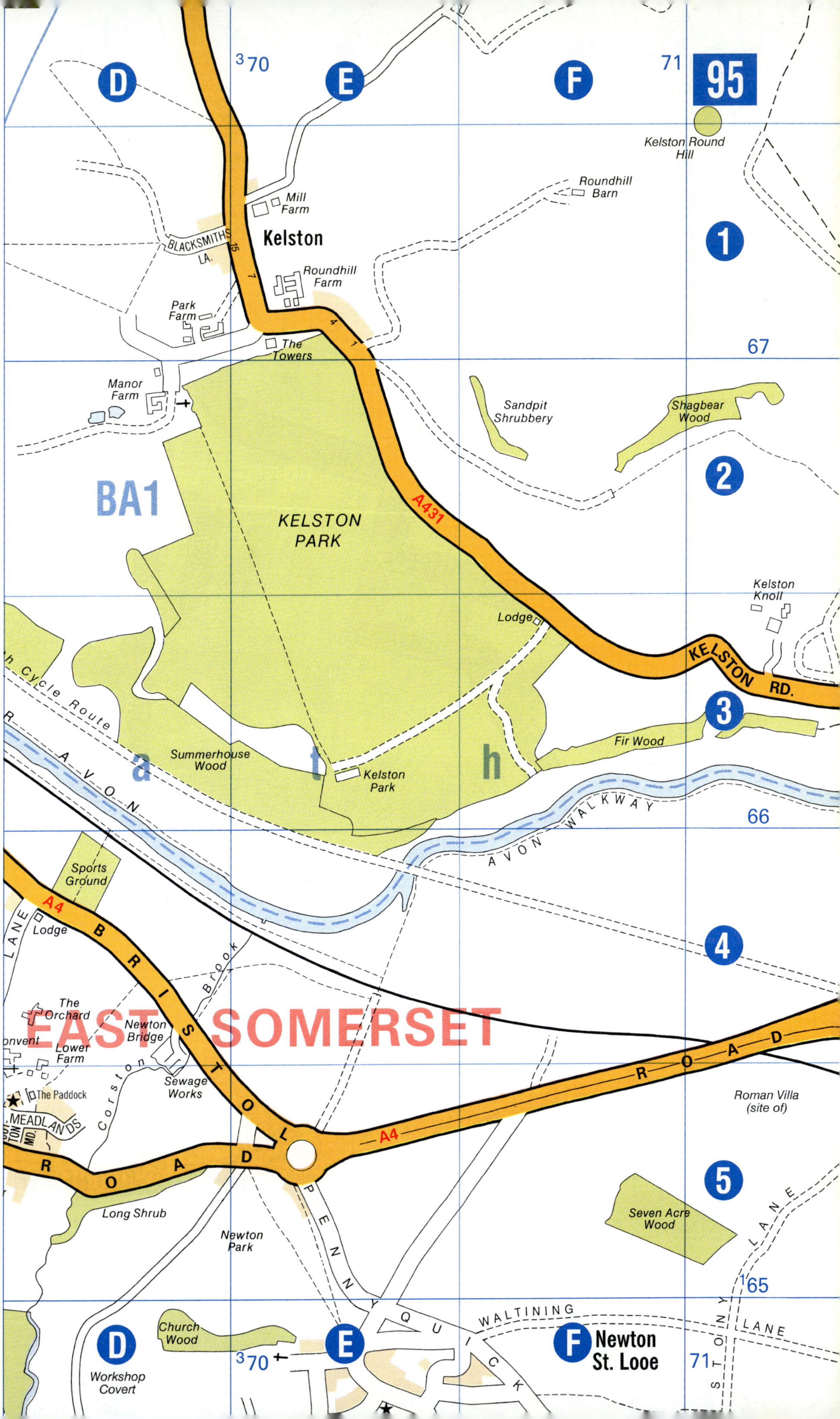

D
E
F
370
71
Kelston Round Hill
Roundhill Barn
Mill Farm
Kelston
BLACKSMITHS LA.
Roundhill Farm
Park Farm
The Towers
67
Manor Farm
Sandpit Shrubbery
Shagbear Wood
BA1
KELSTON PARK
A431
Kelston Knoll
Lodge
KELSTON RD.
Fir Wood
Summerhouse Wood
Kelston Park
AVON
AVON WALKWAY
66
Sports Ground
A4
Lodge
LANE
BRISTOL
Brook
The Orchard
EAST SOMERSET
Newton Bridge
Lower Farm
Sewage Works
The Paddock
MEADLANDS
Corston
ROAD
A4
Roman Villa (site of)
Seven Acre Wood
Long Shrub
Newton Park
PENNY QUICK
LANE
65
WALTINING LANE
STONY
Church Wood
Workshop Covert
Newton St. Looe
1
2
3
4
5

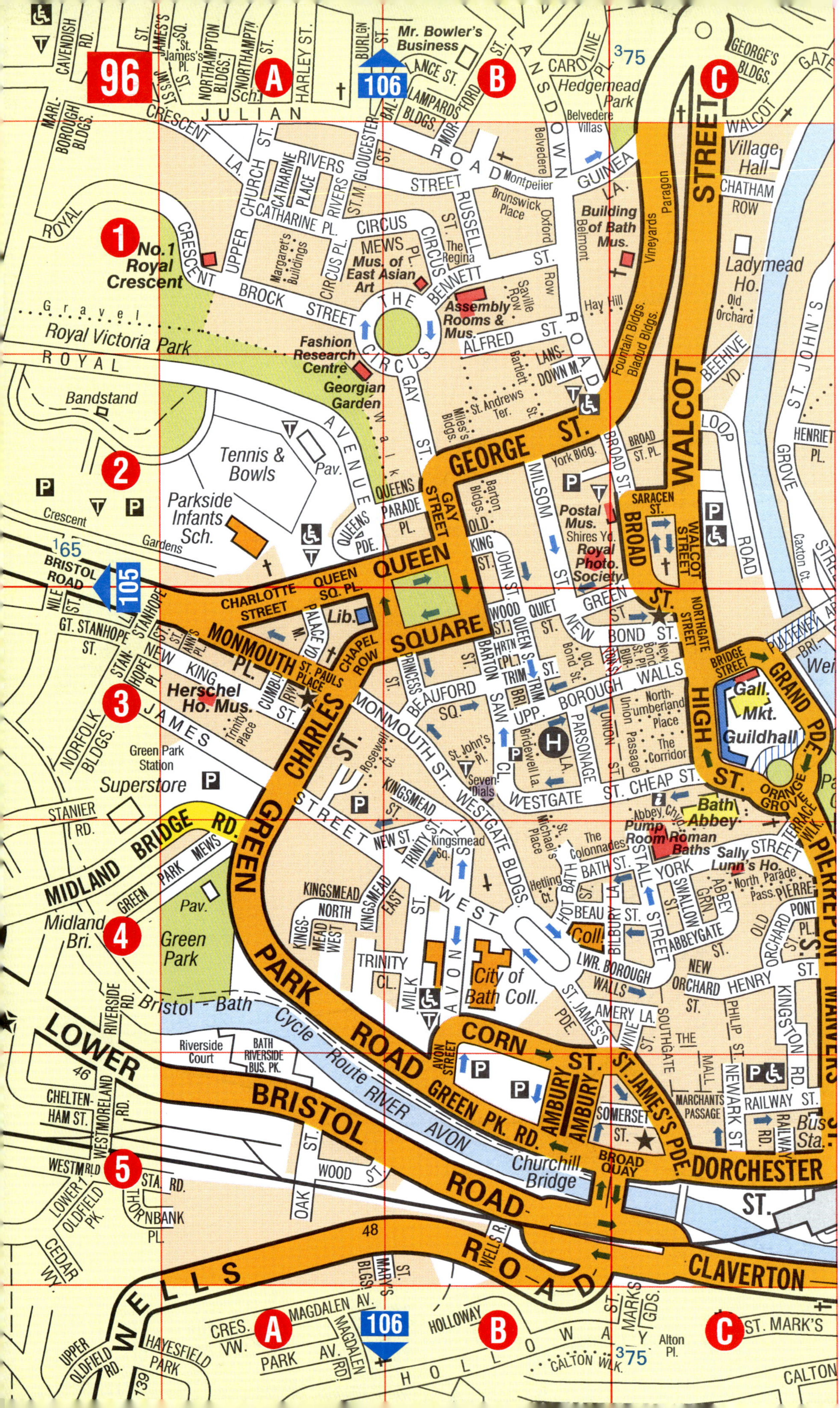

A
B
C
1
2
3
4
5
106
105
375
165
CAVENDISH RD.
MARLBOROUGH BLDGS.
ST. JAMES'S SQ.
St. James's Pl.
NORTHAMPTON BLDGS.
NORTHAMPTON ST.
HARLEY ST.
Sch.
BURLINGTON ST.
Mr. Bowler's Business
LANCE ST.
LAMPARDS BLDGS.
MORFORD ST.
LANSDOWN ROAD
CAROLINE PL.
Hedgemead Park
Belvedere Villas
Belvedere
GEORGE'S BLDGS.
GATE
WALCOT
Village Hall
CHATHAM ROW
JULIAN
CRESCENT LA.
CHURCH ST.
RIVERS ST.
CATHARINE PLACE
CATHARINE PL.
GLOUCESTER ST.
ST. M.
STREET
RUSSELL ST.
Montpelier
Brunswick Place
Oxford Row
GUINEA LA.
Building of Bath Mus.
Belmont
Vineyards
Paragon
STREET
ROYAL CRESCENT
No.1 Royal Crescent
UPPER CHURCH ST.
Margaret's Buildings
CIRCUS PL.
CIRCUS MEWS
Mus. of East Asian Art
The Regina
BENNETT ST.
Assembly Rooms & Mus.
Saville Row
Row
Hay Hill
Ladymead Ho.
Old Orchard
BROCK STREET
THE CIRCUS
ALFRED ST.
ROAD
Fountain Bldgs.
Bladud Bldgs.
Gravel
Royal Victoria Park
ROYAL
Fashion Research Centre
Georgian Garden
Walk
GAY ST.
Bartlett St.
LANSDOWN M.
Miles's Bldgs.
St. Andrews Ter.
BEEHIVE YD.
ST. JOHN'S
Bandstand
Tennis & Bowls
Pav.
AVENUE
GEORGE ST.
York Bldg.
BROAD ST.
BROAD ST. PL.
WALCOT
LOOP
GROVE
HENRIETTA PL.
Crescent
Gardens
Parkside Infants Sch.
QUEENS PDE.
QUEENS PARADE PL.
GAY STREET
Barton Bldgs.
OLD KING ST.
JOHN ST.
MILSOM ST.
Postal Mus.
Shires Yd.
Royal Photo. Society
SARACEN ST.
BROAD ST.
WALCOT STREET
NORTHGATE STREET
ROAD
Caxton Ct.
BRISTOL ROAD
NILE ST.
CHARLOTTE STREET
QUEEN SQ. PL.
QUEEN SQUARE
Lib.
WOOD ST.
QUIET ST.
GREEN ST.
NEW BOND ST.
ST.
GT. STANHOPE ST.
STANHOPE
MONMOUTH PL.
ST. ANN'S PL.
PALACE YD.
CHAPEL ROW
PRINCESS ST.
BARTON ST.
QUEEN ST.
HRTN PL.
TRIM ST.
Old Bond St.
UNION ST.
Burton St.
Bond St.
New
WALLS
BRIDGE STREET
GRAND PDE.
PULTENEY
BRI.
Weir
NEW KING ST.
STANHOPE PL.
Herschel Ho. Mus.
CUMBERLAND RW.
ST. PAULS PLACE
CHARLES ST.
BEAUFORD SQ.
SAW CL.
UPP. BOROUGH
BRI.
Bridewell La.
PARSONAGE LA.
Northumberland Place
Union Passage
The Corridor
HIGH ST.
Gall.
Mkt.
Guildhall
NORFOLK BLDGS.
JAMES
Trinity Place
Green Park Station
Rosewell Ct.
MONMOUTH ST.
St. John's Pl.
Seven Dials
WESTGATE ST.
CHEAP ST.
ORANGE GROVE
TERRACE WLK.
Superstore
STANIER RD.
MIDLAND BRIDGE RD.
STREET
KINGSMEAD ST.
WESTGATE BLDGS.
Michael's Place
Abbey Chyd.
Pump Room
Bath Abbey
Roman Baths
GREEN PARK MEWS
NEW ST.
TRINITY ST.
Kingsmead Sq.
The Colonnades
BATH ST.
STALL STREET
YORK ST.
Sally Lunn's Ho.
North Parade Pass.
STREET
PIERREPONT
Pav.
Green Park
KINGSMEAD NORTH
KINGSMEAD EAST
KINGSMEAD WEST
WEST
Hetling Ct.
HOT BATH ST.
BEAU ST.
BILBURY LA.
SWALLOW ST.
ABBEY GRN.
ABBEYGATE ST.
ORCHARD ST.
PONT PL.
Midland Bri.
TRINITY CL.
MILK ST.
AVON ST.
City of Bath Coll.
Coll.
LWR. BOROUGH WALLS
NEW ORCHARD ST.
HENRY ST.
ST.
RIVERSIDE RD.
Bristol - Bath Cycle Route
AMERY LA.
ST. JAMES'S PDE.
WINE ST.
SOUTHGATE
THE MALL
PHILIP ST.
KINGSTON RD.
MANVERS
LOWER BRISTOL ROAD
46
Riverside Court
BATH RIVERSIDE BUS. PK.
CORN ST.
AVON STREET
AMBURY
ST. JAMES'S PDE.
CHELTENHAM ST.
WESTMORELAND RD.
RIVER AVON
GREEN PK. RD.
SOMERSET ST.
MARCHANTS PASSAGE
NEWARK ST.
RAILWAY ST.
RAILWAY RD.
Bus Sta.
WESTMRLD ST.
WOOD ST.
Churchill Bridge
BROAD QUAY
DORCHESTER ST.
STA. RD.
LOWER OLDFIELD PK.
THORNBANK PL.
OAK ST.
48
WELLS RD.
CLAVERTON
CEDAR WY.
WELLS
ST. MARK'S BLDGS.
ST. MARKS GDS.
CRES. VW.
MAGDALEN AV.
MAGDALEN RD.
PARK AV.
HOLLOWAY
Alton Pl.
ST. MARK'S
CALTON WLK.
CALTON
UPPER OLDFIELD RD.
HAYESFIELD PARK
139

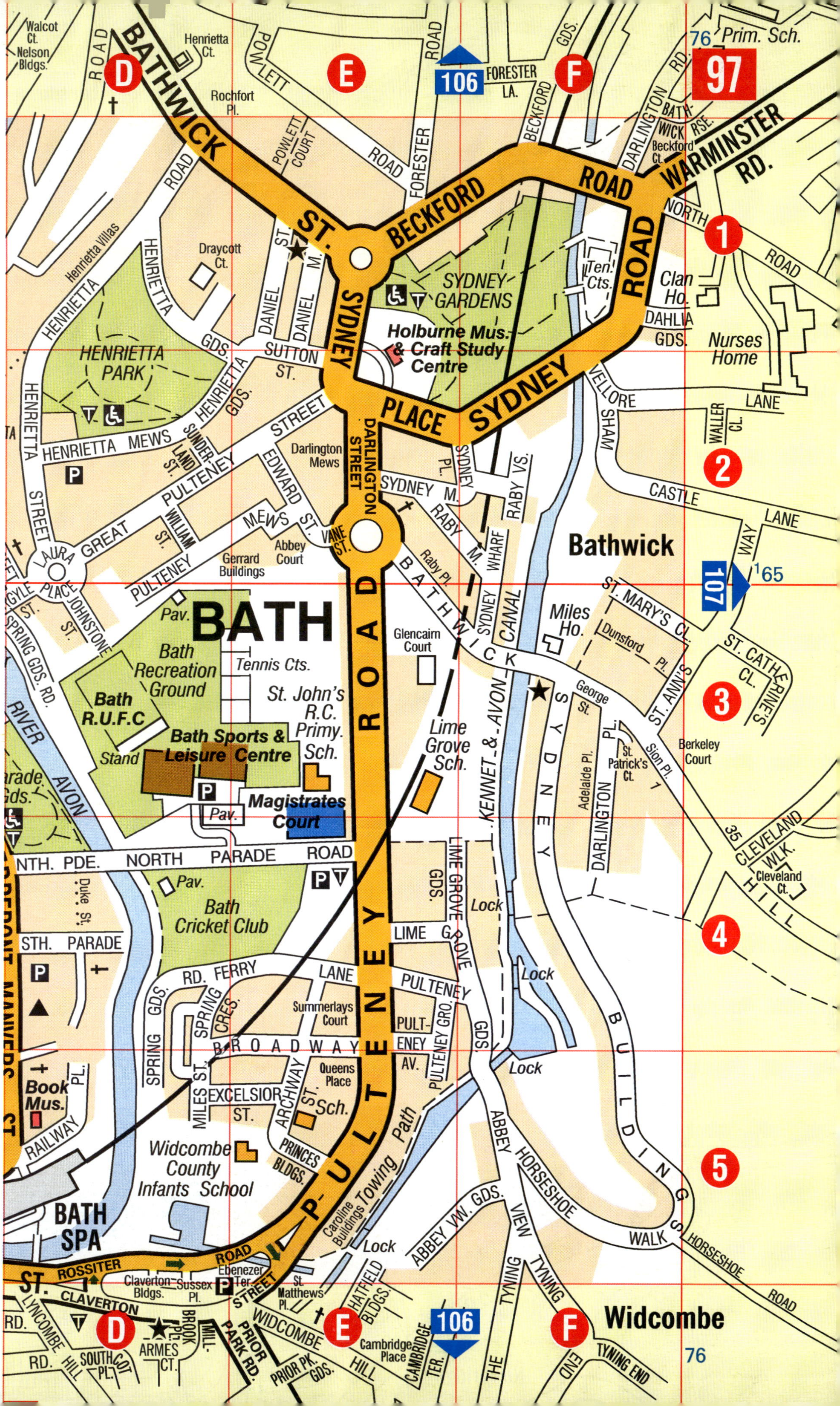

97
76
Prim. Sch.
D
E
F
106
1
2
3
4
5
107
165
Walcot Ct.
Nelson Bldgs.
Henrietta Ct.
Rochfort Pl.
POWLETT ROAD
POWLETT COURT
FORESTER ROAD
FORESTER LA.
BECKFORD GDS.
DARLINGTON RD.
BATHWICK RISE
Beckford Ct.
WARMINSTER RD.
BATHWICK ST.
BECKFORD ROAD
NORTH ROAD
SYDNEY ROAD
SYDNEY GARDENS
Ten. Cts.
Clan Ho.
DAHLIA GDS.
Nurses Home
Holburne Mus. & Craft Study Centre
SYDNEY PLACE
VELLORE LANE
WALLER CL.
SHAM CASTLE LANE
WAY
Henrietta Villas
HENRIETTA ROAD
HENRIETTA GDS.
Draycott Ct.
DANIEL ST.
DANIEL M.
SUTTON ST.
HENRIETTA PARK
HENRIETTA GDS.
HENRIETTA MEWS
HENRIETTA STREET
SUNDERLAND ST.
STREET
GREAT PULTENEY
EDWARD ST.
Darlington Mews
DARLINGTON STREET
SYDNEY M.
SYDNEY PL.
RABY M.
RABY VS.
Raby Pl.
WHARF
VANE ST.
LAURA PLACE
WILLIAM ST.
PULTENEY MEWS
Gerrard Buildings
Abbey Court
Bathwick
ARGYLE ST.
JOHNSTONE ST.
Pav.
BATH
BATHWICK ST.
SYDNEY CANAL
ST. MARY'S CL.
Miles Ho.
Dunsford Pl.
ST. CATHERINE'S CL.
ST. ANN'S PL.
Glencairn Court
Bath Recreation Ground
Tennis Cts.
Bath R.U.F.C
St. John's R.C. Primy. Sch.
ROAD
Lime Grove Sch.
KENNET & AVON
SYDNEY
George St.
St. Patrick's Ct.
Sion Pl.
Berkeley Court
Adelaide Pl.
DARLINGTON
SPRING GDS. RD.
RIVER AVON
Parade Gds.
Stand
Bath Sports & Leisure Centre
Pav.
Magistrates Court
CLEVELAND WLK.
Cleveland Ct.
HILL
35
NTH. PDE.
NORTH PARADE ROAD
Duke St.
Pav.
Bath Cricket Club
GDS.
LIME GROVE
Lock
STH. PARADE
LIME
FERRY LANE
RD.
PULTENEY
Lock
Summerlays Court
PULTENEY GRO.
PULTENEY AV.
GDS.
SPRING CRES.
SPRING GDS.
BROADWAY
Lock
Book Mus.
PIERREPONT PL.
MANVERS ST.
MILES ST.
EXCELSIOR ST.
ARCHWAY ST.
Queens Place
Sch.
RAILWAY
Widcombe County Infants School
PRINCES BLDGS.
PULTENEY ROAD
Towing Path
Caroline Buildings
ABBEY VIEW
HORSESHOE WALK
BUILDINGS
ABBEY VW. GDS.
BATH SPA
ROSSITER ROAD
Lock
HORSESHOE ROAD
ST.
Claverton Bldgs.
Sussex Pl.
Ebenezer Ter.
STREET
St. Matthews Pl.
HATFIELD BLDGS.
TYNING
THE TYNING
CLAVERTON
WIDCOMBE HILL
Cambridge Place
CAMBRIDGE TER.
Widcombe
LYNCOMBE HILL
ARMES CT.
BROOK PL.
MILL
PRIOR PARK RD.
PRIOR PK. GDS.
SOUTHCOT PL.
RD.
TYNING END
76

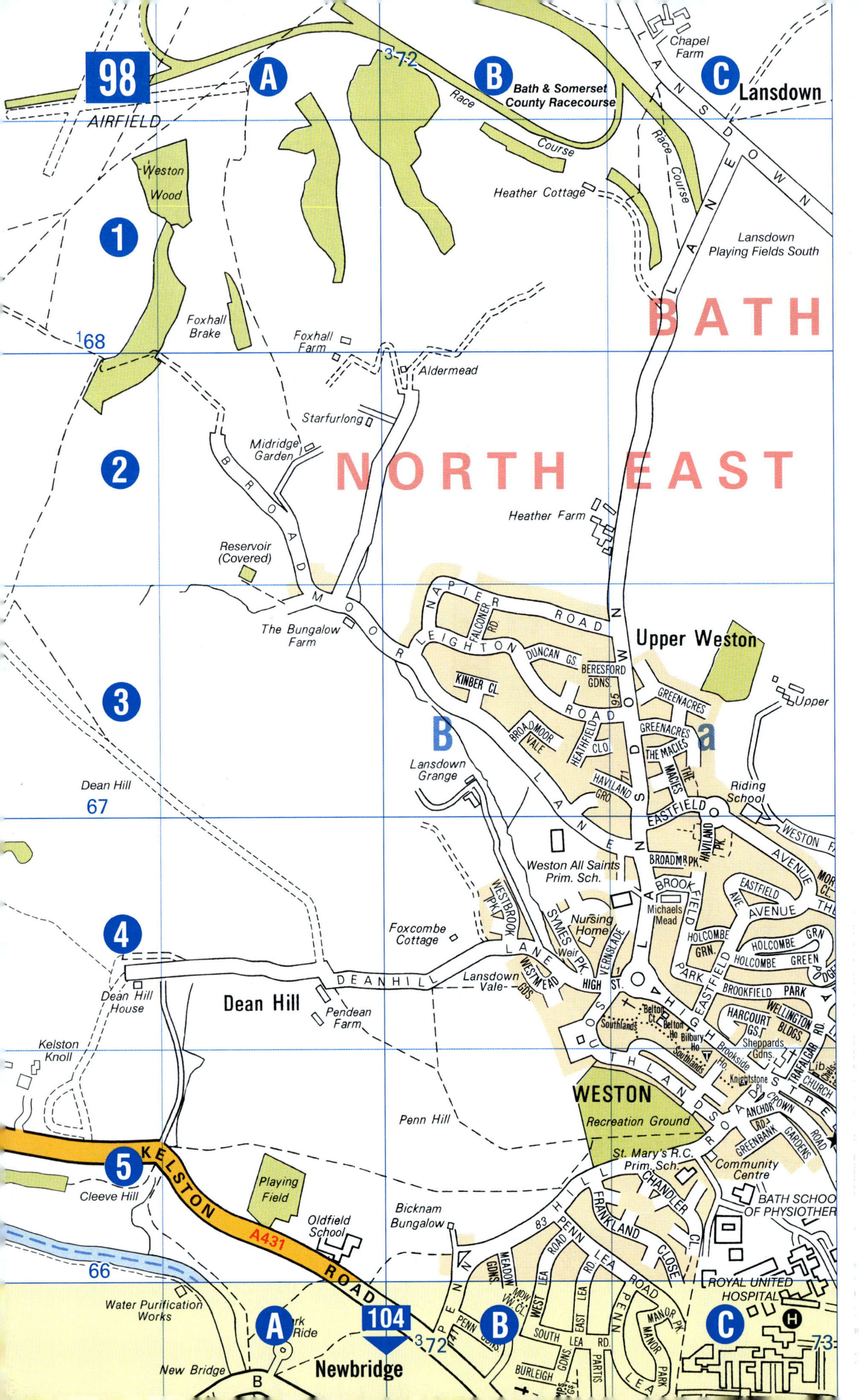
A
B
C
1
2
3
4
5
AIRFIELD
Weston Wood
Foxhall Brake
168
Bath & Somerset County Racecourse
Race Course
Chapel Farm
Lansdown
LANSDOWN
Heather Cottage
Lansdown Playing Fields South
BATH
Foxhall Farm
Aldermead
Starfurlong
Midridge Garden
BROADMOOR
NORTH EAST
Heather Farm
Reservoir (Covered)
The Bungalow Farm
NAPIER ROAD
LEIGHTON ROAD
FALCONER RD.
DUNCAN GS.
BERESFORD GDNS.
KINBER CL.
Upper Weston
GREENACRES
THE MACIES
BROADMOOR VALE
HEATHFIELD CLO.
HAVILAND GRO.
Lansdown Grange
Dean Hill
67
Riding School
EASTFIELD
HAVILAND PK.
BROADMR PK.
WESTON AVENUE
Weston All Saints Prim. Sch.
BROOKFIELD
Michaels Mead
EASTFIELD AVE.
AVENUE
WESTBROOK PK.
SYMES PK.
Nursing Home
VERNSLADE
Weir
HOLCOMBE GRN.
HOLCOMBE GREEN
Foxcombe Cottage
DEAN HILL
Lansdown Vale
WESTMEAD GDS.
HIGH ST.
PARK
BROOKFIELD PARK
WELLINGTON BLDGS.
Dean Hill House
Dean Hill
Pendean Farm
HARCOURT GS.
SOUTHLANDS
Southlands
Belton Ct.
Belton Ho
Bilbury Ho
Sheppards Gdns.
Brookside Ho.
TRAFALGAR RD.
Kelston Knoll
Knightstone Pl.
CROWN
ANCHOR RD.
WESTON
Recreation Ground
Penn Hill
GREENBANK GARDENS
KELSTON ROAD
A431
Playing Field
Cleeve Hill
St. Mary's R.C. Prim. Sch.
CHANDLER CL.
Community Centre
BATH SCHOOL OF PHYSIOTHER
FRANKLAND CLOSE
Oldfield School
Bicknam Bungalow
66
HILL
PENN LEA ROAD
MEADOW GDNS.
MDW VW. CL.
WEST LEA
EAST LEA
SOUTH LEA RD.
MANOR PK.
ROYAL UNITED HOSPITAL
Water Purification Works
Park & Ride
New Bridge
Newbridge
104
372
73
BURLEIGH GDNS.
PARTIS

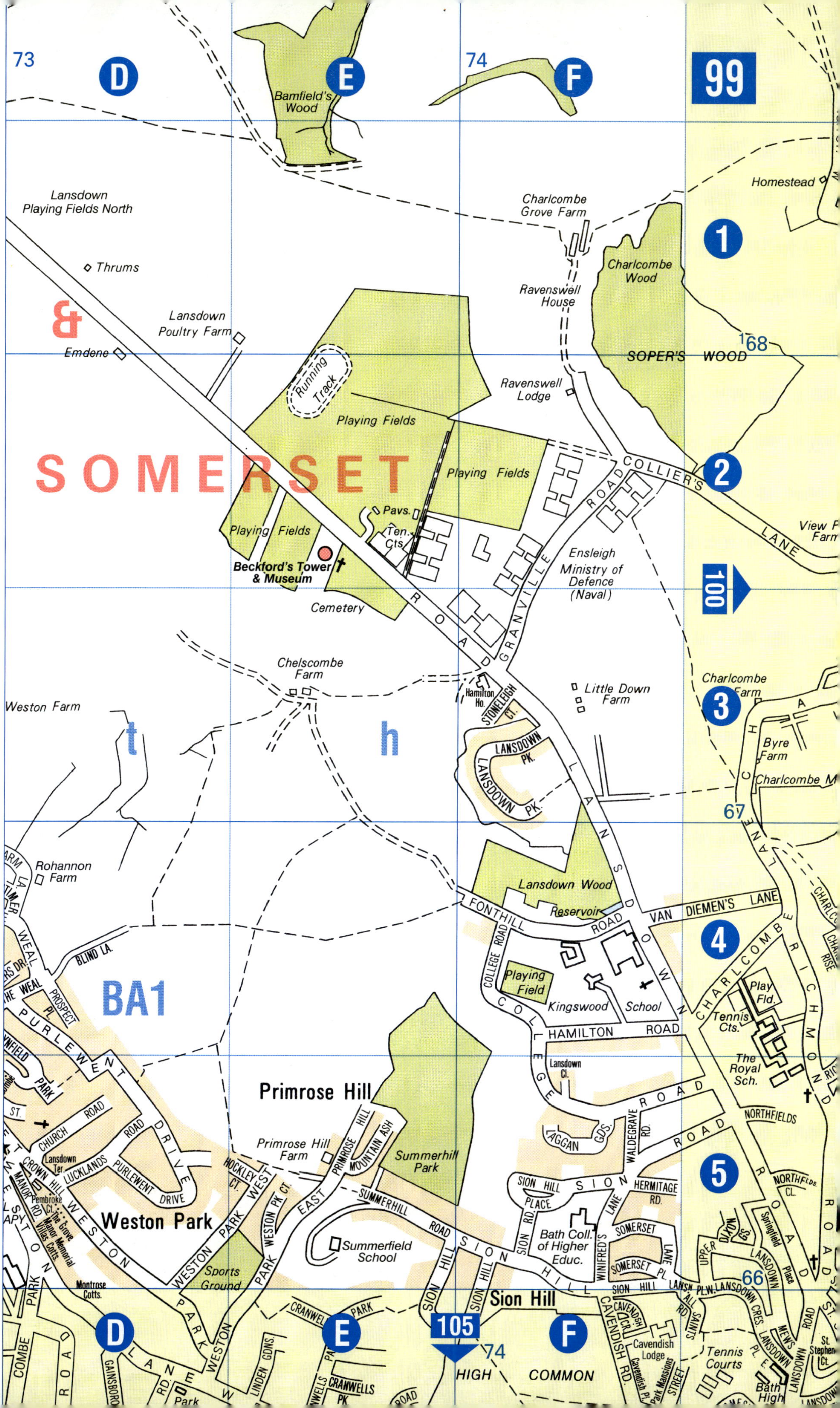
73
74
D
E
F
Bamfield's Wood
Lansdown Playing Fields North
Charlcombe Grove Farm
Homestead
Thrums
Charlcombe Wood
Ravenswell House
Lansdown Poultry Farm
Emdene
168
SOPER'S WOOD
Running Track
Ravenswell Lodge
Playing Fields
SOMERSET
COLLIER'S LANE
ROAD
Playing Fields
Pavs.
Ten. Cts.
Playing Fields
Beckford's Tower & Museum
Ensleigh Ministry of Defence (Naval)
View Farm
100
Cemetery
ROAD
GRANVILLE
Chelscombe Farm
Hamilton Ho.
STONELEIGH CT.
Little Down Farm
Charlcombe Farm
Weston Farm
LANSDOWN PK.
LANSDOWN PK.
Byre Farm
Charlcombe
67
Rohannon Farm
Lansdown Wood
Reservoir
FONTHILL ROAD
VAN DIEMEN'S LANE
LANSDOWN
COLLEGE ROAD
Playing Field
Kingswood School
CHARLCOMBE
Play Fld.
Tennis Cts.
RICHMOND
WEAL
BLIND LA.
PROSPECT PL.
BA1
PURLEWENT
HAMILTON ROAD
Lansdown Cl.
The Royal Sch.
PARK
PURLEWENT DRIVE
Primrose Hill
ROAD
CHURCH ROAD
WALDEGRAVE RD.
NORTHFIELDS
LAGGAN GDS.
Primrose Hill Farm
PRIMROSE HILL
MOUNTAIN ASH
Summerhill Park
ROAD
Lansdown Ter.
LUCKLANDS
PURLEWENT DRIVE
HOCKLEY CT.
WEST
SION HILL PLACE
SION
HERMITAGE RD.
NORTHFIELDS CL.
CROWN HILL
Pembroke Cl.
The Grove
Manor Memorial
Weston Park
WESTON PK CT.
EAST
SUMMERHILL ROAD
LANE
SION RD.
Bath Coll. of Higher Educ.
SOMERSET LANE
Springfield Place
WESTON
Summerfield School
SION HILL
WINIFRED'S
SOMERSET PL.
UPPER
LANSDOWN
Sports Ground
WESTON PARK
PARK
SION HILL
SION HILL
SION HILL
LANSDOWN
Montrose Cotts.
66
Sion Hill
CAVENDISH CR.
CAVENDISH RD.
Cavendish Lodge
ST JAMES'S
Tennis Courts
LANSDOWN CRES.
MEWS
St Stephen's Ct.
CRANWELLS PARK
105
74
COMBE
ROAD
GAINSBOROUGH
LANE
WESTON
LINDEN GDNS.
CRANWELLS PK
HIGH
COMMON
Park Mansions
STREET
Bath High
5
4
3
2
1

100
A
B
C
375
Manor Farm
CHURCH ST.
HIGH ST.
Woolley
Homestead
WOOLLEY LANE
TADWICK LANE
BATH
KENT LA.
BLACKSMITH LA.
Smithy
Pickwick Farm
Manor Farm
Upper Swainswick
Swainswick Prim. Sch.
INNOX LANE
Charlcombe Grove Farm
Charlcombe Wood
Ravenswell House
Crossleaze Farm
Lam Brook
BATH
Little Innox
168
SOPER'S WOOD
NORTH EAST
ROAD
COLLIER'S LANE
View Point Farm
Ensleigh Ministry of Defence (Naval)
99
BA1
Twinfield Farm
Charlcombe Farm
Little Down Farm
CHARLCOMBE LANE
Charlcombe
Hope Cottages
Grange Farm
Byre Farm
Charlcombe Manor
Lower Swainswick
VALLEY VIEW
B
a
67
LANSDOWN ROAD
Lansdown Wood
Reservoir
VAN DIEMEN'S LANE
WHITEWELLS RD.
BATSTONE
UPHILL DRIVE
COXLEY DRIVE
Recreation Ground
CHARLCOMBE WAY
FAIRFIELD AVENUE
Fairfield Park
BAY TREE
St. Mark's Sch.
Kingswood School
Play Fld.
Tennis Cts.
The Royal Sch.
HAMILTON ROAD
COLLEGE ROAD
RICHMOND ROAD
SOLSBURY WAY
RAGLAN LANE
Larkhall
St. Saviours Inf. Sch.
NORTHFIELDS
Richmond Place
St. Stephen's Prim. Sch.
CLAREMONT BLDGS
CLAREMONT ROAD
Beacon Hill
Common
The Towers
SION HILL
Bath Coll. of Higher Educ.
66
Hill
CAVENDISH
COMMON
Cavendish Lodge
Tennis Courts
Bath High
106
375
Kensington Meadows
Villa Fields
LONDON ROAD
A4
Bus Depot
RIVER AVON
Boating

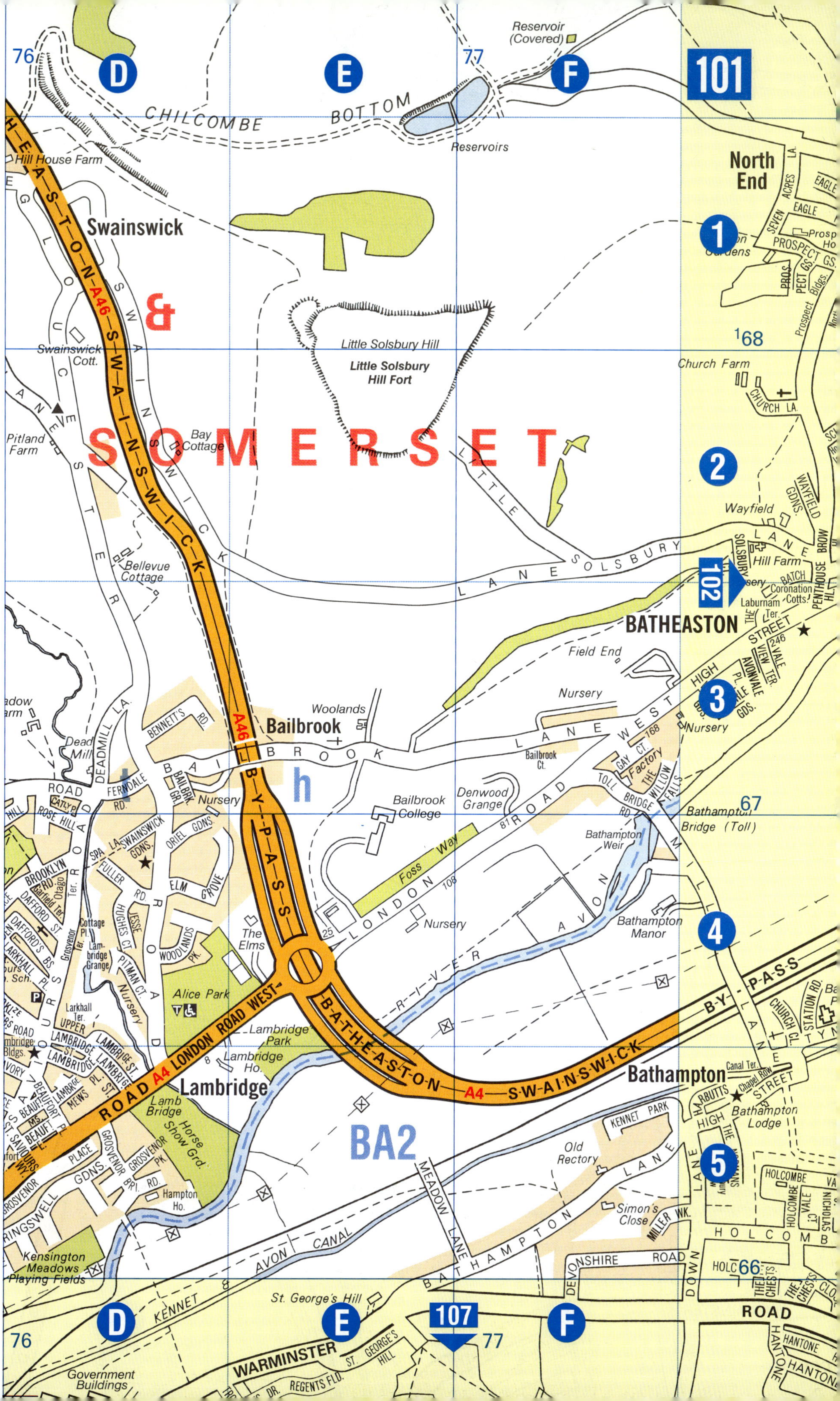
Reservoir (Covered)
76
77
D
E
F
CHILCOMBE BOTTOM
Reservoirs
Hill House Farm
North End
SEVEN ACRES LA.
EAGLE
Prospect GS.
PROSPECT Bldgs.
Swainswick
A46
SWAINSWICK
&
SOMERSET
Little Solsbury Hill
Little Solsbury Hill Fort
Swainswick Cott.
1
2
3
4
5
168
Church Farm
CHURCH LA.
Pitland Farm
Bay Cottage
LITTLE
Wayfield
WAYFIELD GDNS.
SOLSBURY LANE
BROW
Hill Farm
BATCH
Coronation Cotts.
Laburnam Ter.
PENTHOUSE HL.
102
Bellevue Cottage
BATHEASTON
Field End
HIGH STREET
VIEW TER.
AVONVALE
Nursery
Woolands
Bailbrook
BAILBROOK LANE WEST
Baildbrook Ct.
GAY CT.
Factory
THE WILLOW FALLS
TOLL BRIDGE RD.
Dead Mill
DEADMILL LA.
BENNETT'S RD.
FERNDALE RD.
ROAD
ROSE HILL
BAILBRK. GR.
h
Bailbrook College
Denwood Grange
LONDON ROAD
67
Bathampton Bridge (Toll)
Bathampton Weir
Foss Way
SWAINSWICK GDNS.
ORIEL GDNS.
FULLER RD.
ELM GROVE
BROOKLYN RD.
Otago Ter.
Garfield Ter.
DAFFORD ST.
Cottage Pl.
Lambridge Grange
HUGHES CT.
JESSE
PITMAN CT.
WOODLANDS PK.
The Elms
Nursery
BY-PASS
Bathampton Manor
RIVER AVON
Alice Park
Larkhall Ter.
UPPER LAMBRIDGE ST.
LAMBRIDGE
A4 LONDON ROAD WEST
Lambridge Park
Lambridge Ho.
BATHEASTON-SWAINSWICK
A4
Bathampton
Canal Ter.
Chapel Row
HIGH STREET
Bathampton Lodge
CHURCH CL.
STATION RD.
Lambridge
Lamb Bridge
Horse Show Grd.
BEAUFORT
MEWS
ROAD
GROSVENOR PK.
GROSVENOR BRI. RD.
Hampton Ho.
BA2
KENNET PARK
Old Rectory
MEADOW LANE
LANE
Simon's Close
MILLER WK.
HOLCOMBE
HOLCOMBE VALE
NICHOLLS
AVON CANAL
BATHAMPTON
DEVONSHIRE ROAD
DOWN LANE
66
THE CHESTS
Kensington Meadows Playing Fields
GROSVENOR
GDNS.
PLACE
KENNET
St. George's Hill
107
ROAD
HANTONE
WARMINSTER
ST. GEORGE'S HILL
REGENTS FLD.
DR.
Government Buildings

A
B
C
1
2
3
4
5
78
168
67
66
North End
Weir
Radford Farm
Starfall Farm
Eagle Farm
Brook
HOLLIES LA.
OAKFORD LA.
Fairhaven Cotts.
LANE
EAGLE PK.
EAGLE ROAD
SEVEN ACRES LA.
Prospect Ho.
PROSPECT GS.
Easton Gardens
Prospect Bldgs.
Eagle Cotts
BROOKSIDE CL.
STAMBROOK PK.
STEWAY
CATHERINE WAY
Northend Cotts.
LWR. NORTHEND
St. Catherines
Church Farm
CHURCH LA.
SCHOOL LA.
Homelands
Batheaston Prim. Sch.
Whitemore Ct.
BATH & NORTH
ELMHURST ESTATE
Eden Park
The Mount
HIGH BANNERDOWN
Bannerdown Cottages
BANNERDOWN DRI.
EDEN PARK CL.
BANNERDOWN CLO.
BATHEASTON
WAYFIELD GDNS.
Wayfield
LITTLE SOLSBURY LANE
SOLSBURY CT.
Hill Farm
Solsbury Nursery
BATCH
Coronation Cotts.
Laburnam Ter.
THE
BROW
BROW HILL
BROW HILL VS.
PENTHOUSE HL.
POTTS CL.
Football Fld.
COALPIT ROAD
AVON COURT
The Fosse
Weir
VICTORY GDS.
EDEN PARK DRI.
Little Court
COURT GDNS.
Rylstone
Garth
BARNFIELD WAY
WHITE CLO.
FOSSE LANE
BANNERDOWN
PARK LANE
WARLEIGH DRI.
WEST VIEW RD.
MORRIS
LONDON ROAD
EAST
Stam Bridge
HIGH STREET
246
VALE VIEW TER.
AVONVALE PL.
KYRLE GDS.
VICTORIA GDS.
Field End
Nursery
WEST LANE
GAY CT.
Factory
THE WILLOW FALLS
TOLL BRIDGE RD.
Bailbrook Ct.
ROAD
MEADOW
EASTWOODS
WESTWOODS
Box Road Nursery
Avondale House
A4
BOX
B
a
BY-PASS
Bathford Bridge
BATHFORD
Bathford Lodge
OSTLINGS
Vicarage
BRADFORD ROAD
A363
Bathampton Bridge (Toll)
Bathampton Weir
BA2
AVON
Bathampton Farm
SWAINSWICK
BATHEASTON
MILL LANE
CHURCH CL.
STATION RD.
Bathampton Prim. Sch.
TYNING ROAD
Canal Farm
Lower House Farm
CHURCH LA.
CHURCH CL.
COURT LA.
PUMP LANE
Timber Merchants
Canal Ter.
Chapel Row
HARBUTTS
STREET
Bathampton
Bathampton Lodge
KENNET PARK
HIGH
Old Rectory
THE NORMANS
Salisbury View
HOLCOMBE VALE
HOLCOMBE VALE CT.
ST. NICHOLAS
Holcombe Lodge
Simon's Close
MILLER WK.
HOLCOMBE
LANE
DEVONSHIRE ROAD
DOWN
HOLCOMBE GRN.
THE CHESTS
THE CHESS CLOSE
DOWNSIDE CLO.
Holcombe Farm
RIVER AVON
WARLEIGH LANE
Warleigh L
WARMINSTER
A36
ROAD
HANTONE HILL
Warleigh Lodge Farm

101

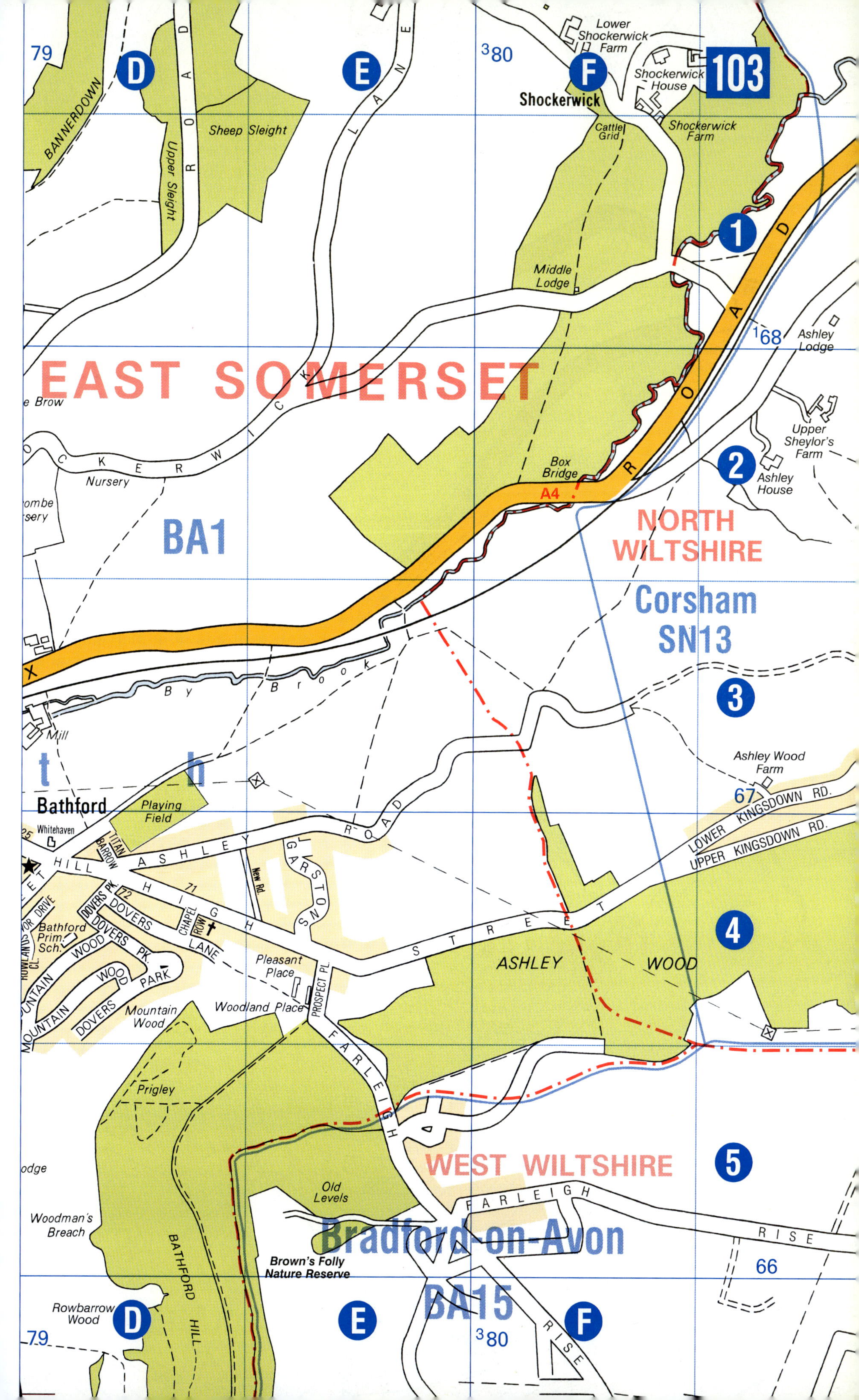

79
D
E
F
380
Lower Shockerwick Farm
Shockerwick House
Shockerwick
Shockerwick Farm
Cattle Grid
BANNERDOWN
Sheep Sleight
Upper Sleight
Middle Lodge
1
168
Ashley Lodge
EAST SOMERSET
Brow
Upper Sheylor's Farm
2
Ashley House
Box Bridge
A4
Nursery
BA1
NORTH WILTSHIRE
Corsham SN13
By Brook
3
Mill
Bathford
Ashley Wood Farm
67
LOWER KINGSDOWN RD.
UPPER KINGSDOWN RD.
Playing Field
Whitehaven
ASHLEY ROAD
HILL
TITAN BARROW
GARSTONS
New Rd.
HIGH STREET
CHAPEL ROW
DOVERS LANE
72
71
Bathford Prim. Sch.
DOVERS PK.
DOVERS PARK
WOOD
MOUNTAIN WOOD
DOVERS
ROWLANDS CL.
Pleasant Place
ASHLEY WOOD
4
Woodland Place
PROSPECT PL.
Mountain Wood
FARLEIGH
Prigley
WEST WILTSHIRE
5
Lodge
Old Levels
FARLEIGH RISE
Woodman's Breach
Bradford-on-Avon
BATHFORD HILL
Brown's Folly Nature Reserve
66
BA15
Rowbarrow Wood
D
E
F
79
380
RISE

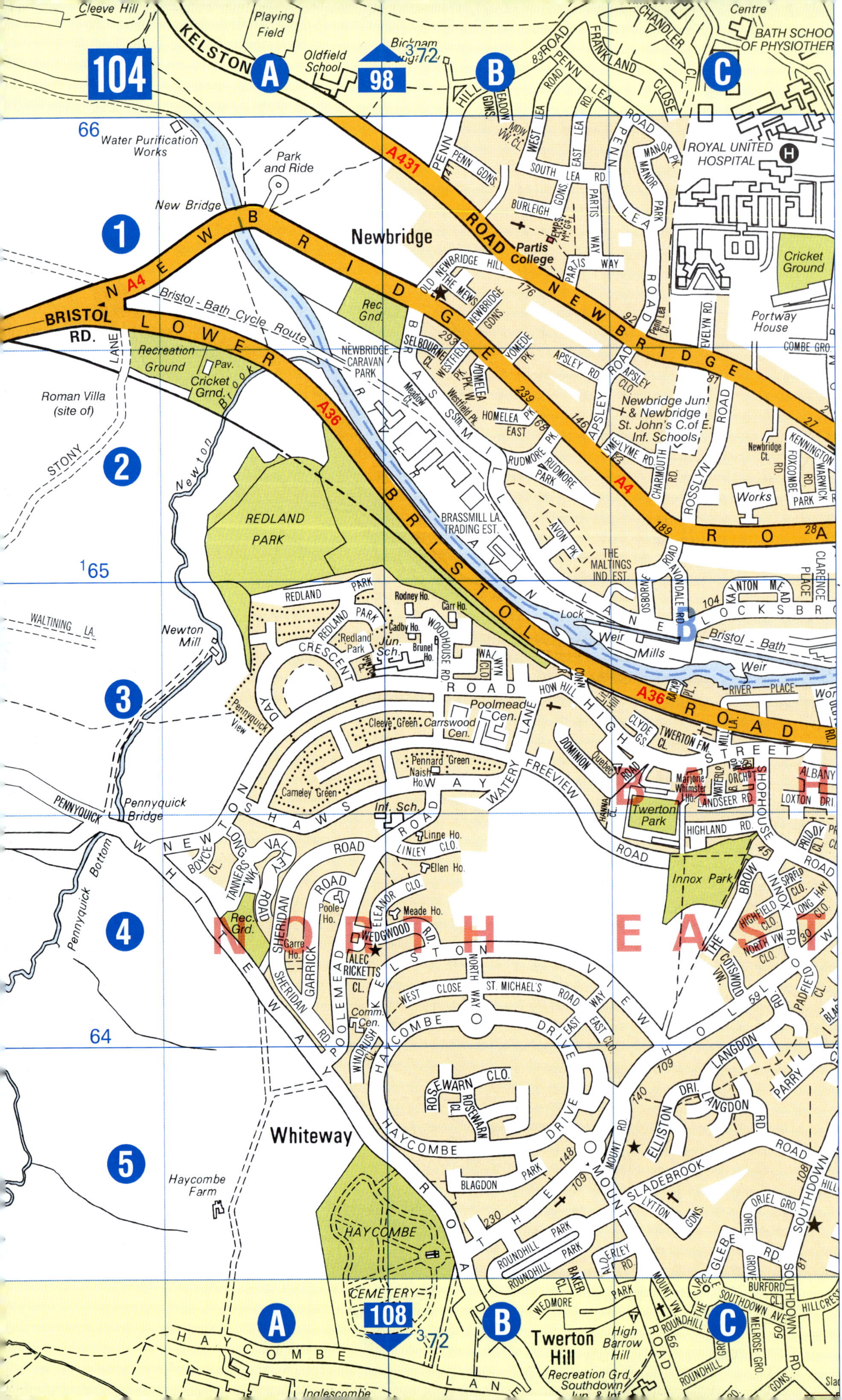

98
108
Newbridge
Whiteway
Twerton Hill
ROYAL UNITED HOSPITAL
BATH SCHOOL OF PHYSIOTHERAPY
Water Purification Works
Park and Ride
New Bridge
Roman Villa (site of)
REDLAND PARK
Newton Mill
Pennyquick Bridge
Haycombe Farm
HAYCOMBE CEMETERY
Innox Park
Twerton Park
Partis College
Portway House
Cricket Ground
Recreation Ground
BRASSMILL LA. TRADING EST.
THE MALTINGS IND. EST.
NEWBRIDGE CARAVAN PARK
Newbridge Jun. & Newbridge St. John's C. of E. Inf. Schools
NEWBRIDGE ROAD
LOWER BRISTOL ROAD
KELSTON ROAD
NEWBRIDGE HILL
HAYCOMBE LANE
WHITEWAY ROAD
NORTH EAST
BATH
Bristol - Bath Cycle Route

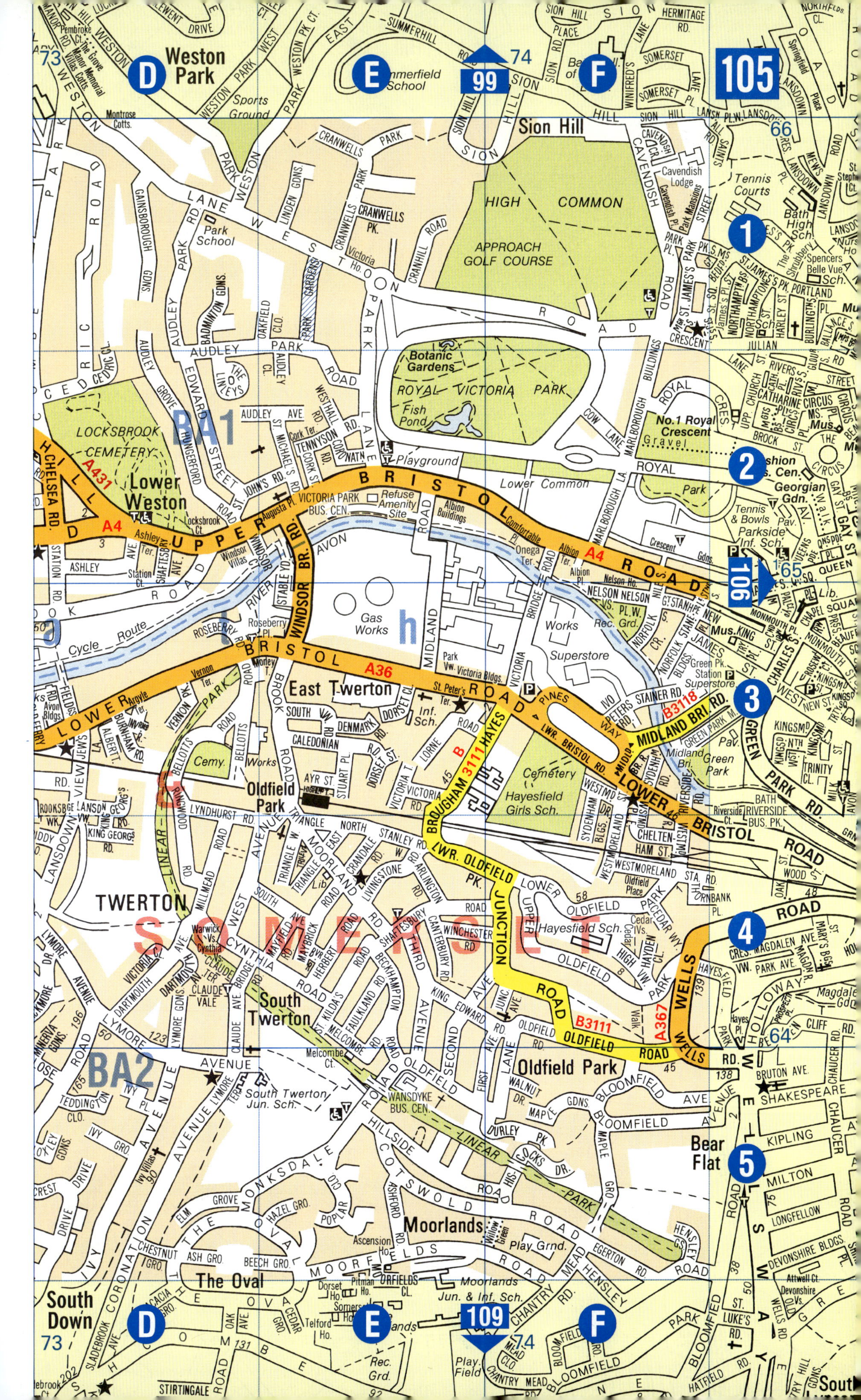

105
99
109
106
Weston Park
Sports Ground
Summerfield School
Sion Hill
High Common
Approach Golf Course
Botanic Gardens
Royal Victoria Park
Fish Pond
Cavendish Lodge
Tennis Courts
Bath High Sch.
Spencers Belle Vue
Park School
Locksbrook Cemetery
Lower Weston
BA1
BA2
Upper Bristol Road
A4
A431
A36
A367
B3111
B3118
Cycle Route
River Avon
Gas Works
Victoria Park Bus. Cen.
Refuse Amenity Site
Lower Common
No.1 Royal Crescent
Royal Crescent
Gravel Walk
Fashion Cen.
Georgian Gdn.
Tennis & Bowls
Parkside Inf. Sch.
Playground
East Twerton
Lower Bristol Road
Works
Superstore
Green Park Station
Green Park
Midland Bri. Rd.
Cemetery
Hayesfield Girls Sch.
Oldfield Park
Twerton
Somerset
Hayesfield Sch.
Cemy.
South Twerton
South Twerton Jun. Sch.
Wansdyke Bus. Cen.
Linear Park
Oldfield Park
Bear Flat
Moorlands
Play Grnd.
Moorlands Jun. & Inf. Sch.
The Oval
South Down
Rec. Grd.
Play. Field
Wells Road
Bath Riverside Bus. Pk.
Junction Road
Wellsway
Shakespeare
Kipling
Milton
Longfellow
Devonshire Bldgs.
Chaucer Rd.

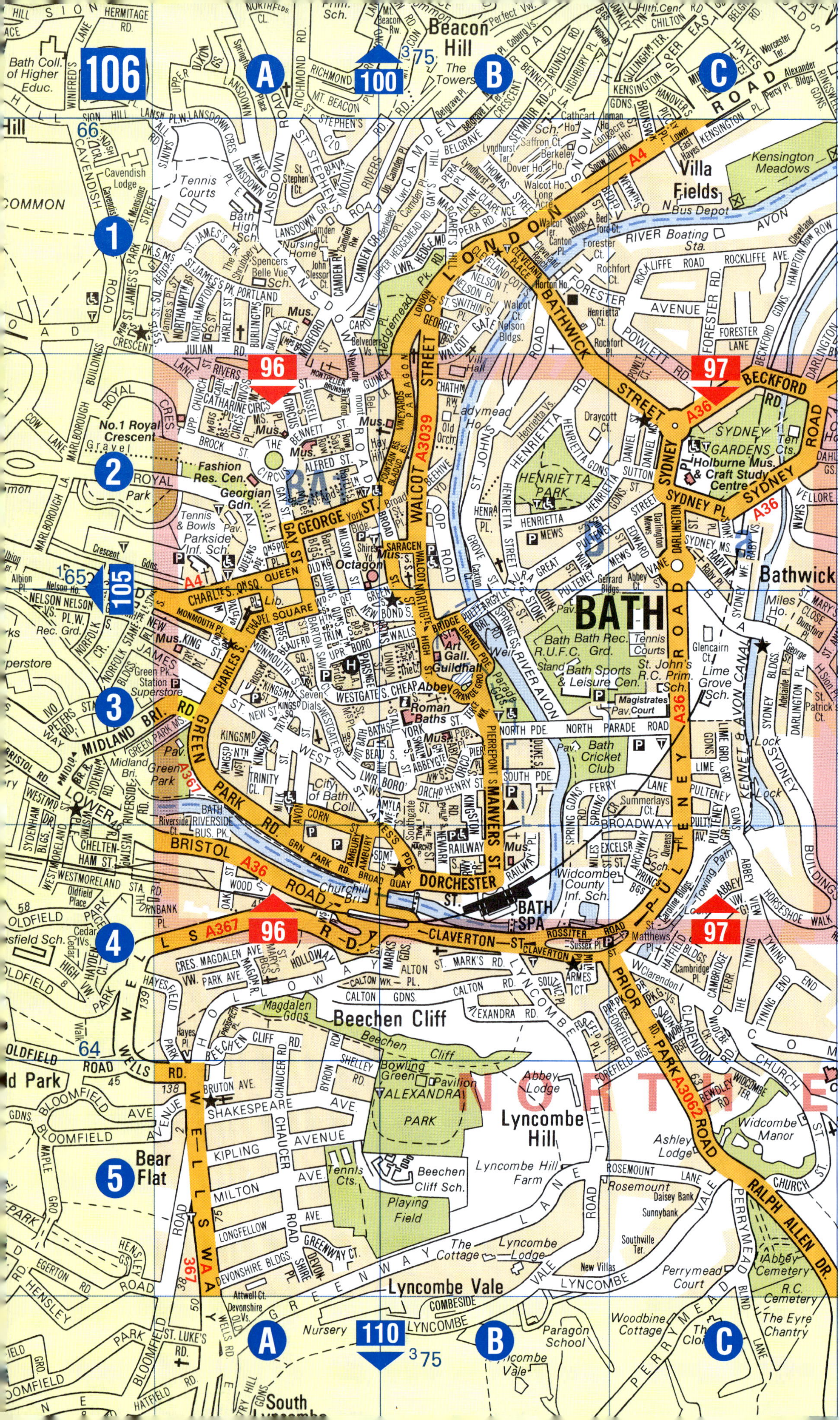

Beacon Hill
The Towers
100
A
B
C
Bath Coll. of Higher Educ.
Cavendish Lodge
Tennis Courts
Bath High Sch.
Nursing Home
Spencers Belle Vue
Villa Fields
Bus Depot
Kensington Meadows
River Boating Sta.
LONDON
ROCKLIFFE ROAD
ROCKLIFFE AVE
FORESTER AVENUE
POWLETT RD
BECKFORD RD
SYDNEY GARDENS
Holburne Mus. & Craft Study Centre
HENRIETTA PARK
Bathwick
96
97
No.1 Royal Crescent
ROYAL CRESCENT
Gravel Walk
Royal Park
Fashion Res. Cen.
Georgian Gdn.
THE CIRCUS
Tennis & Bowls
Parkside Inf. Sch.
QUEEN SQUARE
GEORGE ST
Octagon
WALCOT ST
Ladymead Ho.
BATH
Bath Rec. Grd.
Bath R.U.F.C.
Bath Sports & Leisure Cen.
St. John's R.C. Prim. Sch.
Magistrates Court
Art Gall.
Guildhall
Abbey
Roman Baths
Mus.
Green Park Station & Superstore
Kingsmead
Seven Dials
City of Bath Coll.
Bath Cricket Club
NORTH PARADE ROAD
SOUTH PDE
MANVERS ST.
PIERREPONT ST
Widcombe County Inf. Sch.
GREEN PARK RD.
BRISTOL ROAD
MIDLAND BRI. RD.
Midland Bri. Green Park
DORCHESTER ST.
BATH SPA
CLAVERTON ST
105
1
2
3
4
5
Beechen Cliff
Bowling Green
Pavilion
ALEXANDRA PARK
Lyncombe Hill
Abbey Lodge
Beechen Cliff Sch.
Playing Field
Tennis Cts.
Lyncombe Hill Farm
Rosemount
Bear Flat
WELLS ROAD
WELLSWAY
Lyncombe Vale
The Cottage
Lyncombe Lodge
NORTH
Widcombe Manor
Ashley Lodge
Abbey Cemetery
R.C. Cemetery
The Eyre Chantry
Perrymead Court
RALPH ALLEN DR.
PRIOR PARK ROAD
Woodbine Cottage
Paragon School
110
South Lyncombe

107
101
77
111
77
D
E
F
D
E
F
76
76
66
65
64
1
2
3
4
5
Hampton Ho.
Kensington Meadows Playing Fields
KENNET & AVON CANAL
BATHAMPTON
MEADOW
LANE
Simon's Close
MILLER WK.
DEVONSHIRE ROAD
HOLCOMBE
HOLCOMBE CL.
HOLCOMBE VALE
DOWN
THE CHESTS
St. George's Hill
ROAD
A36
WARMINSTER ROAD
ST. GEORGE'S HILL
REGENTS FLD.
TROSSACHS DR.
HANTONE HILL
Government Buildings
MINSTER WAY
Prim. Sch.
ST. CHRISTOPHER'S CLO.
Parade Grnd.
Ten Cts.
Playing Field
King Edward's School
NORTH ROAD
Nurses Home
LANE
WALLER CL.
CASTLE LANE
WAY
WALK
Chatham Pk.
ST. CATHERINE'S CLO.
Berkeley Ct.
CLEVELAND WALK
Keverstone
BA2
Cleveland Ct.
The Priory
Fiesole Youth Hostel
BATHWICK HILL
Bathwick Wood
Bathampton Warren
BATHAMPTON DOWN
BATH GOLF COURSE
Bathampton Down Reservoir (Covered)
Club House
GOLF COURSE ROAD
Sham Castle
Quantock Ter.
Cotswold Ter.
Mendip Ter.
Conygre Ter.
Woltson Ter.
Eastwood Housing
Playing Fields
ROAD
QUARRY
The Parade
Medical Centre
UNIVERSITY OF BATH
Open Air Theatre
South Building
CONVOCATION AVE.
Sports Pav.
Norwood Playing Fields
To American Museum (Claverton Manor)
THE AVENUE
Claverton Lodge
Upton Ho.
NORTH
Wood Hill Pl.
Oakwood
Woodland Pl.
The Woodlands
Smallcombe Farm
Cemetery
SMALLCOMBE WOOD
Combe Royal
Homefield
COPSELAND
OAKLEY
WOODLAND GROVE
BEECH AVENUE
AVENUE
NORWOOD
R.S.P.C.A. Cat & Dog Home
Widcombe
BATH & NORTH EAST SOMERSET
Beech Vw.
CLARENCE
All Saints Pl.
CLAVERTON CT.
CLAVERTON DOWN ROAD
Hall
QUARRY ROCK GARDENS CARAVAN PARK
Orphan Home
PROSPECT ROAD
MACAULAY BLDGS.
Macaulay
Walden
Violetbank Farm
Fairstowe
Rainbow Wood
Rainbow Wood Farm
CHURCH LANE
Fish
Rainbow Wood

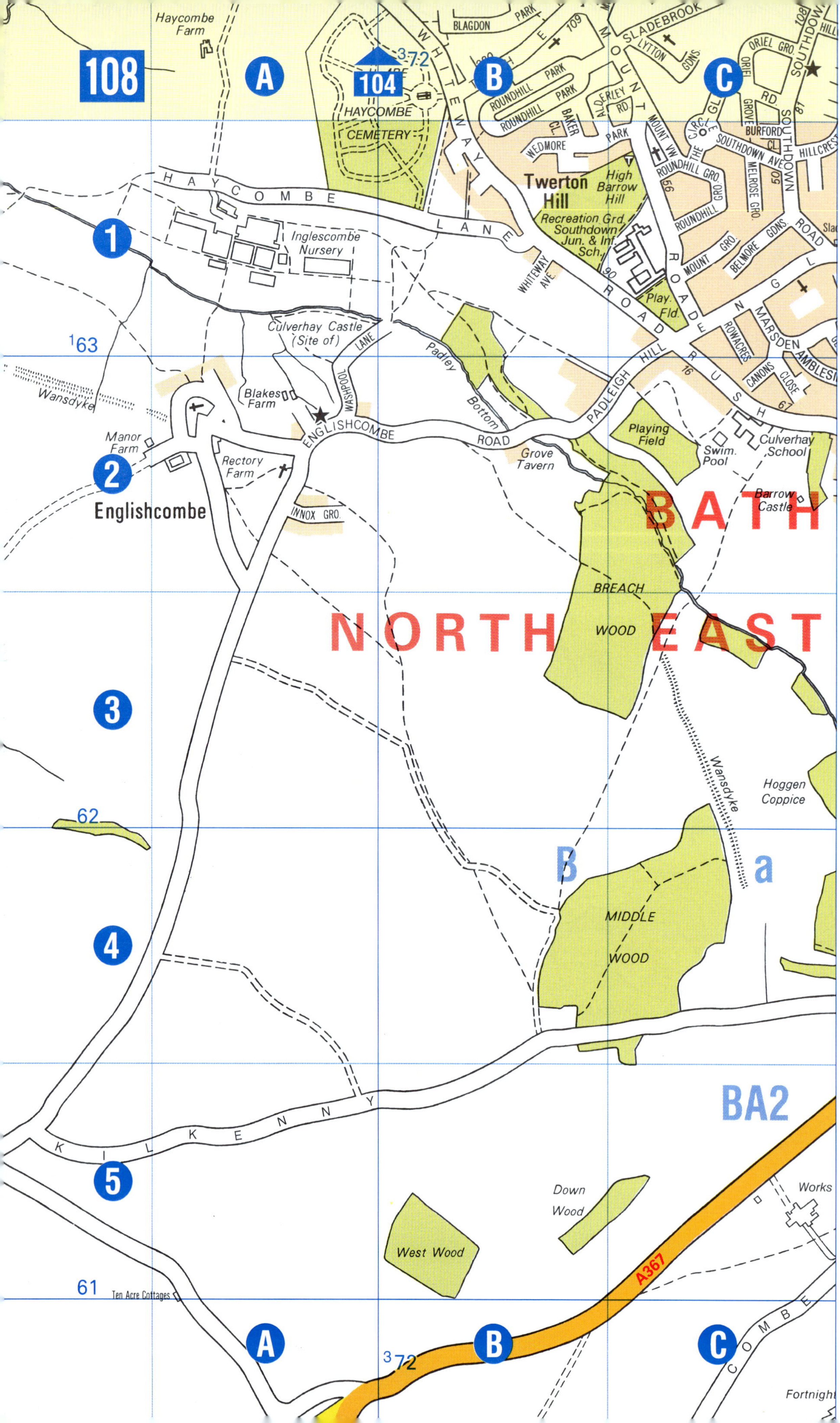
108
104
372
A
B
C
1
2
3
4
5
163
62
61
Haycombe Farm
HAYCOMBE CEMETERY
BLAGDON PARK
SLADEBROOK
LYTTON GDNS.
ORIEL GRO.
SOUTHDOWN
ROUNDHILL PARK
WHITEWAY
MOUNT
WEDMORE
BAKER CL.
ALDERLEY RD.
PARK
MOUNT VW.
THE CIRCLE
BURFORD CL.
SOUTHDOWN AVE.
HILLCREST
Twerton Hill
High Barrow Hill
Recreation Grd.
Southdown Jun. & Inf. Sch.
ROUNDHILL GRO.
MELROSE GRO.
BELMORE GDNS.
MOUNT GRO.
HAYCOMBE LANE
Inglescombe Nursery
WHITEWAY AVE.
ROAD
Play. Fld.
RUSH HILL
Culverhay Castle (Site of)
WASHPOOL LANE
Padley Bottom
PADLEIGH HILL
ROWACRES
MARSDEN
CANONS CLOSE
AMBLESIDE
Wansdyke
Blakes Farm
Manor Farm
ENGLISHCOMBE ROAD
Playing Field
Swim. Pool
Culverhay School
Rectory Farm
Grove Tavern
Englishcombe
INNOX GRO.
Barrow Castle
BATH
NORTH EAST
BREACH WOOD
Hoggen Coppice
B a
MIDDLE WOOD
BA2
KILKENNY
Down Wood
Works
West Wood
A367
Ten Acre Cottages
COMBE
Fortnight

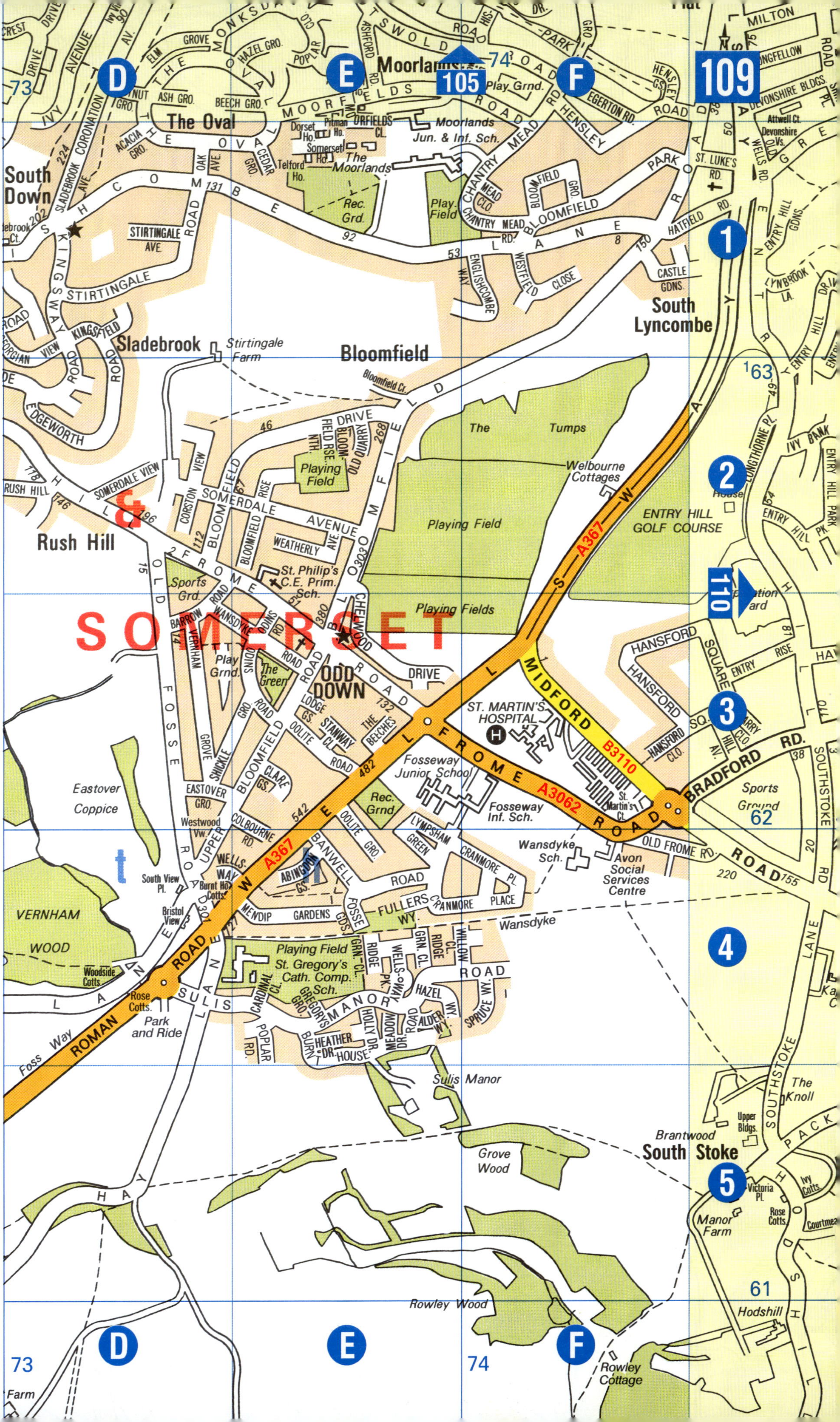
D
E
F
105
Moorlands
73
74
Play Grnd.
The Oval
South Down
Moorlands Jun. & Inf. Sch.
The Moorlands
Rec. Grd.
Play. Field
Dorset Ho.
Pitman Ho.
Somerset Ho.
Telford Ho.
MOORFIELDS ROAD
COMBE ROAD
BLOOMFIELD LANE
CHANTRY MEAD RD.
BLOOMFIELD GRO.
ENGLISHCOMBE WAY
WESTFIELD CLOSE
HENSLEY ROAD
EGERTON RD.
ST. LUKE'S RD.
HATFIELD RD.
CASTLE GDNS.
South Lyncombe
WELLSWAY
ENTRY HILL
LYNBROOK LA.
STIRTINGALE AVE.
STIRTINGALE ROAD
KINGSWAY
Sladebrook
Stirtingale Farm
Bloomfield
Bloomfield Cr.
BLOOMFIELD ROAD
The Tumps
Welbourne Cottages
ENTRY HILL GOLF COURSE
Playing Field
Playing Fields
SOMERDALE AVENUE
SOMERDALE VIEW
RUSH HILL
Rush Hill
EDGEWORTH
WEATHERLY AVE.
St. Philip's C.E. Prim. Sch.
Sports Grd.
SOMERSET
ODD DOWN
CHELWOOD DRIVE
OLD FOSSE ROAD
A367
A3062
B3110
MIDFORD ROAD
WELLSWAY
FROME ROAD
ST. MARTIN'S HOSPITAL
Fosseway Junior School
Fosseway Inf. Sch.
HANSFORD SQUARE
ENTRY RISE
BRADFORD RD.
Sports Ground
62
OLD FROME RD.
SOUTHSTOKE RD.
Wansdyke Sch.
Avon Social Services Centre
110
Eastover Coppice
EASTOVER GRO.
Westwood Vw.
UPPER WELLS
ABINGDON GS.
BANWELL ROAD
MENDIP GARDENS
FULLERS WY.
CRANMORE PLACE
Wansdyke
VERNHAM WOOD
Woodside Cotts.
Rose Cotts.
Park and Ride
ROMAN ROAD
Foss Way
SULIS MANOR ROAD
Playing Field
St. Gregory's Cath. Comp. Sch.
HAZEL ROAD
Sulis Manor
Grove Wood
Rowley Wood
Rowley Cottage
South Stoke
Brantwood
The Knoll
Manor Farm
Hodshill
61
163
Farm

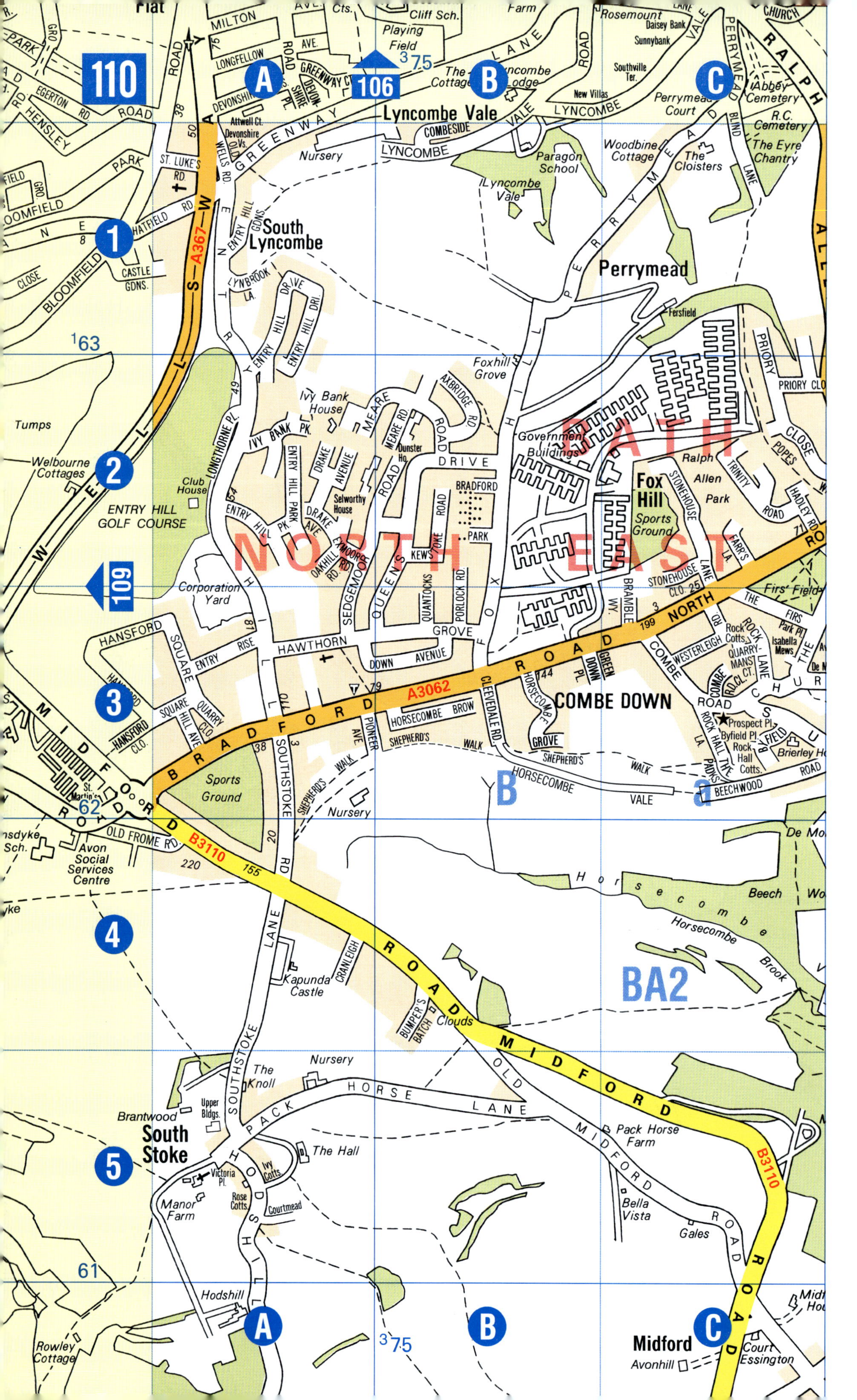
110
106
109
A
B
C
1
2
3
4
5
375
163
62
61
Lyncombe Vale
South Lyncombe
Perrymead
Fox Hill
COMBE DOWN
South Stoke
Midford
NORTH EAST
BATH
BA2
A367
A3062
B3110
WELLS ROAD
BRADFORD ROAD
NORTH ROAD
MIDFORD ROAD
OLD MIDFORD ROAD
PACK HORSE LANE
SOUTHSTOKE ROAD
SOUTHSTOKE LANE
HODSHILL
ENTRY HILL
PERRYMEAD
FOX HILL
GREENWAY
LYNCOMBE
LYNCOMBE VALE
COMBESIDE
MILTON AVE.
LONGFELLOW AVE.
DEVONSHIRE PL.
GREENWAY CT.
ST. LUKE'S RD.
HATFIELD RD.
BLOOMFIELD PARK
BLOOMFIELD CLOSE
CASTLE GDNS.
EGERTON RD
HENSLEY ROAD
ENTRY HILL GDNS.
LYNBROOK LA.
ENTRY HILL DRIVE
LONGTHORNE PL.
IVY BANK PK.
ENTRY HILL PARK
DRAKE AVENUE
MEARE RD.
AXBRIDGE RD.
QUEEN'S DRIVE
BRADFORD PARK
KEWSTOKE ROAD
QUANTOCKS
PORLOCK RD.
EXMOOR RD.
OAKHILL RD.
SEDGEMOOR
HAWTHORN GROVE
DOWN AVENUE
HANSFORD SQUARE
HANSFORD CLO.
ENTRY RISE
QUARRY CLO.
SQUARE HILL AVE.
PIONEER AVE.
HORSECOMBE BROW
SHEPHERD'S WALK
CLEVEDALE RD.
HORSECOMBE GROVE
HORSECOMBE VALE
GREEN DOWN PL.
BRAMBLE WY.
STONEHOUSE LANE
STONEHOUSE CLO.
FARR'S LA.
TRINITY ROAD
HADLEY RD.
POPES CLOSE
PRIORY CLO.
THE FIRS
WESTERLEIGH RD.
COMBE ROAD
ROCK LANE
ROCK HALL LA.
THE PADDS
BEECHWOOD ROAD
CHURCH ST.
BYFIELD
RALPH ALLEN DRIVE
BLIND LANE
CRANLEIGH
BUMPER'S BATCH
OLD FROME RD.
Cliff Sch.
Playing Field
The Cottage
Lyncombe Lodge
Rosemount
Daisey Bank
Sunnybank
Southville Ter.
New Villas
Perrymead Court
Abbey Cemetery
R.C. Cemetery
The Eyre Chantry
Attwell Ct.
Devonshire Vs.
Nursery
Paragon School
Lyncombe Vale
Woodbine Cottage
The Cloisters
Fersfield
Foxhill Grove
Ivy Bank House
Dunster Ho.
Selworthy House
Government Buildings
Ralph Allen Park
Sports Ground
Tumps
Welbourne Cottages
Club House
ENTRY HILL GOLF COURSE
Corporation Yard
Rock Cotts.
Quarry-Mans Ct.
Isabella Mews
Park Pl.
Firs' Field
Prospect Pl.
Byfield Pl.
Rock Hall Cotts.
Brierley Ho.
St. Martin's
Avon Social Services Centre
Horsecombe Brook
Beech Wood
Kapunda Castle
Clouds
The Knoll
Upper Bldgs.
Brantwood
The Hall
Ivy Cotts.
Victoria Pl.
Rose Cotts.
Courtmead
Manor Farm
Pack Horse Farm
Bella Vista
Gales
Hodshill
Rowley Cottage
Court Essington
Avonhill
De Montalt

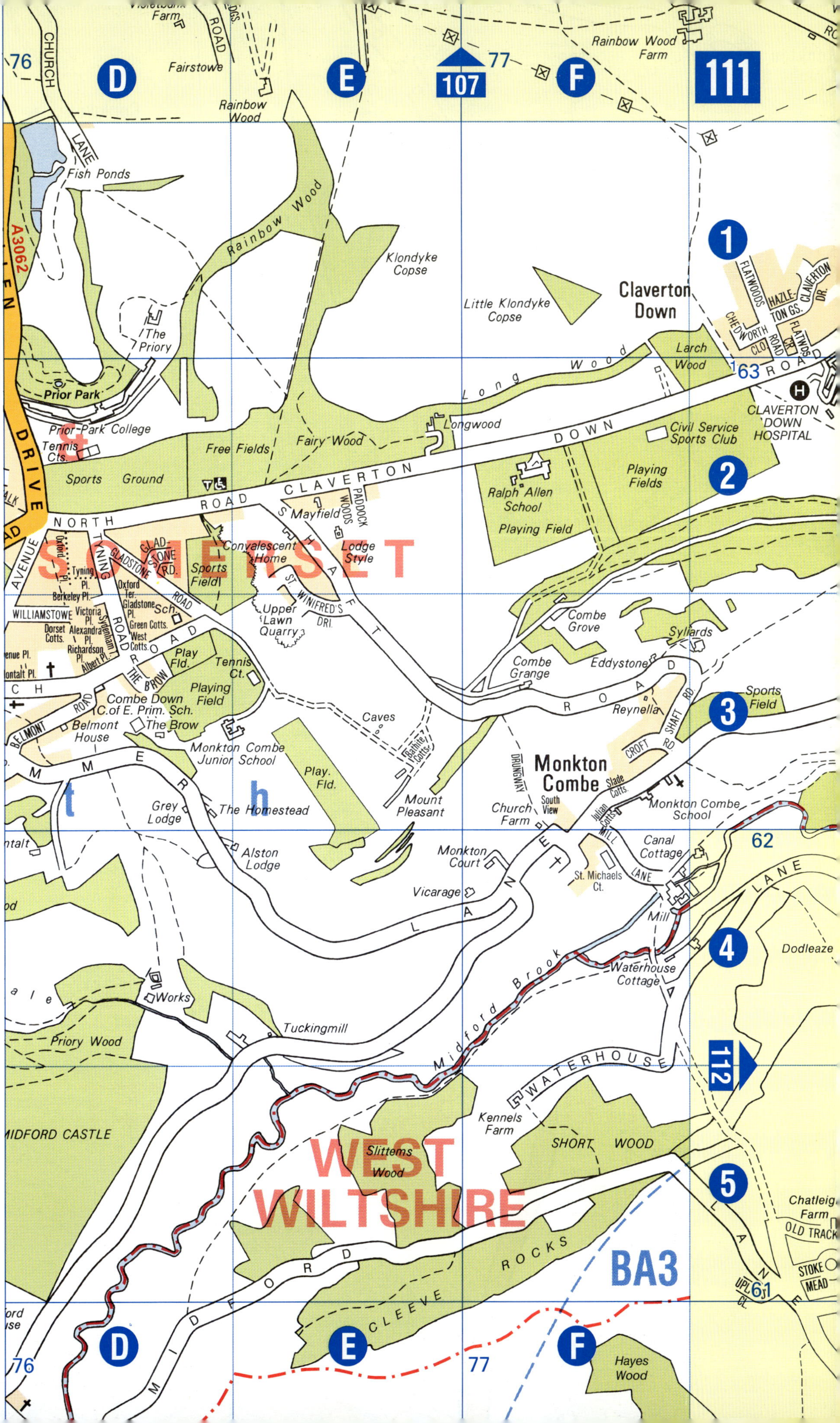
107
112
Claverton Down
Monkton Combe
SOMERSET
WEST WILTSHIRE
BA3
Rainbow Wood Farm
Fairstowe
Rainbow Wood
Fish Ponds
Klondyke Copse
Little Klondyke Copse
The Priory
Prior Park
Prior Park College
Tennis Cts.
Sports Ground
Free Fields
Fairy Wood
Longwood
Long Wood
Larch Wood
CLAVERTON DOWN HOSPITAL
Civil Service Sports Club
Playing Fields
Ralph Allen School
Playing Field
CLAVERTON DOWN ROAD
NORTH ROAD
Mayfield
Convalescent Home
Lodge Style
Sports Field
Upper Lawn Quarry
ST. WINIFRED'S DRI.
Combe Grove
Sylyards
Combe Grange
Eddystone
Reynella
Sports Field
Play Fld.
Tennis Ct.
Playing Field
Combe Down C.of E. Prim. Sch.
Belmont House
The Brow
Monkton Combe Junior School
Caves
Play. Fld.
Mount Pleasant
Church Farm
South View
Monkton Combe School
Grey Lodge
The Homestead
Alston Lodge
Monkton Court
Vicarage
Canal Cottage
St. Michaels Ct.
Mill
Waterhouse Cottage
Dodleaze
Works
Tuckingmill
Priory Wood
Midford Brook
MIDFORD CASTLE
Kennels Farm
SHORT WOOD
Slittems Wood
Chatleigh Farm
OLD TRACK
STOKE MEAD
ROCKS
CLEEVE
MIDFORD ROAD
WATERHOUSE LANE
Hayes Wood
A3062
PRIOR PARK DRIVE
WILLIAMSTOWE
Oxford Pl.
Tyning Pl.
Berkeley Pl.
GLADSTONE RD.
Oxford Ter.
Gladstone Pl.
Green Cotts.
West Cotts.
Victoria Pl.
Alexandra Pl.
Richardson Pl.
Albert Pl.
Dorset Cotts.
BELMONT ROAD
Bathite Cotts.
DRUNGWAY
Slade Cotts.
Julian Cotts.
MILL LANE
SHAFT RD
CROFT RD
FLATWOODS
HAZLETON GS.
CLAVERTON DR.
CHEDWORTH CLO.
76
77
63
62
61
D
E
F
1
2
3
4
5

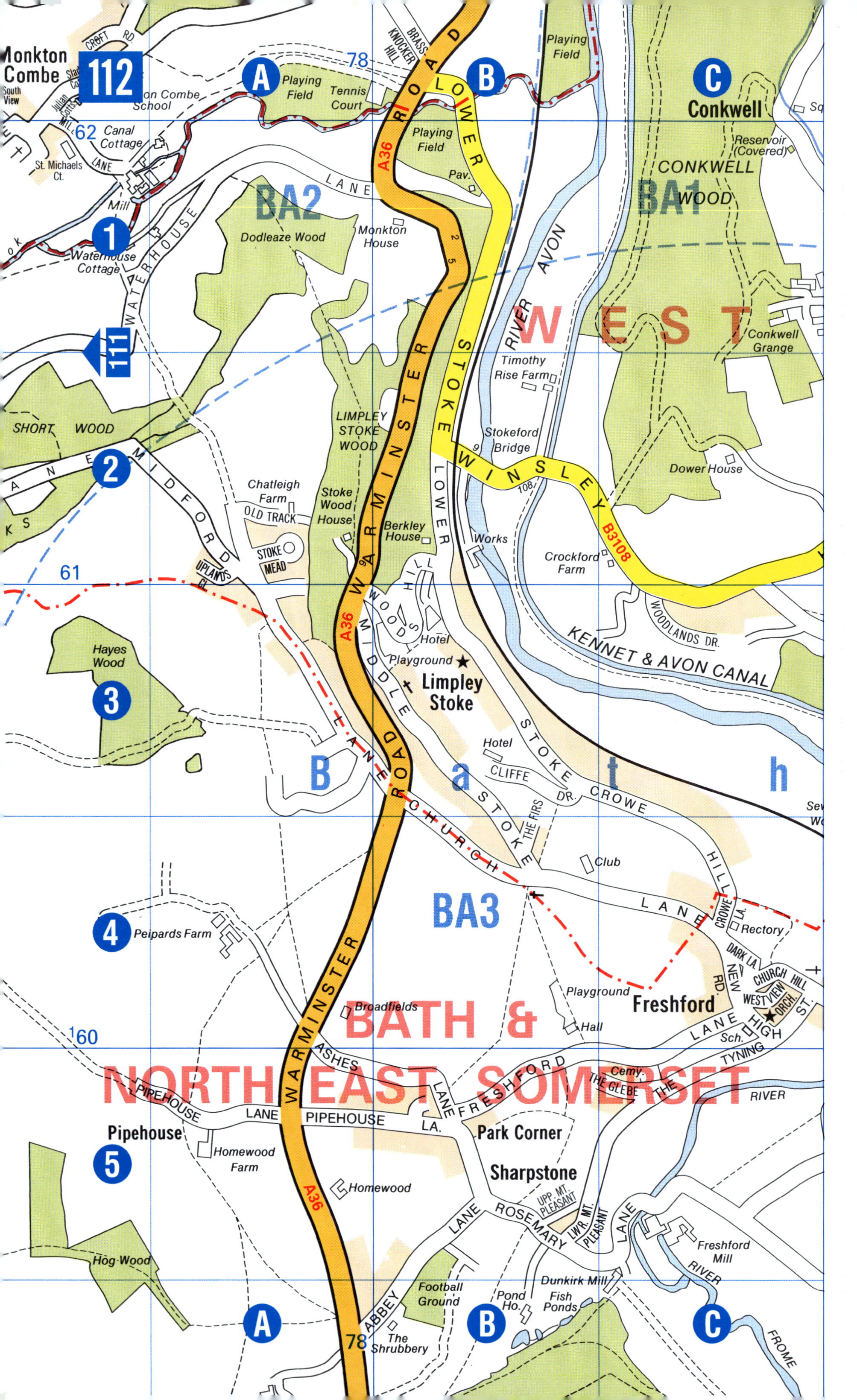
112
111
A
B
C
1
2
3
4
5
78
62
61
160
Monkton Combe
South View
Monkton Combe School
Canal Cottage
St. Michaels Ct.
Mill
Waterhouse Cottage
WATERHOUSE
CROFT RD.
MILL LANE
Playing Field
Tennis Court
Playing Field
Pav.
BRASS KNOCKER HILL
LOWER ROAD
A36
LANE
BA2
Dodleaze Wood
Monkton House
Playing Field
Conkwell
Reservoir (Covered)
CONKWELL WOOD
BA1
RIVER AVON
WEST
Conkwell Grange
Timothy Rise Farm
SHORT WOOD
MIDFORD
LIMPLEY STOKE WOOD
WARMINSTER ROAD
STOKE
Stokeford Bridge
WINSLEY
B3108
Dower House
Chatleigh Farm
OLD TRACK
Stoke Wood House
Berkley House
LOWER
Works
Crockford Farm
STOKE MEAD
UPLANDS CL.
WOODLANDS DR.
KENNET & AVON CANAL
HILL
WOODS
Hotel
Playground
Hayes Wood
MIDDLE
Limpley Stoke
Hotel
CLIFFE
DR.
STOKE
CROWE
LANE
Bath
THE FIRS
CHURCH
Club
HILL
BA3
LANE
CROWE LA.
Rectory
Peipards Farm
DARK LA.
NEW RD.
CHURCH HILL
WESTVIEW
ORCH.
ST.
Playground
Freshford
Broadfields
Hall
HIGH
Sch.
BATH & NORTH EAST SOMERSET
ASHES LANE
FRESHFORD
Cemy.
THE GLEBE
THE TYNING
RIVER
PIPEHOUSE LANE
PIPEHOUSE LA.
Pipehouse
Homewood Farm
Park Corner
Sharpstone
Homewood
ROSEMARY LANE
UPP. MT. PLEASANT
LWR. MT. PLEASANT
LANE
Freshford Mill
RIVER
Hog Wood
Football Ground
Dunkirk Mill
Pond Ho.
Fish Ponds
ABBEY
The Shrubbery
FROME

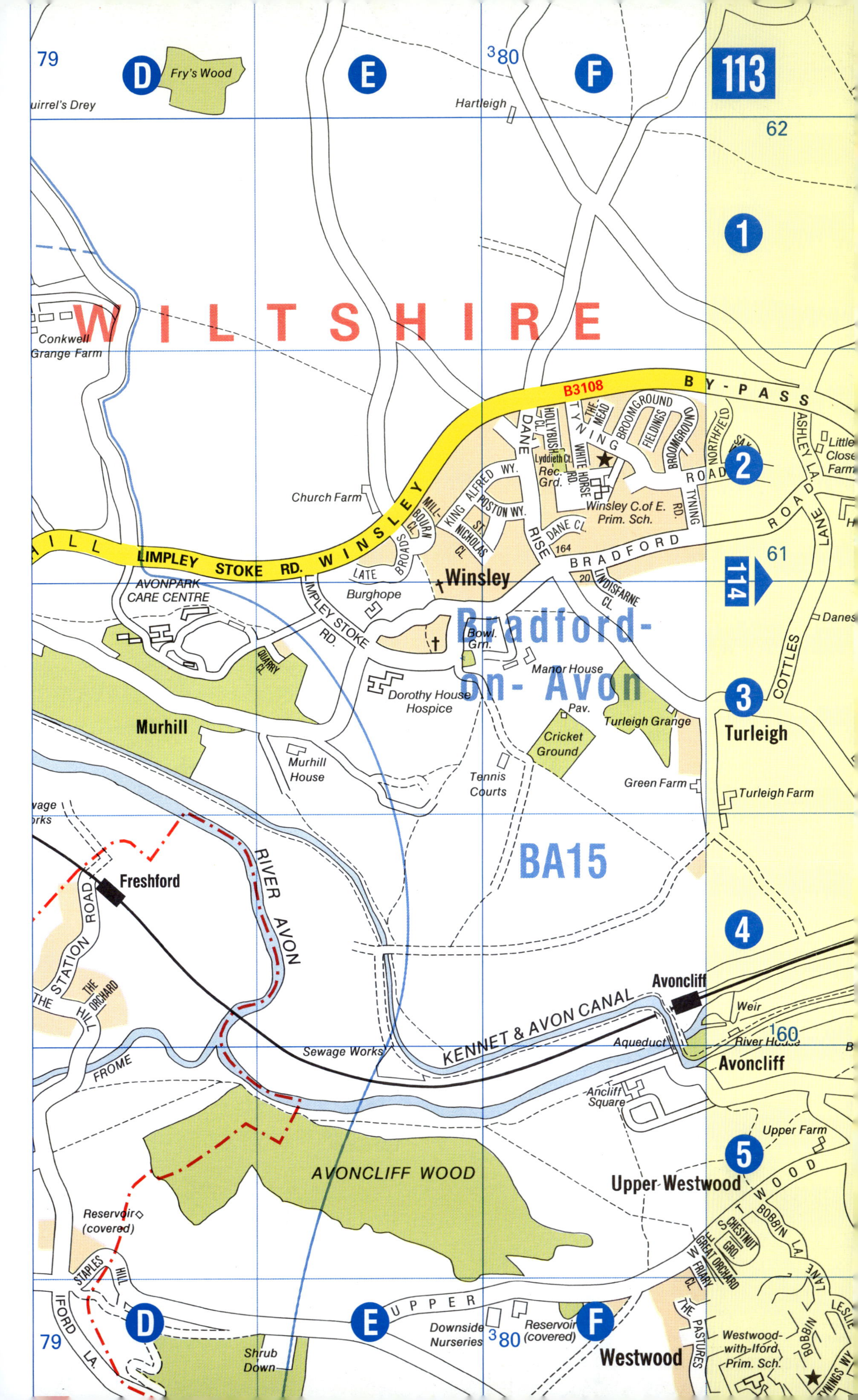
113
D
E
F
79
380
62
61
60
1
2
3
4
5
114
Fry's Wood
Squirrel's Drey
Hartleigh
WILTSHIRE
Conkwell Grange Farm
B3108
BY-PASS
LIMPLEY STOKE RD.
WINSLEY
Church Farm
Little Close Farm
ASHLEY LA.
DANE RISE
HOLLYBUSH CL.
TYNING
THE MEAD
BROOMGROUND
FIELDINGS
NORTHFIELD
WHITE HORSE RD.
Lyddieth Ct.
Rec. Grd.
Winsley C.of E. Prim. Sch.
TYNING RD.
ROAD
KING ALFRED WY.
POSTON WY.
ST. NICHOLAS CL.
MILLBOURN CL.
BROADS
LATE
DANE CL.
BRADFORD ROAD
LINDISFARNE CL.
COTTLES LANE
Winsley
Burghope
AVONPARK CARE CENTRE
QUARRY CL.
LIMPLEY STOKE RD.
Bradford-on-Avon
Bowl. Grn.
Manor House
Dorothy House Hospice
Pav.
Turleigh Grange
Turleigh
Dunes
Murhill
Murhill House
Cricket Ground
Tennis Courts
Green Farm
Turleigh Farm
BA15
Sewage Works
Freshford
STATION ROAD
THE HILL
THE ORCHARD
RIVER AVON
KENNET & AVON CANAL
Avoncliff
Weir
River House
Aqueduct
FROME
Sewage Works
Ancliff Square
Upper Farm
AVONCLIFF WOOD
Upper Westwood
WOOD
BOBBIN LA.
CHESTNUT GRO.
GREAT ORCHARD
FRIARY CL.
W
Reservoir (covered)
STAPLES HILL
IFORD LA.
UPPER
Downside Nurseries
Reservoir (covered)
Westwood
THE PASTURES
Westwood-with-Iford Prim. Sch.
BOBBIN LANE
LESLIE
LYNINGS WY.
Shrub Down

A
B
C
381
Great Ashley Farm
Great Ashley
ASHLEY
62
1
Upp
THE OLD BATCH
ASHLEY
WEST WI
St. Laurence Sch.
WINSLEY
B3108
BY-PASS
THE MEAD
BROOMGROUND
FIELDINGS
TYNING
WHITE HORSE RD.
NORTHFIELD
SAXON WY.
ROAD
ASHLEY LA.
Little Close Farm
Nursery
2
Winsley
Winsley C.of E. Prim. Sch.
TYNING RD.
ROAD
LANE
Hill View Farm
W I N S L E Y
104
90
BEAR
CL.
MAGNON RD.
VIEW
WESTFIELD
DOWNS
DOWNS CL.
BUDBURY
BRADFORD
61
LINDISFARNE CL.
113
Danescroft
MEADOWFIELD
GROVE
LEAZE
RICKFIELD
or House
Pav.
Turleigh Grange
3
COTTLES
Turleigh
Hunterscombe
Bradford-
The Warren
BELCOMBE
Belcombe Court
Green Farm
Turleigh Farm
RIVER
KENNET &
Swing Bridge
Barton Farm Country Park
Sewage Farm
4
BA15
Avoncliff
ON CANAL
Weir
160
Aqueduct
River House
Avoncliff
Becky Addy Wood
JONES
Ancliff Square
Lye Green Farm
Upper Farm
Lye Green
5
WESTWOOD
Upper Westwood
CHESTNUT GRO.
BOBBIN LA.
GREAT ORCHARD
FRIARY CL.
BOBBIN LA.
UPPER
LESLIE RISE
THE PASTURES
Westwood-with-Iford Prim. Sch.
BOBBIN LA.
TYNINGS WAY
Westwood

115
D
E
F
1
2
3
4
5
62
61
160
82
83
LEIGH ROAD
B3105
Northleigh Farm
Leigh Farmhouse
Pav.
Tennis Courts
Playing Fld.
Leigh House Farm
NORTHLEIGH
LEIGH RD.
B3109
Elbury
BATH ROAD
A363
LEIGH PARK ROAD
LEIGH PK. RD.
Bearfield Farm
BRADFORD-ON-AVON HOSPITAL
SLADESBROOK
Leigh Cottage
Woolley Grange Farm
Woolley Green
Woolley Grange
Bearfield Rec. Grd.
WILTSHIRE
HUNTINGDON
Bearfield Buildings
CHRISTCHURCH
PALMER DR.
SLADESBROOK CL.
CEDAR CT.
BANTON CROFT
BAINTON CL.
Play. Field
CHURCH ACRE
HUNTINGDON ST.
HUNTINGDON PL.
RISE
Tennis Courts
Christ Church Prim. Sch.
Comm. Cen.
Bethell Ct.
B3108
ROAD
MOUNT PLEASANT
NEW ROAD
B3109
SAND CL.
WOOLLEY DR.
NATION
CORONATION AV.
WOOLLEY CL.
GRANGE VW.
STREET
Crown Ct.
Woolley
Nursery
TYNING
BUDBURY TYNING
BUDBURY
BUDBURY CL.
BUDBURY RIDGE
BUDBURY PL.
THE WILDERNESS
CONIGRE
PRIORY CLOSE
PRIORY PARK
MASONS LA.
Ivy Ter.
WHITEHILL
HIGHFIELD RD.
KINGSFIELD
KINGSFIELD CL.
Hillcrest Flats
WOOLLEY TER.
CEMETERY
KINGSFIELD GRANGE
SPRINGFIELD
Nursery
Tory
Middle Rank
Tory Pl.
MARKET ST.
THE SHAMBLES
COPPICE HILL
WHITE HEADS LA.
B3107
ST. WOOLLEY
WOOLLEY ST.
HOLT ROAD
Old Court
LA.
B3107
ROAD
Cemy.
WINE STREET
Vine Cotts.
Wine St. Ter.
Rose-mary Steps
DRUCES HILL
CHURCH ST.
NEWTOWN
Bull Pit
Town Bri.
KINGSTON RD.
MILL LA.
SILVER ST.
Mus.
Lib.
The Hall
Kingston Mills
Works
Saltacre Lodge
BRADFORD WOOD LA.
KNAPP
SANDY LEAZE
BELCOMBE PL.
ROAD
BARTON ORCHARD
COACH
Pleasure Grds.
BRIDGE
St. Margaret's Ct.
St. Margaret's Hill
St. Margaret's Villas
BRADFORD-ON-AVON
Swim. Baths
Health Cen.
ST. MARGARET'S
STA. APP.
Lynd-hurst
Bungalows
UP. REGENTS PK.
STREET
Weirside Mill
Upper Mill
The Mill Ho.
GREENLAND MILLS
GREENLAND
Bradford-on-Avon
Bowl. Grn.
Rec. Grd.
Barton Bridge
AVON
RIVER AVON
POUND LA.
REGENTS PL.
JUNCTION RD.
FITZMAURICE PL.
A363
ST. TROWBRIDGE
Barton Farm
Tithe Barn
Victory Field (Play. Fld.)
Club Ho.
BRADFORD-ON-AVON GOLF COURSE
AVON CANAL
Ten. Cts.
Works
Fitzmaurice Prim. Sch.
Clarendon Comp. Sch.
DOWN AVON
AVON CLOSE
VW.
AVONFIELD
AV.
ST. LAURENCE RD.
KINGSTON AV.
AVONFIELD AV.
MYTHERN MDW.
ROAD
VIEW
HILL
SOUTHLEIGH
KENNET GS.
St. Katherine's Quay
POULTON
POULTON RECREATION GROUND
CULVER RD.
ST. ALDHELM RD.
Aldhelm Ct.
SOUTHVIEW CL.
WIDBROOK
SOUTHVILLE
WIDBROOK V.
LODDON WAY
BROOK
ELMS CROSS DR.
THE MALTINGS
SPENCERS ORCHARD
POULTON
STONEFIELD CL.
Bowl. Grn.
Sports Ground
PALAIRET CL.
HENDY CL.
HOBHOUSE CL.
POULTON LA.
DEVERELL CL.
HORTON CL.
FITZMAURICE CL.
MOULTON DRIVE
PIPLAR GROUND
SOUTHWAY
BARN PIECE
FOLLYFIELD
BASSETTS PASTURE
BEDDOE CL.
TOLLPOOL LA.
METHUEN CL.
JOHN RENNIE CL.
Canal Farm
ELMSCROSS SHOPPING CENTRE
B3109
ELMSCROSS BUSINESS PARK
TREENWOOD INDUSTRIAL ESTATE
KENNET & AVON CANAL
ROWDEN
Rowden House
Old Farm
FROME ROAD
ELMS CROSS
Vineyard
Southview Farm
LANE
Widbrook
Widbrook Ho.
Widbrook Bridge
Widbrook Farm
ROAD

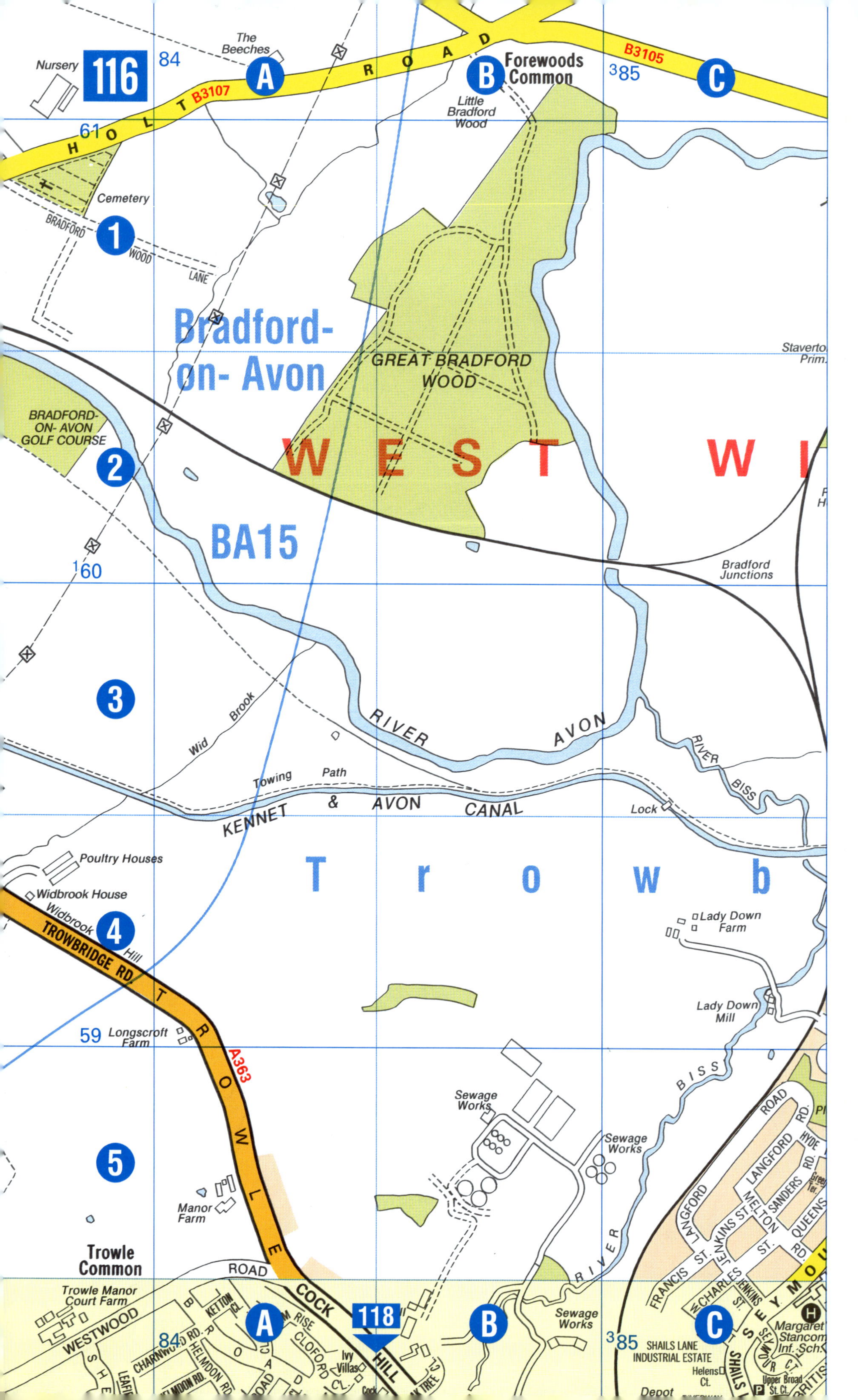
116
Nursery
The Beeches
84
A
B
C
HOLT ROAD
B3107
B3105
Forewoods Common
385
Little Bradford Wood
61
Cemetery
BRADFORD WOOD LANE
1
Bradford-on-Avon
GREAT BRADFORD WOOD
BRADFORD-ON-AVON GOLF COURSE
2
WEST WI
Staverton Prim.
BA15
160
Bradford Junctions
3
RIVER AVON
Wid Brook
RIVER BISS
Towing Path
KENNET & AVON CANAL
Lock
Poultry Houses
Widbrook House
Widbrook Hill
TROWBRIDGE RD.
Trowb
4
Lady Down Farm
Lady Down Mill
59
Longscroft Farm
TROWLE
A363
BISS
Sewage Works
Sewage Works
5
Manor Farm
Trowle Common
ROAD
RIVER
LANGFORD ROAD
HYDE RD.
SANDERS RD.
QUEENS RD
MELTON ST.
JENKINS ST.
FRANCIS ST.
CHARLES ST.
SEYMOUR
Trowle Manor Court Farm
WESTWOOD
KETTON CL.
COCK HILL
118
Ivy Villas
CLOFORD CL.
CHARNWOOD RD.
HELMDON RD.
Sewage Works
SHAILS LANE INDUSTRIAL ESTATE
Helens Ct.
Depot
Margaret Stancomb Inf. Sch.
Upper Broad St. Ct.

D
E
F
86
87
61
160
59
1
2
3
4
5
B3106
Weir
Factory
RIVER AVON
Nasmilco
Staverton
Staverton Farm
ELM CL.
The Square
NEW TERRACE
B3105
C.of E. Sch.
SCHOOL LANE
Playing Field
SMALLBROOK GDNS.
Smallbrook House
Poultry House
Poultry Houses
SCHOOL LA. CL.
MAXCROFT LANE
Maxcroft Farm
Towing Path
KENNET & AVON CANAL
WILTSHIRE
MARSH
HAMMOND WAY
B3106
Hilperton Marsh Farm
DRIVE
SWAN DR.
MARINA
THE SLIPWAY
THESTFIELD DR.
NAVIGATOR CL.
TOWPATH RD.
TUDOR DR.
KINGS
HANOVER CL.
SAXON DR.
STUART CL.
GDS. ROAD
CARISBROOKE CRES.
GARDENS
QUEENS GDS.
PRINCESS
ST. MARY'S CL.
ST. MARY'S GDS.
ST. MARY'S GDNS.
ST. MARY'S GDNS.
B3105 ROAD HILL
MARSHMEAD
NEWLEAZE
GREEN HILL GDS.
STREET
HAMMOND WY.
Depot
CANAL RD.
HORSE ROAD
WYKE ROAD
FARM CL.
POUND
Pound Farm
Hilperton Marsh
Hilperton C.of E. Prim. Sch.
ORIEL CL.
DYMOTT SQ.
Wks.
Works
WAY
HAYES CL.
CANAL ROAD INDUSTRIAL ESTATE
Depot
AVON WY.
TROWBRIDGE INDUSTRIAL ESTATE
Factory
KENNET
Goods Depot
WYTHE CL.
Trowbridge
THE KNAP
CHURCH ST.
ST. MICHAEL'S CL.
NURSERY CL.
Hilperton
Nursery
COPPER BEECHES
GREENWAY GDNS.
VICTORIA ROAD
OSBORNE RD.
ALBERT ROAD
LANE
Warehouse
Factory
BA14
LADYDOWN
CANAL ROAD
PARKLANDS
Seymour Playing Field
AVONVALE RD.
MURRAY RD.
PALMER ROAD
JAMES ST.
Cricket Ground
Pav.
DOWNHAYES RD.
Palmer Gardens
TROWBRIDGE COMMUNITY HOSPITAL
DOWNSIDE PK.
DOWNSIDE VW.
Cemetery
VICTORIA GDNS.
VICTORIA RD.
FULNEY CL.
RAGLETH GR.
MIDDLE
Parochial Jun. Sch.
Playing Field
THE DOWN
ISLINGTON
KENSINGTON CL.
WINDERMERE RD.
CONISTON RD.
MOUNT
RODWELL PK.
ROAD
Nursing Home
CLEVELAND GDNS.
ALBANY CL.
Fieldways
Highfield
TROWBRIDGE ROAD
A361
HILPERTON
HALFWAY CL.
THE BEECHES
Halfway Cottage
GRASMERE
SPRINGFIELD CL.
FULFORD RD.
TRIGG CL.
LOWMEAD
DELAMERE ROAD
KEATES CL.
LOWER CT.
PROSPECT PL.
YORK BUILDINGS
Islington Gdns.
ADCROFT DR.
Charlotte Sq.
CHARLOTTE ST.
CROSS ST.
ST. THOMAS' PASS
TIMBRELL ST.
GEORGE ST.
ST. THOMAS RD.
BELLEFIELD CR.
STANCOMB AV.
SPRINGFIELD
119
KENTON
PEPPERACRE LA.
AVENSCROFT GDNS.
The Prospect

Trowle Common
116
A
B
C
84
385
158
57
56
1
2
3
4
5
Manor Farm
Trowle Manor Court Farm
WESTWOOD ROAD
COCK HILL
A363
BRADFORD ROAD
Cockhill Farm
Ivy Villas
Cock Hill Ho. Ct.
OAK TREE CL.
River Biss
Sewage Works
SHAILS LANE INDUSTRIAL ESTATE
RIVERWAY INDUSTRIAL PARK
THE MALTINGS INDUSTRIAL PARK
RIVER WAY
Depot
Factory
Kitcheners Ct.
Footpath
INNOX MILL CL.
Innox
INNOX RD.
Sub. Hall
Trowbridge
Stallard Rec. Fld.
BRYER ASH BUSINESS PK.
STALLARD ST.
BYTHESEA RD.
Trowbridge Mus.
THE SHIRES SHOP. CEN.
Town Bri.
WICKER HILL
SHAILS LA.
B3106
SEYMOUR RD.
Margaret Stancomb Inf. Sch.
FRANCIS ST.
LANGFORD
CHARLES ST.
JENKINS ST.
WESTCROFT ST.
MELTON
SANDERS
QUEENS
Helens Ct.
Upper Broad St. Ct.
UPPER BROAD ST.
CONIGRE
CHARNWOOD RD.
HELMDON RD.
LEAFIELD PL.
CHEPSTON PL.
SHERBORNE RD.
SHORE PL.
ROSEDALE GDS.
CHILMARK
KINGSLEY PL.
LYNWOOD DR.
KETTON CL.
CLIPSHAM RISE
CLOFORD CL.
BARNACK CL.
ANCASTER CL.
CRANMORE CL.
CRANMORE
CHALFONT CL.
MEADWAY
WOBURN CL.
QUEENS CLUB GDS.
RAMBLER CL.
MERIDIAN WK.
ACACIA
ALBION DR.
Trowle Bridge
Playing Field
St. Augustine's R.C. Sch.
Tennis Cts.
Bowling Green
Pav.
Sch.
ROSSETTI GDS.
CRAWLEY
WARBLER CL.
WREN COURT
NIGHTINGALE
CHAFFINCH DR.
DOVECOTE CL.
SWALLOW DR.
ST. AUGUSTINES RD.
WESTBOURNE GDS.
WESTBOURNE RD.
WEST ST.
A366
Convent
Rec. Grd.
St. John's R.C. Prim. Sch.
BROOK ROAD
BISS MDW.
BERKELEY RD.
CHRISTIN CT.
London Bridge
FARLEIGH AV.
TINING CL.
ARNOLDS HILL
WINGFIELD
TOWER CL.
RICHMOND CL.
HUNGERFORD AV.
BARNES CL.
KEW DR.
MILLINGTON DR.
The John of Gaunt School
Tennis Courts
Playing Field
Stream
Hall
Studley Green
WESTFIELD WAY
GLEBE
ELMDALE CT.
EASTVIEW RD.
ELMDALE RD.
TALBOT RD.
BLAIR ROAD
PITMAN AV.
PITMAN CT.
ALLEN RD.
ROCK RD.
A361
Offices
Works
LANSDOWN CL.
YEOMAN WAY
ALASTAIR CT.
BRADLEY ROAD
COUNTY WAY
Trowbridge Town F.C.
The Homestead
GLOUCESTER RD.
BOND ST. BLDGS.
WATERWORKS RD.
HENDERSON CL.
SURREY PL.
GLADSTONE RD.
PARK ST.
WESLEY ROAD
NEWTOWN
Newtown Cnty. Prim. Sch.
T.A.V.R. Cen.
County Hall
Play. Fld.
MORTIMER ST.
HAVELOCK ST.
FROME RD.
AVENUE RD.
Lambrok
LAMBROK RD.
NORTH
RODSLEIGH
Recn. Gnd.
WESTFIELD CL.
SUMMERLEAZE
Playing Field
Studley Grn. Prim. Sch.
Manor Ct.
Shaftesbury Ct.
MANOR RD.
ST. MARGARETS
WARBURTON CL.
FIELD WAY
ALDEBURGH PL.
LAMBROK CL.
ST. JOHN'S CR.
WEBBERS CT.
FRAMPTON CT.
GAINSBOROUGH RISE
WHITEROW PARK
WHITE-ROW PK.
Garden Cen.
CHURCH LANE
CHURCH FIELDS
Vic.
Trowbridge Sports Centre
Clarendon School
Play. Fld.
Playing Field
Rutland Ct.
RUTLAND CRES.
Trowbridge College
Tennis Cts.
COLLEGE RD.
BEECH GRO.
LABURNUM GRO.
WALNUT GRO.
LARCH GRO.
GROVE RD.
CEDAR GRO.
MAPLE GRO.
LAUREL GRO.
Grove Ct.
CARLTON ROW
THE CLOSE
HOLBROOK
BA14
SYCAMORE GROVE
HAWTHORN GRO.
ALMOND GRO.
LILAC GRO.
WILLOW GRO.
NUT GR.
CHESTNUT GRO.
SILVER BIRCH GRO.
ALDER CL.
The Grove Prim. Sch.
Playing Field
BAYDON CL.
WILTSHIRE DR.
District Council Offs.
SILVER STREET
SILVER MWS.
HAZEL
Upper Studley
County Council Depot
WHITE ROW HILL
FROME ROAD
FIRS HILL
White Row Bridge
Southwick Court Farm
Moat
SANDRINGHAM RD.
WINDSOR DR.
HOLYROOD CL.
BALMORAL RD.
WINTERSLOW RD.
WESTMEAD CR.
MARSTON RD.
BEWLEY RD.
LANGLEY RD.
BROUGHTON RD.
SUMMERDOWN WK.
KINGSDOWN RD.
HEDDINGTON CL.
BOUNDARY RD.
BOUNDARY WK.
WALK
Pav.
Sports Ground
CLYDESDALE
HILPERTON RD.

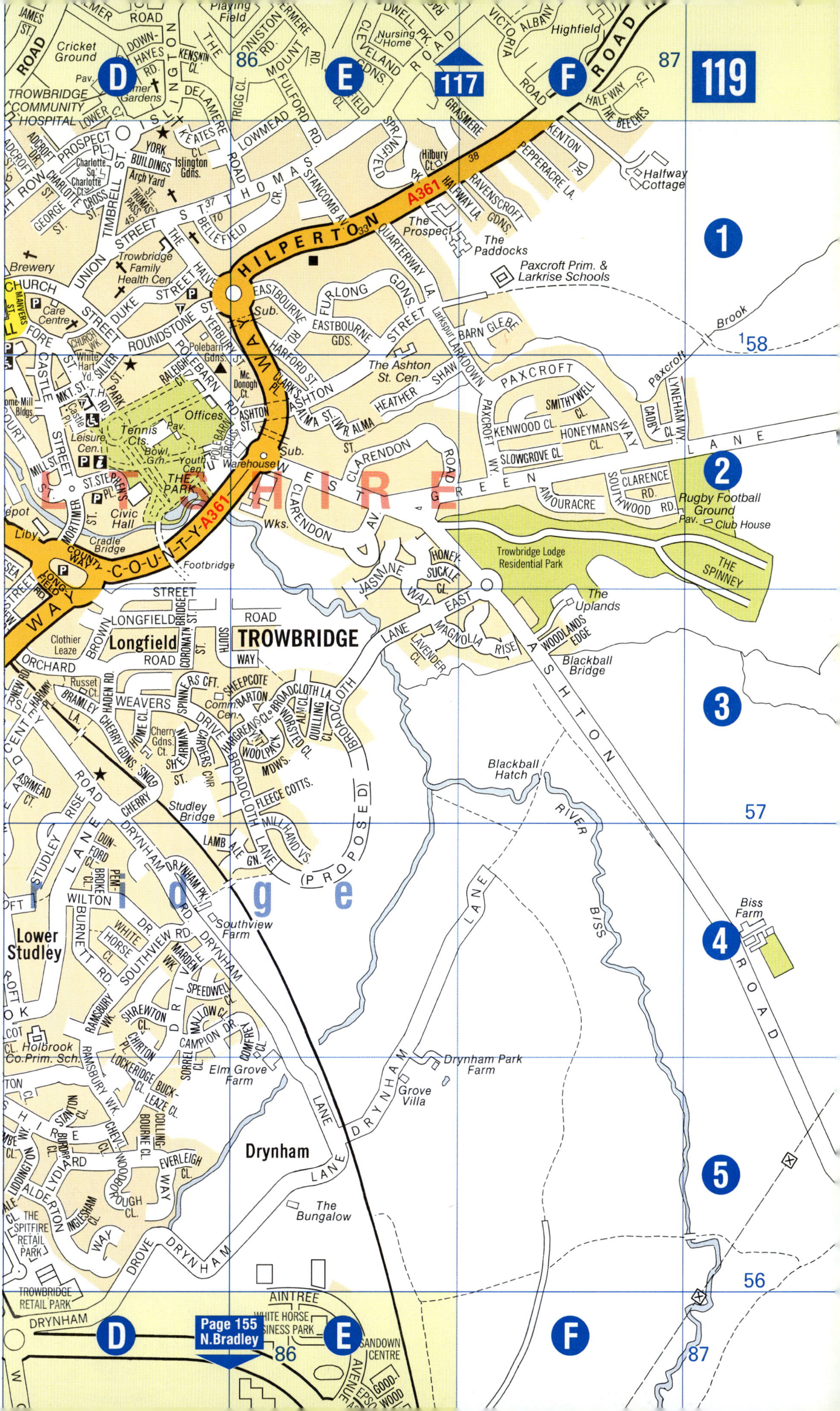
TROWBRIDGE
Longfield
Lower Studley
Drynham
WILTSHIRE
Trowbridge
117
Page 155 N.Bradley
D
E
F
1
2
3
4
5
86
87
58
57
56
HILPERTON ROAD
A361
COUNTY WAY
Cricket Ground
Trowbridge Community Hospital
Playing Field
Nursing Home
Highfield
Halfway Cottage
The Prospect
The Paddocks
Paxcroft Prim. & Larkrise Schools
Brook
The Ashton St. Cen.
Trowbridge Family Health Cen.
Brewery
Care Centre
Leisure Cen.
Tennis Cts.
Bowl. Grn.
Youth Cen.
Offices
Warehouse
Civic Hall
Cradle Bridge
Footbridge
Wks.
Rugby Football Ground
Club House
Trowbridge Lodge Residential Park
THE SPINNEY
The Uplands
Blackball Bridge
Blackball Hatch
RIVER BISS
Biss Farm
ASHTON ROAD
GREEN LANE
WEST ASHTON ROAD
PAXCROFT WAY
LARKDOWN
EAST LANE
Clothier Leaze
Comm. Cen.
Studley Bridge
Southview Farm
Holbrook Co.Prim. Sch.
Elm Grove Farm
Drynham Park Farm
Grove Villa
The Bungalow
DRYNHAM LANE
DRYNHAM ROAD
THE SPITFIRE RETAIL PARK
TROWBRIDGE RETAIL PARK
AINTREE
WHITE HORSE BUSINESS PARK
SANDOWN CENTRE
(PROPOSED)

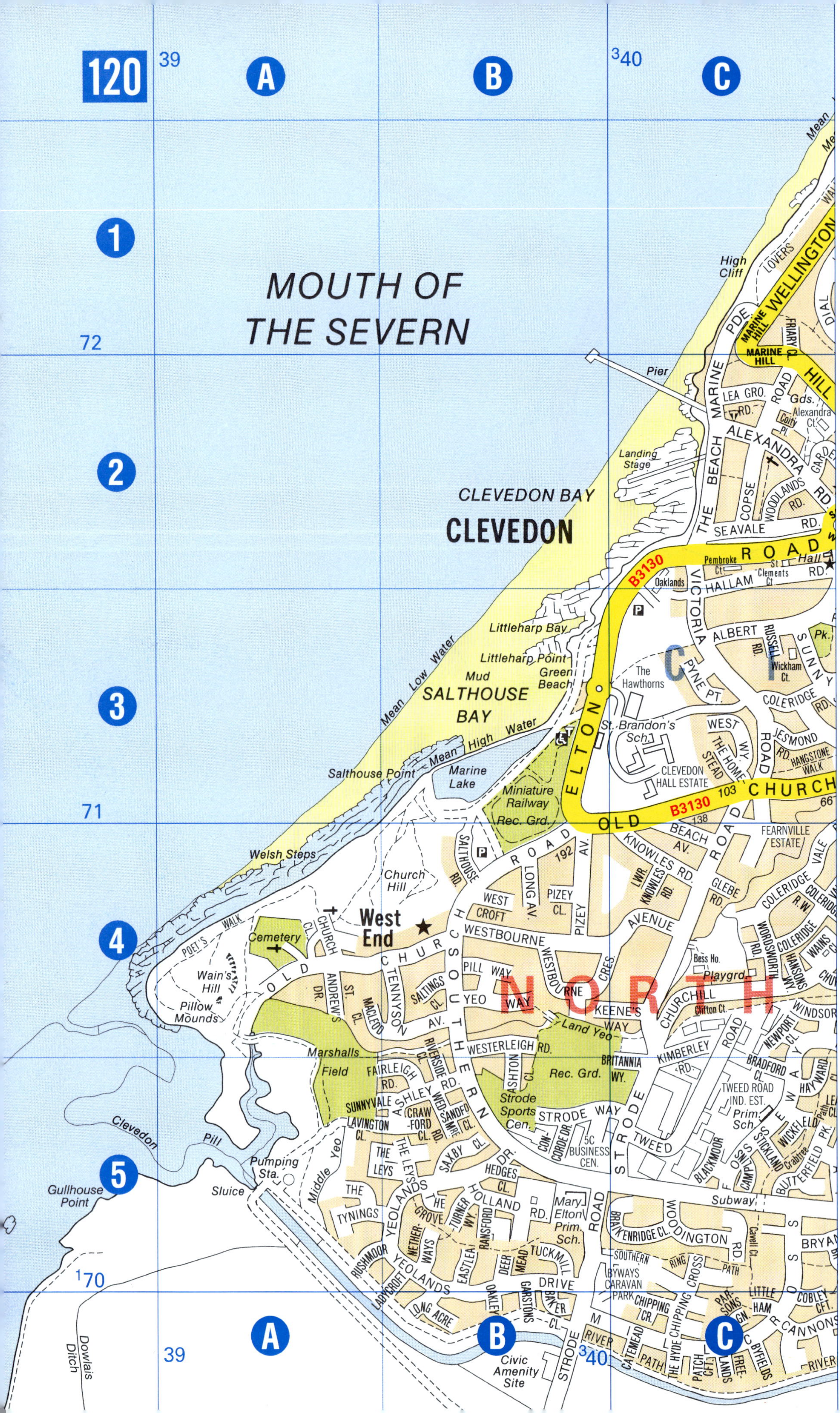

39
A
B
340
C
1
2
3
4
5
72
71
170
MOUTH OF THE SEVERN
CLEVEDON BAY
CLEVEDON
Pier
Landing Stage
High Cliff
WELLINGTON
HILL
MARINE HILL
MARINE PDE.
LOVERS WALK
FRIARY
DIAL
THE BEACH
LEA GRO.
ROAD
Gds.
Alexandra Ct.
ALEXANDRA RD.
COPSE RD.
WOODLANDS RD.
SEAVALE RD.
Pembroke Ct.
ROAD
St Clements Ct.
Hall
RD.
B3130
Oaklands
HALLAM
VICTORIA
ALBERT RD.
RUSSELL
Wickham Ct.
SUNNY
Pk.
Littleharp Bay
Littleharp Point
Green Beach
Mud
SALTHOUSE BAY
Mean Low Water
Mean High Water
The Hawthorns
PYNE PT.
COLERIDGE RD.
ELTON
St. Brandon's Sch.
WEST WY.
THE HOMESTEAD
ROAD
JESMOND RD.
HANGSTONE WALK
Salthouse Point
Marine Lake
Miniature Railway
Rec. Grd.
CLEVEDON HALL ESTATE
103
CHURCH
66
OLD
138
BEACH AV.
FEARNVILLE ESTATE
VALE
Welsh Steps
SALTHOUSE RD.
ROAD
192
LONG AV.
PIZEY CL.
PIZEY AV.
KNOWLES RD.
LWR. KNOWLES RD.
GLEBE RD.
COLERIDGE
Church Hill
WEST CROFT
West End
AVENUE
WORDSWORTH RD.
Bess Ho.
Playgrd.
WAINS
POET'S WALK
Cemetery
CHURCH CL.
CHURCH
SOUTHERN
WESTBOURNE
WESTBOURNE
CRES.
Wain's Hill
Pillow Mounds
OLD
ST. ANDREW'S DR.
ST. CL.
MACLEOD CL.
TENNYSON AV.
SALTINGS CL.
PILL WAY
YEO WAY
NORTH
KEENE'S WAY
CHURCHILL
Clifton Ct.
WINDSOR
Land Yeo
Marshalls Field
WESTERLEIGH RD.
FAIRLEIGH RD.
RIVERSIDE CL.
ASHTON CL.
Rec. Grd.
BRITANNIA WY.
KIMBERLEY RD.
ROAD
NEWPORT CL.
BRADFORD CL.
TWEED ROAD IND. EST.
Prim. Sch.
HAYWARD
SUNNYVALE
ASHLEY RD.
CRAW-FORD CL.
SANDFORD CL.
Strode Sports Cen.
STRODE WAY
STRODE
TWEED
BLACKMOOR
Clevedon Pill
LAVINGTON CL.
THE LEYS
SAXBY CL.
CORBE DR.
5C BUSINESS CEN.
CAMPION
STICKLAND
WICKFIELD
BUTTERFIELD PK.
Crabtree
Pumping Sta.
Sluice
Gullhouse Point
Middle Yeo
THE TYNINGS
YEOLANDS
HEDGES CL.
HOLLAND RD.
Mary Elton Prim. Sch.
ROAD
Subway
THE GROVE
TURNER WY.
BRACKENRIDGE CL.
WOODINGTON RD.
BRYANS
RUSHMOOR
NETHER WAYS
RANSFORD
DEER MEAD
TUCKMILL
SOUTHERN
BYWAYS CARAVAN PARK
RING
CROSS
PATH
Cavell Ct.
LADYCROFT
YEOLANDS
EASTLEA
DRIVE
BAKER CL.
CHIPPING CR.
CHIPPING
PARSONS GN.
LITTLE HAM
COBLEY CFT.
LONG ACRE
OAKLEY
GARSTONS
M
RIVER
STRODE
CATEMEAD
PATH
THE HYDE
PATCH CFT.
LANDS
FREE-
BYFIELDS
CANNONS
RIVER
Civic Amenity Site
Dowlais Ditch

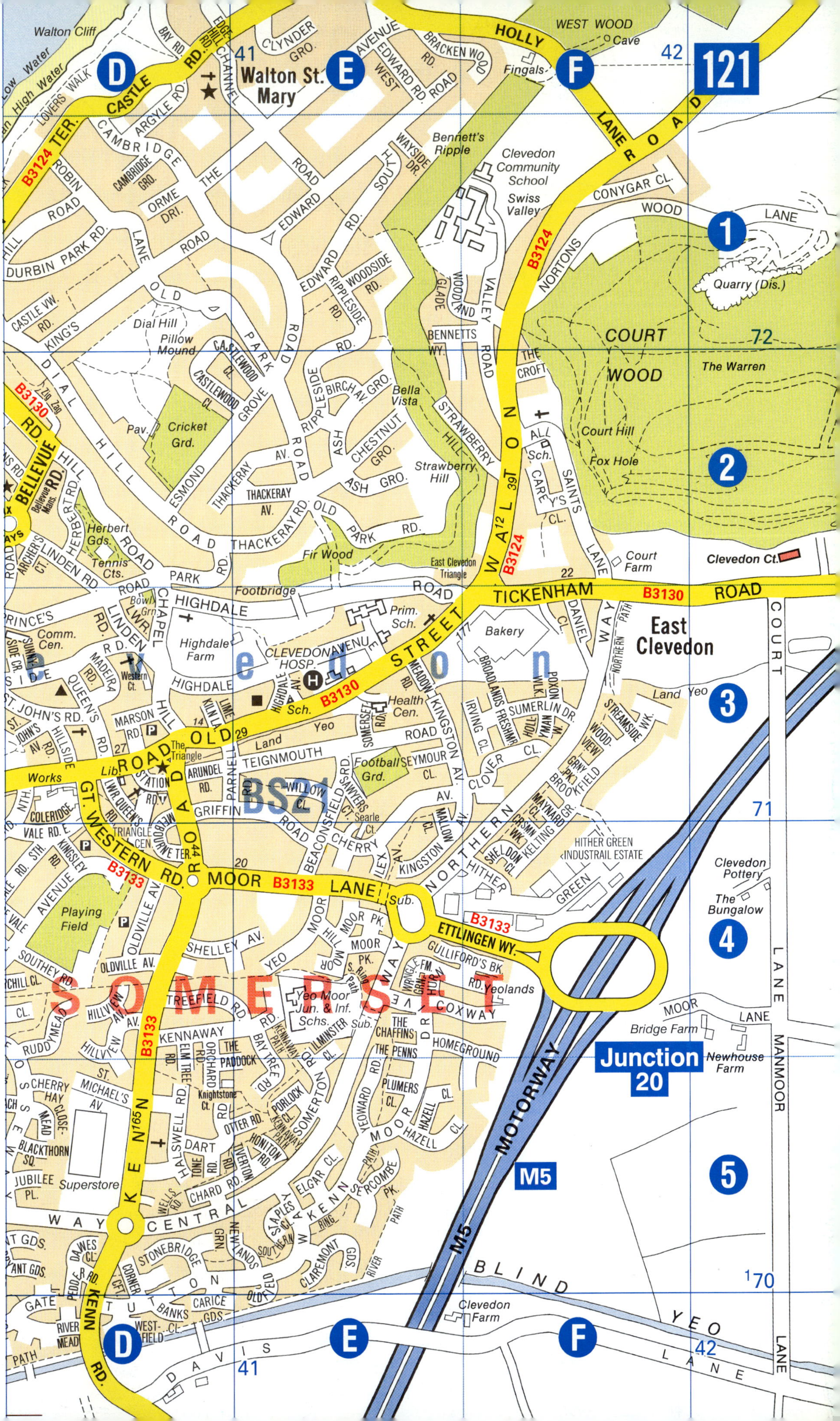
Walton St. Mary
Walton Cliff
High Water
Low Water
HOLLY LANE
WEST WOOD
Cave
Fingals
ROAD
CONYGAR CL.
WOOD LANE
Quarry (Dis.)
COURT WOOD
The Warren
Court Hill
Fox Hole
Clevedon Ct.
Court Farm
Clevedon Community School
Swiss Valley
Bennett's Ripple
NORTONS
WALTON
B3124
THE CROFT
ALL SAINTS
CAREY'S CL.
STRAWBERRY HILL
Strawberry Hill
Bella Vista
Fir Wood
East Clevedon Triangle
TICKENHAM ROAD
B3130
East Clevedon
Bakery
DANIEL CL.
NORTHERN PATH
Land Yeo
STREAMSIDE WK.
WOOD VIEW
BROOKFIELD
Clevedon
CLEVEDON HOSP.
Health Cen.
Football Grd.
Prim. Sch.
HIGHDALE
Highdale Farm
Footbridge
Comm. Cen.
Cricket Grd.
Pav.
Dial Hill
Pillow Mound
Herbert Gds.
Tennis Cts.
BELLEVUE RD.
CASTLE RD.
CASTLE TER.
B3124
CAMBRIDGE RD.
ORME DRI.
DURBIN PARK RD.
OLD PARK ROAD
DIAL HILL ROAD
KING'S
THACKERAY AV.
ESMOND GROVE
BIRCH AV.
CHESTNUT GRO.
ASH GRO.
OLD STREET
OLD ROAD
The Triangle
Lib.
Works
GT. WESTERN RD.
B3133
Playing Field
MOOR LANE
ETTLINGEN WY.
SOMERSET
BS21
TEIGNMOUTH
GRIFFIN ROAD
CHERRY
KINGSTON AV.
NORTHERN WAY
HITHER GREEN
HITHER GREEN INDUSTRAIL ESTATE
Clevedon Pottery
The Bungalow
Yeolands
MOOR LANE
Bridge Farm
Newhouse Farm
Junction 20
MANMOOR LANE
COURT LANE
M5
MOTORWAY
Yeo Moor Jun. & Inf. Schs.
KENN ROAD
KENNAWAY
SHELLEY AV.
OLDVILLE AV.
TREEFIELD RD.
CENTRAL WAY
Superstore
KENN MOOR
BLIND YEO
Clevedon Farm
DAVIS LANE
YEO LANE
Knightstone Ct.
HAZELL CL.
PLUMERS CL.
HOMEGROUND
COXWAY
THE CHAFFINS
THE PENNS
41
42
71
72
170
D
E
F
1
2
3
4
5

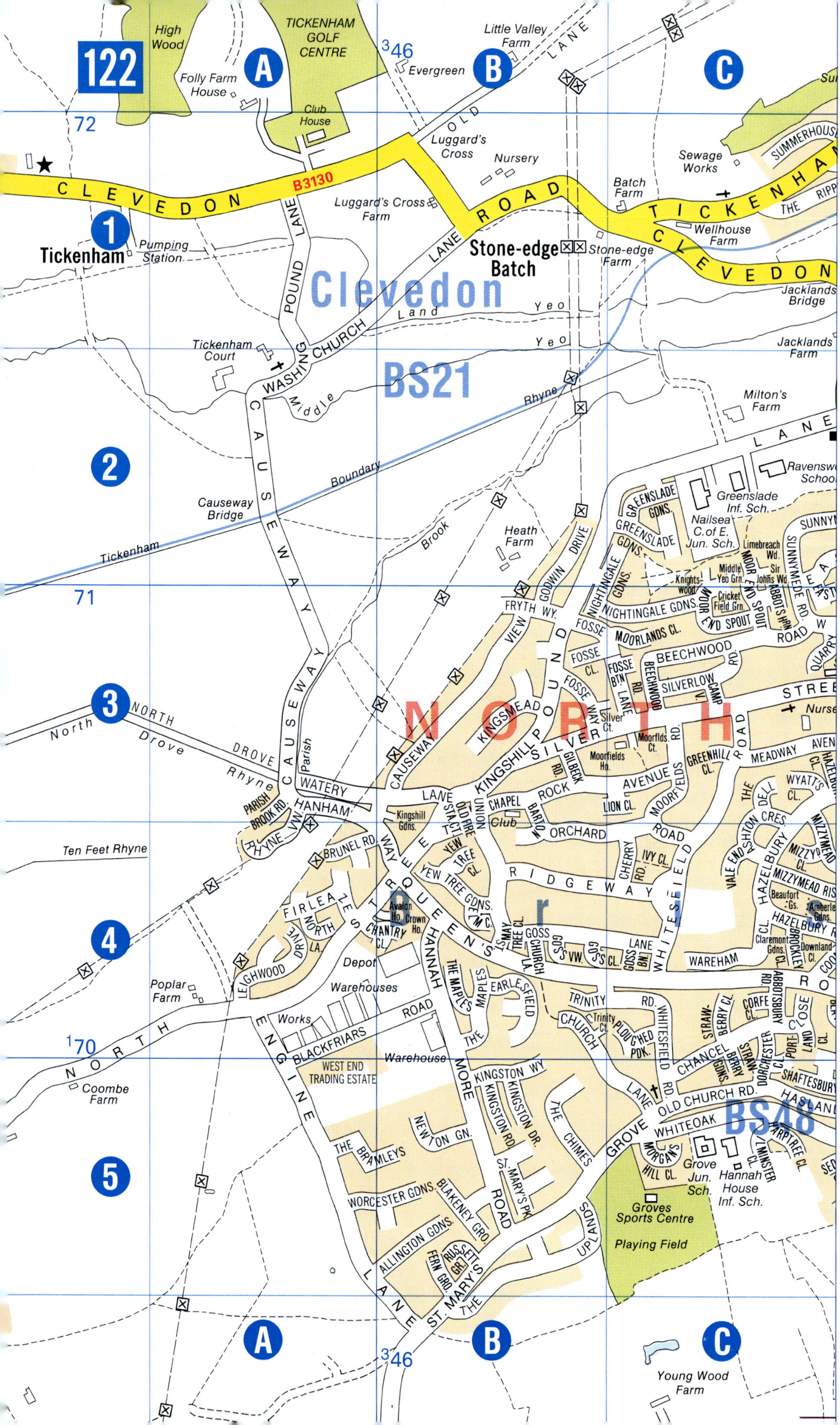

High Wood
TICKENHAM GOLF CENTRE
Folly Farm House
Club House
Little Valley Farm
Evergreen
346
72
71
170
A
B
C
1
2
3
4
5
CLEVEDON
B3130
ROAD
OLD
LANE
POUND LANE
Luggard's Cross
Nursery
Luggard's Cross Farm
Sewage Works
Batch Farm
SUMMERHOUSE
TICKENHAM
CLEVEDON
THE RIPP
Wellhouse Farm
Tickenham
Pumping Station
Stone-edge Batch
Stone-edge Farm
Jacklands Bridge
Clevedon
Land Yeo
Yeo
Jacklands Farm
Tickenham Court
WASHING CHURCH
BS21
Middle Rhyne
Milton's Farm
LANE
Ravenswood School
CAUSEWAY
Boundary
Causeway Bridge
Tickenham Brook
Heath Farm
GREENSLADE GDNS.
Greenslade Inf. Sch.
Nailsea C.of E. Jun. Sch.
SUNNYMEDE RD.
Limebreach Wd.
Knights-wood
Middle Yeo Grn.
Sir Johns Wd.
Cricket Field Grn.
MOOR END SPOUT
ABBOTSHORN
NIGHTINGALE GDNS.
GODWIN DRIVE
FRYTH WY.
VIEW
FOSSE
FOSSE CL.
FOSSE BTN.
FOSSE WAY
FOSSE LANE
MOORLANDS CL.
BEECHWOOD RD.
BEECHWOOD
SILVERLOW
CAMP V.
POUND
KINGSMEAD
STREET
Nurse
NORTH
Silver Ct.
Moorflds. Ct.
Moorfields Ho.
GREENHILL CL.
ROAD
MEADWAY
AVENUE
North Drove
NORTH DROVE Rhyne
Parish
WATERY LANE
KINGSHILL
SILVER
GILBECK RD.
ROCK
AVENUE
MOORFIELDS
THE DELL
WYATT'S CL.
PARISH BROOK RD.
HANHAM
RHYNE VW.
Kingshill Gdns.
STA. CT.
OLD FIRE
UNION
CHAPEL
Club
BARTON
ORCHARD
LION CL.
ROAD
ASHTON CRES.
MIZZYMEAD
Ten Feet Rhyne
BRUNEL RD.
WAY
YEW TREE CL.
YEW TREE GDNS.
RIDGEWAY
CHERRY RD.
IVY CL.
WHITESFIELD
VALE END
HAZELBURY
MIZZYMEAD RISE
Beaufort Gs.
Amberley Gdns.
HAZELBURY R
FIRLEA
NORTH LA.
DRIVE
LESTER
QUEEN'S
Avalon Ho.
Crown Ho.
CHANTRY CL.
M.C.
MAY TREE CL.
GOSS CHURCH LA.
GOSS VW.
GOSS CL.
GOSS LANE
GOSS BN.
WAREHAM
Claremont Gdns.
BROCKLEY
Downland Cl.
ROAD
LEIGHWOOD
Depot
Warehouses
HANNAH
THE MAPLES
EARLESFIELD
TRINITY RD.
Trinity Ct.
CHURCH
PLOUGHED PDK.
WHITESFIELD RD.
STRAWBERRY CL.
CORFE CL.
ABBOTSBURY RD.
CLOSE
PORTLAND CL.
Poplar Farm
Works
ROAD
BLACKFRIARS
ENGINE
Warehouse
WEST END TRADING ESTATE
MORE
KINGSTON WY.
KINGSTON RD.
KINGSTON DR.
THE CHIMES
LANE
CHANCEL
STRAWBERRY GDNS.
DORCHESTER CL.
SHAFTESBURY
HASLAND
OLD CHURCH RD.
NORTH
Coombe Farm
THE BRAMLEYS
NEWTON GN.
GROVE
WHITEOAK
BS48
MORGAN'S HILL CL.
Grove Jun. Sch.
Hannah House Inf. Sch.
HARPTREE CL.
MINSTER CL.
WORCESTER GDNS.
BLAKENEY GRO.
ST. MARY'S PK.
ROAD
UPLANDS
Groves Sports Centre
Playing Field
ALLINGTON GDNS.
RUSSETT GR.
FERN GRO.
THE ST. MARY'S
LANE
Young Wood Farm

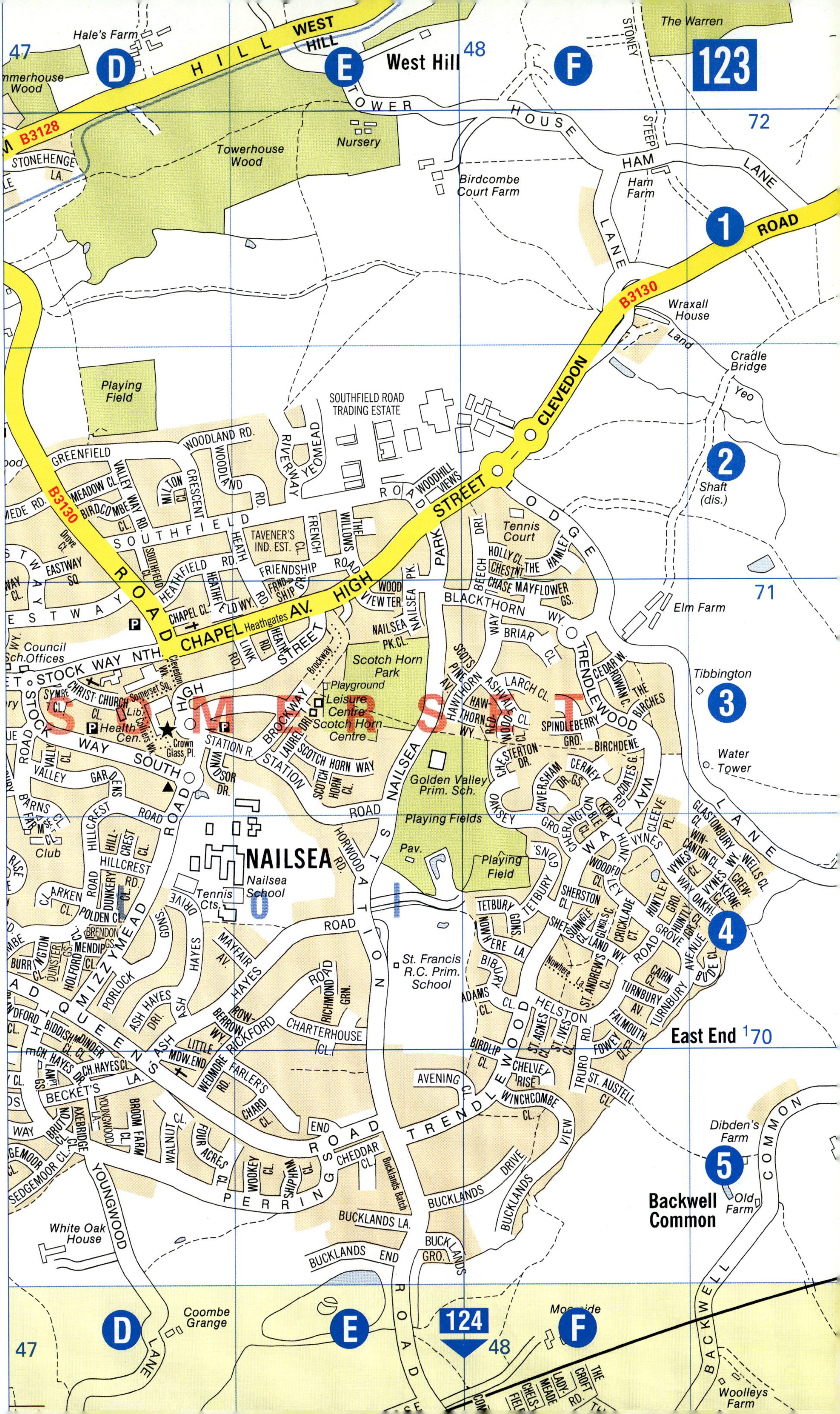
123
47
48
72
71
70
D
E
F
1
2
3
4
5
124
West Hill
WEST HILL
B3128
B3130
Hale's Farm
Summerhouse Wood
The Warren
STONEY STEEP
TOWER HOUSE LANE
HAM LANE
Ham Farm
Birdcombe Court Farm
Towerhouse Wood
Nursery
STONEHENGE LA.
CLEVEDON ROAD
Wraxall House
Land Yeo
Cradle Bridge
Shaft (dis.)
Playing Field
SOUTHFIELD ROAD TRADING ESTATE
GREENFIELD
WOODLAND RD.
RIVERWAY
YEOMEAD
VALLEY WAY RD.
MILTON CL.
CRESCENT
MEADOW CL.
BIRDCOMBE CL.
SOUTHFIELD RD.
TAVENER'S IND. EST.
FRENCH CL.
THE WILLOWS
WOODHILL VIEWS
HIGH STREET
LODGE DRI.
Tennis Court
HOLLY CL.
CHESTNT. CHASE
THE HAMLET
MAYFLOWER GS.
BLACKTHORN WY.
BRIAR CL.
EASTWAY SQ.
EASTWAY
DROVE CL.
HEATHFIELD RD.
FRIENDSHIP ROAD
CHAPEL AV.
Heathgates
CHAPEL CL.
LINK RD.
HEATH RD.
STREET
NAILSEA PK.CL.
Scotch Horn Park
Playground
Leisure Centre
Scotch Horn Centre
Council Offices
STOCK WAY NTH.
STOCK WAY SOUTH
CHRIST CHURCH CL.
Somerset Sq.
Lib.
Health Cen.
Crown Glass Pl.
SOMERSET
STATION ROAD
BROCKWAY
LAUREL DR.
SCOTCH HORN WAY
SCOTCH HORN CL.
WINDSOR DR.
NAILSEA
Nailsea School
Tennis Cts.
Golden Valley Prim. Sch.
Playing Fields
Pav.
Playing Field
HAWTHORN WY.
ASHVALE CL.
LARCH CL.
SPINDLEBERRY GRO.
TRENDLEWOOD WAY
CEDAR W.
ROWAN C.
THE BIRCHES
BIRCHDENE
CHESTERTON DR.
CAVERSHAM DR.
CERNEY GS.
COATES G.
OAKSEY GRO.
CHERINGTON RD.
Elm Farm
Tibbington
Water Tower
GLASTONBURY CL.
WELLS CL.
WINCANTON CL.
VYNES WAY
CREWKERNE CL.
HUNTLEY GRO.
CRICKLADE CT.
SHERSTON CL.
TETBURY GDNS.
WOODFORD CL.
TURNBURY AVENUE
CAIRN CL.
FALMOUTH CL.
FOWEY CL.
TRURO RD.
ST. AUSTELL CL.
HELSTON RD.
ST. AGNES CL.
ST. IVES CL.
St. Francis R.C. Prim. School
East End
HILLCREST RD.
DUNKERY RD.
POLDEN CL.
BRENDON GS.
MENDIP CL.
PORLOCK
MIZZYMEAD ROAD
QUEENS ROAD
ASH HAYES DRI.
MAYFAIR AV.
RICHMOND GRN.
CHARTERHOUSE CL.
RICKFORD
LITTLE MDW.END
WEDMORE RD.
FARLER'S ORCHARD
AVENING CL.
TRENDLEWOOD
WINCHCOMBE CL.
CHELVEY RISE
BIRDLIP CL.
ADAMS CL.
BIBURY
VIEW
BECKET'S LA.
CH. HAYES CL.
BROOM FARM CL.
WALNUT CL.
FOUR ACRES CL.
WOOKEY CL.
SHIPHAM CL.
CHEDDAR CL.
PERRINGS ROAD
Bucklands Batch
BUCKLANDS LA.
BUCKLANDS END
BUCKLANDS GRO.
BUCKLANDS DRIVE
YOUNGWOOD LANE
SEDGEMOOR CL.
AXBRIDGE CL.
White Oak House
Coombe Grange
Mosside
Dibden's Farm
Backwell Common
Old Farm
BACKWELL COMMON
Woolleys Farm
THE CROFT
LADYMEADE
CHELSFIELD

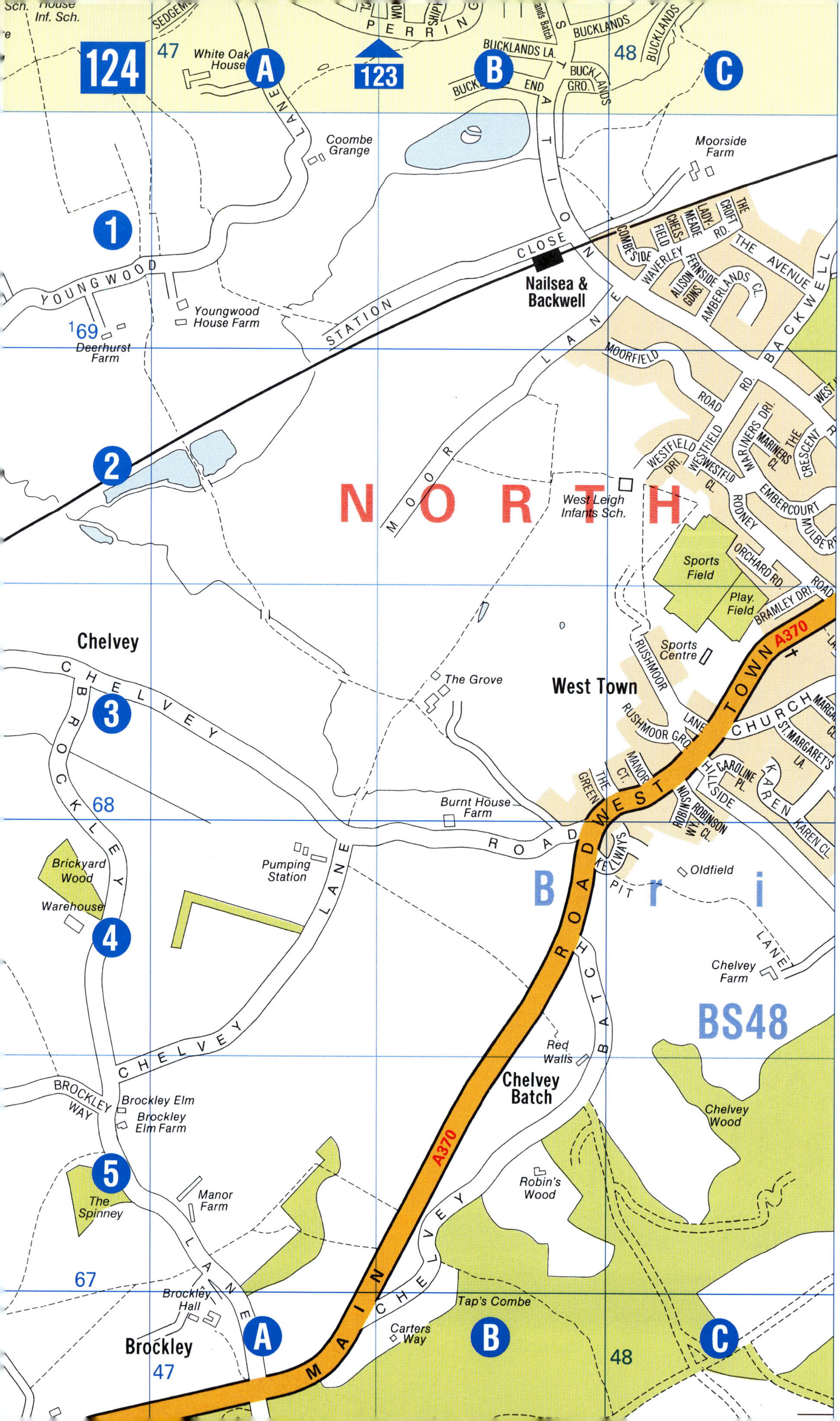
123
A
B
C
1
2
3
4
5
47
48
69
68
67
White Oak House
Coombe Grange
Moorside Farm
Youngwood House Farm
Deerhurst Farm
YOUNGWOOD
LANE
STATION CLOSE
STATION ROAD
Nailsea & Backwell
NORTH
MOOR LANE
West Leigh Infants Sch.
Sports Field
Play. Field
Sports Centre
The Grove
West Town
Chelvey
CHELVEY
BROCKLEY
Burnt House Farm
ROAD
Pumping Station
LANE
Brickyard Wood
Warehouse
CHELVEY
BROCKLEY WAY
Brockley Elm
Brockley Elm Farm
The Spinney
Manor Farm
LANE
Brockley Hall
Brockley
WEST TOWN ROAD
A370
MAIN ROAD
Red Walls
Chelvey Batch
BATCH
CHELVEY
Robin's Wood
Tap's Combe
Carters Way
Oldfield
PIT LANE
Chelvey Farm
BS48
Chelvey Wood
Bri
BUCKLANDS LA.
BUCKLANDS END
BUCKLANDS GRO.
BUCKLANDS
PERRING
COMBE SIDE
WAVERLEY
THE CROFT
LADY-MEADE
CHELS-FIELD
RD.
ALISON GDNS.
FERNSIDE
AMBERLANDS CL.
THE AVENUE
BACKWELL
MOORFIELD ROAD
RD.
WESTFIELD DRI.
WESTFIELD CL.
MARINERS DRI.
MARINERS CL.
THE CRESCENT
RODNEY
EMBERCOURT
ORCHARD RD.
BRAMLEY DRI.
ROAD
RUSHMOOR LANE
RUSHMOOR GRO.
CHURCH
ST. MARGARET'S LA.
CAROLINE PL.
HILLSIDE
KAREN
KAREN CL.
ROBINSON WY.
ROBINSON CL.
THE GREEN
MANOR CT.
KELLWAYS

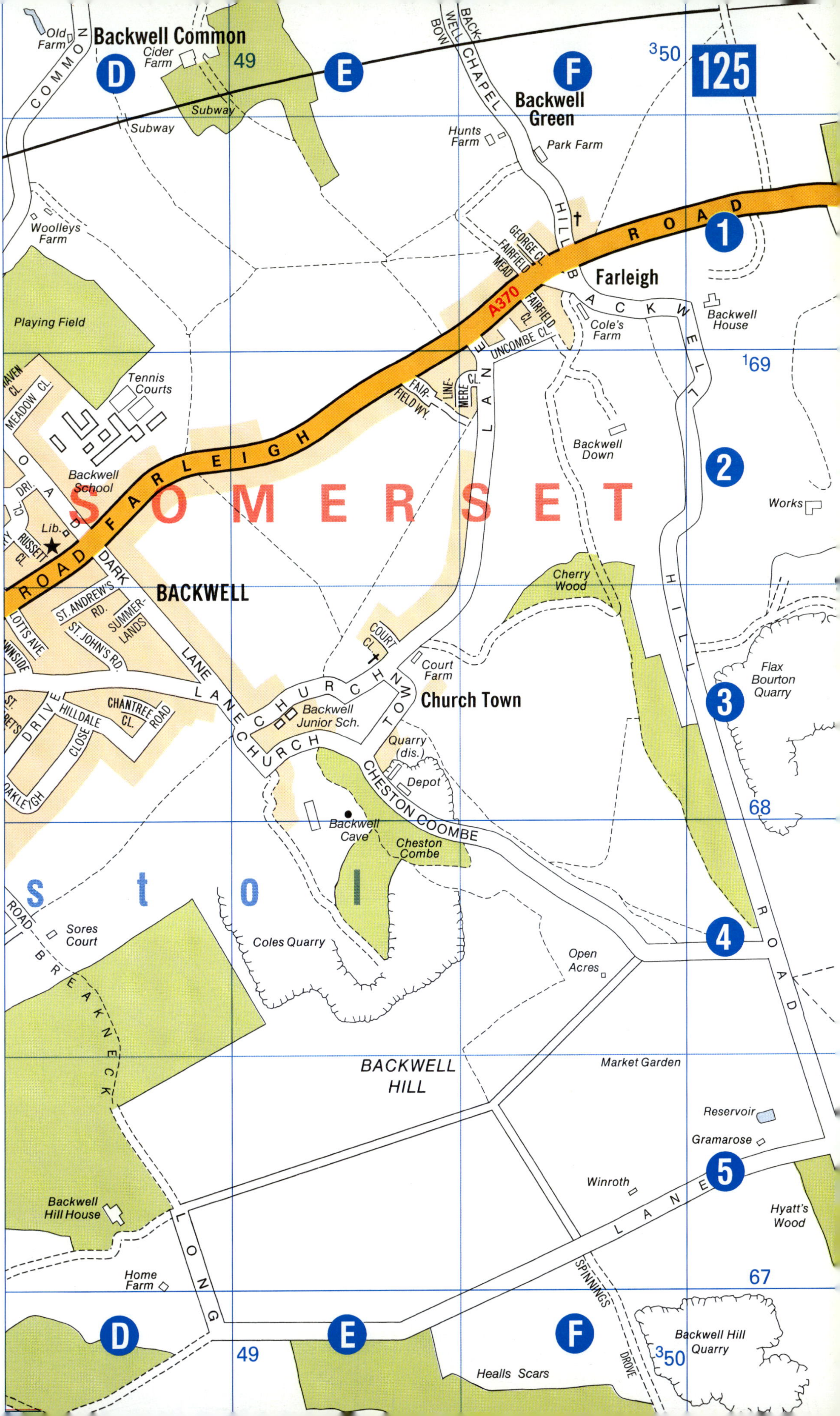
Backwell Common
Old Farm
Cider Farm
COMMON
D
E
F
49
350
Subway
Subway
BACK-WELL BOW
CHAPEL
Backwell Green
Hunts Farm
Park Farm
Woolleys Farm
HILL
GEORGE CL.
FAIRFIELD MEAD
ROAD
1
Farleigh
BACKWELL
Backwell House
A370
FAIRFIELD CL.
UNCOMBE CL.
Cole's Farm
Playing Field
169
Tennis Courts
HAVEN CL.
MEADOW CL.
FAIR-FIELD WY.
LINE-MERE CL.
LANE
Backwell Down
2
Backwell School
DRI.
RUSSETT CL.
Lib.
FARLEIGH ROAD
SOMERSET
Works
Cherry Wood
DARK
BACKWELL
ST. ANDREW'S RD.
SUMMER-LANDS
ST. JOHN'S RD.
LOTTS AVE.
COURT CL.
Court Farm
Flax Bourton Quarry
Church Town
3
HILLDALE
CHANTREY CL.
ROAD
DRIVE
CLOSE
OAKLEIGH
CHURCH LANE
Backwell Junior Sch.
CHURCH
TOWN
Quarry (dis.)
Depot
CHESTON COOMBE
68
Backwell Cave
Cheston Combe
S t o l
ROAD
Sores Court
BREAKNECK
Coles Quarry
Open Acres
4
BACKWELL HILL
Market Garden
Reservoir
Gramarose
5
Winroth
LANE
Backwell Hill House
Hyatt's Wood
LONG
Home Farm
SPINNINGS
67
Backwell Hill Quarry
DROVE
Healls Scars

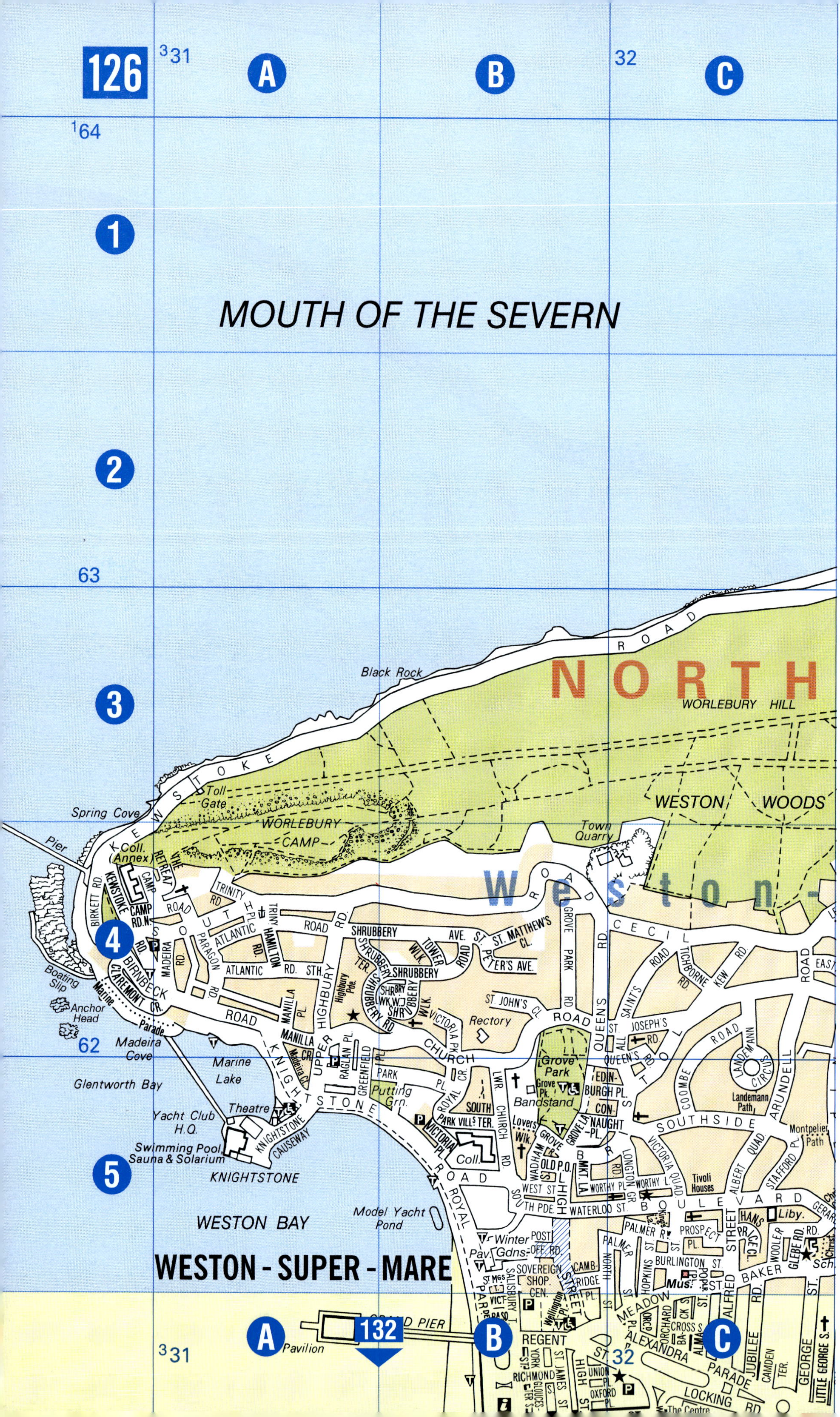

331
A
B
32
C
164
1
2
63
3
4
62
5
MOUTH OF THE SEVERN
NORTH
Weston-
WESTON - SUPER - MARE
WORLEBURY HILL
WESTON WOODS
Black Rock
Spring Cove
Pier
Toll Gate
WORLEBURY CAMP
Coll. Annex
Town Quarry
KEWSTOKE ROAD
SOUTH ROAD
BIRKETT RD
KENSTOKE
CAMP RD.N.
THE RETREAT
TRINITY RD
ATLANTIC RD
ATLANTIC RD. STH.
PARAGON RD
MADEIRA RD
HAMILTON RD
UPPER HIGHBURY RD.
SHRUBBERY AVE.
SHRUBBERY WLK.
SHRUBBERY TER.
SHRUBBERY RD
TOWER WLK.
ST. MATTHEW'S CL.
PETER'S AVE.
GROVE PARK RD
CECIL ROAD
TICHBORNE RD.
KEW RD
EAST
ST. JOHN'S CL
Rectory
Highbury Pde.
MANILLA PL.
MANILLA CR.
BIRNBECK RD
CLAREMONT CR.
Marine Parade
Boating Slip
Anchor Head
Madeira Cove
Marine Lake
Glentworth Bay
Theatre
Yacht Club H.Q.
Swimming Pool Sauna & Solarium
KNIGHTSTONE
KNIGHTSTONE CAUSEWAY
KNIGHTSTONE ROAD
WESTON BAY
Model Yacht Pond
RAGLAN PL.
GREENFIELD PL.
PARK PL.
Putting Grn.
CHURCH RD
VICTORIA PK.
ROYAL CR.
SOUTH TER.
PARK VILLS TER.
VICTORIA PL.
Coll.
LWR. CHURCH RD.
Grove Park
Bandstand
Lovers Wlk.
GROVE LA.
WADHAM ST.
OLD P.O.
MKT. LA.
EDINBURGH PL.
CONNAUGHT PL.
QUEEN'S RD
ALL SAINTS' RD
ST. JOSEPH'S RD
QUEEN'S
COOMBE RD
LANDEMANN CIRCUS
Landemann Path
ARUNDELL RD
SOUTHSIDE
VICTORIA QUAD
ALBERT QUAD
STAFFORD PL.
Montpelier Path
Tivoli Houses
LONGTON GR.
WORTHY PL.
WORTHY LA.
WEST ST.
SOUTH PDE.
WATERLOO ST.
BOULEVARD
HANS PRICE CL.
Liby.
GERARD RD.
GLEBE RD.
WOOLER RD.
PALMER ROW
PALMER ST.
PROSPECT PL.
ORCHARD ST.
NORTH ST.
HOPKINS ST.
BURLINGTON ST.
Mus.
ALFRED ST.
BAKER ST.
POPLAR PL.
Sch.
Winter Gdns.
Pav.
POST OFFICE RD.
SOVEREIGN SHOP. CEN.
SALISBURY TER.
CAMBRIDGE PL.
HIGH STREET
Wellington La.
MEADOW ST.
ORCHARD PL.
CROSS ST.
ALMA ST.
ALEXANDRA PARADE
JUBILEE RD.
CAMDEN TER.
GEORGE ST.
LITTLE GEORGE ST.
GRAND PIER
Pavilion
132
REGENT ST.
YORK ST.
RICHMOND ST.
ST. JAMES ST.
HIGH ST.
UNION PL.
OXFORD ST.
LOCKING RD
The Centre
ROYAL PARADE
331
32

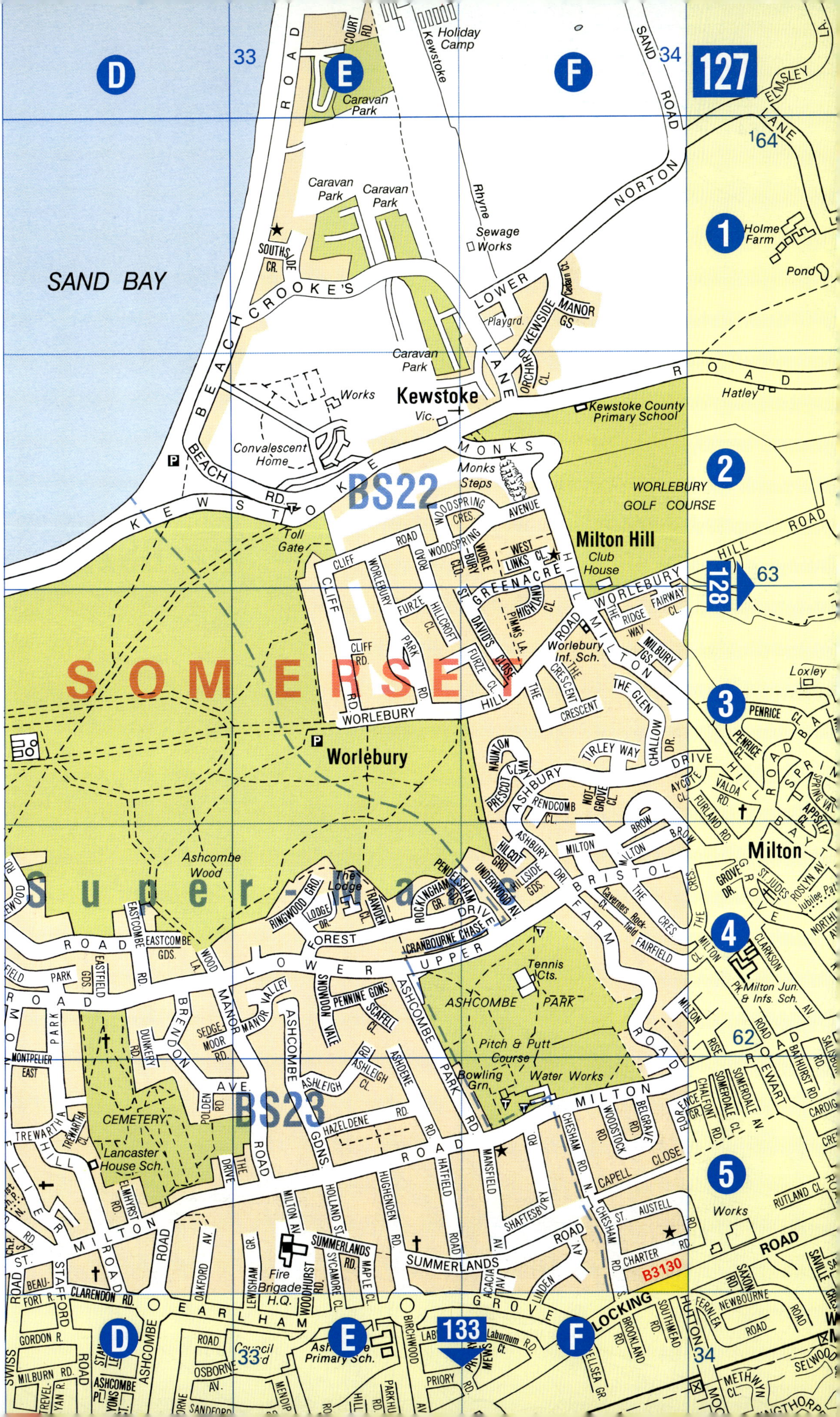
D
E
F
33
34
1
2
3
4
5
SAND BAY
SOMERSET
Super-Mare
BS22
BS23
Holiday Camp
Kewstoke
Caravan Park
Caravan Park
Caravan Park
Caravan Park
ROAD
COURT RD.
SAND ROAD
ELMSLEY LA.
LANE
164
NORTON
Rhyne
Sewage Works
Holme Farm
Pond
SOUTHSIDE CR.
CROOKE'S
LOWER
Playgrd.
KEWSIDE
Cotean Cl.
MANOR GS.
ORCHARD CL.
BEACH
Works
Kewstoke
Vic.
ROAD
Hatley
Kewstoke County Primary School
Convalescent Home
BEACH RD.
KEWSTOKE
Toll Gate
MONKS
Monks Steps
AVENUE
WOODSPRING CRES.
WORLEBURY GOLF COURSE
Milton Hill
Club House
HILL ROAD
128
63
CLIFF
ROAD
WORLEBURY
WOODSPRING
WORLE BURY CLO.
WEST LINKS CL.
GREENACRE
HIGHLAND CL.
PIMMS LA.
ST. DAVID'S CLOSE
FURZE CL.
HILLCROFT CL.
PARK RD.
CLIFF RD.
FURZE CL.
HILL
WORLEBURY
MILTON
THE RIDGE WAY
FAIRWAY CL.
MILBURY GS.
Worlebury Inf. Sch.
THE CRESCENT
CRESCENT
THE GLEN
CHALLOW DR.
Loxley
PENRICE CL.
PENRICE
Worlebury
TIRLEY WAY
DRIVE
AYCOTE CL.
VALDA RD.
FURLAND RD.
SPRING VALE
APPSLEY CL.
BAYHILL ROAD
NAUNTON WAY
PRESCOT CL.
ASHBURY
RENDCOMB CL.
NORTHGROVE CL.
BROW
MILTON BROW
Milton
HILCOT GRO.
ASHBURY DRI.
MILTON
BRISTOL
GROVE DR.
ST JUDES
ROSLYN AV.
Jubilee Path
GROVE
Ashcombe Wood
The Lodge
PENDLESHAM GDS.
UNDERWOOD AV.
HILLSIDE GDS.
FARM
Caveners Cl.
Rockfield
THE CRES
FAIRFIELD
MILTON CL.
CLARKSON AV.
Milton Jun. & Infs. Sch.
RINGWOOD GRO.
LODGE DR.
TRAWDEN CL.
ROCKINGHAM GR.
DRIVE
CRANBOURNE CHASE
FOREST
UPPER
EASTCOMBE RD.
EASTCOMBE GDS.
WOOD LA.
LOWER
ROAD
PARK
EASTFIELD GDS.
FIELD
Tennis Cts.
ASHCOMBE PARK
MONTPELIER EAST
PARK
BRENDON
MANOR
MANOR VALLEY
SEDGEMOOR RD.
ASHCOMBE
SNOWDON VALE
PENNINE GDNS.
SCAFELL CL.
ASHCOMBE PARK RD.
Pitch & Putt Course
Bowling Grn.
Water Works
MILTON RISE
62
EWART ROAD
BATHURST RD
SALISBURY
DUNKERY RD.
POLDEN RD.
AVE.
ASHLEIGH
ASHLEIGH CL.
ASHDENE RD.
HAZELDENE RD.
MILTON
CHALFONT RD.
SOMERDALE CL.
SOMERDALE AV.
CARDIGAN
CHESHAM RD. N.
WOODSTOCK RD.
BELGRAVE RD
FLORENCE GR.
CAPELL CLOSE
TREWARTHA HILL
TREWARTHA CL.
CEMETERY
Lancaster House Sch.
ELMHYRST RD.
THE DRIVE
ROAD
GDNS.
ROAD
HATFIELD RD.
MANSFIELD AV.
SHAFTESBURY ROAD
RUTLAND CL.
Works
ST. AUSTELL RD.
CHESHAM RD.
CHARTER RD.
B3130
ROAD
MILTON ROAD
ROAD
OAKFORD AV.
MILTON AV.
HOLLAND ST.
HUGHENDEN RD.
SUMMERLANDS RD.
SUMMERLANDS
Fire Brigade H.Q.
LEWISHAM GR.
WOODHURST RD.
SYCAMORE CL.
MAPLE CL.
ACACIA AV.
LINDEN AV.
SOUTHMEAD RD.
HUTTON
ST.
STAFFORD ROAD
BEAU-FORT R.
CLARENDON RD.
EARLHAM
GROVE
LOCKING
BROOKLAND RD.
FERNLEA
NEWBOURNE ROAD
SAXON RD.
SAVILLE CRES.
GORDON R.
SWISS ROAD
MILBURN RD.
TREVELYAN R.
ASHCOMBE PL.
LYONS CT.
ROAD
OSBORNE AV.
Council Yd
Ashcombe Primary Sch.
BIRCHWOOD AV.
133
Laburnum Ct.
Laburnum RD.
PRIORY
PRIORY MEWS
ELLSEA GR.
METHWYN CL.
SELWOOD
34

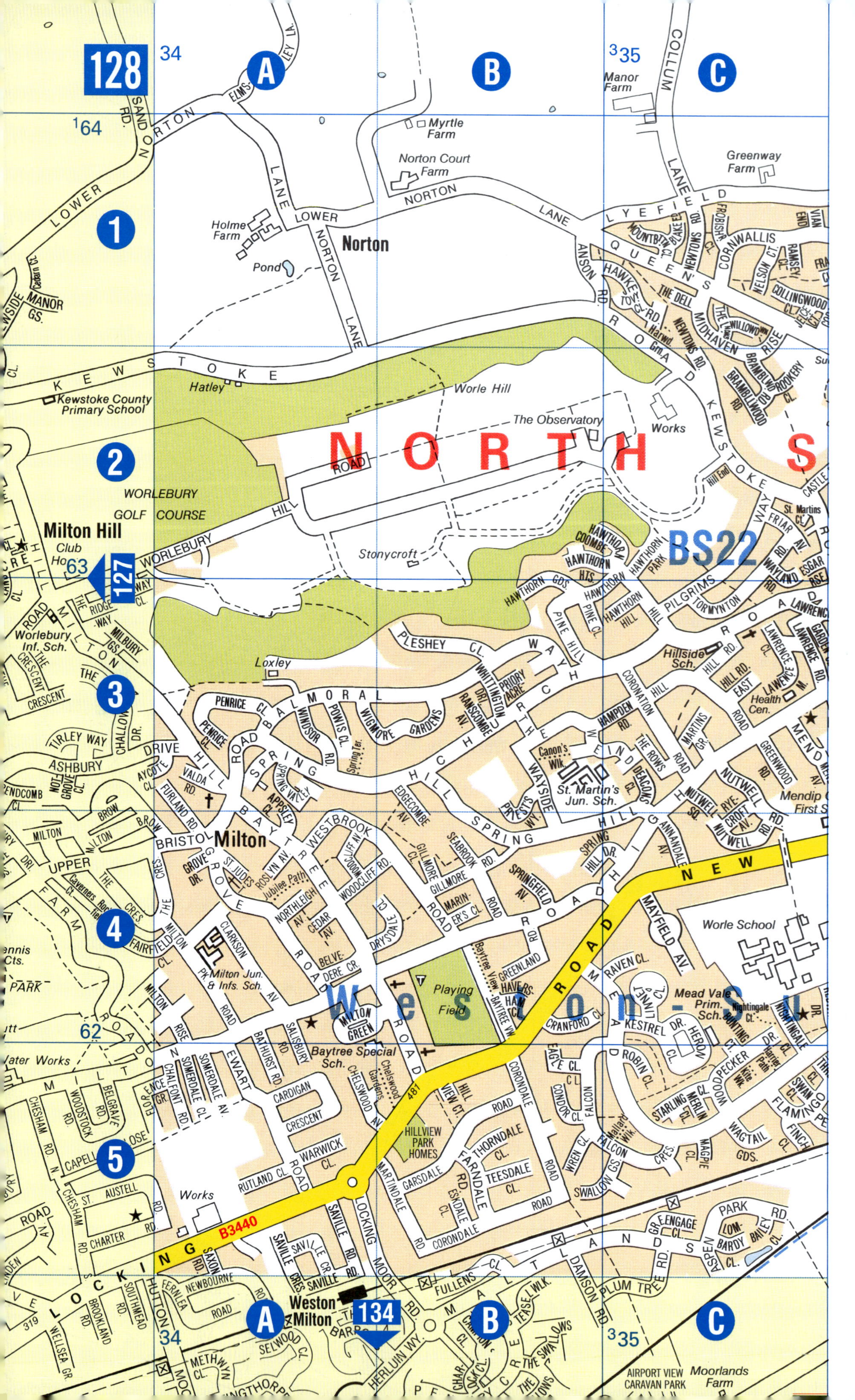
NORTH
BS22
Norton
Milton Hill
Milton
Weston Milton
Worle Hill
The Observatory
Works
Stonycroft
Loxley
Hatley
Kewstoke County Primary School
WORLEBURY GOLF COURSE
Club Ho
Worlebury Inf. Sch.
Myrtle Farm
Norton Court Farm
Manor Farm
Greenway Farm
Holme Farm
Pond
LOWER NORTON LANE
NORTON LANE
KEWSTOKE ROAD
WORLEBURY HILL ROAD
MILTON ROAD
SPRING HILL
BRISTOL ROAD
BAYTREE ROAD
NEW ROAD
LOCKING ROAD
B3440
LYEFIELD RD.
QUEENS RD.
COLLUM LANE
ANSON RD.
CORNWALLIS
MIDHAVEN RISE
BRAMBLEWOOD RD.
HAWTHORN HILL
PILGRIMS WAY
TORMYNTON ROAD
CHURCH ROAD
CORONATION RD.
HAMPDEN RD.
BALMORAL WAY
PLESHEY CL.
PENRICE CL.
WINDSOR RD.
POWIS CL.
WIGMORE GARDENS
WHITTINGTON DR.
PRIORY ACRE
RANSCOMBE AV.
Canon's Wlk.
St. Martin's Jun. Sch.
Hillside Sch.
Health Cen.
St. Martins Cl.
MENDIP AV.
Mendip First S
NUTWELL SQ.
GREENWOOD RD.
WESTBROOK RD.
WOODCLIFF RD.
GILLMORE CL.
SEABROOK RD.
SPRINGFIELD AV.
MARINER'S CL.
Worle School
MAYFIELD AV.
RAVEN CL.
Mead Vale Prim. Sch.
KESTREL DR.
HERON
WOODPECKER
STARLING CL.
MERLIN CL.
FLAMINGO
WAGTAIL GDS.
FALCON CRES.
SWALLOW GS.
CRANFORD CL.
GREENLAND RD.
Baytree View
Playing Field
Milton Jun. & Infs. Sch.
Baytree Special Sch.
MILTON GREEN
CARDIGAN CRESCENT
WARWICK CL.
RUTLAND CL.
HILLVIEW PARK HOMES
FARNDALE RD.
THORNDALE CL.
TEESDALE CL.
CORONDALE RD.
GARSDALE
MARTINDALE RD.
SAVILLE RD.
LOCKING MOOR RD.
LANDS RD.
GREENGAGE CL.
ASPEN PARK RD.
LOMBARDY CL.
DAMSON RD.
PLUM TREE RD.
FULLENS CL.
TEASEL WLK.
THE SWALLOWS
HERLUIN WY.
AIRPORT VIEW CARAVAN PARK
Moorlands Farm
Water Works
PARK
UPPER MILTON
FARM
ASHBURY DRIVE
TIRLEY WAY
CHALLOW DR.
THE CRESCENT
MANOR GS.
ST. AUSTELL RD.
CHARTER RD.
CHESHAM RD.
BELGRAVE RD.
WOODSTOCK RD.
CHALFONT RD.
SOMERDALE AV.
EWART RD.
BATHURST RD.
SALISBURY RD.
CLARKSON AV.
NEWBOURNE RD.
SELWOOD CL.
METHWYN CL.
WELLSEA GR.
BROOKLAND RD.
SOUTHMEAD RD.
HUTTON
34
35
164
63
62
319
481
A
B
C
1
2
3
4
5
127
134

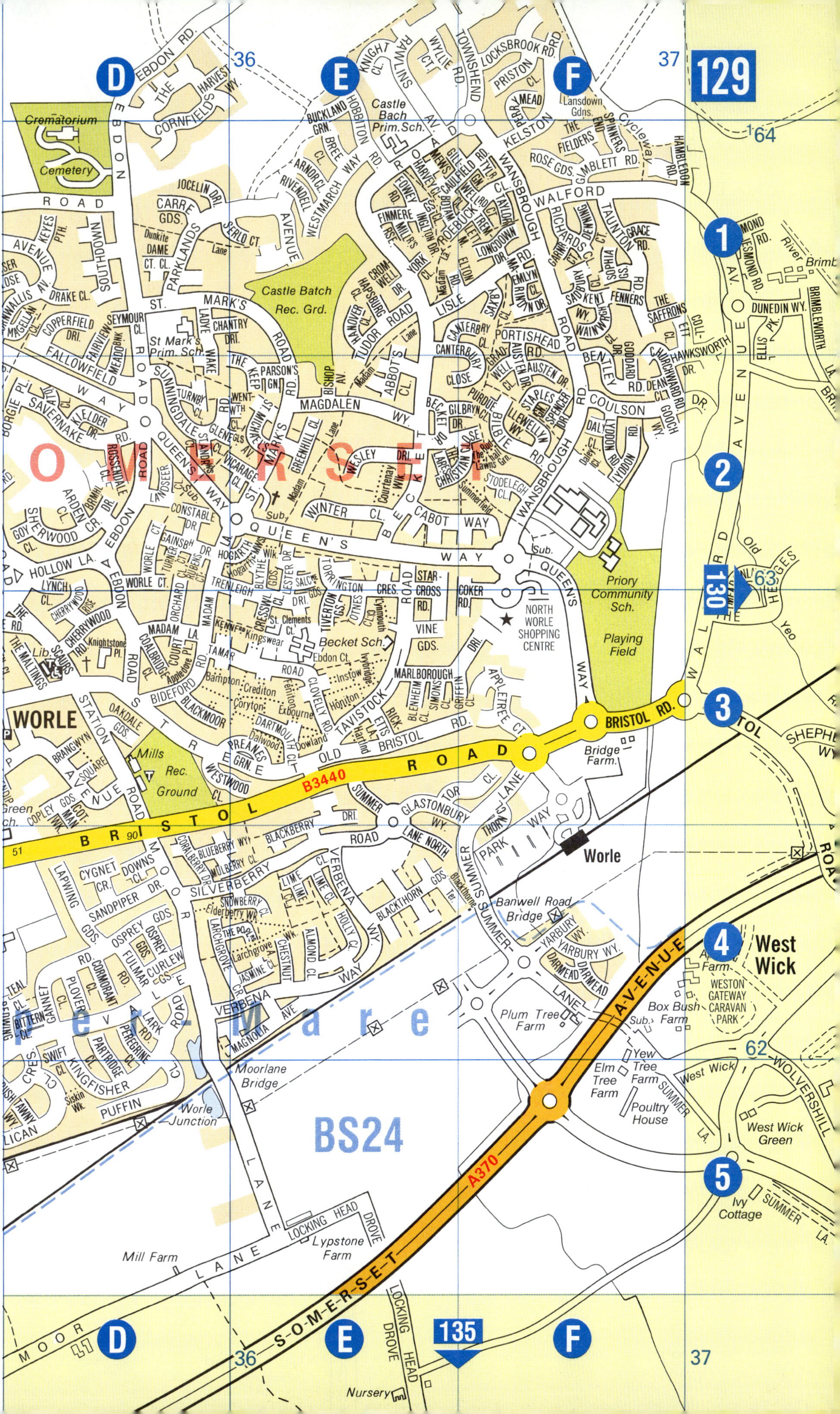
D
E
F
36
37
64
63
62
1
2
3
4
5
130
135
Crematorium
Cemetery
EBDON RD.
THE CORNFIELDS
HARVEST WY.
Castle Bach Prim.Sch.
Castle Batch Rec. Grd.
St Mark's Prim. Sch.
Priory Community Sch.
Playing Field
NORTH WORLE SHOPPING CENTRE
Becket Sch.
WORLE
Mills Rec. Ground
Bridge Farm
Worle
Banwell Road Bridge
Plum Tree Farm
Elm Tree Farm
Yew Tree Farm
Poultry House
Box Bush Farm
WESTON GATEWAY CARAVAN PARK
West Wick
West Wick Green
Ivy Cottage
Moorlane Bridge
Worle Junction
Mill Farm
Lypstone Farm
Nursery
BS24
SOMERSET
Weston-super-Mare
BRISTOL ROAD
B3440
A370
SOMERSET AVENUE
WALFORD AVENUE
QUEEN'S WAY
MAGDALEN WY.
WANSBROUGH RD.
STATION ROAD
MOOR LANE
LOCKING HEAD DROVE
SUMMER LANE
GLASTONBURY WY.
SILVERBERRY ROAD
KELSTON RD.
HAWKSWORTH DR.
DUNEDIN WY.
WOLVERSHILL

37
A
B
C
38
M5
M5 MOTORWAY
Weston-Su
BS22
Lane
Walford
Lansdown Gdns.
The Fielders
Gimblett Rd.
Hambledon Rd.
Taunton Rd.
Richards Cl.
Sophia Gdns.
Sadbury Cl.
Kent Wy.
Fenners
The Saffrons
Bentley Rd.
Goddard Dr.
Churchward Rd.
Hawksworth Dr.
Dean Cl.
Gooch Wy.
Coulson Dr.
Daly Cl.
Lyddon Rd.
Jesmond Rd.
Dunedin Wy.
Ellis Pk.
Brimbleworth La.
Brimbleworth Farm
River Banwell
Walford Avenue
Poplar Farm
Bourton Lane
Grove Farm
Works
Grape Vine Farm
Depot
Road
Priory Community Sch.
Old Yeo
The Meadowlands
The Hedges
Queen's Way
Playing Field
Trelawn Cl.
St. Georges
Vale Cr.
Willow Gdns.
Station Rd.
Rhyne
Willow Close
Shepherd's Wy.
Goosey La.
Bristol Road
B3130
Bridge Farm
Worle
Somerset Avenue
A370
Junction 21
Haybow Farm
Double Farm
New
Poplar Farm
Brick House Farm
Way Wick
Waywick Farm
NORTH S
Yarbury Wy.
Darmead
Lane
West Wick
Apple Farm
Weston Gateway Caravan Park
Box Bush Farm
Sub.
Camping Site
Yew Tree Farm
Elm Tree Farm
Poultry House
Summer La.
West Wick
Wolvershill Road
Westacres Farm
West Wick Green
Old Yeo Rhyne
Ivy Cottage
Summer La.
Blind Yeo Rhyne
Wolvershill Road
Refinery
Eton Lane
1
2
3
4
5
62
63
64
129
136

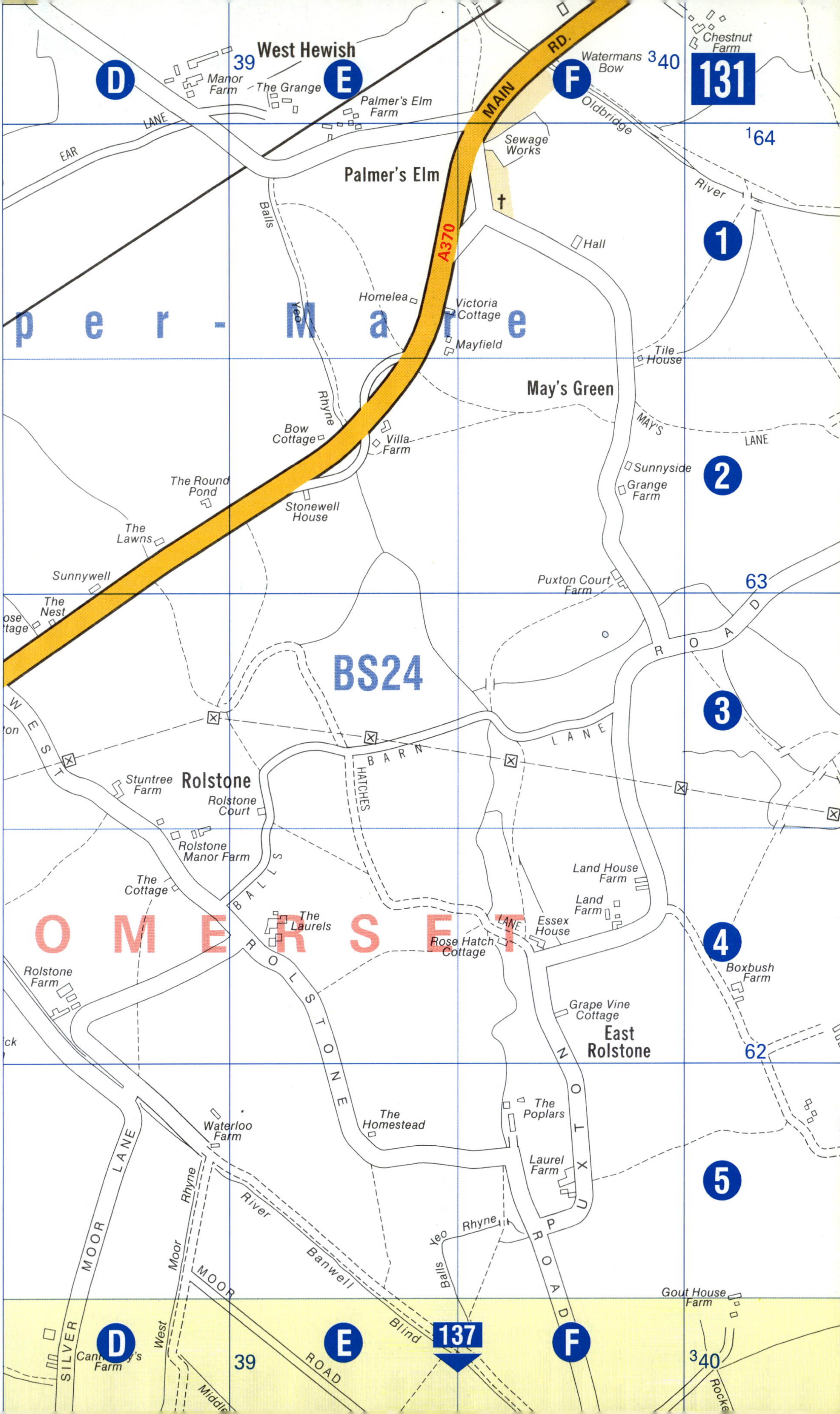

West Hewish
Manor Farm
The Grange
Palmer's Elm Farm
Watermans Bow
Chestnut Farm
Oldbridge
River
MAIN RD.
Sewage Works
EAR LANE
Palmer's Elm
Balls
A370
Hall
Homelea
Victoria Cottage
Mayfield
Yeo
per-Mare
Tile House
May's Green
MAY'S LANE
Rhyne
Bow Cottage
Villa Farm
Sunnyside
Grange Farm
The Round Pond
Stonewell House
The Lawns
Sunnywell
Puxton Court Farm
The Nest
BS24
ROAD
LANE
BARN
HATCHES
WEST
Stuntree Farm
Rolstone
Rolstone Court
Rolstone Manor Farm
BALLS
The Cottage
The Laurels
LANE
Essex House
Rose Hatch Cottage
Land House Farm
Land Farm
OMERSET
ROLSTONE
Boxbush Farm
Rolstone Farm
Grape Vine Cottage
East Rolstone
PUXTON ROAD
The Poplars
The Homestead
Waterloo Farm
Laurel Farm
MOOR LANE
Rhyne
River Banwell
Yeo Rhyne
Moor
Balls
MOOR ROAD
Blind
Gout House Farm
SILVER
West
Middle
Rocke
D
E
F
1
2
3
4
5
39
340
164
63
62
137

WESTON - SUPER - MARE
WESTON
BAY
KNIGHTSTONE
Model Yacht Pond
126
138
A
B
C
1
2
3
4
5
331
32
61
160
59
GRAND PIER
Pavilion
Tropicana Leisure Complex
Model Yacht Pond
Putting Green
Club House
WESTON-SUPER-MARE GOLF COURSE
Uphill Road Sports Ground
The Plantation
Uphill Manor
UPHILL
Westhaven School
Rectory
ROYAL PDE.
MARINE PARADE
BEACH ROAD
UPHILL ROAD NORTH
UPHILL ROAD SOUTH
A370
A3033
REGENT ST.
HIGH ST.
OXFORD ST.
UNION ST.
ST JAMES ST.
RICHMOND ST.
CARLTON ST.
WALLISCOTE RD.
WALLISCOTE ROAD
DOLPHIN SQ.
LOCKING RD.
ALEXANDRA PARADE
STATION RD.
MEADOW ST.
ORCHARD ST.
ALFRED ST.
JUBILEE RD.
CAMDEN TER.
GEORGE ST.
LITTLE GEORGE ST.
BAKER ST.
BURLINGTON ST.
BOULEVARD
WATERLOO ST.
WEST ST.
SOUTH PDE.
SOVEREIGN SHOP. CEN.
The Centre
Superstore
Town Hall
Council Offs.
Clinic
Walliscote Prim. Sch.
Birnbeck Ct.
BEACONSFIELD RD.
GRAHAM RD.
NEVA RD.
Weston-super-Mare
Squash Cen. & Gym.
Sports Ground
SUNNYSIDE ROAD
Ashbrooke School
ELLENBOROUGH PK. NORTH
ELLENBOROUGH PK. SOUTH
Ellenborough Park
Corpus Christi R.C. Prim. Sch.
ALBERT RD.
ALBERT AV.
RIDGEWAY AV.
DICKENSON RD.
PITMAN RD.
ADDICOTT RD.
CLEVEDON ROAD
CLIFTON ROAD
SEVERN ROAD
NEWTON RD.
LANGPORT RD.
WHITECROSS RD.
CLARENCE RD. NORTH
CLARENCE RD. SOUTH
NORTH
Vic.
ST. PAUL'S RD.
EXETER RD.
AVENUE RD.
Clarence Park
Bowling Grns.
Pav.
Cricket Ground
QUANTOCK ROAD
MOORLAND ROAD
Heathgates
CHARLTON ROAD
Sch.
WOODLAND RD.
ELMSLEIGH ROAD
BREAN RD.
BROADOAK ROAD
Broadoak School
Playing Field
DOWN AVENUE
DELAPRE RD.
FRENCHAY RD.
LYNDHURST RD.
SOUTHEND RD.
NITHSDALE RD.
Weston
BS23
DEVONSHIRE ROAD
DROVE ROAD
WHITTING RD.
BEDFORD RD.
SOUTHVILLE RD.
SELBOURNE RD.
ADDISCOMBE RD.
STANHOPE RD.
BOUNDARY CL.
WINDWHISTLE RD.
WINDWHISTLE
Windwhistle Open Space
Cricket Ground
Cricket Ground
BRIDGWATER ROAD
WINGARD CL.
AUBYN AV.
THE PADDOCKS
MOSELEY GRO.
NEW CHURCH RD.

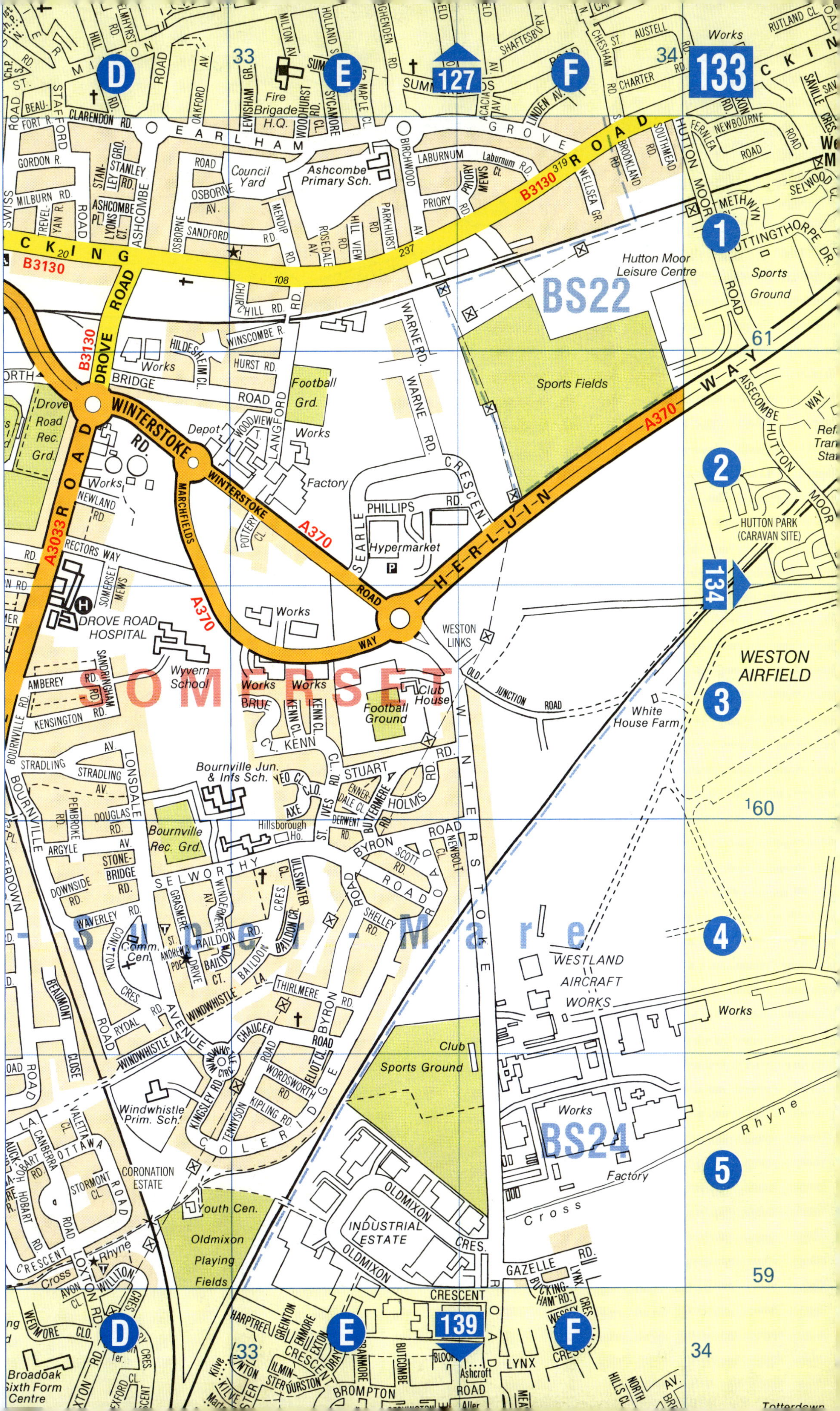

127
134
139
D
E
F
1
2
3
4
5
33
34
61
160
59
BS22
BS24
SOMERSET
Super-Mare
B3130
A370
A3033
WINTERSTOKE ROAD
HERLUIN WAY
DROVE ROAD
EARLHAM GROVE
Fire Brigade H.Q.
Council Yard
Ashcombe Primary Sch.
Hutton Moor Leisure Centre
Sports Fields
Sports Ground
Football Grd.
Works
Factory
Depot
Hypermarket
PHILLIPS RD.
SEARLE CRESCENT
WARNE RD.
MARCHFIELDS
Drove Road Rec. Grd.
DROVE ROAD HOSPITAL
Wyvern School
Football Ground
Club House
WESTON LINKS
OLD JUNCTION ROAD
White House Farm
WESTON AIRFIELD
HUTTON PARK (CARAVAN SITE)
Bournville Jun. & Infs Sch.
Bournville Rec. Grd.
Hillsborough Ho.
SELWORTHY
Comm. Cen.
WESTLAND AIRCRAFT WORKS
Club
Sports Ground
Windwhistle Prim. Sch.
CORONATION ESTATE
Youth Cen.
Oldmixon Playing Fields
INDUSTRIAL ESTATE
OLDMIXON CRES.
OLDMIXON CRESCENT
Rhyne
Cross
GAZELLE RD.
LYNX CRES.
Broadoak Sixth Form Centre
BROMPTON
Ashcroft
CLARENDON RD.
STAFFORD
GORDON R.
MILBURN RD.
OSBORNE AV.
SANDFORD RD.
MENDIP
ROSEDALE AV.
HILL VIEW
PARKHURST
BIRCHWOOD
LABURNUM
Laburnum Ct.
PRIORY RD.
PRIORY MEWS
WELLSEA GR.
BROOKLAND RD.
SOUTHMEAD RD.
HUTTON MOOR ROAD
METHWYN
OTTINGTHORPE DR.
AISECOMBE WAY
HILDESHEIM CL.
WINSCOMBE R.
HURST RD.
LANGFORD
WOODVIEW
POTTERY CL.
RECTORS WAY
NEWLAND RD.
SOMERSET MEWS
SANDRINGHAM RD.
AMBERLEY RD.
KENSINGTON RD.
BOURNVILLE RD.
STRADLING AV.
LONSDALE AV.
PEMBROKE RD.
DOUGLAS RD.
ARGYLE AV.
STONEBRIDGE RD.
DOWNSIDE RD.
WAVERLEY RD.
STUART RD.
HOLMS RD.
BYRON ROAD
SCOTT RD.
SHELLEY RD.
NEWBOLT CL.
WINTERSTOKE ROAD
GRASMERE DRIVE
WINDERMERE AV.
ULLSWATER CL.
BAILDON RD.
BAILDON CT.
THIRLMERE RD.
WINDWHISTLE LA.
AVENUE
CHAUCER ROAD
WORDSWORTH RD.
KIPLING RD.
ELIOT CL.
COLERIDGE
KINGSLEY RD.
TENNYSON
OTTAWA RD.
CANBERRA
STORMONT CL.
HOBART RD.
VALETTA CL.
WILLITON CRES.
AVON CL.
LOXTON RD.
WESTMORE CL.
BUCKINGHAM RD.
WESSEX CRES.
HARPTREE
GREINTON
ENMORE
CRESCENT
BUTCOMBE
DURSTON
KILVE
ILMINSTER
Works

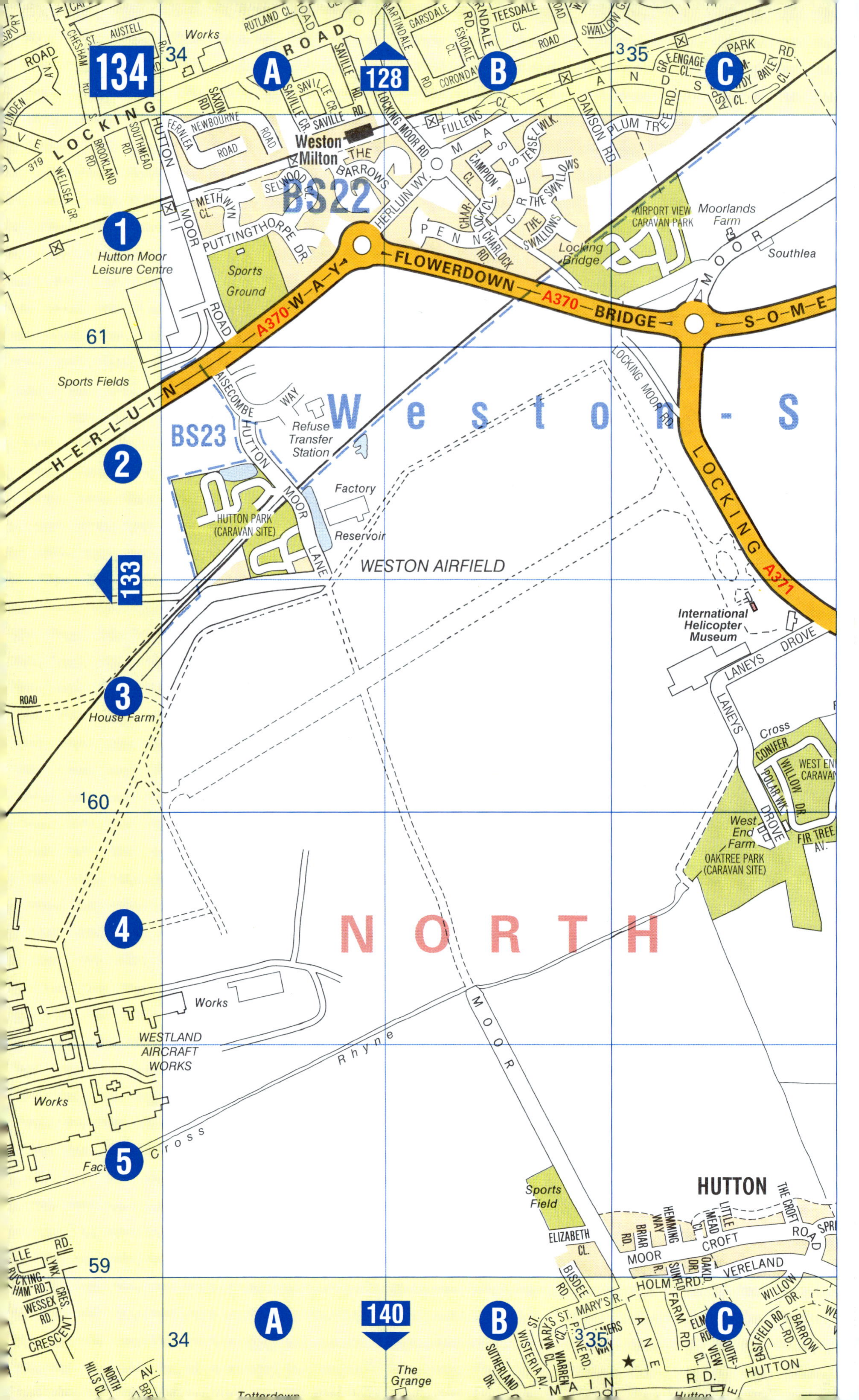
128
133
140
A
B
C
1
2
3
4
5
34
35
61
160
59
LOCKING ROAD
Weston Milton
BS22
BS23
Hutton Moor Leisure Centre
Sports Ground
PUTTINGTHORPE DR.
HUTTON MOOR ROAD
FLOWERDOWN BRIDGE
A370
A371
HERLUIN WAY
AIRPORT VIEW CARAVAN PARK
Moorlands Farm
Southlea
Locking Bridge
MOOR
Sports Fields
AISECOMBE WAY
Refuse Transfer Station
Weston-S
HUTTON PARK (CARAVAN SITE)
Factory
Reservoir
HUTTON MOOR LANE
WESTON AIRFIELD
LOCKING MOOR RD.
LOCKING
International Helicopter Museum
LANEYS DROVE
Cross
CONIFER
WILLOW DR.
POLAR WK.
West End Farm
OAKTREE PARK (CARAVAN SITE)
FIR TREE AV.
House Farm
NORTH
Works
WESTLAND AIRCRAFT WORKS
Rhyne
Cross
MOOR
Sports Field
HUTTON
ELIZABETH CL.
MOOR CROFT
VERELAND ROAD
HOLM RD.
BISDEE RD.
ST. MARY'S R.
SUTHERLAND DR.
WISTERIA AV.
The Grange
MAIN RD.
HUTTON
EASTFIELD RD.
BARROW

D
E
F
36
37
129
136
141
1
2
3
4
5
61
60
59
Dill Farm
LOCKING HEAD DROVE
LANE
AVENUE
A370
Ivy Cottage
SUMMER LA.
Nursery
LOCKING HEAD DROVE
Grumblepill
Rhyne
Jack Plumley's Stone
Locking Head Farm
super-Mare
WOOLVERS WY.
VARSITY WY.
MERRYFIELD RD.
ROAD
ANSON
OXFORD SQUARE
Playground
CANBERRA CRES.
LARKHILL
RUSSELL ROAD
LEEDHAM ROAD
Drove Farm
BS24
Tennis Courts
R.A.F. Locking
LOWER PARADE GROUND RD.
CRANBOROUGH
Locking Farm
MOOR ROAD
A371
Rhyne
Tennis Cts.
Mayfield Farm
FARM PARK
WAY
LOCKING
MEADOW DR.
HOMEFIELD
HOME CL.
MEFIELD
THE ORCHARD
THE ORCHARD CL.
BRAMLEY CL.
BEECHWOOD
BEECHWOOD AV.
BEECHWOOD AVE.
MANOR GDS.
ELM GRO.
ELM TREE
B3368
Stadium
McCRAE
POST OFFICE ROAD
BOWEN
LEAFY WAY
Manor Ct.
Locking Co. Prim. Sch.
Nursery
SOUTH LAWN
RYDAL AVE.
BYRON RD.
GRENVILLE AVE.
Plumley Cr.
Hall
MEADOW DRI.
FAIRACRE CL.
MENDIP RISE
LIME CL.
BIRCH CL.
BYRON CL.
LAWN
THE GREEN
SOUTH LAWN CL.
LYCHGATE PK.
OLD ROAD
BANWELL ROAD
Connemara
SOMERSET
Church Farm
BURY
Hutton and Locking Rhyne
Sewage Works
Ludwell Farm
Karibu
THE
ROAD BANWELL
Elborough
Elborough Farm
Wingfield House
Nursery Gardens
Hill View Farm
Elborough Wood
Engine
NGWOOD GDNS.
LONGLEAZE GDNS.
HILLSIDE WEST
ELMVALE DR.
GARSIDE CL.
ROAD
HILL
BANWELL
CANADA
WINDMILL
Lower Canada
Benthills

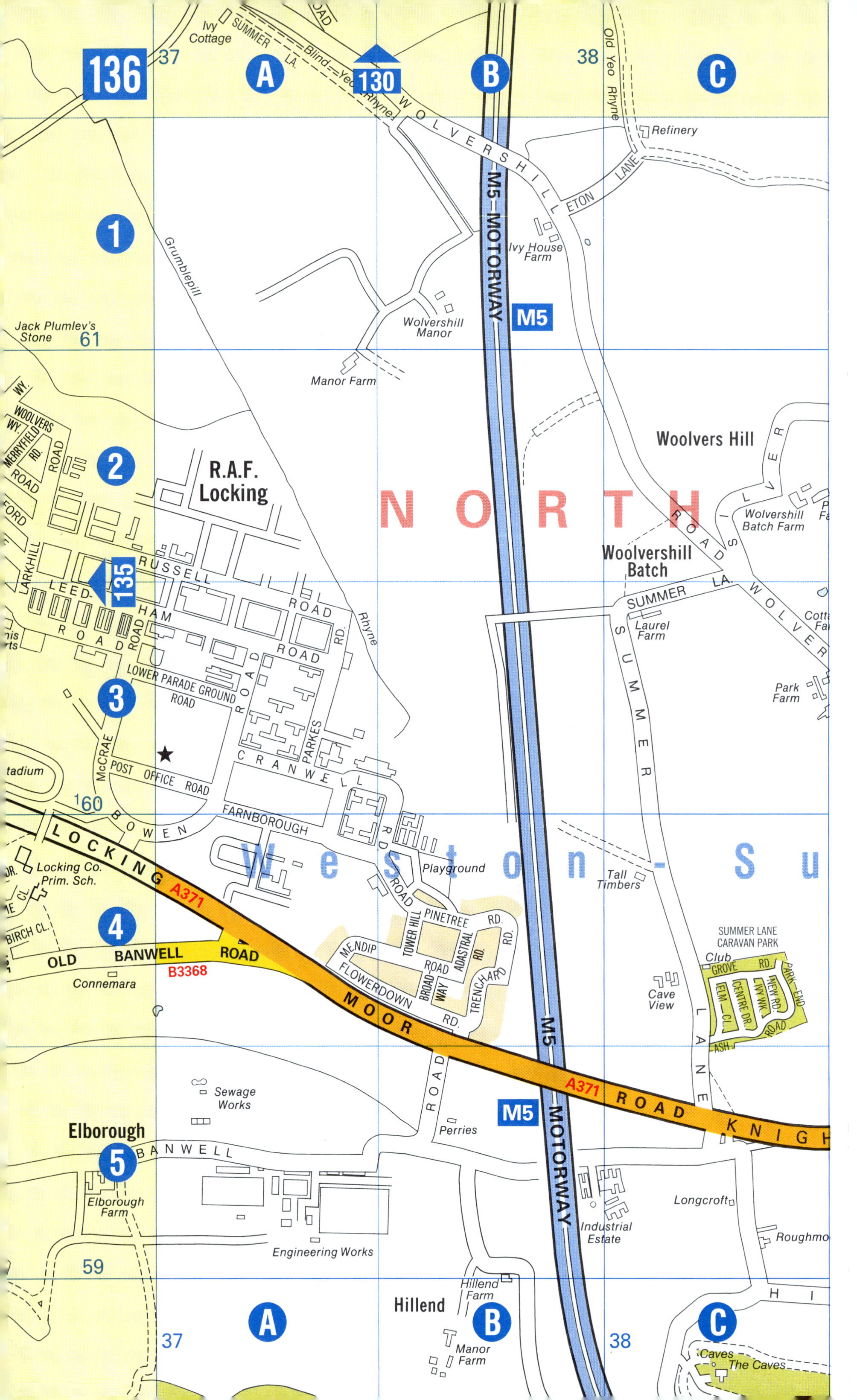

130
135
A
B
C
1
2
3
4
5
37
38
61
160
59
Ivy Cottage
SUMMER LA.
Blind Yeo Rhyne
WOLVERSHILL
M5 MOTORWAY
M5
Old Yeo Rhyne
Refinery
ETON LANE
Ivy House Farm
Grumblepill
Wolvershill Manor
Manor Farm
Jack Plumley's Stone
Woolvers Hill
R.A.F. Locking
NORTH
Wolvershill Batch Farm
Woolvershill Batch
SUMMER LA.
Laurel Farm
RUSSELL ROAD
LEEDHAM ROAD
LARKHILL
WOOLVERS WY.
MERRYFIELD RD.
ROAD
Rhyne
ROAD
RD.
LOWER PARADE GROUND ROAD
PARKES
CRANWELL
McCRAE
POST OFFICE ROAD
BOWEN
FARNBOROUGH
Stadium
Park Farm
SUMMER
LOCKING
A371
Locking Co. Prim. Sch.
Weston-Su
Playground
Tall Timbers
BIRCH CL.
OLD BANWELL ROAD
B3368
Connemara
MENDIP
FLOWERDOWN RD.
TOWER HILL
PINETREE RD.
ADASTRAL RD.
BROAD WAY
TRENCHARD RD.
MOOR
SUMMER LANE CARAVAN PARK
Club
GROVE RD.
PARK END
ELM CL.
CENTRE DR.
IVY WK.
NEW RD.
ROAD
ASH
Cave View
LANE
Sewage Works
ROAD
Perries
A371 ROAD
KNIGH
Elborough
BANWELL
Elborough Farm
Industrial Estate
Longcroft
Roughmo
Engineering Works
Hillend Farm
Hillend
Manor Farm
HI
Caves
The Caves

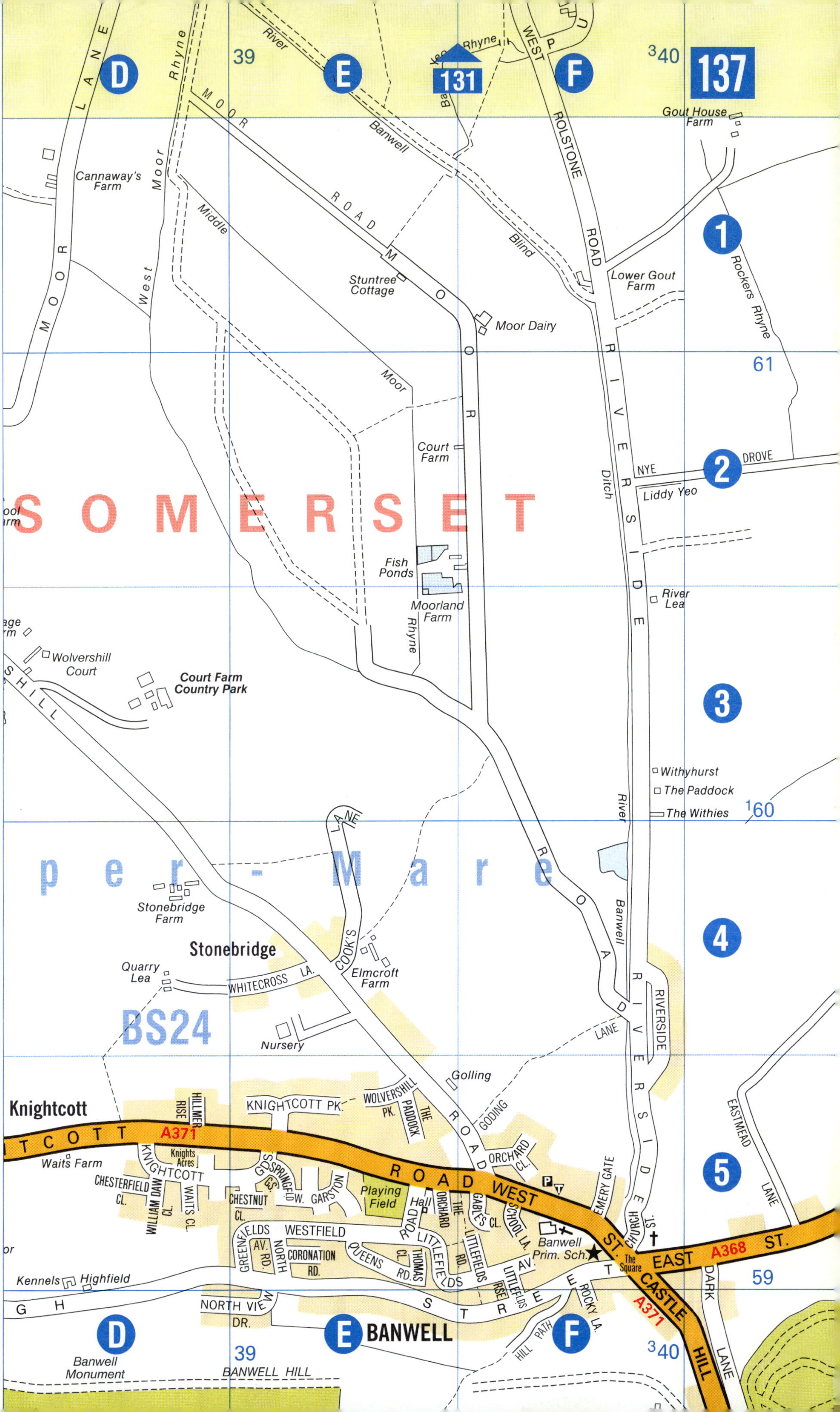
131
Moor Lane
Rhyne
River
Yeo
Rhyne
West
Banwell
Moor Road
Rolstone Road
Gout House Farm
Cannaway's Farm
West Moor Rhyne
Middle Moor
Blind
Stuntree Cottage
Moor Dairy
Lower Gout Farm
Rockers Rhyne
Moor Road
Riverside
Court Farm
Ditch
Nye Drove
Liddy Yeo
SOMERSET
Fish Ponds
Moorland Farm
Rhyne
River Lea
Wolvershill Court
Court Farm Country Park
Shill
Withyhurst
The Paddock
The Withies
River
Weston-super-Mare
Cook's Lane
Banwell
Stonebridge Farm
Stonebridge
Quarry Lea
Whitecross La.
Elmcroft Farm
Riverside
BS24
Nursery
Lane
Golling
Knightcott
Hillmer Rise
Knightcott Pk.
Wolvershill Pk.
The Paddock
Goding
Road
Eastmead Lane
Knightcott Road West
A371
Orchard Cl.
Emery Gate
Knights Acres
Waits Farm
Knightcott
Chesterfield Cl.
William Daw Cl.
Waits Cl.
Gds
Springfield Cl.
Chestnut Cl.
W. Garston
Playing Field
Hall
Orchard Rd.
The Littlefields
Gables Cl.
School La.
Church St.
Road
Banwell Prim. Sch.
Greenfields Av.
North Rd.
Westfield
Coronation Rd.
Queens Rd.
Thomas Cl.
Littlefields Av.
Littlefields Rise
The Square
East St.
A368
Castle Hill
A371
Dark Lane
Kennels
Highfield
High Street
North View Dr.
Rocky La.
Hill Path
Banwell
Banwell Monument
Banwell Hill
Lane
Rd.
D
E
F
1
2
3
4
5
39
340
61
160
59

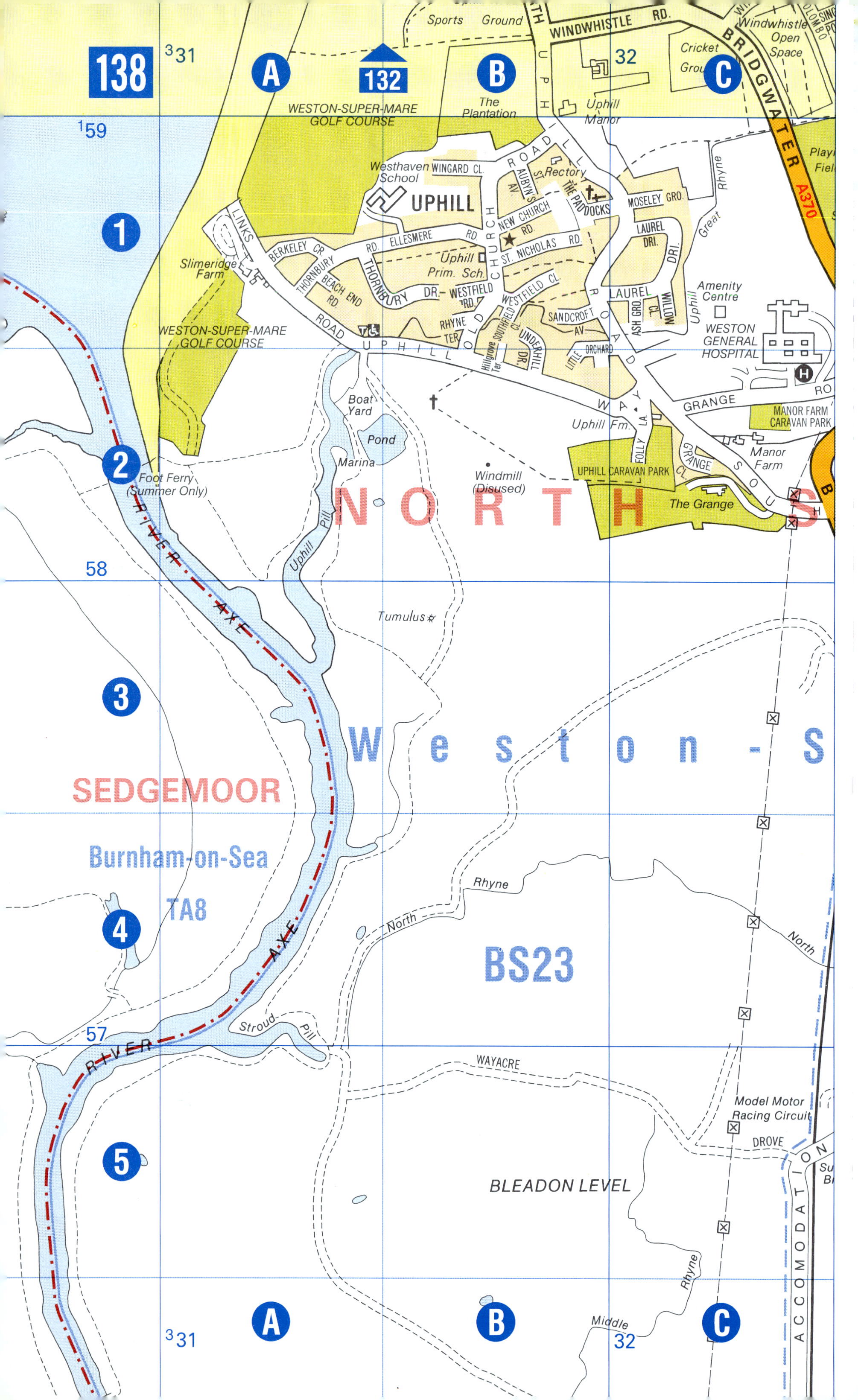

138
132
331
32
A
B
C
1
2
3
4
5
159
58
57
Sports Ground
WINDWHISTLE RD.
Windwhistle Open Space
Cricket Grou
BRIDGWATER
A370
Play Fiel
WESTON-SUPER-MARE GOLF COURSE
The Plantation
Uphill Manor
UPHILL
Westhaven School
WINGARD CL.
ROAD
ST. AUBYN'S AV.
Rectory
THE PADDOCKS
MOSELEY GRO.
NEW CHURCH RD.
ST. NICHOLAS RD.
LAUREL DRI.
Great Rhyne
LINKS
BERKELEY CR.
ELLESMERE RD.
Uphill Prim. Sch.
THORNBURY DR.
THORNBURY
BEACH END RD.
WESTFIELD RD.
WESTFIELD CL.
OLD CHURCH
RHYNE TER.
SOUTHFIELD CL.
SANDCROFT AV.
UNDERHILL DR.
Hillgrove Ter.
LAUREL
ASH GRO.
CL.
WILLOW DRI.
Uphill
Amenity Centre
WESTON GENERAL HOSPITAL
Slimeridge Farm
WESTON-SUPER-MARE GOLF COURSE
ROAD
UPHILL
LITTLE ORCHARD
WAY
GRANGE RO
MANOR FARM CARAVAN PARK
Boat Yard
Pond
Marina
Uphill Fm.
FOLLY LA.
Manor Farm
GRANGE CL.
Foot Ferry (Summer Only)
Windmill (Disused)
UPHILL CARAVAN PARK
The Grange
SOUTH
NORTH
RIVER AXE
Uphill Pill
Tumulus
Weston-S
SEDGEMOOR
Burnham-on-Sea
TA8
Rhyne
North
BS23
North
AXE
Stroud Pill
RIVER
WAYACRE DROVE
Model Motor Racing Circuit
ACCOMODATION
BLEADON LEVEL
Rhyne
Middle

D
E
F
133
33
34
1
2
3
4
5
59
58
57
140
Oldmixon Playing Fields
Youth Cen.
OLDMIXON INDUSTRIAL ESTATE
OLDMIXON CRESCENT
WINTERSTOKE ROAD
GAZELLE RD.
LYNX CRES.
BUCKINGHAM RD.
WESSEX RD.
LYNX CRESCENT
Broadoak Sixth Form Centre
WEDMORE CLO.
LOXTON RD.
WESTBURY CRES.
Christon Ter.
EXFORD CL.
PORLOCK CL.
WESTBURY CRESCENT
Uphill Junction
HARPTREE
GREINTON
ENMORE
EXTON
DRAYTON
ILMINSTER
HINTON
DURSTON
CRESCENT
CRANMORE
BUTCOMBE
BLOOMFD.
Ashcroft
BROMPTON ROAD
Aller Parade
BECKINGTON
BRUTON
AVENUE
UPTON
MONKTON
Oldmixon Prim. Sch.
DUNSTER CRES.
LITTON
RODNEY
SHEPTON
PAWLETT
PENNARD
WALTON
OAKHILL
Milverton
Kilve
Martock
Midford
Meare
MANOR FM. CRES.
MANOR FARM CL.
NORTH HILLS CL.
BRENT AV.
WELL CL.
WOODSIDE
WALSH CL.
Totterdown Farm
OLDMIXON ROAD
BROADWAY
HAMWOOD CL.
WALNUT CL.
St. Mary's Cl.
BARRY CL.
PENARTH DR.
ASHFORD DR.
OLDMIXON
BEECHMOUNT CL.
BEECHMOUNT DR.
FAVERSHAM DR.
ROCHESTER CL.
MAIDSTONE GRO.
LANE
HAYWOOD CL.
HAYWOOD GARDENS
COPSE
Manor House
Hay Wood
HAY WOOD
Oldmixon Copse
BRECON VIEW
WENTWOOD DR.
Oldmixon Bridge
The Tips
THE SPINNEY
BURRINGTON CL.
BURRINGTON AV.
BROCKLEY CL.
BLAGDON CL.
BURNHAM CL.
BURNHAM DRIVE
CRESCENT
Devil's Bri.
SOMERSET
Oldmixon
CHANNEL HEIGHTS
VEITCH CT.
TOTTERDOWN
HIGHFIELD RD.
White Barns
BRUNEL CL.
Flatroof Farm
MENDIP EDGE
BLEADON HILL
ROMAN ROAD
HILLCOTE ESTATE
Highcroft
HILLSIDE RD.
CELTIC
THE PURN RD.
TOLL RD.
PURN LEIGHTON CRES.
SOUTHRIDGE HEIGHTS
BRIDGWATER ROAD
Weston-super-Mare
Coombe Farm
BS24
Purn Hill
Purn House Farm
MANOR GRANGE
BLEADON
CHESTNUT LA.
WAY
Purn
PURN
Purn Farm
Rhyne
A370
BLEADON ROAD
PINE LEA
STH. COMBE
FERN LEA
WHITE GATE CL.
AMESBURY DR.
PEARTREE GDS.
RECTORY LA.
TENTERK CL.
CORONATION RD.
OLD SCHOOL LA.
MULBERRY LA.
BIRCH AV.
WILLOW DR.
ASH
BRIDGE RD.
PURN INTERNATIONAL HOLIDAY PARK
EAST MEAD DROVE
RIVER AXE
Works
Little Down Quarries
Mill
SEDGEMOOR
Bleadon Bridge
RIVER

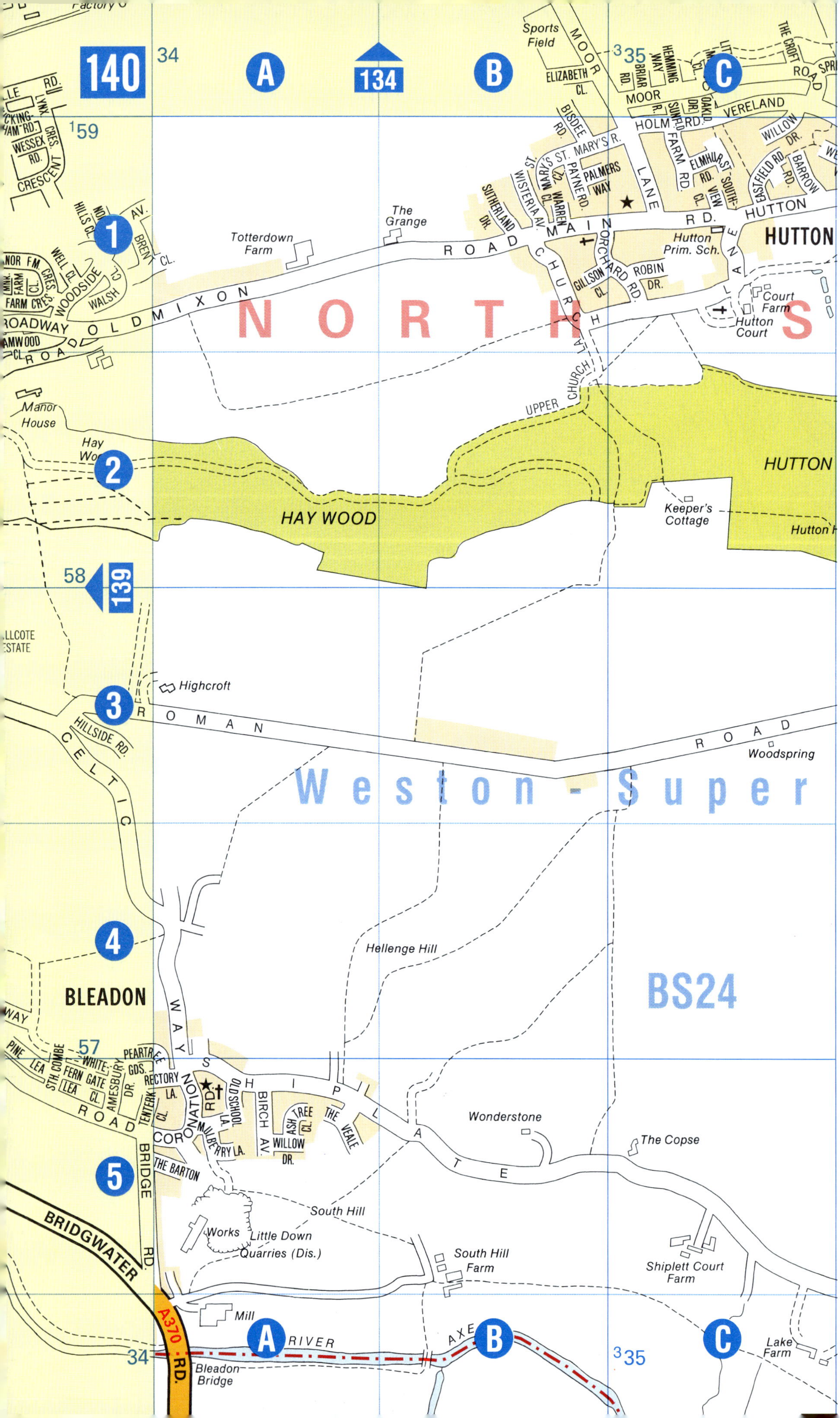
134
139
A
B
C
1
2
3
4
5
34
335
159
58
57
NORTH
Weston - Super
BS24
HUTTON
BLEADON
HAY WOOD
HUTTON
Sports Field
MOOR
ELIZABETH CL.
BRIAR RD.
HEMMING WAY
MOOR
HOLM RD.
SUNFORD
FARM RD.
OAKD. DR.
VERELAND
THE CROFT
ROAD
WILLOW DR.
BARROW
EASTFIELD RD.
ELMHURST RD.
SOUTH-VIEW CL.
BISDEE RD.
ST. MARY'S R.
ST. MARY'S CL.
WISTERIA AV.
SUTHERLAND DR.
PAYNE RD.
WARREN
PALMERS WAY
LANE
MAIN RD.
HUTTON
The Grange
Totterdown Farm
ROAD
OLDMIXON ROAD
BRENT CL.
WALSH CL.
WOODSIDE
WELL CL.
BROADWAY
WESSEX RD.
CRESCENT
LYNX CRES.
CHURCH LANE
UPPER CHURCH LANE
ORCHARD RD.
GILLSON CL.
ROBIN DR.
Hutton Prim. Sch.
Court Farm
Hutton Court
Manor House
Hay Wood
Keeper's Cottage
Hutton H
Highcroft
ROMAN ROAD
HILLSIDE RD.
CELTIC WAY
Woodspring
ALLCOTE ESTATE
Hellenge Hill
WAY
PINE LEA
STH. COMBE
FERN LEA
WHITE-GATE CL.
AMESBURY DR.
PEARTREE GDS.
TENTERK CL.
RECTORY LA.
CORONATION RD.
OLD SCHOOL LA.
MULBERRY LA.
BIRCH AV.
ASH TREE CL.
WILLOW DR.
THE VEALE
SHIPLATE
ROAD
BRIDGE RD.
THE BARTON
Wonderstone
The Copse
South Hill
Works
Little Down Quarries (Dis.)
South Hill Farm
Shiplett Court Farm
BRIDGWATER RD.
A370 RD.
Mill
RIVER AXE
Bleadon Bridge
Lake Farm

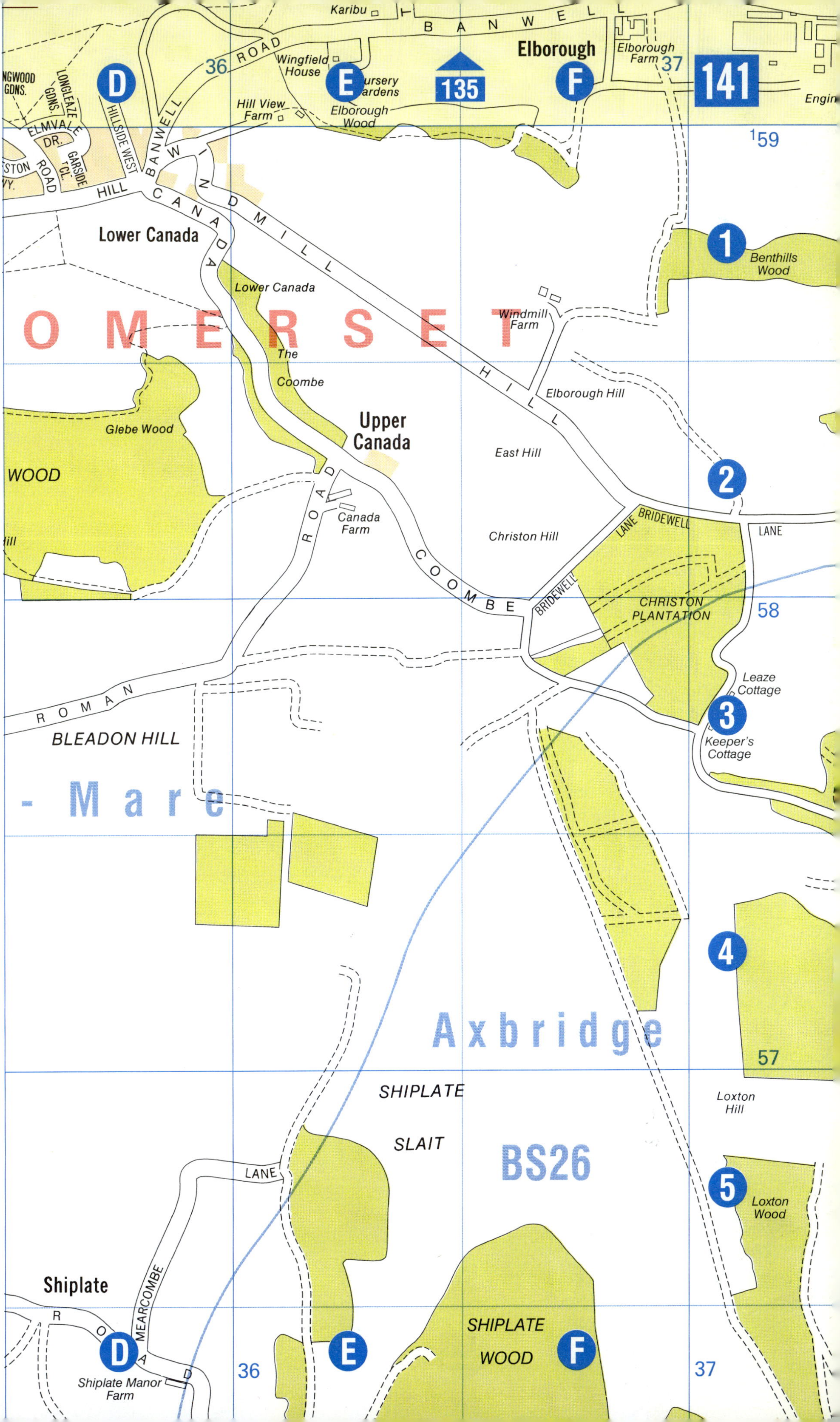

141
135
Karibu
BANWELL
Elborough
Elborough Farm
Wingfield House
Nursery Gardens
Elborough Wood
Hill View Farm
BANWELL ROAD
HILLSIDE WEST
LONGLEAZE GDNS.
ELMVALE DR.
GARSIDE CL.
HILL
WINDMILL HILL
CANADA
Lower Canada
Benthills Wood
Windmill Farm
SOMERSET
The Coombe
Elborough Hill
Glebe Wood
WOOD
Upper Canada
East Hill
ROAD
Canada Farm
Christon Hill
BRIDEWELL LANE
LANE
COOMBE
BRIDEWELL
CHRISTON PLANTATION
Leaze Cottage
Keeper's Cottage
ROMAN
BLEADON HILL
- Mare
Axbridge
SHIPLATE
SLAIT
BS26
Loxton Hill
Loxton Wood
LANE
Shiplate
MEARCOMBE
ROAD
Shiplate Manor Farm
SHIPLATE WOOD
D
E
F
1
2
3
4
5
36
37
159
58
57

142
North End
Horsecastle
YATTON
Yatton
Frost Hill
NORTH SOMERSET
B3133
NORTH END ROAD
HIGH STREET
Moorstreet Bow
Northend Farm
Chestnut Farm
Weeping Ash Farm
Sports Ground
Park Farm
The Grange
Macquarie
Factory
Warehouse
Works
Osmond Bridge
Gasholder
Hillsea
Westmead Rhyne
Middle Rhyne
Stowey Rhyne
Little River
Yatton Jun. & Inf. Schs.
Sports Field
Hall
Cross (Restored)
Lib.
The Batch
Rectory Farm
Cadbury Hill
Land Farm
Congresbury Moor
Gang Wall
Binhay Rhyne
Biddle Street Rhyne
Branch Rhyne
New Rhyne
Middle Elm
BS24
Weston-Super-Mare
WESTON ROAD
CONGRESBURY YEO
WEMBERHAM
MOOR ROAD
STATION RD.
HORSECASTLE FARM ROAD
MENDIP ROAD
CHESCOMBE ROAD
STOWEY PK.
MARKET IND. EST.
144
42
43
67
66
65
A
B
C
1
2
3
4
5

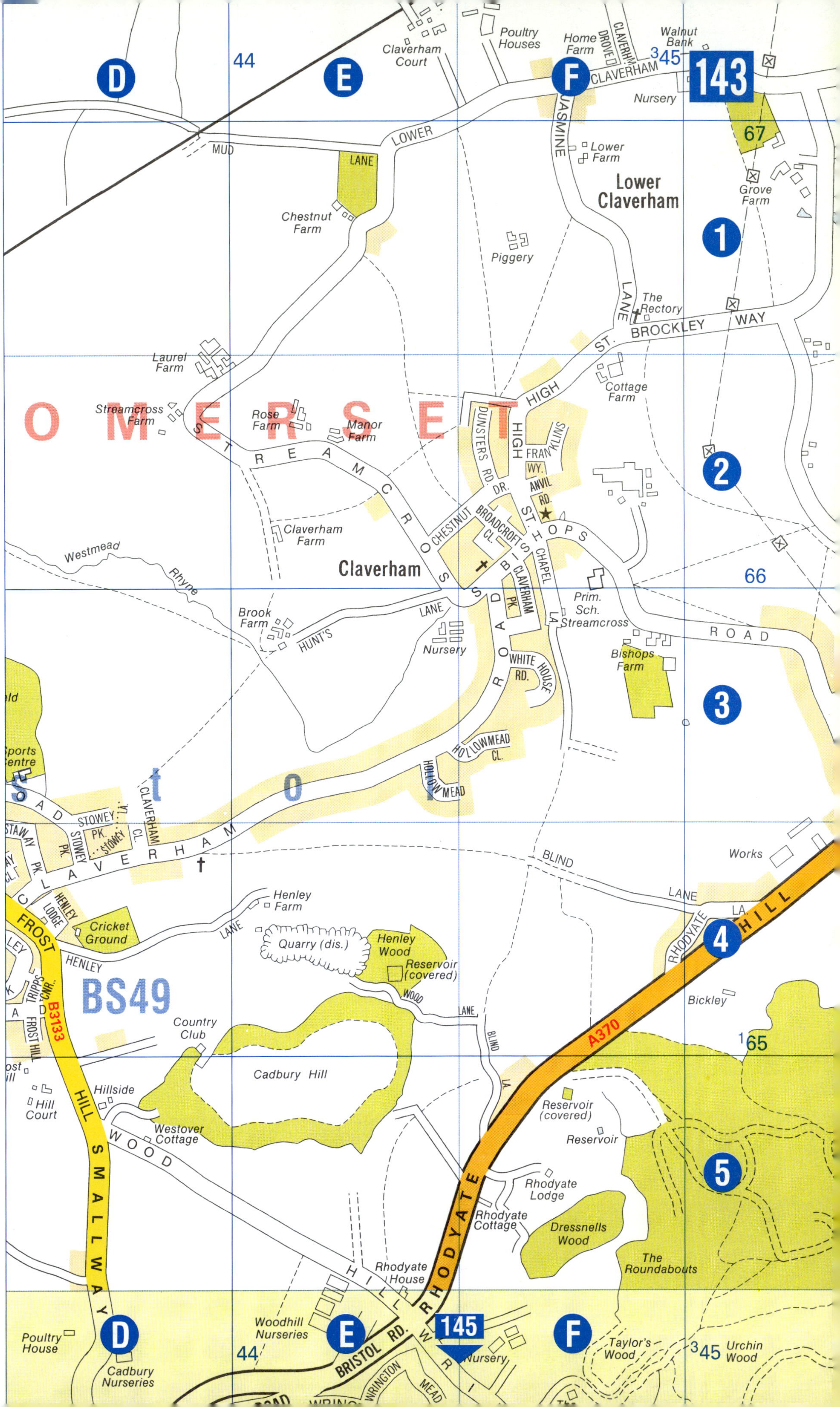

Claverham Court
Poultry Houses
Home Farm
Walnut Bank
Nursery
Lower Claverham
Lower Farm
Grove Farm
Chestnut Farm
Piggery
The Rectory
Laurel Farm
Streamcross Farm
Rose Farm
Manor Farm
Cottage Farm
Claverham Farm
Claverham
Westmead Rhyne
Brook Farm
Nursery
Prim. Sch.
Streamcross
Bishops Farm
Works
Henley Farm
Quarry (dis.)
Henley Wood
Reservoir (covered)
Cricket Ground
BS49
Country Club
Bickley
Cadbury Hill
Hillside
Hill Court
Westover Cottage
Reservoir (covered)
Reservoir
Rhodyate Lodge
Rhodyate Cottage
Dressnells Wood
The Roundabouts
Rhodyate House
Woodhill Nurseries
Poultry House
Cadbury Nurseries
Nursery
Taylor's Wood
Urchin Wood
SOMERSET
Stop
MUD LANE
LOWER CLAVERHAM
CLAVERHAM DROVE
JASMINE LANE
BROCKLEY WAY
HIGH ST.
STREAMCROSS
CHESTNUT DR.
DUNSTERS RD
FRANKLINS WY.
ANVIL RD.
BROADCROFT CL.
BISHOPS ROAD
CHAPEL LA
CLAVERHAM PK.
HUNT'S LANE
WHITE HOUSE RD.
HOLLOWMEAD CL.
HOLLOWMEAD
CLAVERHAM ROAD
STOWEY PK.
CLAVERHAM CL.
HENLEY LODGE
BLIND LANE
RHODYATE LA
HILL
A370
FROST HILL
HENLEY LANE
TRIPPS CNR.
B3133
SMALLWAY
WOOD LANE
WOOD HILL
RHODYATE
BRISTOL RD.
WRINGTON MEAD
44
345
67
66
165
145

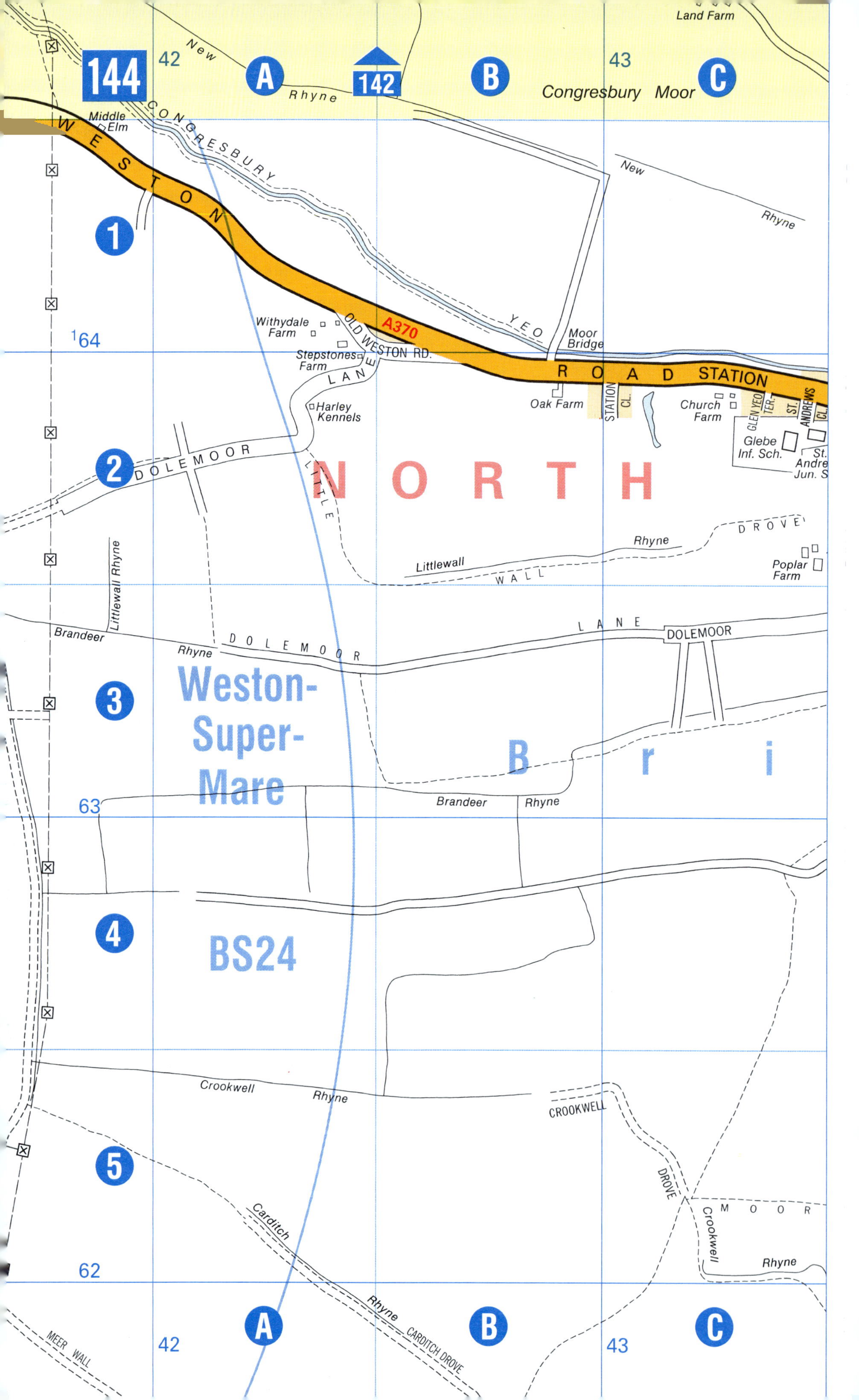

142
A
B
C
42
43
Congresbury Moor
Land Farm
New Rhyne
Middle Elm
WESTON
CONGRESBURY
YEO
New Rhyne
1
164
Withydale Farm
Stepstones Farm
OLD WESTON RD.
LANE
A370
Moor Bridge
ROAD STATION
Harley Kennels
Oak Farm
STATION CL.
Church Farm
GLEN YEO TER.
ST. ANDREWS CL.
Glebe Inf. Sch.
St. Andre Jun. S
2
DOLEMOOR
LITTLE
NORTH
Rhyne
DROVE
Littlewall
WALL
Poplar Farm
Littlewall Rhyne
Brandeer
Rhyne
DOLEMOOR
LANE
DOLEMOOR
3
Weston-Super-Mare
Bri
63
Brandeer
Rhyne
4
BS24
Crookwell
Rhyne
CROOKWELL
DROVE
5
Carditch
MOOR
Crookwell
Rhyne
62
Rhyne
CARDITCH DROVE
MEER WALL

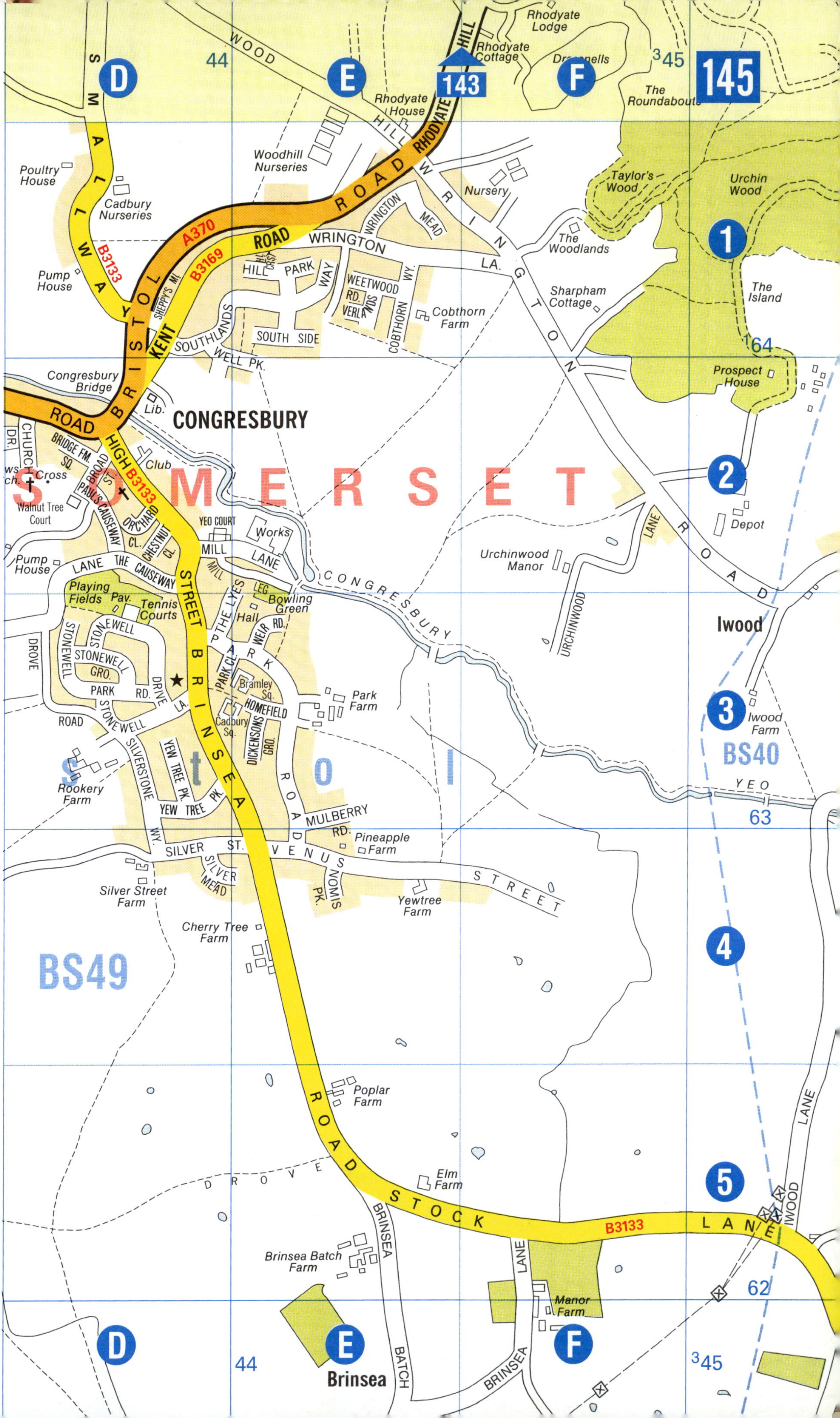
143
D
E
F
44
345
WOOD
HILL
RHODYATE
Rhodyate Lodge
Rhodyate Cottage
Rhodyate House
The Roundabout
Woodhill Nurseries
Poultry House
Cadbury Nurseries
Pump House
SMALLWAY
B3133
A370
B3169
BRISTOL ROAD
KENT ROAD
SHEPPY'S ML.
WRINGTON ROAD
WRINGTON LA.
WRINGTON MEAD
HILL PARK WAY
HILL CRST.
WEETWOOD RD.
VERLANDS
COBTHORN WY.
Cobthorn Farm
SOUTHLANDS
SOUTH SIDE
WELL PK.
Nursery
Taylor's Wood
Urchin Wood
The Woodlands
Sharpham Cottage
The Island
1
64
Prospect House
Congresbury Bridge
Lib.
CONGRESBURY
ROAD
CHURCH DR.
BRIDGE FM. SQ.
BROAD ST.
PAUL'S CAUSEWAY
Cross
Walnut Tree Court
HIGH STREET
Club
ORCHARD CL.
CHESTNUT CL.
YEO COURT
Works
MILL LANE
Pump House
LANE
THE CAUSEWAY
SOMERSET
2
Depot
LANE
Urchinwood Manor
ROAD
CONGRESBURY
URCHINWOOD
Iwood
Playing Fields
Pav.
Tennis Courts
THE LYES
LEG
Bowling Green
Hall
WEIR RD.
STONEWELL
STONEWELL GRO.
PARK RD.
DRIVE
DROVE
PARK
PARK CL.
Bramley Sq.
HOMEFIELD
Cadbury Sq.
DICKENSONS GRO.
Park Farm
ROAD
STONEWELL LA.
BRINSEA
3
Iwood Farm
BS40
Rookery Farm
SILVERSTONE WY.
YEW TREE PK.
YEW TREE PK.
Stoi
MULBERRY RD.
YEO
63
Pineapple Farm
SILVER ST.
VENUS STREET
SILVER MEAD
SIMONS PK.
Silver Street Farm
Yewtree Farm
Cherry Tree Farm
BS49
4
Poplar Farm
ROAD
DROVE
Elm Farm
STOCK LANE
B3133
5
LANE
IWOOD
BRINSEA BATCH
Brinsea Batch Farm
LANE
Manor Farm
62
BRINSEA
D
E
F
44
Brinsea
345

Church Farm
Rec. Grd.
BUTLASS CL.
TIMSBURY RD.
BUNGAY'S HILL
Bungay's Hill Farm
Timsbury Bottom Farm
A
B
C
365
Timsbury Bottom
HIGH ST.
A39
Cemy.
Sch.
High Littleton Ho.
High Littleton
158
Rosewell Fm.
Vicarage
GOOSARD LANE
BROOM HILL LANE
Broom Hill Farm
Jaylands
Poultry Houses
1
Rosedene
LANGFORD'S LANE
Goosard Bridge
ROAD
Sewage Works
BATH & NO
Hanham House
HANHAM LANE
Wiscombe Brake
2
Swimming Pool
SOME
57
Sports Ground
BRISTOL ROAD
New Pit
Tennis Cts.
Bowl. Grn.
South Vw.
Victoria Ter.
BATH
Jubilee Ter.
LITTLEBROOK
GREGORY'S TYNING
BRITTEN'S CL.
HALLATROW
Bristol
Works
Greenhill Farm
3
Plummer's Hill
Cemy.
BROOKSIDE
VALLEY VIEW
WALLENGE CL.
WALLENGE DR.
HILLSIDE CL.
Britten's
ROMAN WY.
SPRINGHILL CL.
BRUMMEL WAY
CAM VIEW
DOWNS WAY
B3355 ROAD
CHURCH ST.
Millward Ter.
ORCHARD RD.
ORCHARD GS.
Hill Ct.
SOMERSET WAY
CHESTNUT CL.
BROOKSIDE CL.
BRITTEN'S LANE
PAULTON
HIGH PARK
High Park Corner
WOODVIEW
WESTVIEW
ROAD
THE PITHAY
ASHLEIGH CL.
Surgery
Ashleigh Ho.
HIGH STREET
Windsor Ter.
Alexandra Ter.
SIMONS CL.
Ham Farm
BS39
Victoria Pl.
New Town
Park Cl.
LAUREL DR.
ASH
MANS GA.
LUDWELLS ORCHD.
Lib.
Lilian Ter.
HAM GRO.
HAM
Poultry Houses
4
FARRINGTON ROAD
ABBOTS FM. CL.
CARTER RD.
PARK RD.
PARK
The Batch
ALEXANDRA PK.
Ham
PAULTON ROAD
SPECKLEMEAD
TENNIS COURT AV.
TENNIS COURT RD.
Swim. Baths
Paulton Jun. & Inf. Schs.
WINTERFIELD ROAD
BLOOMFIELD LA
Bloomfield
PLUMPTRE
GREENVALE RD.
Plumptre Cl.
BADMAN CL.
ELM ROAD
SPRING GROUND RD.
Tenniscourt Cotts.
Football Ground
56
RUDGEWAY RD
WINTERFIELD
Bowl. Grn.
Rec. Grd.
OLD MILLS LANE
Towns End
WINTERFIELD PK.
HIGH ACRE
Poultry Houses
St. Julien Farm
PARK
SALISBURY RD
RUETT LANE
MENDIP CL.
MENDIP
OAKLANDS
ALPINE
ALPINE C.
CLANDOWN RD
Salisbury Farm
FIR TREE AV.
5
Winterfield
B3355
MEADOW RD.
Salisbury
PAULTON HOSPITAL
PHILLIS HILL
A
B
C
Fernlea
365
MONGER LANE
HARTS PADDOCK

150

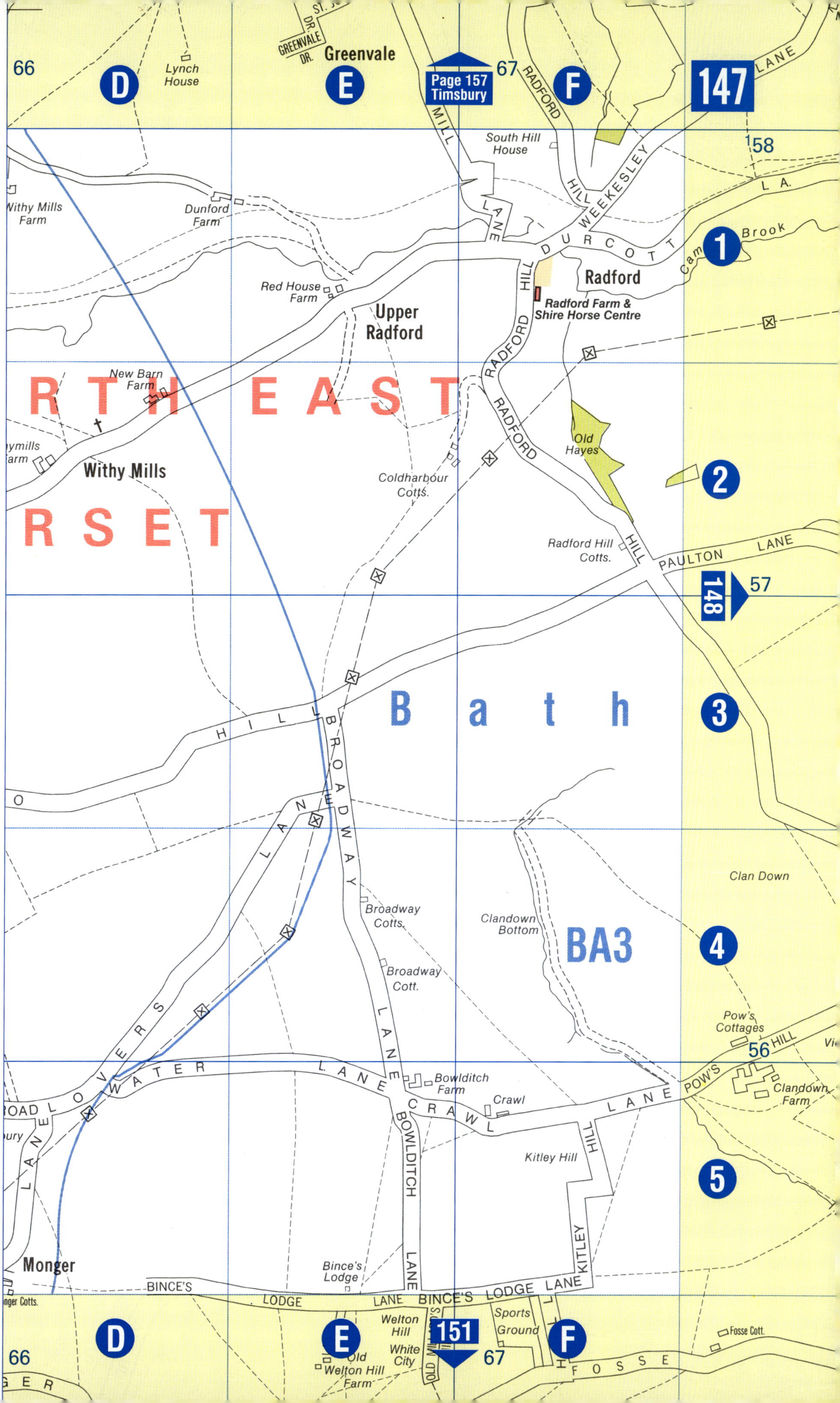
Page 157 Timsbury
Greenvale
GREENVALE DR.
DR.
ST.
Lynch House
66
67
D
E
F
158
MILL LANE
RADFORD HILL
South Hill House
WEEKESLEY LANE
LA.
Brook
Cam
1
DURCOTT
Withy Mills Farm
Dunford Farm
Red House Farm
Upper Radford
Radford
Radford Farm & Shire Horse Centre
HILL
RADFORD
New Barn Farm
NORTH EAST
SOMERSET
Withy Mills
Withy Mills Farm
Coldharbour Cotts.
Old Hayes
RADFORD HILL
2
Radford Hill Cotts.
PAULTON LANE
148
57
HILL
Bath
3
BROADWAY
LANE
Clan Down
Broadway Cotts.
Clandown Bottom
BA3
4
Broadway Cott.
LANE
Pow's Cottages
56
POW'S HILL
LOVERS LANE
WATER LANE
Bowlditch Farm
CRAWL LANE
Crawl
Clandown Farm
ROAD
5
Kitley Hill
HILL
BOWLDITCH LANE
KITLEY HILL
Monger
Bince's Lodge
BINCE'S LODGE LANE
Monger Cotts.
Welton Hill
White City
Old Welton Hill Farm
OLD MILLS LANE
Sports Ground
151
FOSSE
Fosse Cott.
66
67

148
A
B
C
68
1
2
3
4
5
58
57
56
147
152
Radford
Radford Farm & Shire Horse Centre
Camerton
Wicklane
Clandown
BATH & N
SOMERSET
BA3
DURCOTT LANE
WEEKESLEY HILL
Cam Brook
COLLIER CL.
SUNNYVALE
RED LANE
BRIDGE PLACE
ROAD WICK LANE
WHITE
CAM BROOK CL.
DAGLANDS
THE
CAMERTON HILL
Bridge Place Farm
Camerton Court
CAMERTON PARK
Camerton C. of E. Prim. Sch.
Abbey Farm
Rectory
Manor Farm
SKINNER'S HILL
Old Hayes
Parson's Brake
Radford Hill Cotts.
HILL
PAULTON LANE
Glebe Cottage
Well Head Wood
Camerton Farm
Starvelark Wood
Football Ground
Clan Down
NORTH-DOWN RD.
EASTDOWN RD
OVERDALE
DUCHY RD.
PRINCE'S
DUCHY ST.
South View CL.
SMALLCOMBE RD.
SMALL-COMBE CL.
OLD FOSSE RD.
FOSSE WAY
Pow's Cottages
POW'S HILL
Recreation Ground
Vicarage
Clandown Farm
Smallcombe Fm.
Works
LANE
Kitley Hill
KITLEY HILL
LANE
Clandown C.of E. Prim. Sch.
CHAPEL RD.
Chapel Ct.
FOSSE GRN.
Springfield Heights
SPRINGFIELD PL.
CHAPEL LAWNS
Way
Old Pit Ter.
COOMBEND
Rockhill Cottages
BATH NEW RD.
A367
BRISTOL ROAD
Round Hill Cottages
Recreation Ground
Pav.
BATH
MENDIP WY.
Fosse Cott.
FOSSE LANE
Fosse

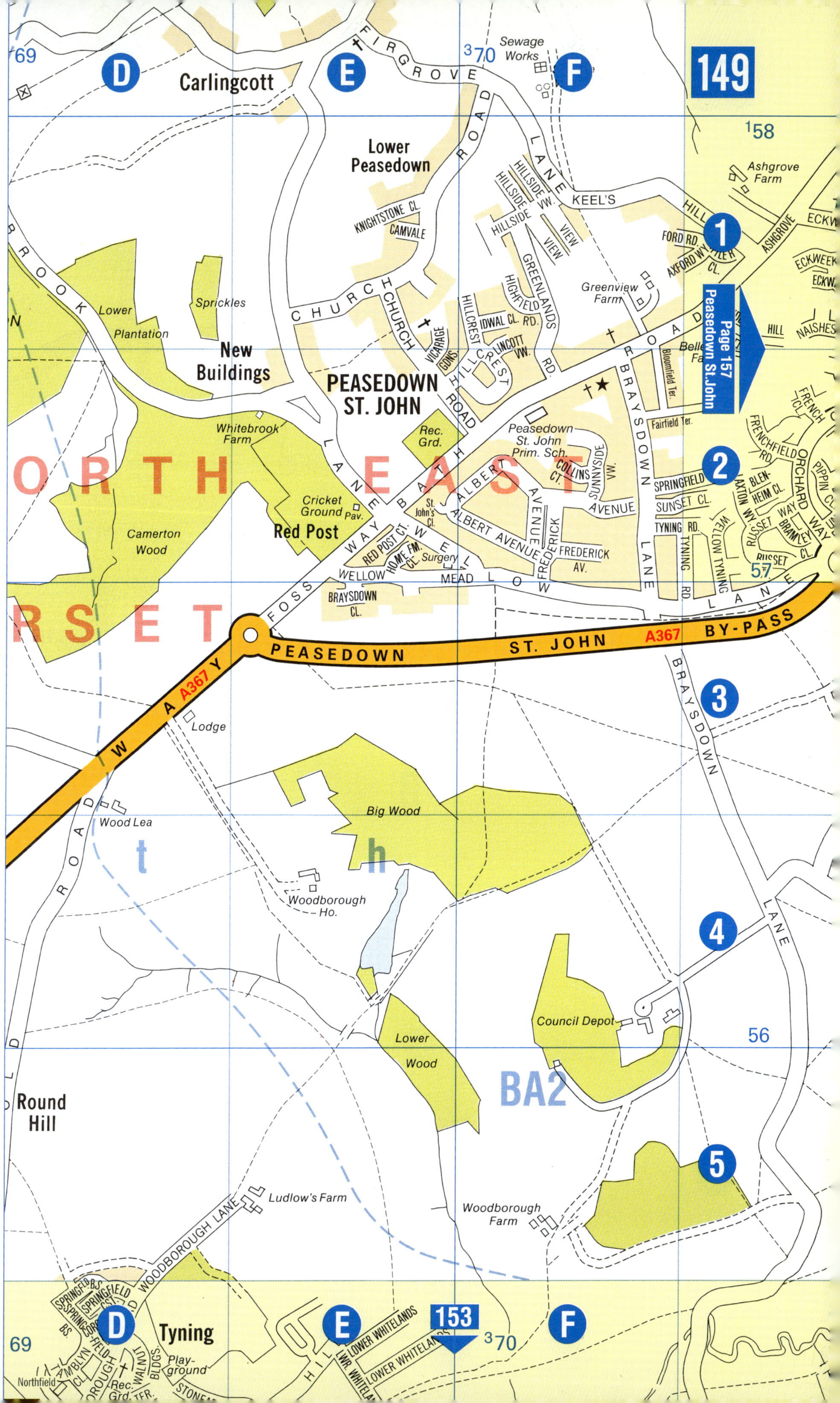
Carlingcott
Sewage Works
FIRGROVE LANE
Lower Peasedown
KNIGHTSTONE CL.
CAMVALE
CHURCH ROAD
KEEL'S HILL
HILLSIDE VW.
HILLSIDE VIEW
GREENLANDS RD.
HIGHFIELD RD.
FORD RD.
AXFORD WY.
TYLER CL.
ASHGROVE
Ashgrove Farm
Greenview Farm
ECKWEEK
HILL
NAISHES
Page 157 Peasedown St.John
BROOK
Lower Plantation
Sprickles
New Buildings
IDWAL CL.
HILLCREST
LINCOTT VW.
VICARAGE GDNS.
PEASEDOWN ST. JOHN
Rec. Grd.
Whitebrook Farm
BATH ROAD
BRAYSDOWN LANE
Bloomfield Ter.
Fairfield Ter.
Peasedown St. John Prim. Sch.
COLLINS CT.
SUNNYSIDE VW.
ALBERT AVENUE
FREDERICK AVENUE
FREDERICK AV.
SPRINGFIELD
SUNSET CL.
TYNING RD.
WELLOW TYNING
FRENCHFIELD RD.
FRENCH CL.
ORCHARD WAY
PIPPIN CL.
BLENHEIM CL.
LAXTON WY.
RUSSET WAY
BRAMLEY CL.
RUSSET
NORTH EAST SOMERSET
Cricket Ground Pav.
Red Post
Camerton Wood
St. John's Cl.
RED POST CT.
HOME FM. CL.
Surgery
WELLOW MEAD
WELLOW LANE
BRAYSDOWN CL.
FOSS WAY
A367
PEASEDOWN ST. JOHN BY-PASS
Lodge
Big Wood
Wood Lea
ROAD
Woodborough Ho.
Council Depot
Lower Wood
BA2
Round Hill
Ludlow's Farm
WOODBOROUGH LANE
Woodborough Farm
Tyning
SPRINGFIELD
CORNFIELD
AMBLYN CL.
ROUGH
WALNUT BLDGS.
Play-ground
Rec. Grd.
Northfield
STONE
LOWER WHITELANDS
LWR. WHITELANDS
HILL
153
D
E
F
1
2
3
4
5
69
370
158
57
56

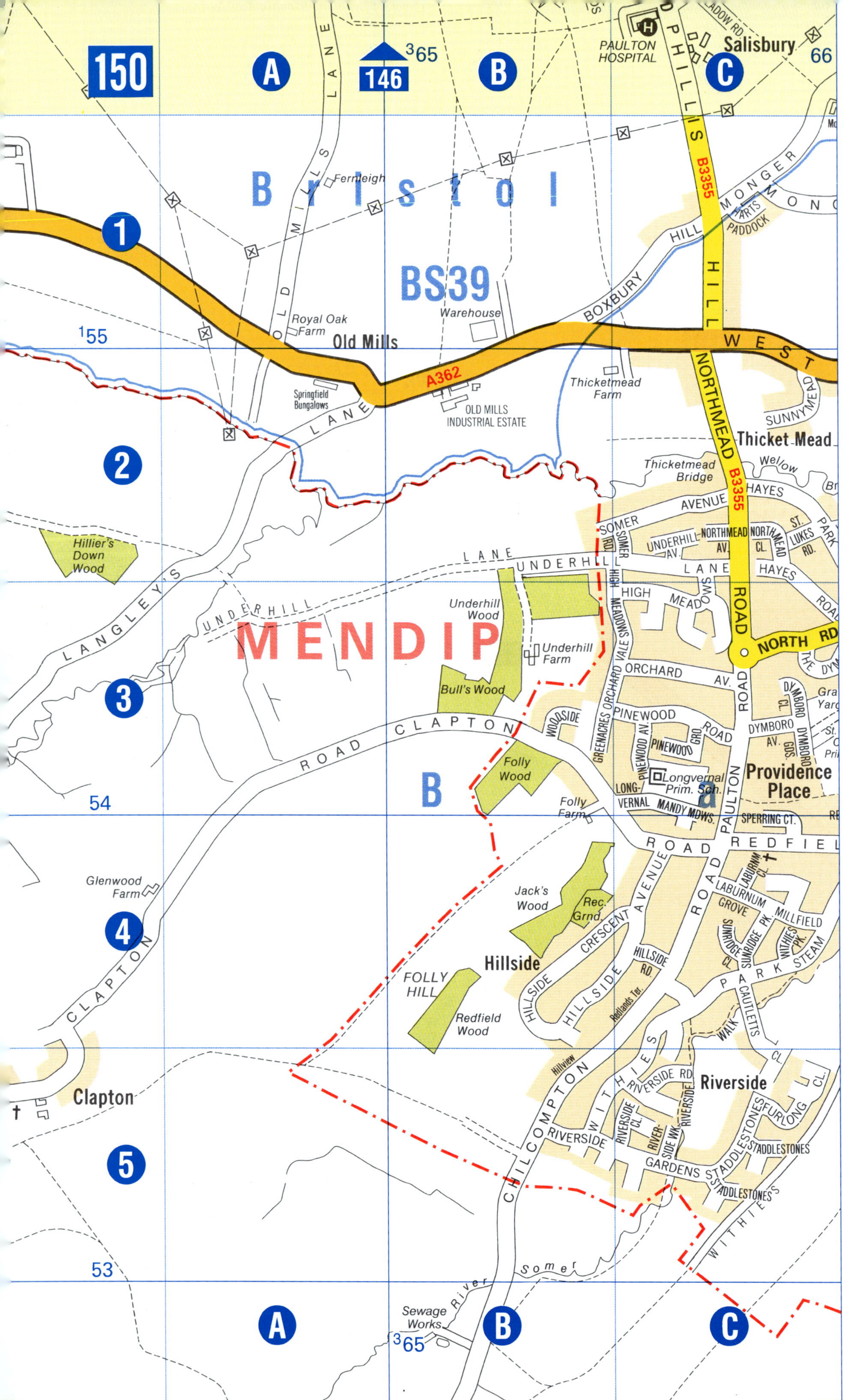
146
A
B
C
1
2
3
4
5
55
54
53
365
66
Bristol
BS39
MENDIP
PAULTON HOSPITAL
Salisbury
Fernleigh
OLD MILLS LANE
Royal Oak Farm
Old Mills
Warehouse
BOXBURY HILL
MONGER
ARTS PADDOCK
B3355
A362
WEST
Springfield Bungalows
LANE
OLD MILLS INDUSTRIAL ESTATE
Thicketmead Farm
NORTHMEAD ROAD
SUNNYMEAD
Thicket Mead
Thicketmead Bridge
Wellow
HAYES
AVENUE
SOMER RD.
UNDERHILL AV.
NORTHMEAD AV.
NORTHMEAD CL.
ST. LUKES RD.
PARK
Hillier's Down Wood
LANGLEY'S LANE
UNDERHILL LANE
HIGH MEADOWS
HAYES ROAD
Underhill Wood
UNDERHILL
Underhill Farm
NORTH RD
ORCHARD AV.
Bull's Wood
CLAPTON ROAD
WOODSIDE
GREENACRES
ORCHARD VALE
PINEWOOD ROAD
PINEWOOD AV.
PINEWOOD GRO.
DYMBORO CL.
DYMBORO AV.
DYMBORO GDS.
Providence Place
Folly Wood
Longvernal Prim. Sch.
LONG-VERNAL
MANDY MDWS.
PAULTON ROAD
SPERRING CT.
Folly Farm
REDFIELD ROAD
LABURNUM CL.
LABURNUM GROVE
MILLFIELD
Glenwood Farm
Jack's Wood
Rec. Grnd
CRESCENT AVENUE
SUNRIDGE CL.
SUNRIDGE PK.
WITHIES PK.
PARK STEAM
CAUTLETTS CL.
FOLLY HILL
Hillside
HILLSIDE
HILLSIDE RD.
Redfield Wood
Redlands Ter.
WALK
Hillview
WITHIES
RIVERSIDE RD.
Riverside
FURLONG
CL.
Clapton
CHILCOMPTON ROAD
RIVERSIDE
RIVERSIDE CL.
RIVERSIDE WK.
STADDLESTONES
GARDENS
River Somer
Sewage Works

D
E
F
147
67
1
2
3
4
5
152
55
54
53
66
Monger
BINCE'S LODGE LANE
Bince's Lodge
Welton Hill
White City
OLD MILLARD'S HILL
Sports Ground
Fosse Cott.
FOSSE LANE
Old Welton Hill Farm
Belle Vue
MILLARD'S HILL
Welton Hill Farm
GREEN TREE RD.
GLADSTONE ST.
Millards Ct.
Manor Farm
BATH & NORTH EAST SOMERSET
WELTON
GREENHILL PL.
GREENHILL RD.
Hillside Vw.
WELTON ROAD
WELLOW BROOK MDW.
Wellow Brook
GELDOFF DR.
BEAUFORT
WHITE CL.
ST. PAUL'S
THOMAS
MEAD ST.
Welton
VALLEY WALK
Wheeler's Hill
MIDSOMER ENTERPRISE PARK
Works
WELTON VALE
ROCK ROAD
Welton Co. Prim. Sch.
BURLINGTON RD.
Florida Ter.
A362
ROAD
FIVE ARCHES CL.
WHEELERS RD.
WHEELERS DR.
STATION ROAD
RADSTOCK ROAD
BERKELEY AVENUE
AVENUE
VIVIEN
ST. JOHN'S CR.
ST. MARK'S RD.
CLEVEDON RD.
Football Ground
Stanley Ct.
RAILWAY VW.
Sunnymount
Lilac Ter.
Hope Ter.
River Somer
Hayes Park
NORTH ROAD
ELM VIEW
NORTH WY.
Play. Fld.
Midsomer Norton Prim. Sch.
CHURCH LA.
PRIORY CL.
POW'S ORCHARD
THE HOLLIES
Council Offs.
Mansbrook Ho.
Chesterfield Ho.
B3355
RACKVERNAL RD.
TYNING
GULLOCK
Sports Centre
MIDSOMER NORTON
HIGH STREET
Lib.
Holly Ct.
SOUTH
PIT ROAD
Primrose Ter.
PRIMROSE LA.
EXCELSIOR T.
THE ISLAND
Town Hall
ST. CHAD'S AV.
ST. CHAD'S GN.
FERN CL.
IVY WALK
Sommervale Sch.
Playing Field
Cricket Ground
Pav.
PARK WAY
PARK
BA3
Playing Field
Norton Hill
Norton Hill School
CHARLTON ROAD
NIGHTINGALE WAY
CHAFFINCH DR.
WOODPECKER AV.
KINGFISHER DR.
LINNET WY.
LARK CL.
BLACKBIRD CL.
ROBIN CL.
Kestrel
LYNDHURST RD.
LYNTON RD.
HAZEL TERRACE
HAZEL GRO.
THE TIMBERS
LYNWOOD CL.
Playing Field
OLD PIT ROAD
KEATS RD.
CHAUCER RD.
LONGFELLOW RD.
KINGSLEY RD.
POETS CORNER
KIPLING RD.
Fosse Way Sch.
Westfield Co. Prim. Sch.
Westfield
SHELLEY RD.
SHAKESPEARE RD.
WESLEY AVENUE
RUSKIN RD.
MILTON RD.
Inner Elm Ter.
ELM TER.
FOSSEWAY GS
FOSSE WAY
ROAD
JUBILEE RD.
BRYANT
Westfield Ter.
WATERSIDE CR.
WATERSIDE WY.
WATERSIDE ROAD
TREE AVENUE
LINCOMBE RD.
Factory
Sunflower Nursery Sch.
ST. PETER'S RD.
WELLS WAY
FOSSE WAY
A367
Play Field
Bowl. Gn.
FOURTH AV.
FIRST AVENUE
THIRD AV.
SECOND AVENUE
WESTFIELD INDUSTRIAL & TRADING ESTATE
Cricket Ground
Bowl. Grn.
CHARLTON PK.
PARK ROAD
SOUTH WAY
St. Benedicts R.C. Prim. Sch.
FOSSEWAY COUNTRY CLUB & GOLF COURSE
CHARLTON LANE
SILVER STREET
B3355
The Gables
Highfields
The Grange
GRANGE END
BOUNDARY CL.
CHARLTON PARK
FOSSEFIELD RD.
FOSSEWAY
MENDIP
The Firs
Playing Field
Club

148
151
68
155
54
53
A
B
C
1
2
3
4
5
NORTH EAST
BATH
Ba
BA3
Prim. Sch.
Springfield Heights
FOSSE GRN.
Old Pit Ter.
Clandown
Recreation Ground
Pav.
Rockhill Cottages
Fosse Cott.
KITLEY
LANE
HILL
FOSSE
LANE
Fosse Way
COOMBEND
BRISTOL ROAD
NEW ROAD
A367
OLD ROAD
MENDIP WY.
Rectory
Market Pl.
County Bri.
Wellow Brook
Wheeler's Hill
MIDSOMER ENTERPRISE PARK
Welton Hollow
Works
RADSTOCK ROAD
SOMERVALE ROAD
A362
Brook
Superstore
Wellow
WELTON ROAD
WELLS ROAD
WELLS HILL
FORTESCUE RD.
THE STREET
Liby.
Youth Cen.
Hall
CHURCH ST.
St. Nicholas Inf. Sch.
Norton Radstock College
Play. Fld.
Tennis Ct.
WHEELERS CL.
FIVE ARCHES CL.
WHEELERS DR.
WHEELERS
Fosseway Cottages
Somer
Coal Depot
HIGHFIELDS
Wells Square
FOSS WAY
FOSSEWAY GS.
AVENUE
SHAKESPEARE RD.
WESLEY
WESLEY AVENUE
WESLEY RD.
WELLS RD.
West Hill
West Hill Gdns.
TERRACE
MAPLE DR.
ALDER T.
WILLOW CL.
THE DRING
ACACIA RD.
PINE WK.
BIRCH
PARK
HOLLY WK.
MAY TREE RD.
West Hill Gardens
CEDAR TER.
CYPRS. TER.
OAK Gdns.
LIME
BEECH
JUBILEE RD.
BRYANT AV.
WEST HILL
Rec. Grd.
Westhill Sports Club
ROWAN CT.
TREE CT.
ASH
ROAD
GLEBELANDS
CHERRY TREE CL.
CHESTNUT CL.
Westfield Ter.
ELM TREE AVENUE
Inner Elm Ter.
ELM TER.
Playing Field
Westfield
Works
Westfield Co. Prim. Sch.
WATERSIDE CR.
WATERSIDE WY.
WATERSIDE ROAD
MAGNOLIA RD.
REDWOOD CL.
Waterside
Recreation Ground
Grove Wood
GROVE
WOOD RD.
HAYDON
HAYDON GA.
Down View
Haydon
KILMERSDON ROAD
HAYDON INDUSTRIAL ESTATE
LARCH CT.
THE LEAZE
LINCOMBE RD.
WAY
WATER
BRIAR CL.
LINDEN CL.
Waterside
Factory
FOSSEWAY
Hall
Play. Field
Bowl. Gn.
FOURTH AV.
FIRST AVENUE
THIRD AV.
SECOND AVENUE
Tyning Farm
Radstock & Midsomer Norton District Museum
Waterside House
WESTFIELD INDUSTRIAL & TRADING ESTATE
CHARLTON
FOSSEWAY COUNTRY CLUB & GOLF COURSE
Golf Course
Waterside Farm
LANE
WATERSIDE

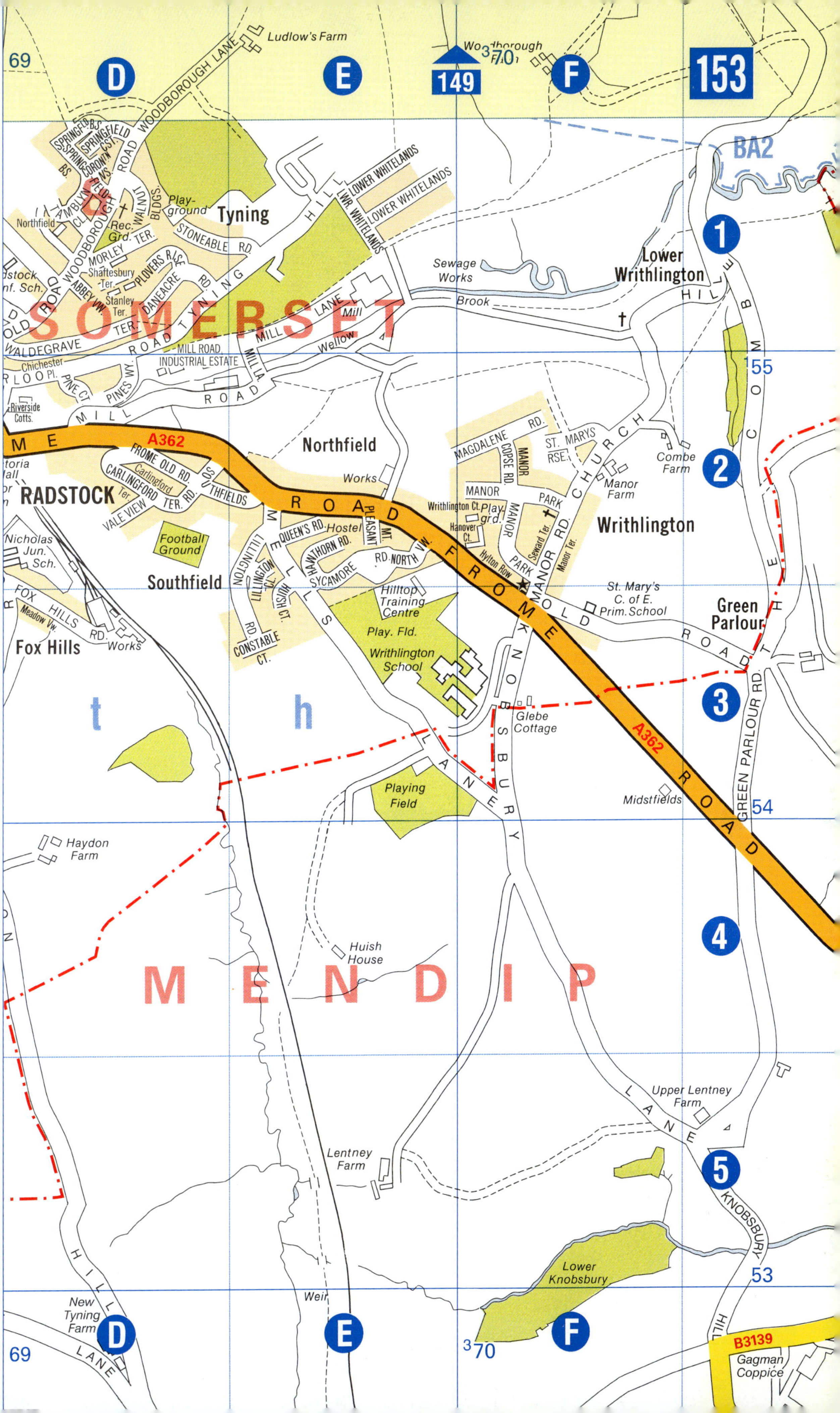

69
D
E
F
149
Ludlow's Farm
Woodborough
370
BA2
1
2
3
4
5
155
54
53
SOMERSET
MENDIP
Tyning
Lower Writhlington
Writhlington
Northfield
RADSTOCK
Southfield
Fox Hills
Green Parlour
WOODBOROUGH LANE
SPRINGFIELD BS.
SPRINGFIELD CRES.
SPRINGFIELD
CORONATION
TAMBLYN CL.
WOODBOROUGH RD.
Northfield
Rec. Grd.
WALNUT BLDGS.
Play-ground
STONEABLE RD.
MORLEY TER.
Shaftesbury Ter.
PLOVERS RISE
ABBEY VW.
Stanley Ter.
DANEACRE RD.
TYNING ROAD
TYNING TER.
WALDEGRAVE TER.
OLD ROAD
Chichester Pl.
LOOP
PINE CT.
PINES WY.
MILL ROAD INDUSTRIAL ESTATE
MILL LANE
MILL LA.
Mill
Wellow
ROAD
Riverside Cotts.
MILL
HILL
LOWER WHITELANDS
WR. WHITELANDS
Sewage Works
Brook
HILL
Combe Farm
Manor Farm
CHURCH
MAGDALENE RD.
ST. MARYS RSE.
COPSE RD.
MANOR
MANOR PARK
Writhlington Ct.
Play grd.
Hanover Ct.
Hylton Row
Seward Ter.
MANOR RD.
Manor Ter.
OLD ROAD
St. Mary's C. of E. Prim. School
THE COMBE
GREEN PARLOUR RD.
A362
FROME ROAD
FROME OLD RD.
Carlingford
CARLINGFORD TER.
VALE VIEW
SOUTHFIELDS
Works
MELLS LANE
MT. PLEASANT
QUEEN'S RD.
Hostel
HAWTHORN RD.
NORTH VW.
SYCAMORE
LILLINGTON CL.
LILLINGTON RD.
HUISH CT.
CONSTABLE CT.
Hilltop Training Centre
Play. Fld.
Writhlington School
Football Ground
Nicholas Jun. Sch.
FOX HILLS RD.
Meadow Vw.
Works
KNOBSBURY LANE
Glebe Cottage
Playing Field
Midstfields
Haydon Farm
Huish House
Upper Lentney Farm
Lentney Farm
Lower Knobsbury
KNOBSBURY HILL
B3139
Gagman Coppice
New Tyning Farm
HILL LANE
Weir

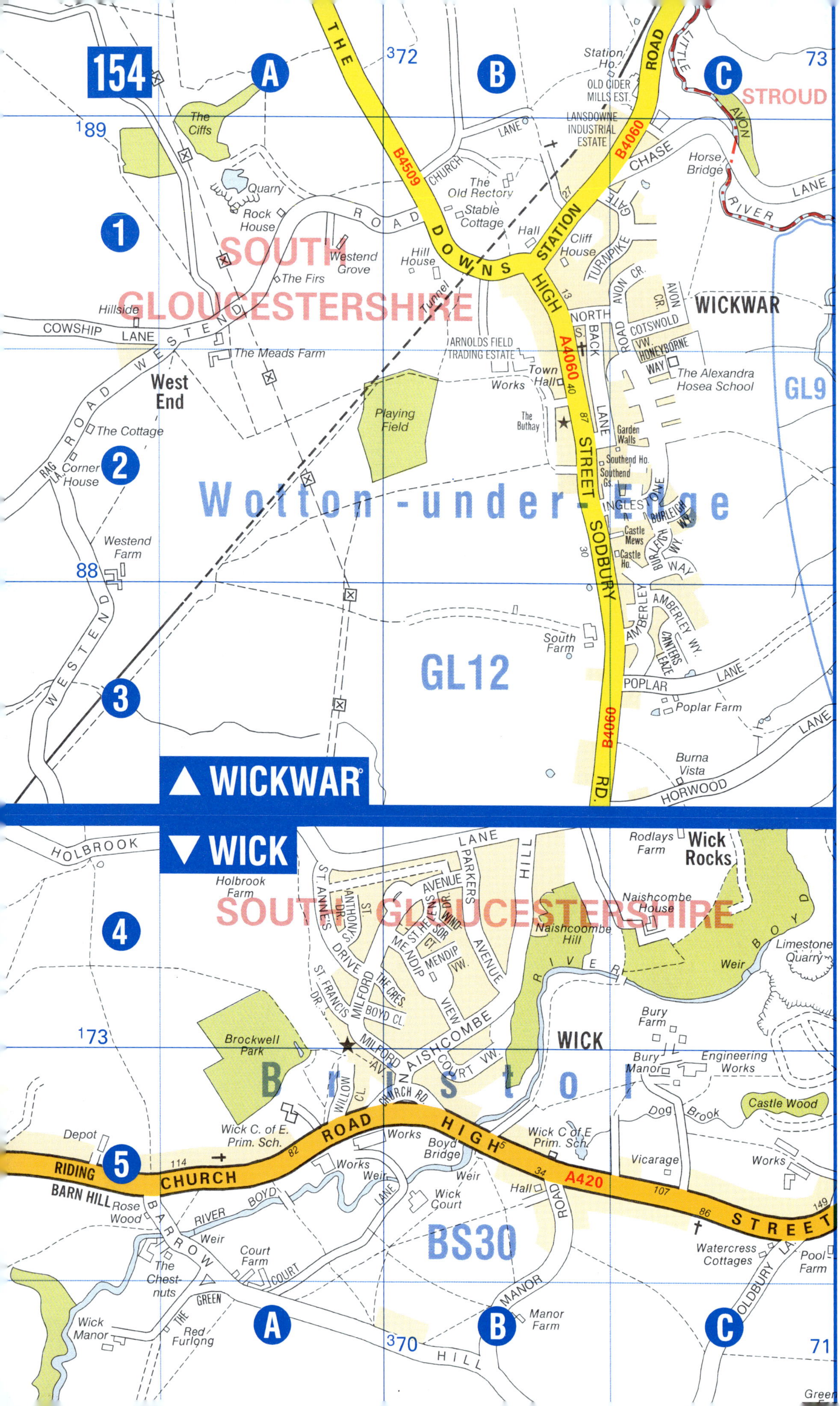

WICKWAR
WICK
SOUTH GLOUCESTERSHIRE
Wotton-under-Edge
Bristol
GL12
GL9
BS30
STROUD
A
B
C
1
2
3
4
5
372
370
73
71
189
88
173
The Ciffs
Quarry
Rock House
Westend Grove
The Firs
Hillside
COWSHIP LANE
WESTEND ROAD
West End
The Meads Farm
The Cottage
RAG LA.
Corner House
Westend Farm
THE DOWNS
B4509
CHURCH LANE
The Old Rectory
Stable Cottage
Hill House
Hall
Tunnel
ARNOLDS FIELD TRADING ESTATE
Playing Field
Works
Town Hall
The Buthay
Station Ho.
OLD CIDER MILLS EST.
LANSDOWNE INDUSTRIAL ESTATE
STATION ROAD
B4060
A4060
HIGH STREET
SODBURY RD.
Cliff House
TURNPIKE
GATE
CHASE
AVON CR.
NORTH
BACK LANE
ROAD
COTSWOLD
VW.
HONEYBORNE WAY
The Alexandra Hosea School
Garden Walls
Southend Ho.
Southend Gs.
INGLESTONE
Castle Mews
Castle Ho.
BURLEIGH WY.
WAY
AMBERLEY
AMBERLEY WY.
CANTERS LEAZE
South Farm
POPLAR LANE
Poplar Farm
Burna Vista
HORWOOD LANE
WICKWAR
LITTLE AVON
Horse Bridge
RIVER LANE
HOLBROOK LANE
Holbrook Farm
ST. ANNE'S DRIVE
ST. ANTHONY'S DR.
AVENUE
PARKERS AVENUE
HILL
ST. HELENS DR.
WINDSOR CT.
MENDIP VW.
MENDIP VIEW
MILFORD
THE CRES.
BOYD CL.
ST. FRANCIS DR.
MILFORD AV.
AISHCOMBE
COURT VW.
WILLOW CL.
CHURCH RD.
Brockwell Park
Wick C. of E. Prim. Sch.
Depot
Rodlays Farm
Wick Rocks
Naishcombe House
Naishcombe Hill
BOYD RIVER
Limestone Quarry
Weir
Bury Farm
Bury Manor
Engineering Works
Castle Wood
Dog Brook
Vicarage
Works
RIDING
BARN HILL
CHURCH ROAD
HIGH STREET
A420
Boyd Bridge
Hall
Wick Court
Rose Wood
BARROW
RIVER BOYD
LANE
Court Farm
COURT
The Chestnuts
THE GREEN
Red Furlong
Wick Manor
MANOR ROAD
Manor Farm
HILL
Watercress Cottages
OLDBURY LA.
Pool Farm
Green

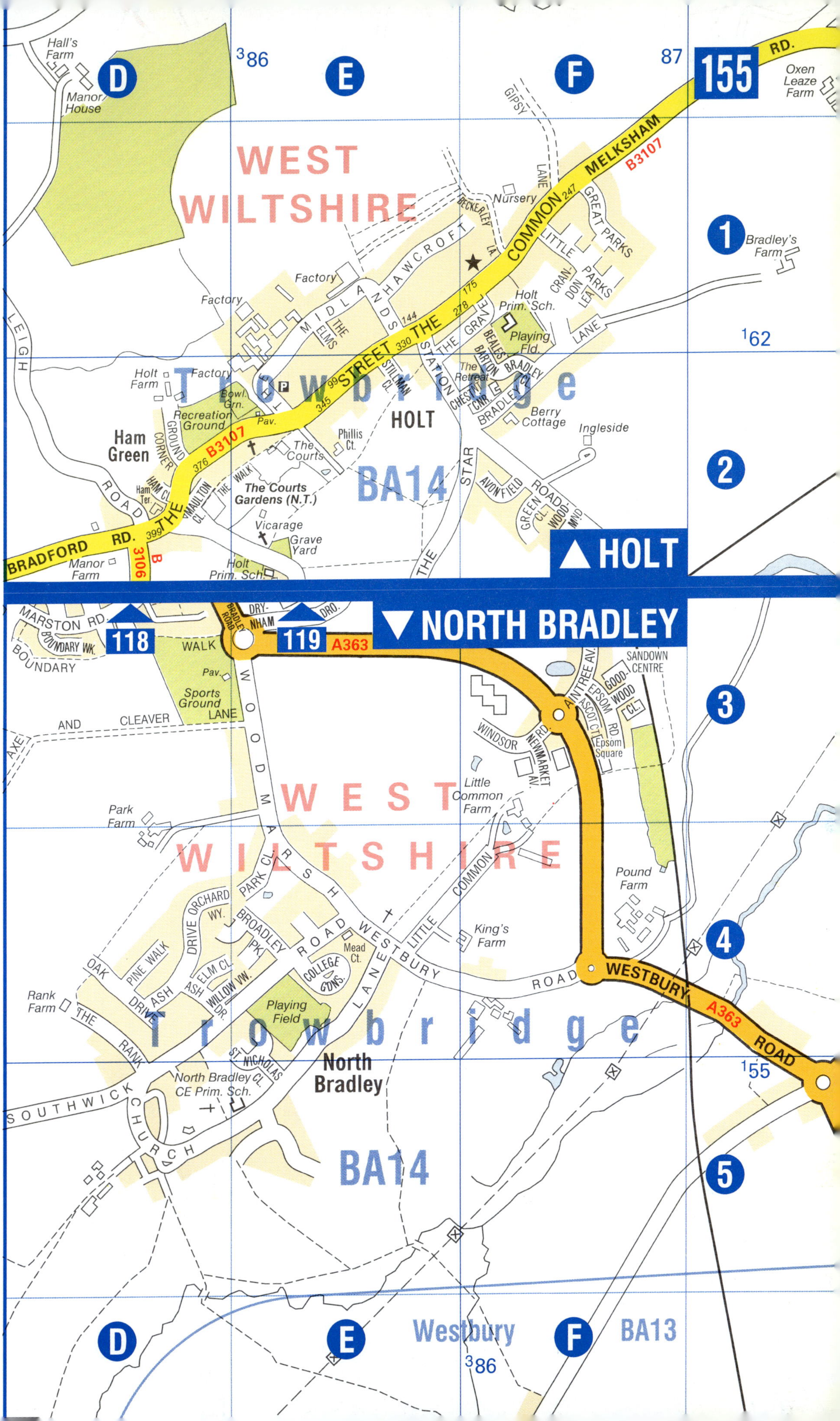
155
D
E
F
386
87
162
155
1
2
3
4
5
HOLT
NORTH BRADLEY
118
119
WEST WILTSHIRE
Trowbridge
BA14
BA13
Westbury
Hall's Farm
Manor House
Oxen Leaze Farm
Bradley's Farm
MELKSHAM RD.
B3107
GIPSY LANE
Nursery
BECKERLEY LA.
COMMON
GREAT PARKS
LITTLE PARKS
CRANDON LEA
LANE
Holt Prim. Sch.
Playing Fld.
HAWCROFT
MIDLANDS
THE ELMS
Factory
THE STREET
STILLMAN CL.
STATION
THE GRAVE
BEALES BARTON
BRADLEY CL.
The Retreat
CHESTNUT CNR.
BRADLEY
Berry Cottage
Ingleside
LEIGH
Holt Farm
Bowl. Grn.
Recreation Ground
Pav.
Ham Green
CORNER GROUND
The Courts
Phillis Ct.
HOLT
The Courts Gardens (N.T.)
Vicarage
Grave Yard
STAR
AVONFIELD
GREEN CL.
WOODMIND
ROAD
HAM CL.
Ham Ter.
MAULTON CL.
THE WALK
BRADFORD RD.
B3106
Manor Farm
Holt Prim. Sch.
THE
MARSTON RD.
BOUNDARY WK.
BOUNDARY
WALK
BRADLEY ROAD
DRYNHAM DRO.
A363
SANDOWN CENTRE
AINTREE AV.
EPSOM RD.
ASCOT CT.
GOODWOOD CL.
Epsom Square
WINDSOR RD.
NEWMARKET AV.
Pav.
Sports Ground
LANE
AXE AND CLEAVER
WOODMARSH
Little Common Farm
Park Farm
PARK CL.
ORCHARD DRIVE
WY.
BROADLEY PK.
LITTLE COMMON
Pound Farm
King's Farm
WESTBURY ROAD
WESTBURY ROAD
A363
Mead Ct.
COLLEGE GDNS.
PINE WALK
ELM CL.
ASH
ASH
WILLOW VW.
DR.
OAK DRIVE
LANE
Playing Field
Rank Farm
THE RANK
ST. NICHOLAS CL.
North Bradley
North Bradley CE Prim. Sch.
SOUTHWICK
CHURCH

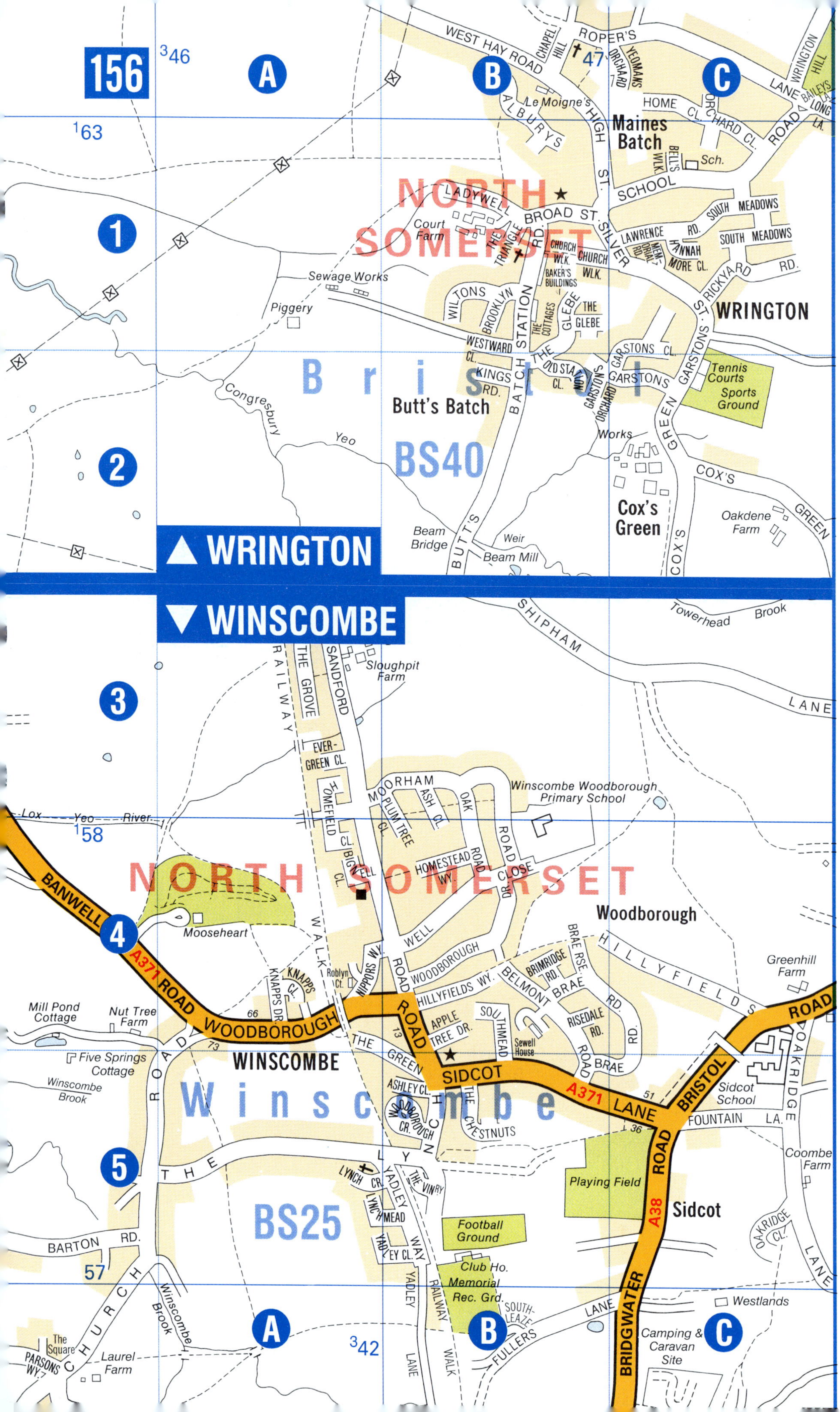
WRINGTON
WINSCOMBE
NORTH SOMERSET
Bristol
BS40
BS25
A
B
C
1
2
3
4
5
346
163
47
158
57
342
WEST HAY ROAD
CHAPEL HILL
ROPER'S
ORCHARD
YEOMANS
WRINGTON HILL
LANE
BAILEYS LA.
LONG LA.
Le Moigne's
ALBURYS
HIGH ST.
HOME CL.
ORCHARD CL.
ROAD
Maines Batch
BELL'S WLK.
Sch.
SCHOOL
LADYWELL
BROAD ST.
SILVER ST.
Court Farm
THE TRIANGLE
RD.
CHURCH WLK.
BAKER'S BUILDINGS
LAWRENCE RD.
MEMORIAL RD.
HANNAH MORE CL.
SOUTH MEADOWS
RICKYARD RD.
Sewage Works
Piggery
WILTONS
BROOKLYN
STATION
THE COTTAGES
GLEBE
THE GLEBE
WESTWARD CL.
KINGS RD.
BATCH
THE OLD STATION CL.
GARSTONS CL.
GARSTONS
GARSTON'S ORCHARD
GREEN
Tennis Courts
Sports Ground
Congresbury
Yeo
Butt's Batch
Works
COX'S
GREEN
Cox's Green
Oakdene Farm
Beam Bridge
BUTT'S
Weir
Beam Mill
SHIPHAM
Towerhead
Brook
LANE
RAILWAY
THE GROVE
SANDFORD
Sloughpit Farm
EVERGREEN CL.
MOORHAM
ASH CL.
OAK
PLUM TREE CL.
Winscombe Woodborough Primary School
ROAD
HOMEFIELD CL.
Lox Yeo River
BIGWELL CL.
HOMESTEAD WY.
CLOSE
DR.
Woodborough
BANWELL
A371
ROAD
Mooseheart
WALK
WELL
WOODBOROUGH
BRAE RSE.
BRIMRIDGE RD.
BELMONT BRAE
HILLYFIELDS
HILLYFIELDS WY.
Greenhill Farm
KNAPPS CL.
KNAPPS DR.
Roblyn Ct.
NIPPORS WY.
APPLE TREE DR.
SOUTHMEAD
RISEDALE RD.
RD.
Mill Pond Cottage
Nut Tree Farm
66
WOODBOROUGH
THE GREEN
Sewell House
ROAD
BRAE
OAKRIDGE
73
WINSCOMBE
13
SIDCOT
51
LANE
BRISTOL
Sidcot School
Five Springs Cottage
Winscombe Brook
ASHLEY CL.
WOODBOROUGH CR.
CHURCH
THE CHESTNUTS
FOUNTAIN LA.
36
Coombe Farm
THE LY
LYNCH CR.
YADLEY
THE VINRY
Playing Field
A38
Sidcot
LYNCH MEAD
YADLEY CL.
WAY
Football Ground
OAKRIDGE CL.
BARTON RD.
Club Ho.
Memorial Rec. Grd.
RAILWAY
SOUTH LEAZE
FULLERS
Westlands
BRIDGWATER
Camping & Caravan Site
Winscombe Brook
The Square
PARSONS WY.
Laurel Farm

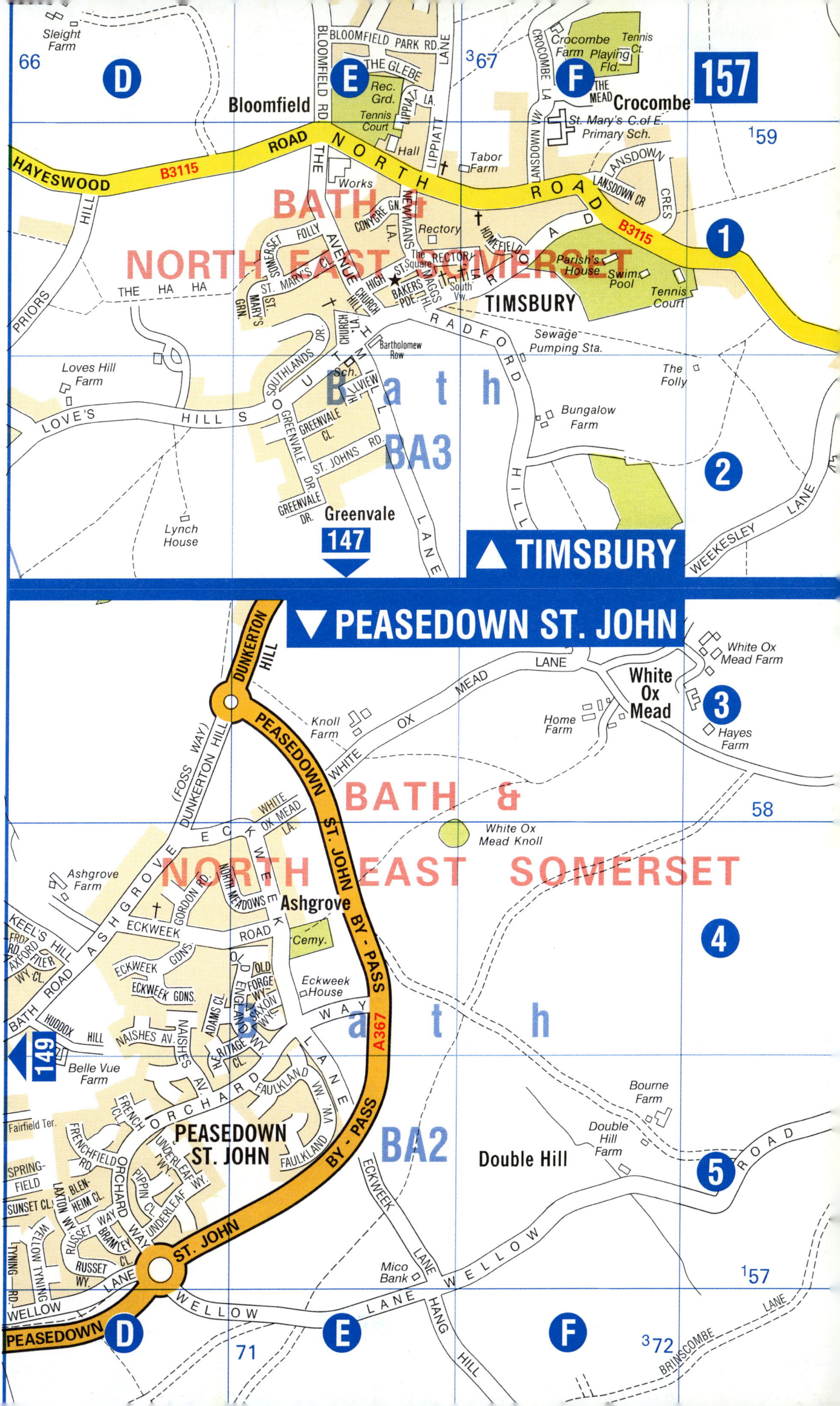
D
E
F
66
367
159
58
157
71
372
1
2
3
4
5
Sleight Farm
Bloomfield
BLOOMFIELD PARK RD.
BLOOMFIELD RD.
THE GLEBE
Rec. Grd.
Tennis Court
LIPPIATT LA.
LIPPIATT LANE
Hall
Crocombe Farm
Tennis Ct.
Playing Fld.
CROCOMBE LA.
THE MEAD
Crocombe
St. Mary's C.of E. Primary Sch.
LANSDOWN VW.
LANSDOWN CRES
LANSDOWN CR
HAYESWOOD ROAD
B3115
NORTH ROAD
THE AVENUE
Works
Tabor Farm
CONYGRE GN.
NEWMANS LA.
Rectory
HOMEFIELD
HILL
FOLLY
SOMERSET SQ.
ST. MARY'S CL.
ST. MARY'S GRN.
THE HA HA
PRIORS HILL
The Square
RECTORY
HIGH ST.
BAKERS PDE.
MAGGS HL.
South Vw.
CHURCH HILL
CHURCH LA.
Parish's House
Swim. Pool
Tennis Court
TIMSBURY
BATH & NORTH EAST SOMERSET
RADFORD HILL
Sewage Pumping Sta.
The Folly
Bartholomew Row
Sch.
SOUTHLANDS DR.
HILLVIEW
Loves Hill Farm
LOVE'S HILL
SOUTH HILL
MILL LANE
Bath
BA3
Bungalow Farm
GREENVALE DR.
GREENVALE CL.
ST. JOHNS RD.
Greenvale
Lynch House
WEEKESLEY LANE
147
▲ TIMSBURY
▼ PEASEDOWN ST. JOHN
DUNKERTON HILL
White Ox Mead Farm
LANE
White Ox Mead
WHITE OX MEAD LANE
Knoll Farm
Home Farm
Hayes Farm
(FOSS WAY)
PEASEDOWN ST. JOHN BY - PASS
WHITE OX MEAD LA.
White Ox Mead Knoll
ECKWEEK LANE
ASHGROVE
Ashgrove Farm
Ashgrove
GORDON RD.
NORTH MEADOWS
ECKWEEK ROAD
Cemy.
KEEL'S HILL
FRD. RD.
AXFORD WY.
FILER CL.
BATH ROAD
ECKWEEK GDNS.
OLD ENGLAND WY.
OLD FORGE WY.
SAXON WY.
Eckweek House
WAY
A367
ADAMS CL.
HERITAGE CL.
HUDDOX HILL
NAISHES AV.
149
Belle Vue Farm
ORCHARD
FAULKLAND VW.
FAULKLAND
FRENCH CL.
Fairfield Ter.
FRENCHFIELD RD.
PEASEDOWN ST. JOHN
BA2
Bourne Farm
Double Hill Farm
Double Hill
ROAD
SPRING-FIELD
SUNSET CL.
BLEN-HEIM CL.
ORCHARD WAY
UNDERLEAF WY.
PIPPIN CL.
LAXTON WY.
RUSSET WAY
BRAMLEY CL.
RUSSET WY.
WELLOW TYNING
TYNING RD.
ECKWEEK LANE
ST. JOHN
LANE
WELLOW
Mico Bank
WELLOW LANE
HANG HILL
BRINSCOMBE LANE
PEASEDOWN

CWMBRAN
A4042
Llandegveth
Tredunnock
Llangybi
Newbridge-on-Usk
Llanfrechta
Ponthir
Caerleon
Malpas
Bettws
NEWPORT
(Casnewydd)
NEWPORT
Transporter Bridge
Tredegar House
Coedkernew
Marshfield
St. Brides Wentlooge
Peterstone Wentlooge
Pye Corner
Nash
Goldcliff
Whitson
Redwick
Llandevenny
Bishton
Llanwern
Magor
Undy
Magor Marsh
Llanmartin
Penhow
Parc-Seymour
Llanvaches
Caerwent
Carrow Hill
Shirenewton
Earlswood
Wentwood
Llanvair Discoed
Itton Common
Mynydd-bach
Crossway Green
Pwllmeyric
Mounton
Newton Green
Mathern
Crick
Caldicot
Rogiet
Portskewett
Sudbrook
Highmoor Hill
St. Arvans
Woodcroft
Tutshill
Tidenham
Sedbury
CHEPSTOW
(Cas-gwent)
Beachley
Severn Road Bridge
Severn Tunnel
SEVERN VIEW
Aust
Redwick
Northwick
Severn Beach
Pilning
Easter Compton
Compton Greenfield
Hallen
Henbury
Shirehampton
Sea Mills
Avonmouth
Portishead
Portishead Point
Woodhill
Redcliff Bay
West Hill
Weston-in-Gordano
North Weston
Clapton-in-Gordano
Easton-in-Gordano
Pill
Ham Green
Abbots Leigh
Clifton
GORDANO
Portbury
Lower Failand
Failand
BRISTOL
Long Ashton
Yanley
Farley
Walton-in-Gordano
Walton Park
CLEVEDON
East Clevedon
Clevedon Ct.
Tickenham
Stone-edge Batch
Wraxall
Nailsea
West End
East End
St. Mary's Grove
Kenn
Chelvey
Farleigh
Flax Bourton
Backwell
Barrow Gurney
Barrow Common
Dundry
East Dundry
Bishopsworth
Headley Park
NORTH SOMERSET
West Town
Brockley
Brockley Combe
Kingston Seymour
North End
Claverham
Horsecastle
Yatton
Cleeve
Goblin Combe
BRISTOL (Lulsgate)
Lulsgate Bottom
Upper Town
Felton
Winford
Chew Magna
Dundry Hill
MOUTH OF THE SEVERN
Portland Grounds
SCALE
approx. 3 miles to 1 inch 1:195,084
0 1 2 3 4 5 Miles
0 1 2 3 4 5 Kilometres
Middle Hope
Sand Point
Sand Bay
Woodspring Priory
Wick St. Lawrence
Iwood
Bourton
Kewstoke
St. George's
Worle
Milton
West Wick
Weston Bay
Sea Life Centre
WESTON-SUPER-MARE
Hutton
Locking
Uphill
Oldmixon
Bleadon
Brean Down
Bleadon Hill
Christon
Loxton
Brean
Brean Leisure Park
Lympsham
Eastertown
Berrow Dunes
Wick
Edingworth
SEDGEMOOR
Berrow
East Brent
Brent Knoll
Battleborough
Edithmead
BURNHAM-ON-SEA
Highbridge
Alstone
Bridgwater Bay
Huntspill
East Huntspill
West Huntspill
Stretcholt
Bason Bridge
Mark Causeway
Mark
Yarrow
Vole
Northwick
Rooks Bridge
Tarnock
Stone Allerton
Chapel Allerton
Badgworth
Weare
Lower Weare
Cross
Biddisham
Compton Bishop
Barton
Winscombe
Sidcot
Shipham
Banwell
Sandford
Churchill
Knightcott
Stonebridge
Court Farm
West Hewish
Hewish
Puxton
Congresbury
Wrington
Lower Langford
Upper Langford
Rowberrow
Burrington
Rickford
Blagdon
Blagdon Lake
Redhill
Cowslip Green
Butcombe
Regil
Chew Stoke
West Town
Nempnett Thrubwell
Chew Valley Lake
Bishop Sutton
Ubley
Compton Martin
West Harptree
East Harptree
Smitham Hill
Greendown
Charterhouse
MENDIP HILLS
Cheddar
Cheddar Gorge
Axbridge
Cheddar Resr.
Cox's Cave
Jacob's Ladder
Bradley Cross
Draycott
Rodney Stoke
Priddy
Nyland Hill
Alston Sutton
Clewer
Crickham
Middle Stoughton
Stoughton Cross
West Stoughton
Blackford
Wedmore
Cocklake
Westham
Sand
Heath House
Bagley
Mudgley
Theale
Panborough
Bleadney
Westbury-sub-Mendip
Easton
Wookey Hole
Wookey Hole Caves & Mill
Ebbor Gorge
Ebbor Rocks
Wookey
Henton
Yarley
Walcombe
Haybridge
Wells
Dulcote
Burcott
Coxley
Dinder
Green Ore
West Horrington
SOMERSET
M4
M48
M49
M5
A4042
A449
A48
A4455
A403
A4
A369
A370
A371
A38
A368
A3033
B4245
B3124
B3128
B3129
B3130
B3133
B3134
B3135
B3139
B3140
B3151
B3371
B3114
TOLL
DANGER AREA

159
Bevington
Shepperdine
Hill
Stone
Woodford
MICHAELWOOD
North Nibley
Southend
Tyndale Mon
Holywell
Coombe
Wotton-under-Edge
Newark Park
Kingscote
Newington Bagpath
Tetbury
Long
Rockhampton
Falfield
Tortworth
Chestnut
Bradley
Charfield
Kingswood
Abbey Gatehouse
Wortley
Alderley
COTSWOLD HILLS
Tresham
Doughton
Oldbury-on-Severn
Lower Morton
Whitfield
Thornbury
Brickpits
Kington
Morton
Cromhall
Hillesley
Lower Kilcott
Leighterton
Westonbirt Arboretum
Westonbirt
Shipton Moyne
Brokenborough
Easton Grey
Elberton
Thornbury
Milbury Heath
Cromhall Common
Nan Tow's Tump
Oldbury on the Hill
Willesley
Knockdown
Oldown Farm
Alveston
Old Down
SOUTH GLOUCESTERSHIRE
Tytherington
West End
Wickwar
Somerset Monument
Upper Kilcott
Olveston
Rudgeway
Bagstone
Didmarton
Sopworth
Malmes
Tockington
Itchington
Earthcott Green
Rangeworthy
Hawkesbury
Hawkesbury Upton
Dunkirk
Sherston
Foxley
WILTSHIRE
Norton
Horton
Horton Court
Little Badminton
Luckington
Luckington Court
Alderton
Corston
Engine Common
Gaunt's Earthcott
Latteridge
Iron Acton
Frampton Cotterell
Goose Green
Yate
Little Sodbury
Old Sodbury
Badminton
Badminton House
Patchway
Bradley Stoke
Winterbourne
Coalpit Heath
Mayshill
Chipping Sodbury
Dodington
Acton Turville
Littleton Drew
Grittleton
Hullavington
Leigh Delamere
Stanton St. Quintin
Filton
Stoke Gifford
Harry Stoke
Westerleigh
Wapley
Codrington
Tormarton
Burton
Kendleshire
Henfield
Nettleton
West Kington
Castle Combe
LEIGH DELAMERE
Kington St. Michael
Horfield
Hambrook
Downend
MANGOTSFIELD
Staple Hill
Broomhill
Stapleton
Fishponds
Soundwell
Shortwood
Pucklechurch
Hinton
Dyrham Park
Dyrham
West Littleton
Yatton Keynell
North Wraxall
Rack Hill
Ford
West Yatton
Hardenhuish
Clay Hill
Siston
Abson
Warmley
Bridgeyate
Doynton
Pennsylvania
Wick
Marshfield
Upper Wraxall
Slaughterford
Giddeahall
Sheldon Manor
Biddestone
Kingswood
Hanham
Avon Valley
Oldland
Conham
Hanham Green
Brislington
Willsbridge
Beach
Sir Bevil Grenville's Monument
Upton Cheyney
Cold Ashton
Tadwick
St. Catherine
Thickwood
Underground Quarry
Colerne
Corsham
Easton
Corsham Court
Knowle
Bitton
KEYNSHAM
Avon Valley
Saltford
North Stoke
Bath
Langridge
Ditteridge
Rudloe
Moor Green
Nottons
Stockwood
Queen Charlton
Woolley
Swainswick
Tower
Charlcombe
Fort NT
Batheaston
Box
Hazelbury Manor
Ashley
Kingsdown
Neston
Gastard
Fox Talbot NT
Whitchurch
Kelston
Weston
Larkhall
Bathford
Wadswick
North Wick
Norton Malreward
Chewton Keynsham
Burnett
Corston
Newton St. Loe
Paris College
Bathampton
Monkton Farleigh
South Wraxall
Atworth
Whitley
Shaw
Beanacre
Woollard
Publow
Pensford
Compton Dando
BATH
Twerton
Hall
Claverton
Combe Down
Prior
Farleigh Wick
Norrington Common
Broughton Gifford
Stone Circles
Stanton Wick
Stanton Prior
Englishcombe
Southdown
Dundas Aqueduct
Bradford Leigh
Great Chalfield Manor
Holt
Kennet & Avon Canal
Hunstrete
Marksbury
Wilmington
Odd Down
Monkton Combe
Limpley Stoke
Woolley Green
The Courts
Staverton
Chelwood
BATH & N.E. SOMERSET
Inglesbatch
Southstoke
Winsley
Turleigh
Tithe Barn
Old Manor
BRADFORD-ON-AVON
Semington
Stowey
Clutton
Farmborough
Priston
Tunley
Midford
Freshford
Barton Farm
Iford Manor
Westwood
Trowle Common
Hilperton
Hilperton Marsh
Great Hinton
High Littleton
Timsbury
Dunkerton
Combe Hay
Twinhoe
Ashton Common
Cameley
Radford
Meadgate
Carlingcott
Peasedown St. John
Wellow
Ford
Charterhouse
Farleigh Hungerford
Upper Studley
TROWBRIDGE
Steeple Ashton
Hinton Blewett
Temple Cloud
Hallatrow
Shire Horse Ctr
Camerton
Shoscombe
Stoney Littleton Long Barrow
Norwood Farm
Norton St. Philip
Wingfield
West Ashton
Farrington Gurney
Paulton
Clandown
Radstock
Foxcote
Tellisford
Southwick
Sherborne
Litton
Midsomer Norton
Welton
Westfield
Faulkland
Rode
Bird Gardens
North Bradley
Yarnbrook
Dunge
Ford
Chewton Mendip
Ston Easton
Clapton
Norton Hill
Norton District
Hemington
Woolverton
Hawkeridge
Woodland Park
Heywood
Edingt
Chilcompton
Emborough
Charlton
Kilmersdon
Hardington
Laverton
Bratton
Bratton Castle
White Horse
East End
Downside
Stratton-on-the-Fosse
Lullington
Buckland Dinham
Beckington
Rudge
Standerwick
Dilton Marsh
Westbury
Binegar
Gurney Slade
Lipyeate
Highbury
Holcombe
Vobster Light Railway
Mells
Great Elm
Oldford
Stonebridge
Berkley
Westbury Leigh
Summer Down
Ashwick
Nettlebridge
Coleford
Leigh-upon-Mendip
Vobster
Whatley
Old Dilton
Upton Scudamore
East Horrington
Maesbury Castle
Oakhill
Stoke St. Michael
Chantry
FROME
Keyford
Chapmanslade
Lane End
Corsley
Weapons Museum
Shepton Mallet
Cranmore Tower
Little Elm
Nunney
Blatchbridge
Corsley Heath
Cley Hill
WARMINSTER
Dewey
Boreham
Downside
Bowlish
Shepton Mallet
Waterlip
Chelynch
Dean
Downhead
Holwell
Leighton
Cloford
Tytherington
West Woodlands
East Woodlands
Longleat
Longhedge
Sambourne
Norton Bavant
Bishopstrow
East Cranmore
Trudoxhill
M4
M5
M32
M48
A4
A36
A37
A38
A46
A350
A361
A420
A432
A433

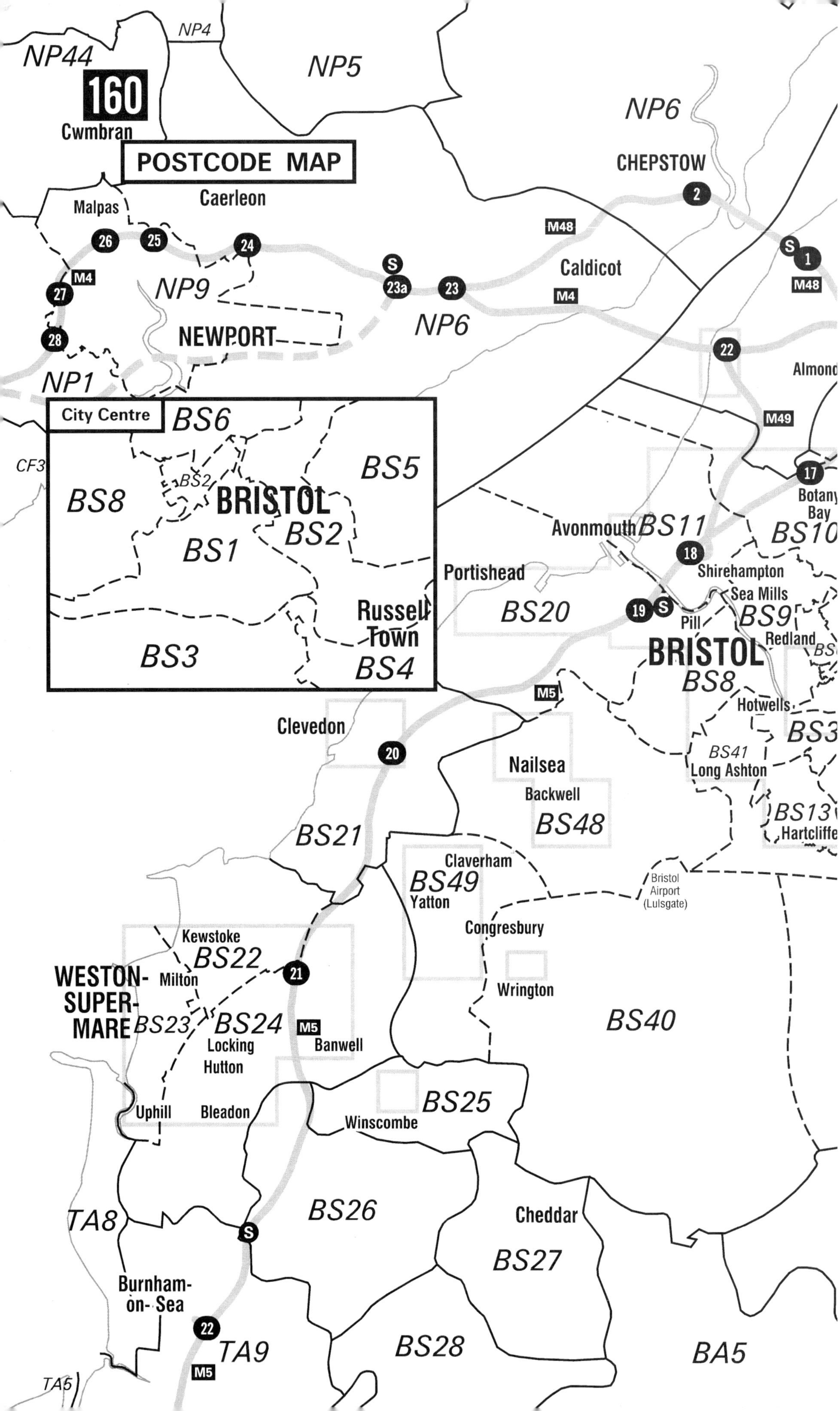
160
POSTCODE MAP
NP44
NP4
NP5
NP6
Cwmbran
CHEPSTOW
Caerleon
Malpas
M48
M4
Caldicot
NP9
NEWPORT
NP6
NP1
Almond
M49
CF3
City Centre
BS6
BS5
BS2
BS8
BRISTOL
BS2
BS1
Russell Town
BS3
BS4
Botany Bay
Avonmouth
BS11
BS10
Portishead
Shirehampton
Sea Mills
BS20
Pill
BS9
Redland
BRISTOL
BS8
Hotwells
M5
BS3
Clevedon
Nailsea
BS41
Long Ashton
Backwell
BS48
BS13
Hartcliffe
BS21
Claverham
BS49
Yatton
Bristol Airport (Lulsgate)
Congresbury
Kewstoke
BS22
WESTON-SUPER-MARE
Milton
Wrington
BS23
BS24
M5
Locking
Banwell
BS40
Hutton
BS25
Uphill
Bleadon
Winscombe
BS26
TA8
Cheddar
BS27
Burnham-on-Sea
BS28
TA9
M5
BA5
TA5

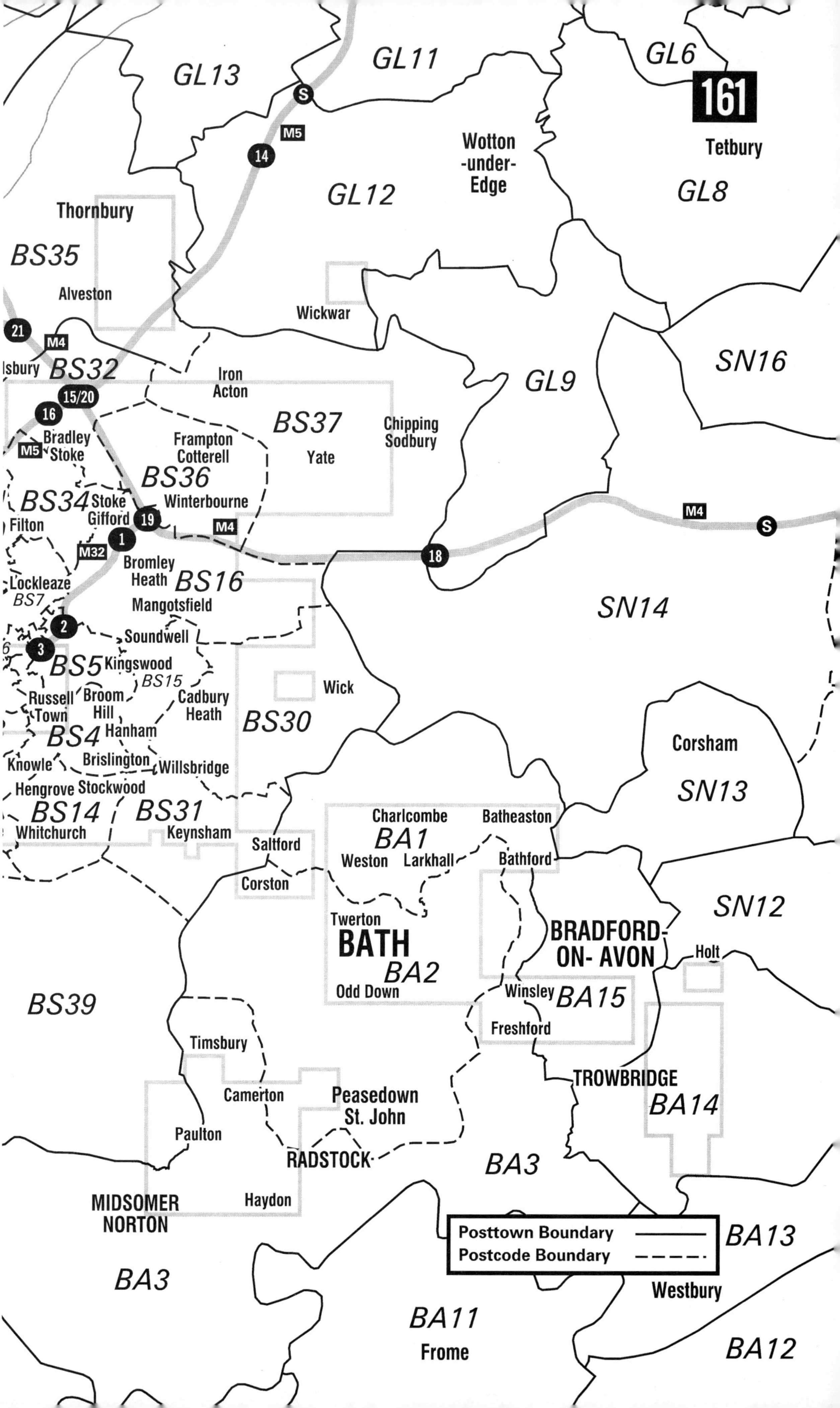
GL13
GL11
GL6
Tetbury
M5
14
Wotton
-under-
Edge
GL12
GL8
Thornbury
BS35
Alveston
Wickwar
21
M4
lsbury
BS32
Iron
Acton
15/20
16
BS37
Chipping
Sodbury
SN16
GL9
Bradley
Stoke
M5
Frampton
Cotterell
Yate
BS36
BS34
Stoke
Gifford
19
Winterbourne
Filton
M4
1
M32
M4
18
Bromley
Heath
BS16
Lockleaze
BS7
Mangotsfield
SN14
2
Soundwell
3
BS5
Kingswood
BS15
Russell
Town
Broom
Hill
Cadbury
Heath
Wick
BS4
Hanham
BS30
Corsham
Knowle
Brislington
Willsbridge
SN13
Hengrove
Stockwood
BS14
BS31
Whitchurch
Keynsham
Charlcombe
Batheaston
BA1
Saltford
Weston
Larkhall
Bathford
Corston
SN12
Twerton
BATH
BRADFORD-
ON- AVON
Holt
BA2
Odd Down
Winsley
BA15
BS39
Freshford
Timsbury
TROWBRIDGE
BA14
Camerton
Peasedown
St. John
Paulton
RADSTOCK
BA3
MIDSOMER
NORTON
Haydon
Posttown Boundary
Postcode Boundary
BA13
BA3
Westbury
BA11
Frome
BA12

INDEX TO PLACES & AREAS

with their map square reference

NOTES

1. Names in this Index shown in CAPITAL LETTERS followed by their Postcode District(s), are Postal Addresses.
2. The places & areas index reference indicates the approximate centre of the town or place and not where the name occurs on the map.

ABBOTS LEIGH. (BS8) —3E **67**
Abson. —5F **65**
ALMONDSBURY. (BS32) —2D **11**
ALVESTON. (BS35) —2B **8**
Alveston Down. —2A **8**
ARNO'S VALE. (BS4) —1D **81**
Ashgrove. —4D **157**
ASHLEY DOWN. (BS7) —3A **58**
ASHTON GATE. (BS3) —1C **78**
Ashton Hill. —4A **94**
Ashton Vale. —3B **78**
Ashton Watering. —5A **76**
AVONCLIFF. (BA15) —4F **113**
AVONMOUTH. (BS11) —3D **37**
AZTEC WEST. (BS32) —4C **10**

BACKWELL. (BS48) —2D **125**
Backwell Common. —1D **125**
Backwell Green. —1F **125**
Bailbrook. —3D **101**
BANWELL. (BS24) —5F **137**
BAPTIST MILLS. (BS2) —5C **58**
BARRS COURT. (BS30) —5B **74**
BARTON HILL. (BS5) —4D **71**
Batch, The. —4B **146**
BATH. (BA1 to BA3) —3B **106**
BATHAMPTON. (BA2) —5A **102**
BATHEASTON. (BA1) —3A **102**
BATHFORD. (BA1) —4D **103**
BATHWICK. (BA2) —2C **106**
Beacon Hill. —5B **100**
Bear Flat. —5A **106**
BEDMINSTER. (BS3) —2E **79**
BEDMINSTER DOWN. (BS13) —5C **78**
Beechen Cliff. —4A **106**
Belle Vue. —1E **151**
Berwick. —3F **23**
BISHOPSTON. (BS7) —4F **57**
BISHOPSWORTH. (BS13) —2C **86**
BITTON. (BS30) —5F **85**
Blackhorse. —4C **46**
Blaise Hamlet. —2F **39**
BLEADON. (BS24) —5A **140**
Bloomfield. —2E **109** (Bath)
Bloomfield. —4B **146** (Paulton)
Bloomfield. —1E **157** (Timsbury)
Botany Bay. —5B **24**
Bower Ashton. —1A **78**
BRADFORD-ON-AVON. (BA15) —3D **115**
BRADLEY STOKE. (BS32) —1E **27**
BRENTRY. (BS10) —1D **41**
BRIDGEYATE. (BS30) —3F **75**
Brinsea. —5E **145**
BRISLINGTON. (BS4) —3A **82**
BRISTOL. (BS1 to BS20) —3F **69**
Britten's. —3C **146**
Broad Mead. —5D **27**
BROCKLEY. (BS48) —5A **124**
Bromley Heath. —3F **45**
Broomhill. —1B **60** (North Bristol)
Broom Hill. —2B **82** (South Bristol)
Burchells Green. —1D **73**
Butts Batch. —2B **156**

Cadbury Heath. —4D **75**
CAMERTON. (BA3) —1B **148**
Canon's Marsh. —4E **69**
CARLINGCOTT. (BA2) —1D **149**
Catbrain. —3D **25**
CHARLCOMBE. (BA1) —3A **100**
CHELVEY. (BS48) —3A **124**
Chelvey Batch. —5B **124**
Chester Park. —5D **61**
CHIPPING SODBURY. (BS37) —5D **19**
Church Town. —3E **125**
CLANDOWN. (BA3) —5B **148**
CLAVERHAM. (BS49) —2F **143**
CLAVERTON DOWN. (BA2) —1F **111**
Clay Bottom. —5F **59**
CLAY HILL. (BS5) —5A **60**
CLEVEDON. (BS21) —3D **121**
CLIFTON. (BS8) —5C **56**
CLIFTON WOOD. (BS8) —4C **68**
COALPIT HEATH. (BS36) —3E **31**
Cockshot Hill. —5A **62**
Colt's Green. —1F **35**
COMBE DOWN. (BA2) —3C **110**
Compton Greenfield. —1B **24**
CONGRESBURY. (BS49) —2D **145**
Conham. —5B **72**
Conkwell. —1C **112**
COOMBE DINGLE. (BS9) —5F **39**
CORSTON. (BA2) —5D **95**
COTHAM. (BS6) —1E **69**
Cox's Green. —2C **156**
Crew's Hole. —3A **72**
Crocombe. —1F **157**
Crofts End. —1A **72**
Crook's Marsh. —1C **22**
Crossways. —2F **7**

Dean Hill. —4A **98**
Dings, The. —4C **70**
Double Hill. —5F **157**
DOWNEND. (BS16) —1A **62**
Drynham. —5E **119**
DUNDRY. (BS41) —4A **86**

East Clevedon. —3F **121**
East End. —4F **123**
EASTER COMPTON. (BS35) —1D **25**
Eastfield. —5D **41**
EASTON-IN-GORDANO. (BS20) —3C **52**
EAST ROLSTONE. (BS24) —4F **131**
East Twerton. —3E **105**
EASTVILLE. (BS5) —5E **59**
Elborough. —5F **135**
Emerson's Green. —1D **63**
Engine Common. —1E **17**
ENGLISHCOMBE. (BA2) —2A **108**

Fairfield Park. —4B **100**
Farleigh. —1F **125**
FILTON. (BS34) —1C **42**
Filwood Park. —4A **80**
FISHPONDS. (BS16) —3C **60**
Flaxpits. —4A **30**
Forewoods Common. —1B **116**
Fox Hills. —3D **153**
FRAMPTON COTTERELL. (BS36) —1C **30**
Frampton End. —1E **31**
FRENCHAY. (BS16) —5D **45**
FRESHFORD. (BA3) —4C **112**
Frogland Cross. —2E **13**
Frost Hill. —4D **143**

GAUNT'S EARTHCOTT. (BS32) —1D **13**
Golden Hill. —2E **57**
Goose Green. —1E **75** (Warmley)
Goose Green. —2A **18** (Yate)
GREAT ASHLEY. (BA15) —1B **114**
Great Stoke. —4B **28**
Green Parlour. —3F **153**
Green Vale. —2E **157**
GROVESEND. (BS35) —5F **7**

Hacket, The. —3F **7**
HALLEN. (BS10) —5E **23**
Ham. —4C **146**
HAMBROOK. (BS16) —2D **45**
Ham Green. —2D **155** (West Wiltshire)
Ham Green. —3F **53** (Woodspring)
HANHAM. (BS15) —5E **73**
Hanham Green. —2D **83**
Harry Stoke. —2A **44**
Hartcliffe. —4E **87**
HAYDON. (BA3) —4C **152**
Hayes Park. —2C **150**
Headley Park. —2D **87**
HENBURY. (BS10) —2A **40**
Henfield. —1F **47**
HENGROVE. (BS14) —2D **89**
HENLEAZE. (BS9) —2D **57**
Hicks Common. —4A **30**
Hicks Gate. —5E **83**
HIGH LITTLETON. (BS39) —1A **146**
Highridge. —1A **86** (Bristol)
Highridge. —4A **86** (Woodspring)
Hillend. —5B **136**
Hillfields. —4D **61**
Hillside. —4B **150**
HILPERTON. (BA14) —4F **117**
HILPERTON MARSH. (BA14) —3E **117**
HOLT. (BA14) —1F **155**
HORFIELD. (BS7) —1A **58**
Horsecastle. —2A **142**
HOTWELLS. (BS8) —5C **68**
HUTTON. (BS24) —1C **140**

Inn's Court. —1F **87**
IRON ACTON. (BS37) —2F **15**
Ivory Hill. —5C **30**
IWOOD. (BS40) —3F **145**

Jeffries Hill. —5C **72**

KELSTON. (BA1) —1E **95**
Kendleshire. —1C **46**
Kensington Park. —2E **81**
KEWSTOKE. (BS22) —2F **127**
KEYNSHAM. (BS31) —2A **92**
KINGSDOWN. (BS2) —2E **69**
KINGSWOOD. (BS15) —2A **74**
Knightcott. —5D **137**
KNOWLE. (BS4 & BS14) —3D **81**
Knowle Park. —4D **81**

Lambridge. —5D **101**
LANSDOWN. (BA1) —1C **98**
LARKHALL. (BA1) —4C **100**
Latteridge. —1C **14**
LAWRENCE WESTON. (BS11) —3C **38**
LEIGH WOODS. (BS8) —4F **67**
Lilliput. —1C **34**
LIMPLEY STOKE. (BA3) —3B **112**
LITTLE STOKE. (BS34) —3F **27**
LOCKING. (BS24) —4E **135**
Lockleaze. —5E **43**
Lodway. —2E **53**
LONG ASHTON. (BS41) —4B **76**
Longfield. —3D **119**
LONGWELL GREEN. (BS30) —2B **84**
Lower Almondsbury. —1C **10**
Lower Canada. —1D **141**
LOWER CLAVERHAM. (BS49) —1F **143**
Lower Easton. —1E **71**
LOWER HAZEL. (BS35) —4A **8**
Lower Knowle. —3A **80**
Lower Peasedown. —1E **149**
Lower Soundwell. —5B **62**
Lower Studley. —4D **119**
Lower Swainswick. —4D **101**
LOWER WESTON. (BA1) —2D **105**
Lower Writhlington. —1F **153**
Lyde Green. —4F **47**
Lye Green. —5B **114**
Lyncombe Hill. —5B **106**
Lyncombe Vale. —1B **110**

Maines Batch. —1C **156**
MANGOTSFIELD. (BS18) —2C **62**
Mayfield Park. —5C **60**
May's Green. —2F **131**
Mayshill. —5A **16**
MIDFORD. (BA2) —5C **110**
MIDSOMER NORTON. (BA3) —3D **151**
MILTON. (BS22) —4A **128**
MILTON HILL. (BS22) —2F **127**
Monger. —1C **150**
MONKTON COMBE. (BA2) —3F **111**
MONTPELIER. (BS6) —5F **57**
Moorend. —2A **46**
Moorfields. —2E **71**
Moorlands. —1E **109**
Morton. —2E **7**
Mount Hill. —4B **74**
Murhill. —3E **113**

NAILSEA. (BS48) —3D **123**
Netham. —4F **71**
Newbridge. —1B **104**
New Buildings. —2D **149**
NEW CHELTENHAM. (BS15) —1B **74**
Newleaze. —2D **43**
New Passage. —1B **20**
NEWTON ST LOE. (BA2) —5F **95**
NEWTOWN. (BS2) —3C **70**
Nibley. —5C **16**
NORTH BRADLEY. (BA14) —4E **155**
North Common. —4F **75**
North Corner. —5B **14**
NORTH END. (BA1) —1A **102** (Batheaston)
North End. —1A **142** (Yatton)
Northfield. —2E **153**
NORTHVILLE. (BS7) —3C **42**
North Weston. —5E **49**
Norton. —1A **128**
Norton Hill. —4E **151**

Odd Down. —3E **109**
Oldfield Park. —4F **105**
Oldland. —1E **85**
OLDLAND COMMON. (BS30) —2E **85**
Old Mills. —1A **150**
Oldmixon. —1F **139**
Oval, The. —1D **109**
Over. —4A **10**
Overhill. —4F **53**

Palmer's Elm. —1E **131**
Park Corner. —5B **112**
Parkfield. —1C **64**
Parkway. —1A **44**
PATCHWAY. (BS34) —3E **27**
PAULTON. (BS39) —4B **146**
PEASEDOWN ST JOHN. (BA2) —2F **149**
Perrymead. —1C **110**
Pilemarsh. —3F **71**
PILL. (BS20) —3E **53**
Pipehouse. —5A **112**
Plummers Hill. —3A **146**
Pomphrey. —2D **63**
PORTBURY. (BS20) —4A **52**
Portbury Wharf. —2C **50**
PORTISHEAD. (BS20) —4F **49**
Potterswood. —3E **73**
Primrose Hill. —5E **99**
Providence. —3B **76**
Providence Place. —3C **150**
PUCKLECHURCH. (BS16) —2D **65**
Purn. —4E **139**
Pye Corner. —1F **45**

QUEEN CHARLTON. (BS31) —5C **90**

RADSTOCK. (BA3) —2C **152**
Ram Hill. —5F **31**
Redcliff Bay. —4A **48**
REDFIELD. (BS5) —2F **71**
REDLAND. (BS6) —4E **57**
Red Post. —2E **149**
Redwick. —1C **20**
Ridge, The. —4B **18**
Ridgeway. —5B **60**
Riverside. —5C **150**
Rocks, The. —1B **18**
Rodford. —2F **33**
Rodway Hill. —3C **62**
Rolstone. —4D **131**
Rose Green. —5F **59**
Round Hill. —5C **148**
RUDGEWAY. (BS35) —5A **8**
Rush Hill. —2D **109**
Russell Town. —3D **71**

ST ANDREWS. (BS6) —5F **57**
ST ANNE'S. (BS4) —5F **71**
ST ANNE'S PARK. (BS4) —5A **72**
ST GEORGE. (BS5) —2B **72**
ST GEORGE'S. (BS22) —3B **130**
ST PAUL'S. (BS2) —2B **70**
ST PHILIP'S MARSH. (BS2) —5D **71**
Salisbury. —5C **146**
SALTFORD. (BS31) —1A **94**
SEA MILLS. (BS9) —1E **55**
SEVERN BEACH. (BS35) —4B **20**
Sharpstone. —5B **112**
Sheepway. —3D **51**
SHIREHAMPTON. (BS11) —1A **54**
Shockerwick. —1F **103**
Shortwood. —2F **63**
Sidcot. —5B **156**
Sion Hill. —5F **99**
Siston. —4B **64**
Siston Common. —1C **74**
Sladebrook. —1D **109**
SNEYD PARK. (BS9) —4F **55**
Somerdale. —1B **92**
SOUNDWELL. (BS16) —4A **62**

SOUTH DOWN. (BA2) —1C **108**
Southfield. —2D **153**
South Lyncombe. —1A **110**
SOUTHMEAD. (BS10) —3E **41**
SOUTH STOKE. (BA2) —5A **110**
South Twerton. —5E **105**
SOUTHVILLE. (BS3) —1E **79**
SPEEDWELL. (BS5) —1C **72**
Stanshawe. —1A **34**
STAPLE HILL. (BS16) —3F **61**
STAPLETON. (BS16) —2F **59**
STAVERTON. (BA14) —1D **117**
STOCKWOOD. (BS14) —3A **90**
Stockwood Vale. —2E **91**
STOKE BISHOP. (BS9) —2F **55**
STOKE GIFFORD. (BS34) —5B **28**
Stonebridge. —4D **137**
Stone-edge Batch. —1B **122**
Stone Hill. —1A **84**
Stover. —4D **17**
Studley Green. —4A **118**
SWAINSWICK. (BA1) —1D **101**

Thicket Mead. —2C **150**
THORNBURY. (BS35) —4C **6**
Thornbury Park. —2C **6**
TICKENHAM. (BS21) —2A **122**
TIMSBURY. (BA3) —1E **157**
Timsbury Bottom. —1C **146**
TOTTERDOWN. (BS3 & BS4) —1B **80**
Towns End. —5B **146**
TROWBRIDGE. (BA14) —2D **119**
Trowle Common. —1A **118**
TURLEIGH. (BA15) —3A **114**
TWERTON. (BA2) —3C **104**
Twerton Hill. —1B **108**
Twomile Hill. —2D **73**
TYNDALL'S PARK. (BS8) —3D **69**
Tyning. —1D **153**

UPHILL. (BS23) —1B **138**
Upper Canada. —2E **141**
Upper Easton. —2D **71**
Upper Eastville. —4A **60**
Upper Knowle. —2D **81**
UPPER MORTON. (BS12) —1E **7**
Upper Soundwell. —4F **61**
Upper Studley. —5A **118**
UPPER SWAINSWICK. (BA1) —1C **100**
Upper Weston. —3C **98**
UPPER WESTWOOD. (BA15) —5A **114**

Victoria Park. —2D **69**
Villa Fields. —1C **106**
Vinney Green. —5C **46**

Walton St Mary. —1D **121**
Wapley. —5A **34**
WARMLEY. (BS30) —2D **75**
Warmley Hill. —2C **74**
Waterside. —3B **152**
Watley's End. —2B **30**
WAY WICK. (BS24) —4C **130**
Webbs Heath. —1F **75**
Welton. —2E **151**
Welton Hollow. —2A **152**
WESTBURY ON TRYM. (BS9 & BS10) —5C **40**
WESTBURY PARK. (BS6) —3C **56**
West End. —4B **120**
WESTERLEIGH. (BS37) —5D **33**
Westfield. —3F **151**
WEST HEWISH. (BS24) —1E **131**
WEST HILL. (BS48) —1E **123** (Nailsea)
WEST HILL. (BS20) —3D **49** (Portishead)
West Hill Gardens. —3A **152**
WESTON. (BA1) —5C **98**
Weston Park. —5D **99**
WESTON-SUPER-MARE. (BS22 to BS24) —5B **126**
West Passage. —2A **154**
WEST TOWN. (BS48) —3C **124**
WEST WICK. (BS24) —4A **130**
WESTWOOD. (BA15) —5A **114**
Wheeler's Hill. —2F **151**
WHITCHURCH. (BS14) —4E **89**
WHITEHALL. (BS5) —1F **71**
White's Hill. —4C **72** (Bristol)
Whiteshill. —1F **45** (Northavon)
Whiteway. —2C **72** (Kingswood)
WHITEWAY. (BA2) —4A **104** (Twerton)
WICK. (BS30) —5B **154**
Wicklane. —1C **148**
Wick Rocks. —4C **154**
WICKWAR. (GL12) —1B **154**
Widbrook. —5F **115**
WIDCOMBE. (BA2) —4C **106**
WILLSBRIDGE. (BS30) —3C **84**
Windmill Hill. —1F **79**
WINSCOMBE. (BS25) —4B **155**
WINSLEY. (BA15) —2F **113**
WINTERBOURNE. (BS36) —3F **29**
WINTERBOURNE DOWN. (BS36) —5A **30**
Winterfield. —5B **146**
Withy Mills. —2D **147**
Withywood. —4B **86**
Wolvers Hill. —2C **136**
Wolvershill Batch. —3C **136**
Woodborough. —4B **156**
Woodhill. —1F **49**
Woodlands. —2E **11**
Woodstock. —3A **74**
Woolley. —2F **115** (Bradford-on-Avon)
WOOLLEY. (BA1) —1A **100** (Swainswick)
Woolley Green. —1F **115**
WORLE. (BS22) —3D **129**
WORLEBURY. (BS40) —3E **127**
WRINGTON. (BS18) —1B **156**
WRITHLINGTON. (BA3) —2F **153**

Yanley. —5D **77**
YATE. (BS37) —5A **18**
Yate Rocks. —1B **18**
YATTON. (BS49) —3C **142**

INDEX TO STREETS

HOW TO USE THIS INDEX

1. Each street name is followed by its Posttown or Postal Locality and then by its map reference; e.g. Abbeydale. *Wint* —3A **30** is in the Winterbourne Postal Locality and is to be found in square 3A on page **30**. The page number being shown in bold type.
   A strict alphabetical order is followed in which Av., Rd., St., etc. (though abbreviated) are read in full and as part of the street name; e.g. Abbotsbury Rd. appears after Abbots Av. but before Abbots Clo.

2. Streets and a selection of Subsidiary names not shown on the Maps, appear in the index in *Italics* with the thoroughfare to which it is connected shown in brackets; e.g. *Abbey Chambers. Bath —3B **106** (off York St.)*

3. The page references shown in brackets indicate those streets that appear on the large scale map pages 4-5 and 96-97; e.g. Abbey Ct. *Bath* —2C **106** (2E **97**) appears in square 2C on page **106** and also appears in the enlarged section in square 2E on page **97**.

GENERAL ABBREVIATIONS

All : Alley
App : Approach
Arc : Arcade
Av : Avenue
Bk : Back
Boulevd : Boulevard
Bri : Bridge
B'way : Broadway
Bldgs : Buildings
Bus : Business
Cvn : Caravan
Cen : Centre
Chu : Church
Chyd : Churchyard
Circ : Circle
Cir : Circus
Clo : Close
Comn : Common
Cotts : Cottages
Ct : Court
Cres : Crescent
Dri : Drive
E : East
Embkmt : Embankment
Est : Estate
Gdns : Gardens
Ga : Gate
Gt : Great
Grn : Green
Gro : Grove
Ho : House
Ind : Industrial
Junct : Junction
La : Lane
Lit : Little
Lwr : Lower
Mnr : Manor
Mans : Mansions
Mkt : Market
M : Mews
Mt : Mount
N : North
Pal : Palace
Pde : Parade
Pk : Park
Pas : Passage
Pl : Place
Quad : Quadrant
Rd : Road
S : South
Sq : Square
Sta : Station
St : Street
Ter : Terrace
Trad : Trading
Up : Upper
Vs : Villas
Wlk : Walk
W : West
Yd : Yard

POSTTOWN AND POSTAL LOCALITY ABBREVIATIONS

Abb L : Abbots Leigh
Alm : Almondsbury
Alv : Alveston
Arn V : Arnos Vale
Ash D : Ashley Down
Asht : Ashton
Ash G : Ashton Gate
Avon : Avoncliff
A'mth : Avonmouth
Azt W : Aztec West
Back : Backwell
Bann : Bannerdown
Ban : Banwell
Bap M : Baptist Mills
Bar C : Barrs Court
Bar H : Barton Hill
Bath : Bath
B'ptn : Bathampton
Bathe : Batheaston
Bathf : Bathford
Bathw : Bathwick
Bedm : Bedminster
Bed D : Bedminster Down
Bishop : Bishopston
B'wth : Bishopsworth
Bit : Bitton
B'don : Bleadon
Brad A : Bradford-on-Avon
Brad S : Bradley Stoke
Bren : Brentry
Brisl : Brislington
Bris : Bristol
B'ley : Brockley
C'ton : Camerton
Charl : Charlcombe
C'vey : Chelvey
Chip S : Chipping Sodbury
Chit : Chittening
C'chu : Christchurch
Clan : Clandown
C'tn : Clapton
Clav : Claverham
Clav D : Claverton Down
Clay H : Clay Hill
C've : Cleeve
Clev : Clevedon
Clif : Clifton
Clif W : Clifton Wood
Clut : Clutton
Coal H : Coalpit Heath
Cod : Codrington
C Down : Combe Down
C Hay : Combe Hay
Cong : Congresbury
C Din : Coombe Dingle
Cor : Corston
Cot : Cotham
Crom : Cromhall
Dod : Dodington
Down : Downend
Dun : Dundry
E Comp : Easter Compton
E'tn : Easton
E'ton G : Easton-in-Gordano
Eastv : Eastville
E Grn : Emersons Green
Eng : Englishcombe
Fail : Failand
Far G : Farrington Gurney
Fil : Filton
Fish : Fishponds
Fram C : Frampton Cotterell
Fren : Frenchay
F'frd : Freshford
G'bnk : Greenbank
Grov : Grovesend
Hall : Hallatrow
H'len : Hallen
Ham : Hambrook
Han : Hanham
Hawk B : Hawkfield Bus. Park
Hay : Haydon
Hen : Henbury
H'gro : Hengrove
Henl : Henleaze
Hew : Hewish
High L : High Littleton
Hil : Hilperton
Hil M : Hilperton Marsh
Holt : Holt
Hor : Horfield
Hot : Hotwells
Hut : Hutton
Iron A : Iron Acton
Kel : Kelston
Ken : Kendleshire
Kew : Kewstoke
Key : Keynsham
Kngdn : Kingsdown (Bath)
K'dwn : Kingsdown (Bristol)
K'wd : Kingswood
Know : Knowle
L'dwn : Lansdown
Lark : Larkhall
Law H : Lawrence Hill
Law W : Lawrence Weston
L Wds : Leigh Woods
Lim S : Limpley Stoke
Lit S : Little Stoke
L Sev : Littleton-upon-Severn
Lock : Locking
L Ash : Long Ashton
L Grn : Longwell Green
Lwr W : Lower Weston
L W'wd : Lower Westwood
Mang : Mangotsfield
Mid : Midford
Mid N : Midsomer Norton
Mil : Milton
Mon C : Monkton Combe
Mont : Montpelier
Nail : Nailsea
New C : New Cheltenham
N Brad : North Bradley
Nthnd : Northend
N'vle : Northville
Old C : Oldland Common
Old S : Old Sodbury
Pat : Patchway
Paul : Paulton
Pea J : Peasedown St John
Pill : Pill
Piln : Pilning
P'bry : Portbury
P'head : Portishead
Puck : Pucklechurch
Rads : Radstock
Redc : Redcliffe
Redf : Redfield
Redl : Redland
Rudg : Rudgeway
St Ag : St Agnes
St And : St Andrews
St Ap : St Annes Park
St Aug : St Augustines
St G : St George
St Geo : St Georges
St Ja : St James
St Jud : St Judes
St Pa : St Pauls
St Ph : St Philips
St Pm : St Philips Marsh
St W : St Werburghs
Salt : Saltford
Sea M : Sea Mills
Sev B : Severn Beach
Shire : Shirehampton
S Park : Sneyd Park
Soun : Soundwell
S'dwn : Southdown
S'mead : Southmead
S'ske : Southstoke
S'vle : Southville
S'wll : Speedwell
Stap H : Staple Hill
Stap : Stapleton
Stav : Staverton
Stoc : Stockwood
Stok B : Stoke Bishop
Stok G : Stoke Gifford
Swain : Swainswick
Tem M : Temple Meads
T'bry : Thornbury
Tic : Tickenham
Tim : Timsbury
Tot : Totterdown
Trow : Trowbridge
Tur : Turleigh
Twer A : Twerton on Avon
Tyn P : Tyndalls Park
Tyth : Tytherington
Uph : Uphill
Up Swa : Upper Swainswick
Up W : Upper Westwood
War : Warmley
W Trym : Westbury-on-Trym
W'bry P : Westbury Park
W'lgh : Westerleigh
W'fld I : Westfield Ind. Est.
W Hill : West Hill
W'ton : Weston
W Mare : Weston-super-Mare
W Town : West Town
W'wd : Westwood
W'chu : Whitchurch
W'hall : Whitehall
Whit B : White Horse Bus. Park
W'way : Whiteway
Wick : Wick
Wick L : Wick St Lawrence
Wickw : Wickwar
Wid : Widcombe
Will : Willsbridge
Wins : Winscombe
W'ley : Winsley
Wint : Winterbourne
Wint D : Winterbourne Down
W'ly : Woolley
Wor : Worle
Worl : Worlebury
Wrax : Wraxall
Wrin : Wrington
Writ : Writhlington
Yarn : Yarnbrook
Yate : Yate
Yat : Yatton

INDEX TO STREETS

*Abbey Chambers. Bath (off York St.) —3B **106***
*Abbey Chu. Ho. Bath —3A **106** (off Hetling Ct.)*
*Abbey Chu. Yd. Bath —3B **106** (off Cheap St.)*
Abbey Clo. *Key* —1A **92**
Abbey Ct. *Bath* —2C **106** (2E **97**)
Abbey Ct. *St Ap* —5B **72**
Abbey Courtyard. *Bath* —3B **106**
Abbeydale. *Wint* —3A **30**
Abbeygate St. *Bath* —3B **106** (4C **96**)
Abbey Grn. *Bath* —3B **106** (4C **96**)
Abbey Ho. *Yate* —2F **33**
Abbey La. *Alv* —1E **9**
Abbey La. *F'frd* —5B **112**
Abbey Pk. *Key* —2B **92**
Abbey Rd. *Bris* —1B **56**
*Abbey St. Bath —3B **106** (off York St.)*
Abbey View. *Bath* —4C **106** (5F **97**)
Abbey View. *Rads* —1D **153**
Abbey View Gdns. *Bath* —4C **106** (5E **97**)
Abbeywood Dri. *Bris* —2E **55**
Abbots Av. *Bris* —1E **83**
Abbotsbury Rd. *Nail* —4C **122**
Abbots Clo. *Bris* —5C **88**
Abbot's Clo. *W Mare* —2E **129**
Abbotsford Rd. *Bris* —1D **69**
Abbots Horn. *Nail* —2C **122**
Abbots Leigh Rd. *Abb L* —2C **66**
Abbots Leigh Rd. *L Wds* —4F **67**
Abbots Rd. *Bris* —2E **83**
Abbots Way. *Bris* —1F **57**
Abbotswood. *Bris* —3F **73**
Abbotswood. *Yate* —2F **33**
Abbott Rd. *Sev B* —5B **20**
Abbotts Farm Clo. *Paul* —4A **146**
Aberdeen Rd. *Bris* —2D **69**
Abingdon Gdns. *Bath* —4E **109**
Abingdon Rd. *Bris* —4C **60**
Ableton Ct. *Brad S* —4B **20**
Ableton La. *H'ley* —1B **22**
Ableton La. *Sev B* —4B **20**
Ableton Wlk. *Bris* —2E **55**
Abon Ho. *Bris* —3E **55**
Abraham Clo. *Bris* —2D **71**
Abraham Fry Ho. *Bris* —3A **74**
Abson Rd. *Puck* —2E **65**
Acacia Av. *Bris* —3E **61**
Acacia Av. *W Mare* —5F **127**
Acacia Clo. *Bris* —4F **61**
Acacia Ct. *Key* —4E **91**
Acacia Cres. *Trow* —2B **118**
Acacia Gro. *Bath* —1D **109**
Acacia M. *Bris* —3F **61**
Acacia Rd. *Bris* —3F **61**
Acacia Rd. *Rads* —3B **152**
Accomodation Rd. *B'don* —5C **138**
Acorn Gro. *Bris* —2A **86**
Acraman's Rd. *Bris* —1E **79**
Acresbush Clo. *Bris* —3C **86**
Acton Rd. *Bris* —4C **60**
Adams Clo. *Pea J* —4D **157**
Adams Gdns. *Fram C* —1E **31**
Adams Hay. *Bris* —4F **81**
Adastral Rd. *Lock* —4B **136**
Adcroft Dri. *Trow* —1D **119**
Adcroft St. *Trow* —1D **119**
Addicott Rd. *W Mare* —2C **132**
Addiscombe Rd. *Bris* —3D **89**
Addiscombe Rd. *W Mare* —4C **132**
Addison Rd. *Bris* —2A **80**
Adelaide Pl. *Bath* —3C **106** (3F **97**)
Adelaide Pl. *Bris* —3B **60**
Adelaide Pl. *E'tn* —2D **71**
Adelaide Ter. *Bris* —3C **60**
Admirals Wlk. *P'head* —3D **49**

Agate St. Bris —2D 79
Aiken St. Bris —4D 71
Ainslie's Belvedere. Bath (off Caroline Pl.) —1A 106
Aintree Av. Whit B —3F 155
Aintree Dri. Bris —3B 46
Air Balloon Rd. Bris —3C 72
Airport Rd. Bris —1B 88
Aisecombe Way. W Mare —2A 134
Akeman Way. Bris —4E 37
Alard Rd. Bris —1B 88
Alastair Ct. Trow —3C 118
Albany Bldgs. Bris —1E 79
Albany Clo. Trow —5F 117
Albany Ga. Stok G —4A 28
Albany Rd. Bath —3C 104
Albany Rd. Bris —1B 70
Albany St. Bris —2E 73
Albany Way. Bris —5E 75
Albermarle Row. Bris —4B 68
Albermarle Ter. Bris —4B 68
Albert Av. Pea J —2F 149
Albert Av. W Mare —2C 132
Albert Cres. Bris —5C 70
Albert Gro. Bris —2B 72
Albert Mill. Key —4B 92
Alberton Rd. Bris —1B 60
Albert Pde. Bris —2F 71
Albert Pk. Bris —1B 70
Albert Pk. Pl. Bris —1A 70
Albert Pl. Bath —3D 111
Albert Pl. Bedm —2E 79
Albert Pl. W Trym —5C 40
Albert Quad. W Mare —5C 126
Albert Rd. Clev —3C 120
Albert Rd. Han —5F 73
Albert Rd. Key —3A 92
Albert Rd. P'head —3F 49
Albert Rd. Sev B —4B 20
Albert Rd. Stap H —2A 62
Albert Rd. St Ph —1C 80
Albert Rd. Trow —4F 117
Albert Rd. W Mare —2C 132
Albert St. Bris —2E 71
Albert Ter. Bris —3B 60
Albert Ter. Twer A —3D 105
Albion Bldgs. Bath —2E 105
Albion Clo. Bris —2B 62
Albion Dockside Est. Bris —5D 69
Albion Dri. Trow —2B 118
Albion Pl. Bath —2F 105
Albion Pl. Bris —4C 70
Albion Pl. St Ph —3B 70 (2F 5)
Albion Rd. Bris —1D 71
Albion St. Bris —2E 71
Albion Ter. Bath —2F 105
Albion Ter. Pat —5D 11
Alburys. Wrin —1B 156
Alcove Rd. Bris —4A 60
Aldeburgh Pl. Trow —4A 118
Alder Clo. Trow —5B 118
Aldercombe Rd. Bris —4E 39
Alderdown Clo. Bris —4C 38
Alder Dri. Bris —1A 72
Alderley Rd. Bath —5B 104
Aldermoor Way. L Grn —1A 84
Alderney Av. Bris —1B 82
Alders, The. Bris —3D 45 (off Marlborough Dri.)
Alder Ter. Rads —2B 152
Alderton Rd. Bris —4A 42
Alderton Way. Trow —5D 119
Alder Way. Bath —4E 109
Aldhelm Ct. Brad A —4F 115
Aldwick Av. Bris —5E 87
Alec Ricketts Clo. Bath —4A 104
Alexander Bldgs. Bath —5C 100
Alexander Way. Yat —4B 142
Alexandra Clo. Bris —3F 61
Alexandra Ct. Clev —2C 120
Alexandra Gdns. Bris —3F 61
Alexandra Pde. W Mare —1C 132
Alexandra Pk. Fish —3B 60
Alexandra Pk. Paul —4B 146
Alexandra Pk. Redl —5E 57
Alexandra Pl. Bath —3D 111
Alexandra Pl. Bris —3F 61
Alexandra Rd. Bath —4B 106
Alexandra Rd. Bed D —1B 86
Alexandra Rd. Clev —2C 120
Alexandra Rd. Clif —2D 69
Alexandra Rd. Coal H —2F 31
Alexandra Rd. Han —5F 73
Alexandra Rd. W Trym —4E 41
Alexandra Ter. Paul —4B 146
Alexandra Way. T'bry —1C 6
Alford Rd. Bris —3E 81
Alfred Hill. Bris —2F 69
Alfred Lovell Gdns. Bris —1C 84
Alfred Pde. Bris —2F 69
Alfred Pl. K'dwn —2E 69
Alfred Pl. Redc —5F 69
Alfred Rd. Bris —2F 79
Alfred Rd. W'bry P —3C 56
Alfred St. Bath —2A 106 (1B 96)
Alfred St. Redf —2E 71
Alfred St. St Ph —4C 70
Alfred St. W Mare —1C 132
Algars Dri. Iron A —3A 16
Algiers St. Bris —2F 79
Alison Gdns. Back —1C 124
Allanmead Rd. Bris —5D 81
Allen Rd. Trow —3B 118
Aller Pde. W Mare —1F 139
Allerton Cres. Bris —4D 89
Allerton Gdns. Bris —3D 89
Allerton Rd. Bris —4C 88
Allfoxton Rd. Bris —4C 58
All Hallows Rd. Bris —2D 71
Allington Dri. Bar C —1B 84
Allington Gdns. Nail —5B 122
Allington Rd. Bris —5E 69
Allison Av. Bris —2A 82
Allison Rd. Bris —2F 81
All Saints Ct. Bris —3F 69 (3C 4)
All Saints Gdns. Bris —2C 68
All Saints La. Bris —3F 69 (2C 4)
All Saints La. Clev —2F 121
All Saints Pl. Bath —4E 107
All Saints Rd. Bath —1A 106
All Saints Rd. Bris —2C 68
All Saints Rd. W Mare —4C 126
All Saints St. Bris —3F 69 (2C 4)
Alma Clo. Bris —2A 74
Alma Ct. Bris —1D 69
Alma Rd. Clif —2C 68
Alma Rd. K'wd —1A 74
Alma Rd. Av. Bris —2D 69
Alma St. Trow —2E 119
Alma St. W Mare —1C 132
Alma Vale Rd. Bris —2C 68
Almeda Rd. Bris —4C 72
Almond Clo. W Mare —4E 129
Almond Gro. Trow —5B 118
Almondsbury Bus. Cen. Alm —3F 11
Almond Way. Bris —2B 62
Almorah Rd. Bris —2A 80
Alpha Rd. Bris —1F 79
Alpine Clo. Paul —5C 146
Alpine Gdns. Bath —1B 106
Alpine Rd. Bris —1E 71
Alpine Rd. Paul —5C 146
Alsop Rd. Bris —2F 73
Alton Pl. Bath —4B 106
Alton Rd. Bris —2B 58
Altringham Rd. Bris —1F 71
Alum Clo. Trow —3E 119
Alverstoke. Bris —1B 88
Alveston Hill. T'bry —1B 8
Alveston Wlk. Bris —5D 39
Alwins Ct. Bar C —1B 84
Amberey Rd. W Mare —3D 133
Amberlands Clo. Back —1C 124
Amberley Clo. Bris —5F 45
Amberley Clo. Key —4A 92
Amberley Gdns. Nail —4C 122
Amberley Rd. Bris —5F 45
Amberley Rd. Pat —1D 27
Amberley Way. Wickw —3C 154
Amble Clo. Bris —3B 74
Ambleside Av. Bris —3D 41
Ambleside Rd. Bath —2C 108
Ambra Vale. Bris —4C 68
Ambra Vale E. Bris —4C 68
Ambra Vale S. Bris —4C 68
Ambra Vale W. Bris —4C 68
Ambrose Rd. Bris —4C 68
Ambury. Bath —4A 106 (5B 96) (in two parts)
Amercombe Wlk. Bris —1F 89
Amery La. Bath —3B 106 (4C 96)
Amesbury Dri. B'don —5F 139
Amouracre. Trow —2F 119
Ancaster Clo. Trow —1A 118
Anchor Clo. St G —4B 72
Anchor La. Bris —4E 69 (4A 4)
Anchor Rd. Bath —5C 98
Anchor Rd. Bris —4D 69
Anchor Rd. K'wd —1C 74
Anchor Way. Pill —3F 53
Ancliff Sq. Avon —3F 115
Andereach Clo. Bris —5D 81
Andover Rd. Bris —3B 80
Angels Ground. St Ap —4B 72
Angers Rd. Tot —1B 80
Anglesea Pl. Bris —5C 56
Anglo Ter. Bath —1B 106 (off London Rd.)
Annandale Av. W Mare —4C 128
Anson Clo. Salt —5F 93
Anson Rd. Kew —1B 128
Anson Rd. Lock —2E 135
Anstey's Rd. Han —5D 73
Anstey St. Bris —1D 71
Anthea Rd. Bris —5A 60
Antona Ct. Bris —5E 37
Antona Dri. Bris —5F 37
Antrim Rd. Bris —1D 57
Anvil Rd. Clav —2F 143
Anvil St. Bris —4B 70
Apex Ct. Alm —3F 11
Apperley Clo. Yate —1F 33
Appleby Wlk. Bris —1F 87
Appledore. W Mare —3D 129
Appledore Clo. Bris —5D 81
Applegate. Bris —1D 41
Appletree Ct. Wor —3F 129
Apple Tree Dri. Wins —4B 156
Appsley Clo. W Mare —3A 128
Apseleys Mead. Brad S —4E 11
Apsley Clo. Bath —2C 104
Apsley Rd. Bath —2B 104
Apsley Rd. Bris —1C 68
Apsley St. Bris —5E 59
Apsley Vs. Bris —1F 69
Arbutus Dri. Bris —5E 39
Arbutus Wlk. Bris —3F 39
Arcade, The. Bris —3A 70 (1D 5)
Arch Clo. L Ash —4B 76
Archer Ct. L Grn —2B 84
Archer's Ct. Clev —2D 121
Archer Wlk. Bris —1A 90
Archfield Rd. Bris —1E 69
Archgrove. L Ash —4B 76
Archway St. Bath —4C 106 (5E 97)
Arch Yd. Trow —1D 119
Arden Clo. Brad S —3A 28
Arden Clo. W Mare —2D 129
Ardenton Wlk. Bris —1C 40
Ardern Clo. Bris —4D 39
Argus Rd. Bris —2E 79
Argyle Av. Bris —5E 59
Argyle Av. W Mare —4D 133
Argyle Dri. Yate —2A 18
Argyle Pl. Bris —4C 68
Argyle Rd. Clev —1D 121
Argyle Rd. Fish —5D 61
Argyle Rd. St Pa —2A 70
Argyle St. Bath —3B 106 (3C 96)
Argyle St. Bedm —1E 79
Argyle St. Eastv —5E 59
Argyle Ter. Bath —3D 105
Arley Cotts. Bris —1F 69
Arley Hill. Bris —1F 69
Arley Pk. Bris —5F 57
Arley Ter. Bris —1A 72
Arlingham Way. Pat —5A 10
Arlington Rd. Bath —4E 105
Arlington Rd. Bris —4F 71
Arlington Vs. Bris —3D 69
Armadale Av. Bris —1A 70
Armada Pl. Bris —1A 70
Armada Rd. Bris —2C 88
Armes Ct. Bath —4B 106
Armoury Sq. Bris —2C 70
Armstrong Clo. T'bry —5E 7
Armstrong Dri. War —5D 75
Armstrong Way. Yate —3C 16
Arnall Dri. Bris —3B 40
Arncliffe Flats. Bris —4E 41
Arndale Rd. W Mare —5B 128
Arneside Rd. Bris —3E 41
Arnold Ct. Chip S —5D 19
Arnolds Field Trad. Est. Wickw —2B 154
Arnolds Hill. Wing —3A 118
Arnolds Way. Yat —2A 142
Arnor Clo. W Mare —1E 129
Arno's St. Bris —2C 80
Arras Clo. Trow —4C 118
Arrowfield Clo. Bris —5C 88
Arthur Skemp Clo. Bris —3D 71
Arthur St. Bris —5C 70
Arthur St. St G —2E 71
Arthurswood Rd. Bris —4C 86
Arundel Clo. Bris —3D 87
Arundel Ct. Bris —4F 57
Arundell Rd. W Mare —5C 126
Arundel Rd. Bath —5B 100
Arundel Rd. Bris —4F 57
Arundel Rd. Clev —3D 121
Arundel Wlk. Key —3F 91
Ascension Ho. Bath —5E 105
Ascot Clo. Bris —3B 46
Ascot Ct. Whit B —3F 155
Ascot Rd. Bris —2F 41
Ashbourne Clo. Bris —4E 75
Ashburton Rd. Bris —3E 41
Ashbury Dri. W Mare —3F 127
Ash Clo. Fish —4E 61
Ash Clo. Lit S —2F 27
Ash Clo. Wins —3B 156
Ash Clo. Yate —3F 17
Ashcombe Cres. Bris —4E 75
Ashcombe Gdns. W Mare —4E 127
Ashcombe Pk. Rd. W Mare —4E 127
Ashcombe Pl. W Mare —1D 133
Ashcombe Rd. W Mare —1D 133
Ashcott. Bris —1B 88
Ash Ct. Bris —3C 88
Ashcroft. W Mare —1F 139
Ashcroft Av. Key —3F 91
Ashcroft Rd. Bris —5E 39
Ashdene Av. Bris —4F 59
Ashdene Rd. W Mare —4E 127
Ashdown Rd. P'head —2C 48
Ash Dri. N Brad —4D 155
Asher La. Bris —3B 70 (1F 5)
Ashes La. F'frd —5A 112
Ashfield Pl. Bris —1B 70
Ashfield Rd. Bris —2D 79
Ashford Dri. W Mare —2E 139
Ashford Rd. Bath —5E 105
Ashford Rd. Pat —2C 26
Ashford Way. Bris —3B 74
Ash Gro. Bath —5D 105
Ash Gro. Bris —4E 61
Ash Gro. Clev —2E 121
Ashgrove. Pea J —4D 157
Ashgrove. T'bry —3D 7
Ash Gro. Uph —1C 138
Ashgrove Av. Abb L —3D 67
Ashgrove Av. Bris —3B 58
Ashgrove Rd. Ash D —3B 58
Ashgrove Rd. Bedm —2D 79
Ashgrove Rd. Redl —1D 69
Ash Hayes Dri. Nail —4D 123
Ash Hayes Rd. Nail —4D 123
Ashland Rd. Bris —4C 86
Ash La. Alm —4A 10
Ashleigh Clo. Paul —3B 146
Ashleigh Clo. W Mare —5E 127
Ashleigh Cres. Yat —3B 142
Ashleigh Ho. Paul —4B 146
Ashleigh Rd. W Mare —5E 127
Ashleigh Rd. Yat —3B 142
Ashley. Bris —2B 74
Ashley Av. Bath —2D 105
Ashley Clo. Brad A —1C 114 (in two parts)
Ashley Clo. Bris —3B 58
Ashley Clo. Wins —5B 156
Ashley Ct. Bris —1B 70
Ashley Ct. Rd. Bris —5B 58
Ashley Down Rd. Bris —2A 58
Ashley Gro. Rd. Bris —5B 58
Ashley Hill. Bris —4B 58
Ashley La. W'ley —2A 114
Ashley Pde. Bris —5B 58
Ashley Pk. Bris —4B 58
Ashley Rd. Bathf —4D 103
Ashley Rd. Brad A —1C 114
Ashley Rd. Bris —1A 70
Ashley Rd. Clev —5B 120
Ashley St. Bris —1C 70
Ashley Ter. Bath —2D 105
Ashley Trad. Est. Bris —5B 58
Ashman Clo. Bris —2C 70
Ashmans Ga. Paul —4B 146
Ashmead. Trow —4C 118
Ashmead Bus. Cen. Key —3D 93
Ashmead Ct. Trow —3D 119
Ashmead Rd. Key —3D 93
Ashmead Way. Bris —5B 68
Ashridge Rd. Alm —3D 11
Ash Rd. Ban —4C 136
Ash Rd. Bris —2A 58
Ashton. Bris —3E 45 (off Harford Dri.)
Ashton Av. Bris —5C 68
Ashton Clo. Clev —5B 120
Ashton Cres. Nail —4C 122
Ashton Dri. Bris —3A 78
Ashton Ga. Rd. Bris —1C 78
Ashton Ga. Ter. Bris —1C 78
Ashton Ga. Underpass. Bris —1B 78
Ashton Rd. Bris —2F 77
Ashton St. Trow —2E 119
Ashton Vale Rd. Bris —2A 78
Ashton Vale Trad. Est. Bris —4B 78
Ashton Way. Key —2A 92
Ash Tree Clo. B'don —5A 140
Ash Tree Ct. Rads —3B 152
Ashvale Clo. Nail —3F 123
Ashville Rd. Bris —1C 78
Ash Wlk. Bren —1D 41
Ashwell Clo. Bris —2A 90
Ashwicke. Bris —2C 88
Aspen Pk. Rd. W Mare —5C 128
Assembly Rooms La. Bris —4F 69 (4B 4)
Astry Clo. Bris —3C 38
Atchley St. Bris —3D 71
Atherston. Bris —5F 75
Athlone Wlk. Bris —4A 80
Atholl Clo. W Mare —2D 129
Atkins Clo. Bris —2A 90
Atlantic Rd. Bris —4E 37
Atlantic Rd. W Mare —4A 126
Atlantic Rd. S. W Mare —4A 126
Atlas Clo. Bris —5C 60
Atlas Rd. Bris —2A 80
Atlas St. Bris —5D 71
Attwell Ct. Bath —5A 106
Atwell Dri. Brad S —4D 11
Atwood Dri. Bris —2D 39
Aubrey Rd. Bris —2D 79
Auburn Av. L Grn —2D 85
Auburn Rd. Bris —5D 57
Auckland Clo. W Mare —5D 133
Audley Av. Bath —2D 105
Audley Clo. Bath —2E 105
Audley Gro. Bath —1D 105
Audley Pk. Rd. Bath —1D 105
Audrey Wlk. Bris —5F 41
Augusta Pl. Bath —2E 105
Austen Dri. W Mare —1F 129
Austen Gro. Bris —4C 42
Aust La. Bris —4C 40
Avalon Clo. Yat —2A 142
Avalon Ho. Nail —4B 122
Avalon Rd. Bris —5D 73
Avebury Rd. Bris —3A 78
Avendall. Bris —5A 38
Avening Clo. Nail —5E 123
Avening Rd. Bris —2C 72
Avenue Pl. C Down —3C 110
Avenue Rd. Trow —2B 118

Avenue, The. Back —1C 124
Avenue, The. Brad S —4E 11
Avenue, The. Clav D —4F 107 (in two parts)
Avenue, The. Clev —1E 121
Avenue, The. Clif —1C 68
Avenue, The. C Down —2D 111
Avenue, The. Key —2A 92
Avenue, The. Lit S —3E 27
Avenue, The. S Park —4A 56
Avenue, The. St And —4A 58
Avenue, The. St G —2B 72
Avenue, The. Tim —1E 157
Avenue, The. Yat —3B 142
Avenue, The. Yate —5F 17
Averay Rd. Bris —3E 59
Avon Bank Ind. Est. Bris —5D 37
Avonbridge Ind. Est. Bris —4F 37
Avon Bldgs. Bath —3D 105 (off Old Ferry Rd.)
Avon Clo. Brad A —4F 115
Avon Clo. Key —2B 92
Avon Clo. St G —4B 72
Avon Clo. W Mare —1D 139
Avon Ct. Bathe —2B 102
Avon Ct. Bris —2D 61
Avon Cres. Bris —5C 68
Avon Cres. Wickw —1C 154 (in two parts)
Avondale Bldgs. Bath —4C 100
Avondale Ct. Bris —5F 55
Avondale Ct. L Grn —3B 84
Avondale Rd. Bath —2C 104
Avondown Clo. Bris —2F 41
Avondown Ct. Bris —3E 79
Avonfield. Holt —2F 155
Avonfield Av. Brad A —4F 115
Avon Gorge Ind. Est. Bris —5E 37
Avon Gro. Bris —5F 55
Avon La. Salt —1B 94
Avonlea. Han —5E 73
Avonleaze. Bris —2D 55
Avonleigh Rd. Bris —3D 79
Avonmeads. Bris —5E 71
Avonmere Residential Pk. Brad S —1E 43
Avon Mill La. Key —2B 92
Avonmouth Rd. Bris —3D 37
Avonmouth Way. A'mth —3D 37
Avonmouth Way. Bris —1A 40
Avon Pk. Bath —2B 104
Avon Pk. Bris —3F 71
Avon Ring Rd. Bris & E Grn —2A 44
Avon Ring Rd. Han & War —5E 83
Avon Rd. Bris —2C 86
Avon Rd. Key —3B 92
Avon Rd. Pill —2E 53
Avonside Rd. Bris —4E 71
Avonside Trad. Est. Bris —4E 71
Avonside Way St Ap —4B 72
Avonsmere Cvn. Pk. Brad S —1E 43
Avon St. Bath —3A 106 (5B 96)
Avon St. Bris —4B 70 (3F 5)
Avon Trad. Est. Bris —5C 70
Avon Vale. Bris —3F 55
Avonvale Pl. Bathe —3A 102
Avonvale Rd. Bris —4D 71
Avonvale Rd. Trow —5D 117
Avon Valley Bus. Pk. Bris —4A 72
Avon View. Bris —2D 83
Avon Way. Bris —2E 55
Avon Way. P'head —3D 49
Avon Way. T'bry —4D 7
Avon Way. Trow —4D 117
Avonwood Clo. Bris —1A 54
Awdelett Clo. Bris —3D 39
Axbridge Clo. Nail —5D 123
Axbridge Rd. Bath —2B 110
Axbridge Rd. Bris —3B 80
Axe Clo. W Mare —3E 133
Axe Ct. T'bry —4C 6
Axford Way. Pea J —4D 157
Aycote Clo. W Mare —3F 127
Aylesbury Cres. Bris —4D 79
Aylesbury Rd. Bris —4D 79
Aylmer Cres. Bris —2D 89
Aylminton Wlk. Bris —2D 39
Ayr St. Bath —3E 105
Aztec Cen. Alm —4C 10
Aztec W. Brad S —4C 10
Aztec W. Bus. Pk. Brad S —4C 10

Backfields. Bris —2A 70
Backfields La. Bris —2A 70
Back La. Coal H —2F 31
Back La. Key —2A 92
Back La. Pill —2E 53 (in two parts)
Back La. Puck —3C 64
Back La. Wickw —1B 154
Bk. of Kingsdown Pde. Bris —2F 69
Back Rd. Bris —1C 78
Bk. Stoke La. Bris —1B 56
Back St. Trow —1C 118
Back St. W Mare —1C 132
Backwell Bow. Back —1E 125
Backwell Comn. Back —1C 124
Backwell Hill Rd. Back —1F 125
Backwell Wlk. Bris —5B 78
Badenham Gro. Bris —4B 38
Baden Rd. K'wd —3C 74 (in two parts)
Baden Rd. St G —3E 71
Bader Clo. Yate —3F 17
Badger Rise. P'head —5A 48
Badgers Clo. Brad S —3F 11
Badgers Dri. Bris —5A 26
Badger's La. Alm —2A 10
Badgers Wlk. Bris —3F 81
Badgeworth. Yate —3F 33
Badman Clo. Paul —4A 146
Badminton. Bris —3E 45 (off Penn Dri.)
Badminton Cen. Yate —4E 17
Badminton Ct. Yate —4E 17
Badminton Gdns. Bath —1D 105
Badminton Rd. Chip S —1F 35
Badminton Rd. Down & Fram C —1A 62
Badminton Rd. St Pa —1B 70
Badminton Rd. Trad. Est. Yate —5D 17
Badminton Wlk. Down —5A 46
Baglyn Av. Bris —4B 62
Bagnell Clo. Bris —3A 90
Bagnell Rd. Bris —3A 90
Bagworth Dri. L Grn —2B 84
Bailbrook Ct. Bath —3F 101
Bailbrook Gro. Bath —3D 101
Bailbrook La. Bath —3D 101
Baildon Ct. W Mare —4D 133
Baildon Cres. W Mare —4E 133
Baildon Rd. W Mare —4D 133
Bailey Clo. W Mare —5C 128
Baileys Ct. Rd. Brad S —3A 28
Baileys La. Wrin —1C 156
Bainton Clo. Brad A —2E 115
Baker Clo. Clev —5B 120
Baker's Bldgs. Wrin —1B 156
Bakersfield. L Grn —2C 84
Bakers Ground. Stok G —4C 28
Bakers Pde. Tim —1E 157
Baker St. W Mare —5C 126
Baker Way. Chip S —1B 34
Balaclava Rd. Bris —4B 60
Baldwin St. Bris —4F 69 (3B 4)
Balfour Rd. Bris —2D 79
Ballance St. Bath —1A 106
Ballast La. Bris —2F 37
Balls Barn La. W Mare —4E 131
Balmain St. Bris —1C 80
Balmoral Clo. Stok G —5F 27
Balmoral Ct. Mang —2C 62
Balmoral Rd. Bris —5B 58
Balmoral Rd. Key —4A 92
Balmoral Rd. L Grn —3B 84
Balmoral Rd. Trow —5B 118
Balmoral Way. W Mare —3A 128
Baltic Pl. Pill —3F 53
Bamfield. Bris —1B 88
Bampton. W Mare —3D 129
Bampton Clo. Bris —1D 87
Bancroft. Brad A —1F 115
Banfield Clo. Bris —4C 38
Bangor Gro. Bris —5B 72
Bangrove Wlk. Bris —4A 38
Banister Gro. Bris —1F 87
Bank Pl. Pill —3F 53
Bank Rd. Bris —2F 73
Bank Rd. Chit —2F 21
Banks Clo. Clev —5D 121
Bankside. Bris —3B 62
Bankside Rd. Bris —2F 81
Bannerdown Clo. Bathe —2C 102
Bannerdown Dri. Bathe —2B 102
Bannerdown Rd. Bathe —3B 102
Bannerleigh La. Bris —4A 68
Bannerleigh Rd. Bris —4A 68
Bannerman Rd. Bris —2D 71
Banner Rd. Bris —1A 70
Bannetts Tree Cres. Alv —2B 8
Bantock Clo. Bris —2F 87
Bantry Rd. Bris —5A 80
Banwell Clo. Bris —5C 78
Banwell Clo. Key —5A 92
Banwell Rd. Bath —4E 109
Banwell Rd. Bris —2C 78
Banwell Rd. Hut —1D 141
Banwell Rd. Wins —4A 156
Baptist St. Bris —1C 70
Barberry Farm Rd. Yat —2B 142
Barbour Gdns. Bris —5F 87
Barbour Rd. Bris —5F 87
Barcroft Clo. Bris —2E 73
Barkers Mead. Yate —1B 18
Barker Wlk. Bris —1C 70
Barkleys Hill. Stap —2E 59
Barlands Ho. Bris —1B 40
Barley Clo. Fram C —1D 31
Barley Clo. Yate —1C 62
Barley Croft. Bris —2B 56
Barnabas St. Bris —1A 70
Barnaby Clo. Mid N —2D 151
Barnack Clo. Trow —1A 118
Barnack Trad. Est. Bedm —4E 79
Barnard Clo. Yat —3C 142
Barnard Wlk. Key —4F 91
Barnes Clo. Trow —3A 118
Barnes St. Bris —2F 71
Barnfield Way. Bathe —2C 102
Barn Glebe. Trow —1F 119
Barnhill Clo. Yate —2C 18
Barnhill Rd. Chip S —5C 18
Barn Owl Way. Stok G —4B 28
Barn Piece. Brad A —5E 115
Barns Clo. Nail —3D 123
Barnstaple Ct. Know —5A 80
Barnstaple Rd. Bris —5A 80
Barnstaple Wlk. Bris —5B 80
Barnwood Clo. Bris —2B 74
Barnwood Rd. Yate —2E 33
Barossa Pl. Bris —5F 69 (5C 4)
Barracks La. Bris —4F 37
Barratt St. Bris —1D 71
Barrington Clo. Bris —5B 62
Barrington Ct. Bris —1B 80
Barrington Ct. K'wd —1A 74
Barrow Hill. Wick —5A 154
Barrow Hill Cres. Bris —5E 37
Barrow Hill Rd. Bris —1E 53
Barrowmead Dri. Bris —4A 38
Barrow Rd. Bath —3D 109
Barrow Rd. Bris —3C 70
Barrow Rd. Hut —1C 140
Barrows, The. W Mare —1A 134
Barr's Ct. Bris —2A 70 (1D 5)
Barrs Ct. Av. Bar C —5C 74
Barrs Ct. Rd. Bar C —5C 74
Barry Clo. Bit —4E 85
Barry Clo. W Mare —2E 139
Barry Rd. Old C —3E 85
Barstaple Ho. Bris —3B 70
Bartholomew Row. Tim —1E 157
Bartlett Ct. Bris —1C 68
Bartlett Dri. Bris —2D 39
Bartlett's Rd. Bris —3E 79
Bartlett St. Bath —2A 106 (2B 96)
Bartley St. Bris —1F 79
Barton Bldgs. Bath —2A 106 (2B 96)
Barton Clo. Alv —2B 8
Barton Clo. Bris —4E 71
Barton Clo. St Ap —4B 72
Barton Clo. Wint —4A 30
Barton Ct. Bath —3B 106 (off Up. Borough Walls)
Barton Grn. Bris —3D 71
Barton Hill Rd. Bris —4D 71
Barton Hill Trad. Est. Bris —4D 71
Barton Ho. Bar H —4E 71
Bartonia Gro. Bris —4F 81
Barton Mnr. Bris —3C 70
Barton Meadow Est. Bris —1E 61
Barton Orchard. Brad A —3D 115
Barton Rd. Bris —4B 70
Barton Rd. Wins —5A 156
Barton St. Bath —3A 106 (3B 96)
Barton St. Bris —2F 69
Barton, The. B'don —5A 140
Barton, The. Bris —1D 83
Barton, The. Cor —5C 94
Barton Vale. Bris —4C 70 (in two parts)
Barwick. Bris —5F 37
Bassetts Pasture. Brad A —5E 115
Batches, The. Bris —3D 79
Batch, The. Bathe —3A 102
Batch, The. Salt —1B 94
Batch, The. Yat —4B 142
Bates Clo. Bris —2C 70
Bathampton La. B'ptn —5E 101
Bath Bldgs. Bris —1A 70
Bath Bus. Cen. Bath —3B 106 (off Up. Borough Walls)
Batheaston Swainswick By-Pass. Swain & Bathe —1C 100
Bathford Hill. Bathf —4C 102
Bath Hill E. Key —3B 92
Bath Hill W. Key —2A 92
Bathings, The. T'bry —4D 7
Bathite Cotts. Bath —3E 111
Bath New Rd. Rads —5B 148
Bath Old Rd. Rads —1C 152
Bath Riverside Bus. Pk. Bath —4A 106 (4A 96)
Bath Rd. Brad A —1D 115
Bath Rd. Brisl —4A 82
Bath Rd. Bris & Tot —5B 70
Bath Rd. B'yate —5F 75
Bath Rd. Key —3B 92
Bath Rd. L Grn —1A 84
Bath Rd. Paul —3B 146
Bath Rd. Pea J —3D 149
Bath Rd. Salt & Cor —5F 93
Bath Rd. T'bry —4C 6
Bath Rd. Will —4D 85
Bath St. Ash G —1C 78
Bath St. Bath —3A 106 (4B 96)
Bath St. Bris —4A 70 (3D 5)
Bath St. Stap H —3A 62
Bathurst Pde. Bris —5F 69
Bathurst Rd. W Mare —4A 128
Bathurst Ter. Bris —5F 69
Bathwell Rd. Bris —1C 80
Bathwick Hill. Bath —3C 106 (2E 97)
Bathwick Rise. Bath —1D 107
Bathwick St. Bath —1B 106
Bathwick Ter. Bath —3C 106
Batley Ct. Bris —1F 85
Batstone Clo. Bath —4C 100
Battenburg Rd. Bris —2C 72
Batten Ct. Chip S —5E 19
Batten Rd. Bris —3D 73
Batten's La. Bris —4C 72
Battersby Way. Bris —2A 40
Battersea Rd. Bris —2E 71
Battery La. P'head —2F 49
Battery Rd. P'head —2F 49
Battson Rd. Bris —3A 90
Baugh Gdns. Bris —3A 46
Baugh Rd. Bris —3A 46
Bawns Pl. Bris —3C 60
Baxter Clo. K'wd —2B 74
Baydon Clo. Trow —5C 118
Bay Gdns. Bris —5E 59
Bayham Rd. Bris —2B 80
Bayleys Dri. Bris —4E 73
Baynham Ct. Han —5D 73
Baynton Ho. Bris —3C 70
Baynton Rd. Bris —1C 78
Bay Rd. Clev —1D 121
Bayswater Av. Bris —3D 57
Bayswater Rd. Bris —5B 42
Bay Tree Clo. Pat —2B 26
Bay Tree Rd. Bath —4B 100
Bay Tree Rd. Clev —4E 121
Baytree Rd. W Mare —4A 128
Baytree View. W Mare (in two parts) —4B 128
Beach Av. Clev —4C 120
Beach Av. Sev B —3A 20
Beach End Rd. Uph —1A 138
Beachgrove Gdns. Bris —3E 61
Beachgrove Rd. Bris —3D 61
Beach Hill. P'head —2E 49
Beachley Wlk. Bris —5F 37
Beach Rd. Kew —2D 127
Beach Rd. Sev B —3A 20
Beach Rd. W Mare —3B 132
Beach Rd. E. P'head —2F 49
Beach Rd. W. P'head —2E 49
Beach, The. Clev —2C 120
Beacon La. Wint —3E 29
Beaconlea. Bris —4F 73
Beacon Rd. Bath —5B 100
Beaconsfield Clo. Bar H —4D 71
Beaconsfield Rd. Clev —4E 121
Beaconsfield Rd. Clif —1C 68
Beaconsfield Rd. Know —2D 81
Beaconsfield Rd. St G —2A 72
Beaconsfield Rd. W Mare —1C 132
Beaconsfield St. Bris —4D 71
Beale Clo. Bris —2A 90
Beales Barton. Holt —2F 155
Beam St. Bris —3E 71
Bean Acre, The. Bris —4F 37
Beanhill Cres. Alv —2B 8
Bean St. Bris —1C 70
Bearbridge Rd. Bris —4B 86
Bear Clo. Brad A —2C 114
Bearfield Bldgs. Brad A —1D 115
Beauchamp Rd. Bris —3F 57
Beauford Sq. Bath —3A 106 (3B 96)
Beaufort. Bris —3E 45 (off Harford Dri.)
Beaufort All. Bris —4B 72
Beaufort Av. Mid N —2D 151
Beaufort Av. Yate —4F 17
Beaufort Bldgs. Bris —3B 68
Beaufort Clo. Bris —3F 71
Beaufort Cres. Stok G —5A 28
Beaufort E. Bath —5D 101
Beaufort Gdns. Nail —4C 122
Beaufort Heights. Bris —3A 72
Beaufort Ho. Bris —3D 71
Beaufort M. Bath —5D 101
Beaufort Pk. Brad S —3F 11
Beaufort Pl. Bath —5D 101
Beaufort Pl. Fren —3D 45
Beaufort Rd. Clif —1C 68
Beaufort Rd. Down —5C 46
Beaufort Rd. Fram C —1C 30
Beaufort Rd. Hor —1B 58
Beaufort Rd. K'wd —1E 73
Beaufort Rd. Stap H —3A 62
Beaufort Rd. St G —3F 71
Beaufort Rd. W Mare —5D 127
Beaufort Rd. Yate —4F 17
Beaufort St. Bedm —3E 79
Beaufort St. E'tn —2C 70
Beaufort Vs. Bath —5C 100
Beaufort W. Bath —5D 101
Beauley Rd. Bris —5D 69
Beaumont Clo. L Grn —2C 84
Beaumont Clo. W Mare —4D 133
Beaumont St. Bris —2C 70
Beaumont Ter. Bris —2C 70
Beau St. Bath —3A 106 (4B 96)
Beaver Clo. Wint —2B 30
Beazer Clo. Bris —4F 61
Beckerley La. Holt —1F 155
Becket Ct. Puck —2D 65
Becket Dri. W Mare —2E 129

Becket Rd. W Mare —2E 129
Becket's La. Nail —5D 123
Beckford Ct. Bath —2C 106 (1F 97) (off Darlington Rd.)
Beckford Gdns. Bath —1C 106 (1F 97)
Beckford Gdns. Bris —5C 88
Beckford Rd. Bath —2C 106 (1E 97)
Beckhampton Rd. Bath —4E 105
Beck Ho. Pat —1C 26
Beckington. W Mare —1E 139
Beckington Rd. Bris —3B 80
Beckington Wlk. Bris —3B 80
Beckspool Rd. Fren & Ham —5D 45
Beddoe Clo. Brad A —5F 115
Bedford Ct. Bath —1B 106
Bedford Cres. Bris —2B 58
Bedford Pl. Bris —2F 69
Bedford Rd. W Mare —4C 132
Bedford St. Bath —1B 106
Bedminster Bri. Bris —1F 79
Bedminster Down Rd. Bris —4C 78
Bedminster Pde. Bris —1F 79
Bedminster Pl. Bris —1F 79
Bedminster Rd. Bris —4D 79
Bedwin Clo. P'head —4B 48
Beech Av. Bath —4F 107
Beech Clo. Alv —2B 8
Beech Clo. Bar C —5C 74
Beech Ct. Bris —3C 88
Beechcroft. Bar G —5A 86
Beechcroft Wlk. Bris —4C 42
Beech Dri. Nail —2F 123
Beechen Cliff Rd. Bath —4A 106
Beechen Dri. Bris —5D 61
Beeches Gro. Bris —3F 81
Beeches Ind. Est. Yate —4D 17
Beeches, The. Bath —3E 109
Beeches, The. Brad S —1F 27
Beeches, The. Bris —4F 55
Beeches, The. Old C —3E 85
Beeches, The. St Ap —5A 72
Beeches, The. Trow —5F 117
Beechfield Clo. L Ash —3E 77
Beech Gro. Bath —5D 105
Beech Gro. Trow —4B 118
Beech Ho. Bris —2E 59
Beech Leaze. Alv —2B 8
Beechmount Clo. W Mare —2E 139
Beechmount Ct. Bris —5D 81
Beechmount Dri. W Mare —2E 139
Beechmount Gro. Bris —5D 81
Beech Rd. Bris —2A 58
Beech Rd. Salt —1A 94
Beech Rd. Yat —3C 142
Beech Ter. Rads —3A 152
Beech View. Bath —4E 107
Beechwood Av. Bris —5F 73
Beechwood Av. Lock —4E 135
Beechwood Clo. Bris —5E 81
Beechwood Dri. P'head —3A 48
Beechwood Rd. Bath —3C 110
Beechwood Rd. Bris —3C 60
Beechwood Rd. E'ton G —3C 52
Beechwood Rd. Nail —3C 122
Beechwood Rd. P'head —3A 48
Bee Hive Trad. Est. Bris —3A 72
Beehive Yd. Bath —2B 106 (2C 96)
Beesmoor Rd. Fram C —3D 31
Begbrook Dri. Bris —1B 60
Begbrook La. Bris —1B 60
Begbrook Pk. Bris —4C 44
Beggar Bush La. Fail —1A 76
Beggarswell Clo. Bris —2B 70
Belcombe Pl. Brad A —3D 115
Belcombe Rd. Brad A —3C 114
Belevue Av. Bris —2C 72
Belfast Wlk. Bris —5A 80
Belfry. War —4D 75
Belfry All. Bris —2C 72
Belfry Av. Bris —2C 72
Belgrave Cres. Bath —1B 106
Belgrave Hill. Bris —5C 56
Belgrave Pl. Bath —5B 100
Belgrave Pl. Bris —3C 68
Belgrave Rd. Bath —5C 100
Belgrave Rd. Bris —2D 69
Belgrave Rd. W Mare —5F 127
Belgrave Ter. Bath —5B 100
Bellamy Av. Bris —4E 87
Bellamy Clo. Bris —5C 72
Belland Dri. Bris —4B 88
Bella Vista Rd. Bath —1A 106
Bell Barn Rd. Bris —1F 55
Bellefield Cres. Trow —1D 119
Bellevue. Bris —4D 69
Belle Vue. Mid N —1E 151
Bellevue Clo. Bris —3B 74
Bellevue Cotts. W Trym —5C 40
Bellevue Ct. Bris —4D 69
Bellevue Cres. Bris —4D 69
Bellevue Mans. Clev —2D 121
Bellevue Pk. Bris —3F 81
Bellevue Rd. Clev —2D 121
Bellevue Rd. E'tn —5E 59
Bellevue Rd. K'wd —3B 74
Bellevue Rd. St G —2C 72
Bellevue Rd. Tot —1B 80
Bellevue Ter. Brisl —3F 81
Bellevue Ter. Clif —4D 69
Bellevue Ter. Tot —1B 80
Bell Hill. Bris —3E 59
Bell Hill Rd. Bris —2C 72
Bellhouse Wlk. Bris —3D 39
Bell La. Bris —3F 69 (2B 4)
Bellotts Rd. Bath —3D 105
Bell Rd. Coal H —3E 31
Bell's Wlk. Wrin —1C 156
Belluton Rd. Bris —2C 80
Bellvue Cotts. Clif —4D 69
Belmont. Bath —2A 106 (1B 96)
Belmont Dri. Stok G —4A 28
Belmont Pk. Bris —3B 42
Belmont Rd. Bath —3D 111
Belmont Rd. Brisl —1E 81
Belmont Rd. St And —5A 58
Belmont Rd. Wins —4B 156
Belmont St. Bris —1D 71
Belmore Gdns. Bath —1C 108
Beloe Rd. Bris —2A 58
Belroyal Av. Bris —2B 82
Belsher Dri. K'wd —4C 74
Belstone Wlk. Bris —5E 79
Belton Ct. Bath —4C 98
Belton Ho. Bath —4C 98
Belton Rd. Bris —1D 71
Belton Rd. P'head —2C 48
Belvedere. Bath —2A 106 (1B 96)
Belvedere Cres. W Mare —4A 128
Belvedere Pl. Bath —1A 106
Belvedere Rd. Bris —4C 56
Belvedere Vs. Bath —1A 106
Belverstone. Bris —2E 73
Belvoir Rd. Bath —4E 105
Belvoir Rd. Bris —5A 58
Bence Ct. Han —4D 73
Benford Clo. Bris —1E 61
Bengough's Almshouses. Bris —3E 69 (1A 4)
Bennett Rd. Bris —3A 72
Bennetts Ct. Yate —5C 18
Bennett's La. Bath —5B 100
Bennett's Rd. Bath —3D 101
Bennett St. Bath —2A 106 (1B 96)
Bennetts Way. Clev —1E 121
Bennett Way. Bris —5B 68
Bensaunt Gro. Bris —5F 25
Bentley Clo. Bris —5B 88
Bentley Rd. W Mare —1F 129
Benville Av. Bris —4E 39
Berchel Ho. Bris —1E 79
Berenda Dri. L Grn —2D 85
Beresford Clo. Salt —2A 94
Beresford Gdns. Bath —3B 98
Berkeley Av. Bishop —4F 57
Berkeley Av. Bris —3E 69
Berkeley Av. Mid N —2D 151
Berkeley Clo. Bris —4B 46
Berkeley Ct. Bath —3D 107
Berkeley Ct. Bris —4F 57
Berkeley Ct. Pat —5B 10
Berkeley Cres. Bris —3D 69
Berkeley Cres. Uph —1A 138
Berkeley Gdns. Key —4A 92
Berkeley Grn. Bris —3D 45
Berkeley Grn. Rd. G'bnk —5E 59
Berkeley Gro. G'bnk —5E 59
Berkeley Ho. Bath —1B 106
Berkeley Ho. Bris —2F 61
Berkeley Pl. Bath —1B 106
Berkeley Pl. Bris —3D 69
Berkeley Pl. C Down —2D 111
Berkeley Rd. Bishop —4F 57
Berkeley Rd. Fish —5C 60
Berkeley Rd. K'wd —3A 74
Berkeley Rd. Stap H —3F 61
Berkeley Rd. Trow —2A 118
Berkeley Rd. W'bry P —3C 56
Berkeleys Mead. Brad S —3B 28
Berkeley Sq. Bris —3E 69
Berkeley St. Bris —4E 59 (in two parts)
Berkshire Rd. Bris —4F 57
Berlington Ct. Bris —5A 70 (5E 5)
Berners Clo. Bris —1F 87
Berrow Wlk. Bris —3A 80
Berry Croft. Bris —1F 79
Berryfield Rd. Brad A —2E 115
Berry La. Bris —1B 58
Berwick Dri. Bris —4A 24
Berwick La. H'len & E Comp —4E 23
Berwick Rd. Bris —5D 59
Beryl Gro. Bris —5E 81
Beryl Rd. Bris —2D 79
Besom La. W'lgh —4E 33
Bess Ho. Clev —4C 120
Bethell Ct. Brad A —2D 115
Bethel Rd. Bris —2B 72
Betjeman Ct. Bar C —5C 74
Bevan Ct. Bris —2C 42
Beverley Av. Bris —3B 46
Beverley Clo. Bris —4D 73
Beverley Gdns. Bris —5F 39
Beverley Rd. Bris —4B 42
Beverstone. Bris —2E 73
Beverston Gdns. Bris —2D 39
Bevington Clo. Pat —5A 10
Bevington Wlk. Pat —5A 10
Bewdley Rd. Bath —5C 106
Bewley Rd. Trow —5C 118
Bexley Rd. Bris —4D 61
Bibstone. Bris —2C 74
Bibury Av. Pat —1D 27
Bibury Clo. Bris —5F 41
Bibury Clo. Nail —4F 123
Bibury Cres. Han —5E 73
Bibury Cres. W Trym —5F 41
Bickerton Clo. Bris —1B 40
Bickford Clo. Bar C —4C 74
Bickley Clo. Bris —3D 83
Biddestone Rd. Bris —4A 42
Biddisham Clo. Nail —4D 123
Biddle St. Yat —4A 142
Bideford Cres. Bris —5B 80
Bideford Rd. W Mare —3D 129
Bidwell Clo. Bris —1D 41
Bifield Clo. Bris —3B 90
Bifield Gdns. Bris —3A 90 (in two parts)
Bifield Rd. Bris —4A 90
Bignell Clo. Wins —4A 156
Bilberry Clo. Bris —4E 39
Bilbie Clo. Bris —5F 41
Bilbie Rd. W Mare —2F 129
Bilbury Ho. Bath —4C 98
Bilbury La. Bath —3B 106 (4C 96)
Bileys Mead Rd. Bris —2E 59
Billand Clo. Bris —5A 86
Bince's Lodge La. Mid N —5D 147
Bindon Dri. Bris —5F 25
Binhay Rd. Yat —4B 142
Binley Gro. Bris —3F 89
Binmead Gdns. Bris —4D 87
Birbeck Rd. Bris —2A 56
Birchall Rd. Bris —3E 57
Birch Av. B'don —5A 140
Birch Av. Clev —2E 121
Birch Clo. Lock —4F 135
Birch Clo. Pat —2A 26
Birch Ct. Key —4E 91
Birch Croft. Bris —5C 88
Birchdale Rd. Bris —5C 80
Birchdene. Nail —3F 123
Birch Dri. Alv —3A 8
Birch Dri. Puck —2D 65
Birches, The. Nail —3F 123
Birch Gro. P'head —4E 49
Birch Rd. K'wd —4A 62
Birch Rd. Rads —3B 152
Birch Rd. S'vle —1D 79
Birch Rd. Yate —4F 17
Birchwood. Bris —5D 41
Birchwood Av. W Mare —1E 133
Birchwood Ct. St Ap —4B 72
Birchwood Rd. Bris —2A 82
Birdale Clo. Bris —1A 40
Birdcombe Clo. Nail —2D 123
Birdlip Clo. Nail —4F 123
Birdwell La. L Ash —4B 76
Birdwell Rd. L Ash —4B 76
Birdwood. Bris —4F 73
Birkdale. War —4C 74
Birkdale. Yate —1A 34
Birkett Rd. W Mare —4A 126
Birkin St. Bris —4C 70
Birnbeck Ct. W Mare —1B 132
Birnbeck Rd. W Mare —4A 126
Bisdee Rd. Hut —5B 134
Bishop Av. W Mare —2E 129
Bishop Manor Rd. Bris —5F 41
Bishop M. Bris —2A 70
Bishop Rd. Bris —3E 57
Bishops Clo. Bris —4A 56
Bishops Ct. Bris —4E 55
Bishops Cove. Bris —3B 86
Bishops Rd. Clav —2F 143
Bishop St. St Pa —2A 70
Bishops Wood. Alm —1E 11
Bishopsworth Rd. Bris —1C 86
Bishop Ter. St Pa —2B 70
Bishopthorpe Rd. Bris —5F 41
Bishport Av. Bris —4C 86
Bishport Clo. Bris —4D 87
Bishport Grn. Bris —5E 87
Bisley. Yate —2E 33
Biss Meadow. Trow —2A 118
Bittern Clo. W Mare —4D 129
Bitterwell Clo. Coal H —1F 47
Bittle Mead. Bris —4B 88
Blackacre. Bris —4E 89
Blackberry Av. Bris —2A 60
Blackberry Dri. W Mare —4E 129
Blackberry Hill. Stap —2A 60
Blackberry La. P'head —5B 48
Blackbird Clo. Mid N —4E 151
Black Boy Hill. Bris —5C 56
Blackdown Ct. Bris —3D 89
Blackdown Rd. P'head —3C 48
Blackfriars. Bris —3F 69 (1B 4)
Blackfriars Rd. Nail —4A 122
Blackhorse Hill. E Comp —1D 25
Blackhorse La. Bris —3B 46 (in two parts)
Blackhorse Pl. Mang —1C 62
Blackhorse Rd. Bris —2F 73
Blackhorse Rd. Mang —5C 46
Blackmoor. Clev —5C 120
Blackmoor. W Mare —3D 129
Blackmoor Rd. Abb L —1A 66
Blackmoors La. Bris —2A 78
Blackmore Dri. Bath —4D 105
Blacksmith La. Up Swa —1C 100
Blacksmiths La. Kel —1D 95
Blackswarth Rd. Bris —3F 71
Blackthorn Clo. Bris —3F 87
Blackthorn Dri. Brad S —2F 27
Blackthorne Ter. W Mare —4E 129
Blackthorn Gdns. W Mare —4E 129
Blackthorn Rd. Bris —3F 87
Blackthorn Sq. Clev —5D 121
Blackthorn Wlk. Bris —5A 62
Blackthorn Way. Nail —3F 123
Blackwell Hill Rd. Back —1F 125
Bladen Clo. P'head —4A 50
Bladud Bldgs. Bath —2B 106 (2C 96)
Blagdon Clo. Bris —3A 80
Blagdon Clo. W Mare —2D 139
Blagdon Pk. Bath —5B 104
Blagrove Clo. Bris —5E 87
Blagrove Cres. Bris —5E 87
Blair Rd. Trow —4A 118
Blaisdon. Yate —2A 34
Blaisdon Clo. Bris —3C 40
Blaise Wlk. Bris —5E 39
Blake End. Kew —1C 128
Blakeney Gro. Nail —5B 122
Blakeney Mills. Yate —5F 17
Blakeney Rd. Bris —1C 58
Blakeney Rd. Pat —5A 10
Blake Rd. Bris —1D 59
Blakes Rd. T'bry —3C 6
Blanchards. Chip S —1F 35
Blandford Clo. Bris —1D 57
Blandford Clo. Nail —4D 123
Bleadon Hill. W Mare —2D 139
Bleadon Rd. B'don —4E 139
Blenheim Clo. Pea J —5D 157
Blenheim Clo. W Mare —3E 129
Blenheim Dri. Bris —5D 27
Blenheim Dri. Yate —3E 17
Blenheim Gdns. Bath —4B 100
Blenheim Rd. Bris —4D 57
Blenheim St. Bris —1C 70
Blenheim Way. P'head —3A 50
Blenman Clo. Bris —5C 44
Blethwin Clo. Bris —3B 40
Blind La. Bath —5C 106
Blind La. Clav —4F 143 (in two parts)
Blind La. W'ton —4D 99
Bloomfield. W Mare —1E 139
Bloomfield Av. Bath —5F 105
Bloomfield Cres. Bath —2E 109
Bloomfield Dri. Bath —2D 109
Bloomfield Gro. Bath —1F 109
Bloomfield La. Paul —4B 146
Bloomfield Pk. Bath —1F 109
Bloomfield Pk. Rd. Tim —1E 157
Bloomfield Rise N. Bath —2E 109
Bloomfield Rd. Bath —2E 109
Bloomfield Rd. Bris —1E 81
Bloomfield Rd. Tim —1E 157
Bloomfield Ter. Pea J —2F 149
Bloucher Pl. Bris —5C 58
Bloy St. Bris —1E 71
Bluebell Clo. T'bry —2E 7
Bluebells, The. Brad S —2A 28
Blueberry Way. W Mare —4D 129
Blythe Gdns. W Mare —2E 129
Boarding Ho. La. Alm —2A 10
Boat Stall La. Bath —3B 106 (off Orange Gro.)
Bobbin La. W'wd —5A 114
Bobbin Pk. Brad A —5A 114
Bockenem Clo. T'bry —5E 7
Bodey Clo. Bris —4C 74
Bodmin Wlk. Bris —4B 80
Bodyce Rd. Alv —2B 8
Boiling Wells La. Bris —4C 58
Bolton Rd. Bris —4A 58
Bond St. Bris —2A 70
Bond St. Trow —3C 118
Bond St. Bldgs. Trow —3B 118
Bonnington Wlk. Bris —4D 43
Bonville Bus. Cen. Bris —3B 82
Bonville Rd. Bris —4A 82
Booth Rd. Bris —1E 79
Boot La. Bris —1F 79
Bordesley Rd. Bris —5C 88
Borgie Pl. W Mare —2D 129
Borleyton Wlk. Bris —4B 86
Borver Gro. Bris —4D 87 (in two parts)
Boscombe Cres. Bris —5B 46
Boston Rd. Bris —4B 42
Boswell Rd. L W'wd —5A 114
Boswell St. Bris —5E 59
Botham Clo. W Mare —1E 129
Botham Dri. Bris —4F 81
Boucher Pl. Bris —5C 58
Boulevard. W Mare —5C 126
Boulters Rd. Bris —4E 87
Boulton's La. Bris —2F 73
Boulton's Rd. Bris —2F 73
Boundary Clo. Mid N —5E 151

Boundary Clo. *W Mare* —5C **132**
Boundary Rd. *Coal H* —2F **31**
Boundary Wlk. *Trow* —5B **118** (in three parts)
Bourchier Gdns. *Bris* —5D **87**
Bourne Clo. *Bris* —2D **73**
Bourne Clo. *Wint* —2A **30**
Bourne Rd. *Bris* —2C **72**
Bourneville Rd. *Bris* —2F **71**
Bournville Rd. *W Mare* —3D **133**
Boursland Clo. *Brad S* —4F **11**
Bourton Av. *Pat* —5E **11**
Bourton Clo. *Pat* —1E **27**
Bourton La. *St Geo* —2B **130**
Bourton Mead. *L Ash* —4D **77**
Bourton Wlk. *Bris* —5C **78**
Bouverie St. *Bris* —2D **71**
Boverton Rd. *Bris* —1D **43**
Bowden Clo. *Bris* —4E **39**
Bowden Pl. *Bris* —5B **46**
Bowden Rd. *Bris* —1A **72**
Bowen Rd. *Lock* —3F **135**
Bower Ashton Ter. *Bris* —1B **78**
Bowerleaze. *Bris* —2E **55**
Bower Rd. *Bris* —2C **78**
Bower Wlk. *Bris* —2A **80**
Bowlditch La. *Mid N* —5E **147**
Bowling Hill. *Chip S* —5C **18**
Bowling Rd. *Chip S* —1D **35**
Bow Mead. *Bris* —3A **90**
Bowness Gdns. *Bris* —4E **41**
Bowood. Bris —3E ***45*** *(off Harford Dri.)*
Bowring Clo. *Bris* —5E **87**
Bowsland. *Brad S* —4A **12**
Bowsland Way. *Brad S* —4E **11**
Bowstreet La. *E Comp* —1C **24**
Boxbury Hill. *Paul* —1B **150**
Box Hedge La. *Coal H* —5A **32**
Box Rd. *Bath* —3C **102**
Box Wlk. *Key* —4E **91**
Boyce Clo. *Bath* —4A **104**
Boyce Dri. *Bris* —5C **58**
Boyce's Av. *Bris* —3C **68**
Boyd Clo. *Wick* —4A **154**
Boyd Rd. *Salt* —5F **93**
Brabazon Rd. *Bris* —2D **43**
Bracewell Gdns. *Bris* —5E **25**
Bracey Dri. *Bris* —1E **61**
Brackenbury Dri. *Stok G* —4B **28**
Brackendene. *Pat* —5E **11**
Bracken Wood Rd. *Clev* —1E **121**
Bracton Dri. *Bris* —3C **88**
Bradeston Gro. *Bris* —5C **44**
Bradford Clo. *Clev* —5C **120**
Bradford Pk. *Bath* —2B **110** (in two parts)
Bradford Rd. *Bathf* —3C **102**
Bradford Rd. *C Down* —3A **110**
Bradford Rd. *Holt* —2D **155**
Bradford Rd. *Trow* —1B **118**
Bradford Rd. *W'ley* —2F **113**
Bradford Wood La. *Brad A* —3F **115**
Bradhurst St. *Bris* —4D **71**
Bradley Av. *Bris* —1A **54**
Bradley Av. *Wint* —4A **30**
Bradley Clo. *Holt* —2F **155**
Bradley Ct. *Bris* —2E **61**
Bradley Cres. *Bris* —1A **54**
Bradley La. *Holt* —2F **155**
Bradley Pavilions. *Brad S* —4E **11**
Bradley Rd. *Pat* —1B **26**
Bradley Rd. *Trow* —3C **118**
Bradley Stoke Way. *Brad S* —3B **28**
Bradstone Rd. *Wint* —4F **29**
Bradville Gdns. *L Ash* —5B **76**
Bradwell Gro. *Bris* —4E **41**
Braemar Av. *Bris* —3B **42**
Braemar Cres. *Bris* —3B **42**
Brae Rise. *Wins* —4B **156**
Brae Rd. *Wins* —4A **156**
Bragg's La. *Bris* —3B **70**
Braikenridge Clo. *Clev* —5C **120**
Braikenridge Rd. *Bris* —1F **81**
Brainsfield. *Bris* —1B **56**
Brake Clo. *Brad S* —3A **28**
Brake Clo. *Bris* —3B **74**
Brake, The. *Coal H* —4E **31**
Brake, The. *Yate* —1A **18**
Brakewell Gdns. *Bris* —4C **88**
Bramble Dri. *Bris* —4E **55**
Bramble La. *Bris* —4E **55**
Brambles, The. *Bris* —4E **87**
Brambles, The. *Key* —5F **91**
Bramble Way. *C Down* —3C **110**
Bramblewood. *Yat* —2B **142**
Bramblewood Rd. *W Mare* —2C **128**
Brambling Wlk. *Bris* —1B **60** (in two parts)
Bramley Clo. *Lock* —4E **135**
Bramley Clo. *Pea J* —5D **157**
Bramley Clo. *Pill* —3E **53**
Bramley Clo. *Yat* —4B **142**
Bramley Ct. *Bar C* —1B **84**
Bramley Dri. *Back* —3C **124**
Bramley La. *Trow* —3D **119**
Bramley Sq. *Cong* —3D **145**
Bramleys, The. *Nail* —5A **122**
Brampton Dri. *Bris* —4F **45**
Brampton Way. *P'head* —3F **49**
Bramshill Dri. *W Mare* —2D **129**
Branche Gro. *Bris* —5F **87**
Brandash Rd. *Chip S* —5E **19**
Brandon Ho. *Bris* —4D **69**
Brandon Steep. *Bris* —4E **69**
Brandon Steps. *Bris* —4E **69**
Brandon St. *Bris* —4E **69**
Brangwyn Gro. *Bris* —2D **59**
Brangwyn Sq. *W Mare* —3D **129**
Branksome Cres. *Bris* —1D **43**
Branksome Dri. *Bris* —1D **43**
Branksome Dri. *Wint* —3A **30**
Branksome Rd. *Bris* —4D **57**
Branscombe Rd. *Bris* —3E **55**
Branscombe Wlk. *P'head* —5B **48**
Branwhite Clo. *Bris* —5D **43**
Brassknocker Hill. *Mon C* —1B **112**
Brassmill La. *Bath* —1B **104**
Brassmill La. Trad. Est. *Bath* —2B **104**
Bratton Rd. *Bris* —1F **87**
Braunton Rd. *Bris* —2E **79**
Braydon Av. *Lit S* —1E **27**
Brayne Ct. *L Grn* —2B **84**
Braysdown Clo. *Pea J* —3E **149**
Braysdown La. *Pea J* —2F **149** (in two parts)
Breaches Ga. *Brad S* —3B **28**
Breaches La. *Key* —4C **92**
Breaches, The. *E'ton G* —2D **53**
Breach Rd. *Bris* —2C **78**
Breakneck. *Back* —4D **125**
Brean Down Av. *Bris* —2D **57**
Brean Down Av. *W Mare* —4B **132**
Brecknock Rd. *Bris* —2C **80**
Brecon Rd. *Bris* —1C **56**
Brecon View. *W Mare* —2E **139**
Bredon. *Yate* —2F **33**
Bredon Clo. *Bris* —3B **74**
Bredon Nook Rd. *Bris* —5E **41**
Bree Clo. *W Mare* —1E **129**
Brendon Av. *W Mare* —4D **127**
Brendon Clo. *Old C* —1E **85**
Brendon Gdns. *Nail* —4D **123**
Brendon Rd. *Bris* —2F **79**
Brendon Rd. *P'head* —3C **48**
Brenner St. *Bris* —5D **59**
Brent Clo. *W Mare* —1F **139**
Brent Rd. *Bris* —2B **58**
Brentry Av. *Bris* —3D **71**
Brentry Hill. *Bris* —3C **40**
Brentry Ho. *Bris* —1D **41**
Brentry La. *Bris* —2C **40**
Brentry Rd. *Bris* —3A **60**
Brereton Way. *Bris* —1D **85**
Brewerton Clo. *Bris* —1E **41**
Briar Clo. *Nail* —3F **123**
Briar Clo. *Rads* —4A **152**
Briarfield Av. *Bris* —5D **73**
Briarleaze. *Rudg* —5A **8**
Briar Mead. *Yat* —2A **142**
Briar Rd. *Hut* —5C **134**
Briarside Rd. *Bris* —1E **41**
Briar Wlk. *Bris* —4E **61**
Briar Way. *Bris* —3D **61**
Briarwood. *Bris* —1B **56**
Briary Rd. *P'head* —3E **49**
Briavels Gro. *Bris* —5B **58**
Briburn M. Bath —3F ***105*** *(off Stanhope Pl.)*
Brick St. *Bris* —3B **70**
Bridewell La. *Bath* —3A **106** (3B **96**)
Bridewell La. *Hut* —3F **141**
Bridewell St. *Bris* —3F **69** (1C **4**)
Bridge Av. *Trow* —2A **118**
Bridge Clo. *Bris* —4E **89**
Bridge Farm Clo. *Bris* —5C **88**
Bridge Farm Sq. *Cong* —2D **145**
Bridgeleap Rd. *Bris* —4B **46**
Bridge Pl. Rd. *C'ton* —1B **148**
Bridge Rd. *Bath* —4D **105**
Bridge Rd. *B'don* —5F **139**
Bridge Rd. *Eastv* —4D **59**
Bridge Rd. *K'wd* —4B **62**
Bridge Rd. *L Wds* —4F **67**
Bridge Rd. *Mang* —3E **63**
Bridge Rd. *W Mare* —2D **133**
Bridge Rd. *Yate* —4C **16**
Bridges Ct. *Fish* —3D **61**
Bridges Dri. *Bris* —1E **61**
Bridge St. *Bath* —3B **106** (3C **96**)
Bridge St. *Brad A* —3E **115**
Bridge St. *Bris* —4A **70** (3C **4**)
Bridge St. *Eastv* —5F **59**
Bridge St. *Trow* —3D **119**
Bridge Valley Rd. *Bris* —2A **68**
Bridge Wlk. *Bris* —4C **42**
Bridge Way. *Fram C* —1D **31**
Bridgewell La. *W Mare* —2F **141**
Bridgman Gro. *Bris* —1E **43**
Bridgwater Rd. *Bris* —2A **86**
Bridgwater Rd. *Uph & B'don* —5C **132**
Bridgwater Rd. *Wins* —5C **156**
Bridle Way. *Alv* —3A **8**
Briercliffe Rd. *Bris* —5F **39**
Brierly Furlong. *Stok G* —1F **43**
Briery Leaze Rd. *Bris* —3C **88**
Brighton Cres. *Bris* —3D **79**
Brighton M. *Bris* —2D **69**
Brighton Pk. *Bris* —2D **71**
Brighton Pl. *Bris* —1F **73**
Brighton Rd. *Bris* —1E **69**
Brighton Rd. *Pat* —1B **26**
Brighton Rd. *W Mare* —2C **132**
Brighton St. *Bris* —1A **70**
Brighton Ter. *Bedm* —3D **79**
Bright St. *Bar H* —3D **71**
Bright St. *K'wd* —2F **73**
Brigstocke Rd. *Bris* —1A **70**
Brimbles. *Bris* —2D **43**
Brimbleworth La. *St Geo* —1A **130**
Brimridge Rd. *Wins* —4B **156**
Brinkworthy Rd. *Bris* —1A **60**
Brinmead Wlk. *Bris* —5B **86**
Brins Clo. *Stok G* —5B **28**
Brinscombe La. *Bath* —5F **157**
Brinsea Batch. *Cong* —5E **145**
Brinsea La. *Cong* —5F **145**
Brinsea Rd. *Cong* —3D **145**
Brinsham La. *Yate* —1C **18**
Briscoes Av. *Bris* —4E **87**
Brislington Hill. *Bris* —3A **82**
Brislington Retail Pk. *Brisl* —4A **82**
Brislington Trad. Est. *Bris* —3B **82**
Bristol Bus. Pk. *Bris* —3A **44**
Bristol Ga. *Bris* —5B **68**
Bristol Hill. *Bris* —3F **81**
Bristol Rd. *Bath* —4D **95**
Bristol Rd. *Cong* —2D **145**
Bristol Rd. *Fram C* —5C **14**
Bristol Rd. *Fren* —4C **44**
Bristol Rd. *Ham* —1F **45**
Bristol Rd. *Key* —2F **91**
Bristol Rd. *Paul* —3B **146**
Bristol Rd. *P'head* —4F **49**
Bristol Rd. *Rads* —5B **148**
Bristol Rd. *T'bry* —5C **6**
Bristol Rd. *W'chu* —3E **89**
Bristol Rd. *Wins* —5C **156**
Bristol Rd. *Wint* —2A **30**
Bristol Rd. *W Mare* —3A **130**
Bristol Rd. Lwr. *W Mare* —5B **126**
Bristol Vale Cen. for Industry. *Bris* —4D **79**
Bristol Vale Trad. Est. *Bris* —5E **79**
Bristol View. *Bath* —4D **109**
Britannia Cres. *Stok G* —4F **27**
Britannia Ho. *Brad S* —2B **42**
Britannia Rd. *E'tn* —1D **71**
Britannia Rd. *K'wd* —2E **73**
Britannia Rd. *Pat* —1F **25**
Britannia Way. *Clev* —5C **120**
British Rd. *Bris* —2D **79**
British Row. *Trow* —1C **118**
British, The. *Yate* —2D **17**
Brittan Pl. *P'bry* —4A **52**
Britten Ct. *L Grn* —1B **84**
Britten's Clo. *Paul* —3C **146**
Britten's Hill. *Paul* —3C **146**
Brixham Rd. *Bris* —3E **79**
Brixton Rd. *Bris* —2D **71**
Brixton Rd. M. *E'tn* —2D **71**
Broadbury Rd. *Bris* —5F **79**
Broadcloth La. *Trow* —3E **119**
Broadcloth La. E. *Trow* —4E **119**
Broad Croft. *Brad S* —4E **11**
Broadcroft Av. *Clav* —2F **143**
Broadcroft Clo. *Clav* —2F **143**
Broadfield Av. *Bris* —2E **73**
Broadfield Rd. *Bris* —5C **80**
Broadlands. *Clev* —3F **121**
Broadlands Av. *Key* —2F **91**
Broadlands Dri. *Bris* —3C **38**
Broad La. *W'lgh* —4F **31**
Broad La. *Yate* —2D **17**
Broadleas. *Bris* —1E **87**
Broadleaze. *Shire* —5F **37**
Broadley Pk. *N Brad* —4E **155**
Broadleys Av. *Bris* —5E **41**
Broadmead. *Bris* —3A **70** (1D **5**)
Broadmead. *Trow* —1A **118**
Broadmead La. *Key* —3D **93**
Broadmead Shopping Cen. *Bris* —3A **70** (1D **5**)
Broadmoor La. *Bath* —2A **98**
Broadmoor Pk. *Bath* —4C **98**
Broadmoor Vale. *Bath* —3B **98**
Broadoak Hill. *Dun* —5B **86**
Broadoak Rd. *Bris* —4B **86**
Broadoak Rd. *W Mare* —5B **132**
Broad Oaks. *Bris* —4A **68**
Broadoak Wlk. *Bris* —3D **61**
Broad Plain. *Bris* —3B **70** (3F **5**)
Broad Quay. *Bath* —4A **106** (5C **96**)
Broad Quay. *Bris* —4F **69** (3B **4**)
Broad Rd. *Bris* —1E **73**
Broadstone Wlk. *Bris* —3F **87**
Broad St. *Bath* —2B **106** (2C **96**)
Broad St. *Bris* —3F **69** (2C **4**)
Broad St. *Chip S* —5D **19**
Broad St. *Cong* —2D **145**
Broad St. *Stap H* —3F **61**
Broad St. *Trow* —1C **118**
Broad St. *Wrin* —1B **156**
Broad St. Pl. *Bath* —2B **106** (2C **96**)
Broad Wlk. *Bris* —3B **80**
Broad Wlk. *P'head* —1A **50**
Broad Wlk. Shopping Precinct. *Bris* —3D **81**
Broadway. *Bath* —3C **106** (4E **97**)
Broadway. *Lock* —4B **136**
Broadway. *Salt* —5F **93**
Broadway. *W Mare* —1D **139**
Broadway. *Yate* —4B **18**
Broadway Av. *Bris* —1F **57**
Broadway La. *Rads* —3E **147**
Broadway Rd. *Bishop* —4F **57**
Broadway Rd. *B'wth* —3B **86**
Broadways Dri. *Bris* —5B **44**
Broad Weir. *Bris* —3A **70** (2E **5**)
Brock End. *P'head* —5A **48**
Brockhurst Gdns. *Bris* —2C **72**
Brockhurst Rd. *Bris* —2C **72**
Brockley Clo. *Lit S* —2E **27**
Brockley Clo. *Nail* —4C **122**
Brockley Clo. *W Mare* —2D **139**
Brockley Combe Rd. *Back* —5A **124**
Brockley Cres. *W Mare* —2D **139**
Brockley La. *B'ley* —3A **124**
Brockley Rd. *Salt* —5F **93**
Brockley Wlk. *Bris* —5C **78**
Brockley Way. *B'ley* —5A **124**
Brockley Way. *Clav* —1F **143**
Brockridge La. *Fram C* —2E **31**
Brocks La. *L Ash* —4B **76**
Brocks Rd. *Bris* —5E **87**
Brock St. *Bath* —2A **106** (1A **96**)
Brockway. *Nail* —3E **123**
Brockworth. *Yate* —3E **33**
Brockworth Cres. *Bris* —1B **60**
Bromley Dri. *Bris* —4F **45**
Bromley Heath Av. *Bris* —4F **45**
Bromley Heath Rd. *Bris* (in two parts) —5F **45**
Bromley Rd. *Bris* —2B **58**
Brompton Clo. *Bris* —2B **74**
Brompton Rd. *W Mare* —1E **139**
Broncksea Rd. *Bris* —3B **42**
Brook Clo. *L Ash* —4D **77**
Brookcote Dri. *Lit S* —3F **27**
Brookdale Rd. *Bris* —2D **87**
Brookfield Av. *Bris* —4F **57**
Brookfield Clo. *Chip S* —4E **19**
Brookfield Pk. *Bath* —4C **98**
Brookfield Rd. *Bris* —5F **57**
Brookfield Rd. *Pat* —1D **27**
Brookfield Wlk. *Clev* —3F **121**
Brookfield Wlk. *Old C* —2E **85**
Brookgate. *Bris* —4A **78**
Brook Hill. *Bris* —1B **70**
Brook Ho. *Lit S* —2E **27**
Brookland Rd. *Bris* —2F **57**
Brookland Rd. *W Mare* —1F **133**
Brook La. *Mont* —1B **70**
Brook La. *Stap* —1A **60**
Brooklea. *Old C* —1D **85**
Brookleaze. *Bris* —1E **55**
Brookleaze Bldgs. *Bath* —4C **100**
Brook Lintons. *Bris* —2F **81**
Brooklyn. *Wrin* —1B **156**
Brooklyn Rd. *Bath* —4D **101**
Brooklyn Rd. *Bris* —5D **79**
Brooklyn St. *Bris* —5B **58**
Brookmead. *T'bry* —5E **7**
Brookridge Ho. *Bris* —1B **40**
Brook Rd. *Bath* —3E **105**
Brook Rd. *Fish* —3C **60**
Brook Rd. *Mang* —1B **62**
Brook Rd. *Mont* —1B **70**
Brook Rd. *St G* —1A **72**
Brook Rd. *S'vle* —1F **79**
Brook Rd. *Trow* —2A **118**
Brook Rd. *War* —2C **74**
Brookside. *Paul* —3B **146**
Brookside. *Pill* —4E **53**
Brookside Clo. *Bathe* —1A **102**
Brookside Clo. *Paul* —3B **146**
Brookside Dri. *Fram C* —1D **31**
Brookside Ho. *Bath* —5C **98**
Brookside Rd. *Bris* —3A **82**
Brook St. *Bris* —3E **71**
Brook St. *Chip S* —5C **18**
Brookthorpe. *Yate* —1F **33**
Brookthorpe Av. *Bris* —3C **38**
Brookview Wlk. *Bris* —1D **87**
Brook Way. *Brad S* —3A **28**
Broom Farm Clo. *Nail* —5D **123**
Broomfield Wlk. *E Grn* —5D **47**
Broomground. *W'ley* —2F **113**
Broom Hill. *Bris* —1A **60**
Broom Hill La. *Clut* —1B **146**
Broomhill Rd. *Brisl* —4B **82**
Brougham Cotts. Bath —4D ***101*** *(off Dafford St.)*
Brougham Hayes. *Bath* —3E **105**

Brougham Pl. Bath —4D 101 (off St Saviours Rd.)
Broughton Ho. Bris —5A 70
Broughton Rd. Holt —5C 118
Brow Hill. Bath —2A 102
Brow Hill Vs. Bath —2A 102
Brownlow Rd. W Mare —4C 132
Brown St. Trow —3D 119
Brow, The. Bath —3D 111 (Church Rd.)
Brow, The. Bath —4C 104 (Innox Rd.)
Broxholme Wlk. Bris —4B 38
Bruce Av. Bris —1E 71
Bruce Rd. Bris —1E 71
Brue Clo. W Mare —3C 132
Brummel Way. Paul —3A 146
Brunel Clo. War —3E 75
Brunel Clo. W Mare —2D 139
Brunel Ct. Yate —4E 17
Brunel Ho. Bath —3B 104
Brunel Lock Rd. Bris —5B 68
Brunel Rd. Bris —5B 78
Brunel Rd. Nail —4A 122
Brunel Way. Ash G & Bris —1B 78
Brunel Way. T'bry —5C 6
Brunswick Pl. Bath —2A 106 (1B 96)
Brunswick Pl. Bris —5B 68
Brunswick Sq. Bris —2A 70
Brunswick St. Bar H —3E 71
Brunswick St. Bath —5C 100
Brunswick St. St Pa —2A 70
Bruton. W Mare —1E 139
Bruton Av. Bath —5A 106
Bruton Av. P'head —3C 48
Bruton Clo. Bris —2B 72
Bruton Clo. Nail —5D 123
Bruton Pl. Bris —3D 69
Bryanson's Clo. Bris —1F 59
Bryant Av. Rads —3A 152
Bryant Gdns. Clev —5C 120
Bryants Clo. Bris —3E 45
Bryants Hill. Bris —4D 73
Bryer-Ash Bus. Pk. Trow —2C 118
Brynland Av. Bris —3A 58
Buchanans Wharf N. Bris —4A 70 (4D 5)
Buchanans Wharf S. Bris —4A 70 (4D 5)
Buckingham Dri. Stok G —5A 28
Buckingham Gdns. Bris —1A 62
Buckingham Ho. Brad S —2B 42
Buckingham Pde. T'bry —3C 6
Buckingham Pl. Clif —3C 68
Buckingham Pl. Down —1A 62
Buckingham Rd. Bris —5F 71
Buckingham Rd. W Mare —5F 133
Buckingham St. Bris —3E 79
Buckingham Vale. Bris —2C 68
Buckland Grn. W Mare —1E 129
Bucklands Batch. Nail —5E 123
Bucklands Dri. Nail —5E 123
Bucklands End. Nail —5E 123
Bucklands Gro. Nail —5E 123
Bucklands La. Nail —5E 123
Bucklands View. Nail —5F 123
Buckleaze Clo. Trow —5D 119
Budbury Circ. Brad A —2D 115
Budbury Clo. Brad A —2D 115
Budbury Heights. Brad A —2D 115
Budbury Pl. Brad A —2D 115
Budbury Ridge. Brad A —2D 115
Budbury Tyning. Brad A —2C 114
Bude Av. Bris —2C 72
Bude Clo. Nail —4F 123
Bude Rd. Bris —1D 43
Bullens Clo. Brad S —4F 11
Buller Rd. Bris —3E 81
Bull La. Bris —4B 72
Bull La. Pill —3E 53
Bull Pit. Brad A —3E 115
Bumper's Batch. Bath —4B 110
Bungay's Hill. Paul —1B 146
Bunting Ct. W Mare —4C 128
Burbank Clo. L Grn —2C 84
Burchells Av. Bris —1D 73
Burchells Grn. Clo. Bris —1D 73
Burchells Grn. Rd. Bris —1D 73
Burcott Rd. Bris —4E 21
Burden Clo. Brad S —3B 28
Burderop Clo. Trow —5D 119
Burfoote Gdns. Bris —4A 90
Burfoote Rd. Bris —4A 90
Burford Av. Pat —1E 27
Burford Clo. Bath —1C 108
Burford Clo. P'head —4A 50
Burford Gro. Bris —2B 54
Burgage Clo. Chip S —1D 35
Burgess Grn. Clo. St Ap —3A 72
Burghill Rd. W Trym —3C 40
Burghley Rd. Bris —5A 58
Burgis Rd. Bris —2F 89
Burleigh Gdns. Bath —1B 104
Burleigh Way. Wickw —2C 154
Burley Av. Bris —2B 62
Burley Cres. Bris —1B 62
Burley Gro. Bris —1B 62
Burlington Pl. Bath —2A 106 (off Julian Rd.)
Burlington Rd. Bris —5D 57
Burlington Rd. Mid N —2F 151
Burlington St. Bath —1A 106
Burlington St. W Mare —5C 126
Burnbush Clo. Bris —2A 90
Burnell Dri. Bris —2B 70
Burnett Rd. Trow —4D 119
Burney Way. L Grn —2C 84
Burnham Clo. Bris —1B 74
Burnham Clo. W Mare —2D 139
Burnham Dri. Bris —1B 74
Burnham Dri. W Mare —2D 139
Burnham Rd. Bath —3D 105
Burnham Rd. Bris —1F 53
Burnside Clo. Bris —2E 41
Burnt Ho. Cotts. Bath —4D 109
Burnt House Rd. Bath —4E 109
Burrington Av. W Mare —2D 139
Burrington Clo. Nail —4D 123
Burrington Clo. W Mare —2D 139
Burrington Wlk. Bris —5C 78
Burrough Way. Wint —4A 30
Burton Clo. Bris —5A 70
Burton Ct. Bris —3D 69
Burton St. Bath —3B 106 (3C 96)
Burwalls Rd. Bris —4A 68
Bury Ct. Clo. Bris —3C 38
Bury Hill. Wint —1B 46
Bury, The. Lock —5E 135
Bush Av. Lit S —3E 27
Bush Ct. Alv —2A 8
Bush Ct. Bris —1B 80
Bush Ind. Est. Bris —2F 71
Bush La. Bris —1D 79
Bushy Ho. Bris —2B 80
Bushy Pk. Bris —2B 80
Butcombe. W Mare —1E 139
Butcombe Wlk. Bris —3D 89
Buthay, The. Wickw —2B 154
Butlass Clo. High L —1A 146
Butlers Clo. Bris —4B 72
Butterfield Clo. Bris —5A 42
Butterfield Pk. Clev —5C 120
Butterfield Rd. Bris —5A 42
Buttermere Rd. W Mare —3E 133
Butterworth Ct. Bris —1F 87
Butt La. T'bry —1D 7
Button Clo. Bris —2C 88
Butt's Batch. Wrin —2B 156
Buxton Wlk. Bris —4C 42
Byfield. C Down —3C 110
Byfield Bldgs. Bath —3C 110 (off Byfield Pl.)
Byfield Pl. Bath —3C 110
Byfields. Clev —5C 120
Byron Clo. Lock —4E 135
Byron Pl. Bris —3D 69
Byron Pl. Stap H —3A 62
Byron Rd. Bath —5A 106
Byron Rd. Lock —4E 135
Byron Rd. W Mare —4E 133
Byron St. Redf —3E 71
Byron St. St Pa —1C 70
Bythesea Rd. Trow —2C 118
Byways Cvn. Pk. Clev —5C 120
Byzantine Ct. Bris —5F 69

Cabot Clo. Salt —5F 93
Cabot Clo. Yate —5B 18
Cabot Ct. Bris —3B 42
Cabot Grn. Bris —3D 71
Cabot Ho. T'bry —4D 7
Cabot Rise. P'head —3C 48
Cabot Way. Bris —5B 68
Cabot Way. Pill —4F 53
Cabot Way. W Mare —2E 129
Cabstand. P'head —2F 49
Cadbury Farm Rd. Yat —4B 142
Cadbury Heath Rd. Bris —5C 74
Cadbury Rd. Key —5A 92
Cadbury Rd. P'head —4F 49
Cadbury Sq. Cong —3D 145
Cadby Clo. Trow —2F 119
Cadby Ho. Bath —3B 104
Caddick Clo. Bris —5B 62
Cade Clo. K'wd —4B 74
Cade Clo. Stok G —4A 28
Cadogan Rd. Bris —5C 80
Caen Rd. Bris —2F 79
Caernarvon Rd. Key —4E 91
Caine Rd. Bris —5B 42
Cains Clo. Bris —4A 74
Cairn Clo. Nail —4F 123
Cairns Ct. Bris —3E 57
Cairns Cres. Bris —1B 70
Cairns Rd. Bris —2D 57
Cala Trad. Est. Bris —2B 78
Calcott Rd. Bris —3C 80
Caldbeck Clo. Bris —2F 41
Calder Clo. Key —4C 92
Caldicot Clo. Bris —2E 39
Caldicot Clo. Will —3D 85
Caledonia M. Bris —3B 68
Caledonian Rd. Bath —3E 105
Caledonia Pl. Bris —4B 68
California Rd. Old C —2C 84
Callard Ho. Bris —3B 60
Callicroft Rd. Pat —2C 26
Callington Rd. Bris —4D 81
Callowhill Ct. Bris —3A 70 (1D 5)
Calton Gdns. Bath —4A 106
Calton Rd. Bath —4B 106
Calton Wlk. Bath —4A 106
Camberley Dri. Fram C —1B 30
Camberley Rd. Bris —5E 79 (in two parts)
Camborne Rd. Bris —5C 42
Cambrian Dri. Yate —3F 17
Cambridge Cres. Bris —5C 40
Cambridge Gro. Clev —1D 121
Cambridge Pk. Bris —4D 57
Cambridge Pl. Bath —4C 106
Cambridge Pl. W Mare —5B 126
Cambridge Rd. Bris —3F 57
Cambridge Rd. Clev —1D 121
Cambridge St. Redf —3E 71
Cambridge St. Tot —1B 80
Cambridge Ter. Bath —4C 106
Cam Brook Clo. C'ton —1A 148
Camden Ct. Bath —1A 106
Camden Cres. Bath —1A 106
Camden Rd. Bath —1B 106
Camden Rd. Bris —5D 69
Camden Row. Bath —1A 106 (in two parts)
Camden Ter. Bath —1B 106 (off Camden Rd.)
Camden Ter. Bris —4C 68
Camden Ter. W Mare —1C 132
Cameley Grn. Bath —3A 104
Camelford Rd. Bris —5F 59
Cameron Wlk. Bris —1E 59
Cameroons Clo. Key —4A 92
Camerton Clo. Salt —1A 94
Camerton Hill. C'ton —1B 148
Camerton Rd. Bris —1F 71
Campbells Farm Dri. Bris —3B 38
Campbell St. Bris —1A 70
Campian Wlk. Bris —2F 87
Campion Clo. T'bry —2E 7
Campion Clo. W Mare —1B 134
Campion Dri. Brad S —4F 11
Campion Dri. Trow —4D 119
Camplins. Clev —5C 120
Camp Rd. Bris —3B 68
Camp Rd. W Mare —4A 126
Camp Rd. N. W Mare —4A 126
Camp View. Nail —3C 122
Camp View. Wint D —5A 30
Camvale. Pea J —1E 149
Camview. Paul —3A 146
Camwal Ind. Est. Bris —5C 70
Camwal Rd. Bris —5C 70
Canada Coombe. Hut —1D 141
Canada Way. Bris —5C 68
Canal Rd. Trow —5D 117
Canal Rd. Ind. Est. Trow —4D 117
Canal Ter. B'ptn —5A 102
Canberra Cres. Lock —2F 135
Canberra Gro. Bris —5D 27
Canberra Rd. W Mare —5D 133
Canford La. Bris —5F 39
Canford Rd. Bris —4B 40
Cann La. Bris —4F 75
Cannons Ga. Clev —5C 120
Cannon St. Bedm —1E 79
Cannon St. Bris —2F 69
Canons Clo. Bath —2C 108
Canons Clo. Wint —2A 30
Canons Ho. Bris —5E 69 (5A 4)
Canons Rd. Bris —5E 69 (5A 4)
Canon St. Bris —2E 71
Canon's Wlk. Bris —5A 62
Canon's Wlk. W Mare —3B 128
Canons Way. Bris —4E 69
Canowie Rd. Bris —4D 57
Cantell Gro. Bris —3B 90
Canterbury Clo. W Mare —1E 129
Canterbury Clo. Yate —3A 18
Canterbury Rd. Bath —4E 105
Canterbury St. Bar H —4D 71
Canters Leaze. Wickw —3C 154
Cantock's Clo. Bris —3E 69 (2A 4)
Canton Pl. Bath —1B 106
Canvey Clo. Bris —5A 42
Canynge Ho. Bris —5A 70
Canynge Rd. Bris —2B 68
Canynge Sq. Bris —2B 68
Canynge St. Bris —4A 70 (4D 5)
Capel Clo. Bris —2D 75
Capell Clo. W Mare —5F 127
Capel Rd. Bris —3D 39
Capenor Clo. P'head —4E 49
Capgrave Clo. Bris —2C 82
Capgrave Cres. Bris —2C 82
Caraway Gdns. Bris —5E 59
Carders Corner. Trow —3D 119
Cardigan Cres. W Mare —5A 128
Cardigan La. Bris —1D 57
Cardigan Rd. Bris —1D 57
Cardill Clo. Bris —5C 78
Cardinal Clo. Bath —4E 109
Carditch Drove. Cong —5B 144
Carey's Clo. Clev —2F 121
Carice Gdns. Clev —5D 121
Carisbrooke Cres. Trow —2E 117
Carisbrooke Rd. Bris —5F 79
Carlingford Ter. Rads —2D 153
Carlingford Ter. Rd. Rads —2D 153
Carlow Rd. Bris —5A 80
Carlton Ct. Bris —5C 40
Carlton Mans. N. W Mare (off Beach Rd.) —1B 132
Carlton Mans. S. W Mare (off Beach Rd.) —1B 132
Carlton Pk. Bris —2E 71
Carlton Row. Trow —4C 118
Carlton St. W Mare —1B 132
Carlyle Rd. Bris —1E 71
Carmarthen Clo. Yate —2B 18
Carmarthen Gro. Will —4D 85
Carmarthen Rd. Bris —1C 56
Carnarvon Rd. Bris —5E 57
Caroline Bldgs. Bath —4C 106 (5E 97)
Caroline Clo. Key —4E 91
Caroline Pl. Back —3C 124
Caroline Pl. Bath —1A 106
Carpenters La. Key —3A 92
Carpenters Shop La. Bris —1A 62
Carre Gdns. W Mare —1D 129
Carr Ho. Bath —3B 104
Carrick Ho. Bris —4B 68 (off Hotwell Rd.)
Carrington Rd. Bris —1C 78
Carsons Rd. Mang —4D 63
Carter Rd. Paul —4A 146
Carter Wlk. Brad S —1F 27
Cart La. Bris —4A 70 (4E 5)
Cartledge Rd. Bris —1E 71
Cashmore Ho. Bris —3D 71
Caslon Ct. Bris —5A 70
Cassell Rd. Bris —2E 61
Cassey Bottom La. Bris —3C 72
Castle Clo. Bris —2F 39
Castle Ct. T'bry —3C 6
Castle Farm Rd. Bris —3D 83
Castle Gdns. Bath —1F 109
Castle Hill. Ban —5F 137
Castle Ho. Wickw —2C 154
Castle M. Wickw —2C 154
Castle Pl. Trow —2D 119
Castle Rd. Bris —5F 61
Castle Rd. Clev —1D 121
Castle Rd. Old C —2E 85
Castle Rd. Puck —1E 65
Castle Rd. W Mare —2C 128
Castle St. Bris —3A 70 (2E 5)
Castle St. T'bry —2B 6
Castle St. Trow —2D 119
Castle View Rd. Clev —1D 121
Castlewood Clo. Clev —2D 121
Caswell Hill. P'bry —5D 51
Caswell La. P'bry —5E 51
Catbrain Hill. Bris —3D 25
Catbrain La. Bris —3D 25
Catemead. Clev —5C 120
Cater Rd. Bris —2C 86
Catharine Pl. Bath —2A 106 (1A 96)
Cathcart Ho. Bath —1B 106
Cathedral Sq. Bris —4E 69 (4A 4)
Catherine Mead St. Bris —1E 79
Catherine St. A'mth —4E 37
Catherine Way. Bathe —2B 102
Catley Gro. L Ash —4D 77
Cato St. Bris —5D 59
Catsley Pl. Bath —3D 101
Cattistock Dri. Bris —4C 72
Cattle Mkt. Rd. Bris —5B 70 (5F 5)
Cattybrook Rd. Mang & (in two parts) E Grn —2F 63
Cattybrook St. Bris —2D 71
Caulfield Rd. W Mare —1F 129
Causeway. Tic & Nail —2A 122
Causeway, The. Coal H —2F 31
Causeway, The. Cong —2D 145
Causeway, The. Yat —4C 142
Causeway View. Nail —3B 122
Causley Dri. Bar C —5B 74
Cautletts Clo. Mid N —4C 150
Cavan Wlk. Bris —4F 79
Cave Ct. Bris —2A 70
Cave Dri. Bris —1F 61
Cavell Ct. Clev —5C 120
Cavendish Clo. Salt —5F 93
Cavendish Cres. Bath —1F 105
Cavendish Gdns. Bris —3E 55
Cavendish Lodge Bath —1F 105
Cavendish Pl. Bath —1F 105
Cavendish Rd. Bath —1F 105
Cavendish Rd. Bris —2C 56
Cavendish Rd. Pat —1B 26
Caverners Ct. W Mare —4F 127
Caversham Dri. Nail —3F 123
Cave St. Bris —2A 70
Caxton Ct. Bath —2B 106 (2C 96)
Caxton Ga. Bris —5A 70
Cecil Av. Bris —1B 72

Cecil Rd. *Clif* —2B **68**
Cecil Rd. *K'wd* —2F **73**
Cecil Rd. *W Mare* —4C **126**
Cedar Av. *W Mare* —4A **128**
Cedar Clo. *L Ash* —4B **76**
Cedar Clo. *Old C* —1D **85**
Cedar Clo. *Pat* —2B **26**
Cedar Ct. *Brad A* —1E **115**
Cedar Ct. *Bris* —3E **55**
Cedar Dri. *Key* —4F **91**
Cedar Gro. *Bath* —1E **109**
Cedar Gro. *Bris* —2F **55**
Cedar Gro. *Trow* —4B **118**
Cedar Hall. *Bris* —4E **45**
Cedarhurst Rd. *P'head* —5A **48**
Cedarn Ct. *W Mare* —1F **127**
Cedar Pk. *Bris* —2F **55**
Cedar Row. *Bris* —1B **54**
Cedars, The. *Bris* —4F **55**
Cedars Way. *Wint* —4F **29**
Cedar Ter. *Rads* —3A **152**
Cedar Vs. *Bath* —4F **105**
Cedar Wlk. *Bath* —4F **105**
(in two parts)
Cedar Way. *Bath* —4F **105**
Cedar Way. *Nail* —3F **123**
Cedar Way. *P'head* —4D **49**
Cedar Way. *Puck* —2D **65**
Cedric Clo. *Bath* —2D **105**
Cedric Rd. *Bath* —2D **105**
Celandine Clo. *T'bry* —2E **7**
Celestine Rd. *Yate* —3E **17**
Celia Ter. *St Ap* —4B **72**
Celtic Way. *B'don* —3F **139**
Cemetery La. *Brad A* —2F **115**
Cemetery Rd. *Bris* —2C **80**
Cennick Av. *Bris* —1A **74**
Centaurus Rd. *Pat* —2E **25**
Central Av. *Bris* —5E **73**
Central Trad. Est. *Bris* —1D **81**
Central Way. *Clev* —5D **121**
Centre Dri. *Ban* —4C **136**
Centre, The. *Key* —3A **92**
Centre, The. *W Mare* —1C **132**
Ceres Clo. *L Grn* —3B **84**
Cerimon Ga. *Stok G* —4A **28**
Cerney Gdns. *Nail* —3F **123**
Cerney La. *Bris* —2A **54**
Cesson Clo. *Chip S* —1E **35**
Chadleigh Gro. *Bris* —1F **87**
Chaffinch Dri. *Mid N* —4E **151**
Chaffinch Dri. *Trow* —2A **118**
Chaffins, The. *Clev* —4E **121**
Chaingate La. *Iron A* —1B **16**
Chakeshill Clo. *Bris* —1E **41**
Chakeshill Dri. *Bris* —1E **41**
Chalcombe Clo. *Lit S* —1E **27**
Chalcroft Ho. *Bris* —1C **78**
Chalcroft Wlk. *Bris* —4A **86**
Chalet, The. *Bris* —1B **40**
Chalfont Clo. *Trow* —2A **118**
Chalfont Rd. *W Mare* —5A **128**
Chalford Clo. *Yate* —1F **33**
Chalks Rd. *Bris* —2F **71**
Challender Av. *Bris* —2B **40**
Challoner Ct. *Bris* —5F **69** (5B **4**)
Challow Dri. *W Mare* —3F **127**
Champion Rd. *Bris* —5B **62**
Champneys Av. *Bris* —1B **40**
Chancel Clo. *Bris* —4F **55**
Chancel Clo. *Nail* —4C **122**
Chancery St. *Bris* —3D **71**
Chandag Rd. *Key* —4B **92**
Chandler Clo. *Bath* —5C **98**
Chandos Bldgs. Bath —*3A* ***106***
(off Westgate Bldgs.)
Chandos Rd. *Bris* —1D **69**
Chandos Rd. *Key* —1A **92**
Chandos Trad. Est. *Bris* —5C **70**
Channel Heights. *W Mare* —2D **139**
Channells Hill. *W Trym* —4C **40**
Channel Rd. *Clev* —1D **121**
Channel View Cres. *P'head* —3D **49**
Channel View Rd. *P'head* —3D **49**
Channon's Hill. *Bris* —3B **60**
Chantree Rd. *Bris* —4F **41**
Chantry Clo. *Nail* —4B **122**
Chantry Dri. *W Mare* —1D **129**
Chantry Gro. *Bris* —2E **39**
Chantry La. *Down* —3B **46**
Chantry Mead Rd. *Bath* —1F **109**
Chantry Rd. *Bris* —1D **69**
Chantry Rd. *T'bry* —2C **6**
Chapel Av. *Nail* —3D **123**
Chapel Barton. *Bedm* —3D **79**
Chapel Barton. *Nail* —3B **122**
Chapel Clo. *Bris* —2D **75**
Chapel Clo. *Nail* —3D **123**
Chapel Ct. Bath —*3A* ***106***
(off Westgate Bldgs.)
Chapel Ct. *Rads* —5B **148**
Chapel Gdns. *Bris* —3C **40**
Chapel Grn. La. *Bris* —5D **57**
Chapel Hill. *Back* —1F **125**
Chapel Hill. *Clev* —3D **121**
Chapel Hill. *Wrin* —1B **156**
Chapel La. *Clav* —2F **143**
Chapel La. *Clay H* —5A **60**
Chapel La. *Fish* —3C **60**
Chapel La. *Fren* —5E **45**
Chapel La. *Law W* —2D **39**
Chapel La. *War* —2D **75**
Chapel Lawns. *Clan* —5B **148**
Chapel Rd. *B'wth* —2C **86**
Chapel Rd. *Clan* —5B **148**
Chapel Rd. *E'tn* —1D **71**
Chapel Rd. *Han* —5E **73**
Chapel Row. *Bath* —3A **106** (3A **96**)
Chapel Row. *B'ptn* —5A **102**
Chapel Row. *Bathf* —4D **103**
Chapel Row. *Pill* —3E **53**
Chapel St. *Bris* —5C **70**
Chapel St. *T'bry* —4C **6**
Chapel Way. *St Ap & Avon V* —4A **72**
Chaplin Rd. *Bris* —1D **71**
Chapter St. *Bris* —2A **70**
Charbon Ga. *Stok G* —4B **28**
Charborough Ct. *Brad S* —2C **42**
Charborough Rd. *Bris* —2B **42**
Charbury Wlk. *Bris* —2A **54**
Chard Clo. *Nail* —5E **123**
Chard Ct. *Bris* —2D **89**
Chard Rd. *Clev* —5D **121**
Chardstock Av. *Bris* —4E **39**
Charfield. *Bris* —2C **74**
Charfield Rd. *Bris* —3E **41**
Chargrove. *Bris* —4F **75**
Chargrove. *Yate* —2F **33**
Charis Av. *Bris* —5E **41**
Charlcombe La. *Lark* —4A **100**
Charlcombe Rise. *Bath* —4A **100**
Charlcombe View Rd. *Bath* —4B **100**
Charlcombe Way. *Bath* —4A **100**
Charlecombe Ct. *W Trym* —1B **56**
Charlecombe Rd. *Bris* —1B **56**
Charles Av. *Stok G* —5A **28**
Charles Clo. *T'bry* —1D **7**
Charles Pl. *Bris* —4C **68**
Charles Rd. *Bris* —1D **43**
Charles St. *Bath* —3A **106** (3A **96**)
Charles St. *Bris* —2F **69**
Charles St. *Trow* —1C **118**
Charlock Clo. *W Mare* —1B **134**
Charlock Rd. *W Mare* —1B **134**
Charlotte Ct. *Trow* —1D **119**
Charlotte Sq. *Trow* —1D **119**
Charlotte St. *Bath* —2A **106** (3A **96**)
Charlotte St. *Bris* —2B **70**
(Meadow St.)
Charlotte St. *Bris* —3E **69**
(Park St.)
Charlotte St. *Trow* —1D **119**
Charlotte St. S. *Bris* —4E **69**
Charlton Av. *Bris* —2C **42**
Charlton Av. *W Mare* —4B **132**
Charlton Comn. *Bris* —5F **25**
Charlton Ct. *Pat* —5B **10**
Charlton Gdns. *Bris* —5F **25**
Charlton La. *Bris* —1C **40**
Charlton La. *Mid N* —5F **151**
Charlton Mead Ct. *Bris* —5F **25**
Charlton Mead Dri. *Bris* —1F **41**
Charlton Pk. *Key* —3F **91**
Charlton Pk. *Mid N* —5E **151**
Charlton Pl. *Bris* —5F **25**
Charlton Rd. *Key* —5E **91**
Charlton Rd. *K'wd* —1D **73**
Charlton Rd. *Mid N* —4E **151**
Charlton Rd. *W Mare* —4B **132**
Charlton Rd. *W Trym* —3C **40**
Charlton St. *Bris* —3D **71**
Charlton View. *P'head* —3E **49**
Charminster Rd. *Bris* —4D **61**
Charmouth Rd. *Bath* —2C **104**
Charnell Rd. *Stap H* —3A **62**
Charnhill Brow. *Mang* —3C **62**
Charnhill Cres. *Mang* —3B **62**
Charnhill Dri. *Mang* —3B **62**
Charnhill Ridge. *Mang* —3C **62**
Charnhill Vale. *Mang* —3B **62**
Charnwood. *Mang* —3C **62**
Charnwood Rd. *Bris* —4D **89**
Charnwood Rd. *Trow* —1A **118**
Charterhouse Clo. *Nail* —4E **123**
Charterhouse Rd. *Bris* —2F **71**
Charter Rd. *W Mare* —5F **127**
Charter Wlk. *Bris* —2C **88**
Chase La. *K'wd* —1C **154**
Chase Rd. *Bris* —5F **61**
Chase, The. *Bris* —4E **61**
Chatcombe. *Yate* —2A **34**
Chatham Pk. *Bath* —3D **107**
Chatham Row. *Bath* —2B **106** (1C **96**)
Chatsworth Pk. *T'bry* —1D **7**
Chatsworth Rd. *Arn V* —1E **81**
Chatsworth Rd. *Fish* —4D **61**
Chatterton Grn. *Bris* —4B **88**
Chatterton Ho. Bris —*5A* ***70***
(off Ship La.)
Chatterton Rd. *Yate* —5F **17**
Chatterton Sq. *Bris* —5B **70**
Chatterton St. *Bris* —5B **70**
Chaucer Rd. *Bath* —5A **106**
Chaucer Rd. *Rads* —4E **151**
Chaucer Rd. *W Mare* —4E **133**
Chaundey Gro. *Bris* —3D **87**
Chavenage. *Bris* —1C **74**
Cheapside. *Bris* —2B **70**
Cheapside St. *Bris* —1B **80**
Cheap St. *Bath* —3B **106** (3C **96**)
Cheddar Clo. *Nail* —5E **123**
Cheddar Gro. *Bris* —5C **78**
Chedworth. *Bris* —4A **62**
Chedworth. *Yate* —2D **33**
Chedworth Clo. *Clav D* —1F **111**
Chedworth Rd. *Bris* —1C **58**
Cheese La. *Bris* —4A **70** (3E **5**)
Chelford Gro. *Pat* —1D **27**
Chelmer Gro. *Key* —4B **92**
Chelmsford Wlk. *Bris* —5B **72**
Chelscombe. *Bath* —5C **98**
Chelsea Clo. *Key* —3C **92**
Chelsea Ho. Bath —*1B* ***106***
(off Snow Hill)
Chelsea Pk. *Bris* —2E **71**
Chelsea Rd. *Bath* —2D **105**
Chelsea Rd. *Bris* —1D **71**
Chelsfield. *Back* —1C **124**
Chelston Rd. *Bris* —1F **87**
Chelswood Av. *W Mare* —5A **128**
Chelswood Gdns. *W Mare* —5B **128**
Cheltenham La. *Bris* —5A **58**
Cheltenham Rd. *Bris* —5F **57**
Cheltenham Rd. *Bris* —1A **74**
Cheltenham St. *Bath* —4F **105**
Chelvey Batch. *B'ley* —5B **124**
Chelvey La. *W Town* —5A **124**
Chelvey Rise. *Nail* —5F **123**
Chelvey Rd. *C'vey & W Town* —3A **124**
Chelvy Clo. *Bris* —5F **87**
Chelwood Dri. *Bath* —3E **109**
Chelwood Rd. *Bris* —5F **37**
Chelwood Rd. *Salt* —1A **94**
Chepston Pl. *Trow* —1A **118**
Chepstow Pk. *Bris* —3B **46**
Chepstow Rd. *Bris* —5F **79**
Chepstow Wlk. *Key* —3F **91**
Chequers Clo. *Old C* —2E **85**
Chequers Ct. *Brad S* —2C **28**
Cherington. *Bris* —5D **73**
Cherington. *Yate* —3F **33**
Cherington Rd. *Bris* —5E **41**
Cherington Rd. *Nail* —4F **123**
Cheriton Pl. *War* —4E **75**
Cheriton Pl. *W Trym* —5D **41**
Cherry Av. *Clev* —4E **121**
Cherry Clo. *Yat* —3B **142**
Cherry Garden La. *Old C* —2D **85**
Cherry Garden Rd. *Bit* —4E **85**
Cherry Gdns. *Bit* —4E **85**
Cherry Gdns. *Hil* —3D **119**
(in two parts)
Cherry Gdns. Ct. *Trow* —3D **119**
Cherry Gro. *Mang* —1C **62**
Cherry Gro. *Yat* —3B **142**
Cherry Hay. *Clev* —5D **121**
Cherry La. *Bris* —2A **70**
Cherry Orchard La. *Bris* —2B **72**
Cherry Rd. *Chip S* —5C **18**
Cherry Rd. *L Ash* —3B **76**
Cherry Rd. *Nail* —4C **122**
Cherrytree Clo. *Bris* —5E **61**
Cherry Tree Clo. *Key* —4E **91**
Cherry Tree Clo. *Rads* —3B **152**
Cherrytree Ct. *Puck* —2E **65**
Cherrytree Cres. *Bris* —5E **61**
Cherrytree Rd. *Bris* —5E **61**
Cherry Wood. *Old C* —3D **85**
Cherrywood Rise. *W Mare* —3D **129**
Cherrywood Rd. *W Mare* —3D **129**
Chertsey Rd. *Bris* —1D **69**
Cherwell Clo. *T'bry* —5D **7**
Cherwell Rd. *Key* —4C **92**
Chescombe Rd. *Yat* —4B **142**
Chesham Rd. N. *W Mare* —5F **127**
Chesham Rd. S. *W Mare* —5F **127**
Chesham Way. *Bris* —1F **73**
Cheshire Clo. *Yate* —3A **18**
Chesle Clo. *P'head* —5A **48**
Cheslefield. *P'head* —5A **48**
Chesle Way. *P'head* —5A **48**
Chessel Clo. *Brad S* —4E **11**
Chessel St. *Bris* —2D **79**
Chessington Av. *Bris* —3D **89**
Chesterfield Av. *Bris* —5A **58**
Chesterfield Clo. *Ban* —5D **137**
Chesterfield Ho. *Mid N* —3E **151**
Chesterfield Rd. *Down* —2A **62**
Chesterfield Rd. *St And* —5A **58**
Chestermaster Clo. *Alm* —1C **10**
Chester Pk. Rd. *Bris* —5D **61**
Chester Rd. *Bris* —1A **72**
Chesters. *Bris* —1C **84**
Chester St. *Bris* —5D **59**
Chesterton Dri. *Nail* —3F **123**
Chestertons, The. *B'ptn*
(in two parts) —5A **102**
Chestnut Av. *W Mare* —4E **129**
Chestnut Chase. *Nail* —2F **123**
Chestnut Clo. *Ban* —5E **137**
Chestnut Clo. *Bris* —3A **90**
Chestnut Clo. *Cong* —2D **145**
Chestnut Clo. *Paul* —3B **146**
Chestnut Clo. *Rads* —3B **152**
Chestnut Corner. *Trow* —2F **155**
Chestnut Ct. *Mang* —2C **62**
Chestnut Dri. *Chip S* —5C **18**
Chestnut Dri. *Clav* —2E **143**
Chestnut Dri. *T'bry* —3D **7**
Chestnut Gro. *Bath* —5D **105**
Chestnut Gro. *Clev* —2E **121**
Chestnut Gro. *Trow* —4B **118**
Chestnut Gro. *Up W* —5A **114**
Chestnut Ho. *Bris* —4F **87**
Chestnut La. *B'don* —4F **139**
Chestnut Rd. *Down* —1F **61**
Chestnut Rd. *K'wd* —4B **62**
Chestnut Rd. *L Ash* —3D **77**
Chestnuts, The. *Wins* —5B **156**
Chestnut Wlk. *Bris* —2C **86**
Chestnut Wlk. *Salt* —1A **94**
Chestnut Way. *Bris* —4B **62**
Cheston Coombe. *Back* —3E **125**
Chestwood Ho. *Bris* —4E **71**
Chetwode Clo. *Bris* —1F **41**
Chevening Clo. *Stok G* —3F **81**
Cheverell Clo. *Trow* —5D **119**
Cheviot Dri. *T'bry* —4F **7**
Cheviot Way. *Old C* —5E **75**
Chewton Clo. *Bris* —4D **61**
Cheyne Rd. *Bris* —1F **55**
Chichester Ho. *Bris* —4B **72**
Chichester Pl. *Rads* —2D **153**
Chichester Way. *Yate* —3F **17**
Chilcompton Rd. *Mid N* —5B **150**
Chillington Ct. *Pat* —5A **10**
Chilmark Rd. *Trow* —1A **118**
Chiltern Clo. *Bris* —4D **89**
Chiltern Clo. *War* —5E **75**
Chiltern Pk. *T'bry* —4E **7**
Chiltern Pl. *Bris* —4E **75**
Chilton Rd. *Bath* —5C **100**
Chilton Rd. *Bris* —5C **80**
Chilwood Clo. *Iron A* —3A **16**
Chimes, The. *Nail* —5C **122**
Chine, The. *Bris* —2F **59**
Chine View. *Bris* —4B **46**
Chiphouse Rd. *Bris* —4B **62**
Chipperfield Dri. *Bris* —1B **74**
Chipping Cross. *Clev* —5C **120**
Chipping Edge Ind. Est. *Chip S* —5E **19**
Chippings, The. *Bris* —2F **59**
Chirton Pl. *Trow* —4D **119**
Chisbury St. *Bris* —4E **59**
Chittening Rd. *Chit* —2A **22**
Chock La. *Bris* —5C **40**
Christchurch Av. *Bris* —2F **61**
Christ Chu. Clo. *Nail* —3D **123**
Christ Chu. Cotts. Bath
(off Julian Rd.) —*1A* ***106***
Christchurch La. *Bris* —1F **61**
Christ Chu. Path. N. *W Mare* —5D **127**
Christ Chu. Path. S. *W Mare* —5C **126**
Christchurch Rd. *Brad A* —1E **115**
Christchurch Rd. *Bris* —3C **68**
Christian Clo. *W Mare* —2E **129**
Christina Ter. *Bris* —5C **68**
Christin Ct. *Trow* —2A **118**
Christmas Steps. *Bris* —3F **69** (2B **4**)
Christmas St. *Bris* —3F **69** (2B **4**)
Christon Ter. *W Mare* —1D **139**
Chubb Clo. *Bar C* —5B **74**
Church Acre. *Brad A* —2D **115**
Church Av. *E'tn* —1D **71**
Church Av. *Stok B* —3A **56**
Church Av. *War* —3F **75**
Church Clo. *B'ptn* —4A **102**
Church Clo. *Bathf* —4C **102**
Church Clo. *Bris* —2A **40**
Church Clo. *Clev* —4A **120**
Church Clo. *Fram C* —1D **31**
Church Clo. *P'head* —3F **49**
Church Clo. *Yat* —4C **142**
Church Ct. *Mid N* —3D **151**
Churchdown Wlk. *Bris* —2A **54**
Church Dri. *Bris* —2A **72**
Church Dri. *Cong* —2D **145**
Churches. *Brad A* —2C **114**
Churchfarm Clo. *Yate* —3B **18**
Church Farm Paddock. *Bit* —1F **93**
Church Fields. *Trow* —5A **118**
Church Hayes Clo. *Nail* —5D **123**
Church Hayes Dri. *Nail* —4D **123**
Church Hill. *Bris* —3F **81**
Church Hill. *F'frd* —4C **112**
Church Hill. *Tim* —1E **157**
Church Hill. *Writ* —2F **153**
Churchill Av. *Clev* —4C **120**
Churchill Clo. *Bar C* —5C **74**
Churchill Clo. *Clev* —4C **120**
Churchill Dri. *Bris* —5F **39**
Churchill Rd. *Bris* —1E **81**
Churchill Rd. *W Mare* —1E **133**

Churchlands. N Brad —5E 155
Churchlands Rd. Bris —3D 79
Church La. Back —3C 124
Church La. Bedm —2F 79 (in two parts)
Church La. Bit —1F 93
Church La. Bris —4A 70 (4E 5)
Church La. Clif —4D 69
Church La. Coal H —3E 31
Church La. Down —3B 46 (in two parts)
Church La. Ham —2A 46
Church La. Hen —2A 40
Church La. Hut —1B 140
Church La. Lim S & F'frd —3B 112
Church La. L Ash —3E 77
Church La. Mid N —3D 151
Church La. Nail —4B 122 (in two parts)
Church La. N Brad —5D 155
Church La. Nthnd —2A 102
Church La. Paul —3B 146 (off Church St.)
Church La. St G —2F 71
Church La. Tic —1A 122
Church La. Tim —1E 157
Church La. Trow —4A 118
Church La. W'chu —5D 89
Church La. Wickw —1B 154
Church La. Wid —5D 107
Church La. Wint —3E 29
Church La. Yat —4B 142
Church Leaze. Bris —1F 53
Church Meadows. W'chu —4E 89
Church Pde. Bris —3A 82
Church Path. Bris —5B 58 (Ashley Hill)
Church Path. Bris —5C 68 (Hotwell Rd.)
Church Path. Bris —2E 79 (New John St.)
Churchpath Rd. Pill —3E 53
Church Pl. Pill —3E 53
Church Rd. Abb L —2C 66
Church Rd. Alm —1C 10
Church Rd. Bedm —1E 79
Church Rd. B'wth —3B 86
Church Rd. Bit —5F 85
Church Rd. C Down —3C 110
Church Rd. Dun —5A 86
Church Rd. E Comp —1C 24
Church Rd. E'ton G —3C 52
Church Rd. Fil —1C 42
Church Rd. Fram C —5C 14
Church Rd. Fren —5D 45
Church Rd. Han —5D 73
Church Rd. Hor —1A 58
Church Rd. K'wd —2A 74
Church Rd. Law H & St G —3D 71
Church Rd. L Wds —4F 67
Church Rd. Pea J —1E 149
Church Rd. P'bry —4A 52
Church Rd. Sev B —4B 20 (in two parts)
Church Rd. Soun —4F 61
Church Rd. Stok B —4F 55
Church Rd. Stok G —5A 28
Church Rd. T'bry —2C 6
Church Rd. W'chu —4D 89
Church Rd. Wick —5A 154
Church Rd. Wins —5A 156
Church Rd. Wint —5A 30
Church Rd. Wor —3B 128
Church Rd. W'ton —5D 99
Church Rd. W Trym —5C 40
Church Rd. Yat —3C 142
Church Rd. Yate —4A 18 (in two parts)
Church Rd. N. P'head —3F 49
Church Rd. S. P'head —4F 49
Church Sq. Mid N —3D 151
Church St. Ban —5F 137
Church St. Bath —3B 106 (off York St.)
Church St. Bathf —4C 102
Church St. Brad A —3D 115
Church St. Bris —4A 70 (4E 5) (Church La.)
Church St. Bris —4D 71 (Queen Ann Rd.)
Church St. E'tn —1D 71
Church St. Paul —3A 146
Church St. Rads —2C 152
Church St. Trow —1D 119
Church St. Wid —4C 106
Church St. W'ly —1A 100
Church St. W'ton —5C 98
Church Town. Back —3E 125
Church View. Fil —1C 42
Church View. Fish —2F 61
Church Wlk. Pill —3E 53
Church Wlk. Trow —1D 119
Church Wlk. Wrin —1B 156 (in two parts)
Churchward Clo. Han —5D 73
Churchward Rd. W Mare —2F 129
Churchward Rd. Yate —3D 17
Churchways. Bris —4E 89
Churchways Av. Bris —1A 58
Churchways Cres. Bris —1A 58
Churston Clo. Bris —5C 88
Circle, The. Bath —1C 108
Circular Rd. Bris —5A 56
Circus M. Bath —2A 106 (1A 96)
Circus Pl. Bath —2A 106 (1A 96) (in two parts)
Circus, The. Bath —2A 106 (1B 96)
City Bus. Pk. Bris —3C 70
City Rd. Bris —2A 70
Clamp, The. Old C —2E 85
Clanage Rd. Bris —1A 78
Clandown Rd. Paul —5C 146
Clapton La. P'head —5F 49
Clapton Rd. Mid N —4A 150
Clapton Rd. P'bry —5F 51
Clapton Wlk. Bris —2E 55
Clare Av. Bris —4E 57
Clare Gdns. Bath —3E 109
Claremont Av. Bris —4E 57
Claremont Bldgs. Bath —5B 100
Claremont Cres. W Mare —4A 126
Claremont Gdns. Clev —5E 121
Claremont Gdns. Nail —4C 122
Claremont Pl. Bath —5B 100 (off Camden Rd.)
Claremont Rd. Bath —5C 100
Claremont Rd. Bris —4F 57
Claremont St. Bris —1C 70
Claremont Ter. Bath —5C 100 (off Camden Rd.)
Claremont Ter. Bris —3F 71
Claremont Wlk. Bath —5B 100
Clarence Av. Bris —2A 62
Clarence Gdns. Bris —2A 62
Clarence Gro. Rd. W Mare —3C 132
Clarence Pl. Bath —2C 104
Clarence Pl. Bris —2E 69
Clarence Rd. Bris —5A 70
Clarence Rd. K'wd —1D 73
Clarence Rd. Stap H —2F 61
Clarence Rd. St Ph —3C 70
Clarence Rd. Trow —2F 119
Clarence Rd. E. W Mare —3C 132
Clarence Rd. N. W Mare —3B 132
Clarence Rd. S. W Mare —3B 132
Clarence St. Bath —1B 106
Clarence Ter. Bath —4E 107
Clarendon Av. Trow —2E 119
Clarendon Rd. Bath —4C 106
Clarendon Rd. Bris —5E 57
Clarendon Rd. Trow —2E 119
Clarendon Rd. W Mare —5D 127
Clarendon Vs. Bath —4C 106
Clare Rd. Cot —1F 69
Clare Rd. Eastv —5D 59
Clare Rd. K'wd —5E 61
Clare St. Bris —4F 69 (3B 4)
Clare St. Redf —2E 71
Clare Wlk. T'bry —2C 6
Clarke Dri. Bris —5B 44
Clarken Clo. Nail —4D 123
Clarke St. Bris —1F 79 (in two parts)
Clark Pl. Bris —5B 46
Clarkson Av. W Mare —4A 128
Clark's Pl. Trow —2E 119
Clark St. Bris —2C 70
Clatworthy Dri. Bris —1C 88
Claude Av. Bath —4D 105
Claude Ter. Bath —4D 105
Claude Vale. Bath —4D 105
Clavell Rd. Bris —2B 40
Claverham Clo. Yat —3D 143
Claverham Drove. Clav —1F 143
Claverham Pk. Clav —2F 143
Claverham Rd. Bris —2C 60
Claverham Rd. Yat —4D 143
Claverton Bldgs. Bath —4B 106 (5D 97) (off Claverton St.)
Claverton Ct. Bath —4F 107
Claverton Down Rd. Bath —4F 107
Claverton Down Rd. C Down —2E 111
Claverton Rd. Salt —5F 93
Claverton Rd. W. Salt —5F 93
Claverton St. Bath —4B 106 (5C 96)
Clay Bottom. Bris —5F 59
Claydon Grn. Bris —5B 88
Clayfield. Yate —1A 18
Clayfield Rd. Bris —2A 82
Clay Hill. Bris —5A 60
Clay La. Bit —5F 85
Clay La. Pat —2D 27
Clay La. T'bry —3F 7
Claymore Cres. Bris —1D 73
Claypiece Rd. Bris —4B 86
Claypit Hill. Chip S —2D 35
Clay Pit Rd. Bris —4C 56
Claypool Rd. Bris —3F 73
Clayton Clo. P'head —4A 50
Clayton Rd. Bris —2C 68
Clayton St. A'mth —3C 36
Clayton St. E'tn —2D 71
Cleave St. Bris —5C 58
Cleeve Av. Bris —5A 46
Cleeve Ct. Bris —5F 45
Cleevedale. Bris —5F 45
Cleevedale Rd. Bath —3B 110
Cleeve Gdns. Bris —5F 45
Cleeve Grn. Bath —3A 104
Cleeve Gro. Key —3F 91
Cleeve Hill. Bris —5F 45
Cleeve Hill Extension. Bris —1A 62
Cleeve Lawns. Bris —5F 45
Cleeve Lodge Clo. Bris —1A 62
Cleeve Lodge Rd. Bris —5A 46
Cleeve Pk. Rd. Bris —5F 45
Cleeve Pl. Nail —4F 123
Cleeve Quarry. Bris —4F 45
Cleeve Rd. Down —1A 62
Cleeve Rd. Fren —4E 45
Cleeve Rd. Know —2D 81
Cleeve Rd. Yate —5A 18
Cleeve Wood Pk. Bris —4E 45
Cleeve Wood Rd. Bris —4E 45 (in two parts)
Clement St. Bris —2B 70
Clevedale Ct. Bris —5F 45 (off Cleeve Wood Rd.)
Clevedon Hall Est. Clev —3C 120
Clevedon Rd. Bris —3F 57
Clevedon Rd. Fail & L Ash —2A 76
Clevedon Rd. Mid N —2D 151
Clevedon Rd. Nail —2F 123
Clevedon Rd. P'head —5E 49
Clevedon Rd. Tic & Nail —1A 122
Clevedon Rd. W Mare —2B 132
Clevedon Ter. Bris —2F 69
Clevedon Wlk. Nail —3D 123
Cleveland Clo. T'bry —4F 7
Cleveland Cotts. Bath —1B 106
Cleveland Ct. Bath —3D 107
Cleveland Gdns. Trow —5E 117
Cleveland Pl. Bath —1B 106
Cleveland Pl. E. Bath —1B 106 (off Cleveland Pl.)
Cleveland Pl. W. Bath —1B 106 (off Cleveland Pl.)
Cleveland Reach. Bath —1B 106
Cleveland Row. Bath —1C 106
Cleveland Ter. Bath —1B 106 (off London Rd.)
Cleveland Wlk. Bath —3D 107
Cleve Rd. Bris —5C 26
Cleweson Rise. Bris —5B 88
Cliff Ct. Dri. Bris —5D 45
Cliffe Dri. Lim S —3B 112
Clifford Gdns. Bris —1A 54
Clifford Rd. Bris —3E 61
Cliff Rd. W Mare —2E 127
Clift Ho. Rd. Bris —1B 78
Clift Ho. Spur. Bris —1B 78
Clifton Av. W Mare —3C 132
Clifton Clo. Bris —2B 68
Clifton Ct. Bris —4F 55
Clifton Ct. Clev —4C 120
Clifton Down. Bris —2B 68
Clifton Down Rd. Clif —3B 68
Clifton Down Shopping Cen. Bris —1D 69
Clifton Heights. Bris —3D 69
Clifton High Gro. Stok B —2A 56
Clifton Hill. Bris —4C 68
Clifton Pk. Clif —2C 68
Clifton Pk. Rd. Bris —2B 68
Clifton Pl. Bris —2C 70
Clifton Rd. Bris —3C 68
Clifton Rd. W Mare —2B 132
Clifton St. Bedm —2E 79
Clifton St. Bris —3F 71
Clifton St. P'head —5E 49
Clifton Ter. Bris —2E 79
Clifton Vale. Bris —4C 68
Clifton Vale Clo. Bris —4C 68
Clifton View. Bris —1B 80
Clifton Wood Ct. Bris —4D 69
Clifton Wood Cres. Bris —4D 69
Clifton Wood Rd. Bris —4D 69
Clifton Wood Ter. Bris —4C 68
Clift Pl. Bris —5F 69 (5C 4)
Clift Rd. Bris —1C 78
Clinton Rd. Bris —3E 79
Clipsham Rise. Trow —1A 118
Clive Rd. Bris —5E 81
Clockhouse M. P'head —2F 49
Clocktower Yd. Tem M —5B 70
Cloford Clo. Trow —1A 118
Cloisters Rd. Wint —3A 30
Clonmel Rd. Bris —4F 79
Closemead. Clev —5D 121
Close, The. Coal H —3E 31
Close, The. Hen —4B 24
Close, The. Lit S —3E 27
Close, The. Pat —5E 11
Close, The. Soun —4F 61
Close, The. T'bry —4C 6
Clothier Leaze Trow —3D 119
Clothier Rd. Brisl —3B 82
Clouds Hill Av. Bris —2A 72
Clouds Hill Rd. St G —2B 72
Clovelly Clo. Bris —2B 72
Clovelly Rd. Bris —2B 72
Clovelly Rd. W Mare —3E 129
Clover Clo. Clev —3F 121
Cloverdale Dri. L Grn —2C 84
Clover Ground. Bris —4D 41
Cloverlea Rd. BS15 —1E 85
Clover Leaze. Lit S —3F 27
Clyde Av. Key —4B 92
Clyde Gdns. Bath —3C 104
Clyde Gdns. Bris —4D 73
Clyde Gro. Bris —2B 42
Clyde La. Bris —5E 57
Clyde M. Redl —5E 57
Clyde Pk. Bris —5D 57
Clyde Rd. Fram C —1D 31
Clyde Rd. Know —2C 80
Clyde Rd. Redl —5D 57
Clydesdale Clo. Bris —2C 88
Clydesdale Clo. Trow —5C 118
Clyde Ter. Bedm —2E 79
Clyde Ter. Know —2C 80
Clynder Gro. Clev —1E 121
Coach Rd. Brad A —3D 115
Coalbridge Clo. W Mare —3D 129
Coaley Rd. Bris —2F 53
Coalpit Rd. Bathe —2B 102
Coalsack La. Wint —1D 47
Coalville Rd. Coal H —2F 31
Coape Rd. Bris —3B 90
Coates Gro. Nail —3F 123
Coates Wlk. Bris —2F 87
Cobbe Ho. Bris —1B 70
Cobblestone M. Bris —2C 68
Cobden St. Bris —3D 71
Coberley. Bris —4E 73
Cobhorn Dri. Bris —4B 86
Cobley Croft. Clev —5C 120
Cobourg Rd. Bris —1B 70
Cobthorn Way. Cong —1E 145
Coburg Vs. Bath —5B 100
Cock Hill. Trow —1A 118
Cock Hill Ho. Ct. Trow —1A 118
Cock Rd. Bris —4A 74
Codrington Pl. Bris —3C 68
Codrington Rd. Bris —4F 57
Cody Ct. Han —5D 73
Cogan Rd. Bris —4A 62
Cogmill La. Iron A —2B 14
Cogsall Rd. Bris —2B 90
Coity Pl. Clev —2C 120
Coker Rd. W Mare —2F 129
Colbourne Rd. Bath —3E 109
Colchester Cres. Bris —1F 87
Coldharbour La. Bris —2A 44
Coldharbour Rd. Bris —4D 57
Coldpark Gdns. Bris —3A 86
Coldpark Rd. Bris —3A 86
Coldrick Clo. Bris —5B 88
Colebrook Rd. Bris —2E 73
Coleford Rd. Bris —4F 41
Cole Mead. Bris —3D 87
Coleridge Rd. Bris —4E 59
Coleridge Rd. Clev —3C 120
Coleridge Rd. W Mare —5D 133
Coleridge Vale Rd. E. Clev —3D 121
Coleridge Vale Rd. N. Clev —4C 120
Coleridge Vale Rd. S. Clev —4C 120
Coleridge Vale Rd. W. Clev —4C 120
Cole Rd. Bris —4D 71
Colesborne Clo. Yate —1F 33
Coleshill Dri. Bris —3D 87
Colin Clo. T'bry —3C 6
College Av. Bris —2C 60
College Ct. Bris —2C 60
College Fields. Bris —2B 68
College Grn. Bris —4E 69 (3A 4) (in three parts)
College Ho. Bris —4F 69 (off Orchard St.)
College La. Bris —4E 69 (3A 4)
College Pk. Dri. Bris —3B 40
College Rd. Bath —4F 99
College Rd. Clif —2B 68
College Rd. Fish —2C 60
College Rd. Trow —4A 118
College Rd. W Trym —5C 40
College Sq. Bris —4E 69
College St. Bris —4E 69
College View. Bath —5B 100
Collegge Gdns. Trow —4E 155
Collett Clo. Bris —5D 73
Collett Clo. W Mare —1A 130
Collett Way. Yate —3E 17
Collier Clo. C'ton —1A 148
Collier's La. Charl —2F 99
Colliers Wlk. Nail —3D 123
Collingbourne Clo. Trow —5D 119
Collingwood Av. Bris —1A 74
Collingwood Clo. Salt —2A 94
Collingwood Clo. W Mare —1C 128
Collingwood Rd. Bris —1D 69
Collin Rd. Bris —1F 81
Collins Av. Lit S —3E 27
Collins Bldgs. Salt —1A 94
Collins La. Bris —1A 60
Collinson Rd. Bris —3D 87
Collins St. Bris —4D 37
Colliter Cres. Bris —3C 78
Collum La. Kew —1C 128
Colne Grn. Key —4C 92
Coln Sq. T'bry —4D 7

Colombo Cres. *W Mare* —5C **132**
*Colonnades, The. Bath —3A **106** (4B **96**) (off Bath St.)*
Colston Av. *Bris* —4F **69** (3B **4**)
Colston Cen. *Bris* —3F **69** (2B **4**)
Colston Clo. *Bris* —4F **61**
Colston Clo. *Wint D* —5A **30**
Colston Ct. *Bris* —4F **57**
Colston Dale. *Bris* —3A **60**
*Colston Fort. Bris —2F **69** (off Montague Pl.)*
Colston Hill. *Bris* —3F **59**
Colston Pde. *Bris* —5A **70** (5D **5**)
Colston Pl. *Bris* —4A **70** (3E **5**)
Colston Rd. *Bris* —1E **71**
Colston St. *Bris* —4F **69** (2B **4**)
Colston St. *Soun* —4F **61**
Colthurst Dri. *Bris* —5A **74**
Colwyn Rd. *Bris* —1E **71**
Combe Av. *P'head* —2E **49**
Combe Fields. *P'head* —2E **49**
Combe Gro. *Bath* —1C **104**
Combe Hay La. *Eng* —5C **108**
Combe Pk. *Bath* —2D **105**
Combermere. *T'bry* —4E **7**
Combe Rd. *Bath* —3C **110**
Combe Rd. *P'head* —3F **49**
Combe Rd. Clo. *Bath* —3C **110**
Combeside. *Back* —1C **124**
Combeside. *Bath* —1B **110**
Combe, The. *Rads* —3F **153**
Combfactory La. *Bris* —2D **71**
Comb Paddock. *Bris* —5D **41**
Comfortable Pl. *Bath* —2F **105**
Comfrey Clo. *Trow* —4E **119**
Commercial Rd. *Bris* —5F **69**
Common E., The. *Brad S* —5F **11**
Commonfield Rd. *Bris* —3D **39**
Common La. *E'ton G* —4D **53** (in two parts)
Common Mead La. *Ham* —3C **44**
Common Rd. *Bris* —2D **83**
Common Rd. *Wint* —2B **30**
Common, The. *Bris* —5D **45**
Common, The. *Holt* —1E **155**
Common W., The. *Pat* —5D **11**
Compton Dri. *Bris* —5E **39**
Compton Grn. *Key* —4A **92**
Compton St. *Bris* —3E **71**
Comyn Wlk. *Bris* —2C **60**
Concorde Dri. *Bris* —3D **41**
Concorde Dri. *Clev* —5B **120**
Concorde Ho. *Brad S* —2B **42**
Concorde Rd. *Pat* —2A **26**
Concourse, The. *Bris* —3A **82**
Condor Clo. *W Mare* —5B **128**
Condor Ho. *Bris* —5E **43**
Condover Rd. *Bris* —2B **82**
Conduit Pl. *Bris* —1C **70**
Conduit Rd. *Bris* —1C **70**
Coneygree. *Bris* —2B **86**
Congleton Rd. *Bris* —1F **71**
Conham Hill. *Bris* —5C **72**
Conham Rd. *Bris* —5B **72**
Conham Vale. *Bris* —5B **72**
Conifer Clo. *Down* —1F **61**
Conifer Clo. *Fram C* —5C **14**
Conifer Way. *Lock* —3C **134**
Conigre. *Trow* —1C **118**
Conigre Hill. *Brad A* —2D **115**
Coniston Av. *Bris* —1A **56**
Coniston Clo. *Bris* —4F **75**
Coniston Cres. *W Mare* —4D **133**
Coniston Rd. *Pat* —1A **26**
Coniston Rd. *Trow* —5E **117**
Connaught Pl. *W Mare* —5B **126**
Connaught Rd. *Bris* —5A **80**
Connection Rd. *Bath* —3B **104**
Constable Clo. *Key* —2B **92**
Constable Dri. *W Mare* —2D **129**
Constable Rd. *Bris* —1D **59**
Constable St. *Bath* —2D **105**
Constantine Av. *Stok G* —4A **28**
Constitution Hill. *Bris* —4C **68**
Convent Clo. *Bris* —1E **39**
Convocation Av. *Bath* —4F **107**
Conway Grn. *Key* —5C **92**
Conway Rd. *Brisl* —1E **81**
Conygar Clo. *Clev* —1F **121**
Conygre Grn. *Tim* —1E **157**
Conygre Gro. *Bris* —5D **27**
Conygre Rd. *Bris* —1C **42**
Conygre Ter. *Bath* —3F **107**
Cook Clo. *Old C* —1E **85**
Cook Ct. *C Down* —2D **111**
Cooks Clo. *Brad S* —3E **11**
Cooks Folly Rd. *Bris* —4F **55**
Cook's La. *Ban* —4E **137**
Cooks La. *Coal H* —1F **47**
Cooksley Rd. *Bris* —2E **71**
Cook St. *Bris* —4D **37**
Cookworthy Clo. *Bris* —3D **71**
Coombe Av. *T'bry* —2C **6**
Coombe Bri. Av. *Bris* —1F **55**
Coombe Clo. *Bris* —1F **39**
Coombe Clo. *P'head* —3F **49**
Coombe Dale. *Bris* —1E **55**
Coombe Gdns. *Bris* —1A **56**
Coombe La. *Bris* —5F **39**
Coombe La. *E'ton G* —5C **52**
Coombend. *Rads* —5B **148**
Coombe Rd. *Bris* —5E **59**
Coombe Rd. *Nail* —4C **122**
Coombe Rd. *W Mare* —5C **126**
Coombes Way. *Bris* —1F **85**
Coombe Way. *Hen* —3B **40**
Coomb Rocke. *Bris* —5F **39**
Cooperage La. *Bris* —5D **69**
Cooperage Rd. *Bris* —3F **71**
Co-operation Rd. *Bris* —1E **71**
Cooper Rd. *Bris* —5B **40**
Cooper Rd. *T'bry* —5C **6**
Coopers Dri. *Yate* —1B **18**
Coots, The. *Bris* —2A **90**
Copeland Dri. *Bris* —3D **89**
Cope Pk. *Alm* —1E **11**
Copford La. *L Ash* —4D **77**
Copley Ct. *Bris* —5A **74**
Copley Gdns. *Bris* —1D **59**
Copley Gdns. *W Mare* —3D **129**
Copper Beeches. *Trow* —4F **117**
Copperfield Dri. *W Mare* —1D **129**
Coppice Hill. *Brad A* —2E **115**
Coppice, The *Brad S* —2A **28**
Coppice, The. *Bris* —4A **86**
Coppice Wood. *Trow* —2F **119**
Copse Clo. *W Mare* —2E **139**
Copseland. *Bath* —4E **107**
Copse Rd. *Bris* —2D **81**
Copse Rd. *Clev* —2C **120**
Copse Rd. *Key* —4E **93**
Coralberry Dri. *W Mare* —4D **129**
Corbet Clo. *Bris* —2D **39**
Cordwell Wlk. *Bris* —5F **41**
Corey Clo. *Bris* —1B **70**
Corfe Clo. *Nail* —4C **122**
Corfe Cres. *Key* —4A **92**
Corfe Pl. *Will* —4D **85**
Corfe Rd. *Bris* —1F **87**
Coriander Dri. *Brad S* —3C **28**
Coriander Wlk. *Bris* —5E **59**
Corinthian Ct. *Bris* —5A **70** (5E **5**)
Corkers Hill. *St G* —4B **72**
*Cork Pl. Bath —2E **105** (off Cork St.)*
Cork St. *Bath* —2E **105**
Cork Ter. *Bath* —2E **105**
*Cormandel Heights Bath (off Camden Rd.) —1B **106***
Cormorant Clo. *W Mare* —4D **129**
Corner Croft. *Clev* —5D **121**
Cornfield Clo. *Pat* —5E **11**
Cornfields, The. *Wick L* —1D **129**
Cornhill Dri. *Bris* —1C **88**
Cornish Gro. *Bris* —2A **90**
Cornish Rd. *Bris* —3F **89**
Cornish Wlk. *Bris* —2A **90**
Cornleaze. *Bris* —3C **86**
Corn St. *Bath* —3A **106** (4B **96**)
Corn St. *Bris* —4F **69** (3C **4**)
Cornwall Cres. *Yate* —2B **18**
Cornwallis Av. *Bris* —4C **68**
Cornwallis Av. *W Mare* —1C **128**
Cornwallis Cres. *Bris* —4B **68**
Cornwallis Gro. *Bris* —4B **68**
Cornwall Rd. *Bris* —3F **57**
Coronation Av. *Bath* —1D **109**
Coronation Av. *Brad A* —2F **115**
Coronation Av. *Bris* —3C **60**
Coronation Av. *Key* —4F **91**
Coronation Clo. *Bris* —5C **74**
Coronation Cotts. *Bathe* —3A **102**
Coronation Est. *W Mare* —5D **133**
Coronation Pl. *Bris* —4F **69** (3C **4**)
Coronation Rd. *Ban* —5E **137**
Coronation Rd. *Bath* —2E **105**
Coronation Rd. *B'don* —5A **140**
Coronation Rd. *Down* —2A **62**
Coronation Rd. *K'wd* —3B **74**
Coronation Rd. *S'vle* —1C **78**
Coronation Rd. *War* —5C **74**
Coronation Rd. *W Mare* —3C **128**
Coronation St. *Trow* —3D **119**
Coronation Vs. *Rads* —1D **153**
Corondale Rd. *W Mare* —5B **128**
Corridor, The. *Bath* —3B **106** (3C **96**)
Corsley Wlk. *Bris* —5B **80**
Corston. *W Mare* —1E **139**
Corston La. *Cor* —5C **94**
Corston View. *Bath* —2D **109**
Corston Wlk. *Bris* —5F **37**
Coryton. *W Mare* —3E **129**
Cossham Clo. *T'bry* —2D **7**
Cossham Rd. *Bris* —2F **71**
Cossham Rd. *Yate* —3E **65**
Cossham St. *Mang* —2C **62**
Cossham Wlk. *Bris* —1C **72**
Cossington Rd. *Bris* —4B **80**
Cossins Rd. *Bris* —4D **57**
Costers Clo. *Alv* —2B **8**
Costiland Dri. *Bris* —2B **86**
Cote Bank Ho. *Bris* —5D **41**
Cote Dri. *Bris* —3C **56**
Cote Ho. La. *Bris* —2C **56**
Cote La. *Bris* —2C **56**
Cote Lea Pk. *Bris* —5D **41**
Cote Paddock. *Bris* —3B **56**
Cote Pk. *Bris* —1A **56**
Cote Rd. *Bris* —2C **56**
Cotham Brow. *Bris* —1F **69**
Cotham Gdns. *Bris* —1D **69**
Cotham Gro. *Bris* —1F **69**
Cotham Hill. *Bris* —1D **69**
Cotham Lawn Rd. *Bris* —1E **69**
Cotham Pk. *Bris* —1E **69**
Cotham Pk. N. *Bris* —1E **69**
Cotham Pl. *Bris* —1E **69**
Cotham Rd. *Bris* —2E **69**
Cotham Rd. S. *Bris* —2F **69**
Cotham Side. *Bris* —1F **69**
Cotham Vale. *Bris* —1E **69**
Cotman Wlk. *Bris* —1D **59**
Cotman Wlk. *W Mare* —3D **129**
Cotrith Gro. *Bris* —1A **40**
Cotswold Clo. *P'head* —4F **49**
Cotswold Ct. *Chip S* —5D **19**
Cotswold Rd. *Bath* —5E **105**
Cotswold Rd. *Bris* —2F **79**
Cotswold Rd. *Chip S* —1D **35**
Cotswold Ter. *Bath* —3F **107**
Cotswold View. *Bath* —4C **104**
Cotswold View. *Fil* —1C **42**
Cotswold View. *K'wd* —5F **61**
Cotswold View. *Wickw* —1C **154**
Cottage Pl. *Bath* —4D **101**
Cottage Pl. *Bris* —2F **69**
Cottages, The. *Wrin* —1B **156**
Cottington Ct. *Bris* —5A **74**
Cottisford Rd. *Bris* —3D **59**
Cottle Gdns. *Bris* —2B **90**
Cottle Rd. *Bris* —2B **90**
Cottles La. *Tur* —3A **114**
Cotton Mead. *Cor* —5D **95**
Cottonwood Dri. *L Grn* —2C **84**
Cottrell Av. *Bris* —5D **61**
Cottrell Rd. *Bris* —4E **59**
Coulson Dri. *W Mare* —2F **129**
Coulsons Clo. *Bris* —5C **88**
Coulson's Rd. *Bris* —5B **88**
Coulson Wlk. *Bris* —5E **61**
Counterpool Rd. *Bris* —3E **73**
Counterslip. *Bris* —4A **70** (3D **5**)
Counterslip Gdns. *Bris* —2E **89**
Countess Wlk. *Bris* —1F **59**
County St. *Bris* —1C **80**
County Way. *Trow* —2D **119**
Court Av. *Stok G* —4B **28**
Court Av. *Yat* —4B **142**
Court Clo. *Back* —3E **125**
Court Clo. *Bris* —5A **42**
Court Clo. *P'head* —4F **49**
Courtenay Cres. *Bris* —1F **87**
Courtenay Rd. *Key* —5A **92**
Courtenay Wlk. *W Mare* —2E **129**
Court Farm Rd. *Bris* —5B **88**
Court Farm Rd. *L Grn* —4F **83**
Courtfield Gro. *Bris* —3C **60**
Court Gdns. *Bathe* —2B **102**
Court Hay. *E'ton G* —3C **52**
Courtlands. *Key* —3A **92**
Courtlands. *Pat* —5E **11**
Courtlands La. *Bris* —1A **78**
Court La. *Bathf* —4C **102**
Court La. *Clev* —3F **121**
Court La. *Wick* —5A **154**
Courtmead. *Bath* —5A **110**
Courtney Rd. *Bris* —3A **74**
Courtney Way. *Bris* —3B **74**
Court Pl. *W Mare* —3D **129**
Court Rd. *Fram C* —1B **30**
Court Rd. *Hor* —5B **42**
Court Rd. *Kew* —1E **127**
Court Rd. *K'wd* —3F **73**
Court Rd. *Old C* —2D **85**
Courtside. *Bris* —3B **74**
Courtside M. *Bris* —1E **69**
Court St. *Trow* —2D **119**
Court View. *Wick* —5B **154**
Court View Clo. *Alm* —1C **10**
Courtyard, The. *Alm* —3F **11**
Courville Clo. *Alv* —3B **8**
Cousins Clo. *Bris* —1F **39**
Cousins La. *Bris* —3B **72**
Cousins M. *St Ap* —4B **72**
Couzens Ct. *Chip S* —4D **19**
Couzens Pl. *Stok G* —4B **28**
Coventry Wlk. *Bris* —4B **72**
Cowdray Rd. *Bris* —1F **87**
Cowhorn Hill. *Old C* —5E **75**
Cow La. *Bath* —2F **105**
Cowler Wlk. *Bris* —4B **86**
Cowling Dri. *Bris* —3E **89**
Cowling Rd. *Bris* —3F **89**
Cowmead Wlk. *Bris* —5C **58**
Cowper Rd. *Bris* —1E **69**
Cowper St. *Bris* —3E **71**
Cowship La. *Crom* —1A **154**
Cox Ct. *Bar C* —1B **84**
Coxgrove Hill. *Puck* —1B **64**
Coxley Dri. *Bath* —4C **100**
Cox's Grn. *Wrin* —2C **156**
Coxway. *Clev* —4E **121**
Crabtree Path. *Clev* —5C **120**
Crabtree Wlk. *Bris* —5F **59**
Craddock Clo. *Bris* —1C **84**
Cranberry Wlk. *Bris* —4E **39**
Cranbourne Chase. *W Mare* —4E **127**
Cranbourne Rd. *Pat* —2B **26**
Cranbrook Rd. *Bris* —3E **57**
Crandale Rd. *Bath* —4E **105**
Crandell Clo. *Bris* —5B **24**
Crandon Lea. *Holt* —1F **155**
Crane Clo. *Bris* —2D **75**
Cranford Clo. *W Mare* —4B **128**
Cranham. *Yate* —2E **33**
Cranham Clo. *Bris* —5B **62**
Cranham Dri. *Pat* —5E **11**
Cranham Rd. *Bris* —4E **41**
Cranhill Rd. *Bath* —1E **105**
Cranleigh. *Bath* —4A **110**
Cranleigh Ct. Rd. *Yate* —4F **17**
Cranleigh Gdns. *Bris* —3A **56**
Cranleigh Rd. *Bris* —3D **89**
Cranmore. *W Mare* —1E **139**
Cranmore Av. *Key* —2F **91**
Cranmore Clo. *Trow* —1A **118**
Cranmore Cres. *Bris* —3F **41**
Cranmore Pl. *Bath* —4E **109**
Cranside Av. *Bris* —3E **57**
Cransley Cres. *Bris* —5E **41**
Crantock Av. *Bris* —5D **79**
Crantock Dri. *Alm* —1D **11**
Crantock Rd. *Yate* —5F **17**
Cranwell Gro. *Bris* —3C **88**
Cranwell Rd. *Lock* —3A **136**
Cranwells Pk. *Bath* —1E **105**
Crates Clo. *K'wd* —2A **74**
Craven Clo. *L Grn* —5B **74**
Craven Way. *Bar C* —5B **74**
Crawford Clo. *Clev* —5B **120**
Crawley Cres. *Trow* —2A **118**
Crawl La. *Clan* —5E **147**
Craydon Gro. *Bris* —3F **89**
Craydon Rd. *Bris* —3F **89**
Craydon Wlk. *Bris* —3F **89**
Crediton. *W Mare* —3E **129**
Crediton Cres. *Bris* —4B **80**
Crescent Cen., The. *Bris* —4A **70** (3E **5**)
Crescent Gdns. *Bath* —2F **105**
Crescent La. *Bath* —1F **105**
Crescent Rd. *Bris* —1E **61**
Crescent, The. *Back* —2C **124**
Crescent, The. *Henl* —1E **57**
Crescent, The. *Mil* —4F **127**
Crescent, The. *Sea M* —1E **55**
Crescent, The. *Soun* —4F **61**
Crescent, The. *Wick* —4B **154**
Crescent, The. *Worl* —3F **127**
Crescent View. *Bath* —4A **106**
Cresswell Clo. *W Mare* —3E **129**
Crest, The. *Bris* —3E **81**
Creswicke Av. *Bris* —5E **73**
Creswicke Rd. *Bris* —1F **87**
Crewkerne Clo. *Nail* —4F **123**
Crews Hole Rd. *Bris* —3F **71**
Cribbs Causeway. *Bris* —5B **24**
Cribbs Causeway Cen. *Bris* —3C **24**
Cribbs Causeway Shopping Cen. *Pat* —3F **25**
Cribbs Retail Pk. *Pat* —3F **25**
Cricket Field Grn. *Nail* —3C **122**
Cricklade Ct. *Nail* —4F **123**
Cricklade Rd. *Bris* —3A **58**
Cripps Rd. *Bris* —2E **79**
Crispin La. *T'bry* —3C **6**
Crispin Way. *Bris* —5B **62**
Crockerne Dri. *Pill* —4E **53**
*Crockerne Ho. Pill —2F **53** (off Underbanks)*
Crocombe La. *Tim* —1F **157**
Croft Av. *Bris* —3E **59**
Croft Clo. *Bit* —5F **85**
Crofton Av. *Bris* —1B **58**
Croft Rd. *Bath* —5C **100**
Croft Rd. *Mon C* —3F **111**
Crofts End Rd. *Bris* —1A **72**
Croft, The. *Back* —1C **124**
Croft, The. *Bris* —2B **62**
Croft, The. *Clev* —2F **121**
Croft, The. *Hut* —5C **134**
Croft, The. *Old C* —2E **85**
Croft, The. *Trow* —4C **118**
Croft View. *Bris* —1E **57**
Crokeswood Wlk. *Bris* —3C **38**
Crome Rd. *Bris* —5D **43**
Cromer Rd. *Bris* —5E **59**
Cromer Rd. *W Mare* —3C **132**
Cromwell Ct. *Bris* —5A **74**
Cromwell Dri. *W Mare* —1E **129**
Cromwell Rd. *St And* —5F **57**
romwell Rd. *St G* —2C **72**
Cromwells Hide. *Bris* —2A **60**
Cromwell St. *Bris* —2E **79**
Crooke's La. *Kew* —1E **127**
Crookwell Drove. *Cong* —5C **144**
Croomes Hill. *Bris* —1F **61**
Cropthorne Rd. *Bris* —3C **42**
Cropthorne Rd. S. *Bris* —4C **42**
Crosby Row. *Clif* —4C **68**
Crosscombe Dri. *Bris* —5D **87**
Crosscombe Wlk. *Bris* —5D **87**
Cross Elms La. *Bris* —2A **56**
Crossfield Rd. *Bris* —4A **62**
Cross Lanes. *Pill* —3D **53** (in two parts)
Crossleaze Rd. *Bris* —2E **83**
Crossley Clo. *Wint* —2B **30**

Crossman Av. *Wint* —4A **30**
Crossman Wlk. *Clev* —3F **121**
Cross St. *Bris* —1E **73**
Cross St. *Key* —1B **92**
Cross St. *Trow* —1D **119**
Cross St. *W Mare* —1C **132**
Cross Tree Gro. *Brad S* —1F **27**
Cross Wlk. *Bris* —2C **88**
Crossways Rd. *Bris* —4C **80**
Crossways Rd. *T'bry* —3E **7**
Crowe Hill. *Lim S & F'frd* —3C **112**
Crowe La. *F'frd* —4C **112**
Crow La. *Bris* —4F **69** (3C **4**)
Crow La. *Hen* —2B **40**
Crown Ct. *Brad A* —2F **115**
Crowndale Rd. *Bris* —2C **80**
Crown Gdns. *Bris* —3D **75**
Crown Glass Pl. *Nail* —3D **123**
Crown Hill. *Bath* —5D **99**
Crown Hill. *Bris* —2B **72**
Crown Hill Wlk. *Bris* —1B **72**
Crown Ho. *Nail* —4B **122**
Crown Ind. Est. *War* —3E **75**
Crown La. *Bris* —4F **61**
Crownleaze. *Bris* —4F **61**
Crown Rd. *Bath* —5C **98**
Crown Rd. *Bris* —5F **61**
Crown Rd. *War* —4E **75**
Crows Gro. *Brad S* —3F **11**
Crowther Pk. *Bris* —3C **58**
Crowther Rd. *Bris* —3C **58**
Crowthers Av. *Yate* —3A **18**
Crowther St. *Bris* —2D **79**
Croydon St. *Bris* —2D **71**
Crunnis, The. *Brad S* —3A **28**
Crusty La. *Pill* —2E **53**
Cuckoo La. *Wint D* —1B **46**
Cuffington Av. *Bris* —1F **81**
Culverhill Rd. *Chip S* —5C **18**
Culver Rd. *Brad A* —4F **115**
Culvers Rd. *Key* —2A **92**
Culver St. *Bris* —4E **69** (3A **4**)
Culverwell Rd. *Bris* —4C **86**
Cumberland Basin Rd. *Bris* —4B **68**
Cumberland Clo. *Bris* —5C **68**
Cumberland Gro. *Bris* —5B **58**
*Cumberland Ho. Bath —3F **105** (off Norfolk Cres.)*
Cumberland Pl. *Bris* —4B **68**
Cumberland Rd. *Bris* —5B **68**
Cumberland Row. *Bath* —3A **106** (3A **96**)
Cumberland St. *Bris* —2A **70**
Cumbria Clo. *T'bry* —3F **7**
Cunningham Gdns. *Bris* —2D **61**
Cunnington Clo. *Will* —4D **85**
Curland Gro. *Bris* —3D **89**
Curlew Clo. *Bris* —1B **60**
Curlew Gdns. *W Mare* —4D **129**
Curtis La. *Stok G* —5C **28**
Custom Clo. *Bris* —1C **88**
Cutler Rd. *Bris* —2B **86**
Cygnet Cres. *W Mare* —4D **129**
Cynthia Rd. *Bath* —4D **105**
Cynthia Vs. *Bath* —4D **105**
Cypress Ct. *Bris* —4F **55**
Cypress Gdns. *Bris* —4A **68**
Cypress Gro. *Bris* —1E **57**
Cypress Ter. *Rads* —3A **152**
Cyrus Ct. *E Grn* —5D **47**

Dafford's Bldgs. *Bath* —4D **101**
*Dafford's Pl. Bath —4D **101** (off Dafford St.)*
Dafford St. *Bath* —4D **101**
Daglands, The. *C'ton* —1A **148**
Dahlia Gdns. *Bath* —2C **106** (1F **97**)
Daisey Bank. *Bath* —5C **106**
Daisy Rd. *Bris* —5E **59**
Dakin Clo. *Bris* —4A **80**
Dakota Dri. *Bris* —4C **88**
Dalby Av. *Bris* —1F **79**
Dale St. *Bris* —2B **72** (Hudd's Hill Rd.)
Dale St. *Bris* —2B **70** (Newfoundland St.)
Daley Clo. *W Mare* —2F **129**
Dalkeith Av. *Bris* —1E **73**
Dalrymple Rd. *Bris* —1A **70**
Dalston Rd. *Bris* —1D **79**
Dalton Sq. *Bris* —2A **70**
Dalwood. *W Mare* —3E **129**
Dame Ct. Clo. *W Mare* —1D **129**
Dampier Rd. *Bris* —2C **78**
Damson Rd. *W Mare* —5B **128**
Danbury Cres. *Bris* —3E **41**
Danbury Wlk. *Bris* —3E **41**
Dancey Mead. *Bris* —1B **86**
Daneacre Rd. *Rads* —1D **153**
Dane Clo. *W'ley* —2F **113**
Dane Rise. *W'ley* —2F **113**
Dangerfield Av. *Bris* —2B **86**
Daniel Clo. *Clev* —3F **121**
Daniel M. *Bath* —2C **106** (1E **97**)
Daniel St. *Bath* —2C **106** (2E **97**)
Dapp's Hill. *Key* —3B **92**
Dark La. *Back* —2D **125**
Dark La. *Ban* —5F **137**
Dark La. *Bris* —4C **40**
Dark La. *Mid N* —4C **112**
Darley Clo. *Bris* —1F **39**
Darlington M. *Bath* —2C **106** (2E **97**)
Darlington Pl. *Bath* —3C **106** (4F **97**)
Darlington Rd. *Bath* —2C **106** (1F **97**)
Darlington St. *Bath* —2C **106** (2E **97**)
Darmead. *W Mare* —4F **129**
Darnley Av. *Bris* —1B **58**
Dart Clo. *T'bry* —4C **6**
Dartmoor St. *Bris* —1D **79**
Dartmouth Av. *Bath* —4D **105**
Dartmouth Clo. *W Mare* —3E **129**
Dartmouth Wlk. *Key* —4F **91**
Dart Rd. *Clev* —5D **121**
Daubeny Clo. *Bris* —2D **61**
Davenport Clo. *L Grn* —3C **84**
Daventry Rd. *Bris* —4A **80**
Davey St. *Bris* —1B **70**
David's Clo. *Alv* —3B **8**
David's La. *Alv* —3B **8**
David's Rd. *Bris* —1E **89**
David St. *Bris* —3B **70** (2F **5**)
David Thomas Houses. *Bris* —5A **58**
Davies Dri. *St Ap* —5B **72**
Davin Cres. *Pill* —4E **53**
Davis Clo. *Bar C* —5B **74**
Davis Ct. *T'bry* —2D **7**
Davis La. *Clev* —5D **121**
Davis St. *Bris* —4D **37**
Dawes Clo. *Clev* —5D **121**
Dawley Clo. *Wint* —2A **30**
Dawlish Rd. *Bris* —3F **79**
Dawn Rise. *Bris* —1B **74**
Day Cres. *Bath* —3A **104**
Day's Rd. *St Ph* —4C **70**
Deacon Clo. *Wint* —4A **30**
Deacons Clo. *W Mare* —3C **128**
Deadmill La. *Swain* —3D **101**
Dean Av. *T'bry* —2D **7**
Dean Clo. *Bris* —5D **73**
Dean Clo. *W Mare* —2F **129**
Dean Ct. *Yate* —3E **17**
Dean Cres. *Bris* —1E **79** (in two parts)
Deanery Clo. *K'wd* —2D **75**
Deanery Rd. *Bris* —4E **69**
Deanery Rd. *War* —2C **74**
Deanhill La. *Bath* —4A **98**
Dean La. *Bris* —1E **79**
Deanna Ct. *Bris* —1A **62**
Dean Rd. *Bris* —4E **21**
Dean Rd. *Yate* —3E **17**
Deans Dri. *S'wll* —5C **60**
Deans Mead. *Bris* —4C **38**
Deans, The. *P'head* —4D **49**
Dean St. *Bris* —1E **79**
Dean St. *St Pa* —2A **70**
De Beccas La. *E'ton G* —3D **53**
De Clifford Rd. *Bris* —2E **39**
Deep Coombe Rd. *Bris* —3C **78**
Deep Pit Rd. *Bris* —1A **72**
Deerhurst. *Bris* —5A **62**
Deerhurst. *Yate* —1E **33**
Deering Clo. *Bris* —3D **39**
Deer Mead. *Clev* —5B **120**
Deerswood. *Bris* —5C **62**
Delabere Av. *Bris* —2D **61**
Delamere Rd. *Trow* —5D **117**
Delapre Rd. *W Mare* —5B **132**
De La Warre Ct. *St Ap* —4B **72**
Delius Gro. *Bris* —1F **87**
Dell, The. *Brad S* —2A **28**
Dell, The. *Bris* —5E **75**
Dell, The. *Nail* —3C **122**
Dell, The. *W Mare* —1C **128**
Dell, The. *W Trym* —2B **56**
Delvin Rd. *Bris* —4E **41**
De Montalt Pl. *C Down* —3C **110**
Denbigh St. *Bris* —1B **70**
Dene Clo. *Key* —5B **92**
Dene Rd. *Bris* —4E **89**
Denleigh Clo. *Bris* —4C **88**
Denmark Av. *Bris* —4E **69** (3A **4**)
Denmark Pl. *Bris* —4A **58**
Denmark Rd. *Bath* —3E **105**
Denmark St. *Bris* —4E **69** (3A **4**)
Denning Ct. *W Mare* —1F **129**
Dennisworth. *Puck* —2D **65**
Dennor Pk. *Bris* —1D **89**
Denny Clo. *P'head* —3C **48**
Denny Isle Dri. *Sev B* —4B **20**
Denny View. *P'head* —3B **48**
Denny View Rd. *Abb L* —2B **66**
Denston Dri. *P'head* —4A **50**
Denston Wlk. *Bris* —1C **86**
Dentwood Gro. *Bris* —5D **39**
Derby Rd. *Bris* —4A **58**
Derby St. *Bris* —2F **71**
Derham Clo. *Yat* —3B **142**
Derham Pk. *Yat* —3B **142**
Derham Rd. *Bris* —3C **86**
Derhill Ter. *Bath* —3F **107**
Dermot St. *Bris* —1B **70**
Derricke Rd. *Bris* —2B **90**
Derrick Rd. *Bris* —2F **73**
Derry Rd. *Bris* —3D **79**
Derwent Clo. *Pat* —1C **26**
Derwent Ct. *T'bry* —4E **7**
Derwent Gro. *Key* —3C **92**
Derwent Rd. *Bris* —1B **72**
Derwent Rd. *W Mare* —3E **133**
Devaney Clo. *St Ap* —5B **72**
Deverell Clo. *Brad A* —5F **115**
Deveron Gro. *Key* —4C **92**
Deverose Ct. *Bris* —1A **84**
Devon Gro. *Bris* —2E **71**
Devon Rd. *Bris* —1E **71**
Devonshire Bldgs. *Bath* —5A **106**
Devonshire Dri. *P'head* —3B **48**
Devonshire Pl. *Bath* —5A **106**
Devonshire Rd. *B'ptn* —5F **101**
Devonshire Rd. *Bris* —3D **57**
Devonshire Rd. *W Mare* —5C **132**
Devonshire Vs. *Bath* —1A **110**
Dial Hill Rd. *Clev* —2D **121**
Dial La. *Bris* —1F **61**
Diamond Rd. *Bris* —3B **72**
Diamond St. *Bris* —2E **79**
Dibden Clo. *Bris* —4C **46**
Dibden La. *E Grn* —5C **46**
Dibden Rd. *Bris* —4C **46**
Dickens Clo. *Bris* —4C **42**
Dickenson Rd. *W Mare* —2C **132**
Dickensons Gro. *Cong* —3E **145**
Didsbury Clo. *Bris* —3B **40**
Dighton Ga. *Stok G* —4A **28**
Dighton St. *Bris* —2F **69**
Dillon Ct. *Bris* —3F **71**
Dinder Clo. *Nail* —4D **123**
Dingle Clo. *Bris* —1E **55**
Dingle Rd. *Bris* —5F **39**
Dingle, The. *Bris* —5F **39**
Dingle, The. *Wint* —1B **46**
Dingle, The. *Yate* —2B **18**
Dingle View. *Bris* —5E **39**
Dinglewood Clo. *Bris* —5F **39**
Dings Wlk. *Bris* —4C **70**
Dixon Gdns. *Bath* —5A **100**
Dixon Rd. *Bris* —3B **82**
Dock Ga. La. *Bris* —5C **68**
Docks Ind. Est. *Chit* —1F **21**
Doctor White's Clo. *Bris* —5A **70**
Dodington La. *Dod* —3D **35**
Dodington Rd. *Chip S* —2D **35**
Dodisham Wlk. *Bris* —1D **61**
Dodmore Crossing. *W'lgh* —5D **33**
Dodsmoor La. *Alv* —3D **9**
Dolemoor La. *Cong* (in two parts) —2A **144**
Dolman Clo. *Bris* —1A **40**
Dolphin Sq. *W Mare* —1B **132**
Dominion Rd. *Bath* —3B **104**
Dominion Rd. *Bris* —4B **60**
Donald Rd. *Bris* —1B **86**
Doncaster Rd. *Bris* —3D **41**
Donegal Rd. *Bris* —4F **79**
Dongola Av. *Bris* —3A **58**
Dongola Rd. *Bris* —3A **58**
Donnington Wlk. *Key* —4F **91**
Doone Rd. *Bris* —4B **42**
Dorcas Av. *Stok G* —4B **28**
Dorchester Clo. *Nail* —5C **122**
Dorchester Rd. *Bris* —5C **42**
Dorchester St. *Bath* —4B **106** (5C **96**)
Dorester Clo. *Bris* —5E **25**
Dorian Clo. *Bris* —5A **42**
Dorian Rd. *Bris* —4A **42**
Dormer Clo. *Coal H* —3F **31**
Dormer Rd. *Bris* —4D **59**
Dorset Clo. *Bath* —3E **105**
Dorset Cotts. *Bath* —3D **111**
Dorset Gro. *Bris* —5C **58**
Dorset Ho. *Bath* —1E **109**
Dorset Rd. *K'wd* —1F **73**
Dorset Rd. *W Trym* —1D **57**
Dorset St. *Bath* —3E **105**
Dorset St. *Bris* —2D **79**
Dorset Way. *Yate* —3C **18**
Douglas Rd. *Hor* —5B **42**
Douglas Rd. *K'wd* —3F **73**
Douglas Rd. *W Mare* —3D **133**
Doulton Way. *Bris* —3D **89**
Dovecote. *Yate* —1A **34**
Dovecote Clo. *Trow* —2B **118**
Dovedale. *T'bry* —5E **7**
Dove La. *Redf* —3E **71**
Dove La. *St Pa* —2B **70**
Dovercourt Rd. *Bris* —2C **58**
Dover Ho. *Bath* —1B **106**
*Dover Pl. Bath —5B **100** (off Seymour Rd.)*
Dover Pl. *Bris* —3D **69**
Dover Pl. Cotts. *Bris* —3D **69**
Dovers La. *Bathf* —4D **103**
Dovers Pk. *Bathf* —4D **103**
Dove St. *Bris* —2F **69**
Dove St. S. *Bris* —2F **69**
Doveswell Gro. *Bris* —4C **86**
Doveton St. *Bris* —1F **79**
Dovey Ct. *Bris* —5E **75**
Dowdeswell Clo. *Bris* —1B **40**
Dowding Rd. *Bath* —5C **100**
Dowland. *W Mare* —3E **129**
Dowland Clo. *Bris* —2F **87**
Dowling Rd. *Bris* —5F **87**
Down Av. *Bath* —3B **110**
Downavon. *Brad A* —4E **115**
Down Clo. *P'head* —3B **48**
Downend Pk. *Bris* —2B **58**
Downend Pk. Rd. *Bris* —2F **61**
Downend Rd. *Down* —2D **61**
Downend Rd. *Hor* —2B **58**
Downend Rd. *K'wd* —1F **73**
Downfield. *Key* —3F **91**
Downfield Clo. *Alv* —2A **8**
Downfield Dri. *Fram C* —1D **31**
Downfield Lodge. *Bris* —1C **68**
Downfield Rd. *Bris* —1C **68**
Downhayes Rd. *Trow* —5D **117**
Downland Clo. *Nail* —4C **122**
Down La. *B'ptn* —5A **102**
Down Leaze. *Alv* —2B **8**
Downleaze. *Down* —4F **45**
Downleaze. *P'head* —3C **48**
Downleaze. *Stok B* —4B **56**
Downleaze Dri. *Chip S* —1C **34**
Downman Rd. *Bris* —2C **58**
Down Rd. *Alv* —2A **8**
Down Rd. *P'head* —5A **48**
Down Rd. *Wint D* —5A **30**
Downs Clo. *Alv* —2B **8**
Downs Clo. *Brad A* —2C **114**
Downs Clo. *W Mare* —4D **129**
Downs Cote Av. *Bris* —1B **56**
Downs Cote Dri. *Bris* —1B **56**
Downs Cote Gdns. *Bris* —1C **56**
Downs Cote Pk. *Bris* —1C **56**
Downs Cote View. *Bris* —1C **56**
Downside. *P'head* —3E **49**
Downside Clo. *Bar C* —4B **74**
Downside Clo. *B'ptn* —5A **102**
Downside Pk. *Trow* —5E **117**
Downside Rd. *Bris* —1C **68**
Downside Rd. *W Mare* —4D **133**
Downside View. *Trow* —5E **117**
Downs Pk. E. *Bris* —2C **56**
Downs Pk. W. *Bris* —2C **56**
Downs Rd. *Bris* —1C **56**
Downs, The. *P'head* —4D **49**
Downs, The. *Wickw* —1A **154**
Downs View. *Brad A* —2C **114**
Downsway. *Paul* —3A **146**
Down, The. *Alv* —2A **8**
Down, The. *Trow* —5D **117**
Downton Rd. *Bris* —4F **79**
Down View. *Bris* —4B **58**
Down View. *Rads* —4C **152**
Dowry Pl. *Bris* —4B **68**
Dowry Rd. *Bris* —4C **68**
Dowry Sq. *Bris* —4C **68**
Dragon Ct. *Bris* —1A **72**
Dragon Rd. *Wint* —4F **29**
Dragons Hill Clo. *Key* —3B **92**
Dragons Hill Ct. *Key* —3B **92**
Dragons Hill Gdns. *Key* —3B **92**
Dragonswell Rd. *Bris* —2C **40**
Dragon Wlk. *Bris* —1B **72**
Drake Av. *Bath* —2A **110**
Drake Clo. *Salt* —5F **93**
Drake Clo. *W Mare* —1D **129**
Drake Rd. *Bris* —2C **78**
Drakes Way. *P'head* —3C **48**
Draycot Pl. *Bris* —5F **69**
Draycott Ct. *Bath* —2B **106** (1D **97**)
Draycott Rd. *Bris* —2B **58**
Draydon Rd. *Bris* —5E **79**
Drayton. *W Mare* —1E **139**
Drayton Clo. *Bris* —5D **81**
Drayton Rd. *Bris* —4E **39**
Dring, The. *Rads* —2B **152**
Drive, The. *H'gro* —2E **89**
Drive, The. *Henl* —2D **57**
Drive, The. *W Mare* —5D **127**
Drove Ct. *Nail* —2D **123**
Drove Rd. *Cong* —3D **145**
Drove Rd. *W Mare* —3C **132**
Drove, The. *P'bry* —1E **51**
Druce's Hill. *Brad A* —2D **115**
Druett's Clo. *Bris* —5A **42**
Druid Clo. *Stok B* —2A **56**
Druid Hill. *Bris* —2A **56**
Druid Rd. *Bris* —3F **55**
Druid Stoke Av. *Bris* —2E **55**
Druid Woods. *Bris* —2E **55**
Druid Wood St. *Bris* —2F **55**
Drummond Ct. *L Grn* —1B **84**
Drummond Rd. *Fish* —4B **60**
Drummond Rd. *St Pa* —1A **70**
Drungway. *Bath* —3F **111**
Dryham Clo. *Bris* —2B **74**
Dryleaze. *Key* —1A **92**
Dryleaze. *Yate* —1A **18**
Dryleaze Rd. *Bris* —1B **60**
Drynham Drove. *Trow* —3E **155**
Drynham La. *Trow* —4D **119**
Drynham Pk. *Trow* —4D **119**
Drynham Rd. *Trow* —4D **119**
Drysdale Clo. *W Mare* —4B **128**
Dubber's La. *Bris* —5A **60**
Dublin Cres. *Bris* —1D **57**
Duchess Rd. *Bris* —1C **68**
Duchess Way. *Bris* —2F **59**
Duchy Clo. *Rads* —4B **148**
Duchy Rd. *Rads* —4B **148**
Ducie Rd. *Law H* —3D **71**
Ducie Rd. *Stap H* —2A **62**
Duckmoor Rd. *Bris* —1C **78**
Duckmoor Yd. *Bris* —1C **78**
Dudley Clo. *Key* —4A **92**
Dudley Ct. *Bar C* —1B **84**

Dudley Gro. Bris —4C 42
Dugar Wlk. Bris —4E 57
Duke St. Bath —3B 106 (4D 97)
Duke St. Trow —1D 119
Dulverton Rd. Bris —3F 57
Dumaine Av. Stok G —4A 28
Dumfries Pl. W Mare —3C 132
Duncan Gdns. Bath —3B 98
Duncombe La. Bris —5C 60
Duncombe Rd. Bris —1D 73
Dundas Clo. Bris —2A 40
Dundonald Rd. Bris —4D 57
Dundridge Gdns. Bris —4C 72
Dundridge La. Bris —4C 72
Dundry Clo. Bris —4A 74
Dundry View. Bris —4C 80
Dunedin Way. St Geo —1A 130
Dunford Clo. Trow —4D 119
Dunford Rd. Bris —2F 79
Dunkeld Av. Bris —2B 42
Dunkerry Rd. Bris —2F 79
Dunkerton Hill. Bath —3D 157
Dunkery Clo. Nail —4D 123
Dunkery Rd. W Mare —4D 127
Dunkirk Rd. Bris —4B 60
Dunkite La. W Mare —1D 129
Dunmail Rd. Bris —2E 41
Dunmore St. Bris —1B 80
Dunsford Pl. Bath —3C 106 (3F 97)
Dunster Cres. W Mare —1D 139
Dunster Gdns. Nail —4D 123
Dunster Gdns. Will —3D 85
Dunster Ho. Bath —2B 110
Dunster Rd. Bris —5B 80
Dunster Rd. Key —4F 91
Dunsters Rd. Clav —2F 143
Durban Rd. Pat —1B 26
Durban Way. Yat —2B 142
Durbin Pk. Rd. Clev —1D 121
Durbin Wlk. Bris —2C 70
Durcott La. Mid N —1F 147
Durdham Ct. Bris —4C 56
Durdham Pk. Bris —4C 56
Durham Gro. Key —4F 91
Durham Rd. Bris —5C 58
Durleigh Clo. Bris —1C 86
Durley Hill. Key —5D 83
Durley La. Key —1E 91
Durley Pk. Bath —5F 105
Durley Pk. Key —1E 91
Durnford Av. Bris —1C 78
Durnford St. Bris —1C 78
Dursley Clo. Yate —5A 18
Dursley Rd. Bris —2F 53
Dursley Rd. Trow —3C 118
Durston. W Mare —1E 139
Durville Rd. Bris —2D 87
Durweston Wlk. Bris —5E 81
Dutton Clo. Bris —2F 89
Dutton Rd. Bris —2F 89
Dutton Wlk. Bris —2F 89
Dyers Clo. Bris —4F 87
Dyer's La. Iron A —3C 16
Dylan Thomas Ct. Bar C —5C 74
Dymboro Av. Mid N —3C 150
Dymboro Clo. Mid N —3C 150
Dymboro Gdns. Mid N —3C 150
Dymboro, The. Mid N —3C 150
Dymott Sq. Hil —4F 117
Dyrham. Bris —3E 45
(off Harford Dri.)
Dyrham Clo. Henl —1F 57
Dyrham Clo. K'wd —2B 74
Dyrham Clo. T'bry —1D 7
Dyrham Pde. Pat —1E 27
Dyrham Rd. Bris —2B 74
Dyrham View. Puck —3E 65
Dysons Clo. Yat —3B 142

Eagle Clo. W Mare —5B 128
Eagle Cotts. Bath —1A 102
Eagle Cres. Puck —3E 65
Eagle Dri. Pat —1A 26
Eagle Pk. Bathe —1A 102
Eagle Rd. Bathe —1A 102
Eagle Rd. Bris —3F 81
Eagles, The. Yat —3B 142
Eagles Wood Bus. Pk. Alm —3E 11
Earlesfield. Nail —4B 122
Earlham Gro. W Mare —1D 133
Earl Russell Way. Bris —3D 71
Earls Mead. Bris —3A 60
Earlstone Clo. Bris —1C 84
Earlstone Cres. Bris —1C 84
Earl St. Bris —2F 69
Earthcott Rd. Brad S —5F 9
Easedale Clo. Bris —2F 41
Eastbourne Av. Bath —5C 100
Eastbourne Gdns. Trow —1E 119
Eastbourne Rd. Bris —1D 71
Eastbourne Rd. Trow —1E 119
Eastbourne Vs. Bath —5C 100
Eastbury Clo. T'bry —3D 7
Eastbury Rd. Bris —3C 60
Eastbury Rd. T'bry —3D 7
E. Clevedon Triangle. Clev —2E 121
East Clo. Bath —4B 104
Eastcombe Gdns. W Mare —4D 127
Eastcombe Rd. W Mare —4D 127
Eastcote Pk. Bris —3D 89
E. Croft. Bris —5E 41
Eastdown Rd. Clan —4B 148
E. Dundry Rd. Bris —5B 88
Eastfield. Bris —5D 41
Eastfield Av. Bath —3C 98
Eastfield Gdns. W Mare —4D 127
Eastfield Pk. W Mare —4C 126
Eastfield Rd. Cot —5F 57
Eastfield Rd. Hut —1C 140
Eastfield Rd. W Trym —5C 40
Eastfield Ter. Bris —5D 41
Eastgate Cen. Bris —4D 59
Eastgate Rd. Bris —4D 59
East Gro. Bris —1B 70
Eastlake Clo. Bris —5D 43
Eastland Av. T'bry —2D 7
Eastland Rd. T'bry —2D 7
Eastlea. Clev —5B 120
E. Lea Rd. Bath —1B 104
Eastleigh Clo. Bris —3A 62
Eastleigh Rd. Stap H —4A 62
Eastleigh Rd. W Trym —3F 41
Eastlyn Rd. Bris —5D 79
East Mead. Mid N —2E 151
E. Mead Drove. B'don —5D 139
Eastmead La. Ban —5F 137
Eastmead La. Bris —3A 56
Eastnor Rd. Bris —5C 88
Easton Bus. Cen. Bris —2D 71
Easton Hill Rd. T'bry —2E 7
Easton Rd. Bris —3C 70
Easton Rd. Pill —3E 53
Easton Way. Bris —1C 70
Eastover Clo. Bris —4C 40
Eastover Gro. Bath —3D 109
East Pde. Bris —1E 55
East Pk. Bris —5E 59
East Pk. Dri. Bris —5E 59
East Pk. Trad. Est. Bris —1F 71
E. Priory Clo. Bris —5C 40
Eastridge Dri. Bris —3B 86
E. Shrubbery. Bris —5D 57
East St. A'mth —3C 36
East St. Ban —5F 137
East St. Bedm —2E 79
East St. St Pa —2B 70
East View. Mang —1B 62
Eastview Rd. Trow —3A 118
Eastville. Bath —5C 100
East Wlk. Yate —5A 18
East Way. Bath —4B 104
Eastway. Nail —2C 122
Eastway Clo. Nail —2C 122
Eastway Sq. Nail —2D 123
Eastwood Cres. Bris —1B 82
E. Wood Pl. P'head —1F 49
Eastwood Rd. Bris —1B 82
Eastwoods. Bathf —3C 102
Eaton Clo. Bris —3A 90
Eaton Clo. Fish —3D 61
Eaton Cres. Bris —2C 68
Eaton St. Bris —2E 79
Ebdon Ct. W Mare —3E 129
Ebdon Rd. W Mare —1D 129
Ebenezer La. Bris —1F 55
(in two parts)
Ebenezer St. Bris —3F 71
Ebenezer Ter. Bath —4B 106 (5E 97)
(off Rossiter Rd.)
Eccleston Ho. Bris —4D 71
Eckweek Gdns. Pea J —4D 157
Eckweek La. Pea J —4E 157
(in two parts)
Eckweek Rd. Pea J —4D 157
Eden Gro. Bris —3B 42
Eden Pk. Cl. Bathe —2B 102
Eden Pk. Dri. Bathe —2B 102
Eden Ter. Bath —4D 101
Eden Vs. Bath —4D 101
(off Dafford's Bldgs.)
Edgar Bldgs. Bath —2A 106
(off George St.)
Edgecombe Av. W Mare —3B 128
Edgecombe Clo. Bris —1B 74
Edgecumbe Rd. Bris —5F 57
Edgefield Clo. Bris —5B 88
Edgefield Rd. Bris —5B 88
Edgehill Rd. Clev —1D 121
Edgeware Rd. Stap H —3F 61
Edgeware Rd. S'vle —1E 79
Edgewood Clo. Bris —5D 81
Edgewood Clo. L Grn —2C 84
Edgeworth. Yate —3E 33
Edgeworth Rd. Bath —2D 109
Edinburgh Pl. W Mare —5C 126
Edinburgh Rd. Key —4A 92
Edington Gro. Bris —2C 40
Edmund Clo. Bris —1F 61
Edmund Ct. Puck —1D 65
Edna Av. Bris —2A 82
Edward Bird Ho. Bris —5E 43
Edward Rd. Arn V —1D 81
Edward Rd. Clev —1E 121
Edward Rd. K'wd —2A 74
Edward Rd. S. Clev —1E 121
Edward Rd. W. Clev —1E 121
Edward St. Bathw —2C 106 (2E 97)
Edward St. Eastv —5F 59
Edward St. Lwr W —2D 105
Edward St. Redf —2E 71
Effingham Rd. Bris —5A 58
Egerton Brow. Bris —3F 57
Egerton La. Bris —3F 57
Egerton Rd. Bath —5F 105
Egerton Rd. Bris —3F 57
Eggshill La. Yate —5F 17
Eighth Av. Bris —4D 43
Eirene Ter. Pill —3F 53
Elberton. Bris —2C 74
Elberton Rd. Bris —5D 39
Elborough Av. Yat —3B 142
Elbury Av. Bris —5E 61
Elcombe Clo. Trow —5C 118
Elderberry Wlk. Bris —2E 41
Elderberry Wlk. W Mare —4D 129
Elderwood Dri. L Grn —2C 84
Elderwood Rd. Bris —1D 89
Eldon Pl. Bath —4C 100
Eldon Ter. Bris —2F 79
Eldonwall Trad. Est. Bris —5E 71
Eldon Way. Bris —5E 71
Eldred Clo. Bris —2F 55
Eleanor Clo. Bath —4A 104
Eleventh Av. Bris —3D 43
Elfin Rd. Bris —2C 60
Elgar Clo. Bris —2F 87
Elgar Clo. Clev —5E 121
Elgin Av. Bris —3B 42
Elgin Croft. Bris —4D 87
Elgin Pk. Bris —5D 57
Elgin Rd. Bris —5D 61
Eliot Clo. W Mare —5E 133
Eliot Dri. Bris —3C 42
Elizabeth Clo. Hut —5B 134
Elizabeth Clo. T'bry —4E 7
Elizabeth Cres. Stok G —5A 28
Elizabeth's M. St Ap —4B 72
Elkstone Wlk. Bit —3E 85
Ellacombe Rd. L Grn —3A 84
Ellan Hay Rd. Brad S —3C 28
Ellbridge Clo. Bris —2F 55
Ellenborough Cres. W Mare —2C 132
Ellenborough La. Bris —1A 54
Ellenborough Pk. N. W Mare —2B 132
Ellenborough Pk. Rd. W Mare —2C 132
Ellenborough Pk. S. W Mare —2B 132
Ellen Ho. Bath —4B 104
Ellesmere. T'bry —4D 7
Ellesmere Rd. Bris —5F 81
Ellesmere Rd. K'wd —2F 73
Ellesmere Rd. Uph —1B 138
Ellfield Clo. Bris —2B 86
Ellicks Clo. Brad S —4A 12
Ellicott Rd. Bris —1B 58
Ellinghurst Clo. Bris —2C 40
Elliot Pl. Trow —1A 118
Elliott Av. Bris —3E 45
Ellis Av. Bris —5C 78
Ellis Pk. St Geo —1A 130
Elliston Dri. Bath —5C 104
Elliston La. Bris —5E 57
Elliston Rd. Bris —5E 57
Ellsbridge Clo. Key —3D 93
Ellsworth Rd. Bris —1B 40
Elm Clo. Ban —4C 136
Elm Clo. Chip S —5C 18
Elm Clo. Lit S —3A 28
Elm Clo. Nail —4B 122
Elm Clo. N Brad —4D 155
Elm Clo. Stav —1D 117
Elm Clo. Yat —4B 142
Elm Ct. Bris —3C 88
Elm Ct. Key —4E 91
Elmcroft Cres. Bris —3C 58
Elmdale Ct. Trow —3A 118
Elmdale Cres. T'bry —3D 7
Elmdale Gdns. Bris —3C 60
Elmdale Rd. Bedm —3D 79
Elmdale Rd. Trow —3A 118
Elmdale Rd. Tyn P —2D 69
Elmfield. Brad A —2D 115
Elmfield. Bris —4A 74
Elmfield Clo. Bris —4A 74
Elmfield Rd. Bris —4C 40
Elm Gro. Bath —5D 105
Elm Gro. Lock —4D 135
Elm Gro. Swain —4D 101
Elmgrove Av. Bris —2D 71
Elmgrove Dri. Yate —4B 18
Elmgrove Pk. Cot —1F 69
Elmgrove Rd. Fish —4A 60
Elmgrove Rd. Redl —1F 69
Elm Hayes. Bris —2B 86
Elmhirst Gdns. Yate —4C 18
Elmhurst Av. Bris —4F 59
Elmhurst Est. Bathe —2B 102
Elmhurst Gdns. L Ash —4B 76
Elmhurst Rd. Hut —1C 140
Elmhyrst Rd. W Mare —5D 127
Elming Down Clo. Lit S —3F 27
Elm La. Bris —5D 57
Elmlea Av. Bris —2B 56
Elmleigh Av. Mang —2D 63
Elmleigh Clo. Mang —2D 63
Elmleigh Rd. Mang —2C 62
Elmore. Bris —5B 62
Elmore. Yate —1F 33
Elmore Rd. Bris —1C 58
Elmore Rd. Pat —5B 10
Elm Pk. Fil —2C 42
Elm Rd. Hor —2A 58
Elm Rd. K'wd —4A 74
Elm Rd. Paul —4B 146
Elms Cross. Brad A —5D 115
Elmscross Bus. Pk. Brad A —5D 115
Elms Cross Dri. Brad A —4D 115
Elmscross Shopping Cen. Brad A —5D 115
Elms Gro. Pat —5D 11
Elmsleigh Rd. W Mare —4B 132
Elmsley La. W Mare —1A 128
Elms, The. Brad A —1D 115
Elms, The. Bris —3E 45
Elms, The. Holt —1E 155
Elm Ter. Rads —3F 151
Elm Tree Av. Mang —5C 46
Elm Tree Av. Rads —3A 152
Elmtree Clo. Bris —1F 73
Elmtree Dri. Bris —4B 86
Elm Tree Pk. P'bry —4F 51
Elm Tree Rd. Clev —4D 121
Elm Tree Rd. Lock —3D 135
Elmtree Way. Bris —1F 73
Elmvale Dri. Hut —5D 135
Elm View. Mid N —2E 151
Elm Wlk. P'head —4E 49
Elm Wlk. Yat —4B 142
Elmwood. Yate —1A 34
Elsbert Dri. Bris —2A 86
Elstree Rd. Bris —1A 72
Elton La. Bris —5F 57
Elton Mans. Bris —5F 57
Elton Rd. Bishop —4F 57
Elton Rd. Clev —3B 120
Elton Rd. K'wd —1D 73
Elton Rd. Tyn P —3D 69
Elton Rd. W Mare —1F 129
Elton St. Bris —2B 70
Elvard Clo. Bris —4C 86
Elvard Rd. Bris —3C 86
Elvaston Rd. Bris —2A 80
Ely Gro. Bris —5D 39
Embassy Rd. Bris —1A 72
Embassy Wlk. Bris —1A 72
Embercourt Dri. Back —2C 124
Embleton Rd. Bris —2D 41
Emersons Grn. La. E Grn —1D 63
Emerson Sq. Bris —4C 42
Emerson Way. E Grn —4D 47
Emery Ga. Ban —5F 137
Emery Rd. Bris —3B 82
Emlyn Clo. W Mare —1F 129
Emlyn Rd. Bris —5E 59
Emmanuel Ct. Bris —2C 68
Emmett Wood. Bris —5D 89
Empire Cres. Han —1A 84
Empress Menen Gdns. Bath —1B 104
Emra Clo. Bris —1B 72
Enfield Rd. Bris —4C 60
Engine Comn. Yate —2E 17
Engine Comn. La. Yate —1E 17
Enginehouse La. Key —4C 90
Engine La. Nail —4A 122
England's Cres. Wint —2A 30
Englishcombe La. Bath —1C 108
Englishcombe Rd. Bath —2A 108
Englishcombe Rd. Bris —5E 87
Englishcombe Way. Bath —1F 109
Enmore. W Mare —1E 139
Ennerdale Clo. W Mare —3E 133
Ennerdale Rd. Bris —2F 41
Entry Hill. Bath —1A 110
Entry Hill Dri. Bath —1A 110
Entry Hill Gdns. Bath —1A 110
Entry Hill Pk. Bath —2A 110
Entry Rise. Bath —3A 110
Epney Clo. Pat —5B 10
Epsom Clo. Bris —3B 46
Epsom Rd. Whit B —3F 155
Epsom Sq. Whit B —3F 155
Epworth Rd. Bris —1C 40
Equinox. Brad S —3E 11
Erin Wlk. Bris —5F 79
Ermine Way. Bris —5E 37
Ermleet Rd. Bris —5E 57
Ernest Barker Clo. Bris —3D 71
Ernestville Rd. Bris —4B 60
Ervine Ter. Bris —2B 70
Esgar Rise. W Mare —2C 128
Eskdale. T'bry —5E 7
Eskdale Clo. W Mare —5B 128
Esmond Gro. Clev —2D 121
Esplanade Rd. P'head —2E 49
Essery Rd. Bris —5E 59
Esson Rd. Bris —1D 73
Estcourt Gdns. Stap —2F 59
Estcourt La. Bris —2F 59
Estelle Pk. Bris —5E 59
Estoril. Yate —5B 18
Estune Wlk. L Ash —3C 76
Etloe Rd. Bris —3C 56
Eton La. Lock —1B 136
Eton Rd. Bris —2F 81
Ettlingen Way. Clev —4E 121
Ettricke Dri. Bris —1D 61

Eugene St. St Ja —2F **69**
Eugene St. St Jud —2B **70**
Evans Clo. St Ap —5B **72**
Evans Rd. Bris —5D **57**
Eveleigh Ho. Bath —2B **106** (off Grove St.)
Evelyn Rd. Bath —1C **104**
Evelyn Rd. Bris —4E **41**
Evelyn Ter. Bath —5B **100**
Evenlode Gdns. Bris —2B **54**
Evenlode Way. Key —5C **92**
Everall Dri. W Mare —2E **127**
Evercreech Rd. Bris —4C **88**
Everest Av. Bris —3A **60**
Everest Rd. Bris —3A **60**
Evergreen Clo. Wins —3A **156**
Everleigh Clo. Trow —5D **119**
Eve Rd. Bris —1D **71**
Everson Clo. W Mare —4E **133**
Ewart Rd. W Mare —5A **128**
Exbourne. W Mare —3E **129**
Excelsior St. Bath —4C **106** (5D **97**)
Excelsior Ter. Mid N —3E **151**
Exchange Av. Bris —4F **69** (3C **4**)
Exeter Bldgs. Bris —5D **57**
Exeter Rd. Bris —1D **79**
Exeter Rd. P'head —4A **50**
Exeter Rd. W Mare —3C **132**
Exford Clo. W Mare —1D **139**
Exley Clo. Bris —5E **75**
Exmoor Rd. Bath —2A **110**
Exmoor St. Bris —1D **79**
Exmouth Rd. Bris —4B **80**
Exton. W Mare —1E **139**
Exton Clo. Bris —3D **89**
Eyers La. Bris —3B **70** (1F **5**)

Faber Gro. Bris —4E **87**
Fabian Dri. Stok G —4A **28**
Factory Rd. Wint —2B **30**
Failand Cres. Bris —2E **55**
Failand La. P'bry & Fail —5A **52**
Failand Wlk. Bris —1E **55**
Fairacre Clo. Bris —2D **59**
Fairacre Clo. Lock —4F **135**
Fairacres Clo. Key —3A **92**
Fairfax Ct. Bris —3A **70**
Fairfax St. Bris —3F **69** (2C **4**)
Fairfield Av. Bath —4B **100**
Fairfield Clo. Back —1F **125**
Fairfield Clo. W Mare —4F **127**
Fairfield Mead. Back —1F **125**
Fairfield Pk. Rd. Bath —4A **100**
Fairfield Pl. Bris —1D **79**
Fairfield Rd. Bath —5B **100**
Fairfield Rd. Mont —5B **58**
Fairfield Rd. S'vle —1E **79**
Fairfield Ter. Bath —4B **100**
Fairfield Ter. Pea J —2F **149**
Fairfield View. Bath —4B **100**
Fairfield Way. Back —2E **125**
Fairfoot Rd. Bris —2C **80**
Fairford Clo. Bris —5B **62**
Fairford Cres. Pat —1E **27**
Fairford Rd. Bris —5F **37**
Fair Furlong. Bris —4C **86**
Fairhaven. Yate —5B **18**
Fairhaven Cotts. Bath —1B **102**
Fairhaven Rd. Bris —3E **57**
Fair Lawn. Old C —1C **84**
Fairlawn Av. Brad S —1C **42**
Fairlawn Rd. Bris —5B **58**
Fairleigh Rd. Clev —5A **120**
Fairlyn Dri. Bris —4B **62**
Fairoaks. L Grn —2C **84**
Fairview. W Mare —1D **129**
Fair View Dri. Bris —5E **57**
Fairview Rd. Bris —2B **74**
Fairway. Bris —4F **81**
Fairway Clo. Old C —1D **85**
Fairway Clo. W Mare —3F **127**
Fairway Ind. Cen. Brad S —1B **42**
Fairways. Salt —2A **94**
Falcon Clo. Bris —4B **40**
Falcon Clo. Pat —1A **26**
Falcon Clo. P'head —4F **49**
Falcon Ct. W Trym —1C **56**
Falcon Cres. W Mare —5B **128**
Falcondale Rd. Bris —5B **40**
Falcondale Wlk. Bris —4C **40**
Falcon Dri. Pat —1A **26**
Falconer Rd. Bath —3B **98**
Falcon Wlk. Pat —5A **10**
Falcon Way. T'bry —2E **7**
Falfield Rd. Bris —2E **81**
Falfield Wlk. Bris —4E **41**
Falkland Rd. Bris —5B **58**
Fallodon Ct. Bris —2D **57**
Fallodon Way. Bris —2D **57**
Fallowfield. War —5F **75**
Fallowfield. W Mare —1D **129**
Falmouth Clo. Nail —4F **123**
Falmouth Rd. Bris —3F **57**
Fane Clo. Bris —2C **40**
Fanshawe Rd. Bris —1C **88**
Faraday Rd. Bris —5B **68**
Far Handstones. Bris —1C **84**
Farington Rd. Bris —5F **41**
Farleigh Av. Trow —3A **118**
Farleigh Rise. Bathf & Mon F —5E **103**
Farleigh Rd. Back —1F **125**
Farleigh Rd. Key —4F **91**
Farleigh Wlk. Bris —5C **78**
Farler's End. Nail —5E **123** (in two parts)
Farley Clo. Lit S —2E **27**
Farm Ct. Bris —5A **46**
Farmer Rd. Bris —4A **86**
Farmhouse Clo. Nail —3D **123**
Farm La. E Comp —1C **24**
Farm Rd. Bris —5A **46**
Farm Rd. Hut —1C **140**
Farm Rd. W Mare —4F **127**
Farmwell Clo. Bris —3D **87**
Farnaby Clo. Bris —1E **87**
Farnborough Rd. Lock —4A **136**
Farndale Rd. Bris —4C **72**
Farndale Rd. W Mare —5B **128**
Farne Clo. Bris —2D **57**
Farrant Clo. Bris —2F **87**
Farringford Ho. Bris —5F **59**
Farrington Rd. Paul —4A **146**
Farr's La. Bath —2C **110**
Farrs La. Bris —4F **69** (4B **4**)
Farr St. Bris —4D **37**
Faulkland Rd. Bath —4E **105**
Faulkland View. Pea J —5E **157**
Faversham Dri. W Mare —2E **139**
Fawkes Clo. Bris —2D **75**
Fearnville Est. Clev —4C **120**
Featherstone Rd. Bris —3B **60**
Feeder Rd. Bris —5B **70**
Felix Rd. Bris —2C **70**
Felstead Rd. Bris —3A **42**
Feltham Rd. Puck —2E **65**
Felton Gro. Bris —5B **78**
Fenbrook Clo. Ham —3D **45**
Fenhurst Gdns. L Ash —5B **76**
Feniton. W Mare —3E **129**
Fennell Gro. Bris —2C **40**
Fenners. W Mare —1F **129**
Fenswood Clo. L Ash —4A **76**
Fenswood Mead. L Ash —4A **76**
Fenswood Rd. L Ash —4A **76**
Fenton Clo. Salt —5F **93**
Fenton Rd. Bris —3F **57**
Fermaine Av. Bris —2B **82**
Fernbank Rd. Bris —5E **57**
Fern Clo. Bren —1D **41**
Fern Clo. Mid N —4E **151**
Ferndale Av. L Grn —2B **84**
Ferndale Rd. Bath —3D **101**
Ferndale Rd. Bris —2C **42**
Ferndale Rd. P'head —2F **49**
Ferndene. Brad S —4E **11**
Ferndown. Yate —5A **18**
Ferndown Clo. Bris —5C **38**
Fern Gro. Lit S —1E **27**
Fern Gro. Nail —5B **122**
Fernhill La. Bris —3D **39**
Fernhurst Rd. Bris —1B **72**
Fern Lea. B'don —5F **139**
Fernlea Gdns. E'ton G —3D **53**
Fernlea Rd. W Mare —1A **134**
Fernleaze. Coal H —3E **31**
Fernleigh Ct. Bris —4D **57**
Fern Rd. Bris —2F **61**
Fernside. Back —1C **124**
Fernsteed Rd. Bris —2B **86**
Fern St. Bris —1B **70**
Ferry La. Bath —3B **106** (4E **97**)
Ferry Rd. Bris —4F **83**
Ferry Steps Ind. Est. Bris —1C **80**
Ferry St. Bris —4A **70** (4D **5**)
Fersfield. Bath —1C **110**
Fiddes Rd. Bris —3E **57**
Fielders, The. W Mare —1F **129**
Field Farm Clo. Stok G —5B **28**
Fieldgrove La. Bris —5E **85**
Fieldings. W'ley —2F **113**
Fieldings Rd. Bath —3D **105**
Field La. Bris —2A **84**
Field La. L Sev —4F **9**
Field Marshall Slim Ct. Bris —3B **70** (1F **5**)
Field Rd. Bris —1E **73**
Field View. Bris —2C **70**
Field View Dri. Bris —1E **61**
Field Way. Trow —4A **118**
Fiennes Clo. Bris —3A **62**
Fifth Av. Bris —3C **42**
Fifth Way. Bris —2A **38**
Filby Dri. Lit S —1E **27**
Filer Clo. Pea J —4D **157**
Filton Av. Fil —5D **27**
Filton Av. Hor & Fil —1B **58**
Filton Gro. Bris —1B **58**
Filton Hill. Brad S —5C **26**
Filton La. Brad S —2F **43**
Filton Rd. Fren & Ham —2A **44**
Filton Rd. Hor —5B **42**
Filton Rd. Stok G —2F **43**
Filwood B'way. Bris —5A **80**
Filwood Ct. Bris —4D **61**
Filwood Dri. Bris —2B **74**
Filwood Rd. Bris —3C **60**
Finch Clo. T'bry —2D **7**
Finch Clo. W Mare —5C **128**
Finch Rd. Chip S —1B **34**
Finmere Gdns. W Mare —1E **129**
Fircliff Pk. P'head —1F **49**
Fireclay Rd. Bris —3F **71**
Fire Engine La. Coal H —2F **31**
Firework Clo. Bris —2D **75**
Firfield St. Bris —1C **80**
Firgrove Cres. Yate —4B **18**
Firgrove La. Mid N —1E **149**
Firleaze. Nail —4A **122**
Firs Ct. Key —4E **91**
Firs Hill. Trow —5A **118**
First Av. Bath —5E **105**
First Av. Bris —5A **72**
First Av. P'bry —2A **52**
First Av. W'fld I —4F **151**
Firs, The. Bris —1A **62**
Firs, The. C Hay —3C **110**
Firs, The. Lim S —4B **112**
First Way. Bris —3E **37**
Fir Tree Av. Lock —4C **134**
Fir Tree Av. Paul —5C **146**
Fir Tree Clo. Pat —2A **26**
Firtree La. Bris —4C **72**
Fisher Av. Bris —1C **74**
Fisher Rd. Bris —1C **74**
Fishponds Rd. Eastv & Fish —5E **59**
Fishponds Trad. Est. Bris —5A **60**
Fishpool Hill. Bris —5D **25**
Fitchett Wlk. Bris —1B **40**
Fitzgerald Rd. Bris —2B **80**
Fitzmaurice Clo. Brad A —5F **115**
Fitzmaurice Pl. Brad A —4E **115**
Fitzroy Rd. Bris —5D **61**
Fitzroy St. Bris —1C **80**
Fitzroy Ter. Bris —5D **57**
Five Acre Dri. Bris —5B **44**
Five Arches Clo. Mid N —2A **152**
5C Bus. Cen. Clev —5B **120**
Flamingo Cres. W Mare —5C **128**
Flatwoods Cres. Clav D —1F **111**
Flatwoods Rd. Clav D —1F **111**
Flaxman Clo. Bris —1D **59**
Flaxpits La. Wint —3F **29**
Fleece Cotts. Trow —3E **119**
Florence Gro. W Mare —5F **127**
Florence Pk. Alm —1E **11**
Florence Pk. Bris —3D **57**
Florence Rd. Bris —4A **62**
Florida Ter. Mid N —2F **151**
Flowerdown Bri. W Mare —1B **134**
Flowerdown Rd. Lock —4A **136**
Flowers Hill. Bris —5A **82**
Flowers Hill Clo. Bris —4A **82**
Flowers Hill Trad. Cen. Bris —4A **82**
Flowers Ind. Est. Bris —4B **82**
Flowerwell Rd. Bris —3D **87**
Folleigh Dri. L Ash —3D **77**
Folleigh La. L Ash —3D **77**
Folliot Clo. Bris —4C **44**
Folly Bri. Clo. Yate —4F **17**
Follyfield. Brad A —5E **115**
Folly La. Bris —3C **70**
Folly La. W Mare —2C **138**
Folly Rd. Iron A —2B **14**
Folly, The. Bris —5B **46**
Folly, The. Salt —2B **94**
Fontana Clo. L Grn —2D **85**
Fonthill Rd. Bath —4F **99**
Fonthill Rd. Bris —2F **41**
Fonthill Way. Bit —3D **85**
Fontmell Ct. Bris —1F **89**
Fontwell Dri. Bris —3B **46**
Footes La. Fram C —2D **31**
Footshill Clo. Bris —4E **73**
Footshill Dri. Bris —3E **73**
Footshill Gdns. Bris —4E **73**
Footshill Rd. Bris —4E **73**
Forde Clo. Bar C —5B **74**
Fordell Pl. Bris —2C **80**
Ford Rd. Pea J —1F **149**
Ford St. Bris —4E **71**
Forefield Pl. Bath —4B **106**
Forefield Rise. Bath —5B **106**
Forefield Ter. Bath —4C **106**
Forest Av. Bris —4D **61**
Forest Dri. Bren —1E **41**
Forest Dri. W Mare —4E **127**
Forest Edge. Bris —1E **83**
Forester Av. Bath —1B **106**
Forester Ct. Bath —1B **106**
Forester La. Bath —1C **106**
Forester Rd. Bath —2C **106** (1E **97**)
Forester Rd. P'head —4F **49**
Forest Hills. Alm —1D **11**
Fore St. Trow —1D **119**
Forest Rd. Fish —4D **61**
Forest Rd. K'wd —3F **73**
Forest Wlk. Fish —4D **61**
Forest Wlk. K'wd —3E **73**
Forge End. P'bry —4A **52**
Fortescue Rd. Rads —2C **152**
Fortfield Rd. Bris —4C **88**
Forty Acre La. Alv —4B **8**
Forum Bldgs. Bath —4B **106** (off St James's Pde.)
Fosse Barton. Nail —3C **122**
Fosse Clo. Nail —3B **122**
Fossedale Av. Bris —2E **89**
Fossefield Rd. Mid N —5E **151**
Fosse Gdns. Bath —4E **109**
Fosse Grn. Rads —5B **148**
Fosse La. Bathe —2B **102**
Fosse La. Mid N —1F **151**
Fosse La. Nail —3B **122** (in two parts)
Fosseway. Clev —5C **120**
Fosseway. Mid N —5E **151**
Fosse Way. Nail —3B **122**
Fosseway Ct. Bris —3C **68**
Fosseway Gdns. Rads —3A **152**
Fosseway S. Mid N —5E **151**
Fosseway, The. Bris —3C **68**
Fossway. Clan —5B **148**
Foss Way. Mid N —3A **152**
Foster's Almshouses. Bris —3F **69** (2B **4**)
Foster St. Bris —5D **59**
Foundry La. Bris —5B **60**
Fountain Bldgs. Bath —2B **106** (2C **96**)
Fountain Ct. Brad S —3E **11**
Fountain Ct. Yate —2F **33** (off Abbotswood)
Fountaine Ct. Bris —5E **59**
Fountain Hill. Bris —1B **68**
Fountain La. Wins —5C **156**
Fountains Dri. Bar C —4B **74**
Four Acre Av. Bris —4A **46**
Fouracre Cres. Bris —3A **46**
Four Acre Rd. Bris —3A **46**
Four Acres. Bris —4A **86**
Four Acres Clo. Bris —4B **86**
Four Acres Clo. Nail —5D **123**
Fourth Av. Bris —3C **42**
Fourth Av. W'fld I —4A **152**
Fourth Way. Bris —3F **37**
Fowey Clo. Nail —4F **123**
Fowey Rd. W Mare —1E **129**
Fox Av. Yate —4F **17**
Foxborough Gdns. Brad S —4F **11**
Fox Clo. St Ap —5B **72**
Foxcombe Rd. Bath —2C **104**
Foxcombe Rd. Bris —4D **89**
Foxcote. Bris —3B **74**
Foxcote Rd. Bris —2C **78**
Fox Ct. L Grn —2B **84**
Foxcroft Clo. Brad S —2B **28**
Foxcroft Rd. Bris —2F **71**
Fox Den Rd. Stok G —1F **43**
Foxe Rd. Fram C —1C **30**
Foxfield Av. Brad S —4F **11**
Foxglove Clo. Stap —3A **60**
Foxglove Clo. T'bry —2E **7**
Fox Hill. Bath —3B **110**
Fox Hills Rd. Rads —3D **153**
Fox & Hounds La. Key —3B **92**
Fox Ho. Bris —2A **82**
Fox Rd. Bris —1D **71**
Fraley Rd. Bris —5C **40**
Frampton Ct. L Grn —1B **84**
Frampton Ct. Trow —4A **118**
Frampton Cres. Bris —3E **61**
Frampton End Rd. Fram C —1E **31**
Frampton End Rd. Yate —4F **15**
Frances Greeves Ct. Bris —3B **40**
Francis Fox Rd. W Mare —1C **132**
Francis Pl. L Grn —1B **84**
Francis Rd. Bedm —3E **79**
Francis Rd. W Trym —4E **41**
Francis St. Trow —1C **118**
Francombe Gro. Bris —1A **58**
Frankland Clo. Bath —5B **98**
Frankley Bldgs. Bath —5C **100**
Frankley Ter. Bath —5C **100** (off Snow Hill)
Franklin Ct. Bris —5A **70** (5E **5**)
Franklins Way. Clav —2F **143**
Franklyn La. Bris —1B **70**
Franklyn St. Bris —1B **70**
Fraser Clo. W Mare —1D **129**
Fraser St. Bris —2F **79**
Frayne Rd. Bris —1C **78**
Frederick Av. Pea J —2F **149**
Frederick Pl. Bris —3D **69**
Frederick St. Bris —1C **80**
Freeland Bldgs. Bris —5E **59**
Freeland Pl. Bris —4B **68**
Freelands. Clev —5C **120**
Freeling Ho. Bris —5A **70**
Freemantle Gdns. Eastv —4E **59**
Freemantle Rd. Bris —4E **59**
Freestone Rd. Bris —4C **70**
Free Tank. Bris —4B **70**
Freeview Rd. Bath —3B **104**
Fremantle La. Bris —1F **69**
Fremantle Rd. Bris —1F **69**
Fremantle Sq. Bris —1F **69**
Frenchay Clo. Bris —5D **45**
Frenchay Comn. Bris —5D **45**
Frenchay Hill. Bris —5E **45**
Frenchay Pk. Rd. Bris —1A **60**
Frenchay Rd. Bris —5E **45**
Frenchay Rd. W Mare —4C **132**
French Clo. Nail —2E **123**
French Clo. Pea J —5D **157**
Frenchfield Rd. Pea J —5D **157**
Freshfield Way. Bris —2D **73**
Freshford Ho. Bris —5A **70** (5D **5**)
Freshford La. F'frd —5B **112**
Freshland Way. Bris —2D **73**
Freshmoor. Clev —3F **121**
Friar Av. W Mare —2C **128**

Friars. *Bris* —3A **70**
Friars Ho. *Yate* —2F **33**
Friary Clo. *Clev* —1C **120**
Friary Clo. *Up W* —5F **113**
Friary Grange Pk. *Wint* —3A **30**
Friary Rd. *Bris* —3F **57**
Friary Rd. *P'head* —3D **49**
Friendly Row. *Pill* —2E **53**
Friendship Gro. *Nail* —3E **123**
Friendship Rd. *Bris* —3B **80**
Friendship Rd. *Nail* —2E **123**
Friezewood Rd. *Bris* —1C **78**
Fripp Clo. *Bris* —4D **71**
Frobisher Av. *P'head* —3C **48**
Frobisher Clo. *P'head* —3C **48**
Frobisher Clo. *W Mare* —1C **128**
Frobisher Rd. *Bris* —2C **78**
Frog La. *Bris* —4E **69** (3A **4**)
Frog La. *Coal H* —1A **32**
Frogmore St. *Bris* —4E **69** (3A **4**)
Frome Bank Gdns. *Wint D* —1A **46**
Frome Ct. *T'bry* —4D **7**
Frome Glen. *Wint D* —5A **30**
Frome Old Rd. *Rads* —2D **153**
Frome Pl. *Bris* —1A **60**
Frome Rd. *Bath* —2D **109**
Frome Rd. *Brad A* —5D **115**
Frome Rd. *Chip S* —5E **19**
Frome Rd. *Trow* —5A **118**
Frome Rd. *Writ* —2C **152**
Fromeside Pk. *Bris* —5D **45**
Frome St. *Bris* —2B **70**
Frome Valley Rd. *Bris* —1B **60**
Frome View. *Fram C* —2D **31**
Frome Vs. *Bris* —5E **45**
Frome Way. *Wint* —4A **30**
Froomshaw Rd. *Bris* —5C **44**
Frost Hill. *Yat* —4D **143**
Fry Ct. *Bris* —1E **79**
Fry's Clo. *Bris* —3F **59**
Fry's Hill. *Brisl* —3F **81**
Fry's Hill. *Bris* —1A **74**
Frys Leaze. *Bath* —4C **100**
Fryth Way. *Nail* —3B **122**
Fulford Rd. *Bris* —3D **87**
Fulford Rd. *Trow* —5E **117**
Fulford Wlk. *Bris* —3D **87**
Fullens Clo. *W Mare* —1B **134**
Fuller Rd. *Bath* —4D **101**
Fullers La. *Wins* —5B **156**
Fullers Way. *Bath* —4E **109**
Fulmar Clo. *T'bry* —2E **7**
Fulmar Rd. *W Mare* —4D **129**
Fulney Clo. *Trow* —5F **117**
Funchal Vs. *Bris* —3C **68**
Furber Ct. *Bris* —4D **73**
Furber Ridge. *Bris* —4D **73**
Furber Rd. *Bris* —3D **73**
Furber Vale. *Bris* —4D **73**
Furland Rd. *W Mare* —3A **128**
Furlong Clo. *Mid N* —5C **150**
Furlong Gdns. *Trow* —1E **119**
Furlong, The. *Bris* —2F **57**
Furnwood. *Bris* —4C **72**
Furze Clo. *W Mare* —3F **127**
Furze Rd. *Bris* —4E **61**
Furze Rd. *W Mare* —3E **127**
Furzewood Rd. *Bris* —2B **74**
Fussell Ct. *Bris* —2B **74**
Fylton Croft. *Bris* —5D **89**

Gable Rd. *Bris* —1C **70**
Gables Clo. *Ban* —5F **137**
Gadshill Dri. *Stok G* —4A **28**
Gadshill Rd. *Bris* —4E **59**
Gages Clo. *Bris* —3B **74**
Gages Rd. *Bris* —3A **74**
Gainsborough Dri. *W Mare* —2D **129**
Gainsborough Gdns. *Bath* —1D **105**
Gainsborough Rise. *Trow* —4A **118**
Gainsborough Rd. *Key* —3B **92**
Gainsborough Sq. *Bris* —5D **43**
Galleries Shopping Cen. *Bris* —3A **70** (1D **5**)
Gallivan Clo. *Lit S* —1D **27**
Galway Rd. *Bris* —4A **80**
Gander Clo. *Bris* —3D **87**
Gannet Rd. *W Mare* —4D **129**
Garamond Ct. *Redc* —5A **70**
Garden Clo. *Bris* —2E **55**
Garden Clo. *W Mare* —3C **128**
Garden Ct. *Bris* —2C **68**
Gardeners Wlk. *L Ash* —4D **77**
Gardens Rd. *Clev* —2C **120**
Garden Walls. *Wickw* —2C **154**
Gardner Av. *Bris* —1B **86**
Gardner Rd. *P'head* —2F **49**
Garfield Rd. *Bris* —2C **72**
Garfield Ter. *Bath* —4D **101**
Garner Ct. *W Mare* —1F **129**
Garnet St. *Bris* —2D **79**
Garnett Pl. *Bris* —5B **46**
Garoner Way. *P'bry* —2B **52**
Garre Ho. *Bath* —4A **104**
Garrett Dri. *Brad S* —2F **27**
Garrick Rd. *Bath* —4A **104**
Garsdale Rd. *W Mare* —5B **128**
Garside St. *Paul* —5C **146**
Garstons. *Bathf* —4E **103**
Garstons. *Clev* —5B **120**
Garstons. *Wrin* —2C **156**
Garstons Clo. *Wrin* —1C **156**
Garstons Orchard. *Wrin* —2B **156**
Garstons, The. *P'head* —4F **49**
Garth Rd. *Bris* —5C **78**
Gasferry Rd. *Bris* —5D **69**
(in two parts)
Gaskins, The. *Bris* —2C **58**
Gas La. *Bris* —4C **70**
Gaston Av. *Key* —2B **92**
Gastons, The. *Bris* —4C **38**
Gatcombe Dri. *Stok G* —5A **28**
Gatcombe Rd. *Bris* —3D **87**
Gatehouse Av. *Bris* —3C **86**
Gatehouse Clo. *Bris* —3C **86**
Gatehouse Ct. *Bris* —3C **86**
Gatehouse Way. *Bris* —3C **86**
Gatesby Mead. *Stok G* —4A **28**
Gathorne Cres. *Yate* —4F **17**
Gathorne Rd. *Bris* —1D **79**
Gatton Rd. *Bris* —1C **70**
Gaunts Clo. *P'head* —4B **48**
Gaunt's Earthcott La. *Alm* —1D **13**
Gaunts La. *Bris* —4E **69** (3A **4**)
Gaunts Rd. *Chip S* —1D **35**
Gay Ct. *Bath* —3F **101**
Gay Elms Rd. *Bris* —4C **86**
Gayner Rd. *Bris* —3C **42**
Gay's Hill. *Bath* —1B **106**
Gay's Rd. *Bris* —1D **83**
Gay St. *Bath* —2A **106** (2A **96**)
Gaywood Ho. *Bris* —2D **79**
Gazelle Rd. *W Mare* —5F **133**
Gazzard Clo. *Wint* —2A **30**
Gazzard Rd. *Wint* —2A **30**
Gee Moors. *Bris* —3B **74**
Gefle Clo. *Bris* —5D **69**
Geldof Dri. *Mid N* —2D **151**
Geoffrey Clo. *Bris* —2A **86**
George Clo. *Back* —1F **125**
George & Dragon La. *Bris* —3F **71**
George's Bldgs. *Bath* —1B **106**
George's Pl. *Bath* —3C **106**
George's Rd. *Bath* —5B **100**
George St. *Bath* —2A **106** (2B **96**)
George St. *Bathw* —3C **106** (3F **97**)
George St. *Bris* —2E **71**
George St. *P'head* —5E **49**
George St. *Trow* —1D **119**
George St. *W Mare* —1C **132**
George Whitefield Ct. *Bris* —3A **70** (1E **5**)
Georgian View. *Bath* —1D **109**
Gerald Rd. *Bris* —2C **78**
Gerard Rd. *W Mare* —5C **126**
Gerrard Bldgs. *Bath* —2C **106** (2E **97**)
Gerrish Av. *Stap H* —2B **62**
Gerrish Av. *W'hall* —2E **71**
Gibbsfold Rd. *Bris* —5E **87**
Gibson Rd. *Bris* —1F **69**
Giffard Ho. *Lit S* —3F **27**
Gifford Cres. *Lit S* —3E **27**
Gifford Rd. *Bris* —5B **24**
Gilbeck Rd. *Nail* —3B **122**
Gilbert Rd. *K'wd* —1F **73**
Gilbert Rd. *Redf* —2E **71**
Gilberyn Dri. *W Mare* —2F **129**
Gilda Clo. *Bris* —3E **89**
Gilda Cres. *Bris* —2D **89**
Gilda Pde. *Bris* —3E **89**
Gilda Sq. E. *Bris* —3D **89**
Gilda Sq. W. *Bris* —3D **89**
Gillard Clo. *K'wd* —2D **73**
Gillard Rd. *Bris* —2D **73**
Gill Av. *Bris* —2D **61**
Gillebank Clo. *Bris* —3F **89**
Gillingham Hill. *Bris* —5D **73**
Gillingham Ter. *Bath* —5C **100**
Gillingstool. *T'bry* —4D **7**
Gillmews. *W Mare* —1F **129**
Gillmore Clo. *W Mare* —4B **128**
Gillmore Rd. *W Mare* —4B **128**
Gillson Clo. *Hut* —1B **140**
Gilpin Clo. *K'wd* —5B **62**
Gilray Clo. *Bris* —1D **59**
Gilroy Clo. *L Grn* —2D **85**
Gilslake Av. *Bris* —1D **41**
Gilton Ho. *Bris* —3A **82**
Gimblett Rd. *W Mare* —1F **129**
Gingell Clo. *Bris* —4B **74**
Gingell's Grn. *Bris* —2C **72**
Gipsies Plat. *Brad S* —4B **20**
Gipsy La. *Trow* —1F **155**
Gipsy Patch La. *Lit S* —3D **27**
Glades, The. *Bris* —5A **60**
Gladstone Dri. *Bris* —4A **62**
Gladstone La. *Fram C* —2E **31**
Gladstone Pl. *C Down* —2D **111**
Gladstone Rd. *Bath* —2D **111**
Gladstone Rd. *Bris* —2D **89**
Gladstone Rd. *K'wd* —1F **73**
Gladstone Rd. *Trow* —3B **118**
Gladstone St. *Bedm* —2D **79**
Gladstone St. *Mid N* —1E **151**
Gladstone St. *Redf* —3F **71**
Gladstone St. *Stap H* —4F **61**
Glaisdale Rd. *Bris* —2C **60**
Glanville Gdns. *Bris* —3A **74**
Glass Ho. La. *Bris* —5D **71**
Glastonbury Clo. *L Grn* —5B **74**
Glastonbury Clo. *Nail* —4F **123**
Glastonbury Way. *W Mare* —3E **129**
Glebe Av. *P'head* —4A **50**
Glebe Clo. *L Ash* —3E **77**
Glebe Field. *Alm* —1C **10**
Glebelands. *Rads* —3A **152**
Glebelands Rd. *Bris* —1C **42**
Glebe Rd. *Bath* —5C **104**
Glebe Rd. *Bris* —2A **72**
Glebe Rd. *Clev* —4C **120**
Glebe Rd. *L Ash* —4E **77**
Glebe Rd. *P'head* —4A **50**
Glebe Rd. *Trow* —3A **118**
Glebe Rd. *W Mare* —5C **126**
Glebe, The. *F'frd* —5C **112**
Glebe, The. *Tim* —1E **157**
Glebe, The. *Wrin* —1B **156**
Glebe Wlk. *Key* —4E **91**
Gledemoor Dri. *Coal H* —2F **31**
Gleeson Ho. *Bris* —1D **61**
Glena Av. *Bris* —3D **81**
Glenarm Rd. *Bris* —3A **82**
Glenarm Wlk. *Bris* —3A **82**
Glen Av. *Abb L* —2B **66**
Glenavon Ct. *Bris* —3E **55**
Glenavon Pk. *Bris* —3E **55**
Glenburn Rd. *Bris* —1D **73**
Glencairn Ct. *Bath* —3C **106** (3E **97**)
Glencoyne Sq. *Bris* —2E **41**
Glendale. *Clif* —4B **68**
Glendale. *Down* —4A **46**
Glendale. *Fish* —4E **61**
Glendare St. *Bris* —4E **71**
Glendevon Rd. *Bris* —5C **88**
Glen Dri. *Bris* —2F **55**
Gleneagles. *Yate* —5A **18**
Gleneagles Clo. *Nail* —4F **123**
Gleneagles Clo. *W Mare* —2D **129**
Gleneagles Dri. *Bris* —1F **39**
Gleneagles Rd. *War* —4D **75**
Glenfall. *Yate* —2F **33**
Glenfrome Ho. *Eastv* —5D **59**
Glenfrome Rd. *St W & Eastv* —5C **58**
Glen La. *Bris* —3F **81**
Glen Pk. *Eastv* —5E **59**
Glen Pk. *St G* —2C **72**
Glen Pk. Gdns. *Bris* —2C **72**
Glenroy Av. *Bris* —1D **73**
Glenside Clo. *Bris* —5E **45**
Glenside Pk. *Bris* —2A **60**
Glen, The. *Han* —1D **83**
Glen, The. *Redl* —4D **57**
Glen, The. *Salt* —3B **94**
Glen, The. *W Mare* —3F **127**
Glen, The. *Yate* —4A **18**
Glentworth Rd. *Clif* —4D **69**
Glentworth Rd. *Redl* —5E **57**
Glenview Rd. *Bris* —3F **81**
Glenwood. *Bris* —4E **61**
Glenwood Dri. *Old C* —1D **85**
Glenwood Rise. *P'head* —3B **48**
Glenwood Rd. *Bris* —5E **41**
Glen Yeo Ter. *Cong* —2C **144**
Gloster Av. *Bris* —4F **59**
Gloucester Clo. *Stok G* —4F **27**
Gloucester La. *Bris* —3B **70**
Gloucester Mans. *Bris* —5F **57**
Gloucester Pl. *Bris* —3F **69** (1B **4**)
Gloucester Rd. *Alm* —1D **11**
Gloucester Rd. *A'mth* —3C **36**
Gloucester Rd. *Bishop & Hor* —5F **57**
Gloucester Rd. *Pat* —1D **27**
Gloucester Rd. *Rudg* —5A **8**
Gloucester Rd. *Stap H* —4A **62**
Gloucester Rd. *Swain* —1D **101**
Gloucester Rd. *T'bry* —3C **6**
Gloucester Rd. *Trow* —3B **118**
Gloucester Rd. *Wint* —2D **29**
Gloucester Rd. N. *Bris & Fil* —3B **42**
Gloucester Row. *Bris* —3B **68**
Gloucester St. *Bath* —2A **106** (1A **96**)
Gloucester St. *Clif* —3B **68**
Gloucester St. *Eastv* —4F **59**
Gloucester St. *St Pa* —2A **70**
Gloucester St. *W Mare* —1B **132**
Gloucester Ter. *T'bry* —3C **6**
Glyn Vale. *Bris* —4F **79**
Goddard Dri. *W Mare* —1F **129**
Godfrey Ct. *L Grn* —1B **84**
Goding La. *Ban* —5F **137**
Godwin Dri. *Nail* —2B **122**
Goffenton Dri. *Bris* —1D **61**
Goldcrest Rd. *Chip S* —2B **34**
Golden Hill. *Bris* —2F **57**
Goldfinch Way. *Puck* —3E **65**
Goldney Av. *Clif* —4C **68**
Goldney Av. *War* —3E **75**
Goldney La. *Bris* —4C **68**
Goldney Rd. *Bris* —4C **68**
Goldsbury Wlk. *Bris* —3C **38**
Goldsmiths Ho. *Bris* —4B **70** (3F **5**)
Golf Club La. *Salt* —2A **94**
Golf Course La. *Bris* —1B **42**
Golf Course Rd. *Bath* —3D **107**
Gooch Ct. *Old C* —2E **85**
Gooch Way. *W Mare* —2F **129**
Goodeve Pk. *Bris* —4F **55**
(in two parts)
Goodeve Rd. *Bris* —4F **55**
Goodhind St. *Bris* —2C **70**
Goodneston Rd. *Bris* —4C **60**
Goodring Hill. *Bris* —3C **38**
Good Shepherd Clo. *Bris* —3E **57**
Goodwin Dri. *Bris* —4B **88**
Goodwood Clo. *Whit B* —3F **155**
Goodwood Gdns. *Bris* —3B **46**
Goold Clo. *Cor* —4C **94**
Goolden St. *Bris* —2C **80**
Goosard La. *High L* —1A **146**
Goose Acre. *Stok G* —3B **28**
Gooseberry La. *Key* —3B **92**
Goose Grn. *Bris* —1E **75**
Goosegreen. *Fram C* —1E **31**
Goose Grn. *Yate* —2A **18**
Goose Grn. Way. *Yate* —3C **16**
Gooseland Clo. *Bris* —5B **88**
Goosey La. *St Geo* —3A **130**
Gordano Gdns. *E'ton G* —3D **53**
Gordano Rd. *P'bry* —1F **51**
Gordano View. *P'head* —3E **49**
Gordon Av. *Bris* —1F **71**
Gordon Clo. *Bris* —1A **72**
Gordon Rd. *Bath* —4C **106**
Gordon Rd. *Clif* —3D **69**
Gordon Rd. *Pea J* —4D **157**
Gordon Rd. *St Pa* —1B **70**
Gordon Rd. *W'hall* —1F **71**
Gordon Rd. *W Mare* —1D **133**
Gore Rd. *Bris* —2C **78**
Gore's Marsh Rd. *Bris* —3C **78**
Gorham Clo. *Bris* —2E **39**
Gorlands Rd. *Chip S* —5E **19**
Gorlangton Clo. *Bris* —1C **88**
Gorse Cover Rd. *Sev B* —3B **20**
Gorse Hill. *Bris* —4D **61**
Gorse La. *Bris* —4D **69**
Gosforth Rd. *Bris* —2D **41**
Goslet Rd. *Bris* —3A **90**
Goss Barton. *Nail* —4C **122**
Goss Clo. *Nail* —4B **122**
Goss La. *Nail* —4B **122**
Goss View. *Nail* —4B **122**
Gotley Rd. *Bris* —3F **81**
Gott Dri. *Bris* —4F **71**
Goulston Rd. *Bris* —3C **86**
Goulston Wlk. *Bris* —2C **86**
Goulter St. *Bris* —4D **71**
Gourney Clo. *Bris* —2D **39**
Gover Rd. *Han* —2E **83**
Goy Rd. *Pat* —2C **26**
Grace Clo. *Chip S* —5E **19**
Grace Clo. *Yat* —3B **142**
Grace Ct. *Bris* —1F **61**
Grace Dri. *Bris* —1C **74**
Grace Dri. *Mid N* —2D **151**
Grace Pk. Rd. *Bris* —4F **81**
Grace Rd. *Bris* —2E **61**
Grace Rd. *W Mare* —1F **129**
Gradwell Clo. *W Mare* —2F **129**
Graeme Clo. *Bris* —3C **60**
Graham Rd. *Bedm* —2E **79**
Graham Rd. *Down* —1B **62**
Graham Rd. *E'tn* —1D **71**
Graham Rd. *W Mare* —1C **132**
Grainger Ct. *Bris* —5A **38**
Grampian Clo. *Old C* —1E **85**
Granby Ct. *Bris* —4B **68**
Granby Hill. *Bris* —4B **68**
Grand Pde. *Bath* —3B **106** (3C **96**)
Grange Av. *Bris* —5E **73**
Grange Av. *Lit S* —3E **27**
Grange Clo. *Brad S* —4E **11**
Grange Clo. *Uph* —2C **138**
Grange Clo. N. *Bris* —1D **57**
Grange Ct. *Bris* —1D **57**
Grange Ct. *Han* —5F **73**
Grange Ct. Rd. *Bris* —1C **56**
Grange Dri. *Bris* —1E **61**
Grange End. *Mid N* —5E **151**
Grange Pk. *Fren* —4E **45**
Grange Pk. *W Trym* —1D **57**
Grange Rd. *B'wth* —3C **86**
Grange Rd. *Clif* —3C **68**
Grange Rd. *Salt* —5E **93**
Grange Rd. *Uph* —2C **138**
Grange View. *Brad A* —2F **115**
Grangeville Clo. *L Grn* —2D **85**
Grangewood Clo. *Bris* —1E **61**
Granny's La. *Bris* —4A **74**
Grantham La. *Bris* —2E **73**
Grantham Rd. *Bris* —2E **73**
Grantson Clo. *Bris* —3A **82**
Granville Clo. *Bris* —2D **83**
Granville Rd. *Bath* —3F **99**
Granville St. *Bris* —4E **71**
Grasmere. *Trow* —5E **117**
Grasmere Clo. *Bris* —4C **40**
Grasmere Dri. *W Mare* —4D **133**
Grasmere Gdns. *Bris* —4F **75**
Grassington Dri. *Chip S* —1C **34**
Grass Meers Dri. *Bris* —4C **88**
Grassmere Rd. *Yat* —3B **142**
Gratitude Rd. *Bris* —1E **71**
Gravel Hill Rd. *Yate* —3A **18**
(in two parts)
Gravel, The. *Holt* —1E **155**
Gravel Wlk. *Bath* —2F **105**
Graveney Clo. *Bris* —4F **81**
Gray Clo. *Bris* —2A **40**
Grayle Rd. *Bris* —2C **40**

Gt. Ann St. Bris —3B 70
Gt. Bedford St. Bath —1A 106
Gt. Brockeridge. Bris —1B 56
Gt. Dowles. Bris —1C 84
Gt. George St. Bris —4E 69
Gt. George St. St Jud —3B 70 (1F 5)
Gt. Hayles Rd. Bris —1B 88
Gt. Leaze. Bris —1C 84
Gt. Meadow Rd. Brad S —3B 28
Gt. Orchard. Brad A —5A 114
Gt. Park Rd. Alm —3E 11
Great Parks. Holt —1F 155
Gt. Pulteney St. Bath —2B 106 (2D 97)
Gt. Stanhope St. Bath —3F 105
Gt. Stoke Way. Brad S —2F 43
Gt. Western Bus. Pk. Yate —3E 17
Gt. Western La. Bris —4E 71
Gt. Western Rd. Clev —3D 121
Gt. Western Way. Bris —4B 70 (4F 5)
Greenacre. W Mare —2F 127
Greenacre Rd. Bris —5C 88
Greenacres. Bath —3C 98
Greenacres. Bris —5A 40
Greenacres. E Grn —5D 47
Greenacres. Mid N —3B 150
Greenacres Cvn. Site. Coal H —5F 31
Greenbank Av. E. Bris —1E 71
Greenbank Av. W. Bris —1D 71
Greenbank Gdns. Bath —5C 98
Greenbank Rd. G'bnk —5E 59
Greenbank Rd. Han —1F 83
Greenbank Rd. S'vle —5C 68
Greenbank View. Bris —5E 59
Green Clo. Bris —4C 42
Green Clo. Holt —2F 155
Green Cotts. Bath —3D 111
Green Croft. Bris —1C 72
Greendale Rd. Bedm —2A 80
Greendale Rd. Redl —3D 57
Green Dell Clo. Bris —1F 39
Greenditch Av. Bris —3E 87
Greendown. Bris —3C 72
Green Down Pl. Bath —3B 110
Green Dragon Rd. Wint —4F 29
Greenfield Av. Bris —4F 41
Greenfield Cres. Nail —2D 123
Greenfield Pk. P'head —5E 49
Greenfield Pl. W Mare —5A 126
Greenfield Rd. Bris —3F 41
Greenfields Av. Ban —5E 137
Greenfinch Lodge. Bris —1A 60
Greengage Clo. W Mare —5C 128
Green Hayes. Chip S —1E 35
Greenhill Clo. Nail —3C 122
Greenhill Clo. W Mare —2E 129
Greenhill Down. Alv —3B 8
Greenhill Gdns. Alv —3B 8
Greenhill Gdns. Hil —3F 117
Greenhill Gro. Bris —3C 78
Greenhill La. Alv —4A 8
Greenhill La. Bris —3E 39
Greenhill Pde. Alv —2B 8
Greenhill Pl. Mid N —1D 151
Greenhill Rd. Alv —2B 8
Greenhill Rd. Mid N —1D 151
Greenland Mills. Brad A —3F 115
Greenland Rd. W Mare —4B 128
Greenlands Rd. Bris —5A 24
Greenlands Rd. Pea J —1F 149
Greenlands Way. Bris —5A 24
Greenland View. Brad A —3E 115
Green La. Bris —4D 37
Green La. Sev B —3B 20
Green La. Trow —2E 119
Green La. Wint —3E 29
Greenleaze. Bris —4D 81
Greenleaze Av. Bris —3F 45
Greenleaze Clo. Bris —3F 45
Greenmore Rd. Bris —3D 81
Greenore. Bris —3E 73
Green Pk. Ho. Bath —3A 106
Green Pk. M. Bath —3F 105 (off Green Pk.)
Green Pk. Rd. Bath —3A 106 (4A 96)
Greenpark Rd. Bris —3A 42
Green Pk. Station. Bath —3F 105
Green Parlour Rd. Rads —3F 153
Greenplott Rd. Brad S —2A 22
Greenridge Clo. Bris —4A 86
Greens Hill. Bris —4A 60
Green Side. Mang —1C 62
Greenside Clo. Bris —1F 39
Greenslade Gdns. Nail —2C 122
Greensplott Rd. Chit —2A 22
Green St. Bath —2A 106 (3B 96)
Green St. Bris —1B 80
Green Ter. Trow —5C 116
Green, The. Back —3B 124
Green, The. Lock —4E 135
Green, The. New C —5A 62
Green, The. Pill —3A 54
Green, The. Shire —1A 54
Green, The. Stok G —5A 28
Green, The. Wick —5A 154
Green, The. Wins —4A 156
Green Tree Rd. Mid N —1E 151
Greenvale Clo. Tim —2E 157
Greenvale Dri. Tim —2E 157
Greenvale Rd. Paul —4A 146
Greenview. L Grn —3C 84
Green Wlk. Bris —4C 80
Greenway Bush La. Bris —1C 78
Greenway Ct. Bath —5A 106
Greenway Dri. Bris —3F 41
Greenway Gdns. Trow —4E 117
Greenway La. Bath —1A 110
Greenway Pk. Bris —4F 41
Greenway Pk. Clev —3F 121
Greenway Rd. Bris —5D 57
Greenways. Bris —1C 74
Greenways Rd. Yate —3F 17
Greenway, The. Bris —4E 61
Greenwood Clo. Bris —5A 42
Greenwood Dri. Alv —3A 8
Greenwood Rd. Bris —3C 80
Greenwood Rd. W Mare —3C 128
Gregory Ct. Bris —4C 74
Gregory Mead. Yat —2A 142
Gregorys Gro. Bath —4E 109
Gregory's Tyning. Paul —3B 146
Greinton. W Mare —1E 139
Grenville Av. Lock —4E 135
Grenville Clo. Bris —2B 72
Grenville Rd. Bris —4A 58
Greve Ct. Bar C —1B 84
Greville Rd. Bris —1D 79
Greville St. Bris —1E 79
Greyfriars. Bris —3F 69 (1B 4)
Greylands Rd. Bris —1B 86
Greystoke. Bris —3C 40
Greystoke Av. Bris —4C 40
Greystoke Gdns. Bris —4C 40
Greystones. Bris —3A 46
Griffin Clo. W Mare —3F 129
Griffin Rd. Clev —3D 121
Griggfield Wlk. Bris —1B 88
Grimsbury Rd. Bris —2C 74
Grindell Rd. Bris —3F 71
Grinfield Av. Bris —4E 87
Grinfield Ct. Bris —4E 87
Grittleton Rd. Bris —4A 42
Grosvenor Bri. Rd. Bath —5D 101
Grosvenor Pk. Bath —5D 101
Grosvenor Pl. Bath —5D 101
Grosvenor Rd. Bris —1B 70
Grosvenor Ter. Bath —4D 101
Grosvenor Vs. Bath —5C 100
Ground Corner. Holt —2D 155
Grove Av. Bris —5F 69 (5C 4)
Grove Av. Fish —3B 60
Grove Av. W Trym —5E 39
Grove Bank. Bris —3E 45
Grove Ct. Trow —4C 118
Grove Dri. Mil —4A 128
Grove La. W Mare —5B 126
Grove Leaze. Brad A —3C 114
Grove Leaze. Shire —1E 53
Grove Pk. Brisl —3F 81
Grove Pk. Redl —5E 57
Grove Pk. W Mare —5B 126
Grove Pk. Av. Bris —3F 81
Grove Pk. Rd. Bris —3F 81
Grove Pk. Rd. W Mare —4B 126
Grove Pk. Ter. Bris —3B 60
Grove Rd. Ban —4C 136
Grove Rd. C Din —4E 39
Grove Rd. Fish —3B 60
Grove Rd. Mil —4A 128
Grove Rd. Redl —5C 56
Grove Rd. W Mare —5B 126
Grovesend Rd. T'bry —3C 6 (in two parts)
Groves, The. Bris —4F 87
Grove St. Bath —2B 106 (2C 96)
Grove, The. Bath —5D 99
Grove, The. Bris —5F 69 (5B 4)
Grove, The. Clev —5B 120
Grove, The. Pat —1D 27
Grove, The. War —1C 84
Grove, The. Wins —3A 156
Grove View. Bris —1A 60
Grove Wood Rd. Hay —4B 152
Guernsey Av. Bris —1B 82
Guest Av. E Grn —4D 47
Guild Ct. Bris —4A 70 (5D 5)
Guildford Rd. Bris —5A 72
Guinea La. Bath —2A 106 (1B 96)
Guinea La. Bris —2C 60 (in two parts)
Guinea St. Bris —5F 69
Gulliford's Bank. Clev —4E 121
Gullimore Gdns. Bris —4D 87
Gullivers Pl. Chip S —1C 34
Gullock Tyning. Mid N —3E 151
Gullons Clo. Bris —2C 86
Gullon Wlk. Bris —3B 86
Gullybrook La. Bris —4D 71
Gully, The. Wint —2B 30
Gunnings Clo. K'wd —4F 73
Gunter's Hill. Bris —4C 72
Guthrie Rd. Bris —2B 68
Gwilliam St. Bris —2F 79
Gwyn St. Bris —1A 70
Gypsy La. Coal H —2F 47

Haberfield Hill. Pill —5F 53
Haberfield Ho. Bris —4B 68
Hacket La. T'bry —3E 7 (in two parts)
Haden Rd. Trow —3D 119
Hadley Ct. Bris —4D 75
Hadley Rd. Bath —2C 110
Hadrian Clo. Bris —3E 55
Ha Ha, The. Tim —1D 157
Haig Clo. Bris —5D 39
Halbrow Cres. Bris —2E 61
Haldon Clo. Bris —4F 79
Hale Clo. Han —1F 83
Hales Horn Clo. Lit S —3F 27
Halfacre Clo. Bris —5C 88
Halfacre La. Bris —4D 89
Halfway Clo. Trow —5F 117
Halfway La. Trow —1E 119
Halifax Rd. Yate —2F 17
Hallam Rd. Clev —2C 120
Hallards Clo. Bris —4B 38
Hallatrow Rd. Paul —3A 146
Hallen Clo. Bris —1F 39
Hallen Dri. Bris —5E 39
Hallen Rd. H'len —5E 23
Hallets Way. P'head —4F 49
Halliwell Rd. P'head —4A 48
Halls Rd. Bris —2F 73
Hall St. Bris —3D 79
Halsbury Rd. Bris —2F 69
Halsbury Rd. W'bry P —3D 57
Halstock Av. Bris —4B 60
Halston Dri. Bris —2B 70
Halswell Gdns. Bris —4D 87
Halswell Rd. Clev —5D 121
Halt End. Bris —5E 89
Halve, The. Trow —1D 119
Halwyn Clo. Bris —2F 55
Hamble Clo. T'bry —4D 7
Hambledon Rd. W Mare —1A 130
Hambrook La. Stok G & Ham —1B 44
Ham Clo. Holt —2D 155
Ham Grn. Pill —3F 53
Ham Gro. Paul —4B 146
Hamilton Ho. Bath —3F 99
Hamilton Rd. Bath —4F 99
Hamilton Rd. E'tn —2D 71
Hamilton Rd. S'vle —1D 79
Hamilton Rd. W Mare —4A 126
Ham La. Bris —1A 60
Ham La. Dun —5A 86
Ham La. Nail —1F 123
Ham La. Paul —4B 146
Hamlet, The. Nail —2F 123
Hammersmith Rd. Bris —2F 71
Hammond Clo. Bris —4F 81
Hammond Gdns. Bris —5A 40
Hammond Way. Trow —3D 117
Hampden Clo. Yate —2F 17
Hampden Rd. Bris —2D 81
Hampden Rd. W Mare —3C 128
Hampshire Way. Yate —2B 18
Hampstead Rd. Bris —2E 81
Hampton Clo. Bris —5C 74
Hampton Corner. Shire —1A 54
Hampton Ho. Bath —5D 101
Hampton La. Bris —1D 69
Hampton Pk. Bris —1D 69
Hampton Rd. Bris —5D 57
Hampton Row. Bath —1C 106
Hampton St. Bris —1F 73
Hampton View. Bath —5C 100
Ham Ter. Trow —2D 155
Hamwood Clo. W Mare —1F 139
Hanbury Clo. Bris —5F 73
Hanbury Rd. Bris —2C 68
Handel Av. Bris —2F 71
Handel Rd. Key —3F 91
Handford Way. L Grn —2D 85
Hanford Ct. Bris —1E 89
Hang Hill. Bath —5E 157
Hangstone Wlk. Clev —3C 120
Hanham Bus. Pk. Han —5D 73
Hanham La. Paul —2C 146
Hanham Mt. Bris —4F 73
Hanham Rd. K'wd —4F 73
Hanham Way. Nail —3A 122
Hanna Clo. Bath —3B 104
Hannah More Clo. Wrin —1C 156
Hannah More Rd. Nail —4B 122
Hanover Clo. Trow —3E 117
Hanover Clo. W Mare —1E 129
Hanover Ct. Bath —4C 100
Hanover Ct. Bris —3A 70 (1E 5)
Hanover Ct. Fil —1C 42
Hanover Ct. Rads —2F 153
Hanover Ho. Bris —3C 70
Hanover Pl. Bath —5C 100 (off London Rd.)
Hanover Pl. Bris —5D 69
Hanover St. Bar H —3E 71
Hanover St. Bath —5C 100
Hanover St. Bris —4F 69 (3B 4)
Hanover Ter. Bath —5C 100 (off Gillingham Ter.)
Hansford Clo. Bath —3F 109
Hansford Sq. Bath —3F 109
Hansons Way. Clev —4C 120
Hans Price Clo. W Mare —5C 126
Hantone Hill. B'ptn —5A 102
Happerton La. E'ton G —5D 53
Hapsburg Clo. W Mare —1E 129
Harbour Rd. P'head —2F 49
Harbour Rd. Trad. Est. P'head —2A 50
Harbour Wall. Bris —3D 55
Harbour Way. Bris —5E 69
Harbury Rd. Bris —5E 41
Harbutts. B'ptn —5A 102
Harcombe Hill. Wint D —5A 30
Harcombe Rd. Wint —4F 29
Harcourt Av. Bris —4C 72
Harcourt Clo. Salt —2A 94
Harcourt Gdns. Bath —4C 98
Harcourt Hill. Bris —4E 57
Harcourt Rd. Bris —3D 57
Hardenhuish Rd. Bris —5F 71
Harden Rd. Bris —3A 90
Harding Pl. Key —3D 93
Hardings Ter. Bris —2B 72
Hardington Dri. Key —5A 92
Hardwick. Yate —2E 33
Hardwick Clo. Brisl —2A 82
Hardwick Clo. War —5F 75
Hardwick Rd. Pill —2E 53
Hardy Av. Bris —1C 78
Hardy Ct. Bar C —5B 74
Hardy Rd. Bris —3D 79
Hareclive Rd. Bris —3D 87
Harefield Clo. Bris —3E 83
Hare Knapp. Brad A —3C 114
Harescombe. Yate —2A 34
Harewood Rd. Bris —1C 72
Harford Clo. Bris —5E 39
Harford Dri. Bris —3E 45
Harford St. Trow —1E 119
Hargreaves Rd. Trow —3E 119
Harington Pl. Bath —3A 106 (3B 96)
Harlech Way. Will —3D 85
Harleston St. Bris —2C 70
Harley Pl. Bris —3B 68
Harley St. Bath —1A 106
Harmer Clo. Bris —1B 40
Harmony Dri. P'head —4B 48
Harmony Pl. Trow —3D 119
Harnhill Clo. Bris —4D 87
Harolds Way. Bris —4E 73
Harptree. W Mare —1E 139
Harptree Clo. Nail —5C 122
Harptree Ct. Bar C —1C 84
Harptree Gro. Bris —3D 79
Harrier Path. W Mare —5C 128
Harrington Av. Bris —2A 90
Harrington Gro. Bris —2A 90
Harrington Rd. Bris —2A 90
Harrington Wlk. Bris —2A 90
Harris Barton. Fram C —2D 31
Harris Ct. L Grn —1B 84
Harris La. Abb L —2B 66
Harrowdene Rd. Bris —2D 81
Harrow Rd. Bris —2F 81
Harry Stoke Rd. Stok G —2A 44
Hartcliffe Rd. Bris —5A 80
Hartcliffe Wlk. Bris —5B 80
Hartcliffe Way. Bris —4E 79
Hartfield Av. Bris —1E 69
Hartgill Clo. Bris —5D 87
Hartington Pk. Bris —5E 57
Hartland. W Mare —3E 129
Hartland Ho. Bris —4E 71
Hartley Clo. Chip S —5E 19
Harts Croft. Yate —2B 18
Harts Paddock. Mid N —1C 150
Harvest Way. W Mare —1D 129
Harvey Clo. W Mare —1E 129
Harvey's La. Bris —2B 72
Harwood Grn. Kew —1C 128
Harwood La. Wickw —3C 154
Haselbury Gro. Salt —2A 94
Haskins Ct. Bar C —1C 84
Haslands. Nail —5C 122
Haslemere Ind. Est. Bris —2E 37
Hassell Dri. Bris —3C 70
Hastings Clo. Bris —4E 79
Hastings Rd. Bris —4E 79
Hatches La. W Mare —3E 131
Hatchet La. Stok G —5A 28
Hatchet Rd. Stok G —4F 27
Hatchmere. T'bry —4E 7
Hatfield Bldgs. Bath —4C 106
Hatfield Rd. Bath —1F 109
Hatfield Rd. W Mare —5E 127
Hatherley. Yate —2A 34
Hatherley Rd. Bris —3A 58
Hathway Wlk. Bris —2C 70
Hatters La. Chip S —5D 19
Havelock Ct. Trow —3C 118
Havelock St. Trow —3C 119
Haven, The. Bris —1A 74
Haversham Clo. W Mare —4B 128
Haverstock Rd. Bris —2C 80
Haviland Gro. Bath —3B 98
Haviland Pk. Bath —4C 98
Havory. Bath —5D 101

Hawarden Ter. Bath —5C 100
Hawburn Clo. Bris —3F 81
Hawcroft. Holt —1E 155
Haweswater. Bris —2D 41
Haweswater Clo. Bris —4F 75
Hawke Rd. Kew —1C 128
Hawkesbury Rd. Bris —4A 60
Hawkeseley Dri. Lit S —3F 27
Hawkesley Dri. Lit S —3F 27
Hawkesworth Rd. Yate —3E 17
Hawkfield Bus. Pk. Hawk B —3F 87
Hawkfield Clo. Hawk B —3F 87
Hawkfield Rd. Bris —3F 87
Hawkfield Way. Hawk B —3F 87
Hawkins Clo. Bris —1E 85
Hawkins Cres. Brad S —1F 27
Hawkins St. Bris —3B 70 (2F 5)
Hawkley Dri. Brad S —3F 11
Hawkridge Dri. Puck —2E 65
Hawksmoor Clo. Bris —2C 88
Hawksworth Dri. Bris —5D 73
Hawksworth Dri. W Mare —1A 130
Hawland Gro. Bath —3B 98
Hawthorn Av. Bris —5D 73
Hawthorn Clo. Pat —1A 26
Hawthorn Clo. P'head —3B 48
Hawthorn Clo. Puck —2E 65
Hawthorn Coombe. W Mare —2C 128
Hawthorn Cres. T'bry —2D 7
Hawthorn Cres. Yat —2A 142
Hawthorne Gdns. Stap H —3B 62
Hawthornes, The. Stap H —3B 62
Hawthorne St. Bris —2C 80
Hawthorn Gdns. W Mare —3B 128
Hawthorn Gro. Bath —3A 110
Hawthorn Gro. Trow —5C 118
Hawthorn Heights. W Mare —2B 128
Hawthorn Hill. W Mare —3C 128
Hawthorn Pk. W Mare —2C 128
Hawthorn Rd. Rads —2E 153
Hawthorns. Key —3A 92
Hawthorns La. Key —3A 92
Hawthorns, The. Clev —3C 120
Hawthorn Way. Nail —3E 123
Hawthorn Way. Stok G —4A 28
Haycombe. Bris —2B 88
Haycombe Dri. Bath —5B 104
Haycombe La. Bath —1A 108
Hayden Clo. Bath —4F 105
Haydock Clo. Bris —3B 46
Haydon Gdns. Bris —2D 59
Haydon Ga. Rads —4C 152
Haydon Hill. Rads —4C 152
Haydon Ind. Est. Rads —4C 152
Hayeley Dri. Brad S —3A 28
Hayes Clo. Bris —3C 70
Hayes Clo. Trow —4E 117
Hayes Ct. Pat —2D 27
Hayesfield Pk. Bath —4A 106
Hayes Pk. Rd. Mid N —2C 150
Hayes Pl. Bath —4A 106
Hayes Rd. Mid N —2C 150
Hayeswood Rd. Tim —1D 157
Hay Hill. Bath —2A 106 (1B 96)
Hay Leaze. Yate —2F 17
Hayleigh Ho. Bris —4E 87
Haymarket, The. Bris —3F 69 (1C 4)
Haymarket Wlk. Bris —2F 69 (off Cannon St.)
Haynes La. Bris —2F 61
Haythorne Ct. Stap H —2B 62
Haytor Pk. Bris —5F 39
Hayward Clo. Clev —5C 120
Hayward Rd. Bar H —3E 71
Hayward Rd. Stap H —3F 61
Haywood Clo. W Mare —2E 139
Haywood Gdns. W Mare —2E 139
Hazel Av. Bris —5D 57
Hazelbury Clo. Nail —3D 123
Hazelbury Dri. Bris —5E 75
Hazelbury Rd. Bris —5E 81
Hazelbury Rd. Nail —4C 122
Hazel Cote Rd. Bris —4D 89
Hazel Cres. T'bry —3E 7
Hazeldene Rd. Pat —2C 26
Hazeldene Rd. W Mare —5E 127
Hazel Gdns. Alv —3A 8
Hazel Gro. Bath —5E 105
Hazel Gro. Bris —4C 42
Hazel Gro. Mid N —4E 151
Hazel Gro. Trow —5B 118
Hazelgrove. Wint —4F 29
Hazel La. Rudg —4A 8
Hazell Clo. Clev —5E 121
Hazel Ter. Mid N —4E 151
Hazelton Rd. Bris —4F 57
Hazel Way. Bath —4E 109
Hazelwood Ct. Bris —4F 55
Hazelwood Rd. Bris —4F 55
Hazleton Gdns. Clav D —1F 111
Headford Av. Bris —3D 73
Headford Rd. Bris —4F 79
Headington Clo. Han —1F 83
Headley Ct. Bris —2D 87
Headley La. Bris —2C 86
Headley Pk. Av. Bris —2D 87
Headley Pk. Rd. Bris —1C 86
Headley Rd. Bris —2C 86
Headley Wlk. Bris —1D 87
Hearn Dri. Fram C —3D 31
Heart Meers. Bris —3D 89
Heath Clo. Wint —3A 30
Heathcote Dri. Coal H —2F 31
Heathcote La. Coal H (off Boundary Rd.) —2F 31
Heathcote Rd. Fish —5D 61
Heathcote Rd. Stap H —2A 62
Heathcote Wlk. Bris —5E 61
Heath Ct. Bris —5F 45
Heather Av. Fram C —3D 31
Heather Clo. Bris —2D 73
Heatherdene. Bris —1B 88
Heather Dri. Bath —4E 109
Heather Shaw. Trow —2E 119
Heathfield Clo. Bath —3B 98
Heathfield Clo. Key —3E 91
Heathfield Cres. Bris —4C 88
Heathfield Rd. Nail —3D 123
Heathfield Way. Nail —2D 123
Heath Gdns. Bris —4F 45
Heath Gdns. Coal H —3E 31
Heathgate. Yat —3B 142
Heathgates. Nail —3E 123
Heathgates. W Mare —4B 132
Heath Ho. La. Stap —3D 59
Heath Ridge. L Ash —3C 76
Heath Rise. Bris —5D 75
Heath Rd. Down —5F 45
Heath Rd. Eastv —4D 59
Heath Rd. Han —1D 83
Heath Rd. Nail —2E 123 (in two parts)
Heath St. Bris —4E 59
Heath Wlk. Bris —5F 45
Heber St. Bris —3E 71
Hebron Rd. Bris —2E 79
Heddington Clo. Trow —5C 118
Hedgemead Clo. Bris —2F 59
Hedgemead Ct. Bath —1B 106 (off Margaret's Hill)
Hedgemead View. Bris —2A 60
Hedges Clo. Clev —5B 120
Hedges, The. St Geo —3A 130
Hedwick Av. Bris —3A 72
Hedwick St. Bris —3A 72
Heggard Clo. Bris —3C 86
Helens Ct. Trow —1C 118
Hellier Wlk. Bris —5E 87
Helmdon Rd. Trow —1A 118
Helston Rd. Nail —4F 123
Hemmings Pde. Bris —3D 71
Hemming Way. Hut —5C 134
Hemplow Clo. Bris —1F 89
Hempton La. Alm —4D 11
Henacre Rd. Bris —4B 38
Henbury Ct. Hen —1A 40
Henbury Gdns. Hen —2A 40
Henbury Hill. W Trym —3B 40
Henbury Rd. Han —5D 73
Henbury Rd. Hen & W Trym —2A 40
Hencliffe Rd. Bris —1F 89
Hencliffe Way. Han —2D 83
Henderson Clo. Trow —3B 118
Henderson Rd. Bris —5D 73
Hendre Rd. Bris —3C 78
Hendy Ct. Yate —1F 33
Henfield Cres. Old C —1D 85
Henfield Rd. Coal H —5E 32
Hengaston St. Bris —3D 79
Hengrove Av. Bris —5D 81
Hengrove La. Bris —5C 80
Hengrove Rd. Bris —3C 80
Hengrove Way. Bris —2D 87
Henleaze Av. Bris —2C 56
Henleaze Gdns. Bris —2C 56
Henleaze Pk. Bris —2E 57
Henleaze Pk. Dri. Bris —1D 57
Henleaze Rd. Bris —2C 56
Henleaze Ter. Bris —5D 41
Henley Gro. Bris —2D 57
Henley La. Yat —4D 143
Henley Lodge. Yat —4D 143
Henley Pk. Yat —4C 142
Hennesy Clo. Bris —5B 88
Henrietta Ct. Bath —1B 106
Henrietta Gdns. Bath —2B 106 (1D 97)
Henrietta M. Bath —2B 106 (2D 97)
Henrietta Pl. Bath —2B 106 (2C 96)
Henrietta Rd. Bath —2B 106 (1D 97)
Henrietta St. Bath —2B 106 (2D 97)
Henrietta St. E'tn —1D 71
Henrietta St. K'dwn —2F 69
Henrietta Vs. Bath —2B 106 (1D 97)
Henry St. Bath —3B 106 (4C 96)
Henry St. Tot —1B 80
Henry Williamson Ct. Bar C —5C 74
Henshaw Clo. Bris —5E 61
Henshaw Rd. Bris —5E 61
Henshaw Wlk. Bris —5E 61
Hensley Gdns. Bath —5F 105
Hensley Rd. Bath —5F 105
Hensman's Hill. Bris —4C 68
Hepburn Rd. Bris —2A 70
Herald Clo. Bris —2F 55
Herapath St. Bris —4E 71
Herbert Cres. Bris —4F 59
Herbert Rd. Bath —4E 105
Herbert Rd. Clev —2D 121
Herbert St. Bris —1E 79 (in two parts)
Herbert St. W'hall —2E 71
Hercules Clo. Lit S —3F 27
Hereford Rd. Bris —5C 58
Hereford St. Bedm —2F 79
Heritage Clo. Pea J —4D 157
Herkomer Clo. Bris —5D 43
Herluin Way. W Mare —2E 133
Hermes Clo. Salt —5F 93
Hermitage Clo. Bris —5A 38
Hermitage Rd. Bath —5F 99
Hermitage Rd. Bris —2F 61
Heron Clo. W Mare —5C 128
Heron Gdns. P'head —4A 50
Heron Rd. Bris —1D 71
Heron Way. Chip S —2B 34
Herridge Clo. Bris —4D 87
Herridge Rd. Bris —4D 87
Hersey Gdns. Bris —5A 86
Hesding Clo. Bris —2E 83
Hestercombe Rd. Bris —2D 87
Hetling Ct. Bath —3A 106 (4B 96)
Heyford Av. Bris —3D 59
Heyron Wlk. Bris —4D 87
Heywood Rd. Pill —3E 53
Heywood Ter. Pill —3E 53
Hicking Ct. K'wd —4A 74
Hicks Av. E Grn —4D 47
Hick's Barton. Bris —2B 72
Hicks Comn. Rd. Wint —4A 30
Hicks Ct. L Grn —1B 84
Hicks Ga. Ho. Key —5D 83
High Acre. Paul —5C 146
Higham St. Bris —1B 80
High Bannerdown. Bathe —2C 102
Highbury Pde. W Mare —4A 126
Highbury Pl. Bath —5B 100
Highbury Rd. Bedm —4E 79
Highbury Rd. Hor —5B 42
Highbury Rd. W Mare —4A 126
Highbury Ter. Bath —5B 100
Highbury Vs. Bath —5B 100 (off Highbury Pl.)
Highbury Vs. Bris —2E 69 (in three parts)
Highcroft. Bris —4E 75
Highdale Av. Clev —3D 121
Highdale Clo. Bris —4D 89
Highdale Rd. Clev —3D 121
High Elm. Bris —4A 74
Highett Dri. Bris —1C 70
Highfield Av. Bris —5F 73
Highfield Clo. Bath —4C 104
Highfield Clo. Stok G —1B 44
Highfield Dri. P'head —5A 48
Highfield Gdns. Bit —3E 85
Highfield Gro. Bris —2F 57
Highfield Rd. Brad A —2E 115
Highfield Rd. Chip S —5C 18
Highfield Rd. Key —5B 92
Highfield Rd. Pea J —1F 149
Highfield Rd. W Mare —2E 139
Highfields. Rads —3A 152
High Gro. Bris —1D 55
Highgrove St. Bris —1C 80
High Kingsdown. Bris —2E 69
Highland Clo. W Mare —3F 127
Highland Cres. Bris —5C 56
Highland Pl. Bris —5C 56
Highland Rd. Bath —4C 104
Highland Sq. Bris —5C 56
Highlands Rd. L Ash —3C 76
Highlands Rd. P'head —3D 49
Highland Ter. Bath —3E 105
High La. Yate —1F 29
Highleaze Rd. Old C —1E 85
Highmead Gdns. Bris —4A 86
High Meadows. Mid N —3C 150
Highmore Gdns. Bris —5E 43
Highnam Clo. Pat —5D 11
High Pk. Bris —4D 81
High Pk. Paul —3A 146
Highridge Cres. Bris —3B 86
Highridge Grn. Bris —1A 86
Highridge Pk. Bris —2B 86
Highridge Rd. Bedm —3D 79
Highridge Rd. B'wth —4A 86
Highridge Wlk. Bris —1A 86
High St. Banwell, Ban —5C 136
High St. Bath, Bath —3B 106 (3C 96)
High St. Bathampton, B'ptn —5A 102
High St. Batheaston, Bathe —3A 102
High St. Bathford, Bathf —4D 103
High St. Bitton, Bit —5F 85
High St. Bristol, Bris —3F 69 (2C 4)
High St. Chipping Sodbury, Chip S —5D 19
High St. Claverham, Clav —2F 143
High St. Clifton, Clif —5C 56
High St. Congresbury, Cong —2D 145
High St. Easton, E'tn —1D 71
High St. Freshford, F'frd —4C 112
High St. Hanham, Han —5E 73
High St. High Littleton, High L —1A 146
High St. Iron Acton, Iron A —2F 15
High St. Keynsham, Key —2A 92
High St. Kingswood, K'wd —2A 74
High St. Midsomer Norton, Mid N —3D 151
High St. Nailsea, Nail —3D 123
High St. Oldland, Old C —2E 85
High St. Paulton, Paul —4B 146
High St. Portbury, P'bry —4A 52
High St. Portishead, P'head —4F 49
High St. Saltford, Salt —1A 94
High St. Shirehampton, Shire —5F 37
High St. Staple Hill, Stap H —3E 61
High St. Thornbury, T'bry —4C 6
High St. Timsbury, Tim —1E 157
High St. Twerton on Avon, Twer A —3B 104
High St. Warmley, War —2D 75
High St. Westbury on Trym, W Trym —5C 40
High St. Weston, W'ton —4B 98
High St. Weston-super-Mare, W Mare —5B 126 (in three parts)
High St. Wick, Wick —5B 154
High St. Wickwar, Wickw —1B 154
High St. Winterbourne, Wint —3F 29
High St. Woolley, W'ly —1A 100
High St. Worle, Wor —4C 128
High St. Wrington, Wrin —1B 156
High St. Yatton, Yat —2B 142
High View. Bath —4F 105
High View. P'head —4C 48
Highview Rd. Bris —5A 62
Highwall La. Q Char —5C 90
Highway. Yate —4B 18
Highwood La. Bren & Pat —3A 26
Highwood Rd. Pat —3A 26
Highworth Cres. Yate —1F 33
Highworth Rd. Bris —4F 71
Hilbury Ct. Trow —1E 119
Hilcot Gro. W Mare —4F 127
Hildesheim Clo. W Mare —1D 133
Hill Av. Bath —3A 110
Hill Av. Bris —2A 80
Hillbrook Rd. T'bry —4E 7
Hill Burn. Bris —1E 57
Hillburn Rd. Bris —3C 72
Hillcote Est. W Mare —3F 139
Hill Ct. Paul —3B 146
Hill Crest. Bris —4D 81
Hill Crest. Cong —1E 145
Hillcrest. Pea J —2F 149
Hillcrest. T'bry —3C 6
Hillcrest Clo. Nail —4D 123
Hillcrest Dri. Bath —5C 104
Hillcrest Flats. Brad A —2E 115
Hillcrest Rd. Nail —4D 123
Hillcrest Rd. P'head —4A 48
Hillcroft Clo. W Mare —3E 127
Hilldale Rd. Back —3D 125
Hill End. W Mare —2C 128
Hill End Dri. Bris —1F 39
Hillfields Av. Bris —5E 61
Hill Gay Clo. P'head —4B 48
Hill Gro. Bris —1E 57
Hillgrove St. Bris —2F 69
Hillgrove St. N. Bris —2F 69
Hillgrove Ter. Uph —1B 138
Hillhouse. Bris —2A 62
Hill Ho. Rd. Bris —1B 62
Hill Lawn. Bris —2F 81
Hillmer Rise. Ban —5D 137
Hillmoor. Clev —4E 121
Hill Pk. Cong —1E 145
Hill Path. Ban —5F 137
Hill Rd. Clev —2C 120
Hill Rd. Dun —5A 86
Hill Rd. W Mare —5D 127
Hill Rd. Wor —3C 128
Hill Rd. E. W Mare —3C 128
Hills Barton. Bris —4C 78
Hillsborough Flats. Bris —4C 68
Hillsborough Ho. W Mare —4E 133
Hillsborough Rd. Bris —1E 81
Hills Clo. Key —3C 92
Hillsdon Rd. Bris —4B 40
Hillside. Clif —4D 69
Hillside. Cot —2E 69

Hillside. Mang —2B 62
Hillside. P'bry —5F 51
Hillside Av. Bris —2E 73
Hillside Av. Mid N —4B 150
Hillside Clo. Fram C —2E 31
Hillside Clo. Paul —3C 146
Hillside Cres. Mid N —4B 150
Hillside Gdns. W Mare —4F 127
Hillside La. Fram C —2E 31
Hillside Rd. Back —3C 124
Hillside Rd. Bath —5E 105
Hillside Rd. B'don —3F 139
Hillside Rd. Bris —3C 72
Hillside Rd. Clev —3D 121
Hillside Rd. L Ash —3D 77
Hillside Rd. Mid N —4C 150
Hillside Rd. P'head —5A 48
Hillside St. Bris —1C 80
Hillside View. Mid N —2D 151
Hillside View. Pea J —1F 149
Hillside W. Hut —5D 135
Hill St. Bris —3E 69
Hill St. Hil —3F 117
Hill St. K'wd —2B 74
Hill St. St G —2B 72
Hill St. Tot —1B 80
Hill St. Trow —1C 118
Hill, The. Alm —2D 11
Hill, The. F'frd —4D 113
Hilltop. P'head —4C 48
Hilltop Gdns. Soun —5F 61 (in two parts)
Hilltop Gdns. St G —3C 72
Hilltop Rd. Bris —5F 61
Hilltop View. Bris —3C 72
Hill View. Clif —4D 69
Hill View. Fil —1C 42
Hill View. Henl —1E 57
Hillview. Mid N —5B 150
Hill View. Soun —5F 61
Hillview. Tim —2E 157
Hillview Av. Clev —4D 121
Hill View Clo. Old C —1E 85
Hill View Ct. W Mare —5B 128
Hillview Pk. Homes. W Mare —5B 128
Hill View Rd. Bath —4C 100
Hill View Rd. Bris —5C 78
Hill View Rd. Puck —2E 65
Hill View Rd. W Mare —1E 133
Hillyfield Rd. Bris —2C 86
Hillyfields. Wins —4C 156
Hillyfields Way. Wins —4B 156
Hilperton Rd. Trow —1E 119
Hilton Ct. Bris —2D 71
Hinton. W Mare —1E 139
Hinton Clo. Bath —3A 104
Hinton Clo. Salt —1A 94
Hinton Dri. Bris —4E 75
Hinton La. Bris —4B 68
Hinton Rd. E'tn —1E 71
Hinton Rd. Fish —3C 60
Hinton Rd. Puck —1F 65
Hiscocks Dri. Bath —5F 105
Hither Grn. Clev —4F 121
Hither Grn. Ind. Est. Clev —4F 121
Hobart Rd. W Mare —5D 133
Hobbiton Rd. W Mare —1E 129
Hobbs Ct. Nail —3E 123 (off Link Rd.)
Hobbs La. Bris —4E 69 (3A 4)
Hobbs La. War —1D 75
Hobhouse Clo. Brad A —5F 115
Hobhouse Clo. Bris —5E 41
Hobwell La. L Ash —2E 77
Hockey's La. Fish —3C 60
Hockley Ct. Bath —5E 99
Hodden La. Puck —2E 65
Hods Hill. S'ske —5A 110
Hogarth M. W Mare —2E 129
Hogarth Wlk. Bris —4D 43
Hogarth Wlk. W Mare —2E 129
Hogues Wlk. Bris —4D 87
Holbeach Way. Bris —5C 88
Holbrook Cres. Bris —4F 87
Holbrook La. Bris —4A 154
Holbrook La. Trow —4C 118
Holcombe. Bris —3C 88
Holcombe Clo. B'ptn —5A 102
Holcombe Grn. Bath —4C 98 (in two parts)
Holcombe Gro. Key —3F 91
Holcombe La. B'ptn —5A 102
Holcombe Vale. B'ptn —5A 102
Holdenhurst Rd. Bris —1E 73
Holders Wlk. L Ash —5B 76
Holford Clo. Nail —4D 123
Holford Ct. Bris —3D 89
Holland Rd. Bath —5C 100
Holland Rd. Clev —5B 120
Holland St. W Mare —5E 127
Hollidge Gdns. Bris —1F 79
Hollies La. Nthnd —1B 102
Hollies Shopping Cen., The. Mid N —3D 151
Hollis Av. P'head —5E 49
Hollis Clo. L Ash —4C 76
Hollis Cres. P'head —5E 49
Hollister's Dri. Bris —5F 87
Holloway. Bath —4A 106
Hollow La. W Mare —2D 129
Hollowmead. Clav —3E 143
Hollowmead Clo. Clav —3F 143
Hollow Rd. Alm —2C 10
Hollow Rd. Bris —2A 74
Hollows, The. Coal H —2E 47
Hollow, The. Bath —4C 104
Hollway Clo. Bris —3A 90
Hollway Rd. Bris —3A 90
Hollybush Clo. W'ley —2F 113
Hollybush La. Bris —2A 56 (in two parts)
Holly Clo. Alv —3A 8
Holly Clo. Nail —2F 123
Holly Clo. Puck —2E 65
Holly Clo. S'wll —5C 60
Holly Clo. W Mare —4E 129
Holly Ct. Mid N —3E 151
Holly Cres. Bris —1A 74
Holly Dri. Bath —4E 109
Holly Grn. Bris —1C 74
Holly Gro. Bris —4E 61
Hollyguest Rd. Bris —4F 73
Holly Hill. Iron A —3A 16
Holly Hill Rd. Bris —2A 74
Holly La. Clev —1F 121
Hollyleigh Av. Bris —2C 42
Holly Lodge Rd. Bris —5B 60
Hollyman Wlk. Clev —3F 121
Hollymead La. Bris —3A 56
Hollyridge. Bris —2E 89
Holly Ridge. P'head —3C 48
Holly Wlk. Key —5F 91
Holly Wlk. Rads —3B 152
Hollywood La. E Comp —1C 24
Hollywood Rd. Bris —2F 81
Holmdale Rd. Bris —1E 43
Holmesdale Rd. Bris —2A 80
Holmes Gro. Bris —2D 57
Holmes Hill Rd. Bris —2B 72
Holmes St. Bris —4D 71
Holmlea Pk. E. Bath —2B 104
Holmlea Pk. W. Bath —2B 104
Holm-Mead La. Bris —1E 93
Holmoak Rd. Key —4E 91
Holm Rd. Hut —1C 140
Holms Rd. W Mare —3E 133
Holmwood. Bris —5E 73
Holmwood Clo. Wint —3F 29
Holmwood Gdns. Bris —4C 40
Holroyd Ho. Bris —2F 79
Holsom Clo. Bris —2A 90
Holsom Rd. Bris —2B 90
Holst Gdns. Bris —1F 87
Holton Rd. Bris —1C 58
Holt Rd. Brad A —1A 116
Holyrood Clo. Stok G —5F 27
Holyrood Clo. Trow —5B 118
Holy Well Clo. St Ap —4A 72
Homeavon Ho. Key —3B 92
Home Clo. Bris —2A 42
Home Clo. Trow —3D 119
Home Clo. Wrin —1C 156
Home Farm Clo. Pea J —2E 149
Home Farm Rd. Abb L —3D 67
Homefield. Cong —3E 145
Homefield. Lock —3D 135
Homefield. T'bry —4E 7
Homefield. Tim —1F 157
Homefield. Yate —3A 18
Homefield Clo. Lock —3E 135
Homefield Clo. Salt —1A 94
Homefield Clo. Wins —3A 156
Homefield Dri. Bris —2C 60
Homefield Rd. Puck —2D 65
Homefield Rd. Salt —1B 94
Home Gdns. Bris —5C 56
Home Ground. Bris —5D 41
Homeground. Clev —4E 121
Home Ground. Shire —5F 37
Homelands. Bath —2A 102
Homelea Pk. E. Bath —2B 104
Homelea Pk. W. Bath —2B 104
Homeleaze Rd. Bris —1F 41
Home Mead. Bris —1A 88 (Creswicke Rd.)
Home Mead. Bris —1C 84 (Earlstone Cres.)
Homemead Dri. Bris —4F 81
Home Mill Bldgs. Trow —2D 119
Home Orchard. Yate —4F 17
Homestead. Bris —5F 89
Homestead. P'head —5A 48
Homestead Gdns. Bris —3D 45
Homestead Rd. Brad S —1B 42
Homestead, The. Clev —3C 120
Homestead, The. Key —5A 92
Homestead, The. Trow —4C 118
Homestead Way. Wins —4B 156
Honeyborne Way. Wickw —2C 154
Honey Garston Clo. Bris —4D 87
Honey Garston Rd. Bris —4D 87
Honey Hill Rd. Bris —2B 74
Honeylands. P'head —5E 49
Honeymans Clo. Trow —2F 119
Honeymead. Bris —2E 89
Honeysuckle Clo. Brad S —4A 12
Honeysuckle Clo. Trow —2E 119
Honeysuckle La. Bris —3A 60
Honey Way. Bris —2B 74
Honiton. W Mare —3E 129
Honiton Rd. Bris —4C 60
Honiton Rd. Clev —5E 121
Hooper Rd. Bris —3F 89
Hoorwood Rd. Nail —4E 123
Hopechapel Hill. Bris —4B 68
Hope Ct. Bris —5D 69
Hope Ho. Pill —2F 53 (off Underbanks)
Hope Rd. Bris —2E 79
Hope Rd. Yate —4C 16
Hope Sq. Bris —4B 68
Hope Ter. Mid N —3E 151
Hopetoun Rd. Bris —4B 58
Hopewell Gdns. Bris —5B 38
Hopkin Clo. T'bry —5E 7
Hopkins St. W Mare —5C 126
Hopland Clo. L Grn —2D 85
Hopp's Rd. Bris —3F 73
Horesham Gro. Bris —3E 87
Horfield Rd. Bris —3F 69 (1B 4)
Horley Rd. Bris —5C 58
Hornbeams, The. Bris —3D 45
Hornbeam Wlk. Key —5E 91
Hornhill Clo. Bris —4D 87
Horsecastle Clo. Yat —2A 142
Horsecastle Farm Rd. Yat —2A 142
Horsecombe Brow. Bath —3B 110
Horsecombe Gro. Bath —3B 110
Horsecombe Vale. Bath —3B 110
Horsecroft Gdns. Bar C —4C 74
Horsefair, The. Bris —3A 70 (1D 5)
Horsepool Rd. Bris —4A 86
Horse Rd. Hil M —3E 117
Horse Shoe Dri. Bris —3E 55
Horseshoe La. Chip S —5D 19
Horseshoe La. T'bry —4C 6 (off Rock St.)
Horseshoe Rd. Bath —4D 107
Horseshoe Wlk. Bath —4C 106 (5F 97)
Horse St. Chip S —5D 19 (in two parts)
Hortham La. G Ear —1F 11
Horton Clo. Brad A —5F 115
Horton Ho. Bath —1B 106
Horton Rd. Chip S —4E 19
Horton St. Bris —3B 70
Horwood Ct. Bar C —1C 84
Horwood La. Wickw —3C 154
Horwood Rd. Nail —4E 123
Hosey Wlk. Bris —3C 86
Hospital Rd. Pill —4F 53
Host St. Bris —3F 69 (2B 4)
Hot Bath St. Bath —3A 106 (4B 96)
Hottom Gdns. Bris —5C 42
Hot Water La. Bris —4B 62
Hotwell Rd. Bris —3A 68
Houlton St. Bris —2B 70
Hounds Clo. Chip S —5D 19
Hounds Rd. Chip S —5D 19
Howard Av. Bris —2A 72
Howard Clo. Salt —5F 93
Howard Rd. Stap H —3F 61
Howard Rd. S'vle —1D 79
Howard Rd. T'bry —2D 7
Howard Rd. W'bry P —3D 57
Howard St. Bris —1A 72
Howecroft Gdns. Bris —3A 56
Howes Clo. Bar C —4C 74
Howett Rd. Bris —3E 71
How Hill. Bath —3B 104
Howsmoor La. E Grn —4D 47
Hoylake. Yate —1A 34
Hoylake Dri. War —4D 75
Huckford La. Ken —5C 30
Huckford Rd. Wint —4A 30
Huckley Way. Brad S —3B 28
Huddox Hill. Pea J —4D 157
Hudd's Hill Gdns. Bris —1B 72
Hudd's Hill Rd. Bris —2B 72
Hudd's Vale Rd. Bris —2A 72
Hudson Clo. Yate —1B 34
Hughenden Rd. Clif —5C 56
Hughenden Rd. Hor —2A 58
Hughenden Rd. W Mare —5E 127
Huish Ct. Rads —3E 153
Hulbert Clo. Bris —3C 82
Hulse Rd. Bris —4F 81
Humberstan Wlk. Bris —4A 38
Humber Way. Bris —4F 21
Humphrey Davy Way. Bris —5B 68
Humphrys Barton. St Ap —5B 72
Hungerford Av. Trow —3A 118
Hungerford Clo. Bris —5A 82
Hungerford Cres. Bris —4A 82
Hungerford Gdns. Bris —5A 82
Hungerford Rd. Bath —2D 105
Hungerford Rd. Bris —4A 82
Hungerford Wlk. Bris —4A 82
Hung Rd. Bris —1A 54
Hunters Clo. Bris —5E 73
Hunters Dri. Bris —1B 74
Hunter's Rd. Bris —5E 73
Hunter's Way. Bris —1E 43
Huntingdon Pl. Brad A —2D 115
Huntingdon Rise. Brad A —1D 115
Huntingdon St. Brad A —2D 115
Huntingham Rd. Bris —4A 86
Huntley Gro. Nail —4F 123
Hunts Ground Rd. Stok G —5C 28
Hunts La. Bris —1A 58
Hunt's La. Clav —3E 143
Hurle Cres. Bris —1C 68
Hurle Rd. Bris —1D 69
Hurlingham Rd. Bris —5B 58
Hurn La. Key —4B 92
Hurn Rd. Clev —4E 121
Hurst Ct. Rads —3E 153
Hurston Rd. Bris —5F 79
Hurst Rd. Bris —5B 80
Hurst Rd. W Mare —2E 133
Hurst Wlk. Bris —5A 80
Hurstwood Rd. Bris —2F 61
Hutton Clo. Bris —5F 39
Hutton Clo. Key —5A 92
Hutton Hill. Hut —1C 140
Hutton Moor Cvn. Pk. W Mare —2A 134
Hutton Moor La. W Mare —2A 134
Hutton Moor Rd. W Mare —1A 134
Huyton Rd. Bris —4A 60
H-Way Cvn. Site. Bris —5D 23
Hyde Av. T'bry —1C 6
Hyde Rd. Trow —5C 116
Hyde, The. Clev —5C 120
Hyland Gro. Bris —4B 40
Hylton Row. Rads —2F 153

Ida Rd. Bris —2E 71
Iddesleigh Rd. Bris —4D 57
Idstone Rd. Bris —3D 61
Idwal Clo. Mid N —1F 149
Iford Clo. Salt —1A 94
Iford La. F'frd —5D 113
Ilchester Cres. Bris —4D 79
Ilchester Rd. Bris —4C 78
Iles Clo. Han —1F 83
Ilex Av. Clev —4E 121
Ilex Clo. Bris —2B 86
Ilminster. W Mare —1E 139
Ilminster Av. Bris —4A 80
Ilminster Clo. Clev —4E 121
Ilminster Clo. Nail —5C 122
Ilsyn Gro. Bris —1F 89
Imber Ct. Clo. Bris —5D 81
Imperial Rd. Know —5E 81
Imperial Rd. Redl —1D 69
Imperial Wlk. Bris —4D 81
Inglesham Clo. Trow —5D 119
Ingleside Rd. Bris —1D 73
Inglestone Rd. Wickw —2C 154
Ingleton Dri. W Mare —1E 129
Ingmire Rd. Bris —4D 59
Inkerman Clo. Bris —5A 42
Inman Ho. Bath —5B 100
Inner Elm Ter. Rads —3F 151
Innox Footpath. Trow —1C 118
Innox Gdns. Bris —3C 86
Innox Gro. Eng —2A 108
Innox La. Up Swa —1C 100
Innox Mill Clo. Trow —1B 118
Innox Rd. Bath —4C 104
Innox Rd. Trow —1B 118
Inn's Ct. Av. Bris —1F 87
Inn's Ct. Dri. Bris —1F 87
Inn's Ct. Grn. Bris —1F 87
Instow. W Mare —3E 129
Instow Rd. Bris —5A 80
Instow Wlk. Bris —5A 80
International Trad. Est. Bris —2D 37
Interplex. Brad S —3E 11
Inverness Rd. Bath —3D 105
Ipswich Dri. Bris —4A 72
Irby Rd. Bris —2C 78
Irena Rd. Bris —4B 60
Ireton Rd. Bris —2D 79
Ironchurch Rd. A'mth —4D 21
Ironmould La. Bris —3C 82
Irving Clo. Bris —3A 62
Irving Clo. Clev —3F 121
Isabella Cotts. Bath —3C 110 (off Rock La.)
Isabella M. Bath —3C 110
Island Gdns. Bris —3E 59
Island, The. Mid N —3D 151
Isleys Ct. L Grn —2B 84
Islington. Trow —5D 117
Islington Gdns. Trow —1D 119
Islington Rd. Bris —1D 79
Ison Hill. Bris —1F 39
Ison Hill Rd. Bris —1F 39
Itchington Rd. Tyth —1F 9
Ivo Peters Rd. Bath —3F 105
Ivor Rd. Bris —2E 71
Ivy Av. Bath —5D 105
Ivy Bank Pk. Bath —2A 110
Ivybridge. W Mare —3E 129
Ivy Clo. Nail —4C 122
Ivy Cotts. S'ske —5A 110
Ivy Ct. P'head —3B 48
Ivy Gro. Bath —5D 105
Ivy La. Bris —4C 60
Ivy Pl. Bath —5D 105
Ivy Ter. Brad A —2E 115
Ivy Ter. Yate —5D 33
Ivy Vs. Bath —5D 105
Ivy Vs. Trow —1A 118

Ivy Wlk. Ban —4C 136
Ivy Wlk. Mid N —4E 151
Ivywell Rd. Bris —4A 56
Iwood La. Cong —5F 145

Jack Knight Ho. Bris —2C 58
Jacobs Ct. Bris —4E 69 (off Queen's Pde.)
Jacobs Ct. Bris —4E 69 (off St George's Rd.)
Jacob St. Bris —3A 70 (2E 5) (in two parts)
Jacob's Wells Rd. Bris —4D 69
Jamaica St. Bris —2A 70
James Clo. Bris —3A 62
James Rd. Bris —4A 62
James St. Bris —2B 70
James St. St W —5C 58
James St. Trow —5D 117
James St. W. Bath —3F 105
Jane St. Bris —3D 71
Jarvis St. Bris —4D 71
Jasmine Clo. W Mare —4E 129
Jasmine Gro. Bris —2E 39
Jasmine La. Clav —1F 143
Jasmine Way. Trow —2E 119
Jasper St. Bris —2D 79
Jean Rd. Bris —3A 82
Jeffery Ct. Bris —4D 75
Jeffries Hill Bottom. Bris —5D 73
Jellicoe Ct. W Mare —1C 128
Jena Ct. Salt —5F 93
Jenkins St. Trow —5C 116
Jenner Clo. Chip S —1F 35
Jersey Av. Bris —1B 82
Jesmond Rd. Clev —3C 120
Jesmond Rd. St Geo —1A 130
Jesse Hughes Ct. Bath —4D 101
Jessop Underpass. Bris —1B 78
Jew's La. Bath —3D 105
Jim O'Neil Ho. Bris —5F 37
Jocelin Dri. W Mare —1D 129
Jocelyn Rd. Bris —5B 42
Jockey La. Bris —3C 72
John Cabot Ct. Bris —5C 68
John Carr's Ter. Bris —4D 69
Johnny Ball La. Bris —3F 69 (1B 4)
John Rennie Clo. Brad A —5F 115
John Slessor Ct. Bath —1A 106
Johnson Dri. Bar C —5B 74
Johnsons La. Bris —1F 71
Johnsons Rd. Bris —1E 71
Johnstone St. Bath —3B 106 (3D 97)
John St. Bath —2A 106 (2B 96)
John St. Bris —3F 69 (2C 4)
John St. K'wd —2E 73
John St. St W —5C 58
John Wesley Rd. Bris —4D 73
Jones Clo. Yat —2A 142
Jones Hill. Brad A —5C 114
Jordan Wlk. Brad S —1F 27
Joy Hill. Bris —4B 68
Jubilee Cotts. Bris —5B 78
Jubilee Cres. Mang —5C 46
Jubilee Dri. T'bry —3E 7
Jubilee Gdns. Yate —4C 18
Jubilee Ho. Pat —1E 27
Jubilee Path. W Mare —4A 128
Jubilee Pl. Clev —5D 121
Jubilee Pl. Redc —5F 69 (5C 4)
Jubilee Rd. Bap M —1C 70
Jubilee Rd. K'wd —4A 62
Jubilee Rd. Know —3E 81
Jubilee Rd. Rads —3A 152
Jubilee Rd. St G —3B 72
Jubilee Rd. W Mare —1C 132
Jubilee St. Bris —4B 70
Jubilee Ter. Paul —3B 146
Jubilee Way. Bris —2D 37
Julian Clo. Bris —4A 56
Julian Cotts. Bath —3F 111
Julian Rd. Bath —1A 106
Julian Rd. S Park —4A 56
Julius Rd. Bris —4F 57
Junction Av. Bath —4F 105
Junction Rd. Bath —4F 105
Junction Rd. Brad A —3E 115
Juniper Ct. Bris —5E 59
Jupiter Rd. Pat —2F 25
Justice Av. Salt —1A 94
Justice Rd. Bris —4B 60
Jutland Rd. Bris —3D 37

Karen Clo. Back —3C 124
Karen Dri. Back —3C 124
Kathdene Gdns. Bris —4B 58
Kaynton Mead. Bath —3C 104
Keates Clo. Trow —1D 119
Keats Rd. Rads —4F 151
Keble Av. Bris —4B 86
Keed's La. L Ash —4B 76
Keedwell Hill. L Ash —4B 76
Keel Clo. St G —4B 72
Keel's Hill. Pea J —1F 149
Keene's Way. Clev —4B 120
Keep, The. Bris —5F 75
Keep, The. W Mare —2E 129
Keinton Wlk. Bris —2C 40
Kellaway Av. Bris —2E 57
Kellaway Cres. Bris —1F 57
Kellways. Back —4B 124
Kelston Clo. Yate —2F 33
Kelston Gdns. Bris —4F 41
Kelston Gdns. W Mare —1F 129
Kelston Gro. Bris —4A 74
Kelston Rd. Bath —5A 98
Kelston Rd. Bris —4F 41
Kelston Rd. Kel —3F 95
Kelston Rd. Key —3F 91
Kelston Rd. W Mare —1F 129
Kelston View. Bath —4A 104
Kelston Wlk. Bris —3E 61
Kelting Gro. Clev —4F 121
Kemble Clo. Bris —4A 74
Kemble Clo. Nail —3F 123
Kemble Gdns. Bris —2A 54
Kemperleye Way. Brad S —2F 27
Kempes Clo. L Ash —3C 76
Kempton Clo. Down —3B 46
Kempton Clo. T'bry —1C 6
Kencot Wlk. Bris —5D 87
Kendall Gdns. Bris —3F 61
Kendall Rd. Stap H —3F 61
Kendal Rd. Hor —5C 42
Kendon Dri. Bris —5F 41
Kenilworth. Yate —1B 34
Kenilworth Clo. Key —4F 91
Kenilworth Dri. Will —3D 85
Kenilworth Rd. Bris —1E 69
Kenmare Rd. Bris —4A 80
Kenmore Cres. Bris —3A 42
Kenmore Dri. Bris —3A 42
Kenmore Gro. Bris —3A 42
Kennard Clo. Bris —3E 73
Kennard Rise. Bris —2E 73
Kennard Rd. Bris —2E 73
Kennaway Path. Clev —4E 121
Kennaway Rd. Clev —4D 121
Kenn Clo. W Mare —3E 133
Kennedy Ho. Yate —5B 18
Kennedy Way. Yate —5A 18
Kennel Lodge Rd. Bris —1A 78
Kennet Gdns. Brad A —4E 115
Kenneth Rd. Bris —3F 81
Kennet Pk. B'ptn —5F 101
Kennet Rd. Key —4C 92
Kennet Way. T'bry —4E 7
Kennet Way. Trow —4D 117
Kennford. W Mare —3D 129
Kennington Av. Bishop —3A 58
Kennington Av. K'wd —1F 73
Kennington Rd. Bath —2C 104
Kennion Rd. Bris —3C 72
Kennmoor Clo. Bris —4C 74
Kenn Moor Dri. Clev —5E 121
Kenn Moor Rd. Yat —2B 142
Kenn Rd. Bris —3C 72
Kenn Rd. Clev —5D 121
Kensal Av. Bris —2A 80
Kensal Rd. Bris —2A 80
Kensington Clo. T'bry —2C 6
Kensington Clo. Trow —5D 117
Kensington Ct. Bath —5C 100
Kensington Ct. Bris —3C 68
Kensington Gdns. Bath —5C 100
Kensington Pk. Bris —1C 70
Kensington Pk. Rd. Bris —3E 81
Kensington Pl. Bath —1C 106
Kensington Pl. Bris —3C 68
Kensington Rd. Bris —3F 61
Kensington Rd. Redl —1E 69
Kensington Rd. St G —2C 72
Kensington Rd. W Mare —3D 133
Kensit Clo. Bris —4B 74
Kent Av. Yate —3B 18
Kent Clo. Stok G —5F 27
Kent La. Bath —1C 100
Kenton Dri. Trow —1F 119
Kenton M. Bris —2E 57
Kent Rd. Bris —4A 58
Kent Rd. Cong —1D 145
Kents Grn. Bris —5A 62
Kent St. Bris —2E 79
Kent Way. W Mare —1F 129
Kenwood Clo. Trow —2F 119
Keppel Clo. Salt —5F 93
Kerry Rd. Bris —4A 80
Kersteman Rd. Bris —5E 57
Kestrel Clo. Chip S —2B 34
Kestrel Clo. Pat —1A 26
Kestrel Clo. T'bry —2E 7
Kestrel Dri. Puck —3E 65
Kestrel Dri. W Mare —4C 128
Kestrel Pl. Mid N —4E 151
Keswick Wlk. Bris —2E 41 (in two parts)
Ketch Rd. Bris —2B 80
Ketton Clo. Trow —1A 118
Kew Dri. Trow —3A 118
Kew Rd. W Mare —4C 126
Kewside. Kew —1F 127
Kewstoke Rd. Bath —2B 110
Kewstoke Rd. Bris —3A 56
Kewstoke Rd. Kew & Wor —2D 127
Kewstoke Rd. W Mare —4A 126
Kew Wlk. Bris —5E 81
Keyes Path. W Mare —1D 129
Keynsham By-Pass. Key —5E 83
Keynsham Rd. Key & Will —2B 92
Keys Av. Bris —5B 42
Kielder Dri. W Mare —2D 129
Kilbirnie Rd. Bris —5C 88
Kilburn St. Bris —2D 71
Kildare Rd. Bris —4F 79
Kilkenny La. Eng —5A 108
Kilkenny St. Bris —4B 70
Kilmersdon Rd. Bris —4D 87
Kilmersdon Rd. Rads —4B 152
Kilminster Rd. Bris —5F 37
Kiln Clo. Bris —5D 61
Kilnhurst Clo. L Grn —3B 84
Kilve. W Mare —1D 139 (in two parts)
Kilvert Clo. Bris —5F 71
Kimberley Av. Bris —2E 61
Kimberley Clo. Bris —5B 46
Kimberley Cres. Bris —2E 61
Kimberley Rd. Bris —1F 73
Kimberley Rd. Clev —4C 120
Kimberley Rd. Fish —2E 61 (in two parts)
Kinber Clo. Bath —3B 98
King Alfred Way. W'ley —2E 113
King Dick's La. Bris —2B 72
King Edward Clo. Bris (in two parts) —2C 88
King Edward Rd. Bath —4E 105
Kingfisher Clo. T'bry —2E 7
Kingfisher Dri. Bris —1A 60
Kingfisher Dri. Mid N —4E 151
Kingfisher Rd. Chip S —1C 34
Kingfisher Rd. W Mare —4D 129
King Georges Rd. Bath —4D 105
King George's Rd. Bris —3B 86
King John's Rd. Bris —5D 61
King Rd. Bris —4E 81
King Rd. Av. A'mth —2D 37
Kingrove Cres. Chip S —1E 35
Kingrove La. Chip S —1E 35
Kings Av. Bishop —3E 57
Kings Av. Han —1D 83
Kings Bus. Pk. Bris —4E 71
King's Chase Shopping Cen. K'wd —2F 73
Kingscote. Yate —3F 33
Kingscote Pk. Bris —4D 73
Kings Ct. Lit S —3E 27
Kings Ct. Clo. Bris —3C 88
Kingsdown Pde. Bris —2F 69
Kingsdown Rd. Trow —5C 118
Kingsdown View. Bath —5B 100
King's Dri. Bishop —2E 57
Kings Dri. Han —1D 83
Kingsfield. Bath —1D 109
Kingsfield. Brad A —2E 115
Kingsfield Clo. Brad A —2E 115
Kingsfield Grange Rd. Brad A —2F 115
Kingsfield La. L Grn —5A 74 (in two parts)
Kings Gdns. Trow —2E 117
Kings Head La. Bris —1A 86
Kingshill. Nail —3B 122
Kingshill Gdns. Nail —3B 122
Kingshill Rd. Bris —4D 81
Kingsholme Rd: K'wd —1F 73
Kingsholm Rd. S'mead —4F 41
Kingsland Bri. Bris —4C 70
Kingsland Clo. Bris —4C 70
Kingsland Rd. Bris —4C 70
Kingsland Trad. Est. Bris —3B 70
Kings La. Puck —2B 64
King's La. W Mare —5C 126
Kingsleigh Clo. Bris —3B 74
Kingsleigh Gdns. Bris —3B 74
Kingsleigh Pk. Bris —3B 74
Kingsley Pl. Trow —1A 118
Kingsley Rd. Clev —4D 121
Kingsley Rd. Cot —5F 57
Kingsley Rd. G'bnk —1E 71
Kingsley Rd. Rads —3F 151
Kingsley Rd. W Mare —5D 133
Kingsmarsh Ho. Bris —3D 71
Kingsmead. Nail —3B 122
Kingsmead Ct. Bath —3A 106 (off Kingsmead N.)
Kingsmead E. Bath —3A 106 (4A 96)
Kingsmead N. Bath —3A 106 (4A 96)
Kingsmead Rd. Bris —1C 72
Kingsmead Sq. Bath —3A 106 (4B 96)
Kingsmead St. Bath —3A 106 (3B 96)
Kingsmead Ter. Bath —3A 106 (off Kingsmead E.)
Kingsmead Wlk. Bris —1C 72
Kingsmead W. Bath —3A 106 (4A 96)
Kings M. Bris —2F 69
Kingsmill. Bris —2F 55
Kings Pde. Av. Bris —1D 69
Kings Pde. M. Bris —1C 68
Kings Pk. Av. Bris —4E 71
King Sq. Bris —2F 69
King Sq. Av. Bris —2F 69
King's Rd. Brisl —2E 81
King's Rd. Clev —1D 121
King's Rd. Clif —3C 68
King's Rd. P'head —4B 48
Kings Rd. Wrin —2B 156
Kings Sq. Bit —5F 85
Kingston Av. Brad A —4F 115
Kingston Av. Clev —3E 121
Kingston Av. Salt —5E 93
Kingston Bldgs. Bath —3B 106 (off York St.)
Kingston Clo. Mang —5C 46
Kingston Dri. Mang —5C 46
Kingston Dri. Nail —5B 122
Kingston Pde. Bath —3B 106 (off York St.)
Kingston Rd. Bath —3B 106 (4C 96)
Kingston Rd. Brad A —3E 115
Kingston Rd. Bris —1E 79
Kingston Rd. Nail —5B 122
Kingston Way. Nail —5B 122
Kingstree St. Tot —1C 80
King St. A'mth —3C 36
King St. Bris —4F 69 (4B 4) (Bristol)
King St. Bris —1E 71 (Lower Easton)
King St. K'wd —2D 73
King's Wlk. Bris —1A 86
Kingsway. Bath —1D 109
Kingsway. Lit S —3E 27
Kingsway. P'head —4B 48
Kingsway. St G & K'wd —3D 73
Kingsway Av. K'wd & St G —2D 73
Kingsway Cvn. Pk. P'head —2F 49
Kingsway Cres. Bris —2E 73
Kingsway Shopping Precinct. Bris —4D 73
Kingsway Trailer Cvn. Pk. Wint —1B 46
Kingsway Trailer Pk. War —4D 75
Kingswear. W Mare —3E 129
Kingswear Rd. Bris —4F 79
Kings Weston Av. Bris —5F 37
Kings Weston La. Bris —5E 21
Kings Weston Rd. Law W & Hen —5C 38
Kington La. T'bry —3A 6
King William Av. Bris —4F 69 (4C 4)
King William St. Bris —1D 79
Kinsale Rd. Bris —1E 89
Kinsale Wlk. Bris —4A 80
Kinvara Rd. Bris —5A 80
Kipling Av. Bath —5A 106
Kipling Rd. Bris —3D 43
Kipling Rd. Rads —3F 151
Kipling Rd. W Mare —5E 133
Kirkby Rd. Bris —3C 38
Kirkstone Gdns. Bris —2E 41
Kirtlington Rd. Bris —4D 59
Kitcheners Ct. Trow —1C 118
Kite Hay Clo. Bris —2A 60
Kites Clo. Brad S —4E 11
Kite Wlk. W Mare —5C 128
Kitley Hill. Rads —5F 147
Knapp Rd. T'bry —3D 7
Knapps Clo. Wins —4A 156
Knapps Dri. Wins —4A 156
Knapps La. Bris —5A 60
Knapp, The. Yate —1B 18
Knap, The. Hil —4F 117
Knight Clo. W Mare —1E 129
Knightcott Gdns. Ban —5D 137
Knightcott Pk. Ban —5E 137
Knightcott Rd. Abb L —2B 66
Knightcott Rd. Ban —5C 136
Knighton Rd. Bris —3F 41
Knights Clo. Henl —1D 57
Knightstone Causeway. W Mare —5A 126
Knightstone Clo. Pea J —1E 149
Knightstone Ct. Clev —5D 121
Knightstone Pl. Bris —2D 83
Knightstone Pl. W Mare —3D 129
Knightstone Pl. W'ton —5C 98
Knightstone Rd. W Mare —4A 126
Knightstone Sq. Bris —2E 89
Knightswood. Nail —2C 122
Knightwood Rd. Stok G —4B 28
Knobsbury Hill. Mid N —5F 153
Knobsbury La. Writ —3F 153
Knole Clo. Alm —2B 10
Knole La. Bris —1C 40
Knole Pk. Alm —3B 10
Knoll Ct. Bris —4F 55
Knoll Hill. Bris —4F 55
Knoll, The. P'head —1F 49
Knovill Clo. Bris —2D 39
Knowle Rd. Bris —2B 80
Knowles Rd. Clev —4C 120
Knowsley Rd. Bris —4A 60
Kyght Clo. War —2C 74
Kylross Av. Bris —3D 89
Kynges Mill Clo. Bris —5C 44
Kyrle Gdns. Bathe —3A 102

Labbott, The. Key —3A 92
Laburnam Ter. Bathe —3A 102

Laburnum Clo. *Mid N* —4C **150**
Laburnum Ct. *W Mare* —1F **133**
Laburnum Gro. *Bris* —3D **61**
Laburnum Gro. *Mid N* —4C **150**
Laburnum Gro. *Trow* —4B **118**
Laburnum Rd. *Bris* —5E **73**
Laburnum Rd. *W Mare* —1E **133**
Laburnum Wlk. *Key* —5E **91**
Lacey Rd. *Bris* —2A **90**
Lacock Dri. *Bar C* —5B **74**
Ladd Clo. *Bris* —3B **74**
Ladden Ct. *T'bry* —4D **7**
Ladies Mile. *Bris* —1B **68**
Ladman Gro. *Bris* —2A **90**
Ladman Rd. *Bris* —2A **90**
Ladycroft. *Clev* —5B **120**
Ladydown. *Trow* —4D **117**
Ladye Wake. *W Mare* —1D **129**
Ladymeade. *Back* —1C **124**
Ladysmith Rd. *Bris* —3D **57**
Ladywell. *Wrin* —1B **156**
Laggan Gdns. *Bath* —5F **99**
Lake Mead Gdns. *Bris* —4B **86**
Lakemead Gro. *Bris* —2B **86**
Lake Rd. *Bris* —5E **41**
Lake Rd. *P'head* —2E **49**
Lakeside. *Bris* —4A **60**
Lake View. *Bris* —4B **60**
Lake View Rd. *Bris* —2F **71**
Lakewood Cres. *Bris* —4D **41**
Lakewood Rd. *Bris* —4D **41**
Lamb Ale Grn. *Trow* —4E **119**
Lambert Pl. *Bris* —2F **87**
Lamb Hill. *Bris* —3B **72**
Lambley Rd. *Bris* —2A **72**
Lambourn Clo. *Bris* —2F **79**
Lambourn Rd. *Key* —4C **92**
Lambridge Bldgs. *Bath* —4D **101**
Lambridge Grange. *Bath* —4D **101**
Lambridge M. *Bath* —5D **101**
Lambridge Pl. *Bath* —5D **101**
Lambridge St. *Bath* —5D **101**
Lambrok Clo. *Trow* —4A **118**
Lambrok Rd. *Trow* —4A **118**
Lambrook Rd. *Bris* —3C **60**
Lamb St. *Bris* —3B **70**
Lamord Ga. *Stok G* —4A **28**
Lampard's Bldgs. *Bath* —1A **106**
Lampeter Rd. *Bris* —5B **40**
Lampton Av. *Bris* —5A **88**
Lampton Gro. *Bris* —5A **88**
Lampton Rd. *L Ash* —4B **76**
Lanaway Rd. *Bris* —1D **61**
Lancashire Rd. *Bris* —4A **58**
Lancaster Clo. *Stok G* —5F **27**
Lancaster Rd. *Bris* —5C **58**
Lancaster Rd. *Yate* —3A **18**
Lancaster St. *Bris* —3E **71**
Landemann Cir. *W Mare* —5C **126**
Landemann Path. *W Mare* —5C **126**
Land La. *Yat* —4C **142**
Landrail Wlk. *Bris* —1B **60**
Landseer Av. *Bris* —1D **59**
Landseer Clo. *W Mare* —2D **129**
Landseer Rd. *Bath* —3C **104**
Land, The. *Coal H* —2E **31**
Lanercost Rd. *Bris* —2E **41**
Lanesborough Rise. *Bris* —1F **89**
Lanes Rd. *L Ash* —5A **86**
Laneys Drove. *Lock* —3C **134**
Langdale Ct. *Pat* —1C **26**
Langdale Rd. *Bris* —3B **60**
Langdon Rd. *Bath* —5C **104**
Langfield Clo. *Bris* —1A **40**
Langford Rd. *Bris* —5B **78**
Langford Rd. *Trow* —5C **116**
Langford Rd. *W Mare* —2E **133**
Langford's La. *Paul* —1A **146**
Langford Way. *Bris* —3A **74**
Langham Rd. *Bris* —3E **81**
Langhill Av. *Bris* —1E **87**
Langley Cres. *Bris* —4A **78**
Langley Rd. *Trow* —5C **118**
Langley's La. *C'tn* —3A **150**
Langport Gdns. *Nail* —5D **123**
Langport Rd. *W Mare* —2C **132**
Langthorn Clo. *Fram C* —2E **31**
Langton Ct. Rd. *Bris* —5F **71**
Langton Pk. *Bris* —1E **79**
Langton Rd. *Bris* —5F **71**
Langton Way *St Ap* —3A **72**
Lansdown. *Yate* —1A **34**
Lansdown Clo. *Bath* —5F **99**
Lansdown Clo. *Bris* —5F **61**
Lansdown Clo. *Trow* —3B **118**
Lansdown Cres. *Bath* —5A **100**
Lansdown Cres. *Tim* —1F **157**
Lansdowne. Bris —3E ***45*** *(off Harford Dri.)*
Lansdowne Ind. Est. *Wickw* —1B **154**
Lansdown Gdns. *W Mare* —1F **129**
Lansdown Gro. *Bath* —1A **106**
Lansdown La. *Bath* —4C **98**
Lansdown M. *Bath* —2A **106** (2B **96**)
Lansdown Pk. *Bath* —3F **99**
Lansdown Pl. *Bris* —3C **68**
Lansdown Pl. *E Grn* —1D **63**
Lansdown Pl. E. *Bath* —1A **106**
Lansdown Pl. W. *Bath* —5A **100**
Lansdown Rd. *Bath* —1C **98**
Lansdown Rd. *Clif* —3C **68**
Lansdown Rd. *E'tn* —1D **71**
Lansdown Rd. *K'wd* —5F **61**
Lansdown Rd. *Puck* —1E **65**
Lansdown Rd. *Redl* —5E **57**
Lansdown Rd. *Salt* —1A **94**
Lansdown Ter. *Bris* —2F **57**
Lansdown Ter. L'dwn —1A ***106*** *(off Lansdown Rd.)*
Lansdown Ter. *W'ton* —5D **99**
Lansdown View. *Bris* —2A **74**
Lansdown View. *Tim* —1F **157**
Lansdown View. *Twer A* —4D **105**
Laphams Ct. *L Grn* —1B **84**
Lapwing Clo. *Brad S* —4F **11**
Lapwing Gdns. *Bris* —1B **60**
Lapwing Gdns. *W Mare* —4D **129**
Larch Clo. *Nail* —3F **123**
Larch Ct. *Rads* —4A **152**
Larches, The. *W Mare* —2E **129**
Larch Gro. *Trow* —4B **118**
Larchgrove Cres. *W Mare* —4D **129**
Larchgrove Wlk. *W Mare* —4E **129**
Larch Rd. *Bris* —4A **62**
Larch Way. *Pat* —2A **26**
Lark Clo. *Mid N* —4E **151**
Larkdown. *Trow* —2F **119**
Larkfield. *Coal H* —2F **31**
Larkhall Pl. *Bath* —4D **101**
Larkhall Ter. *Bath* —4D **101**
Larkhill Rd. *Lock* —3F **135**
Lark Pl. Bath —2E ***105*** *(off Up. Bristol Rd.)*
Lark Rd. *W Mare* —4D **129**
Larks Field. *Bris* —2A **60**
Larksleaze Rd. *L Grn* —3A **84**
Larkspur. *Trow* —1E **119**
Larkspur Clo. *T'bry* —3E **7**
Lasbury Gro. *Bris* —3E **87**
Latchmoor Ho. *Bris* —5C **78**
Late Broads. *W'ley* —2E **113**
Latimer Clo. *Bris* —1A **82**
Latteridge Rd. *Iron A* —1C **14**
Latton Rd. *Bris* —4B **42**
Launceston Av. *Bris* —5D **73**
Launceston Rd. *Bris* —1D **73**
Laura Pl. *Bath* —2B **106** (2D **97**)
Laurel Dri. *Nail* —3E **123**
Laurel Dri. *Paul* —4A **146**
Laurel Dri. *Uph* —1C **138**
Laurel Gdns. *Yat* —2B **142**
Laurel Gro. *Trow* —4C **118**
Laurels, The. *Mang* —1C **62**
Laurel St. *Bris* —2F **73**
Laurel Ter. *Yat* —2B **142**
Laurie Cres. *Bris* —1F **57**
Laurie Lee Ct. *Bar C* —5B **74**
Lavender Clo. *T'bry* —3E **7**
Lavender Clo. *Trow* —3E **119**
Lavender Ct. *Bris* —1B **72**
Lavenham Rd. *Yate* —4D **17**
Lavers Clo. *Bris* —4A **74**
Lavington Clo. *Clev* —5A **120**
Lavington Rd. *Bris* —4D **73**
Lawford Av. *Lit S* —3E **27**
Lawfords Ga. *Bris* —3B **70**
Lawford St. *Bris* —3B **70**
Lawn Av. *Bris* —2D **61**
Lawn Rd. *Bris* —2D **61**
Lawnside. *Back* —3D **125**
Lawns Rd. *Yate* —4A **18**
Lawns, The. *Bris* —5A **38**
Lawns, The. *W Mare* —2F **129**
Lawns, The. *Yat* —2A **142**
Lawnwood Rd. *Bris* —2D **71**
Lawrence Av. *Bris* —1D **71**
Lawrence Clo. *W Mare* —3C **128**
Lawrence Dri. *Yate* —4D **17**
Lawrence Gro. *Bris* —2D **57**
Lawrence Hill. *Bris* —3D **71**
Lawrence Hill Ind. Pk. *Bris* —2D **71**
Lawrence M. *W Mare* —3C **128**
Lawrence Rd. *W Mare* —3C **128**
Lawrence Rd. *Wrin* —1C **156**
Lawrence Weston Rd. *Bris* (in two parts) —5B **22**
Lawson Clo. *Salt* —5E **93**
Laxey Rd. *Bris* —5B **42**
Laxton Way. *Pea J* —5D **157**
Lays Dri. *Key* —4E **91**
Leach Clo. *Clev* —5C **120**
Lea Croft. *Bris* —3C **86**
Leafield Pl. *Trow* —1A **118**
Leafy Way. *Lock* —4F **135**
Lea Gro. Rd. *Clev* —2C **120**
Leaholme Gdns. *Bris* —5C **88**
Leaman Clo. *Chip S* —5C **18**
Leap Vale. *Bris* —4C **46**
Leap Valley Cres. *Bris* —4B **46**
Lear Ct. *Bris* —5D **75**
Leaze, The. *Rads* —4A **152**
Leaze, The. *Yate* —4F **17**
Leda Av. *Bris* —1C **88**
Ledbury Rd. *Bris* —3E **61**
Leechpool Way. *Yate* —1A **18**
Lee Clo. *Pat* —1B **26**
Leedham Rd. *Lock* —3F **135**
Leeming Way. *Bris* —4E **37**
Lees Hill. *Bris* —5A **62**
Leeside. *P'head* —3E **49**
Lees La. *Bris* —5F **75**
Leewood Rd. *W Mare* —4D **127**
Leicester Sq. *Bris* —4F **61**
Leicester St. *Bris* —1F **79**
Leicester Wlk. *Bris* —5B **72**
Leigh Clo. *Bath* —4B **100**
Leigh Pk. Rd. *Brad A* —1E **115**
Leigh Rd. *Brad A* —1E **115**
Leigh Rd. *Bris* —2D **69**
Leigh Rd. *Holt* —1D **155**
Leigh St. *Bris* —1C **78**
Leighton Cres. *W Mare* —3E **139**
Leighton Rd. *Bath* —3B **98**
Leighton Rd. *Know* —3D **81**
Leighton Rd. *S'vle* —1D **79**
Leigh View Rd. *P'head* —1F **49**
Leighwood Dri. *Nail* —4A **122**
Leinster Av. *Know* —1F **87**
Lemon La. *Bris* —2B **70**
Lena Av. *Bris* —1E **71**
Lena St. *Bris* —1D **71**
Lenover Gdns. *Bris* —4D **87**
Leonard La. *Bris* —3F **69** (2B **4**)
Leonard Rd. *Bris* —3E **71**
Leonard's Av. *Bris* —1E **71**
Leopold Rd. *Bris* —5A **58**
Lescren Way. *Bris* —3F **37**
Leslie Rise. *L W'wd* —5A **114**
Lester Dri. *W Mare* —2E **129**
Lewington Rd. *Bris* —3E **61**
Lewins Mead. *Bris* —3F **69** (1B **4**)
Lewin St. *Bris* —3F **71**
Lewis Clo. *Bris* —5F **75**
Lewisham Gro. *W Mare* —5E **127**
Lewis Rd. *Bris* —5C **78**
Lewis St. *Bris* —5D **71**
Lewton La. *Wint* —2A **30**
Leyland Wlk. *Bris* —4B **86**
Leys, The. *Clev* —5B **120**
Leyton Vs. *Bris* —5D **57**
Liberty Ind. Pk. *Bris* —4C **78**
Lichfield Rd. *Bris* —4A **72**
Liddington Way. *Trow* —5D **119**
Like Kiln Clo. *Brad S* —2F **43**
Lilac Clo. *Bris* —3E **41**
Lilac Ct. *Key* —5E **91**
Lilac Gro. *Trow* —5B **118**
Lilac Ter. *Mid N* —2F **151**
Lilian Ter. *Paul* —4B **146**
Lillian St. *Bris* —2E **71**
Lillington Clo. *Rads* —2E **153**
Lillington Rd. *Rads* —2E **153**
Lilliput Av. *Chip S* —1C **34**
Lilliput Ct. *Chip S* —1C **34**
Lilstock Av. *Bris* —3B **58**
Lilton Wlk. *Bris* —4C **78**
Lilymead Av. *Bris* —2B **80**
Limebreach Wood. *Nail* —2C **122**
Lime Clo. *Bren* —1D **41**
Lime Clo. *Lock* —4F **135**
Lime Clo. *W Mare* —4E **129**
Lime Ct. *Key* —4E **91**
Lime Croft. *Yate* —2B **18**
Lime Gro. *Alv* —2A **8**
Lime Gro. *Bath* —3C **106** (4E **97**)
Lime Gro. Gdns. *Bath* —3C **106** (4E **97**)
Lime Kiln Gdns. *Brad S* —3F **11**
Lime Kiln La. *Clev* —3D **121**
Limerick Rd. *Bris* —5E **57**
Lime Rd. *Bedm* —1D **79**
Lime Rd. *Han* —5C **72**
Limes, The. Bris —3D ***45*** *(off Wellington Pl.)*
Lime Ter. *Rads* —3A **152**
Lime Tree Gro. *Pill* —4F **53**
Lime Trees Rd. *Bris* —2F **57**
Limpley Stoke Rd. *W'ley* —2D **113**
Lincoln Clo. *Key* —4E **91**
Lincoln St. *Bris* —3D **71**
Lincombe Av. *Bris* —1F **61**
Lincombe Rd. *Bris* —1E **61**
Lincombe Rd. *Rads* —4A **152**
Lincott View. *Pea J* —1F **149**
Linden Av. *W Mare* —5F **127**
Linden Clo. *Fish* —5C **60**
Linden Clo. *Rads* —4B **152**
Linden Clo. *Stoc* —2A **90**
Linden Clo. *Wint* —3A **30**
Linden Dri. *Brad S* —2A **28**
Linden Gdns. *Bath* —1E **105**
Linden Ho. *Bris* —2E **59**
Linden Pl. *Trow* —1B **118**
Linden Rd. *Clev* —2D **121**
Linden Rd. *W'bry P* —3D **57**
Lindens, The. *W Mare* —1C **128**
Lindisfarne Clo. *W'ley* —2F **113**
Lindon Ho. *Bris* —2A **82**
Lindrea St. *Bris* —2D **79**
Lindsay Rd. *Bris* —3C **58**
Linemere Clo. *Back* —2F **125**
Lines Way. *Bris* —5E **89**
Lingfield Pk. *Down* —2B **46**
Link Rd. *Brad S* —1B **42**
Link Rd. *Nail* —3E **123**
Link Rd. *P'head* —3E **49**
Link Rd. *Yate* —5B **18**
Link Rd. W. *Pat* —3D **25**
Links Rd. *Uph* —1A **138**
Linley Clo. *Bath* —4B **104**
Linley Ho. Bath —4B ***106*** *(off Henry St.)*
Linleys, The. *Bath* —2D **105**
Linne Ho. *Bath* —4B **104**
Linnell Clo. *Bris* —1D **59**
Linnet Clo. *Pat* —1A **26**
Linnet Clo. *W Mare* —4C **128**
Linnet Way. *Bris* —1F **89**
Linnet Way. *Mid N* —4E **151**
Linsey Clo. *P'head* —4B **48**
Lintern Cres. *Bris* —4D **75**
Lintham Dri. *Bris* —4B **74**
Lion Clo. *Nail* —3C **122**
Lipgate Pl. *P'head* —5F **49**
Lippiatt La. *Tim* —1E **157**
Lisburn Rd. *Bris* —4A **80**
Lisle Rd. *W Mare* —1E **129**
Lister Gro. *L W'wd* —5A **114**
Litfield Pl. *Bris* —3B **68**
Litfield Rd. *Bris* —2B **68**
Lit. Ann St. *Bris* —2B **70**
Lit. Birch Croft. *Bris* —5C **88**
Lit. Bishop St. *Bris* —2A **70**
Littlebrook. *Paul* —3B **146**
Lit. Caroline Pl. *Bris* —5B **68**
Lit. Common. *N Brad* —4E **155**
Littlecross Ho. *Bris* —1D **79**
Littledean. *Yate* —2A **34**
Lit. Dowles. *Bris* —1C **84**
Littlefields Av. *Ban* —5E **137**
Littlefields Rise. *Ban* —5F **137**
Littlefields Rd. *Ban* —5F **137**
Lit. George St. *Bris* —2B **70**
Lit. George St. *W Mare* —1C **132**
Lit. Green La. *Sev B* —3B **20**
Lit. Halt. *P'head* —4A **48**
Lit. Ham. *Clev* —5C **120**
Lit. Hayes. *Bris* —2D **61**
Lit. Headley Clo. *Bris* —1D **87**
Lit. Hill. *Bath* —3B **104**
Lit. King St. *Bris* —4F **69** (4C **4**)
Lit. Mead. *Bris* —3D **39**
Lit. Mead Clo. *Hut* —5C **134**
Lit. Meadow. *Brad S* —3C **28**
Lit. Meadow End. *Nail* —4D **123**
Lit. Orchard. *Uph* —2B **138**
Lit. Paradise. *Bris* —1F **79**
Little Parks. *Holt* —1F **155**
Lit. Parr Clo. *Stap* —2E **59**
Lit. Paul St. *Bris* —2E **69**
Lit. Solsbury La. *Bathe* —2F **101**
Lit. Stanhope St. *Bath* —3F **105**
Lit. Stoke La. *Lit S* —3F **27**
Lit. Stoke Rd. *Bris* —3A **56**
Lit. Thomas St. *Bris* —4A **70** (3D **5**)
Littleton Ct. *Pat* —5B **10**
Littleton Rd. *Bris* —3F **79**
Littleton St. *Bris* —1E **71**
Lit. Wall Drove. *Cong* —2A **144**
Lit. Withey Mead. *Bris* —1A **56**
Littlewood Clo. *Bris* —5D **89**
Litton. *W Mare* —1E **139**
Livingstone Rd. *Bath* —4E **105**
Llewellyn Ct. *Bris* —4C **40**
Llewellyn Way. *W Mare* —2F **129**
Lmbardy Clo. *W Mare* —5C **128**
Lockemor Rd. *Bris* —4B **88**
Lockeridge Clo. *Trow* —5D **119**
Lock Gdns. *Bris* —1A **86**
Locking Head Drove. *W Mare* (in two parts) —5E **129**
Locking Moor Rd. *W Mare* (in two parts) —5A **128**
Locking Rd. *W Mare* —1C **132**
Lockingwell Rd. *Key* —3E **91**
Lockleaze Rd. *Bris* —1C **58**
Locksacre. *Alv* —1C **8**
Locksbrook Ct. *Bath* —2D **105**
Locksbrook Rd. *Bath* —3C **104**
Locksbrook Rd. *W Mare* —1F **129**
Lock's La. *Iron A* —2A **14**
Locks Yd. Cvn. Site. *Bris* —4D **79**
Loddon Way. *Brad A* —4F **115**
Lodge Causeway. *Bris* —4B **60**
Lodge Clo. *Yat* —3B **142**
Lodge Ct. *Bris* —3A **56**
Lodge Dri. *L Ash* —3D **77**
Lodge Dri. *Old C* —3E **85**
Lodge Dri. *W Mare* —4E **127**
Lodge Gdns. *Bath* —3E **109**
Lodge Hill. *Bris* —5E **61**
Lodge La. *Nail* —2F **123**
Lodge Pl. *Bris* —3F **69** (2A **4**)
Lodge Rd. *Bris* —5E **61**
Lodge Rd. *Puck* —5D **65**
Lodge Rd. *Yate* —3C **16** (in two parts)
Lodgeside Av. *Bris* —1E **73**
Lodgeside Gdns. *Bris* —1E **73**
Lodge St. *Bris* —3E **69** (2A **4**)

Lodge Wlk. *Bris* —1F **61**
Lodore Rd. *Bris* —3B **60**
Lodway. *E'ton G* —3D **53**
Lodway Clo. *Pill* —2E **53**
Lodway Gdns. *Pill* —3E **53**
Lodway Rd. *Bris* —3E **81**
Logan Rd. *Bris* —4F **57**
Logus Ct. *L Grn* —1B **84**
Lombard St. *Bris* —1F **79**
Lomond Rd. *Bris* —3B **42**
London Rd. *Bath* —1B **106**
London Rd. *St Pa* —1B **70**
London Rd. *War* —3E **75**
London Rd. E. *Bathe* —3A **102**
London Rd. W. *Bath* —4D **101**
London St. *Bath* —1B **106**
London St. *Bris* —2F **73**
Longacre. *Bath* —1B **106**
Long Acre. *Clev* —5B **120**
Longacre Ho. *Bath* —1B **106**
Longacre Rd. *Bris* —5C **88**
Long Acres Clo. *Bris* —5F **39**
Long Ashton By-Pass. *L Ash* —5C **76**
Long Ashton Rd. *L Ash* —4C **76**
Long Av. *Clev* —4B **120**
Long Barnaby. *Mid N* —2D **151**
Long Beach Rd. *L Grn* —2C **84**
Long Clo. *Brad S* —3A **28**
Long Clo. *Bris* —1E **61**
Long Croft. *Bris* —1F **17**
Long Croft. *Yate* —2F **17**
Long Cross. *Bris* —4A **38**
Longden Rd. *Bris* —1B **62**
Longdown Ct. *Bris* —3A **90**
Longdown Dri. *W Mare* —1F **129**
Long Eaton Dri. *Bris* —5D **81**
Longfellow Av. *Bath* —5A **106**
Longfellow Rd. *Rads* —4F **151**
Longfield Rd. *Bris* —4A **58**
Longfield Rd. *Trow* —3D **119**
Longford. *Yate* —1E **33**
Longford Av. *Bris* —4F **41**
Long Handstones. *Bris* —1C **84**
Long Hay Clo. *Bath* —4C **104**
Longhills Hostel. *Bris* —5C **60**
Long La. *Back* —5D **125**
Long La. *Wrin* —1C **156**
Longleat Clo. *Bris* —2E **57**
Longleaze Gdns. *Hut* —5D **135**
Longman Clo. *Bris* —2A **74**
Long Mead. *Yate* —1A **18**
Longmead Av. *Bris* —2F **57**
Longmead Croft. *Bris* —4B **86**
Long Meadow. *Bris* —2F **59**
Longmeadow Rd. *Key* —4E **91**
Longmoor Rd. *Bris* —3C **78**
Longney Pl. *Pat* —5B **10**
Long Path. *Bris* —1F **73**
Longreach Gro. *Bris* —1F **89**
Long Rd. *Mang* —2C **62**
Long Row. *Bris* —4A **70** (3D **5**)
Longs Dri. *Yate* —4E **17**
Longthorne Pl. *Bath* —2A **110**
Longton Gro. Rd. *W Mare* —5C **126**
Long Valley Rd. *Bath* —4A **104**
Longvernal. *Mid N* —3C **150**
Longway Av. *Bris* —4B **88**
Longwell Ho. *Bris* —2B **84**
Longwood. *Bris* —3C **82**
Longwood La. *Fail* —1B **76**
Lonsdale Av. *W Mare* —3D **133**
Loop Rd. *Bath* —2B **106** (2C **96**)
Lorain Wlk. *Bris* —2B **40**
Lorne Rd. *Bath* —3E **105**
Lorton Rd. *Bris* —3D **41**
Lotts Av. *Back* —3D **125**
Loughman Clo. *Bris* —2A **74**
Louisa St. *Bris* —4B **70**
Louise Av. *Mang* —2C **62**
Love La. *Chip S* —1C **34**
Love La. *Yate* —2C **18**
Lovelinch Gdns. *L Ash* —4B **76**
Lovell Av. *Old C* —1F **85**
Lovells Hill. *Bris* —5D **73**
Lovells, The. *E'ton G* —3D **53**
Loveringe Clo. *Bris* —5B **24**
Lovers La. *Paul* —5D **147**
Lover's Wlk. *Bris* —5E **57**
Lovers Wlk. *Clev* —1C **120**
Lovers Wlk. *W Mare* —5B **126**
Love's Hill. *Tim* —2D **157**
Lowbourne. *Bris* —2B **88**
Lwr. Alma St. *Trow* —2E **119**
Lwr. Ashley Rd. *E'tn* —1C **70**
Lwr. Ashley Rd. *St Ag* —1B **70**
Lwr. Borough Walls. *Bath* —3A **106** (4B **96**)
Lwr. Bristol Rd. *Bath* —1A **104**
Lwr. Camden Pl. *Bath* —1B **106**
Lwr. Castle St. *Bris* —3A **70** (1E **5**)
Lwr. Chapel La. *Fram C* —3E **31**
Lwr. Chapel Rd. *Bris* —5E **73**
Lwr. Cheltenham Pl. *Bris* —1B **70**
Lwr. Church La. *Bris* —3E **69** (2A **4**)
Lwr. Church Rd. *W Mare* —5B **126**
Lwr. Claverham. *Clav* —1E **143**
Lwr. Clifton Hill. *Bris* —4C **68**
Lwr. Cock Rd. *Bris* —3B **74**
Lwr. College St. *Bris* —4E **69**
Lower Ct. *Trow* —5D **117**
Lwr. Court Rd. *Alm* —1C **10**
Lwr. Down Rd. *P'head* —3E **49**
Lwr. E. Hayes. *Bath* —1C **106**
Lwr. Fallow Clo. *Bris* —5B **88**
Lwr. Gay St. *Bris* —2F **69**
Lwr. Grove Rd. *Bris* —3A **60**
Lwr. Guinea St. *Bris* —5F **69**
Lwr. Hanham Rd. *Bris* —5E **73**
Lwr. Hedgemead Rd. *Bath* —1B **106**
Lwr. High St. *Bris* —4F **37**
Lwr. House Cres. *Bris* —5D **27**
Lwr. Kingsdown Rd. *Kngdn* —4F **103**
Lwr. Knole La. *Bris* —1C **40**
Lwr. Knowles Rd. *Clev* —4C **120**
Lwr. Lamb St. *Bris* —4E **69**
Lwr. Linden Rd. *Clev* —3D **121**
Lwr. Maudlin St. *Bris* —3F **69** (1C **4**)
Lwr. Moor Rd. *Yate* —2A **18**
Lwr. Mount Pleasant. *F'frd* —5B **112**
Lwr. Northend. *Bathe* —1A **102**
Lwr. Norton La. *Kew* —1F **127**
Lwr. Oldfield Pk. *Bath* —4E **105**
Lwr. Parade Ground Rd. *Lock* —3F **135**
Lwr. Park Row. *Bris* —3F **69** (2B **4**)
Lwr. Queen's Rd. *Clev* —3D **121**
Lwr. Redland Rd. *Bris* —5D **57**
Lwr. Sidney St. *Bris* —1C **78**
Lwr. Station App. Rd. *Tem M* —5B **70** (5F **5**)
Lwr. Station Rd. *Fish* —3C **60**
Lwr. Station Rd. *Stap H* —3E **61**
Lwr. Stoke. *Lim S* —1B **112**
Lwr. Stone Clo. *Fram C* —1E **31**
Lwr. Thirlmere Rd. *Pat* —1C **26**
Lwr. Whitelands. *Rads* —1E **153**
Lowlis Clo. *Bris* —1B **40**
Lowmead. *Trow* —1E **119**
Lowther Rd. *Bris* —2E **41**
Loxley Gdns. *Bath* —5D **105**
Loxton Dri. *Bath* —3C **104**
Loxton Rd. *W Mare* —5D **133**
Loxton Sq. *Bris* —2C **88**
Lucas Clo. *Bris* —4F **81**
Luccombe Hill. *Bris* —5D **57**
Luckington Rd. *Bris* —3A **42**
Lucklands Rd. *Bath* —5D **99**
Luckley Av. *Bris* —3E **87**
Luckwell Rd. *Bris* —2D **79**
Lucky La. *Bris* —1F **79**
Ludlow Clo. *Bris* —1B **70**
Ludlow Clo. *Key* —3F **91**
Ludlow Clo. *Will* —3D **85**
Ludlow Ct. *Will* —4D **85**
Ludlow Rd. *Bris* —5C **42**
Ludwell Clo. *Wint* —4F **29**
Ludwells Orchard. *Paul* —4B **146**
Lullington Rd. *Bris* —2D **81**
Lulsgate Rd. *Bris* —5C **78**
Lulworth Cres. *Bris* —4B **46**
Lulworth Rd. *Key* —4A **92**
Lurgan Wlk. *Bris* —4F **79**
Lux Furlong. *Bris* —5D **39**
Luxton St. *Bris* —2D **71**
Lychgate Pk. *Lock* —4E **136**
Lydbrook Clo. *Yate* —1F **33**
Lyddieth Ct. *Brad A* —2F **113**
Lyddington Rd. *Bris* —4B **42**
Lyddon Rd. *W Mare* —2F **129**
Lydford Wlk. *Bris* —3F **79**
Lydiard Croft. *Bris* —1E **83**
Lydiard Way. *Trow* —5D **119**
Lydney Rd. *S'mead* —4F **41**
Lydney Rd. *Stap H* —3A **62**
Lydstep Ter. *Bris* —1E **79**
Lyefield Rd. *Wor* —1C **128**
Lyes, The. *Cong* —3D **145**
Lyme Gdns. *Bath* —2C **104**
Lyme Rd. *Bath* —2C **104**
Lymore Av. *Bath* —4D **105**
Lymore Gdns. *Bath* —4D **105**
Lymore Ter. *Bath* —5D **105**
Lympsham Grn. *Bath* —3E **109**
Lynbrook. *L Ash* —4B **76**
Lynbrook La. *Bath* —1A **110**
Lynch Clo. *W Mare* —2D **129**
Lynch Ct. *L Grn* —1B **84**
Lynch Cres. *Wins* —5A **156**
Lynchmead. *Wins* —5A **156**
Lynch, The. *Wins* —5A **156**
Lyncombe Hill. *Bath* —4B **106**
Lyncombe Vale. *Bath* —5B **106**
Lyncombe Vale Rd. *Bath* —1B **110**
Lyncombe Wlk. *Bris* —5D **61**
Lyndale Av. *Bris* —2F **55**
Lyndale Rd. *Bris* —2F **71**
Lyndale Rd. *Yate* —5F **17**
Lynde Clo. *Bris* —4D **87**
Lyndhurst Bungalows. *Brad A* —3E **115**
Lyndhurst Pl. *Bath* —1B **106**
Lyndhurst Rd. *Bath* —3D **105**
Lyndhurst Rd. *Bris* —5B **40**
Lyndhurst Rd. *Key* —5B **92**
Lyndhurst Rd. *Mid N* —4E **151**
Lyndhurst Rd. *W Mare* —4C **132**
Lyndhurst Ter. *Bath* —1B **106**
Lyneham Way. *Trow* —2F **119**
Lynfield Pk. *Bath* —4D **99**
Lynmouth Clo. *W Mare* —3E **129**
Lynmouth Rd. *Bris* —5B **58**
Lynn Rd. *Bris* —2F **59**
Lynton. *Bris* —2C **74**
Lynton Clo. *P'head* —4A **50**
Lynton Pl. *Bris* —2E **71**
Lynton Rd. *Bris* —4E **79**
Lynton Rd. *Mid N* —4E **151**
Lynton Way. *Bris* —3D **45**
Lynwood Clo. *Mid N* —4D **151**
Lynwood Dri. *Trow* —1A **118**
Lynwood Rd. *Bris* —3D **79**
Lynx Cres. *W Mare* —1F **139**
Lyons Ct. *W Mare* —1D **133**
Lyons Ct. Rd. *Bris* —1F **89**
Lyppiatt Rd. *Bris* —2F **71**
Lyppincourt Rd. *Bris* —1C **40**
Lysander Rd. *W Trym & Pat* —3D **25**
Lysander Wlk. *Stok G* —4A **28**
Lytchet Dri. *Bris* —4B **46**
Lytes Cary Rd. *Key* —5A **92**
Lytham Ho. *Bris* —4F **81**
Lytton Gdns. *Bath* —5C **104**
Lytton Gro. *Bris* —4C **42**
Lytton Gro. *Key* —3C **92**
Lyveden Gdns. *Bris* —3D **87**
Lyvedon Way. *L Ash* —4D **77**

McAdam Way. *Bris* —5B **68**
Macaulay Bldgs. *Wid* —5D **107**
Macaulay Rd. *Bris* —4C **42**
McCrae Rd. *Lock* —3F **135**
McDonogh Ct. *Trow* —2E **119**
Macey's Rd. *Bris* —5F **87**
Machin Clo. *Bris* —1B **40**
Machin Gdns. *Bris* —1C **40**
Machin Rd. *Bris* —1B **40**
Macies, The. *Bath* —3C **98**
Mackie Av. *Bris* —2D **43**
Mackie Gro. *Bris* —2D **43**
Mackie Rd. *Bris* —2D **43**
McLaren Rd. *Bris* —3D **37**
Macleod Clo. *Clev* —4A **120**
Macqurie Clo. *Yat* —2A **142**
Macrae Ct. *Bris* —2A **74**
Madam La. *W Mare* —3D **129** (in two parts)
Madeira Ct. *W Mare* —4A **126**
Madeira Rd. *Clev* —3D **121**
Madeira Rd. *W Mare* —4A **126**
Madeline Rd. *Bris* —4B **60**
Madison Clo. *Yate* —4F **17**
Maesbury. *Bris* —4A **74**
Maesbury Rd. *Key* —5A **92**
Maesknoll Rd. *Bris* —2C **80**
Magdalen Av. *Bath* —4A **106**
Magdalene Pl. *Bris* —1B **70**
Magdalene Rd. *Rads* —2F **153**
Magdalen Rd. *Bath* —4A **106**
Magdalen Way. *W Mare* —2E **129**
Magellan Clo. *W Mare* —1D **129**
Maggs Clo. *Bris* —1F **41**
Maggs Hill. *Tim* —1E **157**
Maggs La. *C'chu* —4D **89**
Maggs La. *Clay H* —5A **60**
Magnolia Av. *W Mare* —4E **129**
Magnolia Rise *Trow* —3E **119**
Magnolia Rd. *Rads* —3B **152**
Magnon Rd. *Brad A* —2C **114**
Magpie Bottom La. *K'wd* —4E **73**
Magpie Bottom La. *St G & K'wd* —4D **73**
Magpie Clo. *W Mare* —5C **128**
Maidenhead Rd. *Bris* —5F **87**
Maiden Way. *Bris* —4E **37**
Maidstone Gro. *W Mare* —2E **139**
Maidstone St. *Bris* —2B **80**
Main Rd. *B'ley* —5A **124**
Main Rd. *E Comp* —1C **24**
Main Rd. *Hew* —1F **131**
Main Rd. *Hut* —1B **140**
Main Rd. *Yate* —2E **63**
Main View. *Coal H* —2F **31**
Maisemore. *Yate* —3F **33**
Maisemore Av. *Pat* —5D **11**
Makin Clo. *Bris* —5E **75**
Malago Rd. *Bris* —2E **79**
Malago Vale Est. *Bris* —2E **79**
Malago Wlk. *Bris* —4A **86**
Maldowers La. *Bris* —1C **72**
Mallard Clo. *Brad S* —4F **11**
Mallard Clo. *Bris* —1B **72**
Mallard Clo. *Chip S* —1C **34**
Mallard Wlk. *W Mare* —5C **128**
Mallow Clo. *Clev* —3E **121**
Mallow Clo. *T'bry* —2E **7**
Mallow Clo. *Trow* —4D **119**
Mall, The. *Bath* —4B **106** (4C **96**)
Mall, The. *Bris* —3B **68**
Malmains Dri. *Bris* —3D **45**
Malmesbury Clo. *Bris* —3E **57**
Malmesbury Clo. *L Grn* —5B **74**
Malthouse, The. *Bris* —5B **58**
Maltings Ind. Est., The. *Bath* —3C **104**
Maltings, Ind. Pk., The. *Trow* —1B **118**
Maltings, The. *Brad A* —4E **115**
Maltings, The. *W Mare* —3D **129**
Maltlands. *W Mare* —1B **134**
Malvern Bldgs. *Bath* —4B **100**
Malvern Ct. *Bris* —3B **72**
Malvern Dri. *Bris* —5E **75**
Malvern Dri. *T'bry* —4E **7**
Malvern Rd. *Brisl* —2F **81**
Malvern Rd. *St G* —3B **72**
Malvern Rd. *W Mare* —3C **132**
Malvern Ter. *Bath* —5B **100**
Malvern Vs. Bath —5B ***100***
(off Belgrave Cres.)
Mancroft Av. *Bris* —5A **38**
Mandy Meadows. *Mid N* —3C **150**
Mangotsfield Rd. *Bris & Mang* —3B **62**
Manilla Cres. *W Mare* —4B **126**
Manilla Pl. *W Mare* —4A **126**
Manilla Rd. *Bris* —3C **68**
Manmoor La. *Clev* —5F **121**
Manor Clo. *Coal H* —3E **31**
Manor Clo. *E'ton G* —3C **52**
Manor Clo. *Trow* —4A **118**
Manor Clo., The. *Abb L* —2C **66**
Manor Copse Rd. *Writ* —2F **153**
Manor Ct. *Back* —3C **124**
Manor Ct. *Bris* —3A **60**
Manor Ct. *Lock* —4E **135**
Manor Ct. *Trow* —4A **118**
Manor Court Dri. *Bris* —5A **42**
Manor Dri. *Bathf* —4D **103**
Manor Farm Cvn. Pk. *W Mare* —2C **138**
Manor Farm Clo. *W Mare* —1F **139**
Manor Farm Cotts. *Brad S* —5E **11**
Manor Farm Cres. *W Mare* —1F **139**
Manor Gdns. *Kew* —1F **127**
Manor Gdns. *Lock* —4E **135**
Manor Gdns. Ho. *Bris* —2B **60**
Manor Grange. *B'don* —4F **139**
Manor Gro. *Mang* —3C **62**
Manor Gro. *Pat* —4D **11**
Manor La. *Abb L* —2B **66**
Manor La. *Wint* —2B **30**
Manor Pk. *Bath* —1C **104**
Manor Pk. *Bris* —4D **57**
Manor Pk. *Rads* —2F **153**
Manor Pl. *Bris* —3E **45**
Manor Rd. *Abb L* —4B **66**
Manor Rd. *Bath* —5D **99**
Manor Rd. *Bishop* —3A **58**
Manor Rd. *B'wth* —2B **86**
Manor Rd. *Fish* —2B **60**
Manor Rd. *Key* —5B **92**
Manor Rd. *Trow* —4A **118**
Manor Rd. *Wick* —5B **154**
Manor Rd. *W Mare* —4D **127**
Manor Rd. *Writ* —2F **153**
Manor Rd. *Yate* —3C **62**
Manor Ter. *Rads* —2F **153**
Manor Valley. *W Mare* —4E **127**
Manor Vs. *Bath* —5D **99**
Manor Wlk. *T'bry* —1C **6**
Manor Way. *Chip S* —5E **19**
Mansbrook Ho. *Mid N* —3D **151**
Mansell Clo. *Salt* —5E **93**
Mansfield Av. *W Mare* —5F **127**
Mansfield St. *Bris* —3D **79**
Manston Clo. *Bris* —5E **81**
Manton Clo. *Trow* —5C **118**
Manvers St. *Bath* —3B **106** (4C **96**)
Manvers St. *Trow* —1D **119**
Manworthy Rd. *Bris* —2F **81**
Manx Rd. *Bris* —5B **42**
Maple Av. *Bris* —4E **61**
Maple Av. *T'bry* —3D **7**
Maple Clo. *Bris* —3F **89**
Maple Clo. *Lit S* —2E **27**
Maple Clo. *Old C* —1D **85**
Maple Clo. *W Mare* —5E **127**
Maple Ct. *Bris* —1F **73**
Maple Dri. *Rads* —3B **152**
Maple Gdns. *Bath* —5F **105**
Maple Gro. *Bath* —5F **105**
Maple Gro. *Trow* —4C **118**
Maple Leaf Ct. *Bris* —3C **68**
Mapleleaze. *Bris* —2F **81**
Maplemeade. *Bris* —3E **57**
Maple Rd. *Bris* —2F **57**
Maple Rd. *St Ap* —5F **71**
Maples, The. *Nail* —4B **122**
Maplestone Rd. *Bris* —5C **88**
Maple Wlk. *Key* —4F **91**
Maple Wlk. *Puck* —2E **65**
Mapstone Clo. *Ham* —1D **45**
Marbeck Rd. *Bris* —3D **41**
Marchants Pas. *Bath* —4B **106** (5C **96**)
Marchants Quay. *Bris* —5F **69**
Marchfields Way. *W Mare* —2D **133**
Marconi Rd. *P'head* —3B **48**
Mardale Clo. *Bris* —2E **41**
Marden Rd. *Key* —4C **92**

Marden Wlk. Trow —4D 119
Mardon Rd. Bris —4F 71
Mardyke Ferry Rd. Bris —5D 69
Margaret Rd. Bris —4B 86
Margaret's Bldgs. Bath —2A 106 (1A 96)
Margaret's Hill. Bath —1B 106
Margate St. Bris —2B 80
Marguerite Rd. Bris —5B 78
Marigold Wlk. Bris —3C 78
Marina Dri. Stav —3D 117
Marina Gdns. Bris —4A 60
Marindin Dri. W Mare —1F 129
Marine Hill. Clev —1C 120
Marine Pde. Clev —2C 120
Marine Pde. Pill —2E 53
(in two parts)
Marine Pde. W Mare (Beach Rd.) —3B 132
Marine Pde. W Mare (Claremont Cres.) —4A 126
Mariners Clo. Back —2C 124
Mariner's Clo. W Mare —4B 128
Mariners Dri. Back —2C 124
Mariners Dri. Bris —3F 55
Mariner's Path. Bris —3F 55
Mariners Path. P'head —3A 48
Mariners Way. Pill —2E 53
Marion Rd. Bris —2D 83
Marion Wlk. Bris —3C 72
Marissal Clo. Bris —1A 40
Marissal Rd. Bris —1F 39
Mariston Way. Bris —4E 75
Marjorie Whimster Ho. Bath —3C 104
Market Ind. Est. Yat —2B 142
Market La. W Mare —5B 126
Market Pl. Rads —1C 152
Market Sq. Bris —4E 61
Market St. Brad A —2E 115
Market St. Trow —2D 119
Markham Clo. Bris —5E 37
Mark La. Bris —4E 69 (3A 4)
Marksbury Rd. Bris —3E 79
Marlborough Av. Bris —4A 60
Marlborough Bldgs. Bath —2F 105
Marlborough Dri. Bris —3D 45
Marlborough Dri. W Mare —3E 129
Marlborough Hill. Bris —2F 69
Marlborough Hill Pl. Bris —2F 69
Marlborough La. Bath —2F 105
Marlborough St. Bath —1F 105
Marlborough St. Bris —2F 69
Marlborough St. Eastv —4A 60
Marlepit Gro. Bris —2A 86
Marley Pl. Bris —2B 68
Marlfield Wlk. Bris —1A 86
Marling Rd. Bris —2B 72
Marlwood Dri. Bris —1C 40
Marmaduke St. Bris —2B 80
Marmion Cres. Bris —1A 40
Marne Clo. Bris —3F 89
Marsden Rd. Bath —1C 108
Marshall Ho. Bris —3B 60
Marsham Way. Bris —1B 84
Marsh Clo. Wint —4A 30
Marshfield Pk. Bris —4E 45
Marshfield Rd. Bris —3D 61
Marshfield Way. Bath —5B 100
Marsh La. Asht —3C 78
Marsh La. E'ton G —5A 36
Marsh La. Redf —3E 71
Marshmead. Hil —3F 117
Marsh Rd. Bris —2B 78
Marsh Rd. Hil M —2E 117
Marsh Rd. Yat —3B 142
Marsh St. A'mth —4E 37
Marsh St. Bris —4F 69 (3B 4)
Marshwall La. Alm —1A 10
Marson Rd. Clev —3D 121
Marston Rd. Bris —3D 81
Marston Rd. Trow —3D 155
Martcombe Rd. E'ton G (in three parts) —4C 52
Martin Clo. Pat —1A 26
Martindale Rd. W Mare —5B 128
Martingale Rd. Bris —1F 81
Martin's Clo. Bris —5E 73
Martins Gro. W Mare —3C 128
Martin's Rd. Han —5E 73
Martin St. Bris —2D 79
Martock. W Mare —1D 139
Martock Cres. Bris —4E 79
Martock Rd. Bris —4E 79
Martock Rd. Key —5C 92
Marwood Rd. Bris —5A 80
Marybush La. Bris —3A 70 (2E 5)
Mary Carpenter Pl. Bris —1B 70
Mary Ct. Bris —2F 71 (off Alfred St.)
Marygold Leaze. Bris —1C 84
Mary St. Redf —2F 71
Mascot Rd. Bris —2F 79
Masefield Way. Bris —1C 58
Maskelyne Av. Bris —5F 41
Masonpit Pool La. Yate —1E 29
Masons La. Brad A —2E 115
Masons View. Wint —3B 30
Matchells Clo. St Ap —4A 72
Materman Rd. Stoc —3A 90
Matford Clo. Bris —5F 25
Matford Clo. Wint —4A 30
Matthews Clo. Bris —2B 90
Matthews Rd. Bris —3E 71
Maules La. Ham —2B 44
Maulton Clo. Holt —2D 155
Maunsell Rd. Bris —2D 39
Maurice Rd. Bris —5A 58
Mautravers Clo. Brad S —2F 27
Maxcroft La. Hil M —2E 117
Maxse Rd. Bris —2D 81
Maybank Rd. Yate —5F 17
Maybec Gdns. Bris —4C 72
Maybourne. Bris —3C 82
Maybrick Rd. Bath —4E 105
Maycliffe Pk. Bris —5B 58
Mayfair Av. Nail —4D 123
Mayfield Av. Bris —5C 60
Mayfield Av. W Mare —4C 128
Mayfield Clo. P'head —5F 49
Mayfield Pk. Bris —5C 60
Mayfield Pk. N. Bris —5C 60
Mayfield Pk. S. Bris —5C 60
Mayfield Rd. Bath —4E 105
Mayfields. Key —3A 92
Mayflower Gdns. Nail —3F 123
Maynard Clo. Bris —3E 87
Maynard Clo. Clev —3F 121
Maynard Rd. Bris —3E 87
Mayors Bldgs. Bris —2D 61
Mays Hill. Fram C —5A 16
May's La. W Mare —2F 131
May St. Bris —1E 73
Maytree Av. Bris —1D 87
Maytree Clo. Bris —1D 87
May Tree Clo. Nail —4B 122
May Tree Rd. Rads —3B 152
May Tree Wlk. Key —5E 91
Mayville Av. Bris —1D 43
Maywood Av. Bris —3D 61
Maywood Cres. Bris —3D 61
Maywood Rd. Bris —3E 61
Maze St. Bris —4D 71
Mead Clo. Bath —1F 109
Mead Clo. Bris —1A 54
Mead Ct. N Brad —4E 155
Mead Ct. Wint —3A 30
Mead Ct. Bus. Pk. T'bry —5D 7
Meade Ho. Bath —4B 104
Meadgate. E Grn —5D 47
Meadlands. Cor —5D 95
Mead La. Brad S —3A 28
Mead La. Salt —1B 94
Meadowbank. W Mare —1D 129
Meadow Clo. Back —2D 125
Meadow Clo. Bris —5B 46
Meadow Clo. Nail —2D 123
Meadow Ct. Bath —2B 104
Meadow Ct. Dri. Old C —2E 85
Meadow Croft. W Mare —1F 139
Meadow Dri. Bath —4E 109
Meadow Dri. Lock —4F 135
Meadowfield. Brad A —3C 114
Meadow Gdns. Bath —5B 98
Meadow Gro. Bris —5F 37
Meadowland. Yat —2A 142
Meadowland Rd. Bris —5A 24
Meadowlands. St Geo —2A 130
Meadow La. B'ptn —5E 101
Meadow Mead. Fram C —1D 31
Meadow Mead. Yate —1A 18
Meadow Pk. Bathf —3C 102
Meadow Rd. Chip S —5C 18
Meadow Rd. Clev —3E 121
Meadow Rd. Paul —5C 146
Meadows Clo. P'head —3B 48
Meadow Side. Iron A —2F 15
Meadowside. T'bry —4E 7
Meadowside Dri. Bris —5C 88
Meadows, The. Bris —1F 83
Meadow St. A'mth —3C 36
Meadow St. St Pa —3A 70 (1E 5)
Meadow St. W Mare —1C 132
Meadowsweet Av. Bris —1D 43
Meadowsweet Ct. Stap —2A 60
Meadow Vale. Bris —1C 72
Meadow View. Fram C —2E 31
Meadow View. Rads —3D 153
Meadow View Clo. Bath —1B 104
Meadow Way. Brad S —3A 28
Mead Rise. Bris —5B 70
Mead Rd. Chip S —1E 35
Mead Rd. P'head —5E 49
Mead Rd. Stok G —3A 28
Meads, The. Bris —5B 46 (in two parts)
Mead St. Bris —1B 80
Mead, The. Alv —2B 8
Mead, The. Fil —5D 27
Mead. The, Mid N —1F 157
Mead, The. W'ley —2F 113
Mead Vale. W Mare —4C 128
Meadway. Bris —1E 55
Mead Way. T'bry —5C 6
Meadway. Trow —2A 118
Meadway Av. Nail —3C 122
Mearcombe La. B'don —5D 141
Meardon Rd. Bris —2A 90
Meare. W Mare —1D 139
Meare Rd. Bath —2B 110
Mede Clo. Bris —5A 70
Medical Av. Bris —3E 69 (2A 4)
Medina Clo. T'bry —5D 7
Medway Clo. Key —5C 92
Medway Ct. T'bry —4E 7
Medway Dri. Fram C —3D 31
Medway Dri. Key —5C 92
Meere Bank. Bris —3D 39
Meer Wall. W Mare —5A 144
Meg Thatchers Gdns. Bris —3D 73
Meg Thatcher's Grn. Bris —3D 73
Melbourne Dri. Chip S —5D 19
Melbourne Rd. Bris —3F 57
Melbourne Ter. Clev —3D 121
Melbury Rd. Bris —3B 80
Melcombe Ct. Bath —5E 105
Melcombe Rd. Bath —4E 105
Melita Rd. Bris —4A 58
Melksham Rd. Holt —1F 155
Mellent Av. Bris —5E 87
Mells Clo. Key —5A 92
Mells La. Rads —2E 153
Melrose Av. Bris —2D 69
Melrose Av. Yate —4B 18
Melrose Clo. Yate —4C 18
Melrose Gro. Bath —1C 108
Melrose Pl. Bris —2D 69
Melrose Ter. Bath —4B 100
Melton Cres. Bris —4C 42
Melton Rd. Trow —5C 116
Melville Rd. Bris —1D 69
Melville Ter. Bris —2E 79
Melvin Sq. Bris —4A 80
Memorial Clo. Bris —1D 83
Memorial Cotts. Bath —5D 99
Memorial Rd. Bris —5D 73
Memorial Rd. Wrin —1C 156
Mendip Av. W Mare —3C 128
Mendip Clo. Key —3F 91
Mendip Clo. Nail —4D 123
Mendip Clo. Paul —5B 146
Mendip Clo. Yat —4B 142
Mendip Cres. Bris —4C 46
Mendip Edge. W Mare —3D 139
Mendip Gdns. Bath —4E 109
Mendip Gdns. Yat —4B 142
Mendip Rise. Lock —4F 135
Mendip Rd. Bris —2F 79
Mendip Rd. Lock —4A 136
Mendip Rd. P'head —3C 48
Mendip Rd. W Mare —1E 133
Mendip Rd. Yat —3A 142 (in two parts)
Mendip Ter. Bath —3F 107
Mendip View. Wick —4B 154
Mendip View Av. Bris —4C 60
Mendip Way. Rads —1C 152
Mercer Ct. Bris —5D 81
Merchants Ct. Bris —5C 68
Merchants Quay. Bris —5F 69 (5B 4)
Merchants Rd. Clif —3C 68
Merchant's Rd. Hot —5C 68
Merchant St. Bris —3A 70 (1D 5)
Mercia Dri. Bris —5C 58
Mercier Clo. Yate —4B 18
Meredith Ct. Bris —5C 68
Merfield Rd. Bris —3D 81
Meridian Pl. Bris —3D 69
Meridian Rd. Bris —1E 69
Meridian Ter. Bris —4A 58
Meridian Vale. Bris —3D 69
Meridian Wlk. Trow —2A 118
Meriet Av. Bris —4D 87
Merioneth St. Bris —2B 80
Meriton St. Bris —5D 71
Merlin Clo. Bris —4B 40
Merlin Clo. W Mare —5C 128
Merlin Ct. Bris —5D 41
Merlin Pk. P'head —4B 48
Merlin Ridge. Puck —3E 65
Merlin Rd. Pat —3E 25
Merlin Way. Chip S —1B 34
Merrett Ct. Bris —1D 59
Merrick Ct. Bris —5F 69 (5B 4)
Merrimans Rd. Bris —4F 37
Merryfield Rd. Lock —2F 135
Merryweather Clo. Brad S —1F 27
Merryweathers. Bris —3A 82
Merrywood Clo. Bris —1E 79
Merrywood Rd. Bris —1E 79
Merstham Rd. Bris —5C 58
Merton Rd. Bris —2A 58
Mervyn Rd. Bris —3A 58
Metford Gro. Bris —4D 57
Metford Pl. Bris —4E 57
Metford Rd. Bris —4D 57
Methuen Clo. Brad A —5F 115
Methwyn Clo. W Mare —1A 134
Mews, The. Bath —1B 104
Mezellion Pl. Bath —5C 100 (off Camden Rd.)
Michaels Mead. Bath —4C 98
Middle Av. Bris —4F 69 (4B 4)
Middleford Ho. Bris —4E 87
Middle La. Bath —5C 100
Middle La. Trow —5F 117
Middle Rank. Brad A —2D 115
Middle Rd. Bris —4A 62
Middle Stoke. Lim S —3B 112
Middleton Rd. Bris —4B 38
Middle Yeo Grn. Nail —2C 122
Midford. W Mare —1D 139
Midford La. Mid & Lim S —5D 111
Midford Rd. Bath —3F 109
Midhaven Rise. W Mare —1C 128
Midland Bri. Rd. Bath —3F 105
Midland Rd. Bath —3E 105
Midland Rd. Stap H —3F 61
Midland Rd. St Ph —3B 70
Midlands, The. Holt —2E 155
Midland St. Bris —4B 70
Midland Ter. Bris —4B 60
Midland Way. T'bry —4C 6
Midsomer Enterprise Pk. Mid N —2A 152
Midsummer Bldgs. Bath —4B 100
Milburn Rd. W Mare —1D 133
Milbury Gdns. Worl —3F 127
Mildred St. Bris —3E 71
Miles Ct. Bar C —1B 84
Miles Rd. Bris —1C 68
Miles's Bldgs. Bath —2A 106 (2B 96)
Miles St. Bath —4B 106 (5D 97)
Mile Wlk. Bris —1B 88
Milford Av. Wick —4A 154
Milford St. Bris —1E 79
Milk St. Bath —3A 106 (4B 96)
Millard Clo. Bris —2E 41
Millards Ct. Mid N —1E 151
Millard's Hill. Mid N —1E 151
Mill Av. Bris —4F 69 (4C 4)
Millbank Clo. Bris —2A 82
Millbourn Clo. W'ley —2E 113
Millbrook Av. Bris —2B 82
Millbrook Clo. Bris —4E 75
Millbrook Pl. Bath —4B 106
Millbrook Rd. Yate —4D 17
Mill Clo. Fram C —2E 31
Mill Clo. P'bry —5A 52
Mill Cres. W'lgh —5D 33
Millcross. Clev —5C 120
Millers Clo. Pill —3E 53
Millers Dri. Bris —5E 75
Miller's Rise. W Mare —1E 129
Miller Wlk. B'ptn —5F 101
Millfield. Mid N —4C 150
Millfield. T'bry —2D 7
Millfield Dri. Bris —4E 75
Millground Rd. Bris —4A 86
Millhand Vs. Trow —3E 119
Mill Ho., The. Brad A —3F 115
Milliman Clo. Bris —3F 87
Millington Dri. Trow —3A 118
Mill La. B'ptn —4A 102
Mill La. Bedm —1F 79
Mill La. Bit —5F 85
Mill La. Brad A —3E 115
Mill La. Chip S —5C 18
Mill La. Cong —2D 145
Mill La. Fram C —5D 15
Mill La. Mon C —4F 111
Mill La. Old S —3F 35
Mill La. P'bry —4A 52
Mill La. Rads —1E 153
Mill La. Tim —2E 157
Mill La. Trow —1C 118
Mill La. Twer A —3C 104
Mill La. War —5D 75
Mill Leg. Cong —2D 145
Millmead Ho. Bris —4E 87
Millmead Rd. Bath —4D 105
Millpond St. Bris —1C 70
Mill Pool. Bris —3D 41
Mill Rd. Rads —2D 153
Mill Rd. Wint D —5F 29
Mill Rd. Ind. Est. Rads —1D 153
Mill Steps. Wint D —1A 46
Mill St. Trow —2D 119
Millward Gro. Bris —3E 61
Millward Ter. Paul —3B 146
Milner Grn. Bris —5C 74
Milner Rd. Bris —2B 58
Milsom St. Bath —2A 106 (2B 96)
Milsom St. Bris —2C 70
Milton Av. Bath —5A 106
Milton Av. W Mare —5E 127
Milton Brow. W Mare —4F 127
Milton Clo. Nail —2D 123
Milton Clo. Yate —4F 17
Milton Grn. W Mare —4A 128
Milton Hill. W Mare —3F 127
Milton Pk. Bris —3E 71
Milton Pk. Rd. W Mare —4A 128
Milton Rise. W Mare —4A 128
Milton Rd. Bris —1A 58
Milton Rd. Rads —3F 151
Milton Rd. W Mare —5D 127
Milton Rd. Yate —4F 17
Miltons Clo. Bris —4F 87
Milverton. W Mare —1D 139
Milverton Gdns. Bris —5B 58
Milward Rd. Key —2A 92
Mina Rd. Bris —4B 58
Minehead Rd. Bris —4B 80
Minerva Gdns. Bath —4D 105
Minor's La. H'ley —1C 22
Minsmere Rd. Key —5C 92

Minster Way. Bath —1D **107**
Minton Clo. Bris —3D **89**
Minto Rd. Bris —5B **58**
Minto Rd. Ind. Cen. Bris —5B **58**
Mission Rd. Iron A —2C **16**
Mitchell Ct. Bris —4A **70** (4D **5**)
Mitchell La. Bris —4A **70** (4D **5**)
Mivart St. Bris —5D **59**
Mizzymead Clo. Nail —4C **122**
Mizzymead Rise. Nail —4C **122**
Mizzymead Rd. Nail —4D **123**
Modecombe Gro. Bris —1B **40**
Mogg St. Bris —5C **58**
Molesworth Clo. Bris —4C **86**
Molesworth Dri. Bris —4C **86**
Monger Cotts. Paul —1D **151**
Monger La. Paul & Mid N —1C **150**
Monk Rd. Bris —3F **57**
Monks Av. Bris —2D **73**
Monksdale Rd. Bath —5E **105**
Monks Hill. W Mare —2F **127**
Monks Ho. Yate —2F **33**
Monk's Pk. Av. Bris —3A **42**
Monkton Av. W Mare —1E **139**
Monkton Rd. Bris —1D **83**
Monmouth Clo. P'head —4B **48**
*Monmouth Ct. Bath —3F **105** (off Monmouth Pl.)*
Monmouth Ct. Pill —2E **53**
Monmouth Hill. Alm —2A **10**
Monmouth Pl. Bath —3A **106** (3A **96**)
Monmouth Rd. Bris —3F **57**
Monmouth Rd. Key —3F **91**
Monmouth Rd. Pill —2E **53**
Monmouth St. Bath —3A **106** (3A **96**)
Monmouth St. Bris —2B **80**
Monsdale Clo. Bris —1C **40**
Monsdale Dri. Bris —1C **40**
Montague Clo. Stok G —4A **28**
Montague Hill. Bris —2F **69**
Montague Hill S. Bris —2F **69**
Montague Pl. Bris —2F **69**
Montague Rd. Salt —5E **93**
Montague St. Bris —2F **69**
Montgomery St. Bris —1B **80**
Montpelier. Bath —2A **106** (1B **96**)
Montpelier. W Mare —4D **127**
Montpelier E. W Mare —4D **127**
Montpelier Path. W Mare —5C **126**
Montreal Av. Bris —4B **42**
Montrose Av. Bris —1E **69**
Montrose Cotts. Bath —5D **99**
Montrose Dri. War —4D **75**
Montrose Pk. Bris —3F **81**
Montroy Clo. Bris —1E **57**
Moon St. Bris —2A **70**
Moor Croft Dri. L Grn —2B **84**
Moor Croft Rd. Hut —5C **134**
Moordell Clo. Yate —5F **17**
Moor Drove. Cong —5C **144**
Moorend Gdns. Bris —5B **38**
Moorend Rd. Ham —1F **45**
Moor End Spout. Nail —2C **122**
Moorfield Rd. Back —2C **124**
Moorfields Clo. Bath —1E **109**
Moorfields Ct. Nail —3C **122**
Moorfields Ho. Bris —3E **71**
Moorfields Ho. Nail —3B **122**
Moorfields Rd. Bath —5E **105**
Moorfields Rd. Nail —3C **122**
Moor Gro. Bris —4B **38**
Moorgrove Ho. Bris —4E **39**
Moorham Rd. Wins —3B **156**
Moorhill St. Bris —1D **71**
Moorhouse Cvn. Pk. Bris —5D **23**
Moorhouse La. H'len —4B **22**
Moorings, The. Pill —3E **53**
Moorland Rd. Bath —4E **105**
Moorland Rd. W Mare —4B **132**
Moorland Rd. Yate —5F **17**
Moorlands Clo. Nail —3C **122**
Moorlands Rd. Bris —4B **60** (in two parts)
Moor La. Back —2B **124**
Moor La. Clev —4D **121** (in two parts)
Moor La. Lock & W Mare —1C **134**
Moor La. W Mare —4B **134**
Moor Pk. Clev —4E **121**
Moorpark Av. Yate —5E **17**
Moor Rd. Ban —1E **137**
Moor Rd. Yat —2B **142**
Moorside. Yat —2B **142**
Moravian Rd. Bris —2F **73**
Morden Wlk. Bris —1F **89**
Moreton Clo. Bris —4C **88**
Moreton St. Bris —2B **70**
Morford St. Bath —1A **106** (1B **96**)
Morgan Clo. Salt —5F **93**
Morgans Hill Clo. Nail —5C **122**
Morgan St. Bris —1B **70**
Morley Av. Mang —3C **62**
Morley Clo. Bris —3F **61**
Morley Clo. Lit S —2D **27**
Morley Rd. Stap H —3F **61**
Morley Rd. S'vle —1E **79**
Morley Sq. Bris —3A **58**
Morley St. Bar H —3D **71**
Morley St. Bris —1B **70**
Morley Ter. Bath —3E **105**
Morley Ter. K'wd —1F **73**
Morley Ter. Rads —1D **153**
Mornington Rd. Bris —5C **56**
Morpeth Rd. Bris —5F **79**
Morris La. Bathf —3C **102**
Morris Rd. Bris —2C **58**
Morse Rd. Bris —3E **71**
Mortimer Clo. Bath —4C **98**
Mortimer Rd. Clif —3C **68**
Mortimer Rd. Fil —3D **43**
Mortimer St. Trow —3C **118**
Morton St. Bris —3D **71**
Morton St. T'bry —1D **7**
Morton Way. T'bry —1E **7**
Moseley Gro. Uph —1C **138**
Moulton Dri. Brad A —5E **115**
Mountain Ash. Bath —5E **99**
Mountain Wood. Bathf —4D **103**
Mountbatten Clo. Kew —1C **128**
Mountbatten Clo. Yate —3F **17**
Mt. Beacon. Bath —5B **100**
Mount Beacon Pl. Bath —5A **100**
Mt. Beacon Row. Bath —5B **100**
Mount Clo. Fram C —1B **30**
Mount Cres. Wint —4A **30**
Mount Gdns. Bris —4F **73**
Mount Gro. Bath —1C **108**
Mount Hill Rd. Bris —4E **73**
Mt. Pleasant. Brad A —2E **115**
Mt. Pleasant. H'len —5E **23**
Mt. Pleasant. Pill —3F **53**
Mt. Pleasant. Rads —2E **153**
Mt. Pleasant Ter. Bris —1E **79**
Mount Rd. L'dwn —1A **106**
Mount Rd. S'dwn —5B **104**
Mount, The. Trow —5E **117**
*Mount View. L'dwn —5B **100** (off Beacon Rd.)*
Mount View. S'dwn —1C **108**
Mow Barton. Bris —2B **86**
Mow Barton. Yate —4F **17**
Mowbray Rd. Bris —1E **89**
Mowcroft Rd. Bris —4E **87**
Moxham Dri. Bris —4D **87**
Mud La. Clav —1D **143**
Muirfield. War —4C **74**
Muirfields. Yate —1A **34**
Mulberry Clo. Back —2C **124**
Mulberry Clo. Bris —2A **74**
Mulberry Clo. W Mare —4D **129**
Mulberry Dri. Bris —1B **74**
Mulberry La. B'don —5A **140**
Mulberry Rd. Cong —3E **145**
Mulberry Wlk. Bris —4E **39**
Muller Av. Bris —3B **58**
Muller Rd. Hor & Eastv —1B **58**
Mulready Clo. Bris —1E **59**
Murford Av. Bris —3D **87**
Murford Wlk. Bris —4D **87**
Murray Rd. Trow —5D **117**
Murray St. Bris —1E **79**
Musgrove Clo. Bris —2E **39**
Myrtle Dri. Bris —2A **54**
Myrtle Gdns. Yat —3B **142**
Myrtle Rd. Bris —2E **69**
Myrtle St. Bris —1D **79**
Mythern Meadow. Brad A —4F **115**

Nags Head Hill. Bris —3C **72**
Nailsea Clo. Bris —1C **86**
Nailsea Pk. Nail —3E **123**
Nailsea Pk. Clo. Nail —3E **123**
Nailsworth Av. Yate —5A **18**
Naishcombe Hill. Wick —5B **154**
Naishes Av. Pea J —4D **157**
Naish Ho. Bath —3B **104**
Napier Ct. Bris —5D **69**
Napier Miles Rd. Bris —4C **38**
Napier Rd. A'mth —3D **37**
Napier Rd. Bath —3B **98**
Napier Rd. Eastv —5D **59**
Napier Rd. Redl —5D **57**
Napier Sq. Bris —3C **36**
Napier St. Bris —4D **71**
Narroways Rd. Bris —4C **58**
Narrow La. Bris —4A **62**
Narrow Lewins Mead. Bris —3F **69** (2B **4**)
Narrow Plain. Bris —4A **70** (3E **5**)
Narrow Quay. Bris —5F **69** (5B **4**)
*Narrow Wine S. Trow —2D **119** (off Fore St.)*
Naseby Wlk. Bris —1B **72**
Nash Clo. Key —3C **92**
Nash Dri. Bris —5E **43**
Nasmilco. Stav —1D **117**
Naunton Way. W Mare —3F **127**
Navigator Clo. Trow —3E **117**
Neads Dri. War —5E **75**
Neate Ct. Pat —1E **27**
Neath Rd. Bris —2F **71**
Nelson Bldgs. Bath —1B **106**
Nelson Ct. W Mare —1C **128**
Nelson Ho. Bath —2F **105**
Nelson Ho. Bris —2F **61**
Nelson Pde. Bris —1F **79**
Nelson Pl. Bath —1B **106**
*Nelson Pl. E. Bath —1B **106** (off Nelson Ter.)*
Nelson Pl. W. Bath —3F **105**
Nelson Rd. Bris —2F **61** (in two parts)
Nelson St. Bedm —3C **78**
Nelson St. Bris —3F **69** (2C **4**)
Nelson Ter. Bath —1B **106**
Nelson Vs. Bath —3F **105**
Neston Wlk. Bris —5B **80**
Netham Pk. Ind. Est. Bris —4F **71**
Netham Rd. Bris —3F **71**
Netherways. Clev —5B **120**
Nettlestone Clo. Bris —5A **24**
Nevalan Dri. Bris —4C **72**
Neva Rd. W Mare —2C **132**
Neville Rd. Bris —5A **62**
Nevil Rd. Bris —3A **58**
Newark St. Bath —4B **106** (5C **96**)
Newbolt Clo. W Mare —4E **133**
New Bond St. Bath —3A **106** (3B **96**)
*New Bond St. Pl. Bath —3B **106** (3C **96**) (off New Bond St.)*
Newbourne Rd. W Mare —1A **134**
Newbrick Rd. Stok G —4C **28**
Newbridge Clo. Bris —4F **71**
Newbridge Ct. Bath —2C **104**
Newbridge Gdns. Bath —1B **104**
Newbridge Hill. Bath —1B **104**
Newbridge Rd. Bath —1A **104**
Newbridge Rd. Bris —4F **71**
Newbridge Trad. Est. Bris —5F **71**
New Bristol Rd. W Mare —4C **128**
New Brunswick Av. Bris —3D **73**
New Buildings. Bris —3B **60**
Newbury Rd. Bris —5C **42**
New Charlotte St. Bris —1F **79**
New Cheltenham Rd. Bris —1F **73**
New Church Rd. Uph —1B **138**
Newcombe Dri. Bris —3E **55**
Newcombe Rd. Bris —5B **40**
New Ear La. W Mare —1C **130**
New Engine Rank. Coal H —1F **47**
Newent Av. Bris —3D **73**
New Fosseway Rd. Bris —2D **89**
Newfoundland Rd. Bris —2B **70**
Newfoundland St. Bris —2A **70**
Newfoundland Way. Bris —2B **70**
Newgate. Bris —3A **70** (2D **5**)
Newhaven Pl. P'head —4A **48**
Newhaven Rd. P'head —5A **48**
New John St. Bris —2E **79**
New Kingsley Rd. Bris —4B **70** (3F **5**)
New King St. Bath —3A **106**
Newland Dri. Bris —4C **86**
Newland Rd. Bris —4C **86**
Newland Rd. W Mare —2D **133**
Newlands Av. Coal H —2E **31**
Newlands Clo. P'head —3E **49**
Newlands Grn. Clev —5E **121**
Newlands Hill. P'head —4E **49**
Newlands Rd. Key —4F **91**
Newlands, The. Bris —5D **45**
Newland Wlk. Bris —5C **86**
New La. Alv —2D **9**
New Leaze. Alm —3E **11**
Newleaze. Hil —3F **117**
Newleaze Ho. Brad S —2D **43**
Newlyn Av. Bris —2F **55**
Newlyn Wlk. Bris —4D **81**
Newlyn Way. Yate —4B **18**
Newman Clo. W'lgh —5D **33**
Newmans La. Tim —1E **157**
Newmarket Av. Bris —3F **69** (2C **4**)
Newmarket Av. Whit B —3F **155**
*Newmarket Row. Bath (off Grand Pde.) —3B **106***
Newnham Clo. Bris —1F **89**
Newnham Pl. Pat —5B **10**
New Orchard St. Bath —3B **106** (4C **96**)
Newport Clo. Clev —4C **120**
Newport Clo. P'head —4B **48**
Newport Rd. Pill —2E **53**
Newport St. Bris —2A **80**
Newquay Rd. Bris —4B **80**
New Queen St. Bris —1D **73**
New Queen St. K'wd —1A **80**
New Rd. Ban —4C **136**
New Rd. Bathf —4E **103**
New Rd. Brad A —2E **115**
New Rd. Brad S —1B **42**
New Rd. Bris —2E **43**
New Rd. F'frd —4C **112**
New Rd. Mid N —3D **151**
New Rd. Pill —3E **53**
New Rd. Trow —3C **118**
Newry Wlk. Bris —4A **80**
Newsome Av. Pill —3E **53**
New Stadium Rd. Bris —5D **59**
New Station Rd. Bris —3C **60**
New Station Way. Fish —3C **60**
New St. Bath —3A **106** (4B **96**)
New St. Bris —3B **70** (1F **5**)
New St. Flats. Bris —3B **70** (1F **5**)
New Ter. Stav —1D **117**
New Thomas St. Bris —3B **70** (2F **5**)
Newton Clo. Bris —1C **74**
Newton Dri. Bris —5C **74**
Newton Grn. Nail —5B **122**
Newton Rd. Bath —4A **104**
Newton Rd. Bris —5C **74**
Newton Rd. W Mare —2C **132**
Newtons Rd. Kew —1C **128** (in two parts)
Newton St. Bris —2C **70**
Newtown. Brad A —3D **115**
Newtown. Trow —2C **118**
*New Tyning Ter. Bath —5C **100** (off Fairfield Rd.)*
New Vs. Bath —5C **106**
New Wlk. Bris —5D **73**
New Walls. Tot —1B **80**
Niblett Clo. Bris —4B **74**
Nibletts Hill. Bris —4B **72**
Nibley La. Iron A —3A **16**
Nibley La. Yate —3C **16**
Nibley Rd. Bris —2F **53**
Nicholas La. Bris —4C **72**
Nicholas Rd. Bris —1D **71**
Nicholas St. Bris —1A **80**
Nicholettes. Bris —5F **75**
Nicholls La. Wint —3A **30**
*Nicholl's Pl. Bath —1A **106** (off Lansdown Rd.)*
Nichol's Rd. P'head —2B **48**
Nigel Pk. Bris —5A **38**
Nightingale Clo. Fram C —3C **30**
Nightingale Clo. T'bry —2E **7**
Nightingale Clo. W Mare —4C **128**
Nightingale Ct. W Mare —4C **128**
Nightingale Gdns. Nail —3B **122**
Nightingale La. Wint —2C **30**
Nightingale Rise. P'head —5B **48**
Nightingale Rd. Trow —2A **118**
Nightingale Valley. Bris —5A **72**
Nightingale Way. Mid N —4E **151**
Nile St. Bath —3F **105**
Nine Tree Hill. Bris —1A **70**
Ninth Av. Bris —3D **43**
Nippors Way. Wins —4A **156**
Nithsdale Rd. W Mare —4C **132**
Noble Av. Bris —1E **85**
Nomis Pk. Cong —4E **145**
Nore Gdns. P'head —2E **49**
Nore Pk. Dri. P'head —2B **48**
Nore Rd. P'head —4A **48**
Norfolk Av. Bris —2A **70**
Norfolk Av. St And —5A **58**
Norfolk Bldgs. Bath —3F **105**
Norfolk Cres. Bath —3F **105**
Norfolk Gro. Key —4E **91**
Norfolk Pl. Bris —2E **79**
Norfolk Rd. P'head —4A **50**
Norland Rd. Bris —2B **68**
Norley Rd. Bris —5B **42**
Normanby Rd. Bris —1D **71**
Norman Gro. Bris —5F **61**
Norman Rd. Salt —5F **93**
Norman Rd. St W —5C **58**
Norman Rd. War —2D **75**
Normans, The. B'ptn —5A **102**
Normanton Rd. Bris —5C **56**
Norrisville Rd. Bris —1A **70**
Northampton Bldgs. Bath —1A **106**
Northampton St. Bath —1A **106**
*Northanger Ct. Bath —2B **106** (off Grove St.)*
Northavon Bus. Cen. Yate —3E **17**
Northcote Rd. Clif —1B **68**
Northcote Rd. Down & Mang —1B **62**
Northcote Rd. St G —2A **72**
Northcote St. Bris —1D **71**
North Croft Old C —1F **85**
N. Devon Rd. Bris —2C **60**
Northdown Rd. Rads —4B **148**
N. Drove. Nail —3A **122**
N. East Rd. T'bry —2D **7**
North End. Yat —1A **142**
Northend Av. Bris —5F **61**
Northend Cotts. Bath —1A **102**
Northend Gdns. Bris —5F **61**
Northend Rd. Bris —1A **74**
N. End Rd. Yat —1A **142**
Northern Path. Clev —3F **121**
Northern Way. Clev —4E **121**
Northfield. Rads —1D **153**
Northfield. W'ley —2F **113**
Northfield. Yate —1F **33**
Northfield Av. Bris —5F **73**

Northfield Ho. Bris —1E 79
Northfield Rd. Bris —3D 73
Northfield Rd. P'head —5A 48
Northfields. Bath —5A 100
Northfields Clo. Bath —5A 100
Northgate St. Bath —3B 106 (3C 96)
North Grn. St. Bris —4B 68
North Gro. Pill —3E 53
N. Hills Clo. W Mare —1F 139
North La. Bath —4E 107
North La. Nail —4A 122
Northleach Wlk. Bris —2B 54
N. Leaze. L Ash —3D 77
Northleigh. Brad A —1F 115
Northleigh Av. W Mare —4A 128
Northmead Av. Mid N —2C 150
Northmead Clo. Mid N —2C 150
Northmead La. Iron A —1F 15
N. Meadows. Pea J —4E 157
Northmead Rd. Mid N —2C 150
Northover Clo. Bris —3B 40
Northover Rd. Bris —3B 40
North Pde. Bath —3B 106 (4D 97)
North Pde. Yate —4A 18
North Pde. Bldgs. Bath (off Orchard St.) —3B 106
North Pde. Pas. Bath —3B 106 (4C 96)
North Pde. Rd. Bath —3B 106 (4D 97)
North Pk. Bris —1A 74
North Quay. Bris —4A 70 (3E 5)
North Rd. Ash G —1C 78
North Rd. Ban —5E 137
North Rd. Bath —2D 107 (1F 97)
North Rd. C Down —3C 110
North Rd. Iron A —1D 17
North Rd. L Wds —3F 67
North Rd. Mid N —3C 150
North Rd. St And —5F 57
North Rd. Stok G —5A 28
North Rd. T'bry —2D 7
North Rd. Tim —1E 157
North Rd. Wint —2B 30
North St. Bedm —1C 78
North St. Bris —2A 70
North St. Down —2F 61
North St. Nail —5A 122
North St. Old C —1E 85
North St. Wickw —1B 154
North St. W Mare —5C 126
Northumberland Bldgs. Bath (off Barton St.) —3A 106
Northumberland Pl. Bath —3B 106 (3C 96)
Northumberland Rd. Bris —5E 57
Northumbria Dri. Bris —2D 57
North View. Rads —2E 153
North View. Soun —3F 61
North View. Stap H —2A 62
North View. W'bry P —3C 56
N. View Clo. Bath —4C 104
N. View Dri. Ban —5D 137
Northville Rd. Bris —3B 42
North Wlk. Yate —4A 18
North Way. Bath —4B 104
Northway. Bris —5D 27
North Way. Mid N —3D 151
North Way. Trow —3A 118
Northwick Rd. Bris —4B 42
Northwoods Wlk. Bris —1F 41
N. Worle Shopping Cen. W Mare —3F 129
Norton Clo. Bris —3B 74
Norton La. Kew —1A 128
Norton La. W'chu —5F 89
Norton Rd. Bris —3C 80
Nortons Wood La. Clev —1F 121
Norwich Dri. Bris —4A 72
Norwood Av. Bath —5F 107
Norwood Gro. P'head —3B 48
Norwood Rd. Nail —4E 123
Notgrove Clo. W Mare —3F 127
Nottingham Rd. Bris —4A 58
Nottingham St. Bris —2A 80
Nova Scotia Pl. Bris —5C 68
Nover's Cres. Bris —5E 79
Nover's Hill. Bedm & Know —4E 79
Novers Hill Trad. Est. Bedm —4E 79
Nover's La. Bris —5E 79
Nover's Pk. Clo. Bris —2D 87
Nover's Pk. Dri. Bris —5E 79
Nover's Pk. Rd. Bris —5F 79
Nover's Rd. Bris —5E 79
Nowhere La. Nail —4F 123 (in two parts)
Nugent Hill. Bris —1F 69
Nunney Clo. Key —5A 92
Nursery Clo. Hil —4F 117
Nursery Gdns. Bris —1C 40
Nursery, The. Bris —2D 79
Nutfield Gro. Bris —2D 43
Nutgrove Av. Bris —2A 80
Nuthatch Dri. Bris —1C 60
Nuthatch Gdns. Bris —1C 60
Nutwell Rd. W Mare —3C 128
Nutwell Sq. W Mare —3C 128
Nye Drove. W Mare —2F 137
Nympsfield. Bris —5A 62

Oak Av. Bath —1D 109
Oak Clo. Lit S —2F 27
Oak Clo. Yate —2F 17
Oak Ct. Bris —3C 88
Oakdale Av. Bris —4F 45
Oakdale Clo. Bris —4A 46
Oakdale Ct. Bris —4F 45
Oakdale Gdns. W Mare —3D 129
Oakdale Rd. Bris —5C 80
Oakdale Rd. Down —4A 46
Oakdene Av. Bris —4F 59
Oak Dri. N Brad —4D 155
Oak Dri. P'head —4D 49
Oakenhill Rd. Bris —3A 82
Oakenhill Wlk. Bris —3A 82
Oakfield Clo. Bath —1E 105
Oakfield Gro. Bris —2D 69
Oakfield Pl. Bris —2D 69
Oakfield Rd. Clif —2C 68
Oakfield Rd. Key —5B 92
Oakfield Rd. K'wd —3F 73
Oakford Av. W Mare —5D 127
Oakford La. Bath —1B 102
Oak Gro. E'ton G —3E 53
Oakhanger Dri. Bris —3C 38
Oakhill. W Mare —1E 139
Oakhill Av. Bit —3E 85
Oakhill Clo. Nail —4F 123
Oakhill La. H'len —5E 23
Oakhill Rd. Bath —2A 110
Oak Ho. Bris —4F 87
Oakhurst Rd. Bris —2B 56
Oakland Dri. Hut —5C 134
Oakland Rd. Redl —1D 69
Oakland Rd. St G —2A 72
Oaklands. Clev —2C 120
Oaklands. Paul —5B 146
Oaklands Clo. Mang —2D 63
Oaklands Dri. Alm —2C 10
Oaklands Dri. Bris —4C 44
Oaklands Dri. Old C —3E 85
Oaklands Rd. Mang —2C 62
Oak La. Bris —5B 60
Oakleaze. Coal H —2F 31
Oakleaze Rd. T'bry —3D 7
Oakleigh Av. Bris —1F 71
Oakleigh Clo. Back —3D 125
Oakleigh Gdns. Old C —3E 85
Oakley. Bath —4F 107
Oakley. Clev —5B 120
Oakley Rd. Bris —5B 42
Oakmeade Pk. Bris —3D 81
Oakridge Clo. Bris —3C 74
Oakridge Clo. Wins —5C 156
Oakridge La. Wins —5C 156
Oak Rd. Bris —2A 58
Oak Rd. Wins —3B 156
Oaksey Gro. Nail —3F 123
Oak St. Bath —4A 106 (5A 96)
Oak Ter. Rads —3A 152
Oak Tree Av. Puck —2D 65
Oaktree Clo. Bris —2E 83
Oak Tree Clo. Trow —1B 118
Oaktree Ct. Shire —5A 38
Oaktree Cres. Brad S —4D 11
Oaktree Gdns. Bris —3A 86
Oaktree Pk. Lock —3C 134
Oak Tree Wlk. Key —5F 91
Oakwood Av. Bris —1D 57
Oakwood Rd. Bris —1D 57
Oatlands Av. Bris —2C 88
Oatvale Rd. Bris —3C 88
Oberon Av. Bris —5A 60
Odeon Bldgs. W Mare (off Station Rd.) —1C 132
Odins Rd. Bath —3E 109
Okebourne Clo. Bris —5D 25
Okebourne Rd. Bris —1D 41
Oldacre Rd. Bris —5C 88
Old Ashley Hill. Bris —5B 58
Old Aust Rd. Alm —1E 11
Old Banwell Rd. Lock —4F 135
Old Barrow Hill. Bris —5F 37
Old Batch, The. Brad A —1C 114
Old Bond St. Bath —3A 106 (3B 96)
Old Bread St. Bris —4B 70 (3F 5)
Oldbridge Rd. Bris —5E 89
Old Bristol Rd. Key —1E 91
Old Bristol Rd. W Mare —3E 129
Oldbury Chase. Bris —3C 84
Oldbury Ct. Dri. Bris —1D 61
Oldbury Ct. Rd. Bris —2C 60
Oldbury La. T'bry —1D 7
Oldbury La. Wick —5C 154
Old Church Rd. Clev —4A 120
Old Church Rd. Nail —5C 122
Old Church Rd. Rudg —5A 8
Old Church Rd. Uph —1B 138
Old Cider Mills Est. Wickw —1C 154
Old England Way. Pea J —4E 157
Old Farm La. Bris —4D 73
Old Ferry Rd. Bath —3D 105
Oldfield. Clev —5E 121
Oldfield La. Bath —5E 105
Oldfield Pl. Bath —4F 105
Oldfield Pl. Bris —5B 68
Oldfield Rd. Bath —4F 105
Oldfield Rd. Bris —5C 68
Oldfields La. Alm —1D 13
Old Fire Sta. Ct. Nail —3B 122
Old Forge Way. Bath —4E 157
Old Fosse Rd. Bath —2D 109
Old Fosse Rd. Mid N —5B 148
Old Frome Rd. Bath —4F 109
Old Gloucester Rd. Alv —2C 8
Old Gloucester Rd. Fren & (in two parts) Ham —4D 29
Old Gloucester Rd. Wint —5D 13
Old Junction Rd. W Mare —3F 133
Old King St. Bath —2A 106 (2B 96)
Oldlands Av. Coal H —3E 31
Old La. Tic —1B 122
Old Mkt. St. Bris —3A 70 (2E 5)
Oldmead Wlk. Bris —1A 86
Old Midford Rd. S'ske —5B 110
Old Millard's Hill. Mid N —1E 151
Old Mill Clo. W'lgh —5D 33
Old Mill Rd. P'head —2F 49
Old Mills Ind. Est. Mid N —2B 150
Old Mills La. Paul —1A 150
Oldmixon Cres. W Mare —5E 133
Oldmixon Rd. W Mare —2E 139
Old Newbridge Hill. Bath —1B 104
Old Orchard. Bath —2B 106 (1C 96)
Old Orchard St. Bath —3B 106 (4C 96)
Old Park. Bris —3E 69 (1A 4)
Old Pk. Hill. Bris —3E 69 (2A 4)
Old Park Rd. Bris —5F 37
Old Park Rd. Clev —1D 121
Old Pit Rd. Mid N —4E 151
Old Pit Ter. Clan —5B 148
Old Post Office La. W Mare —5B 126
Old Priory Rd. E'ton G —3D 53
Old Quarry. Bath —2E 109
Old Quarry Rise. Bris —5A 38
Old Quarry Rd. Bris —5F 37
Old Rd. Writ —3F 153
Old School La. B'don —5A 140
Old Sneed Av. Bris —3F 55
Old Sneed Cotts. Bris —3F 55
Old Sneed Pk. Bris —3F 55
Old Sneed Rd. Bris —3F 55
Old Sta. Clo. Wrin —2B 156
Old St. Clev —3D 121
Old Track. Lim S —2A 112
Old Vicarage Ct. Bris —4E 89
Old Vicarage Grn. Key —2A 92
Old Vicarage Pl. Bris —5C 56
Old Vicarage, The. Bris —1A 70
Oldville Av. Clev —4D 121
Old Wells Rd. Bath —1A 110
Old Weston Rd. Cong —1A 144
Olive Gdns. Alv —3A 8
Olveston Rd. Bris —2A 58
Olympus Clo. Lit S —3F 27
Olympus Rd. Pat —1F 25
Onega Ter. Bath —2F 105
Oolite Gro. Bath —3E 109
Oolite Rd. Bath —3E 109
Oram Ct. Bar C —1B 84
Orange Gro. Bath —3B 106 (3C 96)
Orange St. Bris —2B 70
Orchard Av. Bris —4E 69 (3A 4)
Orchard Av. Mid N —3C 150
Orchard Av. T'bry —3D 7
Orchard Boulevd. Old C —1D 85
Orchard Cvn. Site, The. Bris —4F 89
Orchard Clo. Ban —5F 137
Orchard Clo. Cong —2D 145
Orchard Clo. Key —2E 91
Orchard Clo. K'wd —2A 74
Orchard Clo. P'head —3F 49
Orchard Clo. Wor —3D 129
Orchard Clo. Wrin —1C 156
Orchard Clo. W Trym —2B 56
Orchard Clo. Yate —4B 18
Orchard Clo., The. Lock —4D 135
Orchard Ct. Bris —4F 69 (3B 4)
Orchard Ct. Fil —2C 42 (off Gloucester Rd. N.)
Orchard Ct. Redf —3F 71
Orchard Ct. S Park —4E 55
Orchard Ct. Trow —3D 119 (off Orchard Rd.)
Orchard Cres. Bris —5F 37
Orchard Dri. Bris —3C 86
Orchard Gdns. Bris —2B 74
Orchard Gdns. Paul —3B 146
Orchard Grange. T'bry —2C 6
Orchard La. Bris —4E 69 (3A 4)
Orchard La. S Park —3F 55
Orchard Lea. Alv —2C 8
Orchard Lea. Pill —3F 53
Orchard Pl. W Mare —1C 132
Orchard Rd. Back —2C 124
Orchard Rd. Bishop —3A 58
Orchard Rd. Clev —4D 121
Orchard Rd. Coal H —2F 31
Orchard Rd. Hut —1B 140
Orchard Rd. K'wd —2A 74
Orchard Rd. L Ash —4B 76
Orchard Rd. Nail —4B 122
Orchard Rd. Paul —3B 146
Orchard Rd. St G —2B 72
Orchard Rd. Trow —3D 119
Orchard Rd. Yate —2D 65
Orchard Sq. Bris —3F 71
Orchards, The. Bris —3B 74
Orchards, The. Pill —3E 53
Orchard St. Bris —4E 69 (3A 4)
Orchard St. W Mare —1C 132
Orchard Ter. Bath —3C 104
Orchard, The. Ban —5E 137
Orchard, The. Fram C —1E 31
Orchard, The. F'frd —4D 113
Orchard, The. Lock —3E 135
Orchard, The. Stok G —4B 28
Orchard, The. W Trym —5C 40
Orchard Vale. Bris —2B 74
Orchard Vale. Mid N —3B 150
Orchard Way. Bath —5D 157
Orchard Way. N Brad —4D 155
Oriel Clo. Hil —4F 117
Oriel Gdns. Bath —4D 101
Oriel Gro. Bath —5C 104
Orion Dri. Lit S —3F 27
Orland Way. L Grn —2C 84
Orlebar Gdns. Bris —2D 39
Orme Dri. Clev —1D 121
Ormerod Rd. Bris —3A 56
Ormonds Clo. Brad S —4A 12
Ormsley Clo. Lit S —1E 27
Ormstone Ho. Bris —4C 86
Orpen Gdns. Bris —2D 59
Orpen Pk. Alm —3D 11
Orpheus Av. Lit S —3F 27
Orwell Dri. Key —4B 92
Orwell St. Bris —2A 80
Osborne Av. Bris —4B 58
Osborne Av. W Mare —1D 133
Osborne Clo. Stok G —4F 27
Osborne Rd. Bath —3C 104
Osborne Rd. Clif —1C 68
Osborne Rd. Sev B —3A 20
Osborne Rd. S'vle —1E 79
Osborne Rd. Trow —4E 117
Osborne Rd. W Mare —1D 133
Osborne Ter. Bris —3D 79
Osborne Vs. Bris —2E 69
Osprey Ct. Bris —3F 87
Osprey Gdns. W Mare —4D 129
Osprey Pk. T'bry —1E 7
Osprey Rd. Bris —3E 71
Ostlings La. Bathf —4C 102
Otago Ter. Bath —4D 101
Ottawa Rd. W Mare —5D 133
Otterford Clo. Bris —3D 89
Otter Rd. Clev —5D 121
Ottery Clo. Bris —3C 38
Ottrells Mead. Brad S —3E 11
Oval, The. Bath —5D 105
Overdale. Clan —4B 148
Overhill. Pill —3F 53
Over La. E Comp —1D 25
Overndale Rd. Bris —2E 61
Overnhill Ct. Bris —2F 61
Overnhill Rd. Bris —2E 61
Overnhurst Ct. Bris —2F 61
Overton Rd. Bris —5A 58
Owen Gro. Bris —2D 57
Owen Sq. Bris —2E 71
Owen St. Bris —2E 71
Owls Head Rd. Bris —4A 74
Ox Barton. Stok G —3B 28
Oxen Leaze. Brad S —4A 12
Oxford Pl. Bris —4B 68
Oxford Pl. C Down —2D 111
Oxford Pl. E'tn —1D 71
Oxford Pl. W Mare —1B 132
Oxford Row. Bath —2A 106 (1B 96)
Oxford Sq. Lock —2F 135
Oxford St. Bar H —3E 71
Oxford St. Bris —1B 70
Oxford St. K'dwn —2E 69
Oxford St. St Ph —4B 70
Oxford St. Tot —2B 80
Oxford St. W Mare —1B 132
Oxford Ter. C Down —2D 111
Oxleaze. Bris —4F 87
Oxleaze La. Dun —5A 86
Ozleworth. Bris —2C 74

Pack Horse La. S'ske —5A 110
Pacquet Houses. Pill —2F 53 (off Underbanks)
Paddock Clo. Brad S —4F 11
Paddock Garden. Bris —4B 88
Paddock Gdns. Alv —2B 8
Paddocks, The. Cor —3C 110
Paddocks, The. T'bry —3E 7
Paddocks, The. Uph —1B 138
Paddock, The. Ban —5E 137
Paddock, The. Bath —5D 95
Paddock, The. Clev —4D 121
Paddock, The. P'head —4F 49
Paddock Woods. C Down —2E 111
Padfield Clo. Bath —4C 104
Padleigh Hill. Bath —2B 108

Padmore Ct. Bris —3F 71
Padstow Rd. Bris —5B 80
Page Clo. Bris —3B 62
Page Ct. Bris —3B 62
Page Rd. Bris —3F 61
Pages Ct. Yat —3C 142
Pages Mead. Bris —4E 37
Painswick Av. Pat —1D 27
Painswick Dri. Yate —5A 18
Palace Yd. M. Bath —3A 106 (3A 96)
Palairet Clo. Brad A —5E 115
Palmdale Clo. L Grn —2C 84
Palmer Dri. Brad A —1E 115
Palmer Rd. Trow —5D 117
Palmer Row. W Mare —5C 126
Palmers Clo. Bar C —4B 74
Palmers Leaze. Brad S —2C 28
Palmerston Rd. Bris —3D 57
Palmerston St. Bris —2E 79
Palmer St. W Mare —5C 126
Palmers Way. Hut —1B 140
Palmyra Rd. Bris —3D 79
Panorama Wlk. Bris —1C 82
Parade, The. Bath —3F 107
Parade, The. Bris —5C 80
Parade, The. Chip S —5C 18
Parade, The. Pat —5B 10
Parade, The. Shire —1A 54
Paragon. Bath —2B 106 (1C 96)
Paragon Rd. W Mare —4A 126
Paragon, The. Bris —4B 68
Parbrook Ct. Bris —3D 89
Parfitts Hill. Bris —4B 72
Parish Brook Rd. Nail —3A 122
Parish Wharf Trad. Est. P'head —2F 49
Park Av. Azt W —4B 10
Park Av. Bath —4A 106
Park Av. Bedm —2A 80
Park Av. Eastv —4F 59
Park Av. Fram C —3D 31
Park Av. St G —2A 72
Park Av. Wint —2A 30
Park Av. Yat —2B 142
Park Clo. Cong —3D 145
Park Clo. Key —3F 91
Park Clo. K'wd —3A 74
Park Clo. N Brad —4E 155
Park Clo. Paul —4A 146
Park Clo. War —5D 75
Park Cres. Fren —3E 45
Park Cres. War —5D 75
Park Cres. W'hall —2F 71
Park End. Ban —4C 136
Parkers Av. Wick —4B 154
Parkers Clo. Bris —5F 25
Parker St. Bris —2D 79
Parkes Rd. Lock —3A 136
Park Farm Ct. L Grn —1B 84
Parkfield Av. Bris —3F 71
Parkfield Rd. Puck —1C 64
Park Gdns. Bath —1E 105
Park Gro. W'bry P —2E 57
Park Hill. Bris —1A 54
Parkhouse La. Key —5E 91
Parkhurst Av. Bris —3D 61
Parkhurst Rd. W Mare —1E 133
Parklands. Bris —2A 74
Parklands. Trow —5D 117
Parklands Av. W Mare —1D 129
Parklands Rd. Bris —1A 78
Parkland Way. T'bry —1C 6
Park La. Bath —1E 105
Park La. Bris —3E 69 (1A 4)
Park La. Yate —5C 30
Park Mans. Bath —1F 105
Park Pl. Bath —1F 105
Park Pl. Bris —3E 69 (1A 4)
Park Pl. Clif —3D 69
Park Pl. C Down —3C 110
Park Pl. Eastv —4A 60
Park Pl. W Mare —5B 126
Park Rd. Bath —2C 104
Park Rd. Clev —2D 121
Park Rd. Cong —3E 145
Park Rd. Key —3A 92
Park Rd. K'wd —1F 73
Park Rd. N'vle —3B 42
Park Rd. Paul —4A 146
Park Rd. Shire —1A 54
Park Rd. Stap —2F 59
Park Rd. Stap H —2A 62
Park Rd. S'vle —5D 69
Park Rd. T'bry —2B 6
Park Rd. Trow —2D 119
Park Rd. War —5D 75
Park Row. Bris —3E 69
Park Row. Fram C —1C 30
Parkside Av. Wint —3F 29
Parkside Gdns. Bris —3D 59
Parkstone Av. Bris —1B 58
Park St. Bath —1F 105
Park St. Bris —3E 69
Park St. Iron A —2F 15
Park St. St G —2B 72
Park St. Tot —1C 80
(in two parts)
Park St. Trow —3C 118
Park St. Av. Bris —3E 69
Park St. M. Bath —1F 105
Park, The. Brad S —3E 11
Park, The. Fren —3D 45
Park, The. Key —2B 92
Park, The. K'wd —1A 74
Park, The. Will —4D 85
Park, The. Yat —2B 142
Park View. Bath —3E 105
Park View. Bris —3A 74
Park View Av. T'bry —2D 7
Park View Ter. Bris —2A 72
Park Vs. W Mare —5B 126
Parkwall Cres. Bar C —1B 84
Parkwall Rd. Bris —1C 84
Park Way. Bris —5D 75
(Coronation Rd.)
Parkway. Bris —1C 70
(New Foundland Way)
Parkway. Fren —4C 44
Park Way. Mid N —4D 151
Park Way. Wor —4F 129
Parkway Trad. Est. Bris —5C 58
Parkwood Clo. Bris —4B 88
Parliament St. Bris —1C 80
Parnall Cres. Yate —3E 17
Parnall Rd. Bris —4C 60
Parnell Rd. Clev —3D 121
Parrish Clo. Bris —1E 39
Parry Clo. Bath —5C 104
Parry's Clo. Bris —2A 56
Parrys Gro. Stok B —2A 56
Parrys La. Bris —2A 56
Parslows Barton. Bris —3C 72
Parsonage La. Bath —3A 106 (3B 96)
Parsonage Rd. L Ash —3E 77
Parsons Av. Stok G —4B 28
Parsons Grn. Clev —5C 120
Parsons Grn. W Mare —2E 129
Parsons Paddock. Bris —5C 80
Parson St. Bris —3D 79
Partis Way. Bath —1B 104
Partition St. Bris —4E 69
Partridge Clo. W Mare —4D 129
Partridge Clo. Yate —2B 18
Partridge Rd. Puck —3E 65
Passage Leaze. Bris —1F 53
Passage Rd. Bris —4C 24
(in three parts)
Passage St. Bris —4A 70 (3E 5)
Pastures, The. L W'wd —5F 113
Patch Croft. Clev —5C 120
Patchway Trad. Est. Pat —2A 26
Paulman Gdns. L Ash —5B 76
Paul's Causeway. Cong —2D 145
Paul St. Bedm —1F 79
Paul St. Bris —2E 69
Paulto Hill. Paul —3C 146
Paulton Dri. Bris —3E 57
Paulton La. C'ton —3E 147
Paulton Rd. Hall —4A 146
Paulton Rd. Mid N —3C 150
Paultow Av. Bris —2A 80
Paultow Rd. Bris —2A 80
Pavey Clo. Bris —4E 87
Pavey Rd. Bris —4E 87
Pawlett. W Mare —1E 139
Pawlett Rd. Bris —5D 87
Pawlett Wlk. Bris —5E 87
Paxcroft Way. Trow —2F 119
Paybridge Rd. Bris —4B 86
Payne Dri. Bris —2D 71
Payne Rd. Hut —1B 140
Paynes Orchard Cvn. Pk. Bris —4F 25
Peache Ct. Bris —1A 62
Peache Rd. Bris —1A 62
Peacock Rd. W Mare —5A 128
Peacocks La. Bris —2E 73
Pearces Hill. Bris —5D 45
Pearl St. Bris —2D 79
Pearsall Rd. L Grn —3A 84
Peart Clo. Bris —3A 86
Peart Dri. Bris —4A 86
Peartree Gdns. B'don —4F 139
Pear Tree Hey. Yate —1A 18
Peartree La. K'wd —5B 62
Pear Tree La. St G —4D 73
Pear Tree Rd. Brad S —4E 11
Peasedown St John By-Pass. Bath —3E 149
Pedder Rd. Clev —5D 121
Peel St. Bris —2B 70
Pegasus Rd. Pat —2F 25
Peg La. Yate —1C 64
Pelican Clo. W Mare —5D 129
Pemberton Ct. Bris —2D 61
Pembery Rd. Bris —2D 79
Pembroke Av. Bris —1A 54
Pembroke Clo. Trow —4D 119
Pembroke Ct. Bath —5D 99
Pembroke Ct. Clev —2C 120
Pembroke Gro. Bris —3C 68
Pembroke Pl. Bris —5C 68
Pembroke Rd. Clif —1C 68
Pembroke Rd. K'wd —4A 62
Pembroke Rd. P'head —5A 48
Pembroke Rd. Shire —1A 54
Pembroke Rd. S'vle —1E 79
Pembroke Rd. W Mare —3D 133
Pembroke St. Bris —2A 70
Pembroke Vale. Bris —2C 68
Penard Way. Bris —3B 74
Penarth Dri. W Mare —2E 139
Pendennis Av. Bris —2F 61
Pendennis Ho. Bris —2F 61
Pendennis Pk. Bris —3F 81
Pendennis Rd. Bris —2F 61
Pendlesham Gdns. W Mare —4E 127
Pendock Clo. Bit —4E 85
Pendock Ct. E Grn —5D 47
Pendock Rd. Bris —1D 61
Pendock Rd. Wint —4A 30
Penfield Rd. Bris —5C 58
Penlea Ct. Bris —5F 37
Pennard. W Mare —1E 139
Pennard Ct. Bris —3D 89
Pennard Grn. Bath —3B 104
Penn Dri. Bris —3E 45
Penn Gdns. Bath —1B 104
Penngrove. L Grn —2C 84
Penn Hill Rd. Bath —1B 104
Pennine Gdns. W Mare —4E 127
Pennine Rd. Old C —1E 85
Pennlea. Bris —1E 87
Penn Lea Ct. Bath —1C 104
Penn Lea Rd. Bath —5B 98
Penns, The. Clev —4E 121
Penn St. Bris —3A 70 (1E 5)
Pennycress. W Mare —1B 134
Pennyquick. Bath —5E 95
(in two parts)
Pennyquick View. Bath —3A 104
Pennyroyal Gro. Bris —2A 60
Pennywell Rd. Bris —2B 70
Pen Pk. Rd. Bris —1E 41
Penpole Av. Bris —1A 54
Penpole Clo. Bris —5F 37
Penpole La. Bris —5F 37
Penpole Pk. Shire —5A 38
Penpole Pl. Bris —1A 54
Penrice Clo. W Mare —3A 128
Penrith Gdns. Bris —3F 41
Penrose. Bris —1B 88
Penrose Dri. Brad S —2F 27
Pensfield Pk. Bris —5F 25
Pensford Ct. Bris —3F 89
Pentagon, The. Bris —1D 55
Penthouse Hill. Bathe —3A 102
Pentire Av. Bris —2C 86
Pentland Av. T'bry —4F 7
Pepperacre La. Trow —1F 119
Pepys Clo. Salt —2A 94
Pera Pl. Bath —1B 106
Pera Rd. Bath —1B 106
Percival Rd. Bris —2B 68
Percy Pl. Bath —5C 100
Percy Walker Ct. Bris —1E 61
Peregrine Clo. W Mare —4D 129
Perfect View. Bath —5B 100
Perrings, The. Nail —4D 123
Perrinpit Rd. Fram C —2F 13
Perrott Rd. Bris —1C 74
Perry Clo. Wint —4F 29
Perrycroft Av. Bris —2C 86
Perrycroft Rd. Bris —2C 86
Perrymans Clo. Bris —1C 60
Perrymead. Bath —5C 106
Perrymead. W Mare —1F 129
Perry Rd. Bris —3E 69 (2A 4)
Perrys Lea. Brad S —4F 11
Perry St. Bris —2C 70
Pesley Clo. Bris —4C 86
Petercole Dri. Bris —2C 86
Peterson Sq. Bris —5E 87
Peter's Ter. Bris —3D 71
Petersway Gdns. Bris —4C 72
Petherton Clo. Bris —3A 74
Petherton Gdns. Bris —1D 89
Petherton Rd. Bris —5D 81
Petticoat La. Bris —4A 70 (3E 5)
Pettigrove Gdns. Bris —3A 74
Pettigrove Rd. Bris —4A 74
Pevensey Wlk. Bris —1F 87
Peverell Clo. Bris —1B 40
Peverell Dri. Bris —1B 40
Philadelphia Ct. Bris —3A 70 (1E 5)
Philippa Clo. Bris —1C 88
Philip St. Bath —3B 106 (4C 96)
Philip St. Bedm —1F 79
Philip St. St Pm —5D 71
Phillips Rd. W Mare —2E 133
Phillis Ct. Trow —2E 155
Phillis Hill. Paul & Mid N —5C 146
Phippen St. Bris —5A 70 (5D 5)
Phipps St. Bris —1D 79
Phipp St. Clev —3C 120
Phoenix Bus. Pk. Bris —3C 78
Phoenix Gro. Bris —2E 57
Phoenix Ho. Bris —4D 71
Phoenix St. Bris —4D 71
Piccadilly Pl. Bath —5C 100
Pickwick Rd. Bath —4B 100
Picton La. Bris —1A 70
Picton St. Bris —1A 70
Pierrepont Pl. Bath —3B 106 (4C 96)
Pierrepont St. Bath —3B 106 (4C 96)
Pier Rd. P'head —1F 49
Pigeon Ho. Dri. Bris —4F 87
Pigott Av. Bris —4C 86
Pile Marsh. Bris —3F 71
Pilgrims Way. Down —4F 45
Pilgrims Way. Shire —5E 37
Pilgrims Way. W Mare —3C 128
Pilgrims Wharf. St Ap —3A 72
Pilkington Clo. Bris —2E 43
Pillingers Rd. Bris —3E 73
Pill Rd. Abb L —1B 66
Pill Rd. Pill & Abb L —4F 53
Pill St. Pill —3F 53
Pill Way. Clev —4B 120
Pimm's La. W Mare —3F 127
Pine Clo. T'bry —3D 7
Pine Clo. W Mare —3B 128
Pine Ct. Key —4E 91
Pine Ct. Rads —2D 153
Pinecroft. Bris —1B 88
Pinecroft. P'head —2B 48
Pine Gro. Bris —3C 42
Pine Gro. Pl. Bris —4F 57
Pine Hill. W Mare —3B 128
Pine Lea. B'don —4F 139
Pine Ridge Clo. Bris —3E 55
Pine Rd. Bren —1D 41
Pines Rd. Bit —4E 85
Pines, The. Bris —4F 55
Pines Way. Bath —3F 105
Pines Way. Rads —2D 153
Pines Way Ind. Est. Bath —3F 105
Pinetree Rd. Lock —4B 136
Pine Wlk. N Brad —4D 155
Pine Wlk. Rads —3B 152
Pinewood. Bris —1B 74
Pinewood Av. Mid N —3C 150
Pinewood Clo. Bris —5D 41
Pinewood Gro. Mid N —3C 150
Pinewood Rd. Mid N —3C 150
Pinhay Rd. Bris —2D 87
Pinkhams Twist. Bris —3C 88
Pinknash Ct. Yate —2F 33
Pioneer Av. Bath —3A 110
Pipe Ct. Bris —4E 69 (3A 4)
Pipehouse La. F'frd —5A 112
Pipe La. Bris —4E 69 (3A 4)
Pipe La. St Aug —5A 70 (5F 5)
Piper Rd. Yate —3A 18
Piplar Ground. Brad A —5E 115
Pippin Clo. Pea J —5D 157
Pippin Ct. Bar C —1B 84
Pitchcombe. Yate —2E 33
Pitchcombe Gdns. Bris —5F 39
Pitch La. Bris —1F 69
Pitch & Pay La. Bris —4A 56
Pitch & Pay Pk. Bris —4A 56
Pithay Ct. Bris —3F 69 (2C 4)
Pithay, The. Bris —3F 69 (2C 4)
Pithay, The. Paul —3B 146
Pit La. Back —4C 124
Pitman Av. Trow —3B 118
Pitman Ct. Bath —4D 101
Pitman Ct. Trow —3B 118
Pitman Ho. Bath —5E 105
Pitman Rd. W Mare —2C 132
Pit Rd. Mid N —3E 151
Pitt Rd. Bris —2A 58
Pittville Clo. T'bry —1D 7
Pitville Pl. Bris —1D 69
Pixash Bus. Cen. Key —3D 93
Pixash La. Key —3D 93
Pizey Av. Clev —4B 120
Pizey Clo. Clev —4B 120
Plain, The. T'bry —3C 6
Players Clo. Ham —5D 29
Playford Gdns. Bris —4A 38
Pleasant Ho. Bris —2F 61
Pleasant Rd. Bris —2F 61
Pleshey Clo. W Mare —3B 128
Plimsoll Ho. Bris —5A 70
(off Burton Clo.)
Ploughed Paddock. Nail —4C 122
Plover Clo. W Mare —4D 129
Plover Clo. Yate —4E 17
Plovers Rise. Rads —1D 153
Plowright Ho. Bris —5D 73
Plumers Clo. Clev —5E 121
Plumley Cres. Lock —4E 135
Plummer's Hill. Bris —2A 72
Plumpton Ct. Bris —3B 46
Plumptre Clo. Paul —4B 146
Plumptre Rd. Paul —4A 146
Plum Tree Clo. Wins —3B 156
Plum Tree Rd. W Mare —1C 134
Podgers Dri. Bath —4C 98
Podium, The. Bath —2B 106
(off Northgate St.)
Poet's Clo. Bris —2F 71
Poets Corner. Rads —4F 151
Poet's Wlk. Clev —4A 120
Polden Clo. Nail —4D 123
Polden Ho. Bris —2F 79
Polden Rd. P'head —3D 49
Polden Rd. W Mare —5D 127
Polebarn Cir. Trow —2D 119
Polebarn Gdns. Trow —1D 119
Polebarn Rd. Trow —2D 119
Polly Barnes Clo. Han —5D 73
Polly Barnes Hill. Bris —5D 73
Polygon Rd. Bris —4B 68
Polygon, The. Bris —4B 68
Pomfrett Gdns. Bris —3A 90
Pomphrey Hill. Mang —2D 63
Ponsford Rd. Bris —5D 81
Ponting Clo. Bris —1C 72
Poolbarton. Key —2A 92
Poole Ct. Yate —4A 18

Poole Ct. Dri. Yate —4A 18
Poole Ho. Bath —4A 104
Poolemead Rd. Bath —4A 104
Poole St. Bris —4D 37
Pool Ho. Pat —1C 26
Pool Rd. Bris —4A 62
Popes Wlk. Bath —2C 110
Poplar Av. Bris —1F 55
Poplar Clo. Bath —5E 105
Poplar Clo. Bris —4E 75
Poplar Dri. Puck —2D 65
Poplar La. Wickw —3C 154
Poplar Pl. Bris —4C 60
Poplar Pl. W Mare —5C 126
Poplar Rd. Bath —4E 109
Poplar Rd. Bed D —1B 86
Poplar Rd. Han —5C 72
Poplar Rd. S'wll —1B 72
Poplar Rd. War —5E 75
Poplars, The. E'ton G —3D 53
Poplars, The. W Mare —4E 129
Poplar Ter. Bris —2B 74
Poplar Wlk. Lock —3C 134
Porlock Clo. Clev —5E 121
Porlock Clo. W Mare —1D 139
Porlock Gdns. Nail —4D 123
Porlock Rd. Bath —3B 110
Porlock Rd. Bris —2F 79
Portbury Comn. P'head —4A 50
Portbury Gro. Bris —1F 53
Portbury Hundred, The. P'bry —3A 52
Portbury Hundred, The. P'head —4B 50
Portbury La. P'bry —5A 52
Portbury Sawmills Est. P'bry —1B 52
Portbury Wlk. Bris —1F 53
Portbury Way. P'bry —3F 51
Portishead Rd. W Mare —1F 129
Portishead Way. Bris —2A 78
Portland Clo. Nail —4C 122
Portland Ct. Bris —5D 69
Portland Dri. P'head —4A 50
Portland Pl. Bath —1A 106
Portland Pl. Stap H —3F 61
Portland Sq. Bris —2A 70
Portland St. Clif —3B 68
Portland St. K'dwn —2E 69
Portland St. Stap H —4F 61
Portland Ter. Bath —1A 106 (off Harley St.)
Portmeirion Clo. Bris —3D 89
Port Side Clo. St G —4B 72
Port View. Pill —2E 53
Portview Rd. Bris —3D 37
Portwall La. Bris —5A 70 (5D 5)
Portwall La. E. Bris —5A 70 (5E 5)
Portway. A'mth —4E 37
Portway. Bris —5F 55
Portway La. Chip S —4E 19
Post Office La. Bris —2A 72
Post Office Rd. Lock —3F 135
Post Office Rd. W Mare —5B 126
Poston Way. W'ley —2F 113
Pottery Clo. W Mare —2E 133
Potts Clo. Bathe —2A 102
Poulton. Brad A —4E 115
Poulton La. Brad A —5F 115
Pound Dri. Bris —2B 60
Pound Farm Clo. Hil M —3E 117
Pound La. Brad A —3D 115
Pound La. Bris —3B 60
Pound La. Nail —3B 122
Pound Rd. Bris —5B 62
Pound, The. Alm —1C 10
Pountney Dri. Bris —2D 71
Powis Clo. W Mare —3A 128
Powlett Ct. Bath —2C 106 (1E 97)
Powlett Rd. Bath —1C 106
Pow's Hill. Rads —5A 148
Pow's Orchard. Mid N —3D 151
Pow's Rd. Bris —3F 73
Poxon Clo. Trow —1B 118
Poyntz Ct. L Grn —2B 84
Poyntz Rd. Bris —5B 80
Prattens La. Bris —3F 61
Preacher Clo. Bris —4D 73
Preanes Grn. W Mare —3E 129
Precinct, The. P'head —3F 49
Preddy's La. Bris —4C 72
Prescot Clo. W Mare —3F 127
Prescott. Yate —1F 33
Press Moor Dri. Bar C —1B 84
Prestbury. Yate —1F 33
Preston Wlk. Bris —4C 80
Prestwick Clo. Bris —4F 81
Pretoria Rd. Pat —1B 26
Prewett St. Bris —5A 70
Priddy Clo. Bath —4C 104 (in two parts)
Priddy Ct. Bris —3D 89
Priddy Dri. Bris —3D 89
Priests Way. W Mare —3B 128
Priestwood Clo. Bris —1C 40
Primrose Clo. Brad S —4F 11
Primrose Clo. Bris —1E 73
Primrose Dri. T'bry —2E 7
Primrose Hill. Bath —5E 99
Primrose La. Bris —1E 73
Primrose La. Mid N —3E 151
Primrose Ter. Bris —1E 73
Primrose Ter. Mid N —3E 151
Princes Bldgs. Bath —4C 106 (5E 97) (Pulteney Rd.)
Princes Bldgs. Bath —2A 106 (2B 96) (off George St.)
Princes' Bldgs. Bris —4B 68
Princes Ct. L Grn —1B 84
Princes' La. Bris —4B 68
Prince's Pl. Bris —4A 58
Prince's Rd. Clev —3D 121
Princess Clo. Key —4A 92
Princess Gdns. Bris —1F 59
Princess Gdns. Trow —3E 117
Princess Row. Bris —2F 69
Princess Royal Gdns. Bris —2E 71
Princess St. Bedm —1A 80
Princess St. Bris —3C 70
Princes St. Bath —3A 106 (3B 96)
Prince's St. Bris —2B 70
Prince's St. Rads —4B 148
Princess Victoria St. Bris —4B 68
Prince St. Bris —5F 69 (5B 4)
Prior Pk. Bldgs. Bath —4C 106 (off Prior Pk. Rd.)
Prior Pk. Cotts. Bath —4C 106
Prior Pk. Gdns. Bath —4C 106
Prior Pk. Rd. Bath —4C 106
Priors Hill. Tim —1D 157
Prior's Hill Flats. Bris —1F 69
Priors Lea. Yate —5F 17
Priory Acre. W Mare —3B 128
Priory Av. Bris —5C 40
Priory Clo. Bath —2C 110
Priory Clo. Brad A —2D 115
Priory Clo. Mid N —3D 151
Priory Ct. Bris —2E 83
Priory Ct. Rd. Bris —5C 40
Priory Dene. Bris —5C 40
Priory Farm Est. P'bry —5F 51
Priory Gdns. Bris —5F 37
Priory Gdns. E'ton G —3D 53
Priory Gdns. Hor —4B 42
Priory M. W Mare —1F 133
Priory Pk. Brad A —2E 115
Priory Rd. Clif —2D 69
Priory Rd. E'ton G —3D 53
Priory Rd. Key —1A 92
Priory Rd. Know —3D 81
Priory Rd. P'bry —5F 51
Priory Rd. Shire —1F 53
Priory Rd. W Mare —1E 133
Priory Wlk. P'bry —5F 51
Priston Clo. W Mare —1F 129
Pritchard St. Bris —2A 70
Probyn Clo. Bris —5C 44
Pro-Cathedral La. Bris —3D 69
Proctor Clo. Bris —4F 81
Proctor Ho. Bris —5A 70
Promenade, The. Bishop —5F 57
Promenade, The. Bris —2B 68
Prospect Av. K'dwn —2F 69
Prospect Av. K'wd —1D 73
Prospect Bldgs. Bath —1A 102
Prospect Clo. Fram C —1B 30
Prospect Clo. Wint —5A 30
Prospect Cres. Bris —5B 62
Prospect Gdns. Bathe —1A 102
Prospect La. Fram C —1B 30
Prospect Pl. Bath —4A 106 (Beechen Cliff Rd.)
Prospect Pl. Bath —5B 100 (Camden Rd.)
Prospect Pl. Bathf —4E 103
Prospect Pl. Bedm —2E 79
Prospect Pl. Bris —5B 42
Prospect Pl. C Down —3C 110
Prospect Pl. Cot —5F 57
Prospect Pl. Trow —1D 119
Prospect Pl. W'hall —2E 71
Prospect Pl. W Mare —5C 126
Prospect Pl. W'ton —4D 99
Prospect Rd. Bath —5D 107
Prospect Rd. Sev B —5B 20
Providence La. L Ash —2B 76
Providence Pl. Bedm —2F 79
Providence Pl. Bris —4B 70 (3F 5)
Providence Pl. Redf —3E 71
Providence View. L Ash —4C 76
Prudham St. Bris —1E 71
Pucklechurch Trad. Est. Puck —3D 65
Puffin Clo. W Mare —5D 129
Pullens Grn. T'bry —3C 6
Pullin Ct. Bris —1F 85
Pulteney Av. Bath —3C 106 (4E 97)
Pulteney Bri. Bath —3B 106 (3C 96)
Pulteney Gdns. Bath —3C 106 (4E 97)
Pulteney Gro. Bath —4C 106 (5E 97)
Pulteney M. Bath —2B 106 (2D 97)
Pulteney Rd. Bath —4C 106 (5E 97)
Pulteney Ter. Bath —3C 106 (off Pulteney Av.)
Pump La. Bathf —5C 102
Pump La. Bris —5A 70 (5D 5)
Pump Sq. Pill —2F 53
Purcell Wlk. Bris —1F 87
Purdey Rd. Bris —3B 60
Purdown Rd. Bris —2B 58
Purdue Clo. W Mare —2F 129
Purlewent Dri. Bath —4D 99
Purn International Holiday Pk. B'don —5E 139
Purn La. W Mare —3E 139
Purn Rd. W Mare —3D 139
Purn Way. B'don —4E 139
Pursey Dri. Brad S —3B 28
Purton Clo. Bris —4A 74
Purton Rd. Bris —5F 57
Puttingthorpe Dri. W Mare —1A 134
Puxley Clo. Bris —2A 90
Puxton Rd. Hew —5F 131
Pye Croft. Brad S —3A 12
Pyecroft Av. Bris —5D 41
Pylle Hill Cres. Bris —1B 80
Pyne Point. Clev —3C 120
Pynne Clo. Bris —2B 90
Pynne Rd. Bris —3B 90
Pyracantha Wlk. Bris —2C 88

Quadrangle, The. W'lgh —5E 33
Quadrant. Alm —3D 11
Quadrant E. Bris —4E 61
Quadrant, The. Bris —4D 57
Quadrant W. Bris —4E 61
Quaker La. T'bry —3C 6
Quakers Clo. Bris —4F 45
Quakers' Friars. Bris —3A 70 (1D 5)
Quaker's Rd. Bris —3F 45
Quantock Clo. Bris —5E 75
Quantock Rd. Bris —2F 79
Quantock Rd. P'head —3D 49
Quantock Rd. W Mare —4B 132
Quantocks. Bath —3B 110
Quantock Ter. Bath —3F 107
Quarries, The. Alm —1D 11
Quarrington Rd. Bris —2A 58
Quarry Barton. Ham —5E 29
Quarry Clo. Bath —3A 110
Quarry Clo. Lim S —3E 113
Quarry La. Bris —3E 39
Quarry La. Wint D —5A 30
Quarrymans Ct. Bath —3C 110
Quarry Mead. Alv —2A 8
Quarry Rd. Alv —2A 8
Quarry Rd. Bath —4E 107
Quarry Rd. Chip S —5C 18
Quarry Rd. Clif —5C 56
Quarry Rd. Fren —5D 45
Quarry Rd. K'wd —4F 73
Quarry Rd. P'head —4E 49
Quarry Rock Gdns. Cvn. Pk. Bath —5E 107
Quarry Steps. Bris —5C 56
Quarry Way. Nail —3C 122
Quarry Way. Stap —2A 60
Quaterway La. Trow —1E 119
Quayside. Bris —4A 70 (3E 5)
Quayside. St G —4B 72
Quayside Ho. Bris —4D 69
Quay St. Bris —3F 69 (2B 4)
Quebec. Bath —3B 104
Quedgeley. Yate —1E 33
Queen Ann Rd. Bris —4D 71
Queen Charlotte St. Bris —4F 69 (3C 4)
Queen Charlton La. Bris —5F 89
Queen Quay. Bris —4F 69 (4C 4)
Queen's Av. Bris —3D 69
Queens Av. P'head —3E 49
Queens Club Gdns. Trow —2A 118
Queen's Ct. Bris —3D 69 (off Queen's Rd.)
Queensdale Cres. Bris —4C 80
Queensdown Gdns. Bris —2E 81
Queen's Dri. Bath —2B 110
Queen's Dri. Bishop —3E 57
Queens Dri. Han —1D 83
Queens Gdns. Trow —3E 117
Queenshill Rd. Bris —3C 80
Queensholm Av. Bris —3A 46
Queensholm Cres. Bris —3F 45
Queensholm Dri. Bris —3A 46
Queensholme Clo. Bris —3A 46
Queens Pde. Bath —2A 106 (2A 96)
Queen's Pde. Bris —4D 69
Queens Pde. Pl. Bath —2A 106 (2B 96)
Queens Pl. Bath —4C 106 (5E 97)
Queen Sq. Bath —2A 106 (2B 96)
Queen Sq. Bris —4F 69 (4B 4)
Queen Sq. Salt —1B 94
Queen Sq. Av. Bris —4F 69 (4C 4)
Queen Sq. Pl. Bath —2A 106 (2A 96)
Queens Rd. Ash D —3B 58
Queens Rd. Ban —5E 137
Queen's Rd. B'wth —5B 86
Queen's Rd. Clev —3D 121
Queen's Rd. Clif —3C 68
Queens Rd. Key —4F 91
Queens Rd. Know —3E 81
Queen's Rd. Nail —4B 122
Queen's Rd. P'head —4A 48
Queen's Rd. Puck —2D 65
Queen's Rd. Rads —2E 153
Queen's Rd. St G —2B 72
Queens Rd. Trow —5C 116
Queens Rd. War —1C 84
Queen's Rd. W Mare —4B 126
Queen St. A'mth —3C 36
Queen St. Bath —3A 106 (3B 96)
Queen St. Eastv —4F 59
Queen St. K'wd —3D 73
Queen St. St Ph —3A 70 (2E 5)
Queens Wlk. T'bry —1C 6
Queensway. Lit S —3E 27
Queen's Way. P'head —4A 48
Queen's Way. W Mare —1C 128
Queen Victoria Rd. Bris —3C 56
Queen Victoria St. Bris —4C 70
Queenwood Av. Bath —5B 100
Quickthorn Clo. Bris —2C 88
Quiet St. Bath —3A 106 (3B 96)
Quilling Clo. Trow —3E 119
Quilter Gro. Bris —1F 87

Raby M. Bathw —2C 106 (2E 97)
Raby Pl. Bathw —2C 106 (2E 97)
Raby Vs. Bath —2C 106 (2F 97)
Rackfield Pl. Bath —3C 104
Rackham Clo. Bris —1D 59
Rackhay. Bris —4F 69 (3C 4)
Rackvernal Rd. Mid N —3E 151
Radford Hill. Tim —1E 157
Radley Rd. Bris —3D 61
Radnor Rd. Hor —2F 57
Radnor Rd. W Trym —2D 57
Radstock Rd. Mid N —2E 151
Raeburn Rd. Bris —3D 73
Raglan Clo. Bath —4B 100 (off Raglan La.)
Rag La. Wickw —2A 154
Raglan La. Bath —4B 100
Raglan La. Bris —3C 72
Raglan Pl. Bris —4F 57
Raglan Pl. T'bry —4C 6
Raglan Pl. W Mare —5A 126
Raglan Rd. Bris —4F 57
Raglan St. Bath —4B 100
Raglan Ter. Bath —4B 100
Raglan Vs. Bath —4B 100
Raglan Wlk. Key —4F 91
Ragleth Gro. Trow —5E 117
Railton Jones Clo. Stok G —1A 44
Railway Bldgs. Bath —3D 105
Railway Pl. Bath —4B 106 (5D 97)
Railway Rd. Bath —4B 106 (5C 96)
Railway St. Bath —4B 106 (5C 96)
Railway Ter. Bris —3E 61
Railway View. Ham —1F 45
Railway View Pl. Mid N —2E 151
Railway Wlk. Wins —3A 156
Raleigh Clo. Salt —5F 93
Raleigh Ct. Trow —2D 119
Raleigh Rise. P'head —2D 49
Raleigh Rd. Bedm —2C 78
Ralph Allen Dri. Bath —5C 106
Ralph Rd. Bris —3B 58
Rambler Clo. Trow —1A 118
Ram Hill. Coal H —4E 31
Ramsbury Wlk. Trow —4D 119
Ramsey Clo. W Mare —1C 128
Ramsey Rd. Bris —5B 42
Ranchway. P'head —4B 48
Randall Clo. Bris —5B 62
Randall Rd. Bris —4C 68
Randolph Av. Bris —3D 87
Randolph Av. Yate —2F 17
Randolph Clo. Bris —3D 87
Rangers Wlk. Bris —1E 83
Rank, The. N Brad —4D 155
Rannoch Rd. Bris —2B 42
Ranscombe Av. W Mare —3B 128
Ransford. Clev —5B 120
Raphael Ct. Redc —5A 70
Ratcliffe Dri. Stok G —4A 28
Rathbone Clo. Coal H —4E 31
Raven Clo. W Mare —4C 128
Ravendale Dri. L Grn —3C 84
Ravenglass Cres. Bris —2E 41
Ravenhead Dri. Bris —5D 81
Ravenhill Av. Bris —3B 80
Ravenhill Rd. Bris —2B 80
Ravenscourt Rd. Pat —2D 27
Ravenscroft Gdns. Trow —1F 119
Ravenswood. L Grn —2C 84
Ravenswood Rd. Bris —1E 69

Rawlins Av. W Mare —1E 129
Rayens Clo. L Ash —4B 76
Rayens Cross Rd. L Ash —4B 76
Rayleigh Rd. Bris —5F 39
Raymend Rd. Bris —2A 80
Raymend Wlk. Bris —3A 80
Raymill. Bris —3C 82
Raymore Rise. L Ash —5B 76
Raynes Rd. Bris —2C 78
Rectors Way. W Mare —2D 133
Rectory Clo. Yate —3B 18
Rectory Dri. Yat —4C 142
Rectory Gdns. Bris —2A 40
Rectory La. B'don —5A 140
Rectory La. Brad S —1C 42
Rectory La. Tim —1E 157
Rectory Rd. E'ton G —4D 53
Rectory Rd. Fram C —1C 30
Rectory Way. Yat —4C 142
Redcar Ct. Down —3C 46
Redcatch Rd. Bris & Know —2B 80
Redcliff Backs. Bris —4A 70 (4D 5)
Redcliffe Clo. P'head —5A 48
Redcliffe Pde. E. Bris —5F 69 (5C 4)
Redcliffe Pde. W. Bris —5F 69 (5C 4)
Redcliffe Way. Bris (in two parts) —4F 69 (4B 4)
Redcliff Hill. Bris —5A 70
Redcliff Mead La. Bris —5A 70 (5E 5)
Redcliff Pde. Bris —5F 69
Redcliff St. Bris —4A 70 (3D 5)
Redcross La. Bris —3B 70 (1F 5)
Redcross St. Bris —3B 70 (2F 5)
Redding Rd. Bris —5D 59
Reddings, The. Bris —5B 62
Redfield Gro. Mid N —3D 151
Redfield Hill. Old C —1F 85
Redfield Rd. Mid N —4C 150
Redfield Rd. Pat —2D 27
Redford Cres. Bris —5A 86
Redford La. Yate —3E 65
Redford Wlk. Bris —5B 86
Red Hill. C'ton —1B 148
Redhill Clo. Bris —4A 60
Redhill Dri. Bris —4A 60
Red Ho. La. Alm —2D 11
Red Ho. La. Bris —1A 56
Redland Ct. Rd. Bris —4E 57
Redland Grn. Rd. Bris —4D 57
Redland Gro. Bris —5E 57
Redland Hill. Redl —5C 56
Redland Pk. Bath —3A 104 (in two parts)
Redland Pk. Bris —5D 57
Redland Rd. Bris —4C 56
Redland Rd. P'bry —1B 52
Redlands Ter. Mid N —4C 150
Redland Ter. Bris —5D 57
Red Post Ct. Bath —2E 149
Redshelf Wlk. Bris —1E 41
Redwick Clo. Bris —2E 39
Redwick Rd. Piln —1B 20
Redwing Dri. W Mare —4D 129
Redwing Gdns. Bris —1A 60
Redwood Clo. L Grn —2C 84
Redwood Clo. Nail —3F 123
Redwood Clo. Rads —4B 152
Redwood Ho. Bris —5F 87
Redwoods, The. Key —2F 91
Reed Ct. L Grn —1B 84
Reedley Rd. Bris —2A 56
Reedling Clo. Bris —1A 60
Regency Dri. Bris —3C 82
Regent Rd. Bris —1F 79
Regents Clo. T'bry —1C 6
Regents Field. Bath —1E 107
Regent's Pl. Brad A —3E 115
Regent St. Clif —4C 68
Regent St. K'wd —2F 73
Regent St. W Mare —1B 132
Regina, The. Bath —2A 106 (1B 96) (off Bennett St.)
Remenham Dri. Bris —2D 57
Rendcomb Clo. W Mare —3F 127
Rene Rd. Bris —1D 71
Repton Rd. Bris —2E 81
Retreat, The. W Mare —4A 126
Reynold's Clo. Key —3C 92
Reynolds Wlk. Bris —5C 42
Rhode Clo. Key —5C 92
Rhododendron Wlk. Bris —3A 40
Rhodyate Hill. Clav —5E 143
Rhodyate La. C've —4F 143
Rhyne Ter. Uph —1B 138
Rhyne View. Nail —4A 122
Ribblesdale. T'bry —4D 7
Richards Clo. W Mare —1F 129
Richardson Pl. C Down —3D 111
Richeson Clo. Bris —2B 40
Richeson Wlk. Bris —2B 40
Richmond Av. Bris —5B 58
Richmond Av. Stok G —4A 28
Richmond Clo. Bath —5A 100
Richmond Clo. Key —4F 91
Richmond Clo. P'head —3A 50
Richmond Clo. Trow —3A 118
Richmond Ct. Pat —5B 10
Richmond Dale. Bris —5C 56
Richmond Grn. Nail —4E 123
Richmond Heights. Bath —4A 100
Richmond Hill. Bath —5A 100
Richmond Hill. Bris —3D 69
Richmond Hill Av. Bris —3D 69
Richmond La. Bath —5A 100
Richmond La. Bris —3C 68
Richmond M. Bris —3C 68
Richmond Pk. Rd. Bris —3C 68
Richmond Pl. Bath —5A 100
Richmond Rd. Bath —4A 100
Richmond Rd. Bris —1A 70
Richmond Rd. Mang —2C 62
Richmond Rd. Mont —5B 58
Richmond Rd. St G —2A 72
Richmond St. Bris —1B 80
Richmond St. W Mare —1B 132
Richmond Ter. A'mth —3C 36
Richmond Ter. Bath —5B 100 (off Rivers Rd.)
Richmond Ter. Clif —3C 68
Richmond Vs. Bris —3C 36
Ricketts La. W Mare —3E 129
Rickfield. Brad A —3C 114
Rickford Rd. Nail —4E 123
Rickyard Rd. Wrin —1C 156
Ride, The. Bris —1C 74
Ridge Clo. P'head —4C 48
Ridge Green Clo. Bath —4E 109
Ridgehill. Bris —1E 57
Ridgemeade. Bris —4D 89
Ridge, The. Bris —5A 38
Ridge, The. Coal H —2E 31
Ridge, The. Yat —3B 142
Ridge View. L Ash —3D 77
Ridgeway. Fram C —2F 31
Ridgeway. Nail —4B 122
Ridgeway. Yate —4B 18
Ridgeway Av. W Mare —2C 132
Ridgeway Ct. Bris —3C 40
Ridgeway Gdns. Bris —3E 89
Ridgeway La. Bris —4D 89
Ridgeway Pde. Bris —4A 60
Ridgeway Rd. Bris —4A 60
Ridgeway Rd. L Ash —4C 76
Ridge Way, The. W Mare —3F 127
Ridgeway, The. W Trym —3C 40
Ridgewood. Bris —4F 55
Ridgewood. Chip S —5B 18
Riding Barn Hill. Wick —5A 154
Riding Cotts. Chip S —4D 19
Ridingleaze. Bris —3C 38
Ridings Clo. Chip S —5E 19
Ridings Rd. Coal H —3E 31
Ridings, The. Bris —4A 86
Ridings, The. Coal H —3E 31
Ringswell Gdns. Bath —5C 100
Ringwood Cres. Bris —3E 41
Ringwood Gro. W Mare —4E 127
Ringwood Rd. Bath —3D 105
Ripley Rd. Bris —1C 72
Ripon Ct. Down —2B 46
Ripon Rd. Bris —4A 72
Rippleside. P'head —3E 49
Rippleside Rd. Clev —2E 121
Ripple, The. Tic —1C 122
Risdale Rd. Bris —4A 78
Risedale Rd. Wins —4B 156
Rivendell. W Mare —1E 129
Riverland Dri. Bris —4B 86
Riverleaze. Bris —2D 55
Riverleaze. P'head —2B 48
River Mead. Clev —5D 121
River Path. Clev —5B 120
River Pl. Bath —3C 104
River Rd. Chip S —5C 18
River Rd. P'bry —3A 36
Riverside. Ban —2F 137
Riverside Bus. Pk. St Ap —4F 71
Riverside Clo. Bris —2B 54
Riverside Clo. Clev —4B 120
Riverside Clo. Mid N —5C 150
Riverside Cotts. Rads —2D 153
Riverside Ct. Bath —3A 106 (4A 96)
Riverside Ct. St Ap —4B 72
Riverside Dri. Bris —5E 45
Riverside Gdns. Bath —3A 106 (off Kingsmead East.)
Riverside Gdns. Mid N —5B 150
Riverside M. St Ap —4B 72
Riverside Pk. Sev B —4A 20
Riverside Rd. Bath —3F 105
Riverside Rd. Mid N —5C 150
Riverside Steps St Ap —3A 72
Riverside Wlk. Mid N —5C 150
Riverside Wlk. St G —4B 72
Riverside Way. Bris —2E 83
Rivers Rd. Bath —1B 106
Rivers St. Bath —2A 106 (1A 96)
Rivers St. M. Bath —2A 106 (1A 96)
Rivers St. Pl. Bath —2A 106 (off Rivers St.)
River St. Bris —3B 70 (1F 5)
River Ter. Key —3B 92
River View. Bris —2A 60
Riverway. Nail —2E 123
River Way. Trow —1C 118
Riverway Ind. Pk. Trow —1C 118
Riverwood Rd. Bris —3E 45
Riviera Cres. Bris —3A 62
Roath Rd. P'head —3F 49
Robbins Clo. Brad S —3B 28
Robel Av. Fram C —1B 30
Robert Ct. Bris —4A 68
Robert Ct. E Grn —5D 47
Robertson Dri. St Ap —4B 72
Robertson Rd. Bris —5D 59
Robert St. Bar H —3D 71
Robert St. Eastv —5D 59
Robin Clo. Bris —2F 89
Robin Clo. Mid N —4E 151
Robin Clo. W Mare —5C 128
Robin Clo. W Trym —2D 41
Robin Dri. Hut —1C 140
Robin Hood La. Bris —3E 69 (1A 4)
Robinia Wlk. Bris —1B 88
Robin La. Clev —1D 121
Robinson Clo. Back —3C 124
Robinson Dri. Bris —1C 70
Robinson Way. Back —3C 124
Robin Way. Chip S —2B 34
Roblyn Ct. Wins —4A 156
Rochester Clo. W Mare —2E 139
Rochester Rd. Bris —5A 72
Rochfort Ct. Bath —1B 106
Rochfort Pl. Bath —1B 106
Rock Av. Nail —3B 122
Rock Clo. Bris —3A 82
Rock Cotts. Bath —3C 110
Rockfield. W Mare —4F 127
Rock Hall Cotts. Bath —3C 110
Rock Hall La. Bath —3C 110
Rock Ho. Bris —1E 41
Rockingham Gro. W Mare —4E 127
Rockingham Ho. Bris —4C 38
Rockland Gro. Bris —1F 59
Rockland Rd. Bris —5E 45
Rock La. C Down —3C 110
Rock La. Stok G —4B 28
Rockleaze. Bris —5A 56
Rockleaze Av. Bris —4A 56
Rockleaze Ct. Bris —4A 56
Rockleaze Rd. Bris —4A 56
Rockliffe Av. Bath —1C 106
Rockliffe Rd. Bath —1C 106
Rock Rd. Key —3A 92
Rock Rd. Mid N —2E 151
Rock Rd. Trow —3B 118
Rock Rd. Wick —4B 154
Rock Rd. Yat —4C 142
Rockside Av. Bris —4B 46
Rockside Dri. Bris —1D 57
Rockside Gdns. Bris —4B 46
Rockside Gdns. Fram C —1E 31
Rockstowes Way. Bris —1F 41
Rock St. T'bry —4C 6
Rock, The. Bris —2A 82
Rockwell Av. Bris —3D 39
Rockwood Ho. Yate —2C 18
Rocky La. Ban —5F 137
Rodborough. Yate —2E 33
Rodborough Way. Bris —3C 74
Rodbourne Rd. Bris —5F 41
Rodfords Mead. Bris —1C 88
Rodford Way. Yate —2E 33
Rodmead Wlk. Bris —4C 86
Rodmoor Rd. P'head —2F 49
Rodney. W Mare —1E 139
Rodney Av. Bris —2C 72
Rodney Cres. Bris —5D 27
Rodney Ho. Bath —3B 104
Rodney Pl. Bris —3C 68
Rodney Rd. Back —2C 124
Rodney Rd. Bris —1C 72
Rodney Rd. Salt —2A 94
Rodney Wlk. Bris —1C 72
Rodsleigh. Trow —4A 118
Rodway Hill. Mang —3C 62
Rodway Hill Rd. Mang —2C 62
Rodway Rd. Mang —2C 62
Rodway Rd. Pat —1B 26
Rodway View. Bris —4B 62
Rodwell Pk. Trow —5E 117
Roebuck Clo. W Mare —1E 129
Roegate Dri. St Ap —4A 72
Rogers Clo. Bris —5D 75
Rokeby Av. Bris —1E 69
Roman Farm Ct. Bris —2E 39
Roman Rd. B'don —3E 139
Roman Rd. Bris —1D 71
Roman Rd. Eng —4D 109
Roman Wlk. Brisl —2E 81
Roman Wlk. Stok G —4A 28
Roman Way. Bris —3E 55
Roman Way. Paul —3A 146
Romney Av. Bris —2C 58
Ronald Rd. Bris —1B 60
Ronayne Wlk. Bris —1E 61
Rookery Clo. W Mare —2C 128
Rookery Rd. Bris —2B 80
Rookery Way. Bris —4B 88
Rooksbridge Wlk. Bath —3D 105
Roper's La. Wrin —1B 156
Rope Wlk., The. Brad A —3D 115
Rose Acre. Bris —1C 40
Rosebay Mead. Bris —2A 60
Roseberry Pk. Bris —2F 71
Roseberry Pl. Bath —3E 105
Roseberry Rd. Bath —3D 105
Roseberry Rd. Bris —3E 71
Rosebery Av. Bris —1C 70
Rosebery Ter. Bris —4D 69
Rose Clo. Wint D —5A 30
Rose Cotts. C Hay —4D 109
Rose Cotts. S'ske —5A 110
Rosedale Av. W Mare —1E 133
Rosedale Gdns. Trow —1A 118
Rosedale Rd. Bris —4D 61
Rose Gdns. W Mare —1F 129
Rose Grn. Bris —5F 59
Rose Grn. Clo. Bris —5A 60
Rose Grn. Rd. Bris —5F 59
Rose Hill. Bath —4C 100 (in two parts)
Rose La. Coal H —2F 31
Roselarge Gdns. Bris —2C 40
Rosemary Clo. Brad S —2B 28
Rosemary La. Bris —5E 59
Rosemary La. F'frd —5B 112
Rosemary Steps. Brad A —3D 115
Rose Mead. Bris —5C 42
Rosemeare Gdns. Bris —1A 86
Rosemont Ter. Bris —4C 68
Rosemount Ct. Bris —2D 73
Rosemount La. Bath —5C 106
Rosenberg Houses. Bath —3A 106 (off Westgate Bldgs.)
Rose Oak La. Coal H —2F 31
Rose Rd. Bris —3A 72
Rosery Clo. Bris —4C 40
Rosery, The. Bris —4E 61
Rose St. Bris —4A 70 (4F 5)
Roseville Av. L Grn —3C 84
Rose Wlk. Bris —4E 61
Rosewarn Clo. Bath —5B 104
Rosewell Ct. Bath —3A 106 (3A 96)
Rosewood Av. Alv —2A 8
Rosling Rd. Bris —1A 58
Roslyn Av. W Mare —4A 128
Roslyn Rd. Bris —5E 57
Rossall Av. Lit S —3E 27
Rossall Rd. Bris —2F 81
Rossendale Clo. W Mare —2D 129
Rossett Gdns. Trow —2A 118
Rossiter Rd. Bath —4B 106 (5D 97)
Rossiter's La. Bris —4C 72
Rossiter Wood Ct. Bris —2D 39
Rosslyn Rd. Bath —2C 104
Rosslyn Way. T'bry —1D 7
Rounceval St. Chip S —5C 18
Roundhill Gro. Bath —1C 108
Roundhill Pk. Bath —5B 104
Roundmoor Clo. Salt —5F 93
Roundmoor Gdns. Bris —2F 89
Roundstone St. Trow —1D 119
Roundways. Coal H —3E 31
Rousham Rd. Bris —4C 58
Rowacres. Bath —1C 108
Rowacres. Bris —2B 88
Rowan Clo. Bris —5C 60
Rowan Clo. Nail —3F 123
Rowan Ct. Bris —3D 71
Rowan Ct. Rads —3A 152
Rowan Ho. Bris —4F 87
Rowans, The. Bris —3D 45
Rowans, The. P'head —4D 49
Rowan Wlk. Key —4E 91
Rowan Way. Bris —2E 83
Rowberrow. Bris —1B 88
Rowberrow Way. Nail —4D 123
Rowden La. Brad A —5E 115
Rowland Av. Bris —3F 59
Rowlands Clo. Bathf —4D 103
Rowlandson Gdns. Bris —1D 59
Rowley St. Bris —2E 79
Rownham Clo. Bris —1A 78
Rownham Ct. Bris —5C 68
Rownham Hill. Bris —4A 68
Rownham Mead. Bris —5C 68
Rows, The. W Mare —3C 128
Royal Albert Rd. Bris —3C 56
Royal Av. Bath —2F 105
Royal Clo. Bris —1E 39
Royal Cres. Bath —2F 105
Royal Cres. W Mare —5B 126
Royal Fort Rd. Bris —3E 69 (1A 4)
Royal Oak Av. Bris —4F 69 (5B 4)
Royal Pde. W Mare —5B 126
Royal Pk. Bris —3C 68
Royal Portbury Dock Rd. P'bry —3B 52
Royal Rd. Mang —1C 62
Royal York Cres. Bris —4B 68
Royal York M. Bris —4C 68
Royal York Vs. Bris —4C 68
Royate Hill. Bris —5F 59
Roycroft Rd. Bris —2D 43
Roy King Gdns. Bris —4E 75
Royston Wlk. Bris —2F 41
Rozel Rd. Bris —2A 58

Rubens Clo. Key —3C 92
Rubens Ct. W Mare —2D 129
Ruby St. Bris —2D 79
Ruddymead. Clev —4D 121
Rudford Clo. Pat —5D 11
Rudge Clo. K'wd —5B 62
Rudgeway Pk. Rudg —5A 8
Rudgeway Rd. Paul —4B 146
Rudgewood Clo. Bris —4F 87
Rudgleigh Av. Pill —3E 53
Rudgleigh Rd. Pill —3E 53
Rudhall Grn. W Mare —2F 129
Rudhall Gro. Bris —5A 42
Rudmore Pk. Bath —2B 104
Rudthorpe Rd. Bris —2A 58
Ruett La. Far G —5A 146
Ruffet Rd. Wint —1C 46
Rugby Rd. Bris —2F 81
Runnymead Av. Bris —4F 81
Runnymeade. Bris —1A 74
Runswick Rd. Bris —2E 81
Rupert St. Bris —3F 69 (2B 4)
Rupert St. Redf —3E 71
Rush Clo. Brad S —4F 11
Rush Hill. Bath —2C 108
Rushmoor. Clev —5A 120
Rushmoor Gro. Back —3C 124
Rushmoor La. Back —3C 124
Rushton Dri. Coal H —2F 31
Rushy. Bris —1C 84
Ruskin Gro. Bris —4C 42
Ruskin Rd. Rads —3F 151
Russell Av. Bris —3A 74
Russell Gro. Bris —2E 57
Russell Rd. Clev —3C 120
Russell Rd. Fish —5D 61
Russell Rd. Lock —2F 135
Russell Rd. W'bry P —3D 57
Russell St. Bath —2A 106 (1B 96)
Russell Town Av. Bris —2D 71
Russet Ct. Trow —3D 119
Russett Clo. Back —2D 125
Russett Gro. Nail —5B 122
Russet Way. Pea J —5D 157
Russ St. Bris —4B 70
Rustic Pk. Cvn. Site. Sev B —4B 20
Rutherford Clo. L Grn —2C 84
Ruthven Rd. Bris —5A 80
Rutland. Bris —5A 38
Rutland Av. Will —3C 84
Rutland Clo. W Mare —5A 128
Rutland Ct. Trow —4C 118
Rutland Cres. Trow —4C 118
Rutland Rd. Bris —4A 58
Rydal Av. Lock —4D 135
Rydal Rd. W Mare —4D 133
Ryde Rd. Bris —3D 81
Rye Clo. Bris —2A 86
Ryecroft Av. W Mare —3C 128
Ryecroft Rise. L Ash —4D 77
Ryecroft Rd. Fram C —1E 31
Ryedown La. Bit —3E 85
Ryland Pl. Bris —5C 58
Rylestone Clo. Fram C —1B 30
Rylestone Gro. Bris —2B 56
Rysdale Rd. Bris —1B 56

Sabrina Way. Bris —3E 55
Sadbury Clo. W Mare —1F 129
Sadlier Clo. Bris —4B 38
Saffron Clo. W'hall —2E 71
Saffron Ct. Bath —1B 106
Saffrons, The. W Mare —1F 129
Saffron St. Bris —2E 71
Sage Clo. P'head —4A 48
Sages Mead. Brad S —1A 28
St Agnes Av. Bris —3B 80
St Agnes Clo. Nail —4F 123
St Agnes Gdns. Bris —3B 80
St Agnes Wlk. Bris —3B 80
St Aidans Clo. Bris —4D 73
St Aidans Rd. Bris —4C 72
St Albans Rd. Bris —3D 57
St Aldams Dri. Puck —2D 65
St Aldhelm Rd. Brad A —4F 115
St Aldwyn's Clo. Bris —4B 42
St Andrews. War —4D 75
St Andrews. Yate —5B 18
St Andrews Clo. Cong —2C 144
St Andrew's Clo. Nail —4F 123
St Andrews Clo. W Mare —2D 129
St Andrews Dri. Clev —4A 120
St Andrews Ind. Est. Bris —2D 37
St Andrew's Pde. W Mare —4D 133
St Andrew's Rd. A'mth —3D 37
St Andrew's Rd. Back —3D 125
St Andrew's Rd. Bris —1A 70
St Andrews Rd. Mont —1A 70
St Andrews Ter. Bath —2A 106 (2B 96)
St Andrews Wlk. Bris —4C 68
St Annes Av. Key —2F 91
St Annes Clo. Bris —1D 85
St Annes Clo. St G —4B 72
St Anne's Ct. Bris —5F 71
St Anne's Ct. Key —2F 91
St Anne's Dri. Coal H —4E 31
St Annes Dri. Old C —3E 85
St Anne's Dri. Wick —4A 154
St Annes Pk. Rd. Bris —5A 72
St Anne's Rd. St Ap & Avon V —4F 71
St Anne's Rd. St G —4D 73
St Anne's Ter. Bris —5A 72
St Ann's Pl. Bath —3A 106 (3A 96) (off New King St.)
St Ann's Way. Bath —3C 106 (3F 97)
St Anthony's Clo. Mid N —2D 151
St Anthony's Dri. Wick —4A 154
St Aubin's Av. Bris —2B 82
St Aubyn's Av. Uph —1B 138
St Augustine's Clo. P'head —4A 48
St Augustine's Pde. Bris —4F 69 (3B 4)
St Augustines Pl. Bris —4F 69 (off Colston St.)
St Augustines Rd. Key (off Station Rd.) —2B 92
St Augustines Rd. Trow —2B 118
St Augustines Yd. Bris —4E 69 (off Gaunts La.)
St Augustines Yd. Bris —4E 69 (off Orchard La.)
St Austell Clo. Nail —5F 123
St Austell Rd. W Mare —5F 127
St Barnabas Clo. Bris —4B 80
St Barnabas Clo. Mid N —1E 151
St Barnabas Clo. War —3E 75
St Bartholomew's Rd. Bris —4B 58
St Bede's Rd. Bris —5E 61
St Bernards Rd. Bris —1A 54
St Brelades Gro. Bris —5B 72
St Brendans Way. Bris —3D 37
St Briavels Dri. Yate —1F 33
St Cadoc Ho. Key —3B 92
St Catherine Pl. Bris —1F 79 (off East St.)
St Catherine's Clo. Bath —3D 107
St Catherines Ct. Bedm —3D 81
St Catherine's Mead. Pill —4F 53
St Chad's Av. Mid N —3D 151
St Chad's Grn. Mid N —3D 151
St Charles Clo. Mid N —2D 151
St Christopher's Clo. Bath —2D 107
St Clements Ct. Clev —2C 120
St Clement's Ct. Key —4A 92
St Clements Ct. W Mare —3E 129
St Clement's Rd. Key —4A 92 (in two parts)
St David's Av. Bris —5C 74
St David's Clo. W Mare —3F 127
St David's Cres. Bris —4B 72
St David's Rd. T'bry —3D 7
St Dunstan's Rd. Bris —3E 79
St Edward's Rd. Bris —4D 69
St Edyths Rd. Bris —1D 55
St Fagans Ct. Will —3D 85
St Francis Dri. Wick —4A 154
St Francis Dri. Wint —3B 30
St Francis Rd. Bris —1C 78
St Francis Rd. Key —2E 91
St Gabriel's Rd. Bris —2D 71
St Georges Av. St G —4B 72
St Georges Bldgs. Bath (off Up. Bristol Rd.) —2F 105
St George's Hill. B'ptn —1E 107
St Georges Hill. E'ton G —4C 52
St George's Ho. Bris —4D 69 (off St George's Rd.)
St Georges Pl. Bath —2F 105 (off Up. Bristol Rd.)
St George's Rd. Bris —4D 69
St Georges Rd. Key —2F 91
St George's Rd. P'bry —5A 36
St Georges Ter. Trow —2C 118
St Gregory's Rd. Bris —4B 42
St Gregory's Wlk. Bris —4B 42
St Helena Rd. Bris —3D 57
St Helens Dri. Old C —3E 85
St Helens Dri. Wick —4B 154
St Helen's Wlk. Bris —1C 72
St Helier Av. Bris —1B 82
St Hilary Clo. Bris —2F 55
St Ivel Way. Bris —4E 75
St Ives Clo. Nail —4F 123
St Ives Rd. W Mare —4E 133
St James Barton. Bris —2A 70
St James Clo. T'bry —1D 7
St James Pde. Bris —3F 69 (1C 4)
St James Pl. Mang —2C 62
St James's Pde. Bath —3A 106 (4B 96)
St James's Pk. Bath —1A 106
St James's Pl. Bath —1A 106
St James's Sq. Bath —1F 105
St James's St. Bath —1A 106
St James St. Mang —2C 62
St James St. W Mare —1B 132
St John's Av. Clev —3D 121
St John's Bldgs. Bedm —1F 79
St John's Clo. Pea J —2E 149
St John's Clo. W Mare —4B 126
St John's Ct. Key —2A 92
St John's Cres. Bris —3A 80
St John's Cres. Mid N —2D 151
St John's Cres. Trow —4A 118
St John's La. Bris —2E 79
St John's Pl. Bath —3A 106 (3B 96)
St John's Rd. Back —3D 125
St John's Rd. Bathw —2B 106 (2C 96)
St John's Rd. Bedm —2E 79
St John's Rd. Clev —3D 121
St John's Rd. Clif —1C 68
St John's Rd. Lwr W —2D 105
St John's Rd. S'vle —1F 79
St Johns Rd. Tim —2E 157
St John's St. Bris —2E 79
St John St. T'bry —3C 6
St John's Way. Chip S —4D 19
St Joseph's Rd. Bris —1D 41
St Joseph's Rd. W Mare —4C 126
St Judes Ter. W Mare —4A 128
St Katherine's Quay. Brad A —4E 115
St Kenya Ct. Key —3B 92
St Keyna Rd. Key —3A 92
St Kilda's Rd. Bath —4E 105
St Ladoc Rd. Key —2F 91
St Laud Clo. Bris —2F 55
St Laurence Rd. Brad A —4F 115
St Leonard's Rd. G'bnk —5E 59
St Leonard's Rd. Hor —1A 58
St Loe Clo. Bris —5B 88
St Lucia Clo. Bris —4A 42
St Lucia Cres. Bris —5A 42
St Lukes Ct. Bris —1A 80
St Luke's Cres. Bris —1B 80
St Luke's Gdns. Bris —3A 82
St Luke's Rd. Bath —1A 110
St Luke's Rd. Bris —1A 80
St Lukes Rd. Mid N —2C 150
St Luke's Steps. Bris —1B 80
St Luke St. Bris —3D 71
St Margaret's Clo. Back —3C 124
St Margaret's Clo. Key —2F 91
St Margarets Clo. Trow —4A 118
St Margaret's Ct. Brad A —3E 115
St Margaret's Dri. Bris —2E 57
St Margaret's Hill. Brad A —3E 115
St Margarets La. Back —3C 124
St Margaret's Pl. Brad A —3E 115
St Margaret's St. Brad A —3E 115
St Margaret's Ter. W Mare —5B 126
St Margaret's Vs. Brad A —3E 115
St Mark's Av. Bris —5E 59
St Marks Clo. Key —2A 92
St Marks Gdns. Bath —4B 106
St Mark's Grn. Tim —1E 157
St Mark's Gro. Bris —1D 71
St Mark's Rd. Bath —4B 106
St Mark's Rd. Bris —1D 71
St Mark's Rd. Mid N —2D 151
St Mark's Rd. W Mare —1D 129
St Mark's Ter. Bris —1D 71
St Martins. L Ash —4C 76
St Martin's Clo. Bris —3D 81
St Martin's Ct. Bath —3F 109
St Martins Ct. W Mare —2C 128
St Martin's Gdns. Bris —4D 81
St Martin's Rd. Bris —3D 81
St Martin's Wlk. Bris —4D 81
St Mary's Bldgs. Bath —4A 106 (5A 96)
St Mary's Clo. Bath —3C 106 (3F 97)
St Mary's Clo. Hil M —3F 117
St Mary's Clo. Hut —1B 140
St Mary's Clo. Tim —1E 157
St Mary's Ct. W Mare —2E 139
St Mary's Gdns. Hil M —3E 117
St Mary's Gro. Nail —5B 122
St Mary's Pk. Nail —5B 122
St Mary's Pk. Rd. P'head —4E 49
St Marys Rise. Writ —2F 153
St Mary's Rd. Hut —1B 140
St Mary's Rd. L Wds —4F 67
St Mary's Rd. P'head —4E 49
St Mary's Rd. Shire —5E 37
St Mary St. T'bry —4C 6
St Mary's Wlk. Bris —1F 53
St Marys Way. T'bry —3C 6
St Mary's Way. Yate —4B 18
St Matthew's Av. Bris —1F 69
St Matthew's Clo. W Mare —4B 126
St Matthew's Pl. Bath —4C 106
St Matthew's Rd. Bris —2F 69
St Matthias Pk. Bris —3B 70 (1F 5)
St Michael's Av. Clev —5D 121
St Michael's Av. W Mare —2E 129
St Michaels Clo. Bris —3A 58
St Michael's Clo. Hil —4F 117
St Michael's Clo. Wint —2A 30
St Michael's Ct. Bris —2D 73
St Michaels Ct. Mon C —4F 111
St Michael's Hill. Bris —2E 69
St Michael's Pk. Bris —2E 69
St Michael's Pl. Bath —3A 106 (4B 96)
St Michael's Rd. Lwr W —2E 105
St Michael's Rd. W'way —4B 104
St Nicholas Clo. N Brad —4E 155
St Nicholas Clo. W'ley —2E 113
St Nicholas Ct. B'ptn —5A 102
St Nicholas Mkt. Bris —4F 69 (3C 4)
St Nicholas Pk. Bris —1D 71
St Nicholas Rd. St Pa —1B 70
St Nicholas Rd. Uph —1B 138
St Nicholas Rd. W'chu —4E 89
St Nicholas St. Bris —4F 69 (3C 4)
St Oswald's Ct. Bris —4D 57
St Oswald's Rd. Bris —4D 57
St Patrick's Ct. Bath —3C 106 (3F 97)
St Patrick's Ct. Key —3A 92
St Pauls Pl. Bath —3A 106 (3A 96)
St Paul's Pl. Mid N —2D 151
St Paul's Rd. Bris —1F 79
St Paul's Rd. Clif —3D 69
St Paul's Rd. W Mare —3C 132
St Paul St. Bris —2A 70
St Peter's Av. W Mare —4B 126
St Peter's Cres. Fram C —1D 31
St Peter's Rise. Bris —1C 86
St Peter's Rd. Mid N —4F 151
St Peter's Rd. P'head —4F 49
St Peter's Ter. Bath —3E 105
St Peter's Wlk. Bris —1D 57
St Philips Causeway. Bris —4D 71
St Philips Central Ind. Est. Bris —5C 70
St Philips Rd. St Ph —3B 70
St Pierre Dri. War —4D 75
St Ronan's Av. Bris —1E 69
St Saviours Rd. Lark —5D 101
St Saviour's Ter. Bath —5C 100
St Saviours Way. Bath —5D 101
St Silas St. Bris —5C 70
St Stephen's Av. Bris —4F 69 (3B 4)
St Stephens Bus. Cen. War (off Poplar Rd.) —5E 75
St Stephen's Clo. Bath —5A 100
St Stephen's Clo. Bris —2E 41
St Stephen's Clo. Soun —4A 62
St Stephen's Ct. Bath —1A 106
St Stephen's Pl. Bath —1A 106 (off St Stephen's Rd.)
St Stephen's Pl. Trow —2D 119
St Stephen's Rd. Bath —1A 106
St Stephen's Rd. Bris —5F 61
St Stephen's St. Bris —3F 69 (2B 4)
St Swithin's Pl. Bath —1B 106
St Thomas' Pas. Trow —1D 119
St Thomas Rd. Mid N —2E 151
St Thomas Rd. Trow —1E 119
St Thomas St. Bris —4A 70 (3D 5)
St Thomas St. E. Bris —4A 70 (4D 5)
St Vincents Hill. Bris —5C 56
St Vincents Rd. Bris —4C 68
St Vincents Trad. Est. Bris —4F 71
St Werburgh's Pk. Bris —5C 58
St Werburgh's Rd. Bris —5B 58
St Whytes Rd. Bris —5F 79
St Winifred's Dri. C Down —2E 111
Salcombe Gdns. W Mare —2E 129
Salcombe Rd. Bris —4B 80
Salem Rd. Wint —2B 30
Salisbury Av. Bris —2D 73
Salisbury Gdns. Bris —2A 62
Salisbury Pk. Bris —1A 62
Salisbury Rd. Bath —4C 100
Salisbury Rd. Down —1A 62
Salisbury Rd. Paul —5C 146
Salisbury Rd. Redl —5F 57
Salisbury Rd. St Ap —5F 71
Salisbury Rd. W Mare —4A 128
Salisbury St. Bar H —4D 71
Salisbury St. St G —3A 72
Salisbury Ter. W Mare —5B 126
Salisbury View. B'ptn —5A 102

Sally Barn Clo. L Grn —3A 84
Sally Lunns Ho. Bath —3B 106 (off N. Parade Pas.)
Sallysmead Clo. Bris —4D 87
Sallys Way. Wint —2B 30
Saltford Ct. Salt —1A 94
Salthouse Farm Cvn. Pk. Sev B —2B 20
Salthouse Rd. Clev —4B 120
Salthrop Rd. Bris —3A 58
Saltings Clo. Clev —4B 120
Saltmarsh Dri. Bris —3C 38
Saltwell Av. Bris —3E 89
Sambourne La. Pill —2E 53
Samian Way. Stok G —4A 28
Sampson Ho. Bus. Pk. H'ley —2F 23
Sampsons Rd. Bris —4F 87
Samuel St. Bris —2E 71
Samuel White Rd. Bris —2D 83
Samuel Wright Clo. Bris —5F 75
Sanctuary Gdns. Bris —4F 55
Sandbach Rd. Bris —1F 81
Sandbed Rd. Bris —5C 58
Sandburrows Rd. Bris —2A 86
Sandburrows Wlk. Bris —2B 86
Sandcroft. Bris —2B 88
Sandcroft Av. Uph —1B 138
Sanders Rd. Trow —5C 116
Sandford Clo. Clev —5B 120
Sandford Rd. Bris —5C 68
Sandford Rd. Wins —3A 156
Sandford Rd. W Mare —1D 133
Sandgate Rd. Bris —1F 81
Sand Hill. Bris —1E 81
Sandholme Clo. Bris —4A 46
Sandholme Rd. Bris —1E 81
Sandhurst. Yate —1F 33
Sandhurst Clo. Pat —5D 11
Sandhurst Rd. Bris —1F 81
Sandling Av. Bris —5B 42
Sandown Cen. Whit B —3F 155
Sandown Clo. Down —3B 46
Sandown Rd. Brisl —1F 81
Sandown Rd. Fil —1E 43
Sandpiper Dri. W Mare —4D 129
Sandringham Av. Bris —4A 46
Sandringham Pk. Bris —5A 46
Sandringham Rd. Bris —2F 81
Sandringham Rd. L Grn —3B 84
Sandringham Rd. Stok G —4F 27
Sandringham Rd. Trow —5B 118
Sandringham Rd. W Mare —3D 133
Sand Rd. Kew —1F 127
Sands La. Fram C —5B 14
Sandstone Rise Wint —5A 30
Sandwich Rd. Bris —1F 81
Sandy Clo. Brad S —3A 28
Sandy La. Abb L —3A 66
Sandy La. Bris —4E 59
Sandy Leaze. Brad A —3D 115
Sandyleaze. Bris —5A 40
Sandy Lodge. Yate —1A 34
Sandy Pk. Rd. Bris —1E 81
Saracen St. Bath —2B 106 (2C 96)
Sarah St. Law H —3D 71
Sargent St. Bris —1A 80
Sarum Cres. Bris —3E 41
Sassoon Ct. Bar C —5B 74
Satchfield Clo. Bris —2B 40
Satchfield Cres. Bris —2B 40
Satellite Bus. Pk. Bris —3F 71
Sates Way. Bris —1E 57
Saunders Rd. Bris —3A 62
Saunton Wlk. Bris —5A 80
Savages Wood Rd. Brad S —1F 27
Savernake Rd. W Mare —2D 129
Saville Cres. W Mare —5A 128
Saville Ga. Clo. Bris —3B 56
Saville Pl. Bris —4C 68
Saville Rd. Bris —4B 56
Saville Rd. W Mare —5A 128
Saville Row. Bath —2A 106 (1B 96)
Savoy Rd. Bris —1F 81
Saw Clo. Bath —3A 106 (3B 96)
Saw Mill La. T'bry —3C 6
Sawyers Ct. Clev —3E 121
Saxby Clo. Clev —5B 120
Saxby Clo. W Mare —1F 129
Saxon Dri. Trow —3E 117
Saxon Rd. Bris —5C 58
Saxon Rd. W Mare —5A 128
Saxon Way. Bris —5E 11
Saxon Way. Pea J —4E 157
Saxon Way. W'ley —2A 114
Scafell Clo. W Mare —4E 127
Scandrett Clo. Bris —2A 40
Scantleberry Clo. Down —4F 45
Scaurs, The. W Mare —3D 129
School Clo. Bris —4B 88
School Clo. Pat —1E 27
School La. Ban —5F 137
School La. Fren —2A 60
School La. Nthnd —2A 102
School La. Stav —2D 117
School La. Clo. Stav —2D 117
School Rd. Brisl —3A 82
School Rd. Fram C —1B 30
School Rd. K'wd —2E 73
School Rd. Old C —1C 84
School Rd. Tot —2C 80
School Rd. War —2D 85
School Rd. Wrin —1C 156
School Wlk. W'hall —1F 71
School Wlk. Yate —4A 18
School Way. Sev B —4B 20
Scop, The. Alm —1D 11
Scotch Horn Clo. Nail —3E 123
Scotch Horn Way. Nail —3E 123
Scots Pine Av. Nail —3F 123
Scott Ct. Bar C —5B 74
Scott Lawrence Clo. Bris —5C 44
Scott Rd. W Mare —4E 133
Scott Way. Chip S —2B 34
Sea Bank Rd. P'bry —4A 36
Seabrook Rd. W Mare —4B 128
Seagry Clo. Bris —3A 42
Sea Mills La. Bris —3E 55
Searle Ct. Clev —3E 121
Searle Ct. Av. Bris —1A 82
Searle Cres. W Mare —2E 133
Seaton Rd. Bris —1E 71
Seavale Rd. Clev —2C 120
Seaview Rd. P'head —2B 48 (Portishead)
Seaview Rd. P'head —4B 48 (Redcliff Bay)
Seawalls. Bris —5F 55
Seawalls Rd. Bris —5F 55
Second Av. Bath —5E 105
Second Av. W'fld I —5F 151
Second Way. Bris —3F 37
Seddon Rd. Bris —5C 58
Sedgefield Gdns. Bris —3B 46
Sedgemoor Clo. Nail —5D 123
Sedgemoor Rd. Bath —3A 110
Sedgemoor Rd. W Mare —4D 127
Sedgewick. Bris —5A 38
Sefton Pk. Rd. Bris —4A 58
Selborne Rd. Bris —2B 58
Selbourne Clo. Bath —1B 104
Selbourne Rd. W Mare —4C 132
Selbrooke Cres. Bris —1D 61
Selby Rd. Bris —1B 72
Selden Rd. Bris —3A 90
Selkirk Rd. Bris —5E 61
Selley Wlk. Bris —3C 86
Selwood Clo. W Mare —1A 134
Selworthy. Bris —3A 74
Selworthy Clo. Key —3F 91
Selworthy Gdns. Nail —4D 123 (off Mizzymead Rd.)
Selworthy Ho. Bath —2A 110
Selworthy Rd. Bris —3D 81
Selworthy Rd. W Mare —4D 133
Seneca Pl. Bris —3F 71
Seneca St. Bris —2F 71
Sercombe Pk. Clev —5E 121
Serlo Ct. W Mare —1E 129
Serridge La. Coal H —5E 31
Servier St. Bris —5B 58
Seven Acres La. Bathe —1A 102
Seven Dials. Bath —3A 106 (3B 96)
Seventh Av. Bris —3D 43
Severn Av. W Mare —3C 132
Severn Dri. T'bry —2C 6
Severn Grange. Bris —1F 39
Severn Ho. Bris —1F 39
Severnmead. P'head —3B 48
Severn Rd. Chit & H'len —1A 22
Severn Rd. Pill —2E 53
Severn Rd. P'head —3E 49
Severn Rd. Shire —1F 53
Severn Rd. W Mare —3B 132
Severnside Trad. Est. Bris —4E 21
Severn View Rd. T'bry —2D 7
Severn Way. Key —4B 92
Severn Way. Pat —5B 10
Severnwood Gdns. Sev B —5B 20
Sevier St. Bris —5B 58
Seville Rd. P'head —1A 50
Seward Ter. Rads —2F 153
Sewell Ho. Wins —4B 156
Seymour Av. Bris —3A 58
Seymour Clo. Clev —3E 121
Seymour Clo. W Mare —1D 129
Seymour Ct. Trow —1C 118
Seymour Rd. Bath —1B 106
Seymour Rd. Bishop —3A 58
Seymour Rd. E'tn —1C 70
Seymour Rd. K'wd —1F 73
Seymour Rd. Stap H —3F 61
Seymour Rd. Trow —1C 118
Seyton Wlk. Stok G —4A 28
Shackleton Av. Yate —1B 34
Shadwell Rd. Bris —4F 57
Shaftesbury Av. Bath —2D 105
Shaftesbury Av. Bris —1A 70
Shaftesbury Clo. Nail —5C 122
Shaftesbury Ct. Trow —4A 118
Shaftesbury Rd. Bath —4E 105
Shaftesbury Rd. W Mare —5F 127
Shaftesbury Ter. Bris —3F 71
Shaftesbury Ter. Rads —1D 153
Shaft Rd. C Down & Mon C —2E 111
Shaft Rd. Sev B —2B 20
Shails La. Trow —1C 118
Shails La. Ind. Est. Trow —1C 118
Shakespeare Av. Bath —5A 106
Shakespeare Av. Bris —4C 42
Shakespeare Rd. Rads —3F 151
Shaldon Rd. Bris —3C 58
Shallows, The. Salt —1B 94
Shambles, The. Brad A —2E 115
Sham Castle La. Bath —2C 106 (2F 97)
Shamrock Rd. Bris —4F 59
Shanklin Dri. Bris —1D 43
Shannon Ct. T'bry —4E 7
Shapcott Clo. Bris —4D 81
Shaplands. Stok B —3B 56
Sharland Clo. Bris —4A 56
Shaw Clo. Bris —2D 71
Shaws Way. Bath —3A 104
Shearman St. Trow —3D 119
Shearwater Ct. Bris —1B 60
Sheene Rd. Bedm —2E 79
Sheepcote Barton. Trow —3E 119
Sheephouse Cvn. Pk. E'ton G —5A 36
Sheepscroft. Bris —4C 86
Sheepway. P'bry —3D 51
Sheepway La. P'bry —2E 51
Sheepwood Clo. Bris —2C 40
Sheepwood Rd. Bris —2C 40
Sheldare Barton. Bris —3D 73
Sheldon Clo. Clev —4F 121
Sheldrake Dri. Bris —1A 60
Shellard Rd. Bris —1D 43
Shellards La. Alv —3D 9
Shellards Rd. L Grn —2B 84
Shelley Av. Clev —4D 121
Shelley Clo. Bris —2B 72
Shelley Rd. Bath —4A 106
Shelley Rd. Rads —3F 151
Shelley Rd. W Mare —4E 133
Shelley Way. Bris —4C 42
Shellmor Av. Pat —5D 11
Shellmor Clo. Pat —5E 11
Shepherds Clo. Bris —2A 62
Shepherds Wlk. Bath —3A 110
Shepherd's Way. W Mare —3A 130
Sheppard Rd. Bris —1E 61
Sheppards Gdns. Bath —5C 98
Sheppy's Mill. Cong —1D 145
Shepton. W Mare —1E 139
Shepton Wlk. Bris —3E 79
Sherborne Rd. Trow —1A 118
Sherbourne Av. Brad S —3A 28
Sherbourne Clo. Bris —5B 62
Sherbourne St. Bris —2A 72
Sheridan Rd. Bath —4A 104
Sheridan Rd. Bris —3C 42
Sheridan Way. L Grn —3C 84
Sherrings, The. Pat —1D 27
Sherrin Way. Bris —4A 86
Sherston Clo. Bris —2D 61
Sherston Clo. Nail —4F 123
Sherston Rd. Bris —4A 42
Sherwell Rd. Bris —2A 82
Sherwood Clo. Key —3A 92
Sherwood Cres. W Mare —2D 129
Sherwood Rd. Bris —1D 73
Sherwood Rd. Key —3A 92
Shetland Rd. Bris —3F 41
Shetland Way. Nail —4F 123
Shickle Gro. Bath —3D 109
Shields Av. Bris —2C 42
Shiels Dri. Lit S —2F 27
Shilton Clo. Bris —3B 74
Shimsey Clo. Bris —1E 61
Shiners Elms. Yat —3B 142
Shipham Clo. Bris —3D 89
Shipham Clo. Nail —5E 123
Shipham La. Wins —3B 156
Ship Hill. Bris —5D 73
Ship La. Bris —5A 70
Shiplate Rd. B'don —5A 140
Shipley Rd. Bris —4C 40
Shire Gdns. Bris —4F 37
Shirehampton Rd. Bris —1B 54
Shires Yd. Bath —2A 106 (2B 96)
Shire Way. Yate —2E 33
Shockerwick La. Bann —2C 102
Shophouse Rd. Bath —3C 104
Shore Pl. Trow —1A 118
Shorthill Rd. W'lgh —5E 33
Shortlands Rd. Bris —3C 38
Short La. L Ash —3C 76
Short St. Bris —5C 70
Short Way. T'bry —5C 6
Shortwood Hill. Mang —2F 63
Shortwood Northern Link. Yate —1F 63
Shortwood Rd. Bris —5A 88
Shortwood Rd. Puck —3B 64
Shortwood View. Bris —2B 74
Shortwood Wlk. Bris —5A 88
Showering Clo. Bris —3F 89
Showering Rd. Bris —3F 89
Shrewton Clo. Trow —4D 119
Shrophouse Rd. Bath —3C 104
Shrubbery Av. W Mare —4A 126
Shrubbery Cotts. Bris —5D 57
Shrubbery Ct. Stap H —2F 61
Shrubbery Rd. Bris —2F 61
Shrubbery Rd. W Mare —4B 126
Shrubbery Ter. W Mare —4A 126
Shrubbery, The. Bath —1A 106
Shrubbery Wlk. W Mare —4B 126
Shrubbery Wlk. W. W Mare —4B 126
Shuter Rd. Bris —3B 86
Sibland. T'bry —4E 7
Sibland Clo. T'bry —4E 7
Sibland Rd. T'bry —3E 7
Sibland Way. T'bry —4D 7
Sidcot. Bris —3C 82
Sidcot La. Wins —5B 156
Sideland Clo. Bris —2A 90
Sidelands Rd. Bris —1E 61
Sidmouth Gdns. Bris —3F 79
Sidmouth Rd. Bris —3F 79
Signal Rd. Bris —3A 62
Silbury Rise. Key —5A 92
Silbury Rd. Bris —3A 78
Silcox Rd. Bris —4E 87
Silklands Gro. Bris —1E 55
Silverberry Rd. W Mare —4D 129
Silverbirch Clo. Lit S —2F 27
Silver Birch Gro. Trow —5B 118
Silver Ct. Nail —3C 122
Silverhill Rd. Bris —1A 40
Silverlow Rd. Nail —3C 122
Silver Mead. Cong —4D 145
Silver Meadows. Trow —5A 118
Silver Moor La. Ban —2C 136
Silverstone Way. Cong —3D 145
Silver St. Brad A —3E 115
Silver St. Bris —3F 69 (1C 4)
Silver St. Cong —4D 145
Silver St. Mid N —5D 151
Silver St. Nail —3B 122
Silver St. T'bry —3C 6
Silver St. Trow —2D 119
Silver St. Wrin —1C 156
Silver St. La. Trow —5A 118
Silverthorne La. Bris —4C 70
Silverton Ct. Bris —4B 80
Simons Clo. Paul —4C 146
Simons Clo. W Mare —3E 129
Simplex Ind. Est. Bris —1F 85
Sinclair Ho. Bris —3D 69
Singapore Rd. W Mare —5C 132
Sion Hill. Bath —5F 99
Sion Hill. Bris —3B 68
Sion Hill Pl. Bath —5F 99
Sion La. Bris —3B 68
Sion Pl. Bath —3C 106 (3F 97)
Sion Pl. Clif —3B 68
Sion Rd. Bath —5F 99
Sion Rd. Bris —2E 79
Sir John's La. Bris —3D 59
Sir Johns Wood. Nail —2C 122
Siskin Wlk. W Mare —5D 129
Siston Clo. Bris —5C 62
Siston Comn. Bris —5C 62
Siston Hill. Bris —1D 75
Siston La. Bris —2F 75
Siston La. Yate & B'yte —3B 64
Siston Pk. Bris —5C 62
Sixth Av. Bris —3D 43
Six Ways. Clev —2C 120
Skinner's Hill. C'ton —2C 148
Skippon Ct. Bris —5A 74
Sladebrook Av. Bath —1D 109
Sladebrook Ct. Bath —1D 109
Sladebrook Rd. Bath —5C 104
Slade Cotts. Bath —3F 111
Slade Rd. P'head —3F 49
Sladesbrook. Brad A —2E 115
Sladesbrook Clo. Brad A —1E 115
Sleep La. Bris —5F 89
Slimbridge Clo. Yate —2B 34
Slipway, The. Stav —3D 117
Sloan St. Bris —2F 71
Slowgrove Clo. Trow —2F 119
Slymbridge Av. Bris —5C 24
Smallbrook Gdns. Stav —2D 117
Smallcombe Clo. Clan —4B 148
Smallcombe Rd. Clan —4B 148
Small La. Bris —2A 60 (in two parts)
Small St. Bris —3F 69 (2B 4)
Small St. St Ph —5C 70
Smallway. Cong —5D 143
Smarts Grn. Chip S —1E 35
Smeaton Rd. Bris —5B 68
Smithcourt Dri. Lit S —3E 27
Smithmead. Bris —3D 87
Smithywell Clo. Trow —2F 119
Smoke La. Bris —4E 21

Smythe Croft. *Bris* —5C **88**
Smyth Rd. *Bris* —2C **78**
Smyth's Clo. *Bris* —3D **37**
Snarland Gro. *Bris* —4E **87**
Snowberry Clo. *W Mare* —4E **129**
Snowberry Wlk. *Bris* —2A **72**
Snowdon Clo. *Bris* —3B **60**
Snowdon Rd. *Bris* —2B **60**
Snowdon Vale. *W Mare* —4E **127**
Snow Hill. *Bath* —1B **106**
Snow Hill Ho. *Bath* —1B **106**
Soapers La. *T'bry* —4C **6**
Sodbury La. *W'lgh* —4A **34**
Sodbury Rd. *Wickw* —2B **154**
Solent Way. *T'bry* —5E **7**
Solsbury Ct. *Bath* —2A **102**
*Solsbury View. Bath —4B **100** (off Fairfield Pk.)*
Solsbury Way. *Bath* —4B **100** (in three parts)
Somer Av. *Mid N* —2B **150**
Somerby Clo. *Brad S* —2F **27**
Somerdale Av. *Bath* —2D **109**
Somerdale Av. *Bris* —5B **80**
Somerdale Av. *W Mare* —5A **128**
Somerdale Clo. *W Mare* —5A **128**
Somerdale Rd. *Key* —2B **92**
Somerdale Rd. N. *Key* —5B **84**
Somerdale View. *Bath* —2D **109**
Somermead. *Bris* —4E **79**
Somer Rd. *Mid N* —2C **150**
Somerset Av. *Lock* —1C **134**
Somerset Av. *Yate* —3B **18**
Somerset Cres. *Stok G* —4B **28**
Somerset Folly. *Tim* —1E **157**
Somerset Ho. *Bath* —1E **109**
Somerset La. *Bath* —5F **99**
Somerset M. *W Mare* —2D **133**
Somerset Pl. *Bath* —5F **99**
Somerset Rd. *Bris* —2C **80**
Somerset Rd. *Clev* —3E **121**
Somerset Rd. *P'head* —3B **48**
Somerset Sq. *Bris* —5A **70**
Somerset Sq. *Nail* —3D **123**
Somerset St. *Bath* —4B **106** (5C **96**)
Somerset St. *K'dwn* —2F **69**
Somerset St. *Redc* —5A **70** (5E **5**)
Somerset Ter. *Bris* —2F **79**
Somerset Way. *Paul* —3B **146**
Somerton Clo. *Bris* —3A **74**
Somerton Rd. *Bris* —1A **58**
Somerton Rd. *Clev* —5E **121**
Somervale Rd. *Rads* —2A **152**
Somerville Clo. *Salt* —2A **94**
Sommerville Rd. *Bris* —4A **58**
Sommerville Rd. S. *Bris* —5B **58**
Sophia Gdns. *W Mare* —1F **129**
Sorrel Clo. *T'bry* —2E **7**
Sorrel Clo. *Trow* —5D **119**
Soundwell Rd. *Bris* —1E **73**
South Av. *Bath* —4E **105**
South Av. *P'head* —2F **49**
South Av. *Yate* —5D **17**
Southblow Ho. *Bris* —2C **78**
Southbourne Gdns. *Bath* —5C **100**
S. Combe. *B'don* —5F **139**
Southcot Pl. *Bath* —4B **106**
S. Croft. *Bris* —5E **41**
South Dene. *Bris* —1A **56**
Southdown. *W Mare* —1D **129**
Southdown Av. *Bath* —1C **108**
Southdown Rd. *Bath* —5C **104**
Southdown Rd. *Bris* —4B **40**
Southdowns. *Bris* —1C **68**
Southend Gdns. *Wickw* —2B **154**
Southend Ho. *Wickw* —2C **154**
Southend Rd. *W Mare* —4C **132**
Southernhay. *Clif W* —4D **69**
Southernhay. *Stap H* —3E **61**
Southernhay Av. *Bris* —4D **69**
Southernhay Cres. *Bris* —4D **69**
Southern Ring Path. *Clev* (in two parts) —5C **120**
Southern Way. *Clev* —4B **120**
Southey Av. *Bris* —1F **73**
Southey Ct. *Bris* —1F **73**
Southey Rd. *Clev* —4D **121**
Southey St. *Bris* —5B **58**
Southfield. *Rads* —2D **153**
Southfield Av. *Bris* —1A **74**
Southfield Clo. *Nail* —2D **123**
Southfield Clo. *Uph* —1B **138**
Southfield Ct. *Bris* —5C **40**
Southfield Rd. *Cot* —1F **69**
Southfield Rd. *Nail* —2D **123** (in two parts)
Southfield Rd. *W Trym* —5C **40**
Southfields. *Rads* —2D **153**
Southfield Trad. Est. *Nail* —2E **123**
Southgate. *Bath* —3B **106** (4C **96**)
South Grn. St. *Bris* —4B **68**
South Gro. *Bris* —2E **57**
South Gro. *Pill* —3E **53**
S. Hayes. *Bris* —3D **59**
Southlands. *Bath* —4B **98** (in two parts)
Southlands Dri. *Tim* —2E **157**
Southlands Way. *Cong* —1D **145**
South Lawn. *Lock* —4E **135**
S. Lawn Clo. *Lock* —4D **135**
S. Lea Rd. *Bath* —1B **104**
Southleaze. *Wins* —5B **156**
Southleigh. *Brad A* —4D **115**
Southleigh Rd. *Bris* —2D **69**
S. Liberty La. *Bris* —4A **78**
S. Lodge. *Bris* —1F **55**
Southmead. *Wins* —4B **156**
S. Meadows. *Wrin* —1C **156**
Southmead Rd. *W Mare* —1F **133**
Southmead Rd. *W Trym & Fil* —5E **41**
Southover Clo. *Bris* —4C **40**
South Pde. *Bath* —3B **106** (4D **97**)
South Pde. *Bris* —2D **69**
South Pde. *W Mare* —5B **126**
South Pde. *Yate* —5A **18**
*South Pde. Cotts. Bath (off Tyning Rd.) —3D **111***
South Quay. *Bris* —4A **70** (3E **5**)
Southridge Heights. *W Mare* —3E **139**
South Rd. *Bedm* —2E **79**
South Rd. *K'wd* —2F **73**
South Rd. *Mid N* —3D **151**
South Rd. *P'head* —2F **49**
South Rd. *Redl* —5E **57**
South Rd. *Tim* —2E **157**
South Rd. *W Mare* —4A **126**
Southsea Rd. *Pat* —2C **26**
South Side. *Cong* —1E **145**
Southside. *W Mare* —5C **126**
Southside Clo. *Bris* —4D **39**
Southside Cres. *Kew* —1E **127**
Southstoke La. *S'ske* —5A **110**
Southstoke Rd. *Bath* —3A **110**
South St. *Bris* —2D **79**
South Ter. *Bris* —5D **57**
South Ter. *W Mare* —5B **126**
*South View. Bath —5B **100** (off Camden Rd.)*
South View. *Bris* —2A **62**
South View. *Fram C* —2D **31**
South View. *Mid N* —4B **148**
South View. *Mon C* —3F **111**
South View. *Paul* —3B **146**
South View. *P'head* —1F **49**
South View. *Tim* —1E **157**
Southview Clo. *Hut* —1C **140**
S. View Cres. *Coal H* —3F **31**
S. View Pl. *Bath* —4D **109**
S. View Pl. *Mid N* —2E **151**
S. View Rise. *Coal H* —3E **31**
S. View Rd. *Bath* —3E **105**
Southview Rd. *Trow* —4D **119**
Southview Ter. *Yat* —2B **142**
Southville Clo. *Brad A* —4F **115**
Southville Pl. *Bris* —1F **79**
Southville Rd. *Brad A* —4F **115**
Southville Rd. *Bris* —1E **79**
Southville Rd. *W Mare* —4C **132**
Southville Ter. *Bath* —5C **106**
South Wlk. *Yate* —5A **18**
South Way. *Trow* —3D **119**
Southway Dri. *Bris* —5F **75**
Southway Rd. *Brad A* —5E **115**
Southwell St. *Bris* —2E **69**
Southwick Rd. *N Brad* —5D **155**
Southwood Av. *Bris* —4E **39**
Southwood Dri. *Bris* —5D **39**
Southwood Dri. E. *Bris* —4E **39**
Southwood Rd. *Trow* —2F **119**
Sovereign Shopping Cen. *W Mare* —1B **132**
Spa La. *Bath* —4D **101**
Spalding Clo. *Bris* —4C **58**
Spar Rd. *Yate* —4F **17**
Spartley Dri. *Bris* —2B **86**
Spartley Wlk. *Bris* —2B **86**
Specklemead. *Paul* —4A **146**
Speedwell Av. *Bris* —3F **71**
Speedwell Clo. *T'bry* —2E **7**
Speedwell Clo. *Trow* —4D **119**
Speedwell Rd. *Bris* —1B **72**
Spencer Dri. *W Mare* —2F **129**
Spencer Ho. *Bris* —5A **70**
Spencers Belle Vue. *Bath* —1A **106**
Spencers Orchard *Brad A* —5E **115**
Sperring Ct. *Mid N* —4C **150**
Spey Clo. *T'bry* —4D **7**
Spindleberry Gro. *Nail* —3F **123**
Spinners Croft. *Trow* —3D **119**
Spinners End. *W Mare* —1F **129**
Spinney Croft. *Bris* —3B **86**
Spinney, The. *Brad S* —2A **28**
Spinney, The. *Fram C* —2D **31**
Spinney, The. *Trow* —2F **119**
Spinney, The. *W Mare* —2D **139**
Spinnings Drove. *Clev* —5F **125**
Spires View. *Bris* —2A **60**
Spitfire Retail Pk. *Trow* —5D **119**
Spring Cres. *Bath* —3B **106** (4D **97**)
Springfield. *Brad A* —3F **115** (in three parts)
Springfield. *Pea J* —2F **149**
Springfield. *T'bry* —4E **7**
Springfield Av. *Hor* —2B **58**
Springfield Av. *Mang* —1C **62**
Springfield Av. *Shire* —1F **53**
Springfield Av. *W Mare* —4B **128**
Springfield Bldgs. *Rads* —1D **153**
Springfield Bungalows. *Mid N* —2A **150**
Springfield Clo. *Bath* —4C **104**
Springfield Clo. *Mang* —5C **46**
Springfield Clo. *Trow* —5E **117**
Springfield Crest. *Rads* —1D **153**
Springfield Gdns. *Ban* —5E **137**
Springfield Gro. *Bris* —2D **57**
Springfield Heights. *Rads* —5B **148**
Springfield Lawns. *Bris* —1F **53**
Springfield Pk. *Trow* —1E **119**
Springfield Pl. *Bath* —5A **100**
Springfield Pl. *Rads* —5B **148**
Springfield Rd. *Bris* —1F **69**
Springfield Rd. *Mang* —5C **46**
Springfield Rd. *Pill* —3E **53**
Springfield Rd. *P'head* —3D **49**
Springfields. *Fil* —2C **42**
*Spring Gdns. Bath —3B **106** (off Spring Gdns. Rd.)*
Spring Gdns. *Bris* —4C **80**
Spring Gdns. Rd. *Bath* —3B **106** (3D **97**) (in two parts)
Spring Ground Rd. *Paul* —4B **146**
Spring Hill. *K'dwn* —2F **69** (in two parts)
Spring Hill. *K'wd* —5A **62**
Spring Hill. *W Mare* —3A **128**
Springhill Clo. *Paul* —3A **146**
Spring Hill Dri. *W Mare* —4B **128**
Spring La. *Bath* —4C **100**
Springleaze. *Bris* —4C **80**
Springleaze. *Mang* —5C **46**
Spring Rise. *P'head* —5E **49**
Spring St. *Bedm* —1A **80**
Spring St. Pl. *Bris* —1A **80**
Spring Ter. *W Mare* —3A **128**
Spring Vale. *Bath* —4C **100**
Spring Valley. *W Mare* —3A **128**
Springville Clo. *L Grn* —2C **84**
Springwood Dri. *Bris* —1F **39**
Springwood Gdns. *Hut* —5C **134**
Spruce Way. *Bath* —4F **109**
Spruce Way. *Pat* —2A **26**
Sprynham Ho. *Bris* —4C **86**
Square, The. *Alv* —3B **8**
Square, The. *Ban* —5F **137**
Square, The. *Brisl* —3F **81**
Square, The. *Know* —4C **80**
Square, The. *Stap H* —3A **62**
Square, The. *Stav* —1D **117**
Square, The. *Tim* —1E **157**
Square, The. *Wins* —5A **156**
Squires Ct. *L Grn* —1B **84**
Squires Leaze. *T'bry* —2D **7**
Stable Yd. *Bath* —3E **105**
Stackpool Rd. *Bris* —1D **79**
Staddlestones. *Mid N* —5C **150**
Stadium Rd. *Bris* —2E **57**
Stafford Cres. *T'bry* —3C **6**
Stafford Pl. *W Mare* —5C **126**
Stafford Rd. *Bris* —5C **58**
Stafford Rd. *P'head* —4A **50**
Stafford Rd. *W Mare* —5D **127**
Staffords Ct. *Bris* —4C **74**
Stafford St. *Bris* —1F **79**
Stainer Clo. *Bris* —2F **87**
Stallard St. *Trow* —2C **118**
Stall St. *Bath* —3B **106** (4C **96**)
Stambrook Pk. *Bathe* —1B **102**
Stanbridge Clo. *Bris* —1B **62**
Stanbridge Rd. *Bris* —1B **62**
Stanbury Av. *Bris* —2E **61**
Stanbury Rd. *Bris* —2A **80**
Stancomb Av. *Trow* —1E **119**
Standfast Rd. *Bris* —1B **40**
Standish Av. *Pat* —5D **11**
Standish Clo. *Bris* —3B **40**
Standon Way. *Bris* —2E **41**
Stane Way. *Bris* —5E **37**
Stanfast Rd. *Bris* —1B **40**
Stanfield Clo. *Bris* —1D **59**
Stanford Clo. *Fram C* —1B **30**
Stanford Pl. *Bris* —1F **87**
Stanhope Pl. *Bath* —3F **105**
Stanhope Rd. *L Grn* —3B **84**
Stanhope Rd. *W Mare* —5C **132**
Stanhope St. *Bris* —5C **70**
Stanier Rd. *Bath* —3F **105**
Stanley Av. *Bishop* —4A **58**
Stanley Av. *Fil* —2D **43**
Stanley Chase. *Bris* —5F **59**
Stanley Ct. *Mid N* —2E **151**
Stanley Cres. *Bris* —2D **43**
Stanley Gdns. *Old C* —1D **85**
Stanley Gro. *W Mare* —1D **133**
Stanley Hill. *Bris* —1C **80**
Stanley Mead. *Brad S* —4A **12**
Stanley Pk. *Bris* —1E **71**
Stanley Pk. Rd. *Bris* —4A **62**
Stanley Rd. *Cot* —5E **57**
Stanley Rd. *War* —2D **75**
Stanley Rd. *W Mare* —1D **133**
Stanley Rd. W. *Bath* —4E **105**
Stanley St. *Bris* —2E **79**
Stanley St. N. *Bris* —2E **79**
Stanley St. S. *Bris* —2E **79**
Stanley Ter. *Bris* —3E **79**
Stanley Ter. *Rads* —1D **153**
*Stanley Vs. Bath —5B **100** (off Camden Rd.)*
Stanshaw Clo. *Bris* —5C **44**
Stanshawe Cres. *Yate* —5A **18**
Stanshawes Ct. *Yate* —1A **34**
Stanshawes Ct. Dri. *Yate* —1A **34**
Stanshawes Dri. *Yate* —5F **17**
Stanshaw Rd. *Bris* —5C **44**
Stanshaws Clo. *Brad S* —4E **11**
Stanton Clo. *Bris* —1B **74**
Stanton Clo. *Trow* —5D **119**
Stanton Rd. *Bris* —3F **41**
Stanway. *Bit* —4E **85**
Stanway Clo. *Bath* —3E **109**
Staple Gro. *Key* —3F **91**
Staplegrove Cres. *Bris* —3C **72**
Staplehill Rd. *Bris* —2D **61**
Staples Clo. *Clev* —5E **121**
Staples Grn. *W Mare* —2F **129**
Staples Hill. *F'frd* —5D **113**
Staples Rd. *Yate* —4F **17**
Stapleton Clo. *Bris* —2F **59**
Stapleton Rd. *Bris* —2C **70**
Star Barn Rd. *Wint* —2A **30**
Starcross Rd. *W Mare* —2E **129**
Star La. *Bris* —4B **60**
Star La. *Pill* —3E **53**
Starling Clo. *W Mare* —5C **128**
Star, The. *Holt* —2E **155**
States Way. *Bris* —1E **57**
Station App. *Brad A* —3D **115**
Station App. *W Mare* —1D **133**
Station App. Rd. *Bris* —5B **70** (5F **5**)
Station Av. *Bris* —3C **60**
Station Clo. *Back* —1B **124**
Station Clo. *Chip S* —1F **35**
Station Clo. *Cong* —2C **144**
Station Clo. *War* —2E **75**
Station Ct. *Bath* —2D **105**
Station La. *Bris* —3C **58**
Station Rd. *Ash D* —3B **58**
Station Rd. *B'ptn* —4A **102**
Station Rd. *Bris* —3F **81**
Station Rd. *Clev* —3D **121**
Station Rd. *Coal H* —4E **31**
Station Rd. *Cong* —2C **144**
Station Rd. *Fil* —1D **43**
Station Rd. *Fish* —3C **60**
Station Rd. *F'frd* —4D **113**
Station Rd. *Hen* —2A **40**
Station Rd. *Holt* —2E **155**
Station Rd. *Iron A* —3F **15**
Station Rd. *Key* —2A **92**
Station Rd. *K'wd* —3A **62**
Station Rd. *Lit S* —3E **27**
Station Rd. *Lwr W* —2D **105**
Station Rd. *Mid N* —2E **151**
Station Rd. *Mont* —5F **57**
Station Rd. *Nail* —3D **123** (in two parts)
Station Rd. *Pill* —3E **53**
Station Rd. *P'bry* —5F **51**
Station Rd. *P'head* —2F **49**
Station Rd. *Sev B* —4A **20**
Station Rd. *Shire* —2F **53**
Station Rd. *St Ap* —5A **72**
Station Rd. *St Geo* —3A **130**
Station Rd. *War* —3E **75**
Station Rd. *Wickw* —1B **154**
Station Rd. *Wint* —5A **30**
Station Rd. *W Mare* —1C **132**
Station Rd. *Wor* —3D **129**
Station Rd. *Wrin* —1B **156**
Station Rd. *Yat* —2A **142**
Station Rd. *Yate* —4E **17**
Station Way. *Trow* —2C **118**
Statnton Clo. *Bris* —1B **74**
Staunton Fields. *Bris* —5E **89**
Staunton La. *Bris* —4E **89**
Staunton Way. *Bris* —5F **89**
Staveley Cres. *Bris* —2E **41**
Staverton Clo. *Pat* —5D **11**
Staverton Way. *Bris* —3C **74**
Stavordale Gro. *Bris* —2D **89**
Staynes Cres. *K'wd* —2A **74**
Steam Mills. *Mid N* —4C **150**
Stean Bri. Rd. *Lit S* —3F **27**
Steel Ct. *L Grn* —2B **84**
Steel Mills. *Key* —4B **92**
Stella Gro. *Bris* —3C **78**
Stephen's Dri. *Bar C* —5B **74**
Stephen St. *Redf* —2E **71**
Stepney Rd. *Bris* —1E **71**
Stepney Wlk. *Bris* —1E **71**
Stepping Stones, The. *St Ap* —4A **72**
Sterncourt Rd. *Bris* —5C **44**
Steven's Cres. *Bris* —1B **80**
Steway La. *Bathe* —1B **102**
Stibbs Ct. *L Grn* —1B **84**
Stibbs Hill. *Bris* —3C **72**

Stickland. *Clev* —5C **120**
Stidham La. *Key* —2D **93**
Stile Acres. *Bris* —3C **38**
Stillhouse La. *Bris* —1F **79**
Stillingfleet Rd. *Bris* —3E **87**
Stillman Clo. *Bris* —4A **86**
Stillman Clo. *Holt* —2E **155**
Stinchcombe. *Yate* —5A **18**
Stirling Clo. *Yate* —2F **17**
Stirling Rd. *Bris* —1E **81**
Stirling Way. *Key* —4A **92**
Stirtingale Av. *Bath* —1D **109**
Stirtingale Rd. *Bath* —1D **109**
Stock La. *Cong* —5E **145**
Stockton Clo. *Bris* —4B **88**
Stockton Clo. *L Grn* —2D **85**
Stock Way N. *Nail* —3D **123**
Stock Way S. *Nail* —3D **123**
Stockwell Av. *Mang* —1C **62**
Stockwell Clo. *Bris* —5B **46**
Stockwell Dri. *Mang* —1C **62**
Stockwell Glen. *Bris* —5B **46**
Stockwood Cres. *Bris* —3B **80**
Stockwood Hill. *Key* —1E **91**
Stockwood La. *Bris & Key* —4F **89**
Stockwood M. *St Ap* —5B **72**
Stockwood Rd. *Brisl* —5B **82**
Stockwood Rd. *Bris* —3F **89**
Stockwood Vale. *Key* —3C **90**
Stodelegh Clo. *W Mare* —2F **129**
Stoke Bri. Av. *Lit S* —3F **27**
Stoke Cotts. *Bris* —3A **56**
Stokefield Clo. *T'bry* —3C **6**
Stoke Gro. *Bris* —1A **56**
Stoke Hamlet. *Bris* —5B **40**
Stoke Hill. *Bris* —3A **56**
Stoke La. *Pat* —1D **27**
Stoke La. *Stap* —5A **44**
Stoke La. *W Trym* —2A **56**
Stokeleigh Wlk. *Bris* —2E **55**
Stoke Mead. *Lim S* —2A **112**
Stokemead. *Pat* —1E **27**
Stoke Paddock Rd. *Bris* —1F **55**
Stoke Pk. Rd. *Bris* —3A **56**
Stoke Pk. Rd. S. *Bris* —4A **56**
Stoke Rd. *Bris* —4B **56**
Stoke Rd. *P'head* —3F **49**
Stokes Ct. *Bar C* —1C **84**
Stokes Croft. *Bris* —2A **70**
Stoke View. *Bris* —1C **42**
Stoke View Rd. *Bris* —4B **60**
Stoneable Rd. *Rads* —1D **153**
Stoneberry Rd. *Bris* —5D **89**
Stonebridge. *Clev* —5D **121**
Stonebridge Pk. *Bris* —5F **59**
Stonebridge Rd. *W Mare* —4D **133**
Stonechat Gdns. *Bris* —1A **60**
Stonefield Clo. *Brad A* —4F **115**
Stonehenge La. *Tic* —1D **123**
Stonehill. *L Grn* —1F **83**
Stonehouse Clo. *Bath* —2C **110**
Stonehouse La. *Bath* —2C **110**
Stone La. *Wint D* —5A **30**
Stoneleigh Ct. *Bath* —3F **99**
Stoneleigh Cres. *Bris* —3C **80**
Stoneleigh Dri. *Bris* —5B **74**
Stoneleigh Rd. *Bris* —3C **80**
Stoneleigh Wlk. *Bris* —3C **80**
Stones Cotts. *Bris* —5E **23**
Stonewell Dri. *Cong* —3D **145**
Stonewell Gro. *Cong* —3D **145**
Stonewell La. *Cong* —3D **145**
Stonewell Pk. Rd. *Cong* —3D **145**
Stoneyfields. *E'ton G* —3D **53**
Stoneyfields Clo. *E'ton G* —2D **53**
Stoney Hill. *Bris* —3E **69** (2A **4**)
Stoney La. *Bris* —4B **58**
Stoney Steep. *Nail* —1F **123**
Stoney Steep. *P'head* —2E **49**
Stoney Stile Rd. *Alv* —2B **8**
Stony La. *Bath* —5F **95**
(in two parts)
Stormont Clo. *W Mare* —5D **133**
Stothard Rd. *Bris* —5D **43**
Stottbury Rd. *Bris* —4C **58**
Stoulton Gro. *Bris* —1C **40**
Stourden Clo. *Bris* —5C **44**
Stourton Dri. *Bar C* —1B **84**
Stover Rd. *Yate* —3C **16**
Stover Trad. Est. *Yate* —4D **17**
Stowey La. *Yat* —4D **143**
Stowey Pk. *Yat* —3D **143**
Stowey Rd. *Yat* —2B **142**
Stow Ho. *Bris* —2A **54**
Stowick Cres. *Bris* —3E **39**
Stradbrook Av. *Bris* —3D **73**
Stradling Av. *W Mare* —3D **133**
Stradling Rd. *Bris* —2E **39**
Straits Pde. *Bris* —2D **61**
Stratford Clo. *Bris* —5B **88**
Strathmore Rd. *Bris* —1A **58**
Stratton Clo. *Lit S* —1E **27**
Stratton St. *Bris* —2A **70**
Strawberry Clo. *Nail* —4C **122**
Strawberry Cres. *St G* —3A **72**
Strawberry Gdns. *Nail* —4C **122**
Strawberry Hill. *Clev* —2E **121**
Strawberry La. *B'wth* —5A **86**
Strawberry La. *Bris* —3A **72**
Strawbridge Rd. *Bris* —3D **71**
Stream Clo. *Bris* —5F **25**
Streamcross. *Clav* —2D **143**
Streamleaze. *T'bry* —4C **6**
Streamside. *Clev* —3F **121**
Streamside. *Yate* —1B **62**
Streamside Rd. *Chip S* —5C **18**
Streamside Wlk. *Bris* —2A **82**
Streamside Wlk. *T'bry* —1D **7**
Stream, The. *Ham* —2D **45**
Street, The. *Alv* —2D **9**
Street, The. *Holt* —2D **155**
Street, The. *Rads* —2C **152**
Stretford Av. *Bris* —2F **71**
Stretford Rd. *Bris* —1F **71**
Stride Clo. *Sev B* —4B **20**
Strode Comn. *Alv* —2A **8**
Strode Gdns. *Alv* —2A **8**
Strode Rd. *Clev* —5B **120**
Strode Way. *Clev* —5B **120**
Stroud Rd. *Bris* —2A **54**
Stroud Rd. *Pat* —1A **26**
Stuart Clo. *Trow* —3E **117**
Stuart Pl. *Bath* —3E **105**
Stuart Rd. *W Mare* —3E **133**
Stuart St. *Redf* —3E **71**
Studland Ct. *Bris* —1D **57**
Studley Rise. *Trow* —4D **119**
Sturden La. *Ham* —1E **45**
Sturdon Rd. *Bris* —2C **78**
Sturmer Clo. *Yate* —2A **18**
Sturminster Clo. *Bris* —2F **89**
Sturminster Rd. *Bris* —5E **81**
Sulis Manor Rd. *Bath* —4D **109**
Sullivan Clo. *Bris* —2F **87**
Sumerlin Dri. *Clev* —3F **121**
Summer Down Wlk. *Trow* —3D **155**
Summerfield. *W Mare* —2F **129**
Summerfield Cotts. Bath
(off Tyning La.) —*5C* ***100***
Summerfield Rd. *Bath* —5B **100**
Summerfield Ter. *Bath* —5B **100**
Summerhayes. *Bris* —5F **75**
Summer Hill. *Bris* —1C **80**
Summerhill Rd. *Bath* —5E **99**
Summerhill Rd. *Bris* —2A **72**
Summerhill Ter. *Bris* —3B **72**
Summerhouse. *Tic* —1C **122**
Summerlands. *Back* —3D **125**
Summerlands Rd. *W Mare* —5E **127**
Summer La. *Ban & W Mare* —4F **129**
Summer La. *C Down* —3C **110**
Summer La. Cvn. Pk. *Ban* —4C **136**
Summer La. N. *W Mare* —3E **129**
Summerlays Ct. *Bath* —3C **106** (4E **97**)
Summerleaze. *Bris* —4E **61**
Summerleaze. *Key* —1A **92**
Summerleaze. *Trow* —4A **118**
Summers Mead. *Yate* —2A **18**
Summers Rd. *Bris* —1C **70**
Summers Ter. *Bris* —1C **70**
Summer St. *Bris* —1E **79**
Sundays Hill. *Alm* —2C **10**
Sunderland Pl. *Bris* —2D **69**
Sunderland St. *Bath* —2B **106** (2D **97**)
Sundridge Pk. *Yate* —2A **34**
Sunfield Rd. *Hut* —5C **134**
Sunningdale. *Bris* —2D **69**
Sunningdale. *Yate* —1A **34**
Sunningdale Clo. *Nail* —4F **123**
Sunningdale Dri. *War* —4D **75**
Sunningdale Rd. *W Mare* —2D **129**
Sunnybank. *Bath* —5C **106**
Sunny Bank. *Bris* —1D **73**
Sunnybank. *Mang* —1A **62**
Sunnydene. *Bris* —1F **81**
Sunny Hill. *Bris* —5D **39**
Sunnyhill Dri. *Bris* —1A **54**
Sunnyhill Ho. E. Bris
(off Sunnyhill Dri.) —*1A* ***54***
Sunnyhill Ho. W. Bris
(off Sunnyhill Dri.) —*1A* ***54***
Sunnymead. *Key* —5B **92**
Sunnymead. *Mid N* —2C **150**
Sunnymede Rd. *Nail* —2C **122**
Sunnymount. *Mid N* —2E **151**
Sunnyside. *Bris* —2A **56**
Sunnyside. *Fram C* —2D **31**
Sunnyside Cres. *Clev* —3D **121**
Sunnyside La. *Ham* —2E **45**
Sunnyside La. *Yate* —5E **17**
Sunnyside Rd. *Clev* —3C **120**
Sunnyside Rd. *W Mare* —3C **132**
Sunnyside Rd. N. *W Mare* —2C **132**
Sunnyside View. *Pea J* —2F **149**
Sunnyvale. *C'ton* —1B **148**
Sunnyvale. *Clev* —5A **120**
Sunnyvale Dri. *L Grn* —2D **85**
Sunny Wlk. *Bris* —1D **73**
Sunridge. *Bris* —1F **61**
Sunridge Clo. *Mid N* —4C **150**
Sunridge Pk. *Mid N* —4C **150**
Sunrise Gro. *Bris* —1F **81**
Sunset Clo. *Pea J* —2F **149**
Surrey Pl. *Trow* —3C **118**
Surrey Rd. *Bris* —4A **58**
Surrey St. *Bris* —2A **70**
Suspension Bri. Rd. *Bris* —3B **68**
Sussex Pl. *Bath* —4B **106** (5D **97**)
Sussex Pl. *Bris* —1B **70**
Sussex St. *Bris* —4C **70**
Sutherland Av. *Bris* —5A **46**
Sutherland Av. *Yate* —2F **17**
Sutherland Dri. *Hut* —1B **140**
Sutherland Pl. *Bris* —5C **56**
Sutton Av. *Bris* —1F **81**
(in two parts)
Sutton St. *Bath* —2C **106** (1E **97**)
Swainswick. *Bris* —2B **88**
Swainswick Gdns. *Bath* —4D **101**
Swainswick La. *Bath* —1D **101**
Swaish Dri. *Bar C* —1B **84**
Swallow Clo. *Mid N* —4E **151**
Swallow Dri. *Pat* —1A **26**
Swallow Dri. *Trow* —2B **118**
Swallow Gdns. *W Mare* —5B **128**
Swallow Pk. *T'bry* —1E **7**
Swallows Ct. *Stok G* —5A **28**
Swallows, The. *W Mare* —1B **134**
Swallow St. *Bath* —3B **106** (4C **96**)
Swan Clo. *W Mare* —5C **128**
Swan Dri. *Stav* —2D **117**
Swane Rd. *Bris* —2B **90**
Swan La. *Wint* —5D **13**
Swanmoor Cres. *Bris* —5C **24**
Sweets Clo. *Bris* —5A **62**
Sweets Rd. *Bris* —5A **62**
Swift Clo. *W Mare* —4D **129**
Swiss Dri. *Bris* —3B **78**
Swiss Rd. *Bris* —3B **78**
Swiss Rd. *W Mare* —1D **133**
Sycamore Clo. *Han* —2D **83**
Sycamore Clo. *Nail* —3D **123**
Sycamore Clo. *W'hall* —1A **72**
Sycamore Clo. *W Mare* —5E **127**
Sycamore Ct. *Bris* —4A **58**
Sycamore Dri. *Pat* —2A **26**
Sycamore Dri. *T'bry* —3D **7**
Sycamore Gro. *Trow* —4B **118**
Sycamore Rd. *Rads* —2E **153**
Sydenham Bldgs. *Bath* —4F **105**
Sydenham Hill. *Bris* —1F **69**
Sydenham La. *Bris* —1F **69**
Sydenham Rd. *Bath* —3F **105**
Sydenham Rd. *Cot* —1F **69**
Sydenham Rd. *Know* —2C **80**
Sydenham Ter. *C Down* —3D **111**
Sydenham Way. *Bris* —2E **83**
Sydney Bldgs. *Bath* —3C **106** (3F **97**)
Sydney M. *Bath* —2C **106** (2E **97**)
Sydney Pl. *Bath* —2C **106** (1E **97**)
Sydney Rd. *Bath* —2C **106** (2F **97**)
Sydney Row. *Bris* —2F **79**
Sydney Wharf. *Bathw* —3C **106** (3F **97**)
Sylvan Way. *Bris* —1D **55**
Sylvia Av. *Bris* —2B **80**
Symes Av. *Bris* —4E **87**
Symes Pk. *W'ton* —4B **98**
Symington Rd. *Bris* —2D **61**
Syston Way. *Bris* —1F **73**

Tabernacle Rd. *Bris* —4E **73**
Tackley Rd. *Bris* —4D **59**
Tadwick La. *Bath* —1B **100**
Tailor's Ct. *Bris* —3F **69** (2C **4**)
Talbot Av. *Bris* —1D **73**
Talbot Rd. *Bris* —3D **81**
Talbot Rd. *Trow* —3A **118**
Talgarth Rd. *Bris* —3B **58**
Tallis Gro. *Bris* —2F **87**
Tamar Clo. *T'bry* —5E **7**
Tamar Dri. *Key* —4C **92**
Tamar Rd. *Bris* —4E **71**
Tamar Rd. *W Mare* —3D **129**
Tamblyn Clo. *Rads* —1D **153**
Tamsin Ct. *Key* —3A **92**
Tamworth Rd. *Key* —4A **92**
Tankards Clo. *Bris* —3E **69** (1A **4**)
Tanner Clo. *Bar C* —5B **74**
Tanners Ct. *Bris* —3D **45**
Tanners Ct. *T'bry* —4C **6**
Tanners Wlk. *Bath* —4A **104**
Tanorth Clo. *Bris* —5C **88**
Tanorth Rd. *Bris* —5B **88**
Tanyard, The. *Will* —3D **85**
Tapsters. *Bris* —1C **84**
Tarn Ho. *Pat* —1C **26**
Tarnock Av. *Bris* —1B **88**
Tarragon Pl. *Brad S* —2B **28**
Taunton Rd. *W Mare* —1F **129**
Taunton Wlk. *Bris* —5C **42**
Taverner Clo. *Bris* —1F **87**
Tavistock Rd. *Bris* —4B **80**
Tavistock Rd. *W Mare* —3E **129**
Tavistock Wlk. *Bris* —4B **80**
Tawny Way. *W Mare* —5D **129**
Taylor Clo. *K'wd* —2B **74**
Taylor Ct. *W Mare* —1F **129**
Taylor Gdns. *Bris* —4B **86**
Tayman Clo. *Bris* —1A **58**
Tayman Ridge. *Bit* —5F **85**
Taynton Clo. *Bit* —3E **85**
Teal Clo. *Brad S* —4F **11**
Teal Clo. *W Mare* —4D **129**
Teasel Wlk. *W Mare* —1B **134**
Teddington Clo. *Bath* —5D **105**
Teesdale Clo. *W Mare* —5B **128**
Teewell Av. *Bris* —3A **62**
Teewell Clo. *Bris* —3A **62**
Teewell Ct. *Bris* —3A **62**
Teewell Hill. *Bris* —3A **62**
Teignmouth Rd. *Bris* —4B **80**
Teignmouth Rd. *Clev* —3E **121**
Telephone Av. *Bris* —4F **69** (3B **4**)
Telford Ho. *Bath* —1E **109**
Telford Wlk. *Bris* —1C **72**
Templar Rd. *Yate* —3A **18**
Temple Back. *Bris* —4A **70** (3E **5**)
Temple Boulevd. *Bris* —4B **70** (4F **5**)
Temple Ct. *Key* —3A **92**
Temple Ga. *Bris* —5B **70** (5F **5**)
Temple Ga. Ho. *Bris* —5A **70** (5F **5**)
Templeland Rd. *Bris* —3B **86**
Temple St. *Bedm* —3D **79**
Temple St. *Bris* —4A **70** (3D **5**)
(in two parts)
Temple St. *Key* —3A **92**
Temple Trad. Est. *Bris* —5D **71**
Temple Way. *Bris* —4A **70** (4E **5**)
Templeway Ho. *Bris* —4B **70** (3F **5**)
Ten Acre Cotts. *Eng* —5A **108**
Tenby Rd. *Key* —4F **91**
Tenby St. *Bris* —3D **71**
Tennessee Gro. *Bris* —2E **57**
Tennis Ct. Av. *Paul* —4A **146**
Tenniscourt Cotts. *Paul* —4A **146**
Tenniscourt Rd. *Bris* —1C **74**
Tennis Ct. Rd. *Paul* —4A **146**
Tennis Rd. *Bris* —3C **80**
Tennyson Av. *Clev* —4B **120**
Tennyson Clo. *Key* —2B **92**
Tennyson Rd. *Bath* —2E **105**
Tennyson Rd. *Bris* —2A **58**
Tennyson Rd. *W Mare* —5E **133**
Tenterk Clo. *B'don* —5F **139**
Tenth Av. *Bris* —3D **43**
Tereslake Grn. *Bris* —5F **25**
Terrace Wlk. *Bath* —3B **106** (4C **96**)
Terrell Gdns. *Bris* —3F **71**
Terrell St. *Bris* —2F **69**
Tetbury Clo. *Lit S* —1E **27**
Tetbury Gdns. *Nail* —4F **123**
Tetbury Rd. *Bris* —2D **73**
Teviot Rd. *Key* —4C **92**
Tewkesbury Rd. *Bris* —5C **58**
Tewther Rd. *Bris* —5E **87**
Teyfant Rd. *Bris* —4A **88**
Teyfant Wlk. *Bris* —4A **88**
Thackeray Av. *Clev* —2D **121**
Thackeray Rd. *Clev* —2E **121**
Thackeray Wlk. *Bris* —4C **42**
Thanet Rd. *Bris* —3D **79**
Thatcher Clo. *P'head* —4F **49**
Thatchers Clo. *Bris* —3D **73**
There & Back Again La. *Bris* —3E **69**
Theresa Av. *Bris* —3A **58**
Thestfield Dri. *Trow* —3D **117**
Theynes Croft. *L Ash* —4D **77**
Thicket Av. *Bris* —5D **61**
Thicket Rd. *Bris* —3E **61**
Thicket Wlk. *T'bry* —3D **7**
Thiery Rd. *Bris* —3E **81**
Thingwall Pk. *Bris* —4A **60**
Third Av. *Bath* —4E **105**
Third Av. *Bris* —3C **42**
Third Av. *W'fld I* —5A **152**
Third Way. *A'mth* —2D **37**
Thirlmere Ct. *Bris* —4F **75**
Thirlmere Rd. *Pat* —1C **26**
Thirlmere Rd. *W Mare* —4E **133**
Thistle St. *Bris* —2D **79**
Thomas Av. *E Grn* —4D **47**
Thomas Clo. *Ban* —5E **137**
Thomas La. *Bris* —4A **70** (4D **5**)
Thomas Pring Wlk. *Bris* —1C **72**
Thomas St. *Bath* —1B **106**
Thomas St. *Bris* —2A **70**
Thomas St. *Law H* —3D **71**
Thomas St. *St Pa* —1B **70**
Thomas St. N. *Bris* —1F **69**
Thompson Rd. *Bris* —2A **90**
Thomson Rd. *Bris* —2D **71**
Thornbank Pl. *Bath* —4F **105**
Thornbury Dri. *Uph* —1A **138**
Thornbury Hill. *Alv* —1A **8**
Thornbury Ind. Pk. *T'bry* —4D **7**

Thornbury Rd. Alv —2B 8 (in two parts)
Thornbury Rd. Uph —1A 138
Thorn Clo. W Mare —3F 129
Thorn Clo. Yate —5F 17
Thorndale. Bris —2C 68
Thorndale Clo. W Mare —5B 128
Thorndale Ct. Bris —1C 68
Thorndale M. Bris —2C 68
Thornhayes Clo. Fram C —1C 30
Thornhills, The. Fish —1D 61
Thornleigh Rd. Bris —2A 58
Thornmead Gro. Bris —1C 40
Thorns Farm. Yate —5A 18
Thornycroft Clo. Bris —5D 43
Three Queen's La. Bris —4A 70 (4D 5)
Three Wells Rd. Bris —4B 86
Thrissell St. Bris —2C 70
Throgmorton Rd. Bris —5B 80
Thrush Clo. W Mare —5C 128
Thunderbolt Steps. Bris —1C 80
Thurlestone. Bris —2B 88
Thurlow Rd. Bris —5E 59
Thurstons Barton. Bris —1A 72
Tibberton. Bris —2C 74
Tibbott Rd. Bris —3F 89
Tibbott Wlk. Bris —3F 89
Tichborne Rd. Bris —3E 71
Tichborne Rd. W Mare —4C 126
Tickenham Hill. Tic —1C 122
Tickenham Rd. Clev —3F 121
Tide Gro. Bris —4C 38
Tidenham Way. Pat —5B 10
Tiffany Ct. Bris —5A 70 (5E 5)
Tilley Clo. Key —5A 92
Tilling Rd. Bris —5A 42
Tilling Wlk. Bris —5A 42
Tilting Rd. T'bry —2C 6
Timber Dene. Bris —3F 59
Timberscombe Wlk. Bris —3D 89
Timbers, The. Mid N —5E 151
Timbrell St. Trow —1D 119
Timsbury Rd. Bris —3A 80
Timsbury Rd. High L —1A 146
Timsbury Wlk. Bris —3A 80
Tindell Ct. L Grn —1B 84
Tintagel Clo. Key —4F 91
Tintern Av. Bris —2F 71
Tintern Clo. Bar C —4B 74
Tippetts Rd. Bris —4F 73
Tirley Way. W Mare —3F 127
Titan Barrow. Bathf —4D 103
Tiverton Gdns. W Mare —3E 129
Tiverton Rd. Clev —5E 121
Tiverton Wlk. Bris —5C 60
Tivoli Houses. W Mare —5C 126
Tockington La. Alm —1C 10
Toddington Clo. Yate —1F 33
Tolland. W Mare —1E 139
Toll Bri. Rd. Bath —3F 101
Toll Ho. Ct. Bedm —1C 78
Toll Rd. B'don —3D 139
Tone Rd. Clev —5D 121
Tonge Rd. Mid N —4C 150
Tor Clo. W Mare —3E 129
Tormarton Cres. Bris —5B 24
Tormynton Rd. W Mare —3C 128
Toronto Rd. Bris —4B 42
Torpoint Rd. Bris —4F 79
Torrance Clo. Bris —4F 75
Torridge Rd. Key —4C 92
Torrington Av. Bris —5B 80
Torrington Cres. W Mare —2E 129
Tortworth Rd. Bris —2A 58
Tory. Brad A —3D 115
Tory Pl. Brad A —2D 115
Totnes Clo. W Mare —3E 129
Totshill Dri. Bris —5A 88
Totshill Gro. Bris —4A 88
Tottenham Pl. Bris —3D 69
Totterdown Bri. Trad. Est. Bris —1C 80
Totterdown La. W Mare —3E 139
Totterdown Rd. W Mare —4C 132
Touchstone Av. Stok G —4B 28
Tovey Clo. Kew —1C 128
Tower Clo. Trow —3A 118
Tower Hill. Bris —3A 70 (2E 5)
Tower Hill. Lock —4B 136
Tower Ho. La. Wrax —1E 123
Tower La. Bris —3F 69 (2C 4) (in two parts)
Tower La. War —4C 74
Towerleaze. Bris —4F 55
Tower Rd. Bris —1E 73
Tower Rd. P'head —4C 48
Tower Rd. N. Bris —3D 75
Tower Rd. S. Bris —4D 75
Tower St. Bris —4A 70 (4E 5)
Tower Wlk. W Mare —4B 126
Townsend. Alm —2B 10
Townsend Clo. Bris —3B 90
Townsend La. Alm —2B 10
Townsend Rd. Bris —3B 90
Townshend Rd. W Mare —1F 129
Towpath Rd. Trow —3E 117
Tozer's Hill. Bris —3E 81
Tracy Clo. Bris —1B 88 (in two parts)
Trafalgar Rd. Bath —5C 98
Trafalgar Ter. Bris —3D 79
Trafalgar Wlk. Bris —3F 69 (1C 4)
Tralee Wlk. Bris —4F 79
Tramway Rd. Brisl —2E 81
Tranmere Av. Bris —5C 24
Tranmere Gro. Bris —1C 40
Tratman Wlk. Bris —1B 40
Travers Clo. Bris —2F 87
Travers Wlk. Stok G —4A 28
Trawden Clo. W Mare —4E 127
Tredegar Rd. Bris —4D 61
Treefield Pl. Bris —5C 58
Treefield Rd. Clev —4D 121
Tree Leaze. Yate —4B 18
Treenwood Ind. Est. Brad A —5E 115
Tregarth Rd. Bris —4B 78
Trelawn Clo. St Geo —3B 130
Trelawney Av. Bris —2F 71
Trelawney Pk. Bris —2F 81
Trelawney Rd. Bris —1E 69
Tremlett M. W Mare —1F 129
Trenchard Rd. Lock —4B 136
Trenchard Rd. Salt —5F 93
Trenchard St. Bris —3E 69 (2A 4)
Trench La. Alm & Wint —4A 12
Trendlewood Pk. Bris —3A 60
Trendlewood Way. Nail —5E 123
Trenleigh Dri. W Mare —2D 129
Trent Dri. T'bry —5E 7
Trent Gro. Key —4C 92
Trentham Clo. Bris —5C 58
Tresham Clo. Brad S —4F 11
Trevelyan Rd. W Mare —1D 133
Trevelyan Wlk. Bris —1B 40
Trevelyan Wlk. Stok G —4C 28
Trevenna Rd. Bris —4B 78
Treverdowe Wlk. Bris —1F 39
Trevisa Gro. Bris —5E 25
Trevithin Clo. Bris —3E 73
Trewartha Clo. W Mare —5D 127
Trewartha Pk. W Mare —5D 127
Trewint Gdns. Bris —5B 80
Triangle E. Bath —4E 105
Triangle N. Bath —3E 105
Triangle Shopping Cen. Clev —4D 121
Triangle S. Clif —3D 69
Triangle, The. Clev —3D 121
Triangle, The. W Hill —4F 49
Triangle, The. Wrin —1B 156
Triangle Vs. Bath —4E 105
Triangle W. Bath —4E 105
Triangle W. Bris —3D 69
Trident Clo. Bris —3C 46
Trigg Ct. Bath —5A 106
Trim Bri. Bath —3A 106 (3B 96)
Trim St. Bath —3A 106 (3B 96)
Trinder Rd. E'ton G —3D 53
Trinity Clo. Bath —3A 106 (4A 96)
Trinity Ct. Nail —4B 122
Trinity M. Bris —3B 70 (off Old Mkt. St.)
Trinity Pl. Bath —3A 106 (3A 96)
Trinity Pl. W Mare —4A 126 (in two parts)
Trinity Quay. Bris —4B 70 (3F 5)
Trinity Rd. Bath —2C 110
Trinity Rd. Bris —3C 70
Trinity Rd. Nail —4B 122
Trinity Rd. W Mare —4A 126
Trinity St. Bath —3A 106 (4B 96)
Trinity St. Bris —3C 70 (Clarenge Rd.)
Trinity St. Bris —4E 69 (4A 4) (College Grn.)
Trinity Wlk. Bris —3B 70
Trin Mills. Bris —5F 69 (5C 4)
Tripps Corner. Yat —4D 143
Troon. Yate —1A 34
Troon Dri. War —4D 75
Trooper's Hill Rd. Bris —4B 72
Trossachs Dri. Bath —1E 107
Trowbridge Ind. Est. Trow —4D 117
Trowbridge Lodge Residential Pk. Trow —2F 119
Trowbridge Retail Pk. Trow —3E 155
Trowbridge Rd. Brad A (in two parts) —3E 115
Trowbridge Rd. Bris —3E 41
Trowbridge Rd. Hil —5F 117
Trowbridge Wlk. Bris —3E 41
Trowle. Trow —4A 116
Truro Rd. Bris —2D 79
Truro Rd. Nail —5F 123
Trym Cross Rd. Bris —2E 55
Trym Leaze. Bris —2E 55
Trym Rd. Bris —5C 40
Trym Side. Bris —2E 55
Trymwood Clo. Bris —2B 40
Trymwood Pde. Bris —1F 55
Tucker St. Bris —3B 70 (1F 5)
Tuckett Ho. Bris —5E 45
Tuckett La. Bris —5E 45
Tuckmill. Clev —5B 120
Tudor Clo. Old C —2E 85
Tudor Dri. Trow —3E 117
Tudor Rd. E'tn —1E 71
Tudor Rd. Han —5E 73
Tudor Rd. P'head —4A 50
Tudor Rd. St Pa —1B 70
Tudor Rd. W Mare —1E 129
Tuffley Rd. Bris —4E 41
Tugela Rd. Bris —1B 86
Tunstall Clo. Bris —3A 56
Turley Rd. Bris —5F 59
Turnberry. War —4C 74
Turnberry. Yate —1A 34
Turnberry Wlk. Bris —4F 81
Turnbridge Rd. Bris —5E 25
Turnbury Av. Nail —4F 123
Turnbury Clo. W Mare —2D 129
Turner Clo. Key —3C 92
Turner Ct. W Mare —2D 129
Turner Gdns. Bris —1D 59
Turners Ct. L Grn —1B 84
Turner Way. Clev —5B 120
Turnpike Clo. Yate —4A 18
Turnpike Ga. Wickw —1B 154
Turtlegate Av. Bris —4A 86
Turtlegate Wlk. Bris —4A 86
Turville Dri. Bris —1C 58
Tuscany Ho. Bris —4C 56
Tutton Way. Clev —5D 121
Tweed Clo. T'bry —4D 7
Tweed Rd. Clev —5C 120
Tweed Rd. Ind. Est. Clev —5C 120
Tweeny La. Bris —4F 75
Twenty Acres Rd. Bris —2D 41
Twerton Farm Clo. Bath —3C 104
Twickenham Rd. Bris —2E 57
Twickenham Rd. Clev —3F 121
Two Acres Rd. Bris —5C 80
Two Mile Hill Rd. Bris —2C 72
Two Stones La. Chip S —1E 35
Twynings, The. Bris —5A 62
Tybalt Way. Stok G —4A 28
Tyler Clo. Bris —5A 74
Tyler Grn. W Mare —1F 129
Tylers La. Bris —2F 61
Tyler St. Bris —4C 70
Tylers Way. Yate —2B 18
Tyndale Av. Bris —3D 61
Tyndale Av. Yate —3F 17
Tyndale Rd. Bris —5A 62
Tyndale View. T'bry —4C 6
Tyndall Av. Bris —2E 69
Tyndall Rd. Bris —2D 71
Tyndalls Pk. M. Bris —2E 69
Tyndalls Pk. Rd. Bris —2D 69
Tyne Path. Bris —5F 57
Tyne Rd. Bris —4F 57
Tyne St. Bris —5C 58
Tyning Clo. Bris —1C 88
Tyning Clo. Trow —3A 118
Tyning Clo. Yate —4A 18
Tyning End. Bath —4C 106 (5F 97)
Tyning Hill. Rads —1D 153
Tyning La. Bath —5C 100
Tyning Pl. C Down —2D 111
Tyning Rd. B'ptn —4A 102
Tyning Rd. Bris —2B 80
Tyning Rd. C Down —2D 111
Tyning Rd. Pea J —2F 149
Tyning Rd. Salt —2A 94
Tyning Rd. W'ley —2F 113
Tyning's La. Yate —4E 13
Tynings, The. Clev —5A 120
Tynings Way. L W'wd —5A 114
Tyning Ter. Bath —5C 100 (off Fairfield Rd.)
Tyning, The. Bath —4C 106
Tyning, The. Mid N —5C 112
Tynte Av. Bris —5A 88
Tyntesfield Rd. Bris —1C 86
Tyrone Wlk. Bris —5A 80
Tyrrel Way. Stok G —3A 28
Tytherington Rd. Grov —5F 7

Ullswater Clo. Bris —4F 75
Ullswater Clo. W Mare —4E 133
Ullswater Clo. Yate —3A 18
Ullswater Dri. Bath —4B 100
Ullswater Rd. Bris —3D 41
Uncombe Clo. Back —1F 125
Underbanks. Pill —3F 53
Underhill Av. Mid N —2C 150
Underhill Dri. Uph —1B 138
Underhill La. Mid N —3A 150
Underleaf Way. Pea J —5D 157
Underwood Av. W Mare —4F 127
Underwood Clo. Alv —3B 8
Underwood Rd. P'head —5E 49
Unicorn Bus. Pk. Brisl —4F 71
Unicorn Pk. Av. Brisl —5F 71
Union Pas. Bath —3B 106 (3C 96)
Union Pl. W Mare —1B 132
Union Rd. Bedm —1F 79
Union Rd. Bris —4C 70 (in two parts)
Union St. Bath —3B 106 (3C 96)
Union St. Bris —3F 69 (1C 4)
Union St. Nail —3B 122
Union St. Trow —1D 119
Union St. W Mare —1B 132
Unity Ct. Key —2C 92
Unity Rd. Key —3C 92 (in two parts)
Unity St. Bris —4E 69 (3A 4)
Unity St. K'wd —2E 73
Unity St. St Ph —3B 70 (2F 5)
University Clo. Bris —3B 56
University Rd. Bris —3E 69
University Wlk. Bris —3E 69
Uphill Cvn. Pk. Uph —2C 138
Uphill Dri. Bath —4C 100
Uphill Rd. Bris —2B 58
Uphill Rd. N. W Mare —4B 132
Uphill Rd. S. W Mare —5B 132
Uphill Way. Uph —1A 138
Upjohn Cres. Bris —5F 87
Uplands Clo. Lim S —3A 112
Uplands Dri. Salt —2B 94
Uplands Rd. Bris —4E 61
Uplands Rd. Salt —2A 94
Uplands, The. Nail —5B 122
Up. Bath Rd. T'bry —4C 6
Up. Belgrave Rd. Bris —5C 56
Up. Belmont Rd. Bris —4A 58
Up. Berkeley Pl. Bris —3D 69
Up. Bloomfield Rd. Bath —4D 109
Up. Borough Walls. Bath —3A 106 (3B 96)
Up. Bristol Rd. Bath —2D 105
Up. Bristol Rd. W Mare —4E 127
Up. Broad St. Trow —1C 118
Up. Broad St. Ct. Trow —1C 118
Up. Buildings. Bath —5A 110
Up. Byron Pl. Bris —3D 69
Up. Camden Pl. Bath —1B 106
Up. Chapel La. Fram C —2E 31
Up. Cheltenham Pl. Bris —1A 70
Up. Church La. Bris —3E 69 (2A 4)
Up. Church La. Hut —1B 140
Up. Church Rd. W Mare —4A 126
Up. Church St. Bath —2A 106 (1A 96)
Up. Cranbrook Rd. Bris —3D 57
Up. E. Hayes. Bath —5C 100
Up. Hedgemead Rd. Bath —1A 106
Up. Kingsdown Rd. Kngdn —4F 103
Up. Lambridge St. Bath —4D 101
Up. Lansdown M. Bath —5A 100
Up. Maudlin St. Bris —3F 69 (1B 4)
Up. Mill. Brad A —3F 115
Up. Mount Pleasant. F'frd —5B 112
Up. Myrtle Hill. Pill —3E 53
Up. Oldfield Pk. Bath —4F 105
Up. Perry Hill. Bris —1E 79
Up. Regents Pk. Brad A —3E 115
Up. Sandhurst Rd. Bris —1F 81
Up. Station Rd. Bris —3E 61
Up. Stone Clo. Fram C —2E 31
Upper St. Bris —1C 80
Up. Sydney St. Bris —2D 79
Up. Wells St. Bris —3E 69 (2A 4)
Up. Westwood. Brad A —5E 113
Up. York St. Bris —2A 70
Upton. W Mare —1E 139
Upton Rd. Bris —1D 79 (in two parts)
Urchinwood La. Cong —3F 145
Urfords Dri. Bris —1E 61
Usk Ct. T'bry —4D 7

Valda Rd. W Mare —3A 128
Vale Cres. St Geo —3A 130
Vale End. Nail —4C 122
Vale La. Bris —5E 79
Valentine Clo. Bris —3D 89
Valerian Clo. Bris —1B 54
Vale St. Bris —1C 80
Valetta Clo. W Mare —5D 133
Vale View. Rads —2D 153
Vale View Pl. Bath —5C 100
Vale View Ter. Bathe —3A 102
Valley Clo. Nail —3D 123
Valley Gdns. Bris —4B 46
Valley Gdns. Nail —3D 123
Valley Rd. Bris —5C 78
Valley Rd. Clev —1F 121
Valley Rd. L Wds —3E 67
Valley Rd. Mang —2C 62
Valley Rd. P'head —5A 48
Valley Rd. War —4F 75
Valley View Clo. Bath —3C 100
Valley View Rd. Bath —3C 100

Valley View Rd. *Paul* —3B **146**
Valley Wlk. *Mid N* —2E **151**
Valley Way Rd. *Nail* —2D **123**
Valls, The. *Brad S* —3B **28**
Valma Rocks. *Bris* —4C **72**
Van Diemen's La. *Bath* —4F **99**
Vandyck Av. *Key* —2B **92**
Vane St. *Bath* —2C **106** (2E **97**)
Varsity Way. *Lock* —2F **135**
Vassall Ct. *Bris* —2D **61**
Vassall Rd. *Bris* —2D **61**
Vattingstone La. *Alv* —2A **8**
Vaughan Clo. *Bris* —1B **40**
Vauxhall Av. *Bris* —1C **78**
Vauxhall Ter. *Bris* —1C **78**
Vayre Clo. *Chip S* —5E **19**
Veale, The. *B'don* —5A **140**
Veitch Clo. *Salt* —5E **93**
Vellore La. *Bath* —2C **106** (2F **97**)
Ventnor Av. *Bris* —2B **72**
Ventnor Rd. *Fil* —1E **43**
Ventnor Rd. *S'wll & St G* —1B **72**
Venton Ct. Bris —5D **73** *(off Henbury Rd.)*
Venus St. *Cong* —4E **145**
Vera Rd. *Bris* —5B **60**
Verbena Way. *W Mare* —4E **129**
Vereland Rd. *Hut* —5C **134**
Verlands. *Cong* —1E **145**
Vernham Gro. *Bath* —3D **109**
Vernon Clo. *Salt* —5F **93**
Vernon Pk. *Bath* —3D **105**
Vernon St. *Bris* —1B **80**
Vernon Ter. *Bath* —3D **105**
Vernslade. *Bath* —4B **98**
Verrier Rd. *Bris* —3E **71**
Verwood Dri. *Bit* —4E **85**
Vian End. *W Mare* —1C **128**
Vicarage Clo. *W Mare* —2E **129**
Vicarage Ct. *Han* —5D **73**
Vicarage Gdns. *Pea J* —1E **149**
Vicarage Rd. *B'wth* —2B **86**
Vicarage Rd. *Coal H* —3E **31**
Vicarage Rd. *Han* —5D **73**
Vicarage Rd. *L Wds* —3F **67**
Vicarage Rd. *Redf* —2E **71**
Vicarage Rd. *S'vle* —1D **79**
Vicars Clo. *Bris* —3D **61**
Victor Ho. *Lit S* —2E **27**
Victoria Av. *Bris* —3E **71**
Victoria Bri. Rd. *Bath* —3F **105**
Victoria Bldgs. *Bath* —3E **105**
Victoria Clo. *Bath* —4D **105**
Victoria Clo. *P'head* —3F **49**
Victoria Clo. *T'bry* —1C **6**
Victoria Ct. *P'head* —3F **49**
Victoria Cres. *Sev B* —4B **20**
Victoria Gdns. *Bathe* —3A **102**
Victoria Gdns. *Bris* —1F **69**
Victoria Gdns. *Trow* —5E **117**
Victoria Gro. *Bris* —1A **80**
Victoria Ho. *Bath* —1E **105**
Victoria Pde. *Bris* —2E **71**
Victoria Pk. *Fish* —2C **60**
Victoria Pk. *K'wd* —1F **73**
Victoria Pk. *W Mare* —4B **126**
Victoria Pk. Bus. Cen. *Bath* —2E **105**
Victoria Pl. *Bris* —1E **79**
Victoria Pl. *C Down* —3D **111** (Combe Down)
Victoria Pl. *C Down* —5A **110** (South Stoke)
Victoria Pl. Lark —5D **101** *(off St Saviours Rd.)*
Victoria Pl. *Paul* —4A **146**
Victoria Pl. *W Mare* —5B **126**
Victoria Quad. *W Mare* —5C **126**
Victoria Rd. *A'mth* —5D **37**
Victoria Rd. *Bath* —3E **105**
Victoria Rd. *Clev* —2C **120**
Victoria Rd. *Han* —5E **73**
Victoria Rd. *Salt* —5F **93**
Victoria Rd. *St Ph* —5C **70** (in two parts)
Victoria Rd. *Trow* —4E **117**
Victoria Rd. *War* —5E **75**
Victoria Sq. *Bris* —3C **68**
Victoria Sq. *P'head* —3F **49**
Victoria Sq. *W Mare* —1B **132**
Victoria St. *Bris* —4A **70** (3D **5**)
Victoria St. *Stap H* —3F **61**
Victoria Ter. *Bath* —3E **105**
Victoria Ter. *Clif* —4B **68**
Victoria Ter. *Paul* —3B **146**
Victoria Ter. *St Ph* —5D **71**
Victoria Wlk. *Bris* —1F **69**
Victor Rd. *Bris* —2E **79**
Victor St. *Bar H* —4D **71**
Victor St. *Bris* —1C **80**
Victory Gdns. *Bath* —2B **102**
Vigar Gdns. *Bris* —4A **86**
Vigor Rd. *Bris* —3D **87**
Village Clo. *Yate* —5F **17**
Villa Rosa. W Mare —4A **126** *(off Shrubbery Rd.)*
Villiers Rd. *Bris* —1D **71**
Vilner La. *T'bry* —5C **6**
Vimpany Clo. *Bris* —1B **40**
Vimpennys La. *E Comp* —1A **24**
Vincent Clo. *Bris* —2E **39**
Vine Acres. *Bris* —2C **58**
Vine Cottage. *Salt* —1B **94**
Vine Cotts. *Brad A* —3D **115**
Vine Cotts. *Bris* —3C **60**
Vine Gdns. *W Mare* —3E **129**
Vinery, The. *Wins* —5B **156**
Vineyards. *Bath* —2B **106** (1C **96**)
Vining Wlk. *Bris* —2D **71**
Vinny Av. *Bris* —5C **46**
Vintery Leys. *Bris* —5D **41**
Virginia Clo. *Chip S* —5C **18**
Vivian St. *Bris* —2F **79**
Vivien Av. *Mid N* —2D **151**
Vowell Clo. *Bris* —4D **87**
Vynes Clo. *Nail* —4F **123**
Vynes Way. *Nail* —4F **123**
Vyvyan Rd. *Bris* —3C **68**
Vyvyan Ter. *Bris* —3C **68**

Wadehurst Ind. Pk. *Bris* —3C **70**
Wade Rd. *Yate* —3C **16**
Wades Rd. *Bris* —1D **43**
Wade St. *Bris* —2B **70**
Wadham Dri. *Bris* —3D **45**
Wadham St. *W Mare* —5B **126**
Wagtail Gdns. *W Mare* —5C **128**
Wainbrook Dri. *Bris* —5F **59**
Wains Clo. *Clev* —4C **120**
Wainwright Clo. *W Mare* —1F **129**
Waits Clo. *Ban* —5D **137**
Wakedean Gdns. *Yat* —2A **142**
Wakeford Rd. *Bris* —5C **46**
Walcot Bldgs. *Bath* —1B **106**
Walcot Ct. *Bath* —1B **106**
Walcot Ga. *Bath* —1B **106** (1C **96**)
Walcot Ho. *Bath* —1B **106**
Walcot Pde. Bath —1B **106** *(off London Rd.)*
Walcot St. *Bath* —2B **106** (2C **96**)
Walcot Ter. *Bath* —1B **106**
Waldegrave Rd. *Bath* —5F **99**
Waldegrave Ter. *Rads* —1D **153**
Walden Rd. *Key* —4C **92**
Walford Av. *W Mare* —1F **129**
Walker Clo. *Down* —5C **46**
Walker Clo. *E'tn* —2D **71**
Walker St. *K'dwn* —2E **69**
Walker Way. *T'bry* —5C **6**
Walk, The. *Holt* —2D **155**
Wallace Rd. *Bath* —5C **100**
Wallcroft Ho. *Bris* —4C **56**
Wallenge Clo. *Paul* —3C **146**
Wallenge Dri. *Paul* —3B **146**
Waller Ct. *Bris* —2D **73**
Wallingford Rd. *Bris* —1F **87**
Walliscote Av. *Bris* —1E **57**
Walliscote Gro. Rd. *W Mare* —1C **132**
Walliscote Rd. *Bris* —1E **57**
Walliscote Rd. *W Mare* —3B **132**
Walliscote Rd. S. *W Mare* —4B **132**
Wallscourt Rd. *Bris* —2D **43**
Wallscourt Rd. S. *Bris* —3D **43**
Walmsley Ter. Bath —5C **100** *(off Snow Hill)*
Walnut Av. *Yate* —4C **18**
Walnut Bldgs. *Rads* —1D **153**
Walnut Clo. *Bris* —1B **74**
Walnut Clo. *E'ton G* —4C **52**
Walnut Clo. *Key* —4E **91**
Walnut Clo. *Nail* —5D **123**
Walnut Clo. *T'bry* —3E **7**
Walnut Clo. *W Mare* —1F **139**
Walnut Cres. *Bris* —2B **74**
Walnut Dri. *Bath* —5F **105**
Walnut Gro. *Trow* —4B **118**
Walnut La. *Bris* —2C **74**
Walnut Tree Clo. *Alm* —1C **10**
Walnut Tree Ct. *Cong* —2D **145**
Walnut Wlk. *Bris* —2C **86**
Walnut Wlk. *Key* —4E **91**
Walsh Av. *Bris* —1C **88**
Walsh Clo. *W Mare* —1F **139**
Walshe Av. *Chip S* —5E **19**
Walsingham Rd. *Bris* —5A **58**
Walter St. *Bris* —1C **78**
Waltining La. *Bath* —5F **95** (in two parts)
Walton. *W Mare* —1E **139**
Walton Av. *Bris* —5F **71**
Walton Clo. *Bit* —4E **85**
Walton Clo. *Key* —4F **91**
Walton Heath. *Yate* —5B **18**
Walton Rise. *Bris* —4C **40**
Walton Rd. *Bris* —1F **53**
Walton Rd. *Clev* —2F **121**
Walton St. *E'tn* —1D **71**
Walwyn Clo. *Bath* —3B **104**
Walwyn Gdns. *Bris* —5F **87**
Wansbeck Rd. *Key* —4C **92**
Wansbrough Rd. *W Mare* —2F **129**
Wanscow Wlk. *Bris* —1D **57**
Wansdyke Bus. Cen. *Bath* —5E **105**
Wansdyke Ct. *Bris* —3D **89**
Wansdyke Rd. *Bath* —3D **109**
Wansdyke Workshops. *Key* —3C **92**
Wapley Hill. *W'lgh* —4A **34**
Wapley Rank. *W'lgh* —4F **33**
Wapley Rd. *Cod* —5A **34**
Wapping Rd. *Bris* —5F **69** (5B **4**)
Warbler Clo. *Trow* —2B **118**
Warburton Clo. *Trow* —4A **118**
Warden Rd. *Bris* —1E **79**
Wardour Rd. *Bris* —5F **79**
Ware Ct. *Wint* —4F **29**
Wareham Clo. *Nail* —4C **122**
Warleigh Dri. *Bathe* —3B **102**
Warleigh La. *Bath* —5C **102**
Warman Clo. *Bris* —2B **90**
Warman Rd. *Bris* —2B **90**
Warmington Rd. *Bris* —5E **81**
Warminster Rd. *Bath* —1D **107** (1F **97**)
Warminster Rd. *Bris* —5C **58**
Warminster Rd. *Lim S & Mon C* —5A **112**
Warner Clo. *Bris* —4B **74**
Warne Rd. *W Mare* —2E **133**
Warns, The. *Bris* —1C **84**
Warren Clo. *Brad S* —3F **11**
Warren Clo. *Hut* —1B **140**
Warren Gdns. *Bris* —3B **90**
Warren La. *L Ash* —4A **76**
Warren Rd. *Bris* —1D **43**
Warren Way. *Yate* —3A **18**
Warrington Rd. *Bris* —3F **81**
Warwick Av. *Bris* —1D **71**
Warwick Clo. *Will* —3D **85**
Warwick Clo. *W Mare* —5A **128**
Warwick Pl. *T'bry* —3B **6**
Warwick Rd. *Bath* —2C **104**
Warwick Rd. *E'tn* —1D **71**
Warwick Rd. *Key* —4F **91**
Warwick Rd. *Redl* —1D **69**
Warwick Vs. *Bath* —4D **105**
Wasborough. *Bris* —5A **38**
Washingpool La. *Chit* —2A **22**
Washing Pound La. *Bris* —4D **89**
Washing Pound La. *Tic* —2A **122**
Washington Av. *Bris* —1E **71**
Washpool La. *Bath* —2A **108**
Watch Elm Clo. *Brad S* —3A **28**
Watch Ho. Rd. *Pill* —3F **53**
Watchill Av. *Bris* —2B **86**
Watchill Clo. *Bris* —2B **86**
Waterbridge Rd. *Bris* —3B **86**
Watercress Rd. *Bris* —4B **58**
Waterdale Clo. *Bris* —5E **41**
Waterdale Gdns. *Bris* —5E **41**
Waterford Clo. *T'bry* —4E **7**
Waterford Pk. *Rads* —4A **152**
Waterford Rd. *Bris* —1D **57**
Waterhouse La. *Mon C* —5F **111**
Water La. *Bedm* —2B **80**
Water La. *Brisl* —4F **81** (in two parts)
Water La. *Bris* —4A **70** (3E **5**)
Water La. *Mid N* —5D **147**
Water La. *Pill* —3E **53**
Waterloo Bldgs. *Twer A* (in two parts) —3C **104**
Waterloo Houses. Pill —2F **53** *(off Underbanks)*
Waterloo Pl. *Bris* —3C **70**
Waterloo Rd. *Bris* —3B **70**
Waterloo Rd. *Rads* —2C **152**
Waterloo St. *Clif* —3B **68**
Waterloo St. *St Ph* —3B **70**
Waterloo St. *W Mare* —5B **126**
Watermead Clo. Bath —3A **106** *(off Kingsmead West)*
Watermore Clo. *Fram C* —2E **31**
Waterside Cres. *Rads* —3A **152**
Waterside Dri. *Azt W* —5C **10**
Waterside La. *Mid N* —5C **152**
Waterside Pk. *P'head* —4A **48**
Waterside Rd. *Rads* —3A **152**
Waterside Way. *Rads* —3A **152**
Water's La. *Bris* —5C **40**
Waters Rd. *Bris* —2E **73**
Waterworks Rd. *Trow* —3B **118**
Watery La. *Bath* —3B **104**
Watery La. *Nail* —3A **122**
Watery La. *Yate* —1E **17**
Wathen Rd. *Bris* —4B **58**
Wathen St. *Bris* —2F **61**
Watkins Yd. *Bris* —4C **40**
Watleys End Rd. *Wint* —2A **30**
Watling Way. *Bris* —5E **37**
Watson Av. *Bris* —1F **81** (in two parts)
Watson's Rd. *L Grn* —2B **84**
Watters Clo. *Coal H* —3F **31**
Wavell Clo. *Yate* —2F **17**
Waveney Rd. *Key* —5C **92**
Waverley Rd. *Back* —1C **124**
Waverley Rd. *Bris* —1E **69**
Waverley Rd. *Shire* —1A **54**
Waverley Rd. *W Mare* —4D **133**
Waverley St. *Bris* —1C **70**
Wayacre Drove. *W Mare* —5B **138**
Wayfarer Rd. *Bris* —3D **25**
Wayfield Gdns. *Bath* —2A **102**
Wayford Clo. *Key* —5C **92**
Wayland Rd. *W Mare* —2C **128**
Wayleaze. *Coal H* —2F **31**
Wayside. *W Mare* —3B **128**
Wayside Clo. *Fram C* —2D **31**
Wayside Dri. *Clev* —1E **121**
Weal, The. *Bath* —4D **99**
Weare Ct. *Bris* —5C **68**
Weatherly Av. *Bath* —2E **109**
Weatherly Dri. *P'head* —4B **48**
Weavers Dri. *Trow* —3D **119**
Webb Clo. *Bris* —4B **74**
Webbers Ct. *Trow* —4A **118**
Webbs Heath. *Bris* —1F **75**
Webb St. *Bris* —2C **70**
Webbs Wood Rd. *Brad S* —3B **28**
Wedgwood Clo. *Bris* —3D **89**
Wedgwood Rd. *Bath* —4A **104**
Wedgwood Rd. *Bris* —3F **45**
Wedmore Clo. *Bris* —3B **74**
Wedmore Clo. *W Mare* —1D **139**
Wedmore Pk. *Bath* —1B **108**
Wedmore Rd. *Clev* —5B **120**
Wedmore Rd. *Nail* —5D **123**
Wedmore Rd. *Salt* —4F **93**
Wedmore Vale. *Bris* —3A **80**
Weedon Clo. *Bris* —5C **58**
Weekesley La. *Tim* —1F **147**
Weetwood Rd. *Cong* —1E **145**
Weight Rd. *Bris* —3E **71**
Weind, The. *W Mare* —3B **128**
Weir La. *Bris* —4A **66**
Weir Rd. *Cong* —3E **145**
Weirside Mill. *Brad A* —3F **115**
Welland Rd. *Key* —4B **92**
Wellard Clo. *W Mare* —1F **129**
Well Clo. *L Ash* —4D **77**
Well Clo. *Wins* —4B **156**
Well Clo. *W Mare* —1F **139**
Wellgarth Ct. *Bris* —3C **80**
Wellgarth Rd. *Bris* —3C **80**
Wellgarth Wlk. *Bris* —3C **80**
Well Ho. Clo. *Bris* —5A **56**
Wellington Av. *Bris* —1A **70**
Wellington Bldgs. *Bath* —4C **98**
Wellington Cres. *Bris* —1A **58**
Wellington Dri. *Bris* —1F **57**
Wellington Dri. *Yate* —4D **17**
Wellington Hill. *Bris* —1A **58**
Wellington Hill W. *Bris* —5E **41**
Wellington La. *Bris* —1A **70**
Wellington M. *Bris* —2F **53**
Wellington Pk. *Bris* —1C **68**
Wellington Pl. *Bris* —3D **45**
Wellington Pl. *W Mare* —1B **132**
Wellington Rd. *K'wd* —5F **61**
Wellington Rd. *St Pa* —3B **70** (1E **5**)
Wellington Rd. *Yate* —2A **18**
Wellington Ter. *Bris* —4B **68**
Wellington Ter. *Clev* —1C **120**
Wellington Wlk. *Bris* —5E **41**
Well La. *Yat* —3C **142**
Wellow Brook Meadow. *Mid N* —2E **151**
Wellow La. *Pea J* —2E **149**
Wellow Mead. *Pea J* —2E **149**
Wellow Rd. *Bath* —5F **157**
Wellow Tyning. *Pea J* —5D **157**
Well Pk. *Cong* —1D **145**
Well Path. *Brad A* —3D **115**
Wells Clo. *Bris* —3E **89**
Wells Clo. *Nail* —4F **123**
Wellsea Gro. *W Mare* —1F **133**
Wells Hill *Rads* —2C **152**
Wells Rd. *Bath* —4F **105** (5B **96**)
Wells Rd. *Bris & H'gro* —1B **80**
Wells Rd. *Clev* —5D **121**
Wells Rd. *Cor* —5A **94**
Wells Rd. *Rads* —4F **151**
Wells Sq. *Rads* —2A **152**
Wells St. *Bris* —1C **78**
Wellstead Av. *Yate* —5F **17**
Wellsway. *Bath* —4E **109**
Wellsway. *Key* —3B **92**
Wellsway Pk. *Bath* —4E **109**
Welsford Av. *Bris* —3F **59**
Welsford Rd. *Bris* —3E **59**
Welsh Back. *Bris* —4F **69** (4C **4**)
Welton Gro. *Mid N* —1D **151**
Welton Rd. *Rads* —2B **152**
Welton Vale. *Mid N* —2E **151**
Welton Wlk. *Bris* —5E **61**
Wemberham Cres. *Yat* —2A **142**
Wemberham La. *Yat* —3A **142**
Wenmore Clo. *Bris* —3F **45**
Wentforth Dri. *Bris* —5E **61**
Wentwood Dri. *W Mare* —2E **139**
Wentworth. *War* —4C **74**
Wentworth. *Yate* —5A **18**
Wentworth Clo. *W Mare* —2E **129**
Wentworth Rd. *Bris* —4F **57**
Wesley Av. *Bris* —5F **73**
Wesley Av. *Rads* —3F **151**
Wesley Clo. *Bris* —4F **61**
Wesley Clo. *W'hall* —1F **71**
Wesley Dri. *W Mare* —2E **129**
Wesley Hill. *Bris* —1F **73**
Wesley La. *Bris* —5D **75**
Wesley Pl. *Bris* —5C **56**
Wesley Rd. *Bris* —3A **58**
Wesley Rd. *Trow* —3C **118**

Wesley St. Bris —2E 79
Wessex Av. Bris —5B 42
Wessex Ho. Bris —4A 70 (3E 5)
Wessex Rd. W Mare —1F 139
Westacre Clo. Bris —2C 40
W. Ashton Rd. Yarn —3F 119
West Av. Bath —4D 105
Westaway Clo. Yat —4C 142
Westaway Pk. Yat —4D 143
Westbourne Av. Clev —4B 120
Westbourne Av. Key —3A 92
Westbourne Cotts. Bris —5D 45
Westbourne Cres. Clev —4B 120
Westbourne Gdns. Trow —2B 118
Westbourne Gro. Bris —2E 79
Westbourne Pl. Bris —3D 69
Westbourne Rd. Down —4B 46
Westbourne Rd. E'tn —2D 71
Westbourne Rd. Trow —2B 118
Westbourne Ter. Bris —5D 45
West B'way. Bris —1F 57
Westbrooke Ct. Bris —5C 68
Westbrook Pk. W'ton —4B 98
Westbrook Rd. Bris —5F 81
Westbrook Rd. W Mare —4A 128
Westbury Ct. Rd. Bris —5B 40
Westbury Cres. W Mare —1D 139
Westbury Hill. Bris —5C 40
Westbury La. Bris —5D 39
Westbury Pk. Bris —3C 56
Westbury Rd. N Brad —4E 155
Westbury Rd. W Trym & Redl —1C 56
West Clo. Bath —4B 104
W. Coombe. Bris —1F 55
West Cotts. Bath —3D 111
Westcourt Dri. Old C —1D 85
W. Croft. Bris —5E 41
West Croft. Clev —4B 120
Westcroft St. Trow —1C 118
West Dene. Bris —1A 56
W. Dock Rd. P'bry —1A 52
West End. Bedm —5E 69
West End. Bris —2F 69
W. End Farm Cvn. Pk. Lock —3D 135
Westend Rd. Wickw —3A 154
W. End Trad. Est. Nail —4A 122
Westering Clo. Mang —2C 62
Westerleigh Clo. Bris —5B 46
Westerleigh Rd. Bath —3C 110
Westerleigh Rd. Clev —4B 120
Westerleigh Rd. Down & E Grn —1A 62
Westerleigh Rd. Puck —1D 65
Westerleigh Rd. Yate & W'lgh —3D 33
Western Av. Fram C —5C 14
Western Ct. Clev —3D 121
Western Dri. Bris —1A 88
Western Rd. Bris —1A 58
Westfield. Brad A —2C 114
Westfield. Clev —5D 121
Westfield Clo. Back —2C 124
Westfield Clo. Bath —1F 109
Westfield Clo. Bris —5F 73
Westfield Clo. Key —3E 91
Westfield Clo. Trow —4A 118
Westfield Clo. Uph —1B 138
Westfield Dri. Back —2C 124
Westfield Ind. & Trad. Est. Rads —5F 151
Westfield La. Stok G —1A 44
Westfield Pk. Bath —2B 104
Westfield Pk. Bris —1D 69
Westfield Pk. S. Bath —2B 104
Westfield Pl. Bris —3B 68
Westfield Rd. Back —2C 124
Westfield Rd. Ban —5E 137
Westfield Rd. Bris —4C 40
Westfield Rd. Trow —3A 118
Westfield Rd. W Mare —1B 138
Westfield Ter. Rads —3A 152
Westfield Way. Brad S —4F 11
W. Garston. Ban —5E 137
Westgate Bldgs. Bath —3A 106 (3B 96)
Westgate St. Bath —3A 106 (3B 96)
West Gro. Bris —1B 70
Westhall Rd. Bath —2E 105
W. Haven Clo. Back —2C 124
W. Hay Rd. Udl —1B 156
West Hill. P'head —3D 49
West Hill. Wrax —1E 123
W. Hill Gdns. P'head —3E 49
West Hill Gdns. Rads —3A 152
W. Hill Rd. Rads —3A 152
Westland Av. Old C —1E 85
W. Lea Rd. Bath —1B 104
W. Leaze Pl. Brad S —3A 28
Westleigh Clo. S'mead —3F 41
Westleigh Clo. Yate —5E 17
Westleigh Pk. Bris —5C 80
Westleigh Rd. Bris —3E 41
W. Links Clo. W Mare —2F 127
West Mall. Bris —3B 68
Westmarch Way. W Mare —1E 129
Westmead Cres. Trow —5B 118
Westmead Gdns. W'ton —4B 98
Westmead Rd. Bris —3D 73
Westminstere Ct. W Trym —5C 40
Westminster Rd. Bris —2F 71
Westmoreland Dri. Bath —3F 105
Westmoreland Pl. E. Bath —3F 105
Westmoreland Rd. Bath —4F 105
Westmoreland Rd. Bris —4D 57
Westmoreland Sta. Rd. Bath —4F 105
Westmoreland St. Bath —4F 105
Westmorland Ho. Bris —4C 56
Weston Av. Bris —3F 71
Weston Clo. Bris —5E 39
Weston Cres. Bris —1A 58
Weston Farm La. Bath —4D 99
Weston Gateway Cvn. Pk. W Mare —4A 130
Westonian Ct. Bris —3E 55
Weston La. Bath —5D 99
Weston Links. W Mare —3F 133
Weston Pk. Bath —5D 99
Weston Pk. Ct. Bath —5E 99
Weston Pk. E. Bath —1D 105
Weston Pk. W. Bath —5D 99
Weston Rd. Bath —1E 105
Weston Rd. Cong —1A 144
Weston Rd. Fail —5A 76
Weston Rd. L Ash —5A 76
Westons Way. Bris —4B 74
Weston Way. Hut —1D 141
Weston Wood Rd. P'head —5E 49
Westover Clo. Bris —3B 40
Westover Dri. Bris —4C 40
Westover Gdns. Bris —3B 40
Westover Rise. Bris —3C 40
Westover Rd. Bris —3B 40
West Pde. Bris —5E 39
West Pk. Bris —2D 69
West Pk. Rd. Bris —2A 62
W. Point Row. Brad S —3E 11
W. Priory Clo. Bris —5C 40
W. Ridge. Fram C —2E 31
West Rd. Mid N —1C 150
West Rd. Yat —4B 142
W. Rocke Av. Bris —5F 39
W. Rolstone Rd. Hew —3D 131
W. Shrubbery. Bris —5D 57
West St. Ban —5F 137
West St. Bedm —3D 79
West St. K'wd —2F 73
West St. Old C —1E 85
West St. St Ph —3B 70
West St. Trow —2C 118
West St. W Mare —5B 126
W. Town Av. Bris —4F 81
W. Town Ct. Bris —3A 82
W. Town Dri. Bris —4F 81
W. Town Gro. Bris —5F 81
W. Town La. Bris —5D 81
W. Town Pk. Bris —4F 81
W. Town Rd. Back —3C 124
W. Town Rd. Bris —5E 37 (in two parts)
West View. Alv —3A 8
West View. Mang —1C 62
Westview. Paul —4A 146
Westview Orchard Mid N —4C 112
W. View Rd. Bathe —3B 102
W. View Rd. Bris —2D 79
W. View Rd. Key —3A 92
West Wlk. Yate —5A 18 (off Station Rd.)
Westward Clo. Wrin —1B 156
Westward Dri. Pill —3E 53
Westward Gdns. L Ash —3D 77
Westward Rd. Bris —1B 86
West Way. Bris —5F 25
West Way. Clev —3C 120
Westway. Nail —3D 123
Westwood Clo. W Mare —3D 129
Westwood Cres. Bris —4F 71
Westwood Rd. Bris —5F 81
Westwood Rd. Trow —1A 118
Westwoods. Bath —3C 102
Westwood View. Bath —4D 109
Wetherby Ct. Bris —3B 46
Wetherell Pl. Bris —3D 69
Wetlands La. P'head —5E 49
Wexford Rd. Bris —5F 79
Weymouth Rd. Bris —3F 79
Weymouth St. Bath —1C 106
Wharfedale. T'bry —4E 7
Wharf La. P'bry —2D 51
Wharf Rd. Bris —3B 60
Wharnecliffe Clo. Bris —3D 89
Wharnecliffe Gdns. Bris —3D 89
Whatley Ct. Bris —1D 69
Whatley Rd. Bris —1D 69
Wheatfield Dri. Brad S —5E 11
Wheathill Clo. Key —3E 91
Wheelers Clo. Mid N —2A 152
Wheelers Dri. Mid N —2F 151
Wheelers Rd. Mid N —2F 151
Whinchat Gdns. Bris —1B 60
Whippington Ct. Bris —3A 70 (1D 5)
Whitby Rd. Bris —1E 81 (in two parts)
Whitchurch La. B'wth —2C 86 (in two parts)
Whitchurch La. Bris —3F 87
Whitchurch Rd. Bris —2C 86
Whitebeam Ct. Bris —2A 72
Whitebrook La. Pea J —1C 148
Whitecroft Way. Bris —3C 74
Whitecross Av. Bris —2E 89
Whitecross La. Ban —4E 137
Whitecross Rd. W Mare —3C 132
White Dri. P'head —4F 49
Whitefield Av. Han —5F 73
Whitefield Av. S'wll —1C 72
Whitefield Clo. Bathe —2C 102
Whitefield Rd. Bris —1B 72
Whitefields. Chip S —5E 19
Whitefriars. Bris —3F 69 (1B 4)
Whitegate Clo. B'don —5F 139
Whitehall Av. Bris —1A 72
Whitehall Gdns. Bris —1F 71
Whitehall Rd. Bris —2D 71
White Hart Steps. Clif W —4D 69
White Hart Yd. Trow —2D 119
Whitehaven. Bath —4D 103
Whiteheads La. Brad A —2E 115
Whitehill. Brad A —2E 115
White Horse Bus. Pk. Trow —3F 155
White Horse Clo. Trow —4D 119
White Horse Rd. W'ley —2F 113
Whitehouse La. Bris —2F 79
Whitehouse Pl. Bris —1A 80
White Ho. Rd. Clav —3F 143
Whitehouse St. Bris —1A 80
Whiteladies Ga. Bris —1D 69
Whiteladies Rd. Bris —5C 56
Whiteleaze. Bris —4E 41
White Lodge Pk. P'head —2F 49
White Lodge Rd. Bris —3B 62
Whitemead Ho. Bris —2C 78
Whitemore Ct. Bathe —1B 102
Whiteoak Way. Nail —5C 122
White Ox Mead La. Pea J (in two parts) —3E 157
White Row Hill. Trow —5A 118
Whiterow Pk. Trow —4A 118
Whitesfield Rd. Nail —4C 122
White's Hill. Bris —4C 72
Whiteshill. Ham —1F 45
White St. Bris —2B 70
White Tree Rd. Bris —3D 57
Whitewall La. T'bry —2F 7
Whiteway Av. Bath —1B 108
Whiteway Clo. Bris —2C 72
Whiteway Clo. St Ap —4A 72
Whiteway Ct. Bris —2C 72
Whiteway M. Bris —2C 72
Whiteway Rd. Bris —2B 72
Whiteway Rd. W'way —4A 104
Whitewells Rd. Bath —4B 100
Whitewood Rd. Bris —1B 72
Whitfield Clo. Bris —5F 61
Whitfield Rd. T'bry —2D 7
Whiting Rd. Bris —4C 86
Whitland Av. Bris —3D 87
Whitland Rd. Bris —3D 87
Whitley Clo. Yate —3E 17
Whitley Mead. Stok G —1A 44
Whitmead Gdns. Bris —4E 87
Whitmore Av. Bris —2C 82
Whitson St. Bris —2F 69
Whitting Rd. W Mare —4C 132
Whittington Dri. W Mare —3B 128
Whittington Rd. Bris —1E 61
Whittock Rd. Bris —3F 89
Whittock Sq. Bris —1F 89
Whittucks Clo. Bris —1F 83
Whittucks Rd. Han —2E 83
Whitwell Rd. Bris —5D 81
Whytes Clo. Bris —4C 40
Wick Cres. Bris —2F 81
Wicker Hill. Trow —1C 118
Wickets, The. K'wd —5F 61
Wicket, The. Bris —2F 71
Wicketts, The. Bris —3B 42
Wickfield. Clev —5C 120
Wickham Clo. Chip S —1F 35
Wickham Ct. Bris —2F 59
Wickham Ct. Clev —3C 120
Wickham Glen. Bris —2F 59
Wickham Hill. Bris —2F 59
Wickham View. Bris —2F 59
Wick Ho. Clo. Salt —5F 93
Wick La. C'ton —1C 148
Wicklow Rd. Bris —5A 80
Wick Rd. Bris —3F 81
Wickwar Rd. Yate —1C 18
Widbrook Meadow. Trow —2A 118
Widbrook View. Brad A —4F 115
Widcombe. Bris —2C 88
Widcombe Clo. Bris —3C 72
Widcombe Cres. Bath —4C 106
Widcombe Hill. Bath —4C 106
Widcombe Pde. Bath —4B 106 (off Claverton St.)
Widcombe Rise. Bath —4C 106
Widcombe Ter. Bath —5C 106
Wigmore Gdns. W Mare —3A 128
Wigton Cres. Bris —3E 41
Wilbye Gro. Bris —1F 87
Wilcot Clo. Trow —4D 119
Wilcox Clo. Bris —4E 73
Wild Country La. L Ash —5A 76
Wildcroft Ho. Bris —3D 57
Wildcroft Rd. Bris —2D 57
Wilder Ct. Bris —2A 70
Wilderness, The. Brad A —2D 115
Wilder St. St Pa —2A 70
Willada Clo. Bris —3D 79
William Daw Clo. Ban —5D 137
William Mason Clo. Bris —3D 71
Williams Clo. L Grn —2B 84
Williamson Rd. Bris —4B 58
Williamstowe. Bath —3D 111
William St. Bath —2B 106 (2D 97)
William St. Bedm —1A 80
William St. Fish —4D 61
William St. Redf —2E 71
William St. St Pa —1B 70
William St. St Ph —4C 70
William St. Tot —1B 80
Willinton Rd. Bris —1B 88
Willis Rd. Bris —5B 62
Williton Cres. W Mare —1D 139
Willment Way. Bris —3F 37
Willmott Clo. Bris —5B 88
Willoughby Clo. Alv —3B 8
Willoughby Clo. Bris —1D 87
Willoughby Rd. Bris —2A 58
Willowbank. Bris —5E 41
Willow Bed Clo. Bris —1D 61
Willow Clo. Bath —4F 109
Willow Clo. Bris —4F 75
Willow Clo. Clev —3E 121
Willow Clo. L Ash —4B 76
Willow Clo. Pat —2A 26
Willow Clo. P'head —3E 49
Willow Clo. Rads —3B 152
Willow Clo. St Geo —3A 130
Willow Clo. Uph —1C 138
Willow Clo. Wick —5A 154
Willowdown. W Mare —1C 128
Willow Dri. Hut —1C 140
Willow Dri. B'don —5A 140
Willow Dri. Lock —3C 134
Willow Falls, The. Bath —3F 101
Willow Gdns. St Geo —3B 130
Willow Grn. Bath —5F 105
Willow Gro. Bris —5E 61
Willow Gro. Trow —5B 118
Willow Ho. Bris —4F 87
Willow Rd. Bris —2E 83
Willow Shopping Cen., The. Bris —1A 62
Willows, The. Brad S —1F 27
Willows, The. Bris —3D 45
Willows, The. Nail —2E 123
Willows, The. Yate —4F 17
Willow View. N Brad —4D 155
Willow Wlk. Bris —1D 41
Willow Wlk. Key —4F 91
Willow Way. Coal H —3E 31
Willsbridge Hill. Will —3C 84
Wills Dri. Bris —2C 70
Willway St. Bedm —1F 79
Willway St. Bris —3B 70
Wilmot Ct. Bris —4C 74
Wilmots Way. Pill —3F 53
Wilshire Av. Bris —5F 73
Wilson Av. Bris —2B 70
Wilson Pl. Bris —2B 70
Wilson St. Bris —2B 70
Wilton Clo. Bris —4E 41
Wilton Dri. Trow —4D 119
Wilton Gdns. W Mare —1C 132
Wiltons. Wrin —1B 156
Wiltshire Av. Yate —3C 18
Wiltshire Dri. Trow —5C 118
Wiltshire Pl. Bris —4A 62
Wiltshire Way. Bath —4B 100
Wilverley Ind. Est. Bris —4A 82
Wimbledon Rd. Bris —2E 57
Wimborne Rd. Bris —4E 79
Winash Clo. Bris —1F 89
Wincanton Clo. Down —3B 46
Wincanton Clo. Nail —4F 123
Winchcombe Clo. Nail —5F 123
Winchcombe Gro. Bris —2B 54
Winchcombe Rd. Fram C —1D 31
Winchcombe Trad. Est. Bris —1C 80
Winchester Av. Bris —2F 81
Winchester Rd. Bath —4E 105
Winchester Rd. Bris —2F 81
Wincroft. Old C —1E 85 (in two parts)
Windcliff Cres. Bris —4A 38
Windermere. W Trym —2F 41
Windermere Av. W Mare —4D 133
Windermere Rd. Pat —1C 26

Windermere Rd. Trow —5E 117
Windermere Way. Bris —4F 75
Windmill Clo. Bris —1A 80
Windmill Farm Bus. Cen. Bris —1F 79
Windmill Hill. Bris —2F 79
Windmill Hill. Hut —1D 141
Windmill La. Bris —1F 39
Windrush Clo. Bath —5A 104
Windrush Ct. T'bry —4D 7
Windrush Grn. Key —4C 92
Windrush Rd. Key —4C 92
Windsor Av. Bris —4D 73
Windsor Av. Key —4A 92
Windsor Bri. Rd. Bath —3E 105
Windsor Clo. Clev —4C 120
Windsor Clo. Stok G —4A 28
Windsor Ct. Bath —2D 105
Windsor Ct. Bris —4B 68
Windsor Ct. Down —5A 46
Windsor Ct. Wick —4B 154
Windsor Cres. H'len —5E 23
Windsor Dri. Nail —3D 123
Windsor Dri. Trow —5B 118
Windsor Dri. Yate —4F 17
Windsor Gro. Bris —2D 71
Windsor Pl. Bris —4B 68
Windsor Pl. Mang —2C 62
Windsor Rd. Bris —5A 58
Windsor Rd. L Grn —3B 84
Windsor Rd. Whit B —3F 155
Windsor Rd. W Mare —3A 128
Windsor Ter. Clif —4B 68
Windsor Ter. Paul —4B 146
Windsor Ter. Tot —1B 80
Windsor Vs. Bath —2D 105
Windwhistle Circ. W Mare —5D 133
Windwhistle La. W Mare (in three parts) —5C 132
Windwhistle Rd. W Mare —5B 132
Wineberry Clo. Bris —1F 71
Wine St. Bath —3B 106 (4C 96)
Wine St. Brad A —2D 115
Wine St. Bris —3F 69 (2C 4)
Wine St. Ter. Brad A —3D 115
Winfield Rd. Bris —3E 75
Winford Clo. P'head —4A 50
Winford Gro. Bris —5C 78
Wingard Clo. Uph —1B 138
Wingfield Rd. Bris —3A 80
Wingfield Rd. Trow —3A 118
Winifred's La. Bath —5F 99
Winkworth Pl. Bris —1B 70
Winsbury Way. Pat —5E 11
Winscombe Clo. Key —2F 91
Winscombe Rd. W Mare —1E 133
Winsford St. Bris —2C 70
Winsham Clo. Bris —3D 89
Winsley By-Pass. Brad A —2E 113
Winsley Hill. Lim S —2B 112
Winsley Rd. Brad A —2B 114
Winsley Rd. Bris —1F 69
Winterbourne Hill. Wint —4F 29
Winterbourne Rd. Stok G —3A 28
Winterfield Pk. Paul —4B 146
Winterfield Rd. Paul —4B 146
Winterslow Rd. Trow —5B 118
Winterstoke Clo. Bris —3D 79
Winterstoke Ho. Bris —1C 78
Winterstoke Rd. Bris —2B 78
Winterstoke Rd. W Mare —2D 133
Winterstoke Underpass. Bris —1B 78
Winton St. Bris —1B 80
Wintour Ho. Bris —4C 38
Wisteria Av. Chip S —5C 18
Wisteria Av. Hut —1B 140
Witchell Rd. Bris —3E 71
Witch Hazel Rd. Bris —5A 88
Witcombe. Yate —2E 33
Witcombe Clo. Bris —1B 74
Witham Rd. Key —5C 92
Withey Clo. E. Bris —1B 56
Withey Clo. W. Bris —2B 56
Witheys, The. Bris —4E 89
Withies La. Mid N —5C 150
Withies Pk. Mid N —4C 150
Withington Clo. Bit —3E 85
Withleigh Rd. Bris —3D 81
Withy Clo. Trow —4E 117
Withypool Gdns. Bris —3D 89
Withys, The. Pill —4F 53
Withywood Gdns. Bris —3B 86
Withywood Rd. Bris —4B 86
Witney Clo. Salt —5F 93
Woburn Clo. Bar C —5B 74
Woburn Clo. Trow —2A 118
Woburn Rd. Bris —4D 59
Wolferton Rd. Bris —5B 58
Wolfridge Gdns. Bris —5C 24
Wolfridge La. Alv —3A 8
Wolfridge Ride. Alv —3A 8
Wolseley Rd. Bris —4F 57
Woltson Ter. Bath —3F 107
Wolvershill Pk. Ban —5E 137
Wolvershill Rd. Ban —5A 130
Woodbine Rd. Bris —2F 71
Woodborough Clo. Trow —5D 119
Woodborough Cres. Wins —5B 156
Woodborough Dri. Wins —4B 156
Woodborough La. Rads —5D 149
Woodborough Rd. Rads —1D 153
Woodborough Rd. Wins —4A 156
Woodborough St. Bris —1D 71
Woodbridge Rd. Bris —3C 80
Woodbury La. Bris —5C 56
Woodchester. Bris —4A 62
Woodchester. Yate —3A 34
Woodchester Rd. Bris —5E 41
Woodcliff Av. W Mare —4A 128
Woodcliff Rd. W Mare —4A 128
Woodcote. Bris —4F 73
Woodcote Rd. Bris —4D 61
Woodcote Wlk. Bris —5D 61
Woodcroft Av. Bris —1F 71
Woodcroft Clo. Bris —1A 82
Woodcroft Rd. Bris —1A 82
Woodend. Bris —4F 73
Woodend Rd. Fram C —2D 31
Wood End Wlk. Bris —1E 55
Woodfield Rd. Bris —5D 57
Woodford Clo. Nail —4F 123
Woodgrove Rd. Bris —2F 39
Woodhall Clo. Bris —1B 62
Wood Hill. Cong —5D 143
Woodhill Av. P'head —1F 49
Wood Hill Pk. P'head —1F 49
Wood Hill Pl. Bath —4E 107
Woodhill Rd. P'head —2F 49
Woodhill Views. Nail —2E 123
Woodhouse Gro. Bris —1A 58
Woodhouse Rd. Bath —3B 104
Woodhurst Rd. W Mare —1E 133
Woodington Ct. Bar C —1B 84
Woodington Rd. Clev —5C 120
Wood Kilns, The. Yat —2A 142
Woodland Av. Bris —5F 61
Woodland Clo. Bris —5E 61
Woodland Ct. Bris —4E 55
Woodland Glade. Clev —1E 121
Woodland Gro. Bath —4F 107
Woodland Gro. Bris —1F 55
Woodland La. Bris —5F 89
Woodland Pl. Bath —4E 107
Woodland Rise. Bris —3E 69 (2A 4)
Woodland Rd. Clif & Bris (in two parts) —2E 69
Woodland Rd. Nail —2D 123
Woodland Rd. W Mare —4B 132
Woodlands. Alm —3F 11
Woodlands Down —1A 62
Woodlands Cvn. Pk. Brad S —3E 11
Woodlands Ct. Alm —3D 11
Woodlands Dri. Mid N —3C 112
Woodlands Edge. Trow —3F 119
Woodlands La. Alm —4D 11 (in two parts)
Woodlands Pk. Bath —4D 101
Woodlands Pk. Cvn. Site. Brad S —3E 11
Woodlands Rise. Bris —1F 61
Woodlands Rd. Clev —2C 120
Woodlands Rd. P'head —1F 49
Woodland Ter. K'wd —2A 74
Woodland Ter. Redl —5D 57
Woodland Way. Bris —5E 61
Wood La. Clav —4E 143
Wood La. W Mare —4D 127
Woodleaze. Bris —1D 55
Wood Leaze. Chip S —5B 18
Woodleigh. T'bry —3D 7
Woodleigh Gdns. Bris —2E 89
Woodmancote. Yate —1F 33
Woodmancote Rd. Bris —1A 70
Woodmand. Holt —2F 155
Woodmans Clo. Chip S —1D 35
Woodmans Rd. Chip S —1D 35
Woodmans Vale. Chip S —1E 35
Woodmarsh. N Brad —3E 155
Woodmarsh Clo. Bris —4C 88
Woodmead Gdns. Bris —4E 87
Woodmill. Yat —2A 142
Woodnock, The. Bris —2E 41
Woodpecker Av. Mid N —4E 151
Woodpecker Cres. Puck —3E 65
Woodpecker Dri. W Mare —5C 128
Wood Rd. K'wd —2F 73
Woods Hill. Lim S —3B 112
Woodside. Bris —4F 55
Woodside. Mid N —3B 150
Woodside Av. W Mare —1F 139
Woodside Cotts. Bath —4D 109
Woodside Gdns. P'head —3A 48
Woodside Gro. Bris —1F 39
Woodside Rd. Brisl —4A 72
Woodside Rd. Clev —1E 121
Woodside Rd. Coal H —2F 31
Woodside Rd. Down —5E 45
Woodside Rd. K'wd —3E 73
Woodspring Av. W Mare —2E 127
Woodspring Cres. W Mare —2E 127
Woodstock Av. Bris —1E 69
Woodstock Clo. Bris —2B 74
Woodstock Rd. K'wd —2B 74
Woodstock Rd. Redl —5D 57
Woodstock Rd. W Mare —5F 127
Wood St. Bath —4A 106 (5A 96) (Lwr. Bristol Rd.)
Wood St. Bath —3A 106 (3B 96) (Queen Sq.)
Wood St. Bris —5D 59
Woodview. Clev —3F 121
Woodview. Paul —4A 146
Woodview Clo. Bris —5A 38
Wood View Ter. Nail —3E 123
Woodview Ter. W Mare —2E 133
Woodward Dri. Bris —1B 84
Woodwell Rd. Bris —1A 54 (in two parts)
Woodyleaze. Bris —4E 73
Woodyleaze Dri. Bris —4E 73
Wookey Clo. Nail —5E 123
Woolcot St. Bris —5D 57
Wooler Rd. W Mare —5C 126
Woollard La. Bris —5F 89
Woolley Clo. Brad A —2F 115
Woolley Dri. Brad A —2F 115
Woolley La. Bath —1A 100
Woolley Rd. Bris —3A 90
Woolley St. Brad A —3E 115
Woolley Ter. Brad A —2F 115
Woolpack Meadows. Trow —3E 119
Woolvers Way. Lock —2F 135
Wootton Cres. Bris —4A 72
Wootton Pk. Bris —4D 81 (in two parts)
Wootton Rd. Bris —4A 72
Worcester Bldgs. Bath —4C 100
Worcester Clo. Bris —5D 61
Worcester Ct. Bath —4C 100 (off Worcester Pk.)
Worcester Cres. Bris —2C 68
Worcester Gdns. Nail —5A 122
Worcester Pk. Bath —4C 100
Worcester Pl. Bath —4C 100
Worcester Rd. Clif —2C 68
Worcester Rd. K'wd —1F 73
Worcester Ter. Bath —5C 100
Worcester Ter. Bris —2C 68
Worcester Vs. Bath —4C 100
Wordsworth Ho. Pat —1C 26
Wordsworth Rd. Bris —1C 58
Wordsworth Rd. Clev —4C 120
Wordsworth Rd. W Mare —5E 133
Worlds End La. Bris —4D 69
Worlds End La. Key —3E 93
Worlebury Clo. W Mare —2F 127
Worlebury Hill Rd. W Mare —3E 127
Worlebury Pk. Rd. W Mare —2E 127
Worle Ct. W Mare —2D 129
Worrall M. Clif —5C 56
Worrall Rd. Bris —5C 56
Worrell's La. Ham —1F 45
Worsley St. Bris —2F 71
Worsted Clo. Trow —3E 119
Worthing Rd. Pat —1B 26
Worthy La. W Mare —5C 126
Worthy Pl. W Mare —5B 126
Worthys, The. Brad S —3C 28
Wotton Rd. Iron A —2A 16
Wrangle Farm Grn. Clev —4E 121
Wraxall Gro. Bris —5B 78
Wraxall Rd. Bris —4C 74 (in two parts)
Wrenbert Rd. Bris —2F 61
Wren Clo. W Mare —5B 128
Wren Ct. Trow —2B 118
Wren Dri. Bris —1B 60
Wrington Clo. Lit S —2E 27
Wrington Cres. Bris —1C 86
Wrington Hill. Wrin —1C 156
Wrington La. Cong —1E 145
Wrington Mead. Cong —1E 145
Wrington Rd. Cong —1E 145
Writhlington Ct. Rads —2F 153
Wroughton Dri. Bris —4F 87
Wroughton Gdns. Bris —4F 87
Wroxham Dri. Lit S —1E 27
Wyatt Av. Bris —3B 86
Wyatt Clo. Bris —3B 86
Wyatt's Clo. Nail —3C 122
Wyatts View. St Ap —4A 72
Wychwood. Bris —4A 74
Wyck Beck Rd. Bris —5B 24
Wycombe Gro. Bris —3F 81
Wyecliffe Rd. Bris —5D 41
Wye Ct. T'bry —4D 7
Wyecroft Clo. Bris —1F 41
Wyedale Av. Bris —5D 39
Wyke Rd. Trow —4E 117
Wykis Ct. Bris —5A 74
Wyllie Ct. W Mare —1E 129
Wymbush Cres. Bris —3E 87
Wymbush Gdns. Bris —3E 87
Wyndham Cres. Bris —1B 82
Wyndham Cres. E'ton G —3D 53
Wyndham Way. P'head —2F 49
Wynstones, The. Bris —3E 73
Wynter Clo. W Mare —2E 129
Wytherlies Dri. Bris —1B 60

Yadley Clo. Wins —5B 156
Yadley La. Wins —5B 156
Yadley Way. Wins —5B 156
Yanleigh Est. L Ash —5D 77
Yanley La. L Ash —3D 77
Yarbury Way. W Mare —4F 129
Yarn Ter. Trow —3E 119
Yate Rd. Iron A —3A 16
Yate Rocks. Yate —1B 18
Yeaman's Ho. Bris —5A 70
Yelverton Rd. Bris —4A 82
Yeo Clo. W Mare —3E 133
Yeo Ct. Cong —2D 145
Yeolands Dri. Clev —5B 120
Yeo La. L Ash —4B 76
Yeoman's Clo. Bris —2F 55
Yeomanside Clo. Bris —3E 89
Yeomans Orchard. Wrin —1C 156
Yeoman Way. Trow —3C 118
Yeomead. Nail —2E 123
Yeomeads. L Ash —4B 76
Yeo Moor. Clev —4E 121
Yeoward Rd. Clev —5E 121
Yeo Way. Clev —4B 120
Yerbury St. Trow —1D 119
Yewcroft Clo. Bris —4C 88
Yew Tree Clo. Nail —4B 122
Yew Tree Ct. Bris —3D 89
Yew Tree Dri. Bris —4A 62
Yew Tree Gdns. E'ton G —3E 53
Yew Tree Gdns. Nail —4B 122
Yew Tree Pk. Cong —3D 145
Yomede Pk. Bath —1B 104
York Av. Bris —3B 58
York Building. Bath —2A 106 (2B 96)
York Bldgs. Trow —1D 119
York Clo. Down —3B 46
York Clo. Stok G —5F 27
York Clo. W Mare —1E 129
York Clo. Yate —2A 18
York Gdns. Bris —4B 68
York Gdns. Wint —1B 30
York Pl. Bris —4E 69
York Pl. Clif —3D 69
York Rd. Bedm —1A 80
York Rd. E'tn —1E 71
York Rd. Mont —1A 70
York Rd. Stap H —3A 62
York St. Bar H —3E 71
York St. Bath —3B 106 (4C 96)
York St. Bris —2A 70
York St. Clif —5C 56
York St. St W —5B 58
York St. W Mare —1B 132
Youngs Ct. E Grn —4D 47
Youngwood La. Nail —5D 123
Youngwood La. Nail —5D 123

Zed All. Bris —3F 69 (2B 4)
Zetland Rd. Bris —5F 57
Zig Zag. Clev —2D 121
Zion Rd. Bris —2C 70

HOSPITALS and HEALTH CENTRES covered by this atlas.

N.B. Where Hospitals and Health Centres are not named on the map, the reference given is for the road in which they are situated.

BLACKBERRY HILL HOSPITAL —2B **60**
Manor Rd., Fishponds,
Bristol, BS16 2EW
Tel: (0117) 9656061

BRADFORD-ON-AVON COMMUNITY HOSPITAL —1E **115**
Berryfields, Berryfield Rd.,
Bradford on Avon, BA15 1TA
Tel: (01225) 862975

Bradford-on-Avon Family Health Centre —3D **115**
Station App.,
Bradford on Avon,
BA15 1DQ
Tel: (01225) 865660

BRENTRY HOSPITAL —2D **41**
Charlton Rd., Brentry,
Bristol, BS10 6JA
Tel: (0117) 9500500

BRISTOL BUPA HOSPITAL —5C **56**
The Glen, Redland Hill,
Durdham Down,
Bristol, BS6 6UT
Tel: (0117) 9732562

BRISTOL DENTAL HOSPITAL —3F **69** (1B **4**)
Lower Maudlin St.,
Bristol, BS1 2LY
Tel: (0117) 9230050

BRISTOL EYE HOSPITAL —3F **69** (1B **4**)
Lower Mauldin St.,
Bristol, BS1 2LX
Tel: (0117) 9230060

BRISTOL GENERAL HOSPITAL —5F **69**
Guinea St.,
Bristol, BS1 6SY
Tel: (0117) 9265001

BRISTOL ONCOLOGY CENTRE —3F **69** (1B **4**)
Horfield Rd.,
Bristol, BS2 8ED
Tel: (0117) 9230000

BRISTOL ROYAL HOSPITAL FOR SICK CHILDREN —3E **69**
St Michael's Hill,
Bristol, BS2 8BJ
Tel: (0117) 9215411

BRISTOL ROYAL INFIRMARY —3F **69**
Marlborough St.,
Bristol, BS2 8H
Tel: (0117) 9230000

Brooklea Health Centre —5A **72**
Wick Rd., Brislington,
Bristol, BS4 4HU
Tel: (0117) 9711211

BURDEN HOSPITAL —4A **44**
Stoke La., Stapleton,
Bristol, BS16 1QT
Tel: (0117) 9701212

Cadbury Heath Health Centre —5C **74**
Parkwall Rd.,
Cadbury Heath,
Bristol, BS30 8HS
Tel: (0117) 9600129

Charlotte Keel Health Centre —1C **70**
Seymour Rd., Easton,
Bristol, BS5 0UA
Tel: (0117) 9512244

CHESTERFIELD HOSPITAL, THE —4C **68**
3 Clifton Hill,
Bristol, BS8 1BP
Tel: (0117) 9467424

Clevedon Health Centre —3E 121
Old St., Clevedon,
BS21 6DG
Tel: (01275) 871454

CLEVEDON HOSPITAL —3E **121**
Old Street, Clevedon,
BS21 6BS
Tel: (01275) 872212

COSSHAM HOSPITAL —5E **61**
Lodge Rd., Kingswood,
Bristol, BS15 1LF
Tel: (0117) 9671661

DROVE ROAD HOSPITAL —3D **133**
Drove Rd., Weston-Super-Mare,
BS23 3NT
Tel: (01934) 636363

Eastville Health Centre —5E **59**
East Pk., Eastville,
Bristol, BS5 6YA
Tel: (0117) 9511261

Fairfield Park Health Centre —5C **100**
Tyning La., Camden Rd.,
Bath, BA1 6EA
Tel: (01225) 331616

Fishponds Health Centre —3D **61**
Beechwood Rd., Fishponds,
Bristol, BS16 3TD
Tel: (0117) 9656281

FRENCHAY HOSPITAL —4D **45**
Frenchay Park Rd., Frenchay,
Bristol, BS16 1LE
Tel: (0117) 9701212

GROVE ROAD DAY HOSPITAL —5C **56**
Grove Rd., Redland,
Bristol, BS6 6UJ
Tel: (0117) 9730225

HANHAM HALL HOSPITAL —1F **83**
Whittucks Rd., Hanham,
Bristol, BS15 3PU
Tel: (0117) 9085000

Hartcliffe Health Centre —4E **87**
Hareclive Rd., Hartcliffe,
Bristol, BS13 0JP
Tel: (0117) 941020

HEATH HOUSE PRIORY HOSPITAL —3D **59**
Heath House La., off Bell Hill,
Stapleton, Bristol,
BS16 1EQ
Tel: (0117) 9525255

Horfield Health Centre —1C **58**
Lockleaze Rd., Horfield,
Bristol, BS7 9RR
Tel: (0117) 9695391

KEYNSHAM HOSPITAL —4B **92**
St Clement's Rd., Keynsham,
Bristol, BS31 1AG
Tel: (0117) 9862356

Kingswood Health Centre —2A **74**
Alma Rd., Kingswood,
Bristol, BS15 4EJ
Tel: (0117) 9677191

Lawrence Hill Health Centre —3C **70**
Hassell Dri., Lawrence Hill, Bristol,
Avon, BS2 0AN
Tel: (0117) 9555241

Montpelier Health Centre —1A **70**
Bath Buildings, Montpelier,
Bristol, BS6 5PT
Tel: (0117) 9426811

Nailsea Health Centre —3D **123**
Somerset Sq.,
Nailsea, BS19 2EY
Tel: (01275) 856611

PAULTON HOSPITAL —5C **146**
Salisbury Rd.,
Paulton, BS39 7SB
Tel: (01761) 412315

Portishead Health Centre —3F **49**
Victoria Sq., Portishead,
Bristol, BS20 9AQ
Tel: (01275) 847474

ROBERT SMITH UNIT DAY HOSPITAL —3C **68**
Mortimer Rd.,
Bristol, BS8 4EX
Tel: (0117) 9735004

ROYAL NATIONAL HOSPITAL FOR RHEUMATIC DISEASES —3A **106** (3B **96**)
Upper Borough Walls,
Bath, BA1 1RL
Tel: (01225) 465941

ROYAL UNITED HOSPITAL —1C **104**
Combe Pk., Bath,
Avon, BA1 3NG
Tel: (01225) 428331

St George Health Centre —2C **72**
Bellevue Rd., St George,
Bristol, BS5 7PH
Tel: (0117) 9612161

St Johns Lane Health Centre —3A **80**
St Johns La., Bedminster,
Bristol, BS14 8PT
Tel: (0117) 667681

ST MARTIN'S HOSPITAL —3F **109**
Midford Rd., Bath,
BA2 5RP
Tel: (01225) 832383

ST MARY'S HOSPITAL —3D **69**
Upper Byron Pl., Clifton,
Bristol, BS8 1JU
Tel: (0117) 9872727

ST MICHAEL'S HOSPITAL —2E **69**
Southwell St., St Michael's Hill,
Bristol, BS2 8EG
Tel: (0117) 9215411

St Peter's Hospice —3B **80**
St Agnes Av., Knowle,
Bristol, BS4 2DU
Tel: (0117) 9774605

Shirehampton Health Centre —1A **54**
Pembroke Rd., Shirehampton,
Bristol, BS11 0QE
Tel: (0117) 9828181

Southmead Health Centre —2E **41**
Ullswater Rd., Southmead,
Bristol, BS10 6DF
Tel: (0117) 9507000

SOUTHMEAD HOSPITAL —4A **42**
Westbury-on-Trym,
Bristol, BS10 5NB
Tel: (0117) 9505050

Stockwood Health Centre —3A **90**
Hollway Rd., Stockwood,
Bristol, BS14 8PT
Tel: (01275) 833103

Thornbury Health Centre —3D **7**
Eastland Rd., Thornbury,
BS35 1DP
Tel: (01454) 414477

THORNBURY HOSPITAL —3D **7**
Eastland Rd., Thornbury, BS35 1DN
Tel: (01454) 412636

TROWBRIDGE COMMUNITY HOSPITAL —1C **118**
Adcroft St., Trowbridge,
BA14 8PH
Tel: (01225) 752558

Trowbridge Family Health Centre —1D **119**
The Halve, Trowbridge,
BA14 8SA
Tel: (01225) 766161

WESTON GENERAL HOSPITAL —2C **138**
Grange Rd., Uphill,
Weston-Super-Mare,
BS23 4TQ
Tel: (01934) 636363

Whitchurch Health Centre —3C **88**
Armada Rd., Whitchurch,
Bristol, BS8 2PU
Tel: (01275) 839421

Whiteladies Health Centre —1D **69**
Whatley Rd., Clifton,
Bristol, BS8 1NL
Tel: (0117) 9731201

William Bud Health Centre —5F **79**
Leinster Av., Knowle,
Bristol, BS4 1NL
Tel: (0117) 9633152

Worle Health Centre —3C **128**
125 High St., Worle,
Weston-Super-Mare,
BS22 0HB
Tel: (01934) 510510

Yate Health Centre —5A **18**
21 West Wlk., Yate,
Bristol, BS37 4AX
Tel: (01454) 313374

INDEX TO PLACES OF INTEREST

with their map square reference

Arnolfini Gallery. —5F **69**
Ashton Court Visitors Cen. —1F **77**
Assembly Rooms & Costume Museum. —2A **106**
Avon Valley Railway. —4D **85**

Barton Farm Country Park. —4B **114**
Bath Abbey. —3B **106**
Bath Art Gallery. —3B **106**
Bath Guildhall. —3B **106**
Bath & Somerset County Racecourse. —1B **98**
Bath Tourist Info. Cen. —3B **106**
Beckford's Tower & Museum. —2E **99**
Blaise Castle House (Museum). —2A **40**
Book Museum. —4B **106**
Botanic Gardens. —2E **105**
Bradford on Avon Museum. —3E **115**
Brandon Hill Nature Park. —4D **69**
Bristol Cathedral. —4E **69**
Bristol Harbour Railway. —5E **69**
Bristol R.C. Cathedral. —2C **68**
Bristol Tourist Info. Cen. —4F **69**
Bristol Zoo. —1B **68**
Browns Folly Nature Reserve. —5E **103**
Brunel Trust. —5B **70**
Building of Bath Museum. —2B **106**

Cabot Tower. —4D **69**
City Museum & Art Gallery. —3E **69**
Clevedon Court. —2F **121**
Clifton Suspension Bridge. —3A **68**
Court Farm Country Park. —3D **137**
Courts Gardens, The. —2E **155**
Crowe Hall. —5C **106**

Dauphine's of Bristol. —2B **72**

Exploratory Hands-On Science Cen., The. —5B **70**

Fashion Research Cen. —2A **106**
Folk Art Museum. —2A **106**

Georgian Garden. —2A **106**

Harveys Wine Museum. —4E **69**
Herschel House Museum. —3A **106**
Holburne Museum. —2C **106**

Industrial Museum. —5F **69**
International Helicopter Museum. —3C **134**

John Wesley's Chapel. —3A **70**

Kings Weston Down Nature Reserve. —4D **39**

Lawrence Weston Meadows Nature Reserve. —1D **39**
Little Solsbury Hill Fort. —2E **101**

Maritime Heritage Cen. —5E **69**
Mid Sommer Norton Tourist Info. Cen. —3E **151**
Mr Bowler's Business Museum. —1A **106**
Museum of East Asian Art. —2A **106**

Observatory. —3B **68**
Old Station. —5B **70**

Partis College. —1B **104**
Postal Museum. —2B **106**
Prior Park. —2D **111**
Pump Room. —3B ***106***
(off York St.)

Radford Farm & Shire Horse Cen. —1F **147**
Red Lodge. —3E **69**
Roman Baths. —3B **106**
Royal Crescent (No.1). —2A **106**
Royal Photographic Society. —2A **106**

Sally Lunn's House Museum. —3B **106**
S.S. Great Britain. —5D **69**
Stratford Mill. —2A **40**

Temple Church. —4A **70**
Thornbury Castle. —2B **6**
Thornbury Museum. —4C **6**
Thornbury Tourist Info. Cen. —4C **6**
Tithe Barn. —4D **115**
Trowbridge Museum. —2C **118**
Trowbridge Tourist Info. Cen. —2D **119**

Westbury College Gatehouse. —5C **40**
Weston Big Wood Nature Reserve. —5C **48**
Weston-Super-Mare Tourist Info. Cen. —1B **132**
Willsbridge Mill Visitor Cen. —3C **84**
Windmill Hill City Farm. —1F ***79***
(off Clark St.)
Woodspring Museum. —5C **126**

Printed and bound in Great Britain by
Butler & Tanner Ltd, Frome and London